Microsoft Exams Study Guide & Tests

# Microsoft Certification

**David Mayer**

2020-06-11

## ALL IN ONE

# Microsoft Certification

*Complete Step By Step Guide To Pass All Microsoft Exams And Get Certifications*

# How to Get a 50% Discount

If you have come this far and are curious about how to get a unique offer, then you surely understand it is essential for you to take the right Microsoft Certification now. There is no more time to waste; it's time to be certified in the right way according to your skills.

By purchasing this book you will then be entitled to an incredible 50% discount code on all products available at www.Certification-questions.com

It is a unique offer, and you will finally be able to understand which is the Certification required for your career, understand how to take the Exam and what are the prerequisites. Also, you will be able to use the only Simulated Exam that always has the latest questions available with 100% guaranteed success and a money back guarantee policy.

Don't wait, send us a copy to info@Certification-questions.com:

- of your book
- of your purchase receipt

And, we will automatically send you a discount code equal to 50% for the best Exam Simulator available on the market.

Thanks - Certification-questions.com

# Introduction

Certifications are a valuable addition to a brilliant career, and a Microsoft Certification is now a must have!

By adding a Microsoft Certification to your resume, you can make a real difference to your employability and get hired faster because it is proven that Microsoft Certification has allowed human resources to fill job vacancies quickly and in a secure way.

There are currently three types of Microsoft Certifications: MTA, MCSA and MCSE.

Microsoft Technology Associate is a basic Certification intended for people who want to know the fundamental technological concepts. MTA Certification addresses a broad spectrum of basic technical concepts.

Microsoft MCSA (Microsoft Certified Solutions Associate) is intended for people looking for their first job in an information technology environment. This is a prerequisite for other more advanced Microsoft Certifications.

Microsoft MCSE (Microsoft Certified Solutions Expert) is the most advanced Certification, and is intended for IT professionals who wish to demonstrate their ability to develop innovative solutions, both in the office and in the cloud.

But how can you get certified? This guide provides all the necessary information for studying and passing the certification exams.

Whether you are a beginner or an expert, our team will provide you with everything you need to start studying in detail to obtain the right Certification for you.

In this guide we will offer you step by step information on the following topics:

- Microsoft Certification Exam registration procedure
- Microsoft Certification Exam topics
- Benefits of obtaining an Microsoft Certification
- Requirements for Microsoft Certification Exams
- The Certification path describes the knowledge of the technologies and related skills necessary to pass the Exams
- Duration of the Exam
- Exam format
- Certified professional salary in different countries

- Price of Microsoft Certification Exams
- Practical tests
- How to obtain the Certification that best suits your professional growth
- 50% discount on the purchase of the Web And Mobile Simulator available at www.Certification-questions.com
- 100% success guarantee

    The guide contains everything you need to prepare for the official Microsoft Exams, and to master the skills needed to obtain the Certification that best suits your career path.

In addition to that, we will also provide you with everything you need for making the right decision when choosing an Microsoft Certification: The material in this guide helps professionals to choose the right Certification and to improve their knowledge to pass the official Certification Exam quickly and easily. Our team already provides selected and targeted questions \ answer content to consolidate professional preparation through practical tests and training material.

Our guide provides 100% Exam information, ensuring your preparation is solid and detailed. Thanks to this guide, you will obtain all the necessary information for choosing and passing the Certification that best suits your needs within the huge Microsoft Certification Program.

# Copyright

PUBLISHED BY

certificaton-questions.com

Copyright @ 2019 Certification Questions

All rights reserved. No part of the contents in this may be reproduced or transmitted in form by any means (electronic, photocopying, recording, or otherwise) without prior written permission of the publisher.

First Edition

This book is provided to expresses the author's views and opinions. The views and opinions expressed in this book including URLs and other Internet websites referenced may change without notice.

Any trademarks, service marks, product names or named features in this book are assumed to the property of their respective owners and are used only for reference. There is no implied endorsement if the author references one of these terms, logos, or trademarks.

Some examples given are provided for illustration and learning purposes, and are fictitious. No real association or connection is intended or inferred.

# Dedication

Do you know how?

You choose a book then go to the Dedication Page and find that once again the author has dedicated a book to someone else and not to you.

Not this time.

This book is dedicated to the readers, as, without you, there would be no need for this book to have been written.

Hopefully the effort put into producing this resource guide will result in value and success when you sit your certification exam.

This one's for you. Thanks - Certification-questions.com

# Acknowledgments

The world is better, thanks to people who want to develop and guide others. What makes it even better are the people who share the gift of their time to guide future leaders. Thank you to all who strive to grow and help others to grow.

Without the experience and support of my colleagues and team at Certification-questions.com, this book would not exist. You have given me the opportunity to lead a great group of people to become a leader of great leaders. It is a blessed place. Thanks to the Certification-questions.com team.

I want to say thank you to everyone who ever said anything positive to me or taught me something. It was your kind words and actions over the years that drove me to help others in my turn. THANK YOU.

# PREFACE

Are you looking for valid Practice Tests for Microsoft Certification?

This book will guide on how you can pass the Microsoft Certification Exam using Practice Tests.

We will cover a large set of information for Microsoft Certification topics, so you will systemically discover how to pass the Certification exam.

This book will also explore many of your questions, such as:

- Microsoft Exam topics
- What are the essential criteria for passing the Official Microsoft Exam?
- How much Microsoft Exam Cost?
- What is the format of the Microsoft Exam?
- The advantage of Microsoft Exam Certification
- What are the difficulties of Microsoft Exam Certification?

We appreciate you taking the time to read this book, and we are really excited to assist you on your career growth journey.

# How to Use This Book

There are four main components to the present Microsoft Study Guide.

First, the Introduction, in which you will get to know about the importance of Microsoft Certification and Practice Tests.

Secondly, the Table of Contents proves quite helpful for maneuvering through the ebook.

Thirdly, there is the Content, in which you will get to know about the different methods of studying for the Microsoft Certification Exam that will help you to pass the Certification Exam on your first attempt.

Fourthly, the Summary, in which you will read the brief statement or account of the main points of the Microsoft Certification Exam.

# Index

| | |
|---|---|
| HOW TO GET A 50% DISCOUNT | 3 |
| INTRODUCTION | 4 |
| COPYRIGHT | 6 |
| DEDICATION | 7 |
| ACKNOWLEDGMENTS | 8 |
| PREFACE | 9 |
| HOW TO USE THIS BOOK | 10 |
| INDEX | 11 |
| MICROSOFT EXAMS | 15 |
|    CHAPTER 1: 70-412 - CONFIGURING ADVANCED WINDOWS SERVER 2012 SERVICES | 16 |
|       *Exam Guide* | *16* |
|       *Sample Practice Test for 70-412* | *18* |
|    CHAPTER 2: 70-461 - MCSA QUERYING MICROSOFT SQL SERVER 2012/2014 | 33 |
|       *Exam Guide* | *33* |
|       *Sample Practice Test for 70-461* | *33* |
|    CHAPTER 3: 70-480 - MCSD PROGRAMMING IN HTML5 WITH JAVASCRIPT AND CSS3 | 41 |
|       *Exam Guide* | *41* |
|       *Sample Practice Test for 70-480* | *42* |
|    CHAPTER 4: 70-483 - MCSD PROGRAMMING IN C# | 57 |
|       *Exam Guide* | *57* |
|       *Sample Practice Test for 70-483* | *58* |
|    CHAPTER 5: 70-486 - MCSD DEVELOPING ASP.NET MVC WEB APPLICATIONS | 69 |
|       *Exam Guide* | *69* |
|       *Sample Practice Test for 70-486* | *70* |
|    CHAPTER 6: 70-740 - INSTALLATION, STORAGE, AND COMPUTE WITH WINDOWS SERVER 2016 | 146 |
|       *Exam Guide* | *146* |
|       *Sample Practice Test for 70-740* | *147* |
|    CHAPTER 7: 70-742 - IDENTITY WITH WINDOWS SERVER 2016 | 155 |
|       *Exam Guide* | *155* |
|       *Sample Practice Test for 70-742* | *157* |
|    CHAPTER 8: 70-743 - UPGRADING YOUR SKILLS TO MCSA: WINDOWS SERVER 2016 | 170 |
|       *Exam Guide* | *170* |

*Sample Practice Test for 70-743* ........... *171*

## Chapter 9: 70-761 - Querying Data with Transact-SQL ........... 182
*Exam Guide* ........... *182*
*Sample Practice Test for 70-761* ........... *183*

## Chapter 10: 70-762 - Developing SQL Databases ........... 200
*Exam Guide* ........... *200*
*Sample Practice Test for 70-762* ........... *202*

## Chapter 11: 70-778 - Analyzing and Visualizing Data with Microsoft Power BI ........... 231
*Exam Guide* ........... *231*
*Sample Practice Test for 70-778* ........... *233*

## Chapter 12: 98-375 - HTML5 App Development Fundamentals ........... 241
*Exam Guide* ........... *241*
*Sample Practice Test for 98-375* ........... *247*

## Chapter 13: AI-100 - Designing and Implementing an Azure AI Solution ........... 255
*Exam Guide* ........... *255*
*Sample Practice Test for AI-100* ........... *258*

## Chapter 14: AZ-103 - Microsoft Azure Administrator ........... 268
*Exam Guide* ........... *268*
*Sample Practice Test for AZ-103* ........... *270*

## Chapter 15: AZ-104 - Microsoft Azure Administrator ........... 281
*Exam Guide* ........... *281*
*Sample Practice Test for AZ-104* ........... *289*

## Chapter 16: AZ-120 - Planning and Administering Microsoft Azure for SAP Workloads ........... 301
*Exam Guide* ........... *301*
*Sample Practice Test for AZ-120* ........... *309*

## Chapter 17: AZ-203 - Developing Solutions for Microsoft Azure ........... 329
*Exam Guide* ........... *329*
*Sample Practice Test for AZ-203* ........... *332*

## Chapter 18: AZ-204 - Developing Solutions for Microsoft Azure ........... 348
*Exam Guide* ........... *348*
*Sample Practice Test for AZ-204* ........... *354*

## Chapter 19: AZ-220 - Microsoft Azure IoT Developer ........... 375
*Exam Guide* ........... *375*
*Sample Practice Test for AZ-220* ........... *382*

## Chapter 20: AZ-300 - Microsoft Azure Architect Technologies ........... 393
*Exam Guide* ........... *393*
*Sample Practice Test for AZ-300* ........... *402*

## Chapter 21: AZ-301 - Microsoft Azure Architect Design ........... 418
*Exam Guide* ........... *418*
*Sample Practice Test for AZ-301* ........... *421*

## Chapter 22: AZ-303 - Microsoft Azure Architect Technologies (beta) ........... 437

*Exam Guide* .......... *437*
*Sample Practice Test for AZ-303* .......... *444*

## Chapter 23: AZ-400 - Microsoft Azure DevOps Solutions .......... 464
*Exam Guide* .......... *464*
*Sample Practice Test for AZ-400* .......... *467*

## Chapter 24: AZ-500 - Microsoft Azure Security Technologies .......... 477
*Exam Guide* .......... *477*
*Sample Practice Test for AZ-500* .......... *480*

## Chapter 25: AZ-900 - Microsoft Azure Fundamentals .......... 496
*Exam Guide* .......... *496*
*Sample Practice Test for AZ-900* .......... *498*

## Chapter 26: DP-100 - Designing and Implementing a Data Science Solution on Azure .......... 510
*Exam Guide* .......... *510*
*Sample Practice Test for DP-100* .......... *512*

## Chapter 27: DP-200 - Implementing an Azure Data Solution .......... 521
*Exam Guide* .......... *521*
*Sample Practice Test for DP-200* .......... *523*

## Chapter 28: DP-201 - Designing an Azure Data Solution .......... 535
*Exam Guide* .......... *535*
*Sample Practice Test for DP-201* .......... *537*

## Chapter 29: MB-200 - Microsoft Power Platform + Dynamics 365 Core .......... 562
*Exam Guide* .......... *562*
*Sample Practice Test for MB-200* .......... *565*

## Chapter 30: MB-300 - Microsoft Dynamics 365: Core Finance and Operations .......... 572
*Exam Guide* .......... *572*
*Sample Practice Test for MB-300* .......... *576*

## Chapter 31: MB-310 - Microsoft Dynamics 365 Finance .......... 587
*Exam Guide* .......... *587*
*Sample Practice Test for MB-310* .......... *590*

## Chapter 32: MB-330 - Microsoft Dynamics 365 Supply Chain Management .......... 599
*Exam Guide* .......... *599*
*Sample Practice Test for MB-330* .......... *603*

## Chapter 33: MB-901 - Microsoft Dynamics 365 Fundamentals .......... 612
*Exam Guide* .......... *612*
*Sample Practice Test for MB-901* .......... *620*

## Chapter 34: MD-100 - Windows 10 .......... 629
*Exam Guide* .......... *629*
*Sample Practice Test for MD-100* .......... *632*

## Chapter 35: MD-101 - Managing Modern Desktops .......... 649
*Exam Guide* .......... *649*
*Sample Practice Test for MD-101* .......... *651*

Chapter 36: MS-100 - Microsoft 365 Identity and Services ................................................... 667
   *Exam Guide* .................................................................................................................. 667
   *Sample Practice Test for MS-100* .................................................................................. 669
Chapter 37: MS-101 - Microsoft 365 Mobility and Security ................................................. 678
   *Exam Guide* .................................................................................................................. 678
   *Sample Practice Test for MS-101* .................................................................................. 680
Chapter 38: MS-201 - Implementing a Hybrid and Secure Messaging Platform ............... 688
   *Exam Guide* .................................................................................................................. 688
   *Sample Practice Test for MS-201* .................................................................................. 690
Chapter 39: MS-300 - Deploying Microsoft 365 Teamwork ................................................. 701
   *Exam Guide* .................................................................................................................. 701
   *Sample Practice Test for MS-300* .................................................................................. 703
Chapter 40: MS-301 - Deploying SharePoint Server Hybrid .............................................. 723
   *Exam Guide* .................................................................................................................. 723
   *Sample Practice Test for MS-301* .................................................................................. 725
Chapter 41: MS-500 - Microsoft 365 Security Administration ............................................ 745
   *Exam Guide* .................................................................................................................. 745
   *Sample Practice Test for MS-500* .................................................................................. 747
Chapter 42: MS-700 - Managing Microsoft Teams .............................................................. 767
   *Exam Guide* .................................................................................................................. 767
   *Sample Practice Test for MS-700* .................................................................................. 774
Chapter 43: MS-900 - Microsoft 365 Fundamentals ............................................................ 779
   *Exam Guide* .................................................................................................................. 779
   *Sample Practice Test for MS-900* .................................................................................. 781
Chapter 44: PL-900 - Microsoft Power Platform Fundamentals ........................................ 790
   *Exam Guide* .................................................................................................................. 790
   *Sample Practice Test for PL-900* .................................................................................. 797

# SUMMARY ............................................................................................................................. 807

# ABOUT THE AUTHOR ......................................................................................................... 808

# APPENDIX ............................................................................................................................. 809

# Microsoft Exams

**Microsoft Certified Professionals** form a unique community with Microsoft as its hub.Individuals can take advantage of the networking and professional growth opportunities which according to the research is a much more poignant aspect of the value of certification that was previously envisioned. Microsoft also recognizes that the community is an important way to engage with its customer base.

The **Certification-questions.com team** has worked directly with industry experts to provide you with the actual questions and answers from **the latest versions of the Microsoft exam**. Practice questions are proven to be the most effectively way of preparing for certification exams.

Microsoft certified professionals are certified individuals who specialize in Microsoft information technology programs and applications. Experts in the field of Microsoft programs, they focus their technical support skills in various areas, ranging from operating systems, cloud solutions to Web development.

With a certificate, your value increases when you apply for jobs. According to Microsoft your chances of getting **hired increases 5 times**. According to Microsoft, **86% of hiring managers indicate that they prefer job applicants having an IT certificate**. And Microsoft certification is a preference over some unknown computer training institutes' certificates. Eight out of ten Hiring Managers wish to verify the certificates provided by job applicants. Further, according to Microsoft, 64% of IT managers prefer Microsoft certificates to other certificates. Certification, training, and experience are the three main areas that provide better recognition to a person when it comes to promotions and incentives.

We offers an online service that allows students to study through tests questions. The Simulator is built to reflect the final exam structure: It is an excellent study material as it offers the ability to run an online actual exam. Every question is also associated with the solution and each solution is explained in detail.

# Chapter 1: 70-412 - Configuring Advanced Windows Server 2012 Services

## Exam Guide

Configuring Advanced Windows Server 2012 Services 70-412 Exam:

Configuring Advanced Windows Server 2012 Services 70-412 Exam measures your ability to accomplish technical tasks like configuring and manage high availability configure file and storage solutions and failover cluster deployment guide. 70-412 exam is the third exam of a series of three exams that test the skills and knowledge necessary to administer a Windows Server 2012 infrastructure in an enterprise environment. IT Professionals, MCS Expert, and IT Managers usually hold or pursue this certification and you can expect the same job role after completion of this certification.

70-412 Exam topics:

Candidates must know the exam topics before they start of preparation. Because it will really help them in hitting the core. Our **70-412 dumps** will include the following topics:

- Configure and manage high-availability 15-20%
- Configure file and storage solution 15-20%
- Implement business continuity and disaster recovery 15-20%
- Configure Network Services 15-20%
- Configure the Active Directory Infrastructure 15-20%

Certification Path:

The Microsoft MCSA Windows Server 2012 Certification includes only one 70-412 Exam.

Who should take the 70-412 exam:

The Configuring Advanced Windows Server 2012 Services 70-412 Exam certification is an internationally-recognized validation that identifies persons who earn it as possessing skilled in Microsoft Configuring Advanced Windows Server 2012 Services. If a candidate wants significant improvement in career growth needs enhanced knowledge, skills, and talents. The Configuring

Advanced Windows Server 2012 Services 70-412 Exam certification provides proof of this advanced knowledge and skill. If a candidate has knowledge of associated technologies and skills that are required to pass Configuring Advanced Windows Server 2012 Services 70-412 Exam then he should take this exam.

How to study the 70-412 Exam:

Certification-questions.com expert team recommends you to prepare some notes on these topics along with it don't forget to practice Microsoft 70-412 Exam dumps which been written by our expert team, Both these will help you a lot to clear this exam with good marks.

How much 70-412 Exam Cost:

The price of the 70-412 exam is $165 USD.

How to book the 70-412 Exam:

These are following steps for registering the 70-412 exam.
Step 1: Visit to Visit to Microsoft Exam Registration
Step 2: Signup/Login to MICROSOFT account
Step 3: Search for MICROSOFT 70-412 Certifications Exam
Step 4: Select Date and Center of examination and confirm with payment value of 165$

What is the duration of the 70-412 Exam:

- Format: Multiple choices, multiple answers
- Length of Examination: 120 minutes
- Number of Questions: 45-55
- Passing Score: 700/1000

   The benefit in Obtaining the 70-412 Exam Certification:

- After completion of MCSA Windows Server 2012 certification Candidates receive official confirmation from Microsoft that you are now fully certified in their chosen field. This can be now added to their CV, cover letters and job applications.
- When Candidates applying for a job or looking to promotion in their current position, an MCSA Windows Server 2012 certification in the field in which Candidates are applying will put you at the top of the list and make them a desirable candidate for employers.
- Candidates will get in-depth knowledge by completing the courses along with the access to revision materials for 6 months upon completion means they will have a wider skill set when it comes to the various technologies and systems than an uncertified professional. Certified Professional in this particular skill set is 74% more efficient when it comes to completing their tasks in a timely well-executed manner.

- Organization owners invest a lot in their employees when it comes to their training with the goal of making them quicker, more efficient, and more knowledgeable about their role. Certified Professional will reduce the time he spends on tasks, meaning he can get more done this could help reduce company downtime when repairing faults on a system or fixing hardware problems.
- Becoming MCSA Windows Server 2012 means one thing you are worth more to the company and therefore more to yourself in the form of an upgraded pay package. On average an MCSA Windows Server 2012 member of staff is estimated to be worth 30% more to a company than their uncertified professionals.

Difficulty in writing 70-412 Exam:

Microsoft 70-412 exam help Candidates in developing their professionals and academic career and It is a very tough task to pass Microsoft 70-412 exam for those Candidates who have not done hard work and get some relevant Microsoft 70-412 exam preparation material. There are many peoples have passed Microsoft 70-412 exam by following these three things such as look for the latest **Microsoft 70-412 exam dumps**, get relevant **Microsoft 70-412 exam dumps** and develop their knowledge about Microsoft 70-412 exam new questions. At the same time, it can also stress out some people as they found passing Microsoft 70-412 exam a tough task. It is just a wrong assumption as many of the peoples have passed Microsoft 70-412 exam questions. All you have to do is to work hard, get some relevant Microsoft 70-412 exam preparation material and go thoroughly from them. Certification-questions is here to help you with this problem. We have the relevant Microsoft 70-412 exam preparation material which are providing the latest Microsoft 70-412 exam questions with the detailed view of every Microsoft 70-412 exam topic. Certification-questions offered a Microsoft 70-412 exam dumps which are more than enough to pass the Microsoft 70-412 exam questions. We are providing all thing such as **Microsoft 70-412 exam dumps**, Microsoft 70-412 practice test, and Microsoft 70-412 pdf dumps that will help the candidate to pass the exam with good grades.

For more info visit::

70-412 Exam Reference

# Sample Practice Test for 70-412

**Question: 1** *One Answer Is Right*

Your company recently deployed a new Active Directory forest named contoso.com. The first domain controller in the forest runs Windows Server 2012 R2. You need to identify the time-to-live (TTL) value for domain referrals to the NETLOGON and SYSVOL shared folders. Which tool should you use?

**Answers:**

**A)** Ultrasound

**B)** Replmon

**C)** Dfsdiag

**D)** Frsutil

**Solution:** C

**Explanation:**

Explanation: DFSDIAG can check your configuration in five different ways: - Checking referral responses (DFSDIAG /TestReferral) - Checking domain controller configuration - Checking site associations - Checking namespace server configuration - Checking individual namespace configuration and integrity References: https://blogs.technet.microsoft.com/josebda/2009/07/15/five-ways-to-check-your-dfs-namespaces-dfs-n-configuration-with-the-dfsdiag-exe-tool/

**Question: 2** *Multiple Answers Are Right*

HOTSPOT Your network contains an Active Directory forest named contoso.com that contains a single domain. The forest contains three sites named Site1, Site2, and Site3. Domain controllers run either Windows Server 2008 R2 or Windows Server 2012 R2. Each site contains two domain controllers. Site1 and Site2 contain a global catalog server. You need to create a new site link between Site1 and Site2. The solution must ensure that the site link supports the replication of all the naming contexts. From which node should you create the site link? To answer, select the appropriate node in the answer area. Hot Area:

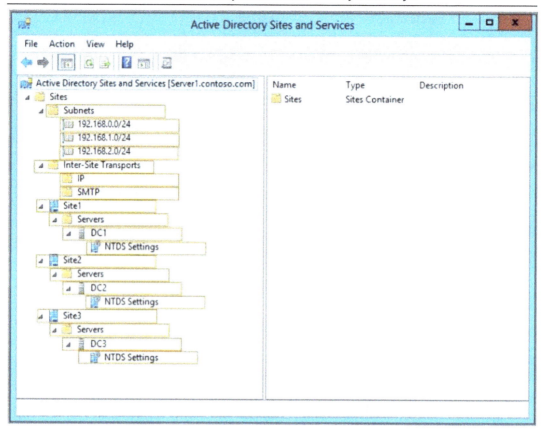

**Answers:**

A)

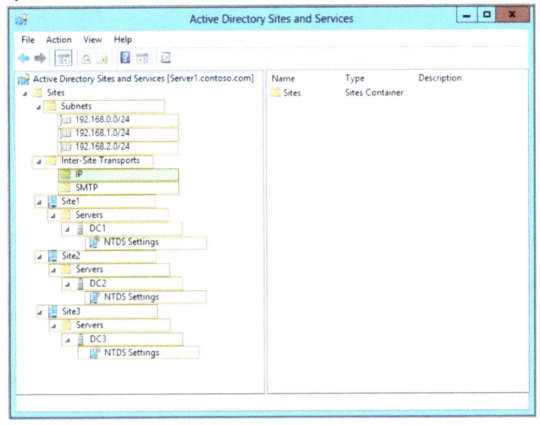

**Solution:** A

**Explanation:**

Explanation: Create a Site Link To create a site link - Open Active Directory Sites and Services. To open Active Directory Sites and Services, click Start, click Administrative Tools, and then click Active Directory Sites and Services. To open Active Directory Sites and Services in Windows Server® 2012, click Start, type dssite.msc. - In the console tree, right-click the intersite transport protocol that you want the site link to use. Use the IP intersite transport unless your network has remote sites where network connectivity is intermittent or end-to-end IP connectivity is not available. Simple Mail Transfer Protocol (SMTP) replication has restrictions that do not apply to IP replication.

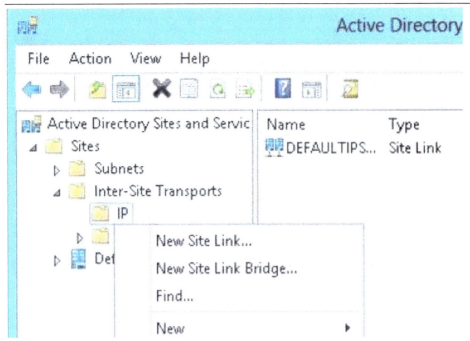

Reference: Create a Site Link p://technet.microsoft.com/en-us/library/cc731294.aspx

**Question: 3** *One Answer Is Right*

Your network contains two Active Directory forests named contoso.com and adatum.com. Contoso.com contains one domain. Adatum.com contains a child domain named child.adatum.com. Contoso.com has a one-way forest trust to adatum.com. Selective authentication is enabled on the forest trust. Several user accounts are migrated from child.adatum.com to adatum.com. Users report that after the migration, they fail to access resources in contoso.com. The users successfully accessed the resources in contoso.com before the accounts were migrated. You need to ensure that the migrated users can access the resources in contoso.com. What should you do?

**Answers:**

A) Replace the existing forest trust with an external trust.

B) Run netdom and specify the /quarantine attribute.

C) Disable SID filtering on the existing forest trust.

D) Disable selective authentication on the existing forest trust.

**Solution:** C

**Explanation:**

Explanation: Security Considerations for Trusts Need to gain access to the resources in contoso.com Disabling SID Filter Quarantining on External Trusts Although it reduces the security of your forest (and is therefore not recommended), you can disable SID filter quarantining for an external trust by using the Netdom.exe tool. You should consider disabling SID filter quarantining only in the following situations: * Users have been migrated to the trusted domain with their SID histories preserved, and you want to grant them access to resources in the trusting domain based on the SID history attribute. Etc. Incorrect Answers: B. Enables administrators to manage Active Directory domains and trust relationships from the command prompt, /quarantine Sets or clears the domain quarantine. D. Selective authentication over a forest trust restricts access to only those users in a trusted forest who have been explicitly given authentication permissions to computer objects (resource computers) that reside in the trusting forest. References: Security Considerations for Trusts https://technet.microsoft.com/en-us/library/cc755321(v=ws.10).aspx

**Question: 4** *Multiple Answers Are Right*

HOTSPOT Your network contains an Active Directory domain named contoso.com. The domain contains domain controllers that run either Windows Server 2003, Windows Server 2008 R2, or Windows Server 2012 R2. You plan to implement a new Active Directory forest. The new forest will be used for testing and will be isolated from the production network. In the test network, you deploy a server named Server1 that runs Windows Server 2012 R2. You need to configure Server1 as a new domain controller in a new forest named contoso.test. The solution must meet the following requirements: - The functional level of the forest and of the domain must be the same as that of contoso.com. - Server1 must provide name resolution services for contoso.test. What should you do? To answer, configure the appropriate options in the answer area. Hot Area:

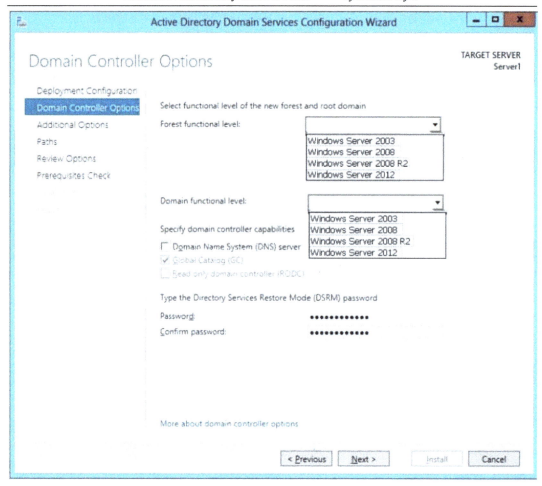

**Answers:**

A)

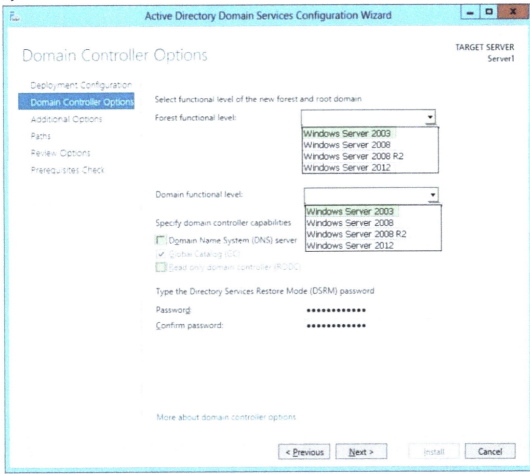

**Solution:** A

**Explanation:**

Explanation: Set the forest function level and the Domain functional level both to Windows Server 2003. Also check Domain Name (DNS) server. Note: * When you deploy AD DS, set the domain and forest functional levels to the highest value that your environment can support. This way, you can use as many AD DS features as possible. For example, if you are sure that you will never add domain controllers that run Windows Server 2003 to the domain or forest, select the Windows Server 2008 functional level during the deployment process. However, if you might retain or add domain controllers that run Windows Server 2003, select the Windows Server 2003 functional level. * You can set the domain functional level to a value that is higher than the forest functional level. For example, if the forest functional level is Windows Server

2003, you can set the domain functional level to Windows Server 2003 or higher. Reference: Understanding Active Directory Domain Services (AD DS) Functional Levels

**Question: 5** *One Answer Is Right*

Your network contains an Active Directory forest named adatum.com. The forest contains a single domain. The domain contains four servers. The servers are configured as shown in the following table.

| Server name | Configuration | Operating system |
| --- | --- | --- |
| DC1 | • Global catalog server<br>• Domain controller<br>• Schema master<br>• DNS server | Windows Server 2003 R2 |
| DC2 | • Domain controller<br>• PDC emulator<br>• DHCP server<br>• DNS server | Windows Server 2003 R2 |
| DC3 | • Infrastructure master<br>• Global catalog server<br>• Domain controller<br>• WINS server | Windows Server 2008 R2 |
| Server1 | • Member server<br>• WINS server<br>• DNS server | Windows Server 2003 R2 |

You need to update the schema to support a domain controller that will run Windows Server 2012 R2. On which server should you run adprep.exe?

**Answers:**

**A)** Server1

**B)** DC3

**C)** DC2

**D)** DC1

**Solution:** B

**Explanation:**

Explanation: We must use the Windows Server 2008 R2 Server. Upgrade Domain Controllers to Windows Server 2012 R2 and Windows Server 2012 You can use adprep.exe on domain controllers that run 64-bit versions of Windows Server 2008 or Windows Server 2008 R2 to upgrade to Windows Server 2012. You cannot upgrade domain controllers that run Windows Server 2003 or 32-bit versions of Windows Server 2008. To replace them, install domain controllers that run a later version of Windows Server in the domain, and then remove the domain controllers that Windows Server 2003. Reference: Upgrade Domain Controllers to Windows Server 2012 R2 and Windows Server 2012, Supported in-place upgrade paths. http://technet.microsoft.com/en-us/library/hh994618.aspx#BKMK_UpgradePaths

**Question: 6** *Multiple Answers Are Right*

HOTSPOT Your network contains three Active Directory forests. The forests are configured as shown in the following table.

| Forest name | Forest functional level |
| --- | --- |
| Contoso.com | Windows Server 2012 R2 |
| Division1.contoso.com | Windows Server 2012 R2 |
| Division2.contoso.com | Windows Server 2012 R2 |

A two-way forest trust exists between contoso.com and divisionl.contoso.com. A two-way forest trust also exists between contoso.com and division2.contoso.com. You plan to create a one-way forest trust from divisionl.contoso.com to division2.contoso.com. You need to ensure that any cross-forest authentication requests are sent to the domain controllers in the appropriate forest after the trust is created. How should you configure the existing forest trust settings? In the table below, identify which configuration must be performed in each forest. Make only one selection in each column. Each correct selection is worth one point. Hot Area:

|  | Division1.contoso.com | Division2.contoso.com |
|---|---|---|
| Add division1.contoso.com as a name suffix routing entry. | ○ | ○ |
| Add division2.contoso.com as a name suffix routing entry. | ○ | ○ |
| Add division1.contoso.com as an exclusion to the name suffix routing entry of contoso.com. | ○ | ○ |
| Add division2.contoso.com as an exclusion to the name suffix routing entry of contoso.com. | ○ | ○ |

**Answers:**

**A)**

|  | Division1.contoso.com | Division2.contoso.com |
|---|---|---|
| Add division1.contoso.com as a name suffix routing entry. | ○ | ● |
| Add division2.contoso.com as a name suffix routing entry. | ○ | ○ |
| Add division1.contoso.com as an exclusion to the name suffix routing entry of contoso.com. | ○ | ○ |
| Add division2.contoso.com as an exclusion to the name suffix routing entry of contoso.com. | ● | ○ |

**Solution:** A

**Explanation:**

Explanation: There will be a one-way forest trust from division1.contoso.com to division2.contoso.com Division1 trusts Division2. Division2 must be able to access resources in Division1. Division1 should not be able to access resources in Division2.

**Question: 7** *One Answer Is Right*

Your network contains an Active Directory forest named contoso.com. The forest contains three domains. All domain controllers run Windows Server 2012 R2. The forest has a two-way realm trust to a Kerberos realm named adatum.com. You discover that users in adatum.com can only access resources in the root domain of contoso.com. You need to ensure that the adatum.com users can access the resources in all of the domains in the forest. What should you do in the forest?

**Answers:**

**A)** Delete the realm trust and create a forest trust.

**B)** Delete the realm trust and create three external trusts.

**C)** Modify the incoming realm trust.

**D)** Modify the outgoing realm trust.

**Solution:** D

**Explanation:**

Explanation: * A one-way, outgoing realm trust allows resources in your Windows Server domain (the domain that you are logged on to at the time that you run the New Trust Wizard) to be accessed by users in the Kerberos realm. * You can establish a realm trust between any non-Windows Kerberos version 5 (V5) realm and an Active Directory domain. This trust relationship allows cross-platform interoperability with security services that are based on other versions of the Kerberos V5 protocol, for example, UNIX and MIT implementations. Realm trusts can switch from nontransitive to transitive and back. Realm trusts can also be either one-way or two- way. Reference: Create a One-Way, Outgoing, Realm Trust

**Question: 8** *One Answer Is Right*

Your network contains an Active Directory forest named contoso.com. The forest contains two domains named contoso.com and childl.contoso.com. The domains contain three domain controllers. The domain controllers are configured as shown in the following table.

| Domain controller name | Operating system | Configuration |
|---|---|---|
| dc1.contoso.com | Windows Server 2008 R2 Service Pack 1 (SP1) | Schema master Domain naming master |
| dc10.child1.contoso.com | Windows Server 2012 R2 | PDC emulator |
| dc11.child1.contoso.com | Windows Server 2008 R2 Service Pack 1 (SP1) | RID master |

You need to ensure that the KDC support for claims, compound authentication, and kerberos armoring setting is enforced in the child1.contoso.com domain. Which two actions should you perform? (Each correct answer presents part of the solution. Choose two.)

**Answers:**

**A)** Upgrade DC1 to Windows Server 2012 R2.

**B)** Upgrade DC11 to Windows Server 2012 R2.

**C)** Raise the domain functional level of childl.contoso.com.

**D)** Raise the domain functional level of contoso.com.

**E)** Raise the forest functional level of contoso.com.

**Solution:** A, D

**Explanation:**

Explanation: The root domain in the forest must be at Windows Server 2012 level. First upgrade DC1 to this level (A), then raise the contoso.com domain functional level to Windows Server 2012 (D). (A) To support resources that use claims-based access control, the principal's domains will need to be running one of the following: - All Windows Server 2012 domain controllers - Sufficient Windows Server 2012 domain controllers to handle all the Windows 8 device authentication requests - Sufficient Windows Server 2012 domain controllers to handle all the Windows Server 2012 resource protocol transition requests to support non-Windows 8 devices. References: What's New in Kerberos Authentication https://technet.microsoft.com/en-us/library/hh831747.aspx.

**Question: 9** *One Answer Is Right*

Your network contains an Active Directory domain named contoso.com. All domain controllers run Windows Server 2012 R2. The domain contains two domain controllers. The domain controllers are configured as shown in the following table.

| Domain controller name | Site name | Configuration |
|---|---|---|
| DC1 | Main | Domain controller |
| DC10 | Branch | Read-only domain controller (RODC) |

You configure a user named User1 as a delegated administrator of DC10. You need to ensure that User1 can log on to DC10 if the network link between the Main site and the Branch site fails. What should you do?

**Answers:**

A) Add User1 to the Domain Admins group.

B) On DC10, modify the User Rights Assignment in Local Policies.

C) Run repadmin and specify the /prp parameter.

D) On DC10, run ntdsutil and configure the settings in the Roles context.

E) Run repadmin and specify /replsingleobject parameter.

F) On DC1, modify the User Rights Assignment in Default Controllers Group Policy object (GPO).

**Solution:** C

**Explanation:**

Explanation: repadmin /prp will allow the password caching of the local administrator to the RODC. This command lists and modifies the Password Replication Policy (PRP) for read-only domain controllers (RODCs). References: RODC Administration
https://technet.microsoft.com/en-us/library/cc755310%28v=ws.10%29.aspx

**Question: 10** *One Answer Is Right*

Your company has offices in Montreal, New York, and Amsterdam. The network contains an Active Directory forest named contoso.com. An Active Directory site exists for each office. All of the sites connect to each other by using the DEFAULTIPSITELINK site link. You need to ensure that only between 20:00 and 08:00, the domain controllers in the Montreal office replicate the Active Directory changes to the domain controllers in the Amsterdam office. The solution must ensure that the domain controllers in the Montreal and the New York offices can replicate the Active Directory changes any time of day. What should you do?

**Answers:**

**A)** Create a new site link that contains Montreal and Amsterdam. Remove Amsterdam from DEFAULTIPSITE1INK. Modify the schedule of DEFAULTIPSITELINK.

**B)** Create a new site link that contains Montreal and Amsterdam. Create a new site link bridge. Modify the schedule of DEFAULTIPSITELINK.

**C)** Create a new site link that contains Montreal and Amsterdam. Remove Amsterdam from DEFAULTIPSITELINK. Modify the schedule of the new site link.

**D)** Create a new site link that contains Montreal and Amsterdam. Create a new site link bridge. Modify the schedule of the new site link.

**Solution:** C

**Explanation:**

Explanation: We create a new site link between Montreal and Amsterdam and schedule it only between 20:00 and 08:00. To ensure that traffic between Montreal and Amsterdam only occurs at this time we also remove Amsterdam from the DEFAULTIPSITELINK. Reference: How Active Directory Replication Topology Works http://technet.microsoft.com/en-us/library/cc755994(v=ws.10).aspx

# Chapter 2: 70-461 - MCSA Querying Microsoft SQL Server 2012/2014

## Exam Guide

70-461 - MCSA Querying Microsoft SQL Server 2012/2014:

The **70-461 exam** is part of the new SQL Server 2012 certification paths leading towards MCSA SQL Server 2012, MCSE SQL Server 2012 and MCSE Business Intelligence. The MCSA certification is the base for the higher level MCSE certifications.

Our 70-461 dumps will include those topics::

- Create database objects (20-25%)
- Work with data (25-30%)
- Modify data (20-25%)
- Troubleshoot and optimize (25-30%)

For more info visit: Microsoft Official 70-461 Exam Reference

High level topics covered by our practice test:

- Create database objects - CREATE, ALTER, DROP, Trigger, Views..
- Work with data - SELECT, sub queries, data types
- Modify data - stored procedures, INSERT, UPDATE, DELETE
- Troubleshoot and Optimize Queries - transactions, indexes, error handling

## Sample Practice Test for 70-461

**Question: 1** *One Answer Is Right*

You develop a Microsoft SQL Server server database that supports an application. The application contains a table that has the following definition: CREATE TABLE Inventory (ItemID int NOT NULL PRIMARY KEY, ItemsInStore int NOT NULL, ItemsInWarehouse int NOT NULL) You need to create a computed column that returns the sum total of the ItemsInStore and ItemsInWarehouse values for each row. Which Transact-SQL statement should you use?

**Answers:**

**A)** ALTER TABLE Inventory ADD TotalItems AS ItemsInStore + ItemsInWarehouse

**B)** ALTER TABLE Inventory ADD ItemsInStore - ItemsInWarehouse = TotalItemss

**C)** ALTER TABLEInventory ADD TotalItems = ItemsInStore + ItemsInWarehouse

**D)** ALTER TABLE Inventory ADD TotalItems AS SUM(ItemsInStore, ItemsInWarehouse);

**Solution:** A

**Explanation:**

Explanation: Reference: http://technet.microsoft.com/en-us/library/ms190273.aspx

**Question: 2** *One Answer Is Right*

You develop a Microsoft SQL Server database. You create a view from the Orders and OrderDetails tables by using the following definition.

```
CREATE VIEW vOrders
WITH SCHEMABINDING
AS
SELECT o.ProductID,
    o.OrderDate,
    SUM(od.UnitPrice * od.OrderQty) AS Amount
FROM OrderDetails AS od INNER JOIN
    Orders AS o ON od.OrderID = o.OrderID
WHERE od.SalesOrderID = o.SalesOrderID
GROUP BY o.OrderDate, o.ProductID
GO
```

You need to improve the performance of the view by persisting data to disk. What should you do?

**Answers:**

**A)** Create anINSTEAD OFtrigger on the view.

**B)** Create anAFTERtrigger on the view.

**C)** Modify the view to use theWITH VIEW_METADATAclause.

**D)** Create a clustered index on the view.

**Solution:** D

**Explanation:**

Explanation: Reference: http://msdn.microsoft.com/en-us/library/ms188783.aspx

**Question: 3** *One Answer Is Right*

Note: This question is part of a series of questions that use the same set of answer choices. An answer choice may be correct for more than one question in the series. You develop a database for a travel application. You need to design tables and other database objects. You create the Airline_Schedules table. You need to store the departure and arrival dates and times of flights along with time zone information. What should you do?

**Answers:**

**A)** Use the CAST function.

**B)** Use the DATE data type.

**C)** Use the FORMAT function.

**D)** Use an appropriate collation.

**E)** Use a user-defined table type.

**F)** Use the VARBINARY data type.

**G)** Use the DATETIME data type.

**H)** Use the DATETIME2 data type.

**I)** Use the DATETIMEOFFSET data type.

**J)** Use the TODATETIMEOFFSET function.

**Solution:** I

**Explanation:**

Explanation: Reference: http://msdn.microsoft.com/en-us/library/ff848733.aspx
http://msdn.microsoft.com/en-us/library/bb630289.aspx

**Question: 4** *One Answer Is Right*

Note: This question is part of a series of questions that use the same set of answer choices. An answer choice may be correct for more than one question in the series. You develop a database for a travel application. You need to design tables and other database objects. You create a stored procedure. You need to supply the stored procedure with multiple event names and their dates as parameters. What should you do?

**Answers:**

**A)** Use the CAST function.

**B)** Use the DATE data type.

**C)** Use the FORMAT function.

**D)** Use an appropriate collation.

**E)** Use a user-defined table type.

**F)** Use the VARBINARY data type.

**G)** Use the DATETIME data type.

**H)** Use the DATETIME2 data type.

**I)** Use the DATETIMEOFFSET data type.

**J)** Use the TODATETIMEOFFSET function.

**Solution: E**

**Question: 5** *One Answer Is Right*

You have a Microsoft SQL Server database that contains tables named Customers and Orders. The tables are related by a column named CustomerID. You need to create a query that meets the following requirements: - Returns the CustomerName for all customers and the OrderDate for any orders that they have placed. - Results must include customers who have not placed any orders. Which Transact-SQL query should you use?

**Answers:**

**A)** SELECT CustomerName, OrderDate FROM Customers RIGHT OUTER JOIN Orders ON Customers.CustomerID = Orders.CustomerID

**B)** SELECT CustomerName, OrderDate FROM Customers JOIN Orders ON Customers.CustomerID = Orders.CustomerID

**C)** SELECT CustomerName, OrderDate FROM Customers CROSS JOIN Orders ON Customers.CustomerID = Orders.CustomerID

**D)** SELECT CustomerName, OrderDate FROM Customers LEFT OUTER JOIN Orders ON Customers.CustomerID = Orders.CustomerID

**Solution:** D

**Explanation:**

Explanation: Reference:http://msdn.microsoft.com/en-us/library/ms177634.aspx

**Question: 6** *One Answer Is Right*

You create a stored procedure that will update multiple tables within a transaction. You need to ensure that if the stored procedure raises a run-time error, the entire transaction is terminated and rolled back. Which Transact-SQL statement should you include at the beginning of the stored procedure?

**Answers:**

**A)** SET XACT_ABORT ON

**B)** SET ARITHABORT ON

**C)** TRY

**D)** BEGIN

**E)** SET ARITHABORT OFF

**F)** SET XACT_ABORT OFF

**Solution:** A

**Explanation:**

Explanation: Reference: http://msdn.microsoft.com/en-us/library/ms190306.aspx
http://msdn.microsoft.com/en-us/library/ms188792.aspx

**Question: 7** *One Answer Is Right*

Your database contains two tables named DomesticSalesOrders and InternationalSalesOrders. Both tables contain more than 100 million rows. Each table has a Primary Key column named SalesOrderId. The data in the two tables is distinct from one another. Business users want a report that includes aggregate information about the total number of global sales and total sales amounts. You need to ensure that your query executes in the minimum possible time. Which query should you use?

**Answers:**

**A)** SELECT COUNT(*) AS NumberOfSales, SUM(SalesAmount) AS TotalSalesAmount FROM ( SELECT SalesOrderId, SalesAmount FROM DomesticSalesOrders UNION ALL SELECT SalesOrderId, SalesAmount FROM InternationalSalesOrders ) AS p

**B)** SELECT COUNT(*) AS NumberOfSales, SUM(SalesAmount) AS TotalSalesAmount FROM ( SELECT SalesOrderId, SalesAmount FROM DomesticSalesOrders UNION SELECT SalesOrderId, SalesAmount FROM InternationalSalesOrders ) AS p

**C)** SELECT COUNT(*) AS NumberOfSales, SUM(SalesAmount) AS TotalSalesAmount FROM DomesticSalesOrders UNION SELECT COUNT(*) AS NumberOfSales, SUM(SalesAmount) AS TotalSalesAmount FROM InternationalSalesOrders

**D)** SELECT COUNT(*) AS NumberOfSales, SUM(SalesAmount) AS TotalSalesAmount FROM DomesticSalesOrders UNION ALL SELECT COUNT(*) AS NumberOfSales, SUM(SalesAmount) AS TotalSalesAmount FROM InternationalSalesOrders

**Solution:** A

**Explanation:**

Explanation: Reference: http://msdn.microsoft.com/en-us/library/ms180026.aspx
http://blog.sqlauthority.com/2009/03/11/sql-server-difference-between-union-vs-union-all-optimalperformance-comparison/

**Question: 8** *One Answer Is Right*

You use a Microsoft SQL Server database. You want to create a table to store Microsoft Word documents. You need to ensure that the documents must only be accessible via Transact-SQL queries. Which Transact-SQL statement should you use?

**Answers:**

**A)** CREATE TABLE DocumentStore ( [Id] INT NOT NULL PRIMARY KEY, [Document] VARBINARY(MAX) NULL ) GO

**B)** CREATE TABLE DocumentStore ( [Id] hierarchyid, [Document] NVARCHAR NOT NULL ) GO

**C)** CREATE TABLE DocumentStore AS FileTable

**D)** CREATE TABLE DocumentStore ( [Id] [uniqueidentifier] ROWGUIDCOL NOT NULL UNIQUE, [Document] VARBINARY(MAX) FILESTREAM NULL ) GO

**Solution:** A

**Explanation:**

Explanation: Reference: http://msdn.microsoft.com/en-us/library/gg471497.aspx
http://msdn.microsoft.com/en-us/library/ff929144.aspx

**Question: 9** *One Answer Is Right*

You administer a Microsoft SQL Server database that contains a table named OrderDetail. You discover that the NCI_OrderDetail_CustomerID non-clustered index is fragmented. You need to reduce fragmentation. You need to achieve this goal without taking the index offline. Which Transact-SQL batch should you use?

**Answers:**

**A)** CREATE INDEX NCI_OrderDetail_CustomerID ON OrderDetail.CustomerID WITH DROP EXISTING

**B)** ALTER INDEX NCI_OrderDetail_CustomerID ON OrderDetail.CustomerID REORGANIZE

**C)** ALTER INDEX ALL ON OrderDetail REBUILD

**D)** ALTER INDEX NCI_OrderDetail_CustomerID ON OrderDetail.CustomerID REBUILD

**Solution:** B

**Explanation:**

Explanation: Reference: http://msdn.microsoft.com/en-us/library/ms188388.aspx

**Question: 10** *One Answer Is Right*

You develop a Microsoft SQL Server database. The database is used by two web applications that access a table named Products. You want to create an object that will prevent the applications from accessing the table directly while still providing access to the required data. You need to ensure that the following requirements are met: - Future modifications to the table definition will not affect the applications' ability to access data. - The new object can accommodate data retrieval and data modification. You need to achieve this goal by using the minimum amount of changes to the existing applications. What should you create for each application?

**Answers:**

**A)** views

**B)** table partitions

**C)** table-valued functions

**D)** stored procedures

**Solution:** A

# Chapter 3: 70-480 - MCSD Programming in HTML5 with JavaScript and CSS3

## Exam Guide

70-480 - MCSD Programming in HTML5 with JavaScript and CSS3: Background to the test:

As you probably know, the 70-480 exam forms part of the MCSD certification path for web developers. That pathway consists of 3 exams; an HTML exam, MVC exam and finally a web services exam. Don't be fooled into thinking that the HTML exam is any easier than the others because it isn't. The exam focus on the user interface side of web development using HTML for structure, CSS for styles and Javascript for interactivity. You must be competent in each of these areas before attempting the exam for yourself. If you're a veteran programmer who already uses MVC (or something similar) then you'll be familiar with most aspects of HTML, CSS and Javascript. This alone will give you the basis for this exam but you'll need to push a little deeper into HTML5 specifics, Javascript classes/inheritance and any CSS3 peculiarities.

Our 70-480 dumps will include those topics::

- Implement and manipulate document structures and objects (24%)
- Implement program flow (25%)
- Access and secure data (26%)
- Use CSS3 in applications (25%)

For more info visit: Microsoft Official 70-480 Exam Reference

Topics::

The topics for 70-480 are split into three major sections: HTML, CSS and Javascript. I found that the exam was evenly split between all three areas, with many questions combining skills between these three areas. For example, you might see a question asking you to modify an elements style using JQuery. To answer that you'd need to understand JQuery (javascript) to modify the style but also the CSS style properties that you need to include as parameters to the method call.

Our story::

Passing the Microsoft70-480 examhas never been faster or easier, now with actual questions and answers, without the messy 70-480 brain dumps that are frequently incorrect. Certification-questions.com Unlimited Access Exams are not only the cheaper way to pass without resorting to **70-480 dumps**, but at only affordable you get access to ALL of the exams from every certification vendor.

What you will find at Certification-questions.com are the latest Microsoft **70-480 dumps** or an Microsoft 70-480 lab. You will find the most advanced, correct and guaranteed Microsoft70-480 practice questionsavailable to man. Simply put, MCSD Programming in HTML5 with JavaScript and CSS3 sample questions of the real exams are the only thing that can guarantee you are ready for your Microsoft 70-480 simulation questions on test day.

# Sample Practice Test for 70-480

**Question: 1** One Answer Is Right

You are developing a customer contact form that will be displayed on a page of a company's website. The page collects information about the customer. If a customer enters a value before submitting the form, it must be a valid email address. You need to ensure that the data validation requirement is met. What should you use?

**Answers:**

**A)**

**B)**

**C)** <

**D)**

**Solution:** D

**Explanation:**

Explanation: The is used for input fields that should contain an e-mail address. Depending on browser support, the e-mail address can be automatically validated when submitted. Some smartphones recognize the email type, and adds ".com" to the keyboard to match email input. Example:

E-mail:

Reference: http://www.w3schools.com/html/html5_form_input_types.asp

**Question: 2** *Multiple Answers Are Right*

DRAG DROP You are developing a form that captures a user's email address by using HTML5 and jQuery. The form must capture the email address and return it as a query string parameter. The query string parameter must display the @ symbol that is used in the email address. You need to implement this functionality. How should you develop the form? (To answer, drag the appropriate code segment to the correct target or targets in the answer area. Each code segment may be used once, more than once, or not at all. You may need to drag the split bar between panes or scroll to view content.) Select and Place:

Code segments:

```
str=$("form").serialize();
str=decodeURIComponent(str);
str=$("form").contents.toString();
str=$("form").toLocaleString();
str=decodeURI(str);
```

Answer Area:

```
<!DOCTYPE html>
<html>
<head>
  <script src="http://code.jquery.com/jquery-latest.js"></script>
</head>
<body>
  <form>
    <input type="text" name="email"/>
    <input type="submit" value="Submit"/>
  </form>
  <script>
    $("form").submit(function () {
      var str;




      return true;
    });
  </script>
</body>
</html>
```

**Answers:**

**A)**

Code segments:
```
str=$("form").contents.toString();
str=$("form").toLocaleString();
str=decodeURI(str);
```

Answer Area:
```
<!DOCTYPE html>
<html>
<head>
    <script src="http://code.jquery.com/jquery-latest.js"></script>
</head>
<body>
    <form>
    <input type="text" name="email"/>
    <input type="submit" value="Submit"/>
    </form>
    <script>
        $("form").submit(function () {
        var str;

        str=$("form").serialize();

        str=decodeURIComponent(str);

        return true;
        });
    </script>
</body>
</html>
```

**Solution:** A

**Explanation:**

Explanation: * The serialize() method creates a URL encoded text string by serializing form values. You can select one or more form elements (like input and/or text area),or the form element itself. The serialized values can be used in the URL query string when making an AJAX request. Example: $("form").serialize(); * decodeURIComponent The decodeURIComponent() function decodes a URI component. Return Value:A String,representing the decoded URI Reference: jQuery serialize() Method http://www.w3schools.com/jquery/ajax_serialize.asp http://www.w3schools.com/jsref/jsref_encodeuri.asp

**Question: 3** *One Answer Is Right*

You are developing a web page that enables customers to upload documents to a web server. The page includes an HTML5 PROGRESS element named progressBar that displays information about the status of the upload. The page includes the following code. (Line numbers are included for reference only.)

```
01 var xhr = new XMLHttpRequest();
02 var progressBar = $("#progressBar");
03
04 function(e) {
05   if (e.lengthComputable) {
06     progressBar.value = (e.loaded / e.total) * 100;
07     progressBar.textContent = progressBar.value;
08 }};
```

An event handler must be attached to the request object to update the PROGRESS element on the page. You need to ensure that the status of the upload is displayed in the progress bar. Which line of code should you insert at line 03?

**Answers:**

**A)** xhr.upload.onloadeddata =

**B)** xhr.upload.onplaying =

**C)** xhr.upload.onseeking =

**D)** xhr.upload.onprogress =

**Solution:** D

**Explanation:**

Explanation: Example: xhr.upload.onprogress = function(evt) { if (evt.lengthComputable) { var percentComplete = parseInt((evt.loaded / evt.total) * 100); console.log("Upload: " + percentComplete + "% complete") } }; Reference: http://stackoverflow.com/questions/3352555/xhr-upload-progress-is-100-from-the-start

**Question: 4** *Multiple Answers Are Right*

HOTSPOT You are developing a web application that retrieves data from a web service. The data being retrieved is a custom binary datatype named bint. The data can also be represented in XML. Two existing methods named parseXml() and parseBint() are defined on the page. The application must: - Retrieve and parse data from the web service using binary format if possible - Retrieve and parse the data from the web service using XML when binary format is not possible You need to develop the application to meet the requirements. What should you do? To answer, select the appropriate options in the answer area. NOTE: Each correct selection ids worth one point. Hot Area:

## Answer Area

```
var request = $.ajax({
  uri: '/',
```

| |
|---|
| if (request.getResponderHeader("ContentType") = = "application/bint") |
| if (type = = "application/bint") |
| if (request.mimeType = = "application/bint") |
| accepts: 'application/bint.text/xml', |
| contentType: 'application/bint, text/xml', |
| dataType: 'application/bint, text/xml', |

```
dataFilter: function (data, type) {
```

| |
|---|
| if (request.getResponderHeader("ContentType") = = "application/bint") |
| if (type = = "application/bint") |
| if (request.mimeType = = "application/bint") |
| accepts: 'application/bint.text/xml', |
| contentType: 'application/bint, text/xml', |
| dataType: 'application/bint, text/xml', |

```
    returm parseBint(data);
  else
    return parseXML(data); {
  },
  success: function (data) {
     start(data);
  }
});
```

Answers:

## A)

**Answer Area**

```
var request = $.ajax({
  uri: '/',
```

[dropdown selection:]
- if (request.getResponderHeader("ContentType") = = "application/bint")
- if (type = = "application/bint")
- if (request.mimeType = = "application/bint")
- **accepts: 'application/bint.text/xml',**  *(highlighted/selected)*
- contentType: 'application/bint, text/xml',
- dataType: 'application/bint, text/xml',

```
  dataFilter: function (data, type) {
```

[dropdown selection:]
- **if (request.getResponderHeader("ContentType") = = "application/bint")**  *(highlighted/selected)*
- if (type = = "application/bint")
- if (request.mimeType = = "application/bint")
- accepts: 'application/bint.text/xml',
- contentType: 'application/bint, text/xml',
- dataType: 'application/bint, text/xml',

```
      return parseBint(data);
    else
      return parseXML(data); {
    },
    success: function (data) {
      start(data);
    }
});
```

**Solution:** A

**Explanation:**

Explanation: * accepts : 'application/bint, text/xml' accepts:'application/bin,text/xml' to accept only XML and binary content in HTML responses. * Use the following condition to check if the html response content is binary: If(request.getResponseHeader ("Content-Type")=="application/bint" * var request = $.ajax({ uri:'/', accepts: 'application/bint, text/xml', datafilter: function(data,type){ if(request.getResponseHeader("Content-Type")=="application/bint") return parseBint(data); else return parseXml(); }, success: function (data) { start(data); } });

**Question: 5** *One Answer Is Right*

You are developing a customer web form that includes the following HTML. A customer must enter a value in the text box prior to submitting the form. You need to add validation to the text box control. Which HTML should you use?

**Answers:**

**A)**

**B)**

**C)**

**D)**

**Solution:** A

**Explanation:**

Explanation: Definition and Usage The required attribute is a boolean attribute. When present, it specifies that an input field must be filled out before submitting the form. Example An HTML form with a required input field:

Username:

Username: Reference: HTML required Attribute
http://www.w3schools.com/tags/att_input_required.asp

**Question: 6** *Multiple Answers Are Right*

DRAG DROP You are developing a web page for runners who register for a race. The page includes a slider control that allows users to enter their age. You have the following requirements: - All runners must enter their age. - Applications must not be accepted from runners less than 18 years of age or greater than 90 years. - The slider control must be set to the average age (37) of all registered runners when the page is first displayed. You need to ensure that the slider control meets the requirements. What should you do? (To answer, drag the appropriate word or number to the correct location in the answer area. Each word or number may be used once, more than once, or not at all. You may need to drag the split bar between panes or scroll to view content.) Select and Place:

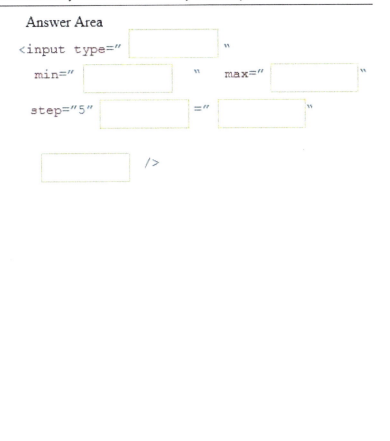

**Answers:**

## A)

**Code segments**

- slider
- 0
- 100
- avgAge()
- default
- optional

**Answer Area**

```
<input type=" range "
       min=" 18 "       max=" 90 "
       step="5" value =" 37 "
       required />
```

**Solution:** A

**Explanation:**

Explanation: Box 1-3: The is used for input fields that should contain a value within a range. Example Box 4-5: Use the value attribute to set the default value Box 6: Definition and Usage The required attribute is a boolean attribute. When present, it specifies that an input field must be filled out before submitting the form. Example Username: Reference: HTML Input Types http://www.w3schools.com/html/html_form_input_types.asp

**Question: 7** *One Answer Is Right*

You have a webpage that includes the following markup:

```
<!DOCTYPE html>
<html>
    <head>
        <script src="jquery.js"></script>
        <script>
        </script>
    </head>
    <body>
        <div id="Div1"></div>
        <span id="Span1"></span>
    </body>
</html>
```

When the page is loaded, the SPAN element must be moved as follows:

```
<div id="Div1"><span id="Span1"></span></div>
```

You need to move the SPAN element and preserve any event handlers attached to the SPAN. Which code segment should you use?

**Answers:**

**A)**
```
document.getElementById("Div1").appendChild(document.getElementById("Span1"))
```

**B)**
```
var moveElement = document.getElementById("Div1");
moveElement.parentNode.appendChild(moveElement);
```

**C)**
```
document.getElementById("Span1").appendChild(document.getElementById("Div1"))
```

**D)**
```
var moveElement = document.getElementById("Span1");
moveElement.parentNode.appendChild(moveElement);
```

**Solution:** A

**Explanation:**

Explanation: Reference: https://www.w3schools.com/jsref/met_node_appendchild.asp

**Question: 8** *One Answer Is Right*

You are developing a customer web form that includes the following HTML. A customer must enter a valid age in the text box prior to submitting the form. You need to add validation to the control. Which code segment should you use?

- A.
  ```
  function validate() {
     var value = $("#txtValue").text();
     var regex = /^[\d\,\.]*$/;
     if (!regex.test(value) || name == "")
        alert("please enter valid value");
     return;
  }
  ```

- B.
  ```
  function validate() {
     var name = $("#txtValue").val();
     if (name == null || name == "")
        alert("please enter valid value");
     return;
  }
  ```

- C.
  ```
  function validate() {
     var name = $("#txtValue").text();
     if (name == null || name == "")
        alert("please enter valid value");
     return;
  }
  ```

- D.
  ```
  function validate() {
     var value = $("#txtValue").val();
     var regex = /^[\d\,\.]*$/;
     if (!regex.test(value) || value == "")
        alert("please enter valid value");
     return;
  }
     return emailPattern.test(userinput);
  }
  ```

**Answers:**

**A)** Option A

**B)** Option B

**C)** Option C

**D)** Option D

**Solution:** D

**Explanation:**

Explanation: .val Return value A string containing the value of the element, or an array of strings if the element can have multiple values

**Question: 9** *One Answer Is Right*

You are developing an application that consumes a Windows Communication Foundation (WCF) service. The application interacts with the service by using the following code. (Line numbers are included for reference only.)

```
01 <script>
02   function getCountry(country) {
03     $.ajax({
04       type: "POST",
05       contentType: "application/json; charset=utf-8",
06       url: "http://contoso.com/Service.svc/GetCountry",
07       data: '{"Country":' + country + '}',
08       dataType: "json",
09       success: OnSuccess,
10       error: OnError
11
12     });
13   }
14   function OnSuccess(data, status) {
15     ...
16   }
17   function OnError(request, status, error) {
18     ...
19   }
20 </script>
```

You need to authenticate to the WCF service. What should you do?

**Answers:**

**A)** At line 11, add the following lines of code: ,username: yourusername ,password: yourpassword

**B)** At line 11, add the following line of code: ,credentials: prompt

**C)** At line 06, replace the code with the following line of code: url: "http://contoso.com/Service.svc/GetCountry? username=username&password=password",

**D)** At line 11, add the following line of code. The username and password will be stored in an XML file. ,credentials: credentials.xml

**Solution:** C

**Question: 10** *One Answer Is Right*

You are developing a customer web form that includes the following HTML.

```
<label id="txtValue"/>
```

Information from the web form is submitted to a web service. The web service returns the following JSON object.

```
{
    "Confirmation": "1234",
    "FirstName": "John"
}
```

You need to display the Confirmation number from the JSON response in the txtValue label field. Which JavaScript code segment should you use?

```
A. $("#txtValue").val = (JSONObject.Confirmation);
B. $("#txtValue").val (JSONObject.Confirmation);
C. $("#txtValue").text = (JSONObject.Confirmation);
D. $("#txtValue").text(JSONObject.Confirmation);
```

**Answers:**

**A)** Option A

**B)** Option B

**C)** Option C

**D)** Option D

**Solution:** D

**Explanation:**

Explanation: Incorrect Answers: A, B: A label object has no value attribute. References: http://api.jquery.com/text/

# Chapter 4: 70-483 - MCSD Programming in C#

## Exam Guide

70-483 - MCSD Programming in C#:

The **70-483 exam** is part of the new MCSD Programming in C# certification. This exam measures your ability to accomplish the below tasks:

- Managing program flow and events
- Asynchronous programming and threading
- Data validation and working with data collections including LINQ
- Handling errors and exceptions
- Working with arrays and collections
- Working with variables, operators, and expressions
- Working with classes and methods
- Decision and iteration statements

Our 70-483 dumps will include those topics::

- Manage Program Flow (25-30%)
- Create and Use Types (25-30%)
- Debug Applications and Implement Security (25-30%)
- Implement Data Access (25-30%)

For more info visit: Microsoft Official 70-483 Exam Reference

High level topics covered by our practice test:

Implement multithreading and asynchronous processing:
Use the Task Parallel library (ParallelFor, Plinq, Tasks); create continuation tasks; spawn threads by using ThreadPool; unblock the UI; use async and await keywords; manage data by using concurrent collections.
Manage multithreading:

Synchronize resources; implement locking; cancel a long-running task; implement thread-safe methods to handle race conditions.

Implement program flow:

Iterate across collection and array items; program decisions by using switch statements, if/then, and operators; evaluate expressions.

Create and implement events and callbacks:

Create event handlers; subscribe to and unsubscribe from events; use built-in delegate types to create events; create delegates; lambda expressions; anonymous methods.

Implement exception handling:

Handle exception types (SQL exceptions, network exceptions, communication exceptions, network timeout exceptions); catch typed vs. base exceptions; implement try-catch-finally blocks; throw exceptions; determine when to rethrow vs. throw; create custom exceptions.

# Sample Practice Test for 70-483

**Question: 1** *One Answer Is Right*

You are developing an application that includes a class named Order. The application will store a collection of Order objects. The collection must meet the following requirements: - Use strongly typed members. - Process Order objects in first-in-first-out order. - Store values for each Order object. - Use zero-based indices. You need to use a collection type that meets the requirements. Which collection type should you use?

**Answers:**

**A)** Queue

**B)** SortedList

**C)** LinkedList

**D)** HashTable

**E)** Array

**Solution:** A

**Explanation:**

Explanation: Queues are useful for storing messages in the order they were received for sequential processing. Objects stored in a Queue are inserted at one end and removed from the other. References: http://msdn.microsoft.com/en-us/library/7977ey2c.aspx

**Question: 2** *One Answer Is Right*

You are developing an application that includes the following code segment. (Line numbers are included for reference only.)

```
01 class Animal
02 {
03   public string Color { get; set; }
04   public string Name { get; set; }
05 }
06 private static IEnumerable<Animal> GetAnimals(string sqlConnectionString)
07 {
08   var animals = new List<Animal>();
09   SqlConnection sqlConnection = new SqlConnection(sqlConnectionString);
10   using (sqlConnection)
11   {
12     SqlCommand sqlCommand = new SqlCommand("SELECT Name, ColorName FROM Animals", sqlConnection);
13
14     using (SqlDataReader sqlDataReader = sqlCommand.ExecuteReader())
15     {
16
17       {
18         var animal = new Animal();
19         animal.Name = (string)sqlDataReader["Name"];
20         animal.Color = (string)sqlDataReader["ColorName"];
21         animals.Add(animal);
22       }
23     }
24   }
25   return animals ;
26 }
```

The GetAnimals() method must meet the following requirements: - Connect to a Microsoft SQL Server database. - Create Animal objects and populate them with data from the database. - Return a sequence of populated Animal objects. You need to meet the requirements. Which two actions should you perform? Each correct answer presents part of the solution. NOTE: Each correct selection is worth one point.

**Answers:**

**A)** Insert the following code segment at line 16: while(sqlDataReader.NextResult())

**B)** Insert the following code segment at line 13: sqlConnection.Open();

**C)** Insert the following code segment at line 13: sqlConnection.BeginTransaction();

**D)** Insert the following code segment at line 16: while(sqlDataReader.Read())

**E)** Insert the following code segment at line 16: while(sqlDataReader.GetValues())

**Solution:** B, D

**Explanation:**

Explanation: - SqlConnection.Open - Opens a database connection with the property settings specified by the ConnectionString. - SqlDataReader.Read - Advances the SqlDataReader to the next record. References: http://msdn.microsoft.com/en-us/library/system.data.sqlclient.sqlconnection.open.aspx http://msdn.microsoft.com/en-us/library/system.data.sqlclient.sqldatareader.read.aspx

**Question: 3** *One Answer Is Right*

You have an assembly named Assembly1 that is written in C#. Assembly1 has a method named Method1. You add a new method named Method2 to Assembly1. Method2 is a newer version of Method1 and must be used by applications in the future. You need to ensure that if a developer builds a project that uses Method1, the developer is notified that Method1 is deprecated. What should you do?

**Answers:**

**A)** Set an #if DEPRECATED preprocessor directive above Method1. Set a #endif preprocessor directive after Method1.

**B)** Set a #pragma warning disable preprocessor inside of Method1.

**C)** Set a #define preprocessor directive above Method1. Set an #if preprocessor directive inside of Method1.

**D)** Set a #warning preprocessor directive inside of Method1.

**Solution:** C

**Explanation:**

Explanation: Explanation: You use #define to define a symbol. When you use the symbol as the expression that's passed to the #if directive, the expression will evaluate to true. Example: #define DEBUG using System; public class TestDefine { static void Main() { #if (DEBUG) Console.WriteLine("Debugging is enabled."); #endif Reference: https://docs.microsoft.com/en-us/dotnet/csharp/language-reference/preprocessor-directives/preprocessor- define

**Question: 4** *One Answer Is Right*

You are developing an application that uses the Microsoft ADO.NET Entity Framework to retrieve order information from a Microsoft SQL Server database. The application includes the following code. (Line numbers are included for reference only.)

```
01 public DateTime? OrderDate;
02 IQueryable<Order> LookupOrdersForYear(int year)
03 {
04   using (var context = new NorthwindEntities())
05   {
06     var orders =
07       from order in context.Orders
08
09       select order;
10     return orders.ToList().AsQueryable();
11   }
12 }
```

The application must meet the following requirements: - Return only orders that have an OrderDate value other than null. - Return only orders that were placed in the year specified in the OrderDate property or in a later year. You need to ensure that the application meets the requirements. Which code segment should you insert at line 08?

**Answers:**

A) Where order.OrderDate.Value != null && order.OrderDate.Value.Year >= year

B) Where order.OrderDate.Value == null && order.OrderDate.Value.Year == year

C) Where order.OrderDate.HasValue && order.OrderDate.Value.Year == year

D) Where order.OrderDate.Value.Year == year

**Solution:** A

**Explanation:**

Explanation: - For the requirement to use an OrderDate value other than null use: OrderDate.Value != null - For the requirement to use an OrderDate value for this year or a later year use: OrderDate.Value >= year

**Question: 5** *Multiple Answers Are Right*

DRAG DROP You are developing an application by using C#. The application includes an array of decimal values named loanAmounts. You are developing a LINQ query to return the values from the array. The query must return decimal values that are evenly divisible by two. The values must be sorted from the lowest value to the highest value. You need to ensure that the query correctly returns the decimal values. How should you complete the relevant code? (To answer, drag the appropriate code segments to the correct locations in the answer area. Each code segment may be used once, more than once, or not at all. You may need to drag the split bar between panes or scroll to view content.) Select and Place:

```
join
from
group
ascending
descending
where
orderby
select
```

```
decimal[] loanAmounts = { 303m, 1000m, 85579m, 501.51m, 603m
   1200m, 400m, 22m };
IEnumerable<decimal> loanQuery =
          amount in loanAmounts
          amount % 2 == 0
          amount
          amount;
```

**Answers:**

**A)**

```
join
group
descending
```

```
decimal[] loanAmounts = { 303m, 1000m, 85579m, 501.51m, 603m
   1200m, 400m, 22m };
IEnumerable<decimal> loanQuery =
   from      amount in loanAmounts
   where     amount % 2 == 0
   orderby   amount ascending
   select    amount;
```

**Solution: A**

**Explanation:**

Explanation: Note: In a query expression, the orderby clause causes the returned sequence or subsequence (group) to be sorted in either ascending or descending order. Examples: // Query for ascending sort. IEnumerable sortAscendingQuery = from fruit in fruits orderby fruit //"ascending" is default select fruit; // Query for descending sort. IEnumerable sortDescendingQuery = from w in fruits orderby w descending select w;

## Question: 6 *One Answer Is Right*

You are developing an application. The application includes a method named ReadFile that reads data from a file. The ReadFile() method must meet the following requirements: -It must not make changes to the data file.- It must allow other processes to access the data file. - It must not throw an exception if the application attempts to open a data file that does not exist. You need to implement the ReadFile() method. Which code segment should you use?

**Answers:**

A) var fs = File.Open(Filename, FileMode.OpenOrCreate, FileAccess.Read,FileShare.ReadWrite);

B) var fs = File.Open(Filename, FileMode.Open, FileAccess.Read,FileShare.ReadWrite);

C) var fs = File.Open(Filename, FileMode.OpenOrCreate, FileAccess.Read,FileShare.Write);

D) var fs = File.ReadAllLines(Filename);

E) var fs = File.ReadAllBytes(Filename);

**Solution:** A

**Explanation:**

Explanation: FileMode.OpenOrCreate - Specifies that the operating system should open a file if it exists; otherwise, a new file should be created. If the file is opened with FileAccess.Read, FileIOPermissionAccess.Read permission is required. If the file access is FileAccess.Write, FileIOPermissionAccess.Write permission is required. If the file is opened with FileAccess.ReadWrite, both FileIOPermissionAccess.Read and FileIOPermissionAccess.Write permissions are required. FileShare.ReadWrite - Allows subsequent opening of the file for reading or writing. If this flag is not specified, any request to open the file for reading or writing (by this process or another process) will fail until the file is closed. However, even if this flag is specified, additional permissions might still be needed to access the file. References: http://msdn.microsoft.com/pl-pl/library/system.io.fileshare.aspx
http://msdn.microsoft.com/en-us/library/system.io.filemode.aspx

## Question: 7 *One Answer Is Right*

You are developing an application. The application converts a Location object to a string by using a method named WriteObject. The WriteObject() method accepts two parameters, a Location object and an XmlObjectSerializer object. The application includes the following code. (Line numbers are included for reference only.)

```
01 public enum Compass
02 {
03     North,
04     South,
05     East,
06     West
07 }
08 [DataContract]
09 public class Location
10 {
11     [DataMember]
12     public string Label { get; set; }
13     [DataMember]
14     public Compass Direction { get; set; }
15 }
16 void DoWork()
17 {
18     var location = new Location { Label = "Test", Direction = Compass.West };
19     Console.WriteLine(WriteObject(location,
20
21     ));
22 }
```

You need to serialize the Location object as a JSON object. Which code segment should you insert at line 20?

**Answers:**

**A)** New DataContractSerializer(typeof(Location))

**B)** New XmlSerializer(typeof(Location))

**C)** New NetDataContractSerializer()

**D)** New DataContractJsonSerializer(typeof(Location))

**Solution:** D

**Explanation:**

Explanation: The DataContractJsonSerializer class serializes objects to the JavaScript Object Notation (JSON) and deserializes JSON data to objects. Use the DataContractJsonSerializer class to serialize instances of a type into a JSON document and to deserialize a JSON document into an instance of a type.

**Question: 8** *One Answer Is Right*

You are developing an application. The application calls a method that returns an array of integers named employeeIds. You define an integer variable named employeeIdToRemove and assign a value to it. You declare an array named filteredEmployeeIds. You have the following requirements: - Remove duplicate integers from the employeeIds array. - Sort the array in order from the highest value to the lowest value. - Remove the integer value stored in the employeeIdToRemove variable from the employeeIds array. You need to create a LINQ query to meet the requirements. Which code segment should you use?

- A. `int[] filteredEmployeeIds = employeeIds.Where(value => value != employeeIdToRemove).OrderBy(x => x).ToArray();`
- B. `int[] filteredEmployeeIds = employeeIds.Where(value => value != employeeIdToRemove).OrderByDescending(x => x).ToArray();`
- C. `int[] filteredEmployeeIds = employeeIds.Distinct().Where(value => value != employeeIdToRemove).OrderByDescending(x => x).ToArray();`
- D. `int[] filteredEmployeeIds = employeeIds.Distinct().OrderByDescending(x => x).ToArray();`

Answers:

A) Option A

B) Option B

C) Option C

D) Option D

Solution: C

**Question: 9** *One Answer Is Right*

An application receives JSON data in the following format:

```
{ "FirstName" : "David",
  "LastName" : "Jones",
  "Values" : [0, 1, 2] }
```

The application includes the following code segment. (Line numbers are included for reference only.)

```
01 public class Name
02 {
03   public int [] Values {get; set; }
04   public string FirstName {get; set; }
05   public string LastName {get; set; }
06 }
07 public static Name ConvertToName (string json)
08 {
09   var ser = new JavaScriptSerializer();
10
11 }
```

You need to ensure that the ConvertToName() method returns the JSON input string as a Name object. Which code segment should you insert at line 10?

**Answers:**

**A)** Return ser.ConvertToType(json);

**B)** Return ser.DeserializeObject(json);

**C)** Return ser.Deserialize(json);

**D)** Return (Name)ser.Serialize(json);

**Solution:** C

**Explanation:**

Explanation: JavaScriptSerializer.Deserialize - Converts the specified JSON string to an object of type T. References: http://msdn.microsoft.com/en-us/library/bb355316.aspx

**Question: 10** *Multiple Answers Are Right*

DRAG DROP You are developing a class named ExtensionMethods. You need to ensure that the ExtensionMethods class implements the IsURL() method on string objects. How should you complete the relevant code? (To answer, drag the appropriate code segments to the correct locations in the answer area. Each code segment may be used once, more than once, or not at all. You may need to drag the split bar between panes or scroll to view content.) Select and Place:

```
public static class ExtensionMethods
```

```
public class ExtensionMethods
```

```
this String str
```

```
String str
```

```
protected static class ExtensionMethods
```

::::::::::::::::

```
{
    public static bool IsUrl(

    )
    {
        var regex = new Regex(
            "(https?://)?([A-Za-z9-0-]*\\.)?([A-Za-z0-9-]*)" +
            "\\.[A-Za-z0-9]*/?.*");
        return regex.IsMatch(str);
    }
}
```

**Answers:**

A)

```
public class ExtensionMethods
```

```
String str
```

```
protected static class ExtensionMethods
```

```csharp
public static class ExtensionMethods
{
    public static bool IsUrl(
        this String str
        )
    {
        var regex = new Regex(
            "(https?://)?([A-Za-z9-0-]*\\.)?([A-Za-z0-9-]*)" +
            "\\.[A-Za-z0-9]*/?.*");
        return regex.IsMatch(str);
    }
}
```

**Solution:** A

**Explanation:**

Explanation:

# Chapter 5: 70-486 - MCSD Developing ASP.NET MVC Web Applications

## Exam Guide

70-486 - MCSD Developing ASP.NET MVC Web Applications:

The **70-486 exam** is part of the new MCSD Developing ASP.NET MVC Web Applications certification. This exam measures your ability to accomplish the below tasks based on this technology: Microsoft Visual Studio 2013, ASP.NET MVC 5.1:

Note also that:

Starting April 30, 2014, the questions on this exam include content covering Visual Studio 2013, MVC5, and updates to Microsoft Azure.
This is a list of covered topics:

- Building Applications with ASP .NET MVC 4
- ASP .NET MVC 5 Fundamentals
- Windows Azure Fundamentals
- Code Contracts

Our 70-486 dumps will include those topics::

- Design the application architecture (15-20%)
- Design the user experience (20-25%)
- Develop the user experience (15-20%)
- Troubleshoot and debug web applications (20-25%)
- Design and implement security (20-25%)

For more info visit: Microsoft Official 70-486 Exam Reference

High level topics covered by our practice test:

This Web Simulator is for Microsoft developers that are ready to start building enterprise web applications and would like to take the 70-486 certification exam. Using the Web Simulator will provide you with training in web development, C Sharp, HTML and CSS, SQL Server, JavaScript, Object Based JavaScript, Model View and Controller, and jQuery.

# Sample Practice Test for 70-486

**Question: 1** *Multiple Answers Are Right*

DRAG DROP You need to implement the Views\RunLog\_CalculatePace.cshtml partial view from Views\Runlog \GetLog.cshtml to display the runner's average mile pace. You have the following markup:

```
<td>
  @Html.DisplayFor(model => log.Time)
</td>
<td>
  Target 1
  Target 2
</td>
<td>
  @Html.ActionLink("Delete", "DeleteLog", new { id = log.Id })
</td>
```

Which markup segments should you include in Target 1 and Target 2 to implement the view? To answer, drag the appropriate markup segments to the correct targets. Each markup segment may be used once, more than once, or not at all. You may need to drag the split bar between panes or scroll to view content. NOTE: Each correct selection is worth one point. Select and Place:

**Markup Segments**

- @Html.Partial(
- @Html.Action(
- "_CalculatePace.cshtml", log)
- "_CalculatePace", log)
- "_CalculatePace")

**Answer area**

Target 1: Markup Segment

Target 2: Markup Segment

## Scenario:

TESTLET-1. Background You are developing an ASP.NET MVC application in Visual Studio that will be used by Olympic marathon runners to log data about training runs. Business Requirements The application stores date, distance, and duration information about a user's training runs. The user can view, insert, edit, and delete records. The application must be optimized for accessibility. All times must be displayed in the user's local time. Technical Requirements Data Access: Database access is handled by a public class named RunnerLog.DataAccess.RunnerLogDb. All data retrieval must be done by HTTP GET and all data updates must be done by HTTP POST. Layout: All pages in the application use a master layout file named \Views\Shared\_Layout.cshtml. Models: The application uses the \Models\LogModel.cs model. Views: All views in the application use the Razor view engine. Four views located in \Views\RunLog are named: - _CalculatePace.cshtml - EditLog.cshtml - GetLog.cshtml - InsertLog.cshtml The application also contains a \Views\Home\Index.cshtml view. Controllers: The application contains a \Controllers\RunLogController.cs controller. Images: A stopwatch.png image is located in the \Images folder. Videos: A map of a runner's path is available when a user views a run log. The map is implemented as an Adobe Flash application and video. The browser should display the video natively if possible, using H264, Ogg, or WebM formats, in that order. If the video cannot be displayed, then the Flash application should be used. Security: You have the following security requirements: - The application is configured to use forms authentication. - Users must be logged on to insert runner data. - Users must be members of the Admin role to edit or delete runner data. - There are no security requirements for viewing runner data. - You need to protect the application against cross-site request forgery. - Passwords are hashed by using the SHA1 algorithm. RunnerLog.Providers.RunLogRoleProvider.cs contains a custom role provider. Relevant portions of the application files follow. (Line numbers are included for reference only.) Application Structure

### Controllers\RunLogController.cs

```
RC01  public class RunLogController : Controller
RC02  {
RC03    public ActionResult GetLog()
RC04    {
RC05      List<LogModel> log = RunnerLogDb.GetLogsFromDatabase();
RC06      return View(log);
RC07    }
RC08
RC09    public ActionResult InsertLog()
RC10    {
RC11      LogModel log = new LogModel();
RC12      log.RunDate = DateTime.Now;
RC13      return View(log);
RC14    }
RC15
RC16    [HttpPost]
RC17    public ActionResult InsertLog(LogModel log)
RC18    {
RC19      RunnerLogDb.InsertLog(log);
RC20      return RedirectToAction("GetLog");
RC21    }
RC22
RC23    public ActionResult DeleteLog(int id)
RC24    {
RC25      RunnerLogDb.DeleteLog(id);
RC26      return RedirectToAction("GetLog");
RC27    }
RC28
RC29    public ActionResult EditLog(int id)
RC30    {
RC31      LogModel log = RunnerLogDb.GetRunnerLog(id);
RC32      return View(log);
RC33    }
RC34  }
```

## Models\LogModel.cs

```
LM01   public class LogModel
LM02   {
LM03     [Required]
LM04     public int Id { get; set; }
LM05
LM06     [Required]
LM07     public DateTime RunDate { get; set; }
LM08
LM09     [Required]
LM10     [Range (0.01, 1000.00)]
LM11     public double Distance { get; set; }
LM12
LM13     [Required]
LM14     public TimeSpan Time { get; set; }
LM15
LM16     public string ShortDate
LM17     {
LM18       get
LM19       {
LM20         return RunDate.ToLocalTime().ToShortDateString();
LM21       }
LM22     }
LM23   }
```

## Views\RunLog\_CalculatePace.cshtml

```
CP01   @model RunnerLog.Models.LogModel
CP02   @(Convert.ToInt32(Model.Time.TotalMinutes / Model.Distance)) Min
CP03   @(Convert.ToInt32(Model.Time.TotalSeconds % 60 / Model.Distance)) Seconds
```

### Views\RunLog\EditLog.cshtml

```
EL01   @model RunnerLog.Models.LogModel
EL02   <h2>Edit Log Item</h2>
EL03   <script src="@Url.Content("~/Scripts/jquery.validate.min.js")"></script>
EL04   <script src="@Url.Content("~/Scripts/jquery.validate.unobtrusive.min.js")"></script>
EL05   @using (Html.BeginForm()) {
EL06      @Html.AntiForgeryToken()
EL07      @Html.ValidationSummary(true)
EL08      <fieldset>
EL09         <legend>LogModel</legend>
EL10         <h3>
EL11            Log Id:  @Model.Id
EL12         </h3>
EL13         <div>
EL14            @Html.LabelFor(model => model.Distance)
EL15         </div>
EL16         <div>
EL17            @Html.EditorFor(model => model.Distance)
EL18            @Html.ValidationMessageFor(model => model.Distance)
EL19         </div>
EL20         <div>
EL21            @Html.LabelFor(model => model.Time)
EL22         </div>
EL23         <div>
EL24            @Html.EditorFor(model => model.Time)
EL25            @Html.ValidationMessageFor(model => model.Time)
EL26         </div>
EL27         <p>
EL28            <input type="submit" value="Save" />
EL29         </p>
EL30      </fieldset>
EL31   }
```

Views\RunLog\GetLog.cshtml

```
GL01    @model List<RunnerLog.Models.LogModel>
GL02    <h2>View Runs </h2>
GL03    <table>
GL04      <tr>
GL05        <th>Id </th>
GL06        <th>Date </th>
GL07        <th>Distance </th>
GL08        <th>Duration </th>
GL09        <th>Avg Mile Pace </th>
GL10      </tr>
GL11      @foreach (RunnerLog.Models.LogModel log in Model)
GL12      {
GL13        <tr>
GL14          <td>
GL15            @Html.DisplayFor(model => log.Id)
GL16          </td>
GL17          <td>
GL18
GL19          </td>
GL20          <td>
GL21            @Html.DisplayFor(model => log.Distance)
GL22          </td>
GL23          <td>
GL24            @Html.DisplayFor(model => log.Time)
GL25          </td>
GL26          <td>
GL27
GL28          </td>
GL29          <td>
GL30            @Html.ActionLink("Edit", "EditLog", new { id = log.Id })
GL31          </td>
GL32          <td>
GL33            @Html.ActionLink("Delete", "DeleteLog", new { id = log.Id })
GL34          </td>
GL35        </tr>
GL36      }
GL37    </table>
```

### Views\RunLog\InsertLog.cshtml

```
IL01  @model RunnerLog.Models.LogModel
IL02  <script src="@Url.Content("~/Scripts/jquery.validate.min.js")"></script>
IL03  <script src="@Url.Content("~/Scripts/jquery.validate.unobtrusive.min.js")"></script>
IL04  @using (Html.BeginForm())
IL05  {
IL06      @Html.ValidationSummary(true)
IL07      <fieldset>
IL08          <legend>LogModel</legend>
IL09
IL10          <div>
IL11              @Html.LabelFor(model => model.RunDate)
IL12          </div>
IL13          <div>
IL14              @Html.EditorFor(model => model.RunDate)
IL15              @Html.ValidationMessageFor(model => model.RunDate)
IL16          </div>
IL17          <div>
IL18              @Html.LabelFor(model => model.Distance)
IL19          </div>
IL20          <div>
IL21              @Html.EditorFor(model => model.Distance)
IL22              @Html.ValidationMessageFor(model => model.Distance)
IL23          </div>
IL24          <div>
IL25              @Html.LabelFor(model => model.Time) HH:MM:SS
IL26          </div>
IL27          <div>
IL28              @Html.EditorFor(model => model.Time)
IL29              @Html.ValidationMessageFor(model => model.Time)
IL30          </div>
IL31          <p>
IL32              <input type="submit" value="Create" />
IL33          </p>
IL34      </fieldset>
IL35  }
```

## Views\Shared\_Layout.cshtml

```
L001  <!DOCTYPE html>
L002  <html lang="en">
L003  <head>
L004    ...
L005  </head>
L006  <body>
L007    ...
L008    <footer>
L009
L010      <script type="text/javascript">
L011        var c = document.getElementById('myCanvas');
L012        var ctx = c.getContext('2d');
L013        ctx.font = '30pt Calibri';
L014        ctx.strokeStyle = 'gray';
L015        ctx.lineWidth = 3;
L016        ctx.strokeText('London 2012', 80, 30);
L017      </script>
L018    </footer>
L019  </body>
L020  </html>
```

**Answers:**

**A)**

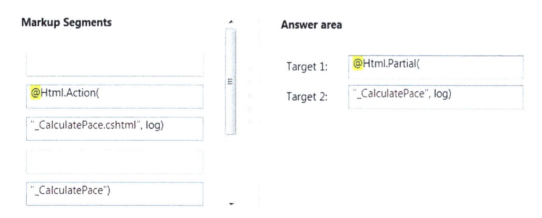

**Solution:** A

**Explanation:**

Explanation: Html.Partial renders the partial view as an HTML-encoded string. This methodresult can be stored in a variable, since it returns string type value. Simple to use and no need to create any action. Like RenderPartial method, Partial method is also useful when the displaying data in the partial view is already in the corresponding view model. References: http://www.dotnettricks.com/learn/mvc/renderpartial-vs-renderaction-vs-partial-vs-action-in- mvc-razor

**Question: 2** *Multiple Answers Are Right*

DRAG DROP You need to ensure that only valid parameters are passed to the EditLog action. You have the following code:

```
routes.MapRoute(
    name: "EditLog",
    Target 1
    Target 2
    {
        controller = "RunLog"
        Target 3
    }
    Target 4
    {
        Target 5
    }
};
```

Which code segments should you include in Target1, Target2, Target3, Target4 and Target5 to build the route? To answer, drag the appropriate code segments to the correct targets. Each code segment may be used once, more than once, or not at all. You may need to drag the split bar between panes or scroll to view content. NOTE: Each correct selection is worth one point. Select and Place:

## Code Segments

- id = @"\d+"
- url:"RunLog/EditLog{id}",
- action = "EditLog",
- defaults:new
- constraints:new

## Answer Area

Target 1:
Target 2:
Target 3:
Target 4:
Target 5:

**Scenario:**

TESTLET-1. Background You are developing an ASP.NET MVC application in Visual Studio that will be used by Olympic marathon runners to log data about training runs. Business Requirements The application stores date, distance, and duration information about a user's training runs. The user can view, insert, edit, and delete records. The application must be optimized for accessibility. All times must be displayed in the user's local time. Technical Requirements Data Access: Database access is handled by a public class named RunnerLog.DataAccess.RunnerLogDb. All data retrieval must be done by HTTP GET and all data updates must be done by HTTP POST. Layout: All pages in the application use a master layout file named \Views\Shared\_Layout.cshtml. Models: The application uses the \Models\LogModel.cs model. Views: All views in the application use the Razor view engine. Four views located in \Views\RunLog are named: - _CalculatePace.cshtml - EditLog.cshtml - GetLog.cshtml - InsertLog.cshtml The application also contains a \Views\Home\Index.cshtml view. Controllers: The application contains a \Controllers\RunLogController.cs controller. Images: A stopwatch.png image is located in the \Images folder. Videos: A map of a runner's path is available when a user views a run log. The map is implemented as an Adobe Flash application and video. The browser should display the video natively if possible, using H264, Ogg, or WebM formats, in that order. If the video cannot be displayed, then the Flash application should be used. Security: You have the following security requirements: - The application is configured to use forms authentication. - Users must be logged on to insert runner data. - Users must be members of the Admin role to edit or delete runner data. - There are no security requirements for viewing runner data. - You need to protect the application against cross-site

request forgery. - Passwords are hashed by using the SHA1 algorithm.
RunnerLog.Providers.RunLogRoleProvider.cs contains a custom role provider. Relevant portions of the application files follow. (Line numbers are included for reference only.)
Application Structure

## Controllers\RunLogController.cs

```
RC01   public class RunLogController : Controller
RC02   {
RC03      public ActionResult GetLog()
RC04      {
RC05         List<LogModel> log = RunnerLogDb.GetLogsFromDatabase();
RC06         return View(log);
RC07      }
RC08
RC09      public ActionResult InsertLog()
RC10      {
RC11         LogModel log = new LogModel();
RC12         log.RunDate = DateTime.Now;
RC13         return View(log);
RC14      }
RC15
RC16      [HttpPost]
RC17      public ActionResult InsertLog(LogModel log)
RC18      {
RC19         RunnerLogDb.InsertLog(log);
RC20         return RedirectToAction("GetLog");
RC21      }
RC22
RC23      public ActionResult DeleteLog(int id)
RC24      {
RC25         RunnerLogDb.DeleteLog(id);
RC26         return RedirectToAction("GetLog");
RC27      }
RC28
RC29      public ActionResult EditLog(int id)
RC30      {
RC31         LogModel log = RunnerLogDb.GetRunnerLog(id);
RC32         return View(log);
RC33      }
RC34   }
```

## Models\LogModel.cs

```
LM01  public class LogModel
LM02  {
LM03    [Required]
LM04    public int Id { get; set; }
LM05
LM06    [Required]
LM07    public DateTime RunDate { get; set; }
LM08
LM09    [Required]
LM10    [Range (0.01, 1000.00)]
LM11    public double Distance { get; set; }
LM12
LM13    [Required]
LM14    public TimeSpan Time { get; set; }
LM15
LM16    public string ShortDate
LM17    {
LM18      get
LM19      {
LM20        return RunDate.ToLocalTime().ToShortDateString();
LM21      }
LM22    }
LM23  }
```

## Views\RunLog\_CalculatePace.cshtml

```
CP01  @model RunnerLog.Models.LogModel
CP02  @(Convert.ToInt32(Model.Time.TotalMinutes / Model.Distance)) Min
CP03  @(Convert.ToInt32(Model.Time.TotalSeconds % 60 / Model.Distance)) Seconds
```

### Views\RunLog\EditLog.cshtml

```
EL01   @model RunnerLog.Models.LogModel
EL02   <h2>Edit Log Item</h2>
EL03   <script src="@Url.Content("~/Scripts/jquery.validate.min.js")"></script>
EL04   <script src="@Url.Content("~/Scripts/jquery.validate.unobtrusive.min.js")"></script>
EL05   @using (Html.BeginForm()) {
EL06      @Html.AntiForgeryToken()
EL07      @Html.ValidationSummary(true)
EL08      <fieldset>
EL09        <legend>LogModel</legend>
EL10        <h3>
EL11          Log Id:  @Model.Id
EL12        </h3>
EL13        <div>
EL14          @Html.LabelFor(model => model.Distance)
EL15        </div>
EL16        <div>
EL17          @Html.EditorFor(model => model.Distance)
EL18          @Html.ValidationMessageFor(model => model.Distance)
EL19        </div>
EL20        <div>
EL21          @Html.LabelFor(model => model.Time)
EL22        </div>
EL23        <div>
EL24          @Html.EditorFor(model => model.Time)
EL25          @Html.ValidationMessageFor(model => model.Time)
EL26        </div>
EL27        <p>
EL28          <input type="submit" value="Save" />
EL29        </p>
EL30      </fieldset>
EL31   }
```

## Views\RunLog\GetLog.cshtml

```
GL01    @model List<RunnerLog.Models.LogModel>
GL02    <h2>View Runs </h2>
GL03    <table>
GL04      <tr>
GL05        <th>Id </th>
GL06        <th>Date </th>
GL07        <th>Distance </th>
GL08        <th>Duration </th>
GL09        <th>Avg Mile Pace </th>
GL10      </tr>
GL11      @foreach (RunnerLog.Models.LogModel log in Model)
GL12      {
GL13        <tr>
GL14          <td>
GL15            @Html.DisplayFor(model => log.Id)
GL16          </td>
GL17          <td>
GL18
GL19          </td>
GL20          <td>
GL21            @Html.DisplayFor(model => log.Distance)
GL22          </td>
GL23          <td>
GL24            @Html.DisplayFor(model => log.Time)
GL25          </td>
GL26          <td>
GL27
GL28          </td>
GL29          <td>
GL30            @Html.ActionLink("Edit", "EditLog", new { id = log.Id })
GL31          </td>
GL32          <td>
GL33            @Html.ActionLink("Delete", "DeleteLog", new { id = log.Id })
GL34          </td>
GL35        </tr>
GL36      }
GL37    </table>
```

Views\RunLog\InsertLog.cshtml

```
IL01  @model RunnerLog.Models.LogModel
IL02  <script src="@Url.Content("~/Scripts/jquery.validate.min.js")"></script>
IL03  <script src="@Url.Content("~/Scripts/jquery.validate.unobtrusive.min.js")"></script>
IL04  @using (Html.BeginForm())
IL05  {
IL06      @Html.ValidationSummary(true)
IL07      <fieldset>
IL08         <legend>LogModel</legend>
IL09
IL10         <div>
IL11            @Html.LabelFor(model => model.RunDate)
IL12         </div>
IL13         <div>
IL14            @Html.EditorFor(model => model.RunDate)
IL15            @Html.ValidationMessageFor(model => model.RunDate)
IL16         </div>
IL17         <div>
IL18            @Html.LabelFor(model => model.Distance)
IL19         </div>
IL20         <div>
IL21            @Html.EditorFor(model => model.Distance)
IL22            @Html.ValidationMessageFor(model => model.Distance)
IL23         </div>
IL24         <div>
IL25            @Html.LabelFor(model => model.Time) HH:MM:SS
IL26         </div>
IL27         <div>
IL28            @Html.EditorFor(model => model.Time)
IL29            @Html.ValidationMessageFor(model => model.Time)
IL30         </div>
IL31         <p>
IL32            <input type="submit" value="Create" />
IL33         </p>
IL34      </fieldset>
IL35  }
```

## Views\Shared\_Layout.cshtml

```
L001    <!DOCTYPE html>
L002    <html lang="en">
L003    <head>
L004      ...
L005    </head>
L006    <body>
L007      ...
L008      <footer>
L009
L010        <script type="text/javascript">
L011          var c = document.getElementById('myCanvas');
L012          var ctx = c.getContext('2d');
L013          ctx.font = '30pt Calibri';
L014          ctx.strokeStyle = 'gray';
L015          ctx.lineWidth = 3;
L016          ctx.strokeText('London 2012', 80, 30);
L017        </script>
L018      </footer>
L019    </body>
L020    </html>
```

**Answers:**

A)

**Code Segments**

**Answer Area**

Target 1: url:"RunLog/EditLog{id}",

Target 2: defaults:new

Target 3: action = "EditLog",

Target 4: constraints:new

Target 5: id = @"\d+"

**Solution:** A

**Explanation:**

Explanation: Routes.MapRoute( name: "EditLog", url: "RunLog/EditLog{id}", defaults: new { controller = "RunLog", action: = "EditLog" } constraints: new { Id = @"\d+" } };

**Question: 3** *Multiple Answers Are Right*

DRAG DROP You need to implement security according to the business requirements. How should you modify RunLogController? (To answer, drag the appropriate code segment to the correct location or locations. Each code segment may be used once, more than once, or not at all. You may need to drag the split bar between panes or scroll to view content.) Select and Place:

```
[Authorize(Roles = "Admin")]

[Authorize]

[Authorize(Users = "Admin")]

[AllowAnonymous]

[Authorize(Users = "*")]
```

```csharp
public class RunLogController : Controller
{

    public ActionResult GetLog()
    ...

    public ActionResult InsertLog()
    ...

    public ActionResult DeleteLog(int id)
    ...

    public ActionResult EditLog(int id)
    ...
}
```

**Scenario:**

TESTLET-1. Background You are developing an ASP.NET MVC application in Visual Studio that will be used by Olympic marathon runners to log data about training runs. Business Requirements The application stores date, distance, and duration information about a user's training runs. The user can view, insert, edit, and delete records. The application must be optimized for accessibility. All times must be displayed in the user's local time. Technical Requirements Data Access: Database access is handled by a public class named RunnerLog.DataAccess.RunnerLogDb. All data retrieval must be done by HTTP GET and all data updates must be done by HTTP POST. Layout: All pages in the application use a master layout file named \Views\Shared\_Layout.cshtml. Models: The application uses the \Models\LogModel.cs model. Views: All views in the application use the Razor view engine. Four views located in \Views\RunLog are named: - _CalculatePace.cshtml - EditLog.cshtml - GetLog.cshtml - InsertLog.cshtml The application also contains a \Views\Home\Index.cshtml view. Controllers: The application contains a \Controllers\RunLogController.cs controller. Images: A stopwatch.png image is located in the \Images folder. Videos: A map of a runner's path is available when a user views a run log. The map is implemented as an Adobe Flash application and video. The browser should display the video natively if possible, using H264, Ogg, or WebM formats, in that order. If the video cannot be displayed, then the Flash application

should be used. Security: You have the following security requirements: - The application is configured to use forms authentication. - Users must be logged on to insert runner data. - Users must be members of the Admin role to edit or delete runner data. - There are no security requirements for viewing runner data. - You need to protect the application against cross-site request forgery. - Passwords are hashed by using the SHA1 algorithm. RunnerLog.Providers.RunLogRoleProvider.cs contains a custom role provider. Relevant portions of the application files follow. (Line numbers are included for reference only.)
Application Structure

## Controllers\RunLogController.cs

```
RC01   public class RunLogController : Controller
RC02   {
RC03     public ActionResult GetLog()
RC04     {
RC05       List<LogModel> log = RunnerLogDb.GetLogsFromDatabase();
RC06       return View(log);
RC07     }
RC08
RC09     public ActionResult InsertLog()
RC10     {
RC11       LogModel log = new LogModel();
RC12       log.RunDate = DateTime.Now;
RC13       return View(log);
RC14     }
RC15
RC16     [HttpPost]
RC17     public ActionResult InsertLog(LogModel log)
RC18     {
RC19       RunnerLogDb.InsertLog(log);
RC20       return RedirectToAction("GetLog");
RC21     }
RC22
RC23     public ActionResult DeleteLog(int id)
RC24     {
RC25       RunnerLogDb.DeleteLog(id);
RC26       return RedirectToAction("GetLog");
RC27     }
RC28
RC29     public ActionResult EditLog(int id)
RC30     {
RC31       LogModel log = RunnerLogDb.GetRunnerLog(id);
RC32       return View(log);
RC33     }
RC34   }
```

## Models\LogModel.cs

```
LM01  public class LogModel
LM02  {
LM03    [Required]
LM04    public int Id { get; set; }
LM05
LM06    [Required]
LM07    public DateTime RunDate { get; set; }
LM08
LM09    [Required]
LM10    [Range (0.01, 1000.00)]
LM11    public double Distance { get; set; }
LM12
LM13    [Required]
LM14    public TimeSpan Time { get; set; }
LM15
LM16    public string ShortDate
LM17    {
LM18      get
LM19      {
LM20        return RunDate.ToLocalTime().ToShortDateString();
LM21      }
LM22    }
LM23  }
```

## Views\RunLog\_CalculatePace.cshtml

```
CP01  @model RunnerLog.Models.LogModel
CP02  @(Convert.ToInt32(Model.Time.TotalMinutes / Model.Distance)) Min
CP03  @(Convert.ToInt32(Model.Time.TotalSeconds % 60 / Model.Distance)) Seconds
```

Views\RunLog\EditLog.cshtml

```
EL01    @model RunnerLog.Models.LogModel
EL02    <h2>Edit Log Item</h2>
EL03    <script src="@Url.Content("~/Scripts/jquery.validate.min.js")"></script>
EL04    <script src="@Url.Content("~/Scripts/jquery.validate.unobtrusive.min.js")"></script>
EL05    @using (Html.BeginForm()) {
EL06      @Html.AntiForgeryToken()
EL07      @Html.ValidationSummary(true)
EL08      <fieldset>
EL09        <legend>LogModel</legend>
EL10        <h3>
EL11          Log Id: @Model.Id
EL12        </h3>
EL13        <div>
EL14          @Html.LabelFor(model => model.Distance)
EL15        </div>
EL16        <div>
EL17          @Html.EditorFor(model => model.Distance)
EL18          @Html.ValidationMessageFor(model => model.Distance)
EL19        </div>
EL20        <div>
EL21          @Html.LabelFor(model => model.Time)
EL22        </div>
EL23        <div>
EL24          @Html.EditorFor(model => model.Time)
EL25          @Html.ValidationMessageFor(model => model.Time)
EL26        </div>
EL27        <p>
EL28          <input type="submit" value="Save" />
EL29        </p>
EL30      </fieldset>
EL31    }
```

## Views\RunLog\GetLog.cshtml

```
GL01    @model List<RunnerLog.Models.LogModel>
GL02    <h2>View Runs </h2>
GL03    <table>
GL04      <tr>
GL05        <th>Id </th>
GL06        <th>Date </th>
GL07        <th>Distance </th>
GL08        <th>Duration </th>
GL09        <th>Avg Mile Pace </th>
GL10      </tr>
GL11      @foreach (RunnerLog.Models.LogModel log in Model)
GL12      {
GL13        <tr>
GL14          <td>
GL15            @Html.DisplayFor(model => log.Id)
GL16          </td>
GL17          <td>
GL18
GL19          </td>
GL20          <td>
GL21            @Html.DisplayFor(model => log.Distance)
GL22          </td>
GL23          <td>
GL24            @Html.DisplayFor(model => log.Time)
GL25          </td>
GL26          <td>
GL27
GL28          </td>
GL29          <td>
GL30            @Html.ActionLink("Edit", "EditLog", new { id = log.Id })
GL31          </td>
GL32          <td>
GL33            @Html.ActionLink("Delete", "DeleteLog", new { id = log.Id })
GL34          </td>
GL35        </tr>
GL36      }
GL37    </table>
```

**Views\RunLog\InsertLog.cshtml**

```
IL01   @model RunnerLog.Models.LogModel
IL02   <script src="@Url.Content("~/Scripts/jquery.validate.min.js")"></script>
IL03   <script src="@Url.Content("~/Scripts/jquery.validate.unobtrusive.min.js")"></script>
IL04   @using (Html.BeginForm())
IL05   {
IL06     @Html.ValidationSummary(true)
IL07     <fieldset>
IL08       <legend>LogModel</legend>
IL09
IL10       <div>
IL11         @Html.LabelFor(model => model.RunDate)
IL12       </div>
IL13       <div>
IL14         @Html.EditorFor(model => model.RunDate)
IL15         @Html.ValidationMessageFor(model => model.RunDate)
IL16       </div>
IL17       <div>
IL18         @Html.LabelFor(model => model.Distance)
IL19       </div>
IL20       <div>
IL21         @Html.EditorFor(model => model.Distance)
IL22         @Html.ValidationMessageFor(model => model.Distance)
IL23       </div>
IL24       <div>
IL25         @Html.LabelFor(model => model.Time) HH:MM:SS
IL26       </div>
IL27       <div>
IL28         @Html.EditorFor(model => model.Time)
IL29         @Html.ValidationMessageFor(model => model.Time)
IL30       </div>
IL31       <p>
IL32         <input type="submit" value="Create" />
IL33       </p>
IL34     </fieldset>
IL35   }
```

## Views\Shared\_Layout.cshtml

```
L001  <!DOCTYPE html>
L002  <html lang="en">
L003  <head>
L004    ...
L005  </head>
L006  <body>
L007    ...
L008    <footer>
L009
L010      <script type="text/javascript">
L011        var c = document.getElementById('myCanvas');
L012        var ctx = c.getContext('2d');
L013        ctx.font = '30pt Calibri';
L014        ctx.strokeStyle = 'gray';
L015        ctx.lineWidth = 3;
L016        ctx.strokeText('London 2012', 80, 30);
L017      </script>
L018    </footer>
L019  </body>
L020  </html>
```

**Answers:**

## A)

```
[Authorize(Roles = "Admin")]

[Authorize]

[Authorize(Users = "Admin")]

[AllowAnonymous]

[Authorize(Users = "*")]
```

```
[Authorize]
public class RunLogController : Controller
{
    [AllowAnonymous]
    public ActionResult GetLog()
    ...

    public ActionResult InsertLog()
    ...
    [Authorize(Roles = "Admin")]
    public ActionResult DeleteLog(int id)

    [Authorize(Roles = "Admin")]
    public ActionResult EditLog(int id)
    ...
}
```

**Solution:** A

**Explanation:**

Explanation:

**Question: 4** *One Answer Is Right*

You need to make the "Distance" header of the table bold in the Views/RunLog/GetLog.cshtml view. Which code segment should you use?

**Scenario:**

TESTLET-1. Background You are developing an ASP.NET MVC application in Visual Studio that will be used by Olympic marathon runners to log data about training runs. Business Requirements The application stores date, distance, and duration information about a user's training runs. The user can view, insert, edit, and delete records. The application must be optimized for accessibility. All times must be displayed in the user's local time. Technical Requirements Data Access: Database access is handled by a public class named RunnerLog.DataAccess.RunnerLogDb. All data retrieval must be done by HTTP GET and all data updates must be done by HTTP POST. Layout: All pages in the application use a master layout file named \Views\Shared\_Layout.cshtml. Models: The application uses the \Models\LogModel.cs model. Views: All views in the application use the Razor view engine. Four views located in \Views\RunLog are named: - _CalculatePace.cshtml - EditLog.cshtml - GetLog.cshtml - InsertLog.cshtml The application also contains a \Views\Home\Index.cshtml view. Controllers: The application contains a \Controllers\RunLogController.cs controller. Images: A stopwatch.png image is located in the \Images folder. Videos: A map of a runner's path is available when a user views a run log. The map is implemented as an Adobe Flash application and video. The browser should display the video natively if possible, using H264, Ogg, or WebM formats, in that order. If the video cannot be displayed, then the Flash application should be used. Security: You have the following security requirements: - The application is configured to use forms authentication. - Users must be logged on to insert runner data. - Users must be members of the Admin role to edit or delete runner data. - There are no security requirements for viewing runner data. - You need to protect the application against cross-site request forgery. - Passwords are hashed by using the SHA1 algorithm. RunnerLog.Providers.RunLogRoleProvider.cs contains a custom role provider. Relevant portions of the application files follow. (Line numbers are included for reference only.) Application Structure

### Controllers\RunLogController.cs

```
RC01  public class RunLogController : Controller
RC02  {
RC03    public ActionResult GetLog()
RC04    {
RC05      List<LogModel> log = RunnerLogDb.GetLogsFromDatabase();
RC06      return View(log);
RC07    }
RC08
RC09    public ActionResult InsertLog()
RC10    {
RC11      LogModel log = new LogModel();
RC12      log.RunDate = DateTime.Now;
RC13      return View(log);
RC14    }
RC15
RC16    [HttpPost]
RC17    public ActionResult InsertLog(LogModel log)
RC18    {
RC19      RunnerLogDb.InsertLog(log);
RC20      return RedirectToAction("GetLog");
RC21    }
RC22
RC23    public ActionResult DeleteLog(int id)
RC24    {
RC25      RunnerLogDb.DeleteLog(id);
RC26      return RedirectToAction("GetLog");
RC27    }
RC28
RC29    public ActionResult EditLog(int id)
RC30    {
RC31      LogModel log = RunnerLogDb.GetRunnerLog(id);
RC32      return View(log);
RC33    }
RC34  }
```

## Models\LogModel.cs

```
LM01   public class LogModel
LM02   {
LM03     [Required]
LM04     public int Id { get; set; }
LM05
LM06     [Required]
LM07     public DateTime RunDate { get; set; }
LM08
LM09     [Required]
LM10     [Range (0.01, 1000.00)]
LM11     public double Distance { get; set; }
LM12
LM13     [Required]
LM14     public TimeSpan Time { get; set; }
LM15
LM16     public string ShortDate
LM17     {
LM18       get
LM19       {
LM20         return RunDate.ToLocalTime().ToShortDateString();
LM21       }
LM22     }
LM23   }
```

## Views\RunLog\_CalculatePace.cshtml

```
CP01   @model RunnerLog.Models.LogModel
CP02   @(Convert.ToInt32(Model.Time.TotalMinutes / Model.Distance)) Min
CP03   @(Convert.ToInt32(Model.Time.TotalSeconds % 60 / Model.Distance)) Seconds
```

Views\RunLog\EditLog.cshtml

```
EL01    @model RunnerLog.Models.LogModel
EL02    <h2>Edit Log Item</h2>
EL03    <script src="@Url.Content("~/Scripts/jquery.validate.min.js")"></script>
EL04    <script src="@Url.Content("~/Scripts/jquery.validate.unobtrusive.min.js")"></script>
EL05    @using (Html.BeginForm()) {
EL06      @Html.AntiForgeryToken()
EL07      @Html.ValidationSummary(true)
EL08      <fieldset>
EL09        <legend>LogModel</legend>
EL10        <h3>
EL11          Log Id:  @Model.Id
EL12        </h3>
EL13        <div>
EL14          @Html.LabelFor(model => model.Distance)
EL15        </div>
EL16        <div>
EL17          @Html.EditorFor(model => model.Distance)
EL18          @Html.ValidationMessageFor(model => model.Distance)
EL19        </div>
EL20        <div>
EL21          @Html.LabelFor(model => model.Time)
EL22        </div>
EL23        <div>
EL24          @Html.EditorFor(model => model.Time)
EL25          @Html.ValidationMessageFor(model => model.Time)
EL26        </div>
EL27        <p>
EL28          <input type="submit" value="Save" />
EL29        </p>
EL30      </fieldset>
EL31    }
```

### Views\RunLog\GetLog.cshtml

```
GL01   @model List<RunnerLog.Models.LogModel>
GL02   <h2>View Runs </h2>
GL03   <table>
GL04     <tr>
GL05       <th>Id </th>
GL06       <th>Date </th>
GL07       <th>Distance </th>
GL08       <th>Duration </th>
GL09       <th>Avg Mile Pace </th>
GL10     </tr>
GL11     @foreach (RunnerLog.Models.LogModel log in Model)
GL12     {
GL13       <tr>
GL14         <td>
GL15           @Html.DisplayFor(model => log.Id)
GL16         </td>
GL17         <td>
GL18
GL19         </td>
GL20         <td>
GL21           @Html.DisplayFor(model => log.Distance)
GL22         </td>
GL23         <td>
GL24           @Html.DisplayFor(model => log.Time)
GL25         </td>
GL26         <td>
GL27
GL28         </td>
GL29         <td>
GL30           @Html.ActionLink("Edit", "EditLog", new { id = log.Id })
GL31         </td>
GL32         <td>
GL33           @Html.ActionLink("Delete", "DeleteLog", new { id = log.Id })
GL34         </td>
GL35       </tr>
GL36     }
GL37   </table>
```

**Views\RunLog\InsertLog.cshtml**

```
IL01  @model RunnerLog.Models.LogModel
IL02  <script src="@Url.Content("~/Scripts/jquery.validate.min.js")"></script>
IL03  <script src="@Url.Content("~/Scripts/jquery.validate.unobtrusive.min.js")"></script>
IL04  @using (Html.BeginForm())
IL05  {
IL06      @Html.ValidationSummary(true)
IL07      <fieldset>
IL08         <legend>LogModel</legend>
IL09
IL10         <div>
IL11            @Html.LabelFor(model => model.RunDate)
IL12         </div>
IL13         <div>
IL14            @Html.EditorFor(model => model.RunDate)
IL15            @Html.ValidationMessageFor(model => model.RunDate)
IL16         </div>
IL17         <div>
IL18            @Html.LabelFor(model => model.Distance)
IL19         </div>
IL20         <div>
IL21            @Html.EditorFor(model => model.Distance)
IL22            @Html.ValidationMessageFor(model => model.Distance)
IL23         </div>
IL24         <div>
IL25            @Html.LabelFor(model => model.Time) HH:MM:SS
IL26         </div>
IL27         <div>
IL28            @Html.EditorFor(model => model.Time)
IL29            @Html.ValidationMessageFor(model => model.Time)
IL30         </div>
IL31         <p>
IL32            <input type="submit" value="Create" />
IL33         </p>
IL34      </fieldset>
IL35  }
```

## Views\Shared\_Layout.cshtml

```
L001  <!DOCTYPE html>
L002  <html lang="en">
L003  <head>
L004    ...
L005  </head>
L006  <body>
L007    ...
L008    <footer>
L009
L010      <script type="text/javascript">
L011        var c = document.getElementById('myCanvas');
L012        var ctx = c.getContext('2d');
L013        ctx.font = '30pt Calibri';
L014        ctx.strokeStyle = 'gray';
L015        ctx.lineWidth = 3;
L016        ctx.strokeText('London 2012', 80, 30);
L017      </script>
L018    </footer>
L019  </body>
L020  </html>
```

**Answers:**

**A)** table>tr{ font-weight:bold; }

**B)** table>th:last-child{ font-weight: bold; }

**C)** table+first-child{ font-weight: bold; }

**D)** table>tr>th:nth-child (2) { font-weight: bold; }

**Solution:** D

**Question: 5** *One Answer Is Right*

You need to extend the edit functionality of RunLogController. Which code segment should you use?

○ A.  [HttpGet]
       [ActionName("EditLog")]
       [ValidateAntiForgeryToken]
       public ActionResult EditLog(LogModel log)
       {
           ...
       }

○ B.  [HttpPost]
       [ActionName("EditLog")]
       public ActionResult EditLogValidated(LogModel log)
       {
           ...
       }

○ C.  [HttpPost]
       [ActionName("EditLog")]
       [ValidateAntiForgeryToken]
       public ActionResult EditLogValidated(LogModel log)
       {
           ...
       }

○ D.  [HttpPost]
       [ActionName("EditLog")]
       [RequireHttps]
       public ActionResult EditLogValidated(LogModel log)
       {
           ...
       }

**Scenario:**

TESTLET-1. Background You are developing an ASP.NET MVC application in Visual Studio that will be used by Olympic marathon runners to log data about training runs. Business Requirements The application stores date, distance, and duration information about a user's training runs. The user can view, insert, edit, and delete records. The application must be optimized for accessibility. All times must be displayed in the user's local time. Technical Requirements Data Access: Database access is handled by a public class named

RunnerLog.DataAccess.RunnerLogDb. All data retrieval must be done by HTTP GETand all data updates must be done by HTTP POST. Layout: All pages in the application use a master layout file named \Views\Shared\_Layout.cshtml. Models: The application uses the \Models\LogModel.cs model. Views: All views in the application use the Razor view engine. Four views located in \Views\RunLog are named: - _CalculatePace.cshtml - EditLog.cshtml - GetLog.cshtml - InsertLog.cshtml The application also contains a \Views\Home\Index.cshtml view. Controllers: The application contains a \Controllers\RunLogController.cs controller. Images: A stopwatch.png image is located in the \Images folder. Videos: A map of a runner's path is available when a user views a run log. The map is implemented as an Adobe Flash application and video. The browser should display the video natively if possible, using H264, Ogg, or WebM formats, in that order. If the video cannot be displayed, then the Flash application should be used. Security: You have the following security requirements: - The application is configured to use forms authentication. - Users must be logged on to insert runner data. - Users must be members of the Admin role to edit or delete runner data. - There are no security requirements for viewing runner data. - You need to protect the application against cross-site request forgery. - Passwords are hashed by using the SHA1 algorithm. RunnerLog.Providers.RunLogRoleProvider.cs contains a custom role provider. Relevant portions of the application files follow. (Line numbers are included for reference only.) Application Structure

**Controllers\RunLogController.cs**

```
RC01    public class RunLogController : Controller
RC02    {
RC03       public ActionResult GetLog()
RC04       {
RC05          List<LogModel> log = RunnerLogDb.GetLogsFromDatabase();
RC06          return View(log);
RC07       }
RC08
RC09       public ActionResult InsertLog()
RC10       {
RC11          LogModel log = new LogModel();
RC12          log.RunDate = DateTime.Now;
RC13          return View(log);
RC14       }
RC15
RC16       [HttpPost]
RC17       public ActionResult InsertLog(LogModel log)
RC18       {
RC19          RunnerLogDb.InsertLog(log);
RC20          return RedirectToAction("GetLog");
RC21       }
RC22
RC23       public ActionResult DeleteLog(int id)
RC24       {
RC25          RunnerLogDb.DeleteLog(id);
RC26          return RedirectToAction("GetLog");
RC27       }
RC28
RC29       public ActionResult EditLog(int id)
RC30       {
RC31          LogModel log = RunnerLogDb.GetRunnerLog(id);
RC32          return View(log);
RC33       }
RC34    }
```

## Models\LogModel.cs

```
LM01   public class LogModel
LM02   {
LM03     [Required]
LM04     public int Id { get; set; }
LM05
LM06     [Required]
LM07     public DateTime RunDate { get; set; }
LM08
LM09     [Required]
LM10     [Range (0.01, 1000.00)]
LM11     public double Distance { get; set; }
LM12
LM13     [Required]
LM14     public TimeSpan Time { get; set; }
LM15
LM16     public string ShortDate
LM17     {
LM18       get
LM19       {
LM20         return RunDate.ToLocalTime().ToShortDateString();
LM21       }
LM22     }
LM23   }
```

## Views\RunLog\_CalculatePace.cshtml

```
CP01   @model RunnerLog.Models.LogModel
CP02   @(Convert.ToInt32(Model.Time.TotalMinutes / Model.Distance)) Min
CP03   @(Convert.ToInt32(Model.Time.TotalSeconds % 60 / Model.Distance)) Seconds
```

Views\RunLog\EditLog.cshtml

```
EL01  @model RunnerLog.Models.LogModel
EL02  <h2>Edit Log Item</h2>
EL03  <script src="@Url.Content("~/Scripts/jquery.validate.min.js")"></script>
EL04  <script src="@Url.Content("~/Scripts/jquery.validate.unobtrusive.min.js")"></script>
EL05  @using (Html.BeginForm()) {
EL06      @Html.AntiForgeryToken()
EL07      @Html.ValidationSummary(true)
EL08      <fieldset>
EL09        <legend>LogModel</legend>
EL10        <h3>
EL11          Log Id:  @Model.Id
EL12        </h3>
EL13        <div>
EL14          @Html.LabelFor(model => model.Distance)
EL15        </div>
EL16        <div>
EL17          @Html.EditorFor(model => model.Distance)
EL18          @Html.ValidationMessageFor(model => model.Distance)
EL19        </div>
EL20        <div>
EL21          @Html.LabelFor(model => model.Time)
EL22        </div>
EL23        <div>
EL24          @Html.EditorFor(model => model.Time)
EL25          @Html.ValidationMessageFor(model => model.Time)
EL26        </div>
EL27        <p>
EL28          <input type="submit" value="Save" />
EL29        </p>
EL30      </fieldset>
EL31  }
```

### Views\RunLog\GetLog.cshtml

```
GL01    @model List<RunnerLog.Models.LogModel>
GL02    <h2>View Runs </h2>
GL03    <table>
GL04      <tr>
GL05        <th>Id </th>
GL06        <th>Date </th>
GL07        <th>Distance </th>
GL08        <th>Duration </th>
GL09        <th>Avg Mile Pace </th>
GL10      </tr>
GL11      @foreach (RunnerLog.Models.LogModel log in Model)
GL12      {
GL13        <tr>
GL14          <td>
GL15            @Html.DisplayFor(model => log.Id)
GL16          </td>
GL17          <td>
GL18
GL19          </td>
GL20          <td>
GL21            @Html.DisplayFor(model => log.Distance)
GL22          </td>
GL23          <td>
GL24            @Html.DisplayFor(model => log.Time)
GL25          </td>
GL26          <td>
GL27
GL28          </td>
GL29          <td>
GL30            @Html.ActionLink("Edit", "EditLog", new { id = log.Id })
GL31          </td>
GL32          <td>
GL33            @Html.ActionLink("Delete", "DeleteLog", new { id = log.Id })
GL34          </td>
GL35        </tr>
GL36      }
GL37    </table>
```

### Views\RunLog\InsertLog.cshtml

```
IL01  @model RunnerLog.Models.LogModel
IL02  <script src="@Url.Content("~/Scripts/jquery.validate.min.js")"></script>
IL03  <script src="@Url.Content("~/Scripts/jquery.validate.unobtrusive.min.js")"></script>
IL04  @using (Html.BeginForm())
IL05  {
IL06     @Html.ValidationSummary(true)
IL07     <fieldset>
IL08        <legend>LogModel</legend>
IL09
IL10        <div>
IL11           @Html.LabelFor(model => model.RunDate)
IL12        </div>
IL13        <div>
IL14           @Html.EditorFor(model => model.RunDate)
IL15           @Html.ValidationMessageFor(model => model.RunDate)
IL16        </div>
IL17        <div>
IL18           @Html.LabelFor(model => model.Distance)
IL19        </div>
IL20        <div>
IL21           @Html.EditorFor(model => model.Distance)
IL22           @Html.ValidationMessageFor(model => model.Distance)
IL23        </div>
IL24        <div>
IL25           @Html.LabelFor(model => model.Time) HH:MM:SS
IL26        </div>
IL27        <div>
IL28           @Html.EditorFor(model => model.Time)
IL29           @Html.ValidationMessageFor(model => model.Time)
IL30        </div>
IL31        <p>
IL32           <input type="submit" value="Create" />
IL33        </p>
IL34     </fieldset>
IL35  }
```

### Views\Shared\_Layout.cshtml

```
L001  <!DOCTYPE html>
L002  <html lang="en">
L003  <head>
L004    ...
L005  </head>
L006  <body>
L007    ...
L008    <footer>
L009
L010      <script type="text/javascript">
L011        var c = document.getElementById('myCanvas');
L012        var ctx = c.getContext('2d');
L013        ctx.font = '30pt Calibri';
L014        ctx.strokeStyle = 'gray';
L015        ctx.lineWidth = 3;
L016        ctx.strokeText('London 2012', 80, 30);
L017      </script>
L018    </footer>
L019  </body>
L020  </html>
```

**Answers:**

**A)** Option A

**B)** Option B

**C)** Option C

**D)** Option D

**Solution:** C

**Question: 6** *Multiple Answers Are Right*

DRAG DROP You need to ensure that the application uses RunLogRoleProvider custom role provider. How should you modify the web.config file? (To answer, drag the appropriate line of code to the correct location or locations. Each line of code may be used once, more than once, or not at all. You may need to drag the split bar between panes or scroll to view content.) Select and Place:

```
"RunnerLog.Providers.RunLogRoleProvider"          <roleManager
"System.Web.Providers.RunLogRoleProvider"                      enabled="true"  >
                                                    <providers>
"System.Web.Providers.DefaultRoleProvider"            <add name="RLRoleProvider"
defaultProvider="DefaultProvider"                       type=
                                                        Application="RunnerLog"/>
defaultProvider="RLRoleProvider"                    </providers>
                                                  </roleManager>
```

**Scenario:**

TESTLET-1. Background You are developing an ASP.NET MVC application in Visual Studio that will be used by Olympic marathon runners to log data about training runs. Business Requirements The application stores date, distance, and duration information about a user's training runs. The user can view, insert, edit, and delete records. The application must be optimized for accessibility. All times must be displayed in the user's local time. Technical Requirements Data Access: Database access is handled by a public class named RunnerLog.DataAccess.RunnerLogDb. All data retrieval must be done by HTTP GETand all data updates must be done by HTTP POST. Layout: All pages in the application use a master layout file named \Views\Shared\_Layout.cshtml. Models: The application uses the \Models\LogModel.cs model. Views: All views in the application use the Razor view engine. Four views located in \Views\RunLog are named: - _CalculatePace.cshtml - EditLog.cshtml - GetLog.cshtml - InsertLog.cshtml The application also contains a \Views\Home\Index.cshtml view. Controllers: The application contains a \Controllers\RunLogController.cs controller. Images: A stopwatch.png image is located in the \Images folder. Videos: A map of a runner's path is available when a user views a run log. The map is implemented as an Adobe Flash application and video. The browser should display the video natively if possible, using H264, Ogg, or WebM formats, in that order. If the video cannot be displayed, then the Flash application should be used. Security: You have the following security requirements: - The application is configured to use forms authentication. - Users must be logged on to insert runner data. - Users must be members of the Admin role to edit or delete runner data. - There are no security requirements for viewing runner data. - You need to protect the application against cross-site request forgery. - Passwords are hashed by using the SHA1 algorithm. RunnerLog.Providers.RunLogRoleProvider.cs contains a custom role provider. Relevant portions of the application files follow. (Line numbers are included for reference only.) Application Structure

## Controllers\RunLogController.cs

```
RC01    public class RunLogController : Controller
RC02    {
RC03      public ActionResult GetLog()
RC04      {
RC05        List<LogModel> log = RunnerLogDb.GetLogsFromDatabase();
RC06        return View(log);
RC07      }
RC08
RC09      public ActionResult InsertLog()
RC10      {
RC11        LogModel log = new LogModel();
RC12        log.RunDate = DateTime.Now;
RC13        return View(log);
RC14      }
RC15
RC16      [HttpPost]
RC17      public ActionResult InsertLog(LogModel log)
RC18      {
RC19        RunnerLogDb.InsertLog(log);
RC20        return RedirectToAction("GetLog");
RC21      }
RC22
RC23      public ActionResult DeleteLog(int id)
RC24      {
RC25        RunnerLogDb.DeleteLog(id);
RC26        return RedirectToAction("GetLog");
RC27      }
RC28
RC29      public ActionResult EditLog(int id)
RC30      {
RC31        LogModel log = RunnerLogDb.GetRunnerLog(id);
RC32        return View(log);
RC33      }
RC34    }
```

## Models\LogModel.cs

```
LM01   public class LogModel
LM02   {
LM03      [Required]
LM04      public int Id { get; set; }
LM05
LM06      [Required]
LM07      public DateTime RunDate { get; set; }
LM08
LM09      [Required]
LM10      [Range (0.01, 1000.00)]
LM11      public double Distance { get; set; }
LM12
LM13      [Required]
LM14      public TimeSpan Time { get; set; }
LM15
LM16      public string ShortDate
LM17      {
LM18         get
LM19         {
LM20            return RunDate.ToLocalTime().ToShortDateString();
LM21         }
LM22      }
LM23   }
```

## Views\RunLog\_CalculatePace.cshtml

```
CP01   @model RunnerLog.Models.LogModel
CP02   @(Convert.ToInt32(Model.Time.TotalMinutes / Model.Distance)) Min
CP03   @(Convert.ToInt32(Model.Time.TotalSeconds % 60 / Model.Distance)) Seconds
```

### Views\RunLog\EditLog.cshtml

```
EL01  @model RunnerLog.Models.LogModel
EL02  <h2>Edit Log Item</h2>
EL03  <script src="@Url.Content("~/Scripts/jquery.validate.min.js")"></script>
EL04  <script src="@Url.Content("~/Scripts/jquery.validate.unobtrusive.min.js")"></script>
EL05  @using (Html.BeginForm()) {
EL06      @Html.AntiForgeryToken()
EL07      @Html.ValidationSummary(true)
EL08      <fieldset>
EL09         <legend>LogModel</legend>
EL10         <h3>
EL11            Log Id:   @Model.Id
EL12         </h3>
EL13         <div>
EL14            @Html.LabelFor(model => model.Distance)
EL15         </div>
EL16         <div>
EL17            @Html.EditorFor(model => model.Distance)
EL18            @Html.ValidationMessageFor(model => model.Distance)
EL19         </div>
EL20         <div>
EL21            @Html.LabelFor(model => model.Time)
EL22         </div>
EL23         <div>
EL24            @Html.EditorFor(model => model.Time)
EL25            @Html.ValidationMessageFor(model => model.Time)
EL26         </div>
EL27         <p>
EL28            <input type="submit" value="Save" />
EL29         </p>
EL30      </fieldset>
EL31  }
```

Views\RunLog\GetLog.cshtml

```
GL01    @model List<RunnerLog.Models.LogModel>
GL02    <h2>View Runs </h2>
GL03    <table>
GL04      <tr>
GL05         <th>Id </th>
GL06         <th>Date </th>
GL07         <th>Distance </th>
GL08         <th>Duration </th>
GL09         <th>Avg Mile Pace </th>
GL10      </tr>
GL11      @foreach (RunnerLog.Models.LogModel log in Model)
GL12      {
GL13         <tr>
GL14            <td>
GL15               @Html.DisplayFor(model => log.Id)
GL16            </td>
GL17            <td>
GL18
GL19            </td>
GL20            <td>
GL21               @Html.DisplayFor(model => log.Distance)
GL22            </td>
GL23            <td>
GL24               @Html.DisplayFor(model => log.Time)
GL25            </td>
GL26            <td>
GL27
GL28            </td>
GL29            <td>
GL30               @Html.ActionLink("Edit", "EditLog", new { id = log.Id })
GL31            </td>
GL32            <td>
GL33               @Html.ActionLink("Delete", "DeleteLog", new { id = log.Id })
GL34            </td>
GL35         </tr>
GL36      }
GL37    </table>
```

### Views\RunLog\InsertLog.cshtml

```
IL01   @model RunnerLog.Models.LogModel
IL02   <script src="@Url.Content("~/Scripts/jquery.validate.min.js")"></script>
IL03   <script src="@Url.Content("~/Scripts/jquery.validate.unobtrusive.min.js")"></script>
IL04   @using (Html.BeginForm())
IL05   {
IL06     @Html.ValidationSummary(true)
IL07     <fieldset>
IL08       <legend>LogModel</legend>
IL09
IL10       <div>
IL11         @Html.LabelFor(model => model.RunDate)
IL12       </div>
IL13       <div>
IL14         @Html.EditorFor(model => model.RunDate)
IL15         @Html.ValidationMessageFor(model => model.RunDate)
IL16       </div>
IL17       <div>
IL18         @Html.LabelFor(model => model.Distance)
IL19       </div>
IL20       <div>
IL21         @Html.EditorFor(model => model.Distance)
IL22         @Html.ValidationMessageFor(model => model.Distance)
IL23       </div>
IL24       <div>
IL25         @Html.LabelFor(model => model.Time) HH:MM:SS
IL26       </div>
IL27       <div>
IL28         @Html.EditorFor(model => model.Time)
IL29         @Html.ValidationMessageFor(model => model.Time)
IL30       </div>
IL31       <p>
IL32         <input type="submit" value="Create" />
IL33       </p>
IL34     </fieldset>
IL35   }
```

## Views\Shared\_Layout.cshtml

```
L001  <!DOCTYPE html>
L002  <html lang="en">
L003  <head>
L004    ...
L005  </head>
L006  <body>
L007    ...
L008    <footer>
L009
L010      <script type="text/javascript">
L011        var c = document.getElementById('myCanvas');
L012        var ctx = c.getContext('2d');
L013        ctx.font = '30pt Calibri';
L014        ctx.strokeStyle = 'gray';
L015        ctx.lineWidth = 3;
L016        ctx.strokeText('London 2012', 80, 30);
L017      </script>
L018    </footer>
L019  </body>
L020  </html>
```

**Answers:**

A)

**Solution:** A

**Explanation:**

Explanation:

**Question: 7** *One Answer Is Right*

If the canvas element is supported by the client browser, the application must display "London 2012" in the footer as text formatted by JavaScript at the end of the _Layout.cshtml file. You need to modify the layout to ensure that "London 2012" is displayed as either formatted text or as plain text, depending on what the client browser supports. Which code segment should you add?

A. ```
<canvas id="myFooter">
   @(Request.Browser.JavaApplets ? new HtmlString("London 2012") : null)
</canvas>
```
B. `<canvas id="myFooter">London 2012</canvas>`
C. `<canvas id="myCanvas">London 2012</canvas>`
D. ```
<canvas id="myCanvas"></canvas>
<p>London 2012</p>
```

**Scenario:**

TESTLET-1. Background You are developing an ASP.NET MVC application in Visual Studio that will be used by Olympic marathon runners to log data about training runs. Business Requirements The application stores date, distance, and duration information about a user's training runs. The user can view, insert, edit, and delete records. The application must be optimized for accessibility. All times must be displayed in the user's local time. Technical Requirements Data Access: Database access is handled by a public class named RunnerLog.DataAccess.RunnerLogDb. All data retrieval must be done by HTTP GET and all data updates must be done by HTTP POST. Layout: All pages in the application use a master layout file named \Views\Shared\_Layout.cshtml. Models: The application uses the \Models\LogModel.cs model. Views: All views in the application use the Razor view engine. Four views located in \Views\RunLog are named: - _CalculatePace.cshtml - EditLog.cshtml - GetLog.cshtml - InsertLog.cshtml The application also contains a \Views\Home\Index.cshtml view. Controllers: The application contains a \Controllers\RunLogController.cs controller. Images: A stopwatch.png image is located in the \Images folder. Videos: A map of a runner's path is available when a user views a run log. The map is implemented as an Adobe Flash application and video. The browser should display the video natively if possible, using H264, Ogg, or WebM formats, in that order. If the video cannot be displayed, then the Flash application should be used. Security: You have the following security requirements: - The application is configured to use forms authentication. - Users must be logged on to insert runner data. - Users must be members of the Admin role to edit or delete runner data. - There are no security requirements for viewing runner data. - You need to protect the application against cross-site request forgery. - Passwords are hashed by using the SHA1 algorithm. RunnerLog.Providers.RunLogRoleProvider.cs contains a custom role provider. Relevant portions of the application files follow. (Line numbers are included for reference only.)

Application Structure

## Controllers\RunLogController.cs

```
RC01    public class RunLogController : Controller
RC02    {
RC03      public ActionResult GetLog()
RC04      {
RC05        List<LogModel> log = RunnerLogDb.GetLogsFromDatabase();
RC06        return View(log);
RC07      }
RC08
RC09      public ActionResult InsertLog()
RC10      {
RC11        LogModel log = new LogModel();
RC12        log.RunDate = DateTime.Now;
RC13        return View(log);
RC14      }
RC15
RC16      [HttpPost]
RC17      public ActionResult InsertLog(LogModel log)
RC18      {
RC19        RunnerLogDb.InsertLog(log);
RC20        return RedirectToAction("GetLog");
RC21      }
RC22
RC23      public ActionResult DeleteLog(int id)
RC24      {
RC25        RunnerLogDb.DeleteLog(id);
RC26        return RedirectToAction("GetLog");
RC27      }
RC28
RC29      public ActionResult EditLog(int id)
RC30      {
RC31        LogModel log = RunnerLogDb.GetRunnerLog(id);
RC32        return View(log);
RC33      }
RC34    }
```

## Models\LogModel.cs

```
LM01    public class LogModel
LM02    {
LM03      [Required]
LM04      public int Id { get; set; }
LM05
LM06      [Required]
LM07      public DateTime RunDate { get; set; }
LM08
LM09      [Required]
LM10      [Range (0.01, 1000.00)]
LM11      public double Distance { get; set; }
LM12
LM13      [Required]
LM14      public TimeSpan Time { get; set; }
LM15
LM16      public string ShortDate
LM17      {
LM18        get
LM19        {
LM20          return RunDate.ToLocalTime().ToShortDateString();
LM21        }
LM22      }
LM23    }
```

## Views\RunLog\_CalculatePace.cshtml

```
CP01    @model RunnerLog.Models.LogModel
CP02    @(Convert.ToInt32(Model.Time.TotalMinutes / Model.Distance)) Min
CP03    @(Convert.ToInt32(Model.Time.TotalSeconds % 60 / Model.Distance)) Seconds
```

Views\RunLog\EditLog.cshtml

```
EL01    @model RunnerLog.Models.LogModel
EL02    <h2>Edit Log Item</h2>
EL03    <script src="@Url.Content("~/Scripts/jquery.validate.min.js")"></script>
EL04    <script src="@Url.Content("~/Scripts/jquery.validate.unobtrusive.min.js")"></script>
EL05    @using (Html.BeginForm()) {
EL06        @Html.AntiForgeryToken()
EL07        @Html.ValidationSummary(true)
EL08        <fieldset>
EL09            <legend>LogModel</legend>
EL10            <h3>
EL11                Log Id:   @Model.Id
EL12            </h3>
EL13            <div>
EL14                @Html.LabelFor(model => model.Distance)
EL15            </div>
EL16            <div>
EL17                @Html.EditorFor(model => model.Distance)
EL18                @Html.ValidationMessageFor(model => model.Distance)
EL19            </div>
EL20            <div>
EL21                @Html.LabelFor(model => model.Time)
EL22            </div>
EL23            <div>
EL24                @Html.EditorFor(model => model.Time)
EL25                @Html.ValidationMessageFor(model => model.Time)
EL26            </div>
EL27            <p>
EL28                <input type="submit" value="Save" />
EL29            </p>
EL30        </fieldset>
EL31    }
```

Views\RunLog\GetLog.cshtml

```
GL01    @model List<RunnerLog.Models.LogModel>
GL02    <h2>View Runs </h2>
GL03    <table>
GL04      <tr>
GL05        <th>Id </th>
GL06        <th>Date </th>
GL07        <th>Distance </th>
GL08        <th>Duration </th>
GL09        <th>Avg Mile Pace </th>
GL10      </tr>
GL11      @foreach (RunnerLog.Models.LogModel log in Model)
GL12      {
GL13        <tr>
GL14          <td>
GL15            @Html.DisplayFor(model => log.Id)
GL16          </td>
GL17          <td>
GL18
GL19          </td>
GL20          <td>
GL21            @Html.DisplayFor(model => log.Distance)
GL22          </td>
GL23          <td>
GL24            @Html.DisplayFor(model => log.Time)
GL25          </td>
GL26          <td>
GL27
GL28          </td>
GL29          <td>
GL30            @Html.ActionLink("Edit", "EditLog", new { id = log.Id })
GL31          </td>
GL32          <td>
GL33            @Html.ActionLink("Delete", "DeleteLog", new { id = log.Id })
GL34          </td>
GL35        </tr>
GL36      }
GL37    </table>
```

Views\RunLog\InsertLog.cshtml

```
IL01  @model RunnerLog.Models.LogModel
IL02  <script src="@Url.Content("~/Scripts/jquery.validate.min.js")"></script>
IL03  <script src="@Url.Content("~/Scripts/jquery.validate.unobtrusive.min.js")"></script>
IL04  @using (Html.BeginForm())
IL05  {
IL06     @Html.ValidationSummary(true)
IL07     <fieldset>
IL08        <legend>LogModel</legend>
IL09
IL10        <div>
IL11           @Html.LabelFor(model => model.RunDate)
IL12        </div>
IL13        <div>
IL14           @Html.EditorFor(model => model.RunDate)
IL15           @Html.ValidationMessageFor(model => model.RunDate)
IL16        </div>
IL17        <div>
IL18           @Html.LabelFor(model => model.Distance)
IL19        </div>
IL20        <div>
IL21           @Html.EditorFor(model => model.Distance)
IL22           @Html.ValidationMessageFor(model => model.Distance)
IL23        </div>
IL24        <div>
IL25           @Html.LabelFor(model => model.Time) HH:MM:SS
IL26        </div>
IL27        <div>
IL28           @Html.EditorFor(model => model.Time)
IL29           @Html.ValidationMessageFor(model => model.Time)
IL30        </div>
IL31        <p>
IL32           <input type="submit" value="Create" />
IL33        </p>
IL34     </fieldset>
IL35  }
```

### Views\Shared\_Layout.cshtml

```
L001    <!DOCTYPE html>
L002    <html lang="en">
L003    <head>
L004    ...
L005    </head>
L006    <body>
L007    ...
L008     <footer>
L009
L010      <script type="text/javascript">
L011        var c = document.getElementById('myCanvas');
L012        var ctx = c.getContext('2d');
L013        ctx.font = '30pt Calibri';
L014        ctx.strokeStyle = 'gray';
L015        ctx.lineWidth = 3;
L016        ctx.strokeText('London 2012', 80, 30);
L017      </script>
L018     </footer>
L019    </body>
L020    </html>
```

**Answers:**

**A)** Option A

**B)** Option B

**C)** Option C

**D)** Option D

**Solution:** C

**Question: 8** *One Answer Is Right*

You need to add an action to RunLogController to validate the users' passwords. Which code segment should you use?

A.
```
public ActionResult Login(string username, string password)
{
    byte[] buffer = Encoding.UTF8.GetBytes(password + username);
    byte[] hash = MD5.Create().ComputeHash(buffer);
    ComparePassword(username, hash);
    return ContextDependentView();
}
```

B.
```
[RequireHttps]
public ActionResult Login(string username, string password)
{
    byte[] buffer = Encoding.UTF8.GetBytes(password + username);
    byte[] hash = SHA1.Create().ComputeHash(buffer);
    ComparePassword(username, hash);
    return ContextDependentView();
}
```

C.
```
public ActionResult Login(string username, string password)
{
    byte[] buffer = Encoding.UTF8.GetBytes(password + username);
    byte[] hash = SHA1.Create().ComputeHash(buffer);
    ComparePassword(username, hash);
    return ContextDependentView();
}
```

D.
```
[RequireHttps]
public ActionResult Login(string username, string password)
{
    byte[] buffer = Encoding.UTF8.GetBytes(password + username);
    byte[] hash = MD5.Create().ComputeHash(buffer);
    ComparePassword(username, hash);
    return ContextDependentView();
}
```

**Scenario:**

TESTLET-1. Background You are developing an ASP.NET MVC application in Visual Studio that will be used by Olympic marathon runners to log data about training runs. Business Requirements The application stores date, distance, and duration information about a user's training runs. The user can view, insert, edit, and delete records. The application must be optimized for accessibility. All times must be displayed in the user's local time. Technical Requirements Data Access: Database access is handled by a public class named RunnerLog.DataAccess.RunnerLogDb. All data retrieval must be done by HTTP GET and all data updates must be done by HTTP POST. Layout: All pages in the application use a master layout file named \Views\Shared\_Layout.cshtml. Models: The application uses the

\Models\LogModel.cs model. Views: All views in the application use the Razor view engine. Four views located in \Views\RunLog are named: - _CalculatePace.cshtml - EditLog.cshtml - GetLog.cshtml - InsertLog.cshtml The application also contains a \Views\Home\Index.cshtml view. Controllers: The application contains a \Controllers\RunLogController.cs controller. Images: A stopwatch.png image is located in the \Images folder. Videos: A map of a runner's path is available when a user views a run log. The map is implemented as an Adobe Flash application and video. The browser should display the video natively if possible, using H264, Ogg, or WebM formats, in that order. If the video cannot be displayed, then the Flash application should be used. Security: You have the following security requirements: - The application is configured to use forms authentication. - Users must be logged on to insert runner data. - Users must be members of the Admin role to edit or delete runner data. - There are no security requirements for viewing runner data. - You need to protect the application against cross-site request forgery. - Passwords are hashed by using the SHA1 algorithm. RunnerLog.Providers.RunLogRoleProvider.cs contains a custom role provider. Relevant portions of the application files follow. (Line numbers are included for reference only.) Application Structure

Controllers\RunLogController.cs

```
RC01    public class RunLogController : Controller
RC02    {
RC03      public ActionResult GetLog()
RC04      {
RC05        List<LogModel> log = RunnerLogDb.GetLogsFromDatabase();
RC06        return View(log);
RC07      }
RC08
RC09      public ActionResult InsertLog()
RC10      {
RC11        LogModel log = new LogModel();
RC12        log.RunDate = DateTime.Now;
RC13        return View(log);
RC14      }
RC15
RC16      [HttpPost]
RC17      public ActionResult InsertLog(LogModel log)
RC18      {
RC19        RunnerLogDb.InsertLog(log);
RC20        return RedirectToAction("GetLog");
RC21      }
RC22
RC23      public ActionResult DeleteLog(int id)
RC24      {
RC25        RunnerLogDb.DeleteLog(id);
RC26        return RedirectToAction("GetLog");
RC27      }
RC28
RC29      public ActionResult EditLog(int id)
RC30      {
RC31        LogModel log = RunnerLogDb.GetRunnerLog(id);
RC32        return View(log);
RC33      }
RC34    }
```

## Models\LogModel.cs

```
LM01   public class LogModel
LM02   {
LM03      [Required]
LM04      public int Id { get; set; }
LM05
LM06      [Required]
LM07      public DateTime RunDate { get; set; }
LM08
LM09      [Required]
LM10      [Range (0.01, 1000.00)]
LM11      public double Distance { get; set; }
LM12
LM13      [Required]
LM14      public TimeSpan Time { get; set; }
LM15
LM16      public string ShortDate
LM17      {
LM18        get
LM19        {
LM20          return RunDate.ToLocalTime().ToShortDateString();
LM21        }
LM22      }
LM23   }
```

## Views\RunLog\_CalculatePace.cshtml

```
CP01   @model RunnerLog.Models.LogModel
CP02   @(Convert.ToInt32(Model.Time.TotalMinutes / Model.Distance)) Min
CP03   @(Convert.ToInt32(Model.Time.TotalSeconds % 60 / Model.Distance)) Seconds
```

Views\RunLog\EditLog.cshtml

```
EL01   @model RunnerLog.Models.LogModel
EL02   <h2>Edit Log Item</h2>
EL03   <script src="@Url.Content("~/Scripts/jquery.validate.min.js")"></script>
EL04   <script src="@Url.Content("~/Scripts/jquery.validate.unobtrusive.min.js")"></script>
EL05   @using (Html.BeginForm()) {
EL06     @Html.AntiForgeryToken()
EL07     @Html.ValidationSummary(true)
EL08     <fieldset>
EL09       <legend>LogModel</legend>
EL10       <h3>
EL11         Log Id:   @Model.Id
EL12       </h3>
EL13       <div>
EL14         @Html.LabelFor(model => model.Distance)
EL15       </div>
EL16       <div>
EL17         @Html.EditorFor(model => model.Distance)
EL18         @Html.ValidationMessageFor(model => model.Distance)
EL19       </div>
EL20       <div>
EL21         @Html.LabelFor(model => model.Time)
EL22       </div>
EL23       <div>
EL24         @Html.EditorFor(model => model.Time)
EL25         @Html.ValidationMessageFor(model => model.Time)
EL26       </div>
EL27       <p>
EL28         <input type="submit" value="Save" />
EL29       </p>
EL30     </fieldset>
EL31   }
```

### Views\RunLog\GetLog.cshtml

```
GL01    @model List<RunnerLog.Models.LogModel>
GL02    <h2>View Runs </h2>
GL03    <table>
GL04      <tr>
GL05        <th>Id </th>
GL06        <th>Date </th>
GL07        <th>Distance </th>
GL08        <th>Duration </th>
GL09        <th>Avg Mile Pace </th>
GL10      </tr>
GL11      @foreach (RunnerLog.Models.LogModel log in Model)
GL12      {
GL13        <tr>
GL14          <td>
GL15            @Html.DisplayFor(model => log.Id)
GL16          </td>
GL17          <td>
GL18
GL19          </td>
GL20          <td>
GL21            @Html.DisplayFor(model => log.Distance)
GL22          </td>
GL23          <td>
GL24            @Html.DisplayFor(model => log.Time)
GL25          </td>
GL26          <td>
GL27
GL28          </td>
GL29          <td>
GL30            @Html.ActionLink("Edit", "EditLog", new { id = log.Id })
GL31          </td>
GL32          <td>
GL33            @Html.ActionLink("Delete", "DeleteLog", new { id = log.Id })
GL34          </td>
GL35        </tr>
GL36      }
GL37    </table>
```

**Views\RunLog\InsertLog.cshtml**

```
IL01  @model RunnerLog.Models.LogModel
IL02  <script src="@Url.Content("~/Scripts/jquery.validate.min.js")"></script>
IL03  <script src="@Url.Content("~/Scripts/jquery.validate.unobtrusive.min.js")"></script>
IL04  @using (Html.BeginForm())
IL05  {
IL06      @Html.ValidationSummary(true)
IL07      <fieldset>
IL08          <legend>LogModel</legend>
IL09
IL10          <div>
IL11              @Html.LabelFor(model => model.RunDate)
IL12          </div>
IL13          <div>
IL14              @Html.EditorFor(model => model.RunDate)
IL15              @Html.ValidationMessageFor(model => model.RunDate)
IL16          </div>
IL17          <div>
IL18              @Html.LabelFor(model => model.Distance)
IL19          </div>
IL20          <div>
IL21              @Html.EditorFor(model => model.Distance)
IL22              @Html.ValidationMessageFor(model => model.Distance)
IL23          </div>
IL24          <div>
IL25              @Html.LabelFor(model => model.Time) HH:MM:SS
IL26          </div>
IL27          <div>
IL28              @Html.EditorFor(model => model.Time)
IL29              @Html.ValidationMessageFor(model => model.Time)
IL30          </div>
IL31          <p>
IL32              <input type="submit" value="Create" />
IL33          </p>
IL34      </fieldset>
IL35  }
```

### Views\Shared\_Layout.cshtml

```
L001    <!DOCTYPE html>
L002    <html lang="en">
L003    <head>
L004      ...
L005    </head>
L006    <body>
L007    ...
L008     <footer>
L009
L010       <script type="text/javascript">
L011          var c = document.getElementById('myCanvas');
L012          var ctx = c.getContext('2d');
L013          ctx.font = '30pt Calibri';
L014          ctx.strokeStyle = 'gray';
L015          ctx.lineWidth = 3;
L016          ctx.strokeText('London 2012', 80, 30);
L017       </script>
L018     </footer>
L019    </body>
L020    </html>
```

**Answers:**

**A)** Option A

**B)** Option B

**C)** Option C

**D)** Option D

**Solution:** B

**Question: 9** *One Answer Is Right*

You need to make all of the rows in the table bold in the Views/RunLog/GetLog.cshtml view. Which code segment should you use?

**Scenario:**

TESTLET-1. Background You are developing an ASP.NET MVC application in Visual Studio that will be used by Olympic marathon runners to log data about training runs. Business Requirements The application stores date, distance, and duration information about a user's training runs. The user can view, insert, edit, and delete records. The application must be optimized for accessibility. All times must be displayed in the user's local time. Technical Requirements Data Access: Database access is handled by a public class named RunnerLog.DataAccess.RunnerLogDb. All data retrieval must be done by HTTP GETand all data updates must be done by HTTP POST. Layout: All pages in the application use a master layout file named \Views\Shared\_Layout.cshtml. Models: The application uses the \Models\LogModel.cs model. Views: All views in the application use the Razor view engine. Four views located in \Views\RunLog are named: - _CalculatePace.cshtml - EditLog.cshtml - GetLog.cshtml - InsertLog.cshtml The application also contains a \Views\Home\Index.cshtml view. Controllers: The application contains a \Controllers\RunLogController.cs controller. Images: A stopwatch.png image is located in the \Images folder. Videos: A map of a runner's path is available when a user views a run log. The map is implemented as an Adobe Flash application and video. The browser should display the video natively if possible, using H264, Ogg, or WebM formats, in that order. If the video cannot be displayed, then the Flash application should be used. Security: You have the following security requirements: - The application is configured to use forms authentication. - Users must be logged on to insert runner data. - Users must be members of the Admin role to edit or delete runner data. - There are no security requirements for viewing runner data. - You need to protect the application against cross-site request forgery. - Passwords are hashed by using the SHA1 algorithm. RunnerLog.Providers.RunLogRoleProvider.cs contains a custom role provider. Relevant portions of the application files follow. (Line numbers are included for reference only.) Application Structure

## Controllers\RunLogController.cs

```
RC01   public class RunLogController : Controller
RC02   {
RC03     public ActionResult GetLog()
RC04     {
RC05       List<LogModel> log = RunnerLogDb.GetLogsFromDatabase();
RC06       return View(log);
RC07     }
RC08
RC09     public ActionResult InsertLog()
RC10     {
RC11       LogModel log = new LogModel();
RC12       log.RunDate = DateTime.Now;
RC13       return View(log);
RC14     }
RC15
RC16     [HttpPost]
RC17     public ActionResult InsertLog(LogModel log)
RC18     {
RC19       RunnerLogDb.InsertLog(log);
RC20       return RedirectToAction("GetLog");
RC21     }
RC22
RC23     public ActionResult DeleteLog(int id)
RC24     {
RC25       RunnerLogDb.DeleteLog(id);
RC26       return RedirectToAction("GetLog");
RC27     }
RC28
RC29     public ActionResult EditLog(int id)
RC30     {
RC31       LogModel log = RunnerLogDb.GetRunnerLog(id);
RC32       return View(log);
RC33     }
RC34   }
```

## Models\LogModel.cs

```
LM01   public class LogModel
LM02   {
LM03     [Required]
LM04     public int Id { get; set; }
LM05
LM06     [Required]
LM07     public DateTime RunDate { get; set; }
LM08
LM09     [Required]
LM10     [Range (0.01, 1000.00)]
LM11     public double Distance { get; set; }
LM12
LM13     [Required]
LM14     public TimeSpan Time { get; set; }
LM15
LM16     public string ShortDate
LM17     {
LM18       get
LM19       {
LM20         return RunDate.ToLocalTime().ToShortDateString();
LM21       }
LM22     }
LM23   }
```

## Views\RunLog\_CalculatePace.cshtml

```
CP01   @model RunnerLog.Models.LogModel
CP02   @(Convert.ToInt32(Model.Time.TotalMinutes / Model.Distance)) Min
CP03   @(Convert.ToInt32(Model.Time.TotalSeconds % 60 / Model.Distance)) Seconds
```

Views\RunLog\EditLog.cshtml

```
EL01    @model RunnerLog.Models.LogModel
EL02    <h2>Edit Log Item</h2>
EL03    <script src="@Url.Content("~/Scripts/jquery.validate.min.js")"></script>
EL04    <script src="@Url.Content("~/Scripts/jquery.validate.unobtrusive.min.js")"></script>
EL05    @using (Html.BeginForm()) {
EL06        @Html.AntiForgeryToken()
EL07        @Html.ValidationSummary(true)
EL08        <fieldset>
EL09           <legend>LogModel</legend>
EL10           <h3>
EL11              Log Id:   @Model.Id
EL12           </h3>
EL13           <div>
EL14              @Html.LabelFor(model => model.Distance)
EL15           </div>
EL16           <div>
EL17              @Html.EditorFor(model => model.Distance)
EL18              @Html.ValidationMessageFor(model => model.Distance)
EL19           </div>
EL20           <div>
EL21              @Html.LabelFor(model => model.Time)
EL22           </div>
EL23           <div>
EL24              @Html.EditorFor(model => model.Time)
EL25              @Html.ValidationMessageFor(model => model.Time)
EL26           </div>
EL27           <p>
EL28              <input type="submit" value="Save" />
EL29           </p>
EL30        </fieldset>
EL31    }
```

### Views\RunLog\GetLog.cshtml

```
GL01    @model List<RunnerLog.Models.LogModel>
GL02    <h2>View Runs </h2>
GL03    <table>
GL04      <tr>
GL05        <th>Id </th>
GL06        <th>Date </th>
GL07        <th>Distance </th>
GL08        <th>Duration </th>
GL09        <th>Avg Mile Pace </th>
GL10      </tr>
GL11      @foreach (RunnerLog.Models.LogModel log in Model)
GL12      {
GL13        <tr>
GL14          <td>
GL15            @Html.DisplayFor(model => log.Id)
GL16          </td>
GL17          <td>
GL18
GL19          </td>
GL20          <td>
GL21            @Html.DisplayFor(model => log.Distance)
GL22          </td>
GL23          <td>
GL24            @Html.DisplayFor(model => log.Time)
GL25          </td>
GL26          <td>
GL27
GL28          </td>
GL29          <td>
GL30            @Html.ActionLink("Edit", "EditLog", new { id = log.Id })
GL31          </td>
GL32          <td>
GL33            @Html.ActionLink("Delete", "DeleteLog", new { id = log.Id })
GL34          </td>
GL35        </tr>
GL36      }
GL37    </table>
```

**Views\RunLog\InsertLog.cshtml**

```
IL01   @model RunnerLog.Models.LogModel
IL02   <script src="@Url.Content("~/Scripts/jquery.validate.min.js")"></script>
IL03   <script src="@Url.Content("~/Scripts/jquery.validate.unobtrusive.min.js")"></script>
IL04   @using (Html.BeginForm())
IL05   {
IL06      @Html.ValidationSummary(true)
IL07      <fieldset>
IL08         <legend>LogModel</legend>
IL09
IL10         <div>
IL11            @Html.LabelFor(model => model.RunDate)
IL12         </div>
IL13         <div>
IL14            @Html.EditorFor(model => model.RunDate)
IL15            @Html.ValidationMessageFor(model => model.RunDate)
IL16         </div>
IL17         <div>
IL18            @Html.LabelFor(model => model.Distance)
IL19         </div>
IL20         <div>
IL21            @Html.EditorFor(model => model.Distance)
IL22            @Html.ValidationMessageFor(model => model.Distance)
IL23         </div>
IL24         <div>
IL25            @Html.LabelFor(model => model.Time) HH:MM:SS
IL26         </div>
IL27         <div>
IL28            @Html.EditorFor(model => model.Time)
IL29            @Html.ValidationMessageFor(model => model.Time)
IL30         </div>
IL31         <p>
IL32            <input type="submit" value="Create" />
IL33         </p>
IL34      </fieldset>
IL35   }
```

### Views\Shared\_Layout.cshtml

```
L001    <!DOCTYPE html>
L002    <html lang="en">
L003    <head>
L004      ...
L005    </head>
L006    <body>
L007      ...
L008      <footer>
L009
L010        <script type="text/javascript">
L011          var c = document.getElementById('myCanvas');
L012          var ctx = c.getContext('2d');
L013          ctx.font = '30pt Calibri';
L014          ctx.strokeStyle = 'gray';
L015          ctx.lineWidth = 3;
L016          ctx.strokeText('London 2012', 80, 30);
L017        </script>
L018      </footer>
L019    </body>
L020    </html>
```

**Answers:**

**A)** Table > th:last-child { font-weight: bold; }

**B)** Table+first-child{ font-weight: bold; }

**C)** Table>tr>th:nth-child{2}{font-weight: bold; }

**D)** Table > tr {font-weight: bold;}

**Solution:** D

**Question: 10** *One Answer Is Right*

You need to display the "miles" unit description after the distance in the GetLog view. Which line of code should you use to replace line GL21? (Each correct answer presents a complete solution. Choose all that apply.)

**Scenario:**

TESTLET-1. Background You are developing an ASP.NET MVC application in Visual Studio that will be used by Olympic marathon runners to log data about training runs. Business Requirements The application stores date, distance, and duration information about a user's training runs. The user can view, insert, edit, and delete records. The application must be optimized for accessibility. All times must be displayed in the user's local time. Technical Requirements Data Access: Database access is handled by a public class named RunnerLog.DataAccess.RunnerLogDb. All data retrieval must be done by HTTP GETand all data updates must be done by HTTP POST. Layout: All pages in the application use a master layout file named \Views\Shared\_Layout.cshtml. Models: The application uses the \Models\LogModel.cs model. Views: All views in the application use the Razor view engine. Four views located in \Views\RunLog are named: - _CalculatePace.cshtml - EditLog.cshtml - GetLog.cshtml - InsertLog.cshtml The application also contains a \Views\Home\Index.cshtml view. Controllers: The application contains a \Controllers\RunLogController.cs controller. Images: A stopwatch.png image is located in the \Images folder. Videos: A map of a runner's path is available when a user views a run log. The map is implemented as an Adobe Flash application and video. The browser should display the video natively if possible, using H264, Ogg, or WebM formats, in that order. If the video cannot be displayed, then the Flash application should be used. Security: You have the following security requirements: - The application is configured to use forms authentication. - Users must be logged on to insert runner data. - Users must be members of the Admin role to edit or delete runner data. - There are no security requirements for viewing runner data. - You need to protect the application against cross-site request forgery. - Passwords are hashed by using the SHA1 algorithm. RunnerLog.Providers.RunLogRoleProvider.cs contains a custom role provider. Relevant portions of the application files follow. (Line numbers are included for reference only.) Application Structure

## Controllers\RunLogController.cs

```
RC01   public class RunLogController : Controller
RC02   {
RC03     public ActionResult GetLog()
RC04     {
RC05       List<LogModel> log = RunnerLogDb.GetLogsFromDatabase();
RC06       return View(log);
RC07     }
RC08
RC09     public ActionResult InsertLog()
RC10     {
RC11       LogModel log = new LogModel();
RC12       log.RunDate = DateTime.Now;
RC13       return View(log);
RC14     }
RC15
RC16     [HttpPost]
RC17     public ActionResult InsertLog(LogModel log)
RC18     {
RC19       RunnerLogDb.InsertLog(log);
RC20       return RedirectToAction("GetLog");
RC21     }
RC22
RC23     public ActionResult DeleteLog(int id)
RC24     {
RC25       RunnerLogDb.DeleteLog(id);
RC26       return RedirectToAction("GetLog");
RC27     }
RC28
RC29     public ActionResult EditLog(int id)
RC30     {
RC31       LogModel log = RunnerLogDb.GetRunnerLog(id);
RC32       return View(log);
RC33     }
RC34   }
```

## Models\LogModel.cs

```
LM01   public class LogModel
LM02   {
LM03     [Required]
LM04     public int Id { get; set; }
LM05
LM06     [Required]
LM07     public DateTime RunDate { get; set; }
LM08
LM09     [Required]
LM10     [Range (0.01, 1000.00)]
LM11     public double Distance { get; set; }
LM12
LM13     [Required]
LM14     public TimeSpan Time { get; set; }
LM15
LM16     public string ShortDate
LM17     {
LM18       get
LM19       {
LM20         return RunDate.ToLocalTime().ToShortDateString();
LM21       }
LM22     }
LM23   }
```

## Views\RunLog\_CalculatePace.cshtml

```
CP01   @model RunnerLog.Models.LogModel
CP02   @(Convert.ToInt32(Model.Time.TotalMinutes / Model.Distance)) Min
CP03   @(Convert.ToInt32(Model.Time.TotalSeconds % 60 / Model.Distance)) Seconds
```

**Views\RunLog\EditLog.cshtml**

```
EL01    @model RunnerLog.Models.LogModel
EL02    <h2>Edit Log Item</h2>
EL03    <script src="@Url.Content("~/Scripts/jquery.validate.min.js")"></script>
EL04    <script src="@Url.Content("~/Scripts/jquery.validate.unobtrusive.min.js")"></script>
EL05    @using (Html.BeginForm()) {
EL06      @Html.AntiForgeryToken()
EL07      @Html.ValidationSummary(true)
EL08      <fieldset>
EL09        <legend>LogModel</legend>
EL10        <h3>
EL11          Log Id: @Model.Id
EL12        </h3>
EL13        <div>
EL14          @Html.LabelFor(model => model.Distance)
EL15        </div>
EL16        <div>
EL17          @Html.EditorFor(model => model.Distance)
EL18          @Html.ValidationMessageFor(model => model.Distance)
EL19        </div>
EL20        <div>
EL21          @Html.LabelFor(model => model.Time)
EL22        </div>
EL23        <div>
EL24          @Html.EditorFor(model => model.Time)
EL25          @Html.ValidationMessageFor(model => model.Time)
EL26        </div>
EL27        <p>
EL28          <input type="submit" value="Save" />
EL29        </p>
EL30      </fieldset>
EL31    }
```

### Views\RunLog\GetLog.cshtml

```
GL01   @model List<RunnerLog.Models.LogModel>
GL02   <h2>View Runs </h2>
GL03   <table>
GL04     <tr>
GL05       <th>Id </th>
GL06       <th>Date </th>
GL07       <th>Distance </th>
GL08       <th>Duration </th>
GL09       <th>Avg Mile Pace </th>
GL10     </tr>
GL11     @foreach (RunnerLog.Models.LogModel log in Model)
GL12     {
GL13       <tr>
GL14         <td>
GL15           @Html.DisplayFor(model => log.Id)
GL16         </td>
GL17         <td>
GL18
GL19         </td>
GL20         <td>
GL21           @Html.DisplayFor(model => log.Distance)
GL22         </td>
GL23         <td>
GL24           @Html.DisplayFor(model => log.Time)
GL25         </td>
GL26         <td>
GL27
GL28         </td>
GL29         <td>
GL30           @Html.ActionLink("Edit", "EditLog", new { id = log.Id })
GL31         </td>
GL32         <td>
GL33           @Html.ActionLink("Delete", "DeleteLog", new { id = log.Id })
GL34         </td>
GL35       </tr>
GL36     }
GL37   </table>
```

**Views\RunLog\InsertLog.cshtml**

```
IL01   @model RunnerLog.Models.LogModel
IL02   <script src="@Url.Content("~/Scripts/jquery.validate.min.js")"></script>
IL03   <script src="@Url.Content("~/Scripts/jquery.validate.unobtrusive.min.js")"></script>
IL04   @using (Html.BeginForm())
IL05   {
IL06       @Html.ValidationSummary(true)
IL07       <fieldset>
IL08           <legend>LogModel</legend>
IL09
IL10           <div>
IL11               @Html.LabelFor(model => model.RunDate)
IL12           </div>
IL13           <div>
IL14               @Html.EditorFor(model => model.RunDate)
IL15               @Html.ValidationMessageFor(model => model.RunDate)
IL16           </div>
IL17           <div>
IL18               @Html.LabelFor(model => model.Distance)
IL19           </div>
IL20           <div>
IL21               @Html.EditorFor(model => model.Distance)
IL22               @Html.ValidationMessageFor(model => model.Distance)
IL23           </div>
IL24           <div>
IL25               @Html.LabelFor(model => model.Time) HH:MM:SS
IL26           </div>
IL27           <div>
IL28               @Html.EditorFor(model => model.Time)
IL29               @Html.ValidationMessageFor(model => model.Time)
IL30           </div>
IL31           <p>
IL32               <input type="submit" value="Create" />
IL33           </p>
IL34       </fieldset>
IL35   }
```

## Views\Shared\_Layout.cshtml

```
L001  <!DOCTYPE html>
L002  <html lang="en">
L003  <head>
L004    ...
L005  </head>
L006  <body>
L007    ...
L008    <footer>
L009
L010      <script type="text/javascript">
L011        var c = document.getElementById('myCanvas');
L012        var ctx = c.getContext('2d');
L013        ctx.font = '30pt Calibri';
L014        ctx.strokeStyle = 'gray';
L015        ctx.lineWidth = 3;
L016        ctx.strokeText('London 2012', 80, 30);
L017      </script>
L018    </footer>
L019  </body>
L020  </html>
```

**Answers:**

**A)** @log.Distance miles

**B)** @Htrml.DisplayFor(model =>log.Distance) miles

**C)** @log.Distance.ToString() @Html.TextArea("miles")

**D)** @Html.DisplayFor(model => log.Distance.ToString() + " miles")

**Solution:** A, B

# Chapter 6: 70-740 - Installation, Storage, and Compute with Windows Server 2016

# Exam Guide

70-740 - Installation, Storage, and Compute with Windows Server 2016:

The **70-740 exam** is part of the Windows Server 2016 Certification. This exam measures your ability to work with Windows Server 2016, Hyper-V and Nano Server.

This certification exam is targeted for professional who perform installation, configuration, general local management and maintenance, storage, and compute functionalities available in Windows Server 2016. Candidates perform general installation tasks, including installing and configuring Nano Server, as well as creating and managing pre configured images for deployment. This is a list of covered topics:

- Windows Server 2016 installation requirements
- Configure \ Install Nano Server
- Create, manage, and maintain images for deployment
- Monitor and Update Windows 2016 and Nano Server
- Data DeDuplication and Server Storage
- Configure and Install Hyper-V and VM
- Deploy and Manage Windows containers
- High availability and disaster recovery with Nano Server technologies
- Manage failover clustering and Load Balancing
- Server installations and Monitoring

    Our 70-740 dumps will include those topics::

- Install Windows Servers in Host and Compute Environments (10-15%)
- Implement Storage Solutions (10-15%)
- Implement Hyper-V (20-25%)
- Implement Windows Containers (5-10%)
- Implement High Availability (30-35%)

- Maintain and Monitor Server Environments (10-15%)

    For more info visit: Microsoft Official 70-740 Exam Reference

High level topics covered by our practice test:

This Web Simulator is for Candidates with experience in Windows 2016 server envorinement, and candidates should have experience with local and server storage solutions including the configuration of disks and volumes, Data Deduplication, High Availability, Disaster Recovery, Storage Spaces Direct, and Failover Clustering solutions. The candidates should also be familiar with managing Hyper-V and Containers as well as maintaining and monitoring servers in physical and compute environments.

The Web Simulator will also help candidate to understand how integrate Hyper-V and Containers. The Web Simulator contains questions regarding the security and administration of Windows 2016 server and core services.

# Sample Practice Test for 70-740

**Question: 1** *One Answer Is Right*

Note: This question is part of a series of questions that present the same scenario. Each question in the series contains a unique solution that might meet the stated goals. Some question sets might have more than one correct solution, while others might not have a correct solution. After you answer a question in this section, you will NOT be able to return to it. As a result, these questions will not appear in the review screen. You have two servers that run Windows Server 2016. You plan to create a Network Load Balancing (NLB) cluster that will contain both servers. You need to configure the network cards on the servers for the planned NLB configuration. Solution: You configure the network cards to be on the same subnet and to have static IP addresses. You configure the cluster to use multicast. Does this meet the goal?

**Answers:**

A) Yes

B) No

**Solution:** A

**Explanation:**

Explanation: Following are the hardware requirements to run an NLB cluster. - All hosts in the cluster must reside on the same subnet. - There is no restriction on the number of network adapters on each host, and different hosts can have a different number of adapters. - Within each cluster, all network adapters must be either multicast or unicast. NLB does not support a mixed environment of multicast and unicast within a single cluster. - If you use the unicast mode, the network adapter that is used to handle client-to-cluster traffic must support changing its media access control (MAC) address. Following are the software requirements to run an NLB cluster. - Only TCP/IP can be used on the adapter for which NLB is enabled on each host. Do not add any other protocols (for example, IPX) to this adapter. - The IP addresses of the servers in the cluster must be static. References: https://technet.microsoft.com/en-us/windows-server-docs/networking/technologies/network-load-balancing

**Question: 2** *One Answer Is Right*

Note: This question is part of a series of questions that present the same scenario. Each question in the series contains a unique solution that might meet the stated goals. Some question sets might have more than one correct solution, while others might not have a correct solution. After you answer a question in this section, you will NOT be able to return to it. As a result, these questions will not appear in the review screen. You have two servers that run Windows Server 2016. You plan to create a Network Load Balancing (NLB) cluster that will contain both servers. You need to configure the network cards on the servers for the planned NLB configuration. Solution: You configure the network cards to be on the same subnet and to have dynamic IP addresses. You configure the cluster to use multicast. Does this meet the goal?

**Answers:**

**A)** Yes

**B)** No

**Solution:** B

**Explanation:**

Explanation: Following are the hardware requirements to run an NLB cluster. - All hosts in the cluster must reside on the same subnet. - There is no restriction on the number of network adapters on each host, and different hosts can have a different number of adapters. - Within each cluster, all network adapters must be either multicast or unicast. NLB does not support a mixed environment of multicast and unicast within a single cluster. - If you use the unicast mode, the network adapter that is used to handle client-to-cluster traffic must support changing its media access control (MAC) address. Following are the software requirements to run an NLB cluster. - Only TCP/IP can be used on the adapter for which NLB is enabled on each host. Do not add any other protocols (for example, IPX) to this adapter. - The IP addresses of the servers in the cluster must be static. References: https://technet.microsoft.com/en-us/windows-server-docs/networking/technologies/network-load-balancing

**Question: 3** *One Answer Is Right*

Note: This question is part of a series of questions that present the same scenario. Each question in the series contains a unique solution that might meet the stated goals. Some question sets might have more than one correct solution, while others might not have a correct solution. After you answer a question in this section, you will NOT be able to return to it. As a result, these questions will not appear in the review screen. You have two servers that run Windows Server 2016. You plan to create a Network Load Balancing (NLB) cluster that will contain both servers. You need to configure the network cards on the servers for the planned NLB configuration. Solution: You configure the network cards to be on the same subnet and to have static IP addresses. You configure the cluster to use unicast. Does this meet the goal?

**Answers:**

**A)** Yes

**B)** No

**Solution:** A

**Explanation:**

Explanation: Following are the hardware requirements to run an NLB cluster. - All hosts in the cluster must reside on the same subnet. - There is no restriction on the number of network adapters on each host, and different hosts can have a different number of adapters. - Within each cluster, all network adapters must be either multicast or unicast. NLB does not support a mixed environment of multicast and unicast within a single cluster. - If you use the unicast mode, the network adapter that is used to handle client-to-cluster traffic must support changing its media access control (MAC) address. Following are the software requirements to run an NLB cluster. - Only TCP/IP can be used on the adapter for which NLB is enabled on each host. Do not add any other protocols (for example, IPX) to this adapter. - The IP addresses of the servers in the cluster must be static. References: https://technet.microsoft.com/en-us/windows-server-docs/networking/technologies/network-load-balancing

**Question: 4** *One Answer Is Right*

Note: This question is part of a series of questions that present the same scenario. Each question in the series contains a unique solution that might meet the stated goals. Some question sets might have more than one correct solution, while others might not have a correct solution. After you answer a question in this section, you will NOT be able to return to it. As a result, these questions will not appear in the review screen. Your network contains an Active Directory forest. You install Windows Server 2016 on 10 virtual machines. You need to deploy the Web Server (IIS) server role identically to the virtual machines. Solution: You use Windows PowerShell Desired State Configuration (DSC) to create a default configuration, and then you apply the configuration to the virtual machines. Does this meet the goal?

**Answers:**

**A)** Yes

**B)** No

**Solution:** A

**Explanation:**

Explanation: DSC gives us a declarative model for system configuration management. What that really means is that we can specify how we want a workstation or server (a 'node') to be configured and we leave it to PowerShell and the Windows Workflow engine to make it happen on those target 'nodes'. We don't have to specify how we want it to happen. The main advantages of DSC are: - To simplify your sysadmin tasks by configuring one or more devices automatically - To be able to configure machines identically with the aim to standardize them - To ensure, at a given time, that the configuration of a machine always be identical to its initial configuration, so as to avoid drift - Deployment on demand as a Cloud strategy, or 'en masse', is largely automated and simplified References: https://www.simple-talk.com/sysadmin/powershell/powershell-desired-state-configuration-the-basics/

**Question: 5** *One Answer Is Right*

Note: This question is part of a series of questions that present the same scenario. Each question in the series contains a unique solution that might meet the stated goals. Some question sets might have more than one correct solution, while others might not have a correct solution. After you answer a question in this section, you will NOT be able to return to it. As a result, these questions will not appear in the review screen. You are a server administrator at a company named Contoso, Ltd. Contoso has a Windows Server 2016 Hyper-V environment configured as shown in the following table.

| Hyper-V host name | Configuration | Virtual switch name |
|---|---|---|
| Host1 | - Uses an Intel processor<br>- Is a member of a SAN named SAN1 | Switch1 |
| Host2 | - Uses an AMD processor<br>- Has local storage only | Switch2 |
| Host3 | - Uses an Intel processor<br>- Is a member of a SAN named SAN1 | Switch1 |
| Host4 | - Uses an Intel processor<br>- Has local storage only | Switch2 |

All of the virtual switches are of the external type. You need to ensure that you can move virtual machines between the hosts without causing the virtual machines to disconnect from the network. Solution: You implement live migration by using Host3 and Host4. Does this meet the goal?

**Answers:**

**A)** Yes

**B)** No

**Solution:** A

**Question: 6** *One Answer Is Right*

Note: This question is part of a series of questions that present the same scenario. Each question in the series contains a unique solution that might meet the stated goals. Some question sets might have more than one correct solution, while others might not have a correct solution. After you answer a question in this section, you will NOT be able to return to it. As a result, these questions will not appear in the review screen. You are a server administrator at a company named Contoso, Ltd. Contoso has a Windows Server 2016 Hyper-V environment configured as shown in the following table.

| Hyper-V host name | Configuration | Virtual switch name |
|---|---|---|
| Host1 | - Uses an Intel processor<br>- Is a member of a SAN named SAN1 | Switch1 |
| Host2 | - Uses an AMD processor<br>- Has local storage only | Switch2 |
| Host3 | - Uses an Intel processor<br>- Is a member of a SAN named SAN1 | Switch1 |
| Host4 | - Uses an Intel processor<br>- Has local storage only | Switch2 |

All of the virtual switches are of the external type. You need to ensure that you can move virtual machines between the hosts without causing the virtual machines to disconnect from the network. Solution: You implement live migration by using Host1 and Host2. Does this meet the goal?

**Answers:**

**A)** Yes

**B)** No

**Solution:** B

**Question: 7** *One Answer Is Right*

Note: This question is part of a series of questions that present the same scenario. Each question in the series contains a unique solution that might meet the stated goals. Some question sets might have more than one correct solution, while others might not have a correct solution. After you answer a question in this section, you will NOT be able to return to it. As a result, these questions will not appear in the review screen. You are a server administrator at a company named Contoso, Ltd. Contoso has a Windows Server 2016 Hyper-V environment configured as shown in the following table.

| Hyper-V host name | Configuration | Virtual switch name |
|---|---|---|
| Host1 | - Uses an Intel processor<br>- Is a member of a SAN named SAN1 | Switch1 |
| Host2 | - Uses an AMD processor<br>- Has local storage only | Switch2 |
| Host3 | - Uses an Intel processor<br>- Is a member of a SAN named SAN1 | Switch1 |
| Host4 | - Uses an Intel processor<br>- Has local storage only | Switch2 |

All of the virtual switches are of the external type. You need to ensure that you can move virtual machines between the hosts without causing the virtual machines to disconnect from the network. Solution: You implement a Hyper-V Replica between Host2 and Host4. Does this meet the goal?

**Answers:**

**A)** Yes

**B)** No

**Solution:** B

**Question: 8** *One Answer Is Right*

Note: This question is part of a series of questions that present the same scenario. Each question in the series contains a unique solution that might meet the stated goals. Some question sets might have more than one correct solution, while others might not have a correct solution. After you answer a question in this section, you will NOT be able to return to it. As a result, these questions will not appear in the review screen. Your network contains an Active Directory forest. You install Windows Server 2016 on 10 virtual machines. You need to deploy the Web Server (IIS) server role identically to the virtual machines. Solution: From a Group Policy object (GPO), you create an application control policy, and then you apply the policy to the virtual machines. Does this meet the goal?

**Answers:**

**A)** Yes

**B)** No

**Solution:** B

**Question: 9** *One Answer Is Right*

Note: This question is part of a series of questions that present the same scenario. Each question in the series contains a unique solution that might meet the stated goals. Some question sets might have more than one correct solution, while others might not have a correct solution. After you answer a question in this section, you will NOT be able to return to it. As a result, these questions will not appear in the review screen. Your network contains an Active Directory forest. You install Windows Server 2016 on 10 virtual machines. You need to deploy the Web Server (IIS) server role identically to the virtual machines. Solution: You create a software installation package, and then you publish the package to the virtual machines by using a Group Policy object (GPO). Does this meet the goal?

**Answers:**

**A)** Yes

**B)** No

**Solution:** B

**Question: 10** *One Answer Is Right*

Note: This question is part of a series of questions that present the same scenario. Each question in the series contains a unique solution that might meet the stated goals. Some question sets might have more than one correct solution, while others might not have a correct solution. After you answer a question in this section, you will NOT be able to return to it. As a result, these questions will not appear in the review screen. You have a server named Server1 that runs

Windows Server 2016. Server1 hosts a line-of-business application named App1. App1 has a memory leak that occasionally causes the application to consume an excessive amount of memory. You need to log an event in the Application event log whenever App1 consumes more than 4 GB of memory. Solution: You create a performance counter data collector. Does this meet the goal?

**Answers:**

A) Yes

B) No

**Solution:** B

# Chapter 7: 70-742 - Identity with Windows Server 2016

## Exam Guide

Identity with Windows Server 2016 70-742 Exam:

**Identity with Windows Server 2016 70-742 Exam** is one of the Microsoft Certified Solutions Associate (MCSA) Level Exam: This exam been designed keeping in mind to validate Candidate skillset in terms of Windows Server knowledge and respective uses mainly focusing over Active Directory, domain Controllers, Group Policy, Organizational Units Etc.

Apart from this it also validate candidates knowledge in terms of configuring and managing Active Directory setup in large enterprises. Candidates planning to write this exam should able to manage identities using the functionalities in Windows Server 2016. Candidates install, configure, manage, and maintain Active Directory Domain Services (AD DS) as well as implement Group Policy Objects (GPOs). Candidates should also be familiar implementing and managing Active Directory Certificate Services (AD CS), Active Directory Federations Services (AD FS), Active Directory Rights Management Services (AD RMS), and Web Application proxy

We think our **Identity with Windows Server 2016 70-742 Exam Practice Test Paper and Dumps** will provide you 100% confidence to make you appear for **Microsoft 70-742 Exam**

This is the list of the contents in our **Identity with Windows Server 2016 70-742 Practice Test:**

- Configure ADDS
- Manage certificates
- Configure ADFS
- Install and configure AD CS
- Manage Group Policy Objects (GPOs)
- Configure Group Policy preferences
- Implement Web Application Proxy (WAP)
- Maintain Active Directory

Identity with Windows Server 2016 (beta) 70-742 Dumps will include below mentioned topics with Exam focused percentage:

- Install and Configure Active Directory Domain Services (AD DS): 20-25%
- Manage and Maintain AD DS: 15-20%
- Create and Manage Group Policy: 25-30%
- Implement Active Directory Certificate Services (AD CS): 10-15%
- Implement Identity Federation and Access Solutions: 15-20%

Identity with Windows Server 2016 70-742 Dumps Provided Study Notes:

Certification-questions.com expert team recommend you to prepare some notes on these topics along with it don't forget to practice **Identity with Windows Server 2016 (beta) 70-742 Dumps** which been written by our expert team, Both these will help you a lot to clear this exam with good marks.

- Active Directory
- Domain Controller
- ADFS
- WAP
- GPO
- Active Directory groups and organizational units (OUs).

Overview about MICROSOFT 70-742 Exam:

- Format: Multiple choice, multiple answer
- Length of Examination: 150 minutes
- Number of Questions: 40-60
- Passing Score: 70-80%
- egistration Fee: 165 USD

Steps for MICROSOFT 70-742 Certifications Exam booking:

- Visit to Microsoft Exam Registration
- Signup/Login to MICROSOFT account
- Search for MICROSOFT 70-742 Certifications Exam
- Select Date and Center of examination and confirm with payment value of 165$

Benefits of having MICROSOFT 70-742 Certifications:

As we know that Active Directory is the brain of the complete IT Infrastructure. Getting a certification like Microsoft 70-742 can enhance the value of a job aspirant as a qualified

Windows Active Directory Administrator. It'd really attract HR to have a look to your CV and definitely it will help you out to have good salaried job in your hand by the end of the day. In such a situation, The relevance of a quality **MICROSOFT 70-742 Exam** study material is extremely important. And so we bring best-in-industry **MICROSOFT 70-742 Exam online course** and **practice tests** for you to help in your exam preparation.

Difficulty in writing MICROSOFT 70-742 Exam:

This exam quite easy to pass as it is one of the foundation level exam, Still ignorance and less study can make you get failed during your first attempt of exam.

Candidates having thorough study and hands-on practice can help you to get prepare for this exam. It is all up to your decision we mean to say a source which you used for 70-742 exam preparation it may be a book or an online source which offered you 70-742. In these days people mostly prefer to buy their study material from an online platform and there are many online websites who are offering **70-742** test questions but they are not verified by experts. So, you have to choose a platform which gives you the best & authentic **Microsoft 70-742 practice test paper & Microsoft 70-742 dumps** and and i.e. only you can have it at **Certification-questions.com** because all their exams are verified by the Subject Matter Expert.

**For more info visit:**
MICROSOFT 70-742 Exam Reference, Microsoft Documents

# Sample Practice Test for 70-742

**Question: 1** *One Answer Is Right*

Note: This question is part of a series of questions that use the same scenario. For you convenience, the scenario is repeated in each question. Each question presents a different goal and answer choices, but the text of the scenario is exactly the same in each question in this series. Start of repeated scenario. You work for a company named Contoso, Ltd. The network contains an Active Directory forest named contoso.com. A forest trust exists between contoso.com and an Active Directory forest named adatum.com. The contoso.com forest contains the objects configured as shown in the following table.

| Object name | Object type | Group scope | Group type |
|---|---|---|---|
| User1 | User | Not applicable | Not applicable |
| User2 | User | Not applicable | Not applicable |
| Computer1 | Computer | Not applicable | Not applicable |
| Group1 | Group | Domain local | Security |
| Group2 | Group | Domain local | Security |
| Group3 | Group | Universal | Security |
| Group4 | Group | Global | Security |
| Group5 | Group | Universal | Security |

Group1 and Group2 contain only user accounts. Contoso hires a new remote user named User3. User3 will work from home and will use a computer named Computer3 that runs Windows 10. Computer3 is currently in a workgroup. An administrator named Admin1 is a member of the Domain Admins group in the contoso.com domain. From Active Directory Users and Computers, you create an organizational unit (OU) named OU1 in the contoso.com domain, and then you create a contact named Contact1 in OU1. An administrator of the adatum.com domain runs the Set-ADUser cmdlet to configure a user named User1 to have a user logon name of User1@litwareinc.com. End of repeated scenario. You need to ensure that User2 can add Group4 as a member of Group5. What should you modify?

**Answers:**

**A)** the group scope of Group5

**B)** the Managed By settings of Group4

**C)** the group scope of Group4

**D)** the Managed By settings of Group5

**Solution:** D

**Question: 2** *One Answer Is Right*

Note: This question is part of a series of questions that use the same scenario. For your convenience, the scenario is repeated in each question. Each question presents a different goal and answer choices, but the text of the scenario is exactly the same in each question in this series. Start of repeated scenario. You work for a company named Contoso, Ltd. The network contains an Active Directory forest named contoso.com. A forest trust exists between contoso.com and an Active Directory forest named adatum.com. The contoso.com forest contains the objects configured as shown in the following table.

| Object name | Object type | Group scope | Group type |
|---|---|---|---|
| User1 | User | Not applicable | Not applicable |
| User2 | User | Not applicable | Not applicable |
| Computer1 | Computer | Not applicable | Not applicable |
| Group1 | Group | Domain local | Security |
| Group2 | Group | Domain local | Security |
| Group3 | Group | Universal | Security |
| Group4 | Group | Global | Security |
| Group5 | Group | Universal | Security |

Group1 and Group2 contain only user accounts. Contoso hires a new remote user named User3. User3 will work from home and will use a computer named Computer3 that runs Windows 10. Computer3 is currently in a workgroup. An administrator named Admin1 is a member of the Domain Admins group in the contoso.com domain. From Active Directory Users and Computers, you create an organizational unit (OU) named OU1 in the contoso.com domain, and then you create a contact named Contact1 in OU1. An administrator of the adatum.com domain runs the Set-ADUser cmdlet to configure a user named User1 to have a user logon name of User1@litwareinc.com. End or repeated scenario. You need to ensure that Admin1 can add Group2 as a member of Group3. What should you modify?

**Answers:**

**A)** Modify the Security settings of Group3.

**B)** Modify the group scope of Group3.

**C)** Modify the group type of Group3.

**D)** Set Admin1 as the manager of Group3.

**E)** Add Admin1 to the Enterprise Admins group

**Solution:** B

**Explanation:**

Explanation: A domain local group (group2) can only be a member of another domain local group. Therefore, we need to change the scope of Group3 from Universal to Domain Local.

**Question: 3** *Multiple Answers Are Right*

HOTSPOT Note: This question is part of a series of questions that use the same scenario. For you convenience, the scenario is repeated in each question. Each question presents a different goal and answer choices, but the text of the scenario is exactly the same in each question in this series.

### Start of repeated scenario

You work for a company named Contoso, Ltd. The network contains an Active Directory forest named contoso.com. A forest trust exists between contoso.com and an Active Directory forest named adatum.com. The contoso.com forest contains the objects configured as shown in the following table.

| Object name | Object type | Group scope | Group type |
|---|---|---|---|
| User1 | User | Not applicable | Not applicable |
| User2 | User | Not applicable | Not applicable |
| Computer1 | Computer | Not applicable | Not applicable |
| Group1 | Group | Domain local | Security |
| Group2 | Group | Domain local | Security |
| Group3 | Group | Universal | Security |
| Group4 | Group | Global | Security |
| Group5 | Group | Universal | Security |

Group1 and Group2 contain only user accounts. Contoso hires a new remote user named User3. User3 will work from home and will use a computer named Computer3 that runs Windows 10. Computer3 is currently in a workgroup. An administrator named Admin1 is a member of the Domain Admins group in the contoso.com domain. From Active Directory Users and Computers, you create an organizational unit (OU) named OU1 in the contoso.com domain, and then you create a contact named Contact1 in OU1. An administrator of the adatum.com domain runs the Set-ADUser cmdlet to configure a user named User1 to have a user logon name of User1@litwareinc.com.

### End of repeated scenario

You need to join Computer3 to the contoso.com domain by using offline domain join. Which commands should you use in the contoso.com domain and on Computer3? To answer, select the appropriate options in the answer area. Hot Area:

Answer Area

The contoso.com domain: ▼
- Add-Computer with the-DomainName parameter
- Djoin.exe with the /provision parameter
- Djoin.exe with the /requestodj parameter
- Net computer with the /add parameter
- Netdom.exe with the join parameter

Computer3: ▼
- Add-Computer with the-DomainName parameter
- Djoin.exe with the /provision parameter
- Djoin.exe with the /requestodj parameter
- Net computer with the /add parameter
- Netdom.exe with the join parameter

**Answers:**

## A)

**Answer Area**

The contoso.com domain:

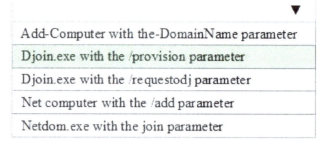

Computer3:

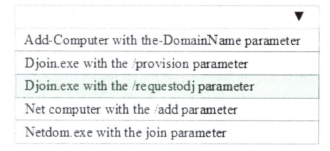

**Solution:** A

**Explanation:**

Explanation:

**Question: 4** *Multiple Answers Are Right*

HOTSPOT Your network contains an Active Directory forest. The forest contains one domain named contoso.com. The domain contains two domain controllers named DC1 and DC2. DC1 holds all of the operations master roles. During normal network operations, you run the following commands on DC2: Move-ADDirectoryServerOperationMasterRole -Identity "DC2" -OperationMasterRole PDCEmulator Move- ADDirectoryServerOperationMasterRole –Identity "DC2" -OperationMasterRole RIDMaster DC1 fails. You remove DC1 from the network, and then you run the following command: Move-ADDirectoryServerOperationMasterRole –Identity "DC2" -OperationMasterRole SchemaMaster For each of the following statements, select Yes if the statement is true. Otherwise, select No. Hot Area:

### Answer Area

| Statements | Yes | No |
|---|---|---|
| DC2 holds the schema master operations role. | ○ | ○ |
| DC2 holds the PDC emulator master operations role. | ○ | ○ |
| Currently, you can add additional domains to the forest. | ○ | ○ |

**Answers:**

**A)**

### Answer Area

| Statements | Yes | No |
|---|---|---|
| DC2 holds the schema master operations role. | ○ | ○ |
| DC2 holds the PDC emulator master operations role. | ○ | ○ |
| Currently, you can add additional domains to the forest. | ○ | ○ |

**Solution:** A

**Explanation:**

Explanation:

**Question: 5** *One Answer Is Right*

Your network contains an Active Directory forest named contoso.com Your company plans to hire 500 temporary employees for a project that will last 90 days. You create a new user account for each employee. An organizational unit (OU) named Temp contains the user accounts for the employees. You need to prevent the new users from accessing any of the resources in the domain after 90 days. What should you do?

**Answers:**

**A)** Run the Get-ADUser cmdlet and pipe the output to the Set-ADUser cmdlet.

**B)** Create a group that contains all of the users in the Temp OU. Create a Password Setting object (PSO) for the new group.

**C)** Create a Group Policy object (GPO) and link the GPO to the Temp OU. Modify the Password Policy settings of the GPO.

**D)** Run the Get-ADOrganizationalUnit cmdlet and pipe the output to the Set-Date cmdlet.

**Solution:** A

**Question: 6** *One Answer Is Right*

Your network contains an Active Directory forest. The forest contains two domains named litwarenc.com and contoso.com. The contoso.com domain contains two domains controllers named LON-DC01 and LON- DC02. The domain controllers are located in a site named London that is associated to a subnet of 192.168.10.0/24 You discover that LON-DC02 is not a global catalog server. You need to configure LON-DC02 as a global catalog server. What should you do?

**Answers:**

**A)** From Active Directory Sites and Services, modify the properties of the 192.168.10.0/24 IP subnet.

**B)** From Windows PowerShell, run the Set-NetNatGlobal cmdlet.

**C)** From Active Directory Sites and Services, modify the NTDS Settings object of LON-DC02.

**D)** From Windows PowerShell, run the Enable-ADOptionalFeature cmdlet.

**E)** From the properties of the LON-DC02 computer account in Active Directory Users and Computers, modify the NTDS settings.

**F)** From the properties of the LON-DC02 computer account in Active Directory Users and Computers, modify the City attribute.

**G)** From the properties of the Domain Controllers organizational unit (OU) in Active Directory Users and Computers, modify the Security settings.

**Solution:** C

**Question: 7** *One Answer Is Right*

Your network contains an Active Directory domain named contoso.com. The domain functional level is Windows Server 2012 R2. You need to secure several high-privilege user accounts to meet the following requirements: - Prevent authentication by using NTLM. - Use Kerberos to verify authentication request to any resources. - Prevent the users from signing in to a client computer if the computer is disconnected from the domain. What should you do?

**Answers:**

**A)** Create a universal security group for the user accounts and modify the Security settings of the group.

**B)** Add the users to the Windows Authorization Access Group group.

**C)** Add the user to the Protected Users group.

**D)** Create a separate organizational unit (OU) for the user accounts and modify the Security settings of the OU.

**Solution:** C

**Question: 8** *Multiple Answers Are Right*

HOTSPOT Your network contains an Active Directory domain named contoso.com. Some user accounts in the domain have the P.O. Box attribute set. You plan to remove the value of the P.O. Box attribute for all of the users by using Ldifde. You have a user named User1 who is located in the Users container. How should you configure the LDIF file to remove the value of the P.O. Box attribute for User1? To answer, select the appropriate options in the answer area. Hot Area:

## Answer Area

dn:

| CN=User1, CN=Users, DC=contoso, DC=com |
|---|
| CN=User1, OU=Users, DC=contoso, DC=com |
| Contoso.com/Users/User1 |
| User1 |

changetype:

| add |
|---|
| delete |
| modify |

delete: postOfficeBox

Answers:

A)

### Answer Area

dn: ▼

| CN=User1, CN=Users, DC=contoso, DC=com |
| CN=User1, OU=Users, DC=contoso, DC=com |
| Contoso.com/Users/User1 |
| User1 |

changetype: ▼

| add |
| delete |
| modify |

delete: postOfficeBox

**Solution:** A

**Explanation:**

Explanation:

**Question: 9** *Multiple Answers Are Right*

DRAG DROP Your company has multiple offices. The network contains an Active Directory domain named contoso.com. An Active Directory site exists for each office. All of the sites connect to each other by using DEFAULTIPSITELINK. The company plans to open a new office. The new office will have a domain controller and 100 client computers. You install Windows Server 2016 on a member server in the new office. The new server will become a domain controller. You need to deploy the domain controller to the new office. The solution must ensure that the client computers in the new office will authenticate by using the local domain controller. Which three actions should you perform next in sequence? To answer, move the appropriate actions from the list of actions to the answer area and arrange them in the correct order. Select and Place:

**Actions**
- Create a new site object.
- Create a new connection object.
- Promote the member server to a domain controller.
- Create a new subnet object.
- Move the server object of the domain controller.

**Answer Area**

Answers:

A)

**Actions**
- Create a new connection object.
- Move the server object of the domain controller.

**Answer Area**
- Create a new site object.
- Create a new subnet object.
- Promote the member server to a domain controller.

**Solution:** A

**Explanation:**

Explanation:

**Question: 10** *One Answer Is Right*

Your network contains an Active Directory forest named contoso.com. Users frequently access the website of an external partner company. The URL of the website is http://partners.adatum.com. The partner company informs you that it will perform maintenance on its Web server and that the IP addresses of the Web server will change. After the change is complete, the users on your internal network report that they fail to access the website. However, some users who work from home report that they can access the website. You need to ensure that your DNS servers can resolve partners.adatum.com to the correct IP address immediately. What should you do?

**Answers:**

**A)** Run dnscmd and specify the CacheLockingPercent parameter.

**B)** Run Set-DnsServerGlobalQueryBlockList.

**C)** Run ipconfig and specify the Renew parameter.

**D)** Run Set-DnsServerCache.

**Solution:** D

# Chapter 8: 70-743 - Upgrading Your Skills to MCSA: Windows Server 2016

## Exam Guide

70-743 - Upgrading Your Skills to MCSA: Windows Server 2016:

The **70-743 exam** is part of the Windows Server 2016 core infrastructure services Certification. This exam measures your ability to work with Windows Server 2016.

This certification exam is targeted for professional who perform installation, configuration, general local management and maintenance, storage, and compute functionalities available in Windows Server 2016 as this exam covers key aspects of installation, storage, compute, networking, and identity functionality available in Windows Server 2016. Candidates perform general installation tasks, including installing and configuring Nano Server, as well as creating and managing pre configured images for deployment. This is a list of covered topics:

- Install, upgrade, and migrate servers and workloads
- Configure \ Install Nano Server
- Create, manage, and maintain images for deployment
- Monitor and Update Windows 2016 and Nano Server
- Data DeDuplication and Server Storage
- Configure and Install Hyper-V and VM
- Deploy and Manage Windows containers
- High availability and disaster recovery with Nano Server technologies
- Manage failover clustering and Load Balancing
- Server installations and Monitoring
- Implement Storage Spaces Direct
- Install and configure DNS servers
- Implement virtual private network (VPN) and DirectAccess solutions and Implement high performance network solutions
- Implement Web Application Proxy (WAP)
- Configure and installa Federation with Active Directory Federation Services (AD FS)

Our 70-743 dumps will include those topics::

- Install Windows Servers in Host and Compute Environments
- Implement Storage Solutions
- Implement Hyper-V
- Implement Windows Containers
- Implement High Availability
- Implement Domain Name System (DNS)
- Implement Network Connectivity and Remote Access Solutions
- Implement an Advanced Network Infrastructure
- Install and Configure Active Directory Domain Services (AD DS)
- Implement identity federation and access solutions

For more info visit: Microsoft Official 70-743 Exam Reference

High level topics covered by our practice test:

This Web Simulator is for Candidates with experience in Windows 2016 server envorinement, and candidates should have experience with local and server storage solutions including the configuration of disks and volumes, Data Deduplication, High Availability, Disaster Recovery, Storage Spaces Direct, and Failover Clustering solutions with Hyper-V and Nano Server technologies. The candidates should also be familiar with managing Hyper-V and Containers as well as maintaining and monitoring servers in physical and compute environments.

The Web Simulator will also help candidate to understand how integrate Hyper-V and Containers. The Web Simulator contains questions regarding the security and administration of Windows 2016 server and core services.

# Sample Practice Test for 70-743

**Question: 1** *One Answer Is Right*

Note: This question is part of a series of a questions that present the same scenario. Each question in the series contains a unique solution that might meet the stated goals. Some questions sets might have more than one correct solutions, while others might not have a correct solution. After you answer a question in this section, you will NOT be able to return to it. As a result, these questions will not appear in the review screen. Your network contains an Active Directory forest named contoso.com. The forest contains a member server named Server1 that runs Windows Server 2016. All domain controllers run Windows Server 2012 R2. Contoso.com has the following configuration.

```
PS C:\> (Get-ADForest).ForestMode
Windows2008R2Forest

PS C:\> (Get-ADDomain).DomainMode
Windows2008R2Domain
PS C:\>
```

You plan to deploy an Active Directory Federation Services (AD FS) farm on Server1 and to configure device registration. You need to configure Active Directory to support the planned deployment. Solution: You upgrade a domain controller to Windows Server 2016. Does this meet the goal?

**Answers:**

**A)** Yes

**B)** No

**Solution:** A

**Explanation:**

Explanation: New installations of AD FS 2016 require the Active Directory 2016 schema (minimum version 85). Upgrading a domain controller will upgrade the schema. Note: upgrading the schema is not the same as upgrading the domain for forest functional level. Upgrading the functional level is not required.

**Question: 2** *One Answer Is Right*

Note: This question is part of a series of questions that present the same scenario. Each question in the series contains a unique solution. Determine whether the solution meets the stated goals. Your network contains an Active Directory domain named contoso.com. The domain contains a DNS server named Server1. All client computers run Windows 10. On Server1, you have the following zone configuration.

```
ZoneName              ZoneType    IsAutoCreated  IsDsIntegrated  IsReverseLookupZone  IsSigned
--------              --------    -------------  --------------  -------------------  --------
_msdcs.contoso.com    Primary     False          True            False                False
0.in-addr.arpa        Primary     True           False           True                 False
127.in-addr.arpa      Primary     True           False           True                 False
255.in-addr.arpa      Primary     True           False           True                 False
adatum.com            Forwarder   False          False           False
contoso.com           Primary     False          True            False                False
fabrikam.com          Primary     False          True            False                True
TrustAnchors          Primary     False          True            False                False
```

You need to ensure that all of the client computers in the domain perform DNSSEC validation for the fabrikam.com namespace. Solution: From Windows PowerShell on Server1, you run the Add-DnsServertrustAnchor cmdlet. Does this meet the goal?

**Answers:**

**A)** Yes

**B)** No

**Solution:** B

**Explanation:**

Explanation: The Add-DnsServerTrustAnchor command adds a trust anchor to a DNS server. A trust anchor (or trust "point") is a public cryptographic key for a signed zone. Trust anchors must be configured on every non- authoritative DNS server that will attempt to validate DNS data. Trust Anchors have no direct relation to DSSEC validation. References: https://docs.microsoft.com/en-us/powershell/module/dnsserver/add-dnsservertrustanchor?view=winserver2012-ps https://technet.microsoft.com/en-us/library/dn593672(v=ws.11).aspx https://docs.microsoft.com/en-us/windows-server/networking/dns/deploy/apply-filters-on-dns-queries

**Question: 3** *One Answer Is Right*

Note: This question is part of a series of questions that present the same scenario. Each question in the series contains a unique solution. Determine whether the solution meets the stated goals. Your network contains an Active Directory domain named contoso.com. The domain contains a DNS server named Server1. All client computers run Windows 10. On Server1, you have the following zone configuration.

```
ZoneName              ZoneType    IsAutoCreated  IsDsIntegrated  IsReverseLookupZone  IsSigned
--------              --------    -------------  --------------  -------------------  --------
_msdcs.contoso.com    Primary     False          True            False                False
0.in-addr.arpa        Primary     True           False           True                 False
127.in-addr.arpa      Primary     True           False           True                 False
255.in-addr.arpa      Primary     True           False           True                 False
adatum.com            Forwarder   False          False           False
contoso.com           Primary     False          True            False                False
fabrikam.com          Primary     False          True            False                True
TrustAnchors          Primary     False          True            False                False
```

You need to ensure that all of the client computers in the domain perform DNSSEC validation for the fabrikam.com namespace. Solution: From a Group Policy object (GPO) in the domain, you add a rule to the Name Resolution Policy Table (NRPT). Does this meet the goal?

**Answers:**

**A)** Yes

**B)** No

**Solution:** A

**Explanation:**

Explanation: The NRPT stores configurations and settings that are used to deploy DNS Security Extensions (DNSSEC), and also stores information related to DirectAccess, a remote access technology. Note: The Name Resolution Policy Table (NRPT) is a new feature available in Windows Server 2008 R2. The NRPT is a table that contains rules you can configure to specify DNS settings or special behavior for names or namespaces. When performing DNS name resolution, the DNS Client service checks the NRPT before sending a DNS query. If a DNS query or response matches an entry in the NRPT, it is handled according to settings in the policy. Queries and responses that do not match an NRPT entry are processed normally. References: https://technet.microsoft.com/en-us/library/ee649207(v=ws.10).aspx https://www.microsoftpressstore.com/articles/article.aspx?p=2756482

**Question: 4** *One Answer Is Right*

Note: This question is part of a series of questions that present the same scenario. Each question in the series contains a unique solution. Determine whether the solution meets the stated goals. Your network contains an Active Directory domain named contoso.com. The domain contains a DNS server named Server1. All client computers run Windows 10. On Server1, you have the following zone configuration.

```
ZoneName              ZoneType   IsAutoCreated  IsDsIntegrated  IsReverseLookupZone  IsSigned
--------              --------   -------------  --------------  -------------------  --------
_msdcs.contoso.com    Primary    False          True            False                False
0.in-addr.arpa        Primary    True           False           True                 False
127.in-addr.arpa      Primary    True           False           True                 False
255.in-addr.arpa      Primary    True           False           True                 False
adatum.com            Forwarder  False          False           False
contoso.com           Primary    False          True            False                False
fabrikam.com          Primary    False          True            False                True
TrustAnchors          Primary    False          True            False                False
```

You need to ensure that all of the client computers in the domain perform DNSSEC validation for the fabrikam.com namespace. Solution: From a Group Policy object (GPO) in the domain, you modify the Network List Manager Policies. Does this meet the goal?

**Answers:**

**A)** Yes

**B)** No

**Solution:** B

**Explanation:**

Explanation: Network List Manager Policies are security settings that you can use to configure different aspects of how networks are listed and displayed on one computer or on many computers. Network List Manager Policies are not related to DNSSEC. References: https://technet.microsoft.com/en-us/library/jj966256(v=ws.11).aspx https://docs.microsoft.com/en-us/windows/device-security/security-policy-settings/network-list-manager- policies

**Question: 5** *One Answer Is Right*

You have a server named Server1 that runs Windows Server 2016. You need to configure Server1 as a multitenant RAS Gateway. What should you install on Server1?

**Answers:**

**A)** the Network Controller server role

**B)** the Remote Access server role

**C)** the Data Center Bridging feature

**D)** the Network Policy and Access Services server role

**Solution:** B

**Explanation:**

Explanation: RAS Gateway - Multitenant. You can deploy RAS Gateway as a multitenant, software-based edge gateway and router when you are using Hyper-V Network Virtualization or you have VM networks deployed with virtual Local Area Networks (VLANs). With the RAS Gateway, Cloud Service Providers (CSPs) and Enterprises can enable datacenter and cloud network traffic routing between virtual and physical networks, including the Internet. With the RAS Gateway, your tenants can use point-so-site VPN connections to access their VM network resources in the datacenter from anywhere. You can also provide tenants with site-to-site VPN connections between their remote sites and your CSP datacenter. In addition, you can configure the RAS Gateway with BGP for dynamic routing, and you can enable Network Address Translation (NAT) to provide Internet access for VMs on VM networks. References: https://technet.microsoft.com/en-us/windows-server-docs/networking/remote-access/remote-access

**Question: 6** *Multiple Answers Are Right*

HOTSPOT You have a server named Server1 that runs Windows Server 2016. Server1 is a Hyper-V host. You have two network adapter cards on Server1 that are Remote Direct Memory Access (RDMA)-capable. You need to aggregate the bandwidth of the network adapter cards for a virtual machine on Server1. The solution must ensure that the virtual machine can use the RDMA capabilities of the network adapter cards. Which commands should you run first? To answer, select the appropriate options in the answer area. Hot Area:

**Answers:**

A)

**Answer Area**

**Solution:** A

**Explanation:**

Explanation: A new feature of Windows Server 2016 is SET (Switch Embedded Teaming). Create a SET team You must create a SET team at the same time that you create the Hyper-V Virtual Switch with the New- VMSwitch Windows PowerShell command. When you create the Hyper-V Virtual Switch, you must include the new EnableEmbeddedTeaming parameter in your command syntax. In the following example, a Hyper-V switch named TeamedvSwitch with embedded teaming and two initial team members is created. New-VMSwitch -Name TeamedvSwitch -NetAdapterName "NIC 1","NIC 2" -EnableEmbeddedTeaming $true References: https://technet.microsoft.com/en-gb/library/mt403349.aspx

**Question: 7** *Multiple Answers Are Right*

DRAG DROP You have a server named Server1 that runs Windows Server 2016. You need to deploy the first cluster node of a Network Controller cluster. Which four cmdlets should you run in sequence? To answer, move the appropriate cmdlets from the list of cmdlets to the answer area and arrange them in the correct order. Select and Place:

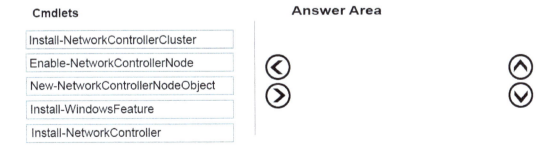

**Answers:**

## A)

**Cmdlets**

Enable-NetworkControllerNode

**Answer Area**

Install-WindowsFeature
New-NetworkControllerNodeObject
Install-NetworkControllerCluster
Install-NetworkController

**Solution:** A

**Explanation:**

Explanation: Deploy Network Controller using Windows PowerShell 1.Install-WindowsFeature Install the Network Controller server role To install Network Controller by using Windows PowerShell, type the following commands at a Windows PowerShell prompt, and then press ENTER. Install-WindowsFeature -Name NetworkController –IncludeManagementTools 2.New-NetworkControllerNodeObject You can create a Network Controller cluster by creating a node object and then configuring the cluster. You need to create a node object for each computer or VM that is a member of the Network Controller cluster. To create a node object, type the following command at the Windows PowerShell command prompt, and then press ENTER. Ensure that you add values for each parameter that are appropriate for your deployment. New-NetworkControllerNodeObject –Name  -Server -FaultDomain -RestInte 3.Install-NetworkControllerCluster To configure the cluster, type the following command at the Windows PowerShell command prompt, and then press ENTER. Ensure that you add values for each parameter that are appropriate for your deployment. Install-NetworkControllerCluster –Node  –ClusterAuthentication … 4.Install-NetworkController To configure the Network Controller application, type the following command at the Windows PowerShell command prompt, and then press ENTER. Ensure that you add values for each parameter that are appropriate for your deployment. Install-NetworkController –Node  –ClientAuthentication References: https://technet.microsoft.com/en-us/library/mt282165.aspx

**Question: 8** *One Answer Is Right*

You have an Active Directory domain that contains several Hyper-V hosts that run Windows Server 2016. You plan to deploy network virtualization and to centrally manage Datacenter Firewall policies. Which component must you install for the planned deployment?

**Answers:**

**A)** the Routing role service

**B)** the Canary Network Diagnostics feature

**C)** the Network Controller server role

**D)** the Data Center Bridging feature

**Solution:** C

**Explanation:**

Explanation: Using Windows PowerShell, the REST API, or a management application, you can use Network Controller to manage the following physical and virtual network infrastructure: * Datacenter Firewall This Network Controller feature allows you to configure and manage allow/deny firewall Access Control rules for your workload VMs for both East/West and North/South network traffic in your datacenter. The firewall rules are plumbed in the vSwitch port of workload VMs, and so they are distributed across your workload in the datacenter. Using the Northbound API, you can define the firewall rules for both incoming and outgoing traffic from the workload VM. You can also configure each firewall rule to log the traffic that was allowed or denied by the rule. * Hyper-V VMs and virtual switches * Remote Access Service (RAS) Multitenant Gateways, Virtual Gateways, and gateway pools * Load Balancers References: https://technet.microsoft.com/en-us/library/dn859239.aspx https://docs.microsoft.com/en-us/windows-server/networking/sdn/technologies/network-controller/network- controller

**Question: 9** *One Answer Is Right*

Note: This question is part of a series of questions that present the same scenario. Each question in the series contains a unique solution that might meet the stated goals. Some questions sets might have more than one correct solutions, while others might not have a correct solution. After you answer a question in this section, you will NOT be able to return to it. As a result, these questions will not appear in the review screen. Your network contains an Active Directory forest named contoso.com. The forest contains a member server named Server1 that runs Windows Server 2016. All domain controllers run Windows Server 2012 R2. Contoso.com has the following configuration:

```
PS C:\> (Get-ADForest).ForestMode
Windows2008R2Forest

PS C:\> (Get-ADDomain).DomainMode
Windows2008R2Domain
PS C:\>
```

You plan to deploy an Active Directory Federation Services (AD FS) farm on Server1 and to configure device registration. You need to configure Active Directory to support the planned deployment. Solution: You run adprep.exe from the Windows Server 2016 installation media. Does this meet the goal?

**Answers:**

**A)** Yes

**B)** No

**Solution:** A

**Explanation:**

Explanation: New installations of AD FS 2016 require the Active Directory 2016 schema (minimum version 85). You can upgrade the schema by running adprep.exe.

**Question: 10** *One Answer Is Right*

You have a server named Server1 that runs Windows Server 2016. The disk configuration for Server1 is shown in the exhibit. (Click the Exhibit button.)

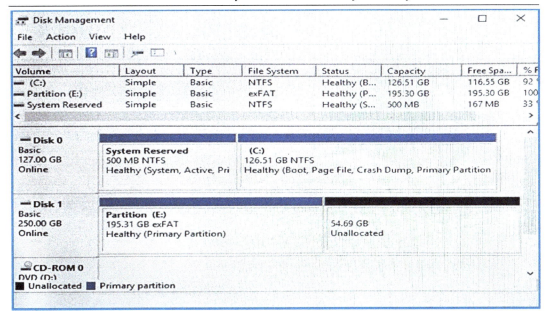

You add Server1 to a cluster. You need to ensure that you can use Disk 1 for Storage Spaces Direct. What should you do first?

**Answers:**

A) Set Disk 1 to offline.

B) Convert Partition (E:) to ReFS.

C) Convert Disk 1 to a dynamic disk.

D) Delete Partition (E:).

**Solution:** D

**Explanation:**

Explanation: The disks used in Storage Spaces Direct cannot contain existing partitions.

# Chapter 9: 70-761 - Querying Data with Transact-SQL

## Exam Guide

70-761 - Querying Data with Transact-SQL:

The **70-761 exam** is part of the Database Core Certification. This exam measures your ability to work with SQL and Transact-SQL.

This certification exam is targeted for professional who perform queries over SQL Server database. The certification is for administrators, system engineers, and developers with one or more years of experience who are seeking to validate their skills and knowledge in writing queries.. This is a list of covered topics:

- Create Transact-SQL SELECT queries, query multiple tables by using joins
- Using subqueries
- Group and pivot data by using queries
- Implement and design database programmability objects by using Transact-SQL
- Error handling and transactions
- Data types

Our 70-761 dumps will include those topics::

- Manage data with Transact-SQL (40-45%)
- Query data with advanced Transact-SQL components (30-35%)
- Program databases by using Transact-SQL (25-30%)

For more info visit: Microsoft Official 70-761 Exam Reference

High level topics covered by our practice test:

This Web Simulator is for Candidates with experience in SQL data queries with relevant work experience in SQL databases. The candidates should also be familiar with the SQL and Transact-SQL.

# Sample Practice Test for 70-761

**Question: 1** *One Answer Is Right*

Note: This question is part of a series of questions that present the same scenario. Each question in the series contains a unique solution that might meet the stated goals. Some question sets might have more than one correct solution, while others might not have a correct solution. After you answer a question in this section, you will NOT be able to return to it. As a result, these questions will not appear in the review screen. You create a table named Products by running the following Transact-SQL statement:

```
CREATE TABLE Products (
    ProductID int IDENTITY(1,1) NOT NULL PRIMARY KEY,
    ProductName nvarchar(100) NULL,
    UnitPrice decimal(18, 2) NOT NULL,
    UnitsInStock int NOT NULL,
    UnitsOnOrder int NULL
)
```

You have the following stored procedure:

```
CREATE PROCEDURE InsertProduct
    @ProductName nvarchar(100),
    @UnitPrice decimal(18,2),
    @UnitsInStock int,
    @UnitsOnOrder int
AS
BEGIN
    INSERT INTO Products(ProductName, ProductPrice, ProductsInStock, ProductsOnOrder)
    VALUES (@ProductName, @UnitPrice, @UnitsInStock, @UnitsOnOrder)
END
```

You need to modify the stored procedure to meet the following new requirements: - Insert product records as a single unit of work. - Return error number 51000 when a product fails to insert into the database. - If a product record insert operation fails, the product information must not be permanently written to the database. Solution: You run the following Transact-SQL statement:

```
ALTER PROCEDURE InsertProduct
@ProductName nvarchar(100),
@UnitPrice decimal(18,2),
@UnitsInStock int,
@UnitsOnOrder int
AS
BEGIN
   SET XACT_ABORT ON
   BEGIN TRY
      BEGIN TRANSACTION
         INSERT INTO Products(ProductName,ProductPrice,ProductsInStock,ProductsOnOrder)
         VALUES (@ProductName,@UnitPrice,@UnitsInStock,@UnitsOnOrder)
      COMMIT TRANSACTION
   END TRY
   BEGIN CATCH
      IF XACT_STATE() <> 0 ROLLBACK TRANSACTION
      THROW 51000, 'The product could not be created.', 1
   END CATCH
END
```

Does the solution meet the goal?

**Answers:**

**A)** Yes

**B)** No

**Solution:** B

**Explanation:**

Explanation: With X_ABORT ON the INSERT INTO statement and the transaction will be rolled back when an error is raised, it would then not be possible to ROLLBACK it again in the IF XACT_STATE() <> 0 ROLLBACK TRANSACTION statement. Note: A transaction is correctly defined for the INSERT INTO ..VALUES statement, and if there is an error in the transaction it will be caughtant he transaction will be rolled back, finally an error 51000 will be raised. Note: When SET XACT_ABORT is ON, if a Transact-SQL statement raises a run-time error, the entire transaction is terminated and rolled back. XACT_STATE is a scalar function thatreports the user transaction state of a current running request. XACT_STATE indicates whether the request has an active user transaction, and whether the transaction is capable of being committed. The states of XACT_STATE are: - 0 There is no active user transaction for the current request. - 1 The current request has an active user transaction. The request can perform any actions, including writing data and committing the transaction. - 2 The current request has an active user transaction, but an error hasoccurred that has caused the transaction to be classified as an uncommittable transaction. References: https://msdn.microsoft.com/en-us/library/ms188792.aspx https://msdn.microsoft.com/en-us/library/ms189797.aspx

**Question: 2** *One Answer Is Right*

Note: This question is part of a series of questions that present the same scenario. Each question in the series contains a unique solution that might meet the stated goals. Some question sets might have more than one correct solution, while others might not have a correct solution. After you answer a question in this section, you will NOT be able to return to it. As a result, these questions will not appear in the review screen. You create a table named Products by running the following Transact-SQL statement:

```
CREATE TABLE Products (
    ProductID int IDENTITY(1,1) NOT NULL PRIMARY KEY,
    ProductName nvarchar(100) NULL,
    UnitPrice decimal(18, 2) NOT NULL,
    UnitsInStock int NOT NULL,
    UnitsOnOrder int NULL
)
```

You have the following stored procedure:

```
CREATE PROCEDURE InsertProduct
    @ProductName nvarchar(100),
    @UnitPrice decimal(18,2),
    @UnitsInStock int,
    @UnitsOnOrder int
AS
BEGIN
    INSERT INTO Products(ProductName, ProductPrice, ProductsInStock, ProductsOnOrder)
    VALUES (@ProductName, @UnitPrice, @UnitsInStock, @UnitsOnOrder)
END
```

You need to modify the stored procedure to meet the following new requirements: - Insert product records as a single unit of work. - Return error number 51000 when a product fails to insert into the database. - If a product record insert operation fails, the product information must not be permanently written to the database. Solution: You run the following Transact-SQL statement:

```
ALTER PROCEDURE InsertProduct
@ProductName nvarchar(100),
@UnitPrice decimal(18,2),
@UnitsInStock int,
@UnitsOnOrder int
AS
BEGIN
    BEGIN TRY
        BEGIN TRANSACTION
            INSERT INTO Products(ProductName,ProductPrice,ProductsInStock,ProductsOnOrder)
            VALUES (@ProductName,@UnitPrice,@UnitsInStock,@UnitsOnOrder)
        COMMIT TRANSACTION
    END TRY
    BEGIN CATCH
        IF @@TRANCOUNT > 0 ROLLBACK TRANSACTION
            IF @@ERROR = 51000
                THROW
    END CATCH
END
```

Does the solution meet the goal?

**Answers:**

**A)** Yes

**B)** No

**Solution:** B

**Explanation:**

Explanation: A transaction is correctly defined for the INSERT INTO .VALUES statement, and if there is an error in the transaction it will be caught ant he transaction will be rolled back. However, error number 51000 will not be returned, as it is only used in an IF @ERROR = 51000 statement. Note: @@TRANCOUNT returns the number of BEGIN TRANSACTION statements that have occurred on the current connection. References: https://msdn.microsoft.com/en-us/library/ms187967.aspx

**Question: 3** *One Answer Is Right*

Note: This question is part of a series of questions that present the same scenario. Each question in the series contains a unique solution that might meet the stated goals. Some question sets might have more than one correct solution, while others might not have a correct solution. After you answer a question in this section, you will NOT be able to return to it. As a result, these questions will not appear in the review screen. You create a table named Products by running the following Transact-SQL statement:

```
CREATE TABLE Products (
    ProductID int IDENTITY(1,1) NOT NULL PRIMARY KEY,
    ProductName nvarchar(100) NULL,
    UnitPrice decimal(18, 2) NOT NULL,
    UnitsInStock int NOT NULL,
    UnitsOnOrder int NULL
)
```

You have the following stored procedure:

```
CREATE PROCEDURE InsertProduct
    @ProductName nvarchar(100),
    @UnitPrice decimal(18,2),
    @UnitsInStock int,
    @UnitsOnOrder int
AS
BEGIN
    INSERT INTO Products(ProductName, ProductPrice, ProductsInStock, ProductsOnOrder)
    VALUES (@ProductName, @UnitPrice, @UnitsInStock, @UnitsOnOrder)
END
```

You need to modify the stored procedure to meet the following new requirements: - Insert product records as a single unit of work. - Return error number 51000 when a product fails to insert into the database. - If a product record insert operation fails, the product information must not be permanently written to the database. Solution: You run the following Transact-SQL statement:

```
ALTER PROCEDURE InsertProduct
@ProductName nvarchar(100),
@UnitPrice decimal(18,2),
@UnitsInStock int,
@UnitsOnOrder int
AS
BEGIN
    BEGIN TRY
        INSERT INTO Products(ProductName, ProductPrice, ProductsInStock, ProductsOnOrder)
            VALUES (@ProductName, @UnitPrice, @UnitsInStock, @UnitsOnOrder)
    END TRY
    BEGIN CATCH
        THROW 51000, 'The product could not be created.', 1
    END CATCH
END
```

Does the solution meet the goal?

**Answers:**

**A)** Yes

**B)** No

**Solution:** A

**Explanation:**

Explanation: If the INSERT INTO statement raises an error, the statement will be caught and an error 51000 will be thrown. In this case no records will have been inserted. Note: You can implement error handling for the INSERT statement by specifying the statement in a TRY... CATCH construct. If an INSERT statement violates a constraint or rule, or if it has a value incompatible with the data type of the column, the statement fails and an error message is returned. References: https://msdn.microsoft.com/en-us/library/ms174335.aspx

**Question: 4** *One Answer Is Right*

Note: This question is part of a series of questions that present the same scenario. Each question in the series contains a unique solution that might meet the stated goals. Some question sets might have more than one correct solution, while others might not have a correct solution. After you answer a question in this section, you will NOT be able to return to it. As a result, these questions will not appear in the review screen. You create a table named Customer by running the following Transact-SQL statement:

```
CREATE TABLE Customer (
    CustomerID int IDENTITY(1,1) PRIMARY KEY,
    FirstName varchar(50) NULL,
    LastName varchar(50) NOT NULL,
    DateOfBirth date NOT NULL,
    CreditLimit money CHECK (CreditLimit < 10000),
    TownID int NULL REFERENCES dbo.Town(TownID),
    CreatedDate datetime DEFAULT(Getdate())
)
```

You must insert the following data into the Customer table:

| Record | First name | Last name | Date of Birth | Credit limit | Town ID | Created date |
|---|---|---|---|---|---|---|
| Record 1 | Yvonne | McKay | 1984-05-25 | 9,000 | no town details | current date and time |
| Record 2 | Jossef | Goldberg | 1995-06-03 | 5,500 | no town details | current date and time |

You need to ensure that both records are inserted or neither record is inserted. Solution: You run the following Transact-SQL statement:

```
INSERT INTO Customer (FirstName, LastName, DateOfBirth, CreditLimit, CreatedDate)
VALUES ('Yvonne', 'McKay', '1984-05-25', 9000, GETDATE())
INSERT INTO Customer (FirstName, LastName, DateOfBirth, CreditLimit, CreatedDate)
VALUES ('Jossef', 'Goldberg', '1995-06-03', 5500, GETDATE())
GO
```

Does the solution meet the goal?

**Answers:**

**A)** Yes

**B)** No

**Solution:** B

**Explanation:**

Explanation: As there are two separate INSERT INTO statements we cannot ensure that both or neither records are inserted.

**Question: 5** *One Answer Is Right*

Note: This question is part of a series of questions that present the same scenario. Each question in the series contains a unique solution that might meet the stated goals. Some question sets might have more than one correct solution, while others might not have a correct solution. After you answer a question in this section, you will NOT be able to return to it. As a result, these questions will not appear in the review screen. You create a table named Customer by running the following Transact-SQL statement:

```
CREATE TABLE Customer (
    CustomerID int IDENTITY(1,1) PRIMARY KEY,
    FirstName varchar(50) NULL,
    LastName varchar(50) NOT NULL,
    DateOfBirth date NOT NULL,
    CreditLimit money CHECK (CreditLimit < 10000),
    TownID int NULL REFERENCES dbo.Town(TownID),
    CreatedDate datetime DEFAULT(Getdate())
)
```

You must insert the following data into the Customer table:

| Record | First name | Last name | Date of Birth | Credit limit | Town ID | Created date |
|---|---|---|---|---|---|---|
| Record 1 | Yvonne | McKay | 1984-05-25 | 9,000 | no town details | current date and time |
| Record 2 | Jossef | Goldberg | 1995-06-03 | 5,500 | no town details | current date and time |

You need to ensure that both records are inserted or neither record is inserted. Solution: You run the following Transact-SQL statement:

```
INSERT INTO Customer (FirstName, LastName, DateOfBirth, CreditLimit, TownID, CreatedDate)
VALUES ('Yvonne', 'McKay', '1984-05-25', 9000, NULL, GETDATE())
INSERT INTO Customer (FirstName, LastName, DateOfBirth, CreditLimit, TownID, CreatedDate)
VALUES ('Jossef', 'Goldberg', '1995-06-03', 5500, NULL, GETDATE())
GO
```

Does the solution meet the goal?

**Answers:**

**A)** Yes

**B)** No

**Solution:** B

**Explanation:**

Explanation: As there are two separate INSERT INTO statements we cannot ensure that both or neither records are inserted.

**Question: 6** *One Answer Is Right*

Note: This question is part of a series of questions that present the same scenario. Each question in the series contains a unique solution that might meet the stated goals. Some question sets might have more than one correct solution, while others might not have a correct solution. After you answer a question in this section, you will NOT be able to return to it. As a result, these questions will not appear in the review screen. You have a database that tracks orders and deliveries for customers in North America. The database contains the following tables: Sales.Customers

| Column | Data type | Notes |
| --- | --- | --- |
| CustomerID | int | primary key |
| CustomerCategoryID | int | foreign key to the Sales.CustomerCategories table |
| PostalCityID | int | foreign key to the Application.Cities table |
| DeliveryCityID | int | foreign key to the Application.Cities table |
| AccountOpenedDate | datetime | does not allow new values |
| StandardDiscountPercentage | int | does not allow new values |
| CreditLimit | decimal(18,2) | null values are permitted |
| IsOnCreditHold | bit | does not allow new values |
| DeliveryLocation | geography | does not allow new values |
| PhoneNumber | nvarchar(20) | does not allow new values<br>data is formatted as follows: 425-555-0187 |

Application.Cities

| Column | Data type | Notes |
| --- | --- | --- |
| CityID | int | primary key |
| LatestRecordedPopulation | bigint | null values are permitted |

Sales.CustomerCategories

| Column | Data type | Notes |
| --- | --- | --- |
| CustomerCategoryID | int | primary key |
| CustomerCategoryName | nvarchar(50) | does not allow null values |

The company's development team is designing a customer directory application. The application must list customers by the area code of their phone number. The area code is defined as the first three characters of the phone number. The main page of the application will be based on an indexed view that contains the area and phone number for all customers. You need to return the area code from the PhoneNumber field. Solution: You run the following Transact-SQL statement:

```
CREATE FUNCTION AreaCode (
    @phoneNumber nvarchar(20)
)
RETURNS
TABLE
WITH SCHEMABINDING
AS
RETURN (
    SELECT TOP 1 @phoneNumber as PhoneNumber, VALUE as AreaCode
    FROM STRING_SPLIT(@phoneNumber, '-')
)
```

Does the solution meet the goal?

**Answers:**

**A)** Yes

**B)** No

**Solution:** B

**Explanation:**

Explanation: The function should return nvarchar(10) and not a TABLE. References: https://sqlstudies.com/2014/08/06/schemabinding-what-why/

**Question: 7** *One Answer Is Right*

Note: This question is part of a series of questions that present the same scenario. Each question in the series contains a unique solution that might meet the stated goals. Some question sets might have more than one correct solution, while others might not have a correct solution. After you answer a question in this section, you will NOT be able to return to it. As a result, these questions will not appear in the review screen. You have a database that tracks orders and deliveries for customers in North America. The database contains the following tables: Sales.Customers

| Column | Data type | Notes |
| --- | --- | --- |
| CustomerID | int | primary key |
| CustomerCategoryID | int | foreign key to the Sales.CustomerCategories table |
| PostalCityID | int | foreign key to the Application.Cities table |
| DeliveryCityID | int | foreign key to the Application.Cities table |
| AccountOpenedDate | datetime | does not allow new values |
| StandardDiscountPercentage | int | does not allow new values |
| CreditLimit | decimal(18,2) | null values are permitted |
| IsOnCreditHold | bit | does not allow new values |
| DeliveryLocation | geography | does not allow new values |
| PhoneNumber | nvarchar(20) | does not allow new values<br>data is formatted as follows: 425-555-0187 |

Application.Cities

| Column | Data type | Notes |
| --- | --- | --- |
| CityID | int | primary key |
| LatestRecordedPopulation | bigint | null values are permitted |

Sales.CustomerCategories

| Column | Data type | Notes |
| --- | --- | --- |
| CustomerCategoryID | int | primary key |
| CustomerCategoryName | nvarchar(50) | does not allow null values |

The company's development team is designing a customer directory application. The application must list customers by the area code of their phone number. The area code is defined as the first three characters of the phone number. The main page of the application will be based on an indexed view that contains the area and phone number for all customers. You need to return the area code from the PhoneNumber field. Solution: You run the following Transact-SQL statement:

```
CREATE FUNCTION AreaCode (
    @phoneNumber nvarchar(20)
)
RETURNS nvarchar(10)
AS
BEGIN
    DECLARE @areaCode nvarchar(max)
    SELECT TOP 1 @areaCode = VALUE FROM STRING_SPLIT(@phoneNumber, '-')
    RETURN @areaCode
END
```

Does the solution meet the goal?

**Answers:**

**A)** Yes

**B)** No

**Solution:** B

**Explanation:**

Explanation: As the result of the function will be used in an indexed view we should use schemabinding. References: https://sqlstudies.com/2014/08/06/schemabinding-what-why/

**Question: 8** *One Answer Is Right*

Note: This question is part of a series of questions that present the same scenario. Each question in the series contains a unique solution that might meet the stated goals. Some question sets might have more than one correct solution, while others might not have a correct solution. After you answer a question in this section, you will NOT be able to return to it. As a result, these questions will not appear in the review screen. You have a database that tracks orders and deliveries for customers in North America. The database contains the following tables:
Sales.Customers

| Column | Data type | Notes |
| --- | --- | --- |
| CustomerID | int | primary key |
| CustomerCategoryID | int | foreign key to the Sales.CustomerCategories table |
| PostalCityID | int | foreign key to the Application.Cities table |
| DeliveryCityID | int | foreign key to the Application.Cities table |
| AccountOpenedDate | datetime | does not allow new values |
| StandardDiscountPercentage | int | does not allow new values |
| CreditLimit | decimal(18,2) | null values are permitted |
| IsOnCreditHold | bit | does not allow new values |
| DeliveryLocation | geography | does not allow new values |
| PhoneNumber | nvarchar(20) | does not allow new values<br>data is formatted as follows: 425-555-0187 |

Application.Cities

| Column | Data type | Notes |
| --- | --- | --- |
| CityID | int | primary key |
| LatestRecordedPopulation | bigint | null values are permitted |

Sales.CustomerCategories

| Column | Data type | Notes |
|---|---|---|
| CustomerCategoryID | int | primary key |
| CustomerCategoryName | nvarchar(50) | does not allow null values |

The company's development team is designing a customer directory application. The application must list customers by the area code of their phone number. The area code is defined as the first three characters of the phone number. The main page of the application will be based on an indexed view that contains the area and phone number for all customers. You need to return the area code from the PhoneNumber field. Solution: You run the following Transact-SQL statement:

```
CREATE FUNCTION AreaCode (
    @phoneNumber nvarchar(20)
)
RETURNS nvarchar(10)
WITH SCHEMABINDING
AS
BEGIN
    DECLARE @areaCode nvarchar(max)
    SELECT @areaCode = value FROM STRING_SPLIT(@phoneNumber, '-')
    RETURN @areaCode
END
```

Does the solution meet the goal?

**Answers:**

**A)** Yes

**B)** No

**Solution:** B

**Explanation:**

Explanation: We need SELECT TOP 1 @areacode =.. to ensure that only one value is returned.

**Question: 9** *One Answer Is Right*

Note: This question is part of a series of questions that use the same scenario. For your convenience, the scenario is repeated in each question. Each question presents a different goal and answer choices, but the text of the scenario is exactly the same in each question in this series. You query a database that includes two tables: Project and Task. The Project table includes the following columns:

| Column name | Data type | Notes |
| --- | --- | --- |
| ProjectId | int | This is a unique identifier for a project. |
| ProjectName | varchar(100) | |
| StartTime | datetime2(7) | |
| EndTime | datetime2(7) | A null value indicates the project is not finished yet. |
| UserId | int | Identifies the owner of the project. |

The Task table includes the following columns:

| Column name | Data type | Notes |
| --- | --- | --- |
| TaskId | int | This is a unique identifier for a task. |
| TaskName | varchar(100) | A nonclustered index exists for this column. |
| ParentTaskId | int | Each task may or may not have a parent task. |
| ProjectId | int | A null value indicates the task is not assigned to a specific project. |
| StartTime | datetime2(7) | |
| EndTime | datetime2(7) | A null value indicates the task is not completed yet. |
| UserId | int | Identifies the owner of the task. |

You plan to run the following query to update tasks that are not yet started: UPDATE Task SET StartTime = GETDATE() WHERE StartTime IS NULL You need to return the total count of tasks that are impacted by this UPDATE operation, but are not associated with a project. What set of Transact-SQL statements should you run?

**Answers:**

A)
```
DECLARE @startedTasks TABLE(ProjectId int)
UPDATE Task SET StartTime = GETDATE() OUTPUT deleted.ProjectId INTO @startedTasks WHERE StartTime is NULL
SELECT COUNT(*) FROM @startedTasks WHERE ProjectId IS NOT NULL
```

B)
```
DECLARE @startedTasks TABLE(TaskId int, ProjectId int)
UPDATE Task SET StartTime = GETDATE() OUTPUT deleted.TaskId, deleted.ProjectId INTO @startedTasks
WHERE StartTime is NULL
SELECT COUNT(*) FROM @startedTasks WHERE ProjectId IS NULL
```

C)
```
DECLARE @startedTasks TABLE(TaskId int)
UPDATE Task SET StartTime = GETDATE() OUTPUT inserted.TaskId, INTO @startedTasks WHERE StartTime is NULL
SELECT COUNT(*) FROM @startedTasks WHERE TaskId IS NOT NULL
```

**D)**

```
DECLARE @startedTasks TABLE(TaskId int)
UPDATE Task SET StartTime = GETDATE() OUTPUT deleted.TaskId, INTO @startedTasks WHERE StartTime is NULL
SELECT COUNT(*) FROM @startedTasks WHERE TaskId IS NOT NULL
```

**Solution:** B

**Explanation:**

Explanation: The WHERE clause of the third line should be WHERE ProjectID IS NULL, as we want to count the tasks that are not associated with a project.

**Question: 10** *Multiple Answers Are Right*

DRAG DROP You need to create a stored procedure to update a table named Sales.Customers. The structure of the table is shown in the exhibit. (Click the exhibit button.)

  **Sales.Customers**

  **Columns**

 **custid (PK, int, not null)**

 **companyname (nvarchar(40), not null)**

 **contactname (nvarchar(30), not null)**

 **contacttitle (nvarchar(30), not null)**

 **address(nvarchar(60), not null)**

 **city (nvarchar(15), not null)**

 **region(nvarchar(15), null)**

 **postalcode (nvarchar(10), null)**

 **country (nvarchar(15), not null)**

 **phone (nvarchar(24), not null)**

 **fax (nvarchar(24), null)**

The stored procedure must meet the following requirements:- Accept two input parameters. - Update the company name if the customer exists. - Return a custom error message if the customer does not exist. Which five Transact-SQL segments should you use to develop the solution? To answer, move the appropriate Transact-SQL segments from the list of Transact-SQL segments to the answer area and arrange them in the correct order. NOTE: More than one order of answer choices is correct. You will receive credit for any of the correct orders you select. Select and Place:

**Transact-SQL segments**

```
UPDATE Sales.Customers
SET companyname = @custID
WHERE custid = @newname
```

```
UPDATE Sales.Customers
SET companyname = @newname
WHERE custid = @custID
```

```
BEGIN THROW 55555, 'The customer ID
does not exist.', 1 END
```

```
CREATE PROCEDURE
Sales.ModCompanyName @custID
int, @newname nvarchar(40) AS
```

```
IF NOT EXISTS (SELECT custid FROM
Sales.Customers WHERE custid =
@custID)
```

```
IF EXISTS (SELECT custid FROM
Sales.Customers
WHERE custid = @custID)
```

```
ROLLBACK TRANSACTION
```

**Answer Area**

**Answers:**

A)

**Solution:** A

**Explanation:**

Explanation:

# Chapter 10: 70-762 - Developing SQL Databases

## Exam Guide

Microsoft Developing SQL Databases 70-762 Exam:

Microsoft Developing SQL Databases 70-762 Exam which is related to MCSA SQL 2016 Database Development Certification. This exam tests candidate knowledge and skills to design and implement indexes, create Stored Procedures, manage isolation levels, optimize concurrency, locking behavior and manage performance for the database instance. Developers and Database Professionals usually hold or pursue this certification and you can expect the same job role after completion of this certification.

70-762 Exam topics:

Candidates must know the exam topics before they start of preparation. Because it will really help them in hitting the core. Our **70-762 dumps** will include the following topics:

- Design and implement database objects 25-30%
- Implement programmability objects 20-25%
- Manage database concurrency 25-30%
- Optimize database objects and SQL infrastructure 20-25%

Certification Path:

The MCSA SQL 2016 Database Development Certification includes only one 70-762 exam.

Who should take the 70-762 exam:

The Microsoft Developing SQL Databases 70-762 Exam certification is an internationally recognized validation that identifies persons who earn it as possessing skilled in MCSA SQL 2016 Database Development. If candidates want significant improvement in career growth needs enhanced knowledge, skills, and talents. The Microsoft Developing SQL Databases 70-762 Exam certification provides proof of this advanced knowledge and skill. If a candidate has knowledge of associated technologies and skills that are required to pass Microsoft Developing SQL Databases 70-762 Exam then he should take this exam.

How to study the 70-762 Exam:

Certification-questions.com expert team recommends you to prepare some notes on these topics along with it don't forget to practice Microsoft MS-900 Exam dumps which been written by our expert team, Both these will help you a lot to clear this exam with good marks.

How much 70-762 Exam Cost:

The price of the 70-762 exam is $165 USD.

How to book the 70-762 Exam:

These are following steps for registering the 70-762 exam.
Step 1: Visit to Microsoft Exam Registration
Step 2: Signup/Login to MICROSOFT account
Step 3: Search for MICROSOFT 70-762 Certifications Exam
Step 4: Select Date and Center of examination and confirm with payment value of $165

What is the duration of the 70-762 Exam:

- Format: Multiple choices, multiple answers
- Length of Examination: 150 minutes
- Number of Questions: 45-60
- Passing Score: 700/1000

The benefit in Obtaining the 70-762 Exam Certification:

- After completion of MCSA SQL, 2016 Database Development Certification candidates receive official confirmation from Microsoft that you are now fully certified in their chosen field. This can be now added to their CV, cover letters and job applications.
- When Candidates applying for a job or looking to promotion in their current position, an MCSA SQL 2016 Database Development certification in the field in which Candidates are applying will put you at the top of the list and make them a desirable candidate for employers.
- Candidates will get in-depth knowledge by completing the courses along with the access to revision materials for 6 months upon completion means they will have a wider skill set when it comes to the various technologies and systems than an uncertified professional. Certified Professional in this particular skill set is 74% more efficient when it comes to completing their tasks in a timely well-executed manner.

- Organization owners invest a lot in their employees when it comes to their training with the goal of making them quicker, more efficient, and more knowledgeable about their role. Certified Professional will reduce the time he spends on tasks, meaning he can get more done this could help reduce company downtime when repairing faults on a system or fixing hardware problems.
- Becoming Microsoft Certified Professional means one thing you are worth more to the company and therefore more to yourself in the form of an upgraded pay package. On average a Microsoft Certified Professional member of staff is estimated to be worth 30% more to a company than their uncertified professionals.

Difficulty in writing 70-762 Exam:

MCSA SQL 2016 Database Development Certification exam has a higher rank in the Information Technology sector. Candidate can add the most powerful Microsoft 70-762 certification on their resume by passing Microsoft 70-762 exam. Microsoft 70-762 is a very challenging exam Candidate will have to work hard to pass this exam. With the help of Certification-questions provided the right focus and preparation material passing this exam is an achievable goal. Certification-Questions provide the most relevant and updated **Microsoft 70-762 exam dumps**. Furthermore, We also provide the Microsoft 70-762 practice test that will be much beneficial in the preparation. Our aims to provide the best Microsoft 70-762 pdf dumps. We are providing all useful preparation materials such as **Microsoft 70-762 dumps** that had been verified by the Microsoft experts, Microsoft 70-762 braindumps and customer care service in case of any problem. These are things are very helpful in passing the exam with good grades.

For more info visit::

Microsoft 70-762 Exam Reference

# Sample Practice Test for 70-762

**Question: 1** *Multiple Answers Are Right*

DRAG DROP Note: This question is part of a series of questions that use the same scenario. For your convenience, the scenario is repeated in each question. Each question presents a different goal and answer choices, but the text of the scenario is exactly the same in each question in this series. You have a database named Sales that contains the following database tables: Customer,

Order, and Products. The Products table and the Order table are shown in the following diagram.

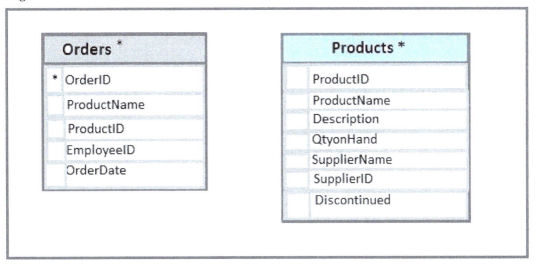

The customer table includes a column that stores the data for the last order that the customer placed. You plan to create a table named Leads. The Leads table is expected to contain approximately 20,000 records. Storage requirements for the Leads table must be minimized. Changes to the price of any product must be less a 25 percent increase from the current price. The shipping department must be notified about order and shipping details when an order is entered into the database. You need to implement the appropriate table objects. Which object should you use for each table? To answer, drag the appropriate objects to the correct tables. Each object may be used once, more than once, or not at all. You may need to drag the split bar between panes or scroll to view content. Select and Place:

**Objects**

- Foreign key constraint
- Instead of trigger
- Check constraint
- Primary key constraint
- Unique constraint
- After insert trigger

**Answer Area**

| Table | Objects |
|---|---|
| Orders | |
| Products | |

**Answers:**

**A)**

**Objects**

| | |
|---|---|
| | Instead of trigger |
| Check constraint | |
| Unique constraint | After insert trigger |

**Answer Area**

| Table | Objects |
|---|---|
| Orders | Foreign key constraint |
| Products | Primary key constraint |

**Solution:** A

**Explanation:**

Explanation: The Products table needs a primary key constraint on the ProductID field. The Orders table needs a foreign key constraint on the productID field, with a reference to the ProductID field in the Products table.

**Question: 2** *Multiple Answers Are Right*

HOTSPOT Note: This question is part of a series of questions that use the same scenario. For your convenience, the scenario is repeated in each question. Each question presents a different goal and answer choices, but the text of the scenario is exactly the same in each question in this series. You have a database named Sales that contains the following database tables: Customer, Order, and Products. The Products table and the Order table are shown in the following diagram.

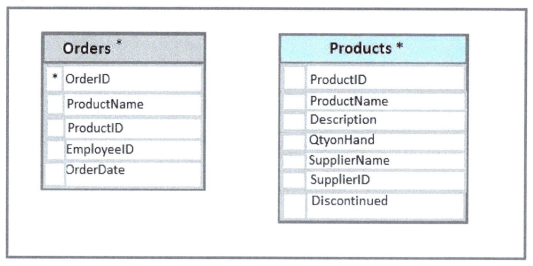

The customer table includes a column that stores the data for the last order that the customer placed. You plan to create a table named Leads. The Leads table is expected to contain approximately 20,000 records. Storage requirements for the Leads table must be minimized. You need to implement a stored procedure that deletes a discontinued product from the Products table. You identify the following requirements: - If an open order includes a discontinued product, the records for the product must not be deleted. - The stored procedure must return a custom error message if a product record cannot be deleted. The message must identify the OrderID for the open order. What should you do? To answer, select the appropriate Transact-SQL segments in the answer area. Hot Area:

**Answer Area**

| Requirement | Transact-SQL segment |
|---|---|
| Handle errors | Try/Parse Select @@error |
| | Begin Tran/Rollback Tran |
| | Try/Catch* |
| Display error message | ERROR_MESSAGE() |
| | PRINT |
| | RAISERROR |
| | RETURN |

**Answers:**

A)

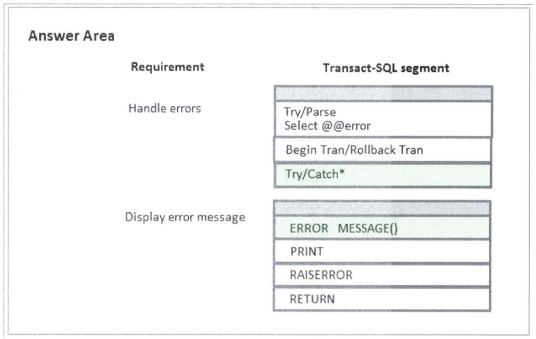

**Solution:** A

**Explanation:**

Explanation: Using TRY...CATCH in Transact-SQL Errors in Transact-SQL code can be processed by using a TRY...CATCH construct. TRY...CATCH can use the following error function to capture error information: ERROR_MESSAGE() returns the complete text of the error message. The text includes the values supplied for any substitutable parameters such as lengths, object names, or times. References: https://technet.microsoft.com/en-us/library/ms179296(v=sql.105).aspx

**Question: 3** *Multiple Answers Are Right*

HOTSPOT Note: This question is part of a series of questions that use the same scenario. For your convenience, the scenario is repeated in each question. Each question presents a different goal and answer choices, but the text of the scenario is exactly the same in each question in this series. You have a database named Sales that contains the following database tables: Customer, Order, and Products. The Products table and the Order table are shown in the following diagram.

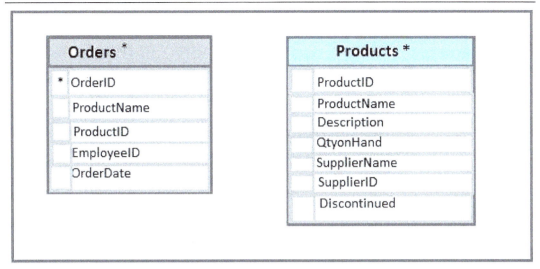

The customer table includes a column that stores the data for the last order that the customer placed. You plan to create a table named Leads. The Leads table is expected to contain approximately 20,000 records. Storage requirements for the Leads table must be minimized. You need to create triggers that meet the following requirements: - Optimize the performance and data integrity of the tables. - Provide a custom error if a user attempts to create an order for a customer that does not exist. - In the Customers table, update the value for the last order placed. - Complete all actions as part of the original transaction. In the table below, identify the trigger types that meet the requirements. NOTE: Make only selection in each column. Each correct selection is worth one point. Hot Area:

| Trigger type | Provide custom | Update Customer table |
| --- | --- | --- |
| AFTER INSERT trigger | ● | ● |
| INSTEAD OF INSERT trigger | ● | ● |
| AFTER UPDATE trigger | ● | ● |
| INSTEAD OF UPDATE trigger | ● | ● |

Answers:

A)

**Answer Area**

| Trigger type | Provide custom | Update Customer table |
|---|---|---|
| AFTER INSERT trigger | ● | ○ |
| INSTEAD OF INSERT trigger | ○ | ○ |
| AFTER UPDATE trigger | ○ | ● |
| INSTEAD OF UPDATE trigger | ○ | ○ |

**Solution:** A

**Explanation:**

Explanation: INSTEAD OF INSERT triggers can be defined on a view or table to replace the standard action of the INSERT statement. AFTER specifies that the DML trigger is fired only when all operations specified in the triggering SQL statement have executed successfully.
References: https://technet.microsoft.com/en-us/library/ms175089(v=sql.105).aspx

**Question: 4** *Multiple Answers Are Right*

HOTSPOT Note: This question is part of a series of questions that use the same scenario. For your convenience, the scenario is repeated in each question. Each question presents a different goal and answer choices, but the text of the scenario is exactly the same in each question in this series. You have a database named Sales that contains the following database tables: Customer, Order, and Products. The Products table and the Order table are shown in the following diagram.

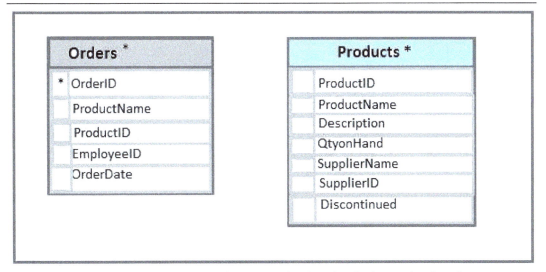

The customer table includes a column that stores the data for the last order that the customer placed. You plan to create a table named Leads. The Leads table is expected to contain approximately 20,000 records. Storage requirements for the Leads table must be minimized. The Leads table must include the columns described in the following table.

| Column name | Description |
|---|---|
| LeadID | This column stores a unique vale that is automatically assigned for each lead. |
| IsCustomer | This column indicates whether the lead is for a current customer. |

The data types chosen must consume the least amount of storage possible. You need to select the appropriate data types for the Leads table. In the table below, identify the data type that must be used for each table column. NOTE: Make only one selection in each column. Hot Area:

## Answer Area

| Data type | LeadID | IsCustomer |
|---|---|---|
| smallint | ● | ● |
| int | ● | ● |
| binary | ● | ● |
| numeric | ● | ● |
| bit | ● | ● |

**Answers:**

A)

## Answer Area

| Data type | LeadID | IsCustomer |
|---|---|---|
| smallint | ● | ○ |
| int | ○ | ○ |
| binary | ○ | ○ |
| numeric | ○ | ○ |
| bit | ○ | ● |

**Solution:** A

**Explanation:**

Explanation: Bit is a Transact-SQL integer data type that can take a value of 1, 0, or NULL. Smallint is a Transact-SQL integer data type that can take a value in the range from -32,768 to 32,767. int, bigint, smallint, and tinyint (Transact-SQL) Exact-number data types that use integer data.

| Data type | Range | Storage |
|---|---|---|
| bigint | -2^63 (-9,223,372,036,854,775,808) to 2^63-1 (9,223,372,036,854,775,807) | 8 Bytes |
| int | -2^31 (-2,147,483,648) to 2^31-1 (2,147,483,647) | 4 Bytes |
| smallint | -2^15 (-32,768) to 2^15-1 (32,767) | 2 Bytes |
| tinyint | 0 to 255 | 1 Byte |

References: https://msdn.microsoft.com/en-us/library/ms187745.aspx
https://msdn.microsoft.com/en-us/library/ms177603.aspx

**Question: 5** *Multiple Answers Are Right*

HOTSPOT Note: This question is part of a series of questions that use the same scenario. For your convenience, the scenario is repeated in each question. Each question presents a different goal and answer choices, but the text of the scenario is exactly the same in each question in this series. You have a database named Sales that contains the following database tables: Customer, Order, and Products. The Products table and the Order table are shown in the following diagram.

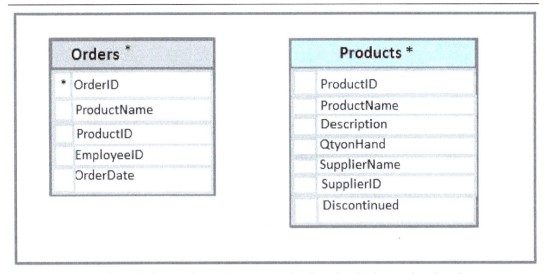

The customer table includes a column that stores the data for the last order that the customer placed. You plan to create a table named Leads. The Leads table is expected to contain approximately 20,000 records. Storage requirements for the Leads table must be minimized. You need to modify the database design to meet the following requirements: - Rows in the Orders table must always have a valid value for the ProductID column. - Rows in the Products table must not be deleted if they are part of any rows in the Orders table. - All rows in both tables must be unique. In the table below, identify the constraint that must be configured for each table. NOTE: Make only one selection in each column. Hot Area:

**Answer Area**

| Constraint | Orders table | Products table |
|---|---|---|
| Check constraint on **OrderID** | ● | ● |
| Foreign key constraint on **ProductID** | ● | ● |
| Check constraint on **ProductID** | ● | ● |
| Foreign key constraint on **OrderID** | ● | ● |

**Answers:**

## A)

### Answer Area

| Constraint | Orders table | Products table |
|---|---|---|
| Check constraint on **OrderID** | ○ | ○ |
| Foreign key constraint on **ProductID** | ● | ○ |
| Check constraint on **ProductID** | ○ | ● |
| Foreign key constraint on **OrderID** | ○ | ○ |

**Solution:** A

**Explanation:**

Explanation: A FOREIGN KEY in one table points to a PRIMARY KEY in another table. Here the foreign key constraint is put on the ProductID in the Orders, and points to the ProductID of the Products table. With a check constraint on the ProductID we can ensure that the Products table contains only unique rows. References: http://www.w3schools.com/sql/sql_foreignkey.asp

**Question: 6** *Multiple Answers Are Right*

DRAG DROP Note: This question is part of a series of questions that use the same scenario. For your convenience, the scenario is repeated in each question. Each question presents a different goal and answer choices, but the text of the scenario is exactly the same in each question in the series. You have a database named Sales that contains the following database tables. Customer, Order, and Products. The Products table and the order table shown in the following diagram.

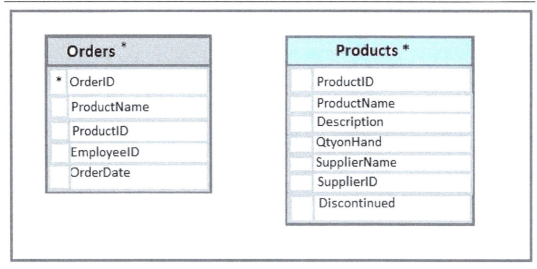

The Customer table includes a column that stores the date for the last order that the customer placed. You plan to create a table named Leads. The Leads table is expected to contain approximately 20,000 records. Storage requirements for the Leads table must be minimized. You need to begin to modify the table design to adhere to third normal form. Which column should you remove for each table? To answer? drag the appropriate column names to the correct locations. Each column name may be used once, more than once, or not at all. You may need to drag the split bar between panes or scroll to view content. Select and Place:

Columns
- ProductID
- ProductName
- Description
- EmployeeID
- OrderDate
- SupplierName
- SupplierID
- Discontinued

Answer Area

| Table | Column to remove |
|---|---|
| Products | Column |
| Orders | Column |

**Answers:**

## A)

**Columns**
- ProductID
- Description
- EmployeeID
- OrderDate
- SupplierID
- Discontinued

**Answer Area**

| Table | Column to remove |
|---|---|
| Products | SupplierName |
| Orders | ProductName |

**Solution:** A

**Explanation:**

Explanation: In the Products table the SupplierName is dependant on the SupplierID, not on the ProductID. In the Orders table the ProductName is dependant on the ProductID, not on the OrderID. Note: A table is in third normal form when the following conditions are met: - It is in second normal form. - All nonprimary fields are dependent on the primary key. Second normal form states that it should meet all the rules for First 1Normnal Form and there must be no partial dependences of any of the columns onthe primary key. First normal form (1NF) sets the very basic rules for an organized database: - Define the data items required, because they become the columns in a table. Place related data items in a table. - Ensure that there are no repeating groups ofdata. - Ensure that there is a primary key. References: https://www.tutorialspoint.com/sql/third-normal-form.htm

**Question: 7** *Multiple Answers Are Right*

HOTSPOT Note: This question is part of a series of questions that use the same scenario. For your convenience, the scenario is repeated in each question. Each question presents a different goal and answer choices, but the text of the scenario is exactly the same in each question in this series. You have a database that contains the following tables: BlogCategory, BlogEntry, ProductReview, Product, and SalesPerson. The tables were created using the following Transact SQL statements:

```sql
CREATE TABLE BlogCategory
(
    CategoryID int NOT NULL PRIMARY KEY,
    CategoryName nvarchar (20)
);

CREATE TABLE BlogEntry
(
    Entry int NOT PRIMARY KEY,
    Entrytitle nvarchar (50),
    Category int NOT NULL FOREIGN KEY REFERENCES BlogCategory (CategoryID)
);

CREATE TABLE dbo.ProductReview
(
    ProductReviewID IDENTITY(1,1) PRIMARY KEY,
    Product int NOT NULL,
    Review varchar (1000) NOT NULL
);

CREATE TABLE dbo.Product
(
    ProductID int Identity(1,1) PRIMARY KEY,
    Name varchar(1000) NOT NULL
);
CREATE TABLE dbo.SalesPerson
(
    SalesPersonID int IDENTITY(1,1) PRIMARY KEY,
    Name varchar (1000) NOT NULL,
    SalesID Money
)
```

You must modify the ProductReview Table to meet the following requirements: - The table must reference the ProductID column in the Product table - Existing records in the ProductReview table must not be validated with the Product table. - Deleting records in the Product table must not be allowed if records are referenced by the ProductReview table. - Changes to records in the Product table must propagate to the ProductReview table. You also have the following database tables: Order, ProductTypes, and SalesHistory, The transact-SQL statements for these tables are not available. You must modify the Orders table to meet the following requirements: - Create new rows in the table without granting INSERT permissions to the table. - Notify the sales person who places an order whether or not the order was completed. You must add the following constraints to the SalesHistory table: - a constraint on the SaleID column that allows the field to be used as a record identifier - a constant that uses the ProductID column to reference the Product column of the ProductTypes table - a constraint on the CategoryID column that allows one row with a null value in the column - a constraint that limits the

SalePrice column to values greater than four Finance department users must be able to retrieve data from the SalesHistory table for sales persons where the value of the SalesYTD column is above a certain threshold. You plan to create a memory-optimized table named SalesOrder. The table must meet the following requirements: - The table must hold 10 million unique sales orders. - The table must use checkpoints to minimize I/O operations and must not use transaction logging. - Data loss is acceptable. Performance for queries against the SalesOrder table that use Where clauses with exact equality operations must be optimized. You need to enable referential integrity for the ProductReview table. How should you complete the relevant Transact-SQL statement? To answer? select the appropriate Transact-SQL segments in the answer area. Hot Area:

Answer Area

Alter Table dbo.ProdectReview

```
WITH CHECK
WITH NOCHECK
ALTER COLUMN ProductId int NULL; ALTER TABLE dbo.ProductReview WITH NOCHECK
ALTER COLUMN ProductId int NULL; ALTER TABLE dbo.ProductReview WITH CHECK
```

ADD CONSTRAINT FK_productReview_Product FOREIGN KEY (ProductID)

REFERENCES Product (productID)

```
ON DELETE NO ACTION
ON DELETE NO ACTION ON UPDATE CASCADE
ON DELETE CASCADE ON UPDATE CASCADE
ON DELETE CASCADE ON UPDATE SET DEFAULT
```

Answers:

A)

Answer Area

Alter Table dbo.ProductReview

```
WITH CHECK
WITH NOCHECK
ALTER COLUMN ProductId int NULL; ALTER TABLE dbo.ProductReview WITH NOCHECK
ALTER COLUMN ProductId int NULL; ALTER TABLE dbo.ProductReview WITH CHECK
```

ADD CONSTRAINT FK_productReview_Product FOREIGN KEY (ProductID)

REFERENCES Product (productID)

```
ON DELETE NO ACTION
ON DELETE NO ACTION ON UPDATE CASCADE
ON DELETE CASCADE ON UPDATE CASCADE
ON DELETE CASCADE ON UPDATE SET DEFAULT
```

**Solution:** A

**Explanation:**

Explanation: Box 1: WITH NOCHECK We should use WITH NOCHECK as existing records in the ProductReview table must not be validated with the Product table. Box 2: ON DELETE NO ACTION ON DELETE NO CASCADE Deletes should not be allowed, so we use ON DELETE NO ACTION. Updates should be allowed, so we use ON DELETE NO CASCADE NO ACTION: the Database Engine raises an error, and the update action on the row in the parent table is rolled back. CASCADE: corresponding rows are updated in the referencing table when that row is updated in the parent table. Note: ON DELETE { NO ACTION | CASCADE | SET NULL | SET DEFAULT } Specifies what action happens to rows in the table that is altered, if those rows have a referential relationship and the referenced row is deleted from the parent table. The default is NO ACTION. ON UPDATE { NO ACTION | CASCADE | SET NULL | SET DEFAULT } Specifies what action happens to rows in the table altered when those rows have a referential relationship and the referenced row is updated in the parent table. The default is NO ACTION. Note: You must modify the ProductReview Table to meet the following requirements: 1. The table must reference the ProductID column in the Product table 2. Existing records in the ProductReview table must not be validated with the Product table. 3. Deleting records in the Product table must not be allowed if records are referenced by the ProductReview table. 4. Changes to records in the Product table must propagate to the ProductReview table. References: https://msdn.microsoft.com/en-us/library/ms190273.aspx https://msdn.microsoft.com/en-us/library/ms188066.aspx

**Question: 8** *Multiple Answers Are Right*

HOTSPOT Note: This question is part of a series of questions that use the same scenario. For your convenience, the scenario is repeated in each question. Each question presents a different goal and answer choices, but the text of the scenario is exactly the same in each question in this series. You have a database that contains the following tables: BlogCategory, BlogEntry, ProductReview, Product, and SalesPerson. The tables were created using the following Transact SQL statements:

```
CREATE TABLE BlogCategory
(
    CategoryID int NOT NULL PRIMARY KEY,
    CategoryName nvarchar (20)
);

CREATE TABLE BlogEntry
(
    Entry int NOT PRIMARY KEY,
    Entrytitle nvarchar (50),
    Category int NOT NULL FOREIGN KEY REFERENCES BlogCategory (CategoryID)
);

CREATE TABLE dbo.ProductReview
(
    ProductReviewID IDENTITY(1,1) PRIMARY KEY,
    Product int NOT NULL,
    Review varchar (1000) NOT NULL
);

CREATE TABLE dbo.Product
(
    ProductID int Identity(1,1) PRIMARY KEY,
    Name varchar(1000) NOT NULL
);
CREATE TABLE dbo.SalesPerson
(
    SalesPersonID int IDENTITY(1,1) PRIMARY KEY,
    Name varchar (1000) NOT NULL,
    SalesID Money
)
```

You must modify the ProductReview Table to meet the following requirements: - The table must reference the ProductID column in the Product table - Existing records in the ProductReview table must not be validated with the Product table. - Deleting records in the Product table must not be allowed if records are referenced by the ProductReview table. - Changes to records in the Product table must propagate to the ProductReview table. You also have the following database tables: Order, ProductTypes, and SalesHistory, The transact-SQL statements for these tables are not available. You must modify the Orders table to meet the following requirements: - Create new rows in the table without granting INSERT permissions to the table. - Notify the sales person who places an order whether or not the order was completed. You must add the following constraints to the SalesHistory table: - a constraint on the SaleID column that allows the field to be used as a record identifier - a constant that uses the ProductID column to reference the Product column of the ProductTypes table - a constraint on the CategoryID column that allows one row with a null value in the column - a constraint that limits the SalePrice column to values greater than four Finance department users must be able to retrieve data from the SalesHistory table for sales persons where the value of the SalesYTD column is above a certain threshold. You plan to create a memory-optimized table named SalesOrder. The table must meet the following requirements: - The table must hold 10 million unique sales orders. - The table must use checkpoints to minimize I/O operations and must not use transaction logging. - Data loss is acceptable. Performance for queries against the SalesOrder table that use Where clauses with exact equality operations must be optimized. You need to create an object that allows finance users to be able to retrieve the required data. The object must not have a negative performance impact. How should you complete the Transact-SQL statements? To answer, select the appropriate Transact-SQL segments in the answer area. Hot Area:

## Answer Area

```
CREATE  [PROCEDURE ▼]  Sales.YTDSalesByPerson
        [TRIGGER    ]
        [FUNCTION   ]
        [VIEW       ]

        (@minYTDSales money)

        [WITH SCHEMABINDING ▼]
        [RETURNS TABLE      ]
        [WITH ENCRYPTION    ]
        [RETURNS INT        ]

AS
RETURN (
   SELECT SalesPersonID, BusinessEntityID, SalesYTD
   FROM Sales.SalesHistory
   WHERE SalesYTD > @minYTDSales
   ORDER BY SalesYTD desc
);
```

Answers:

**A)**

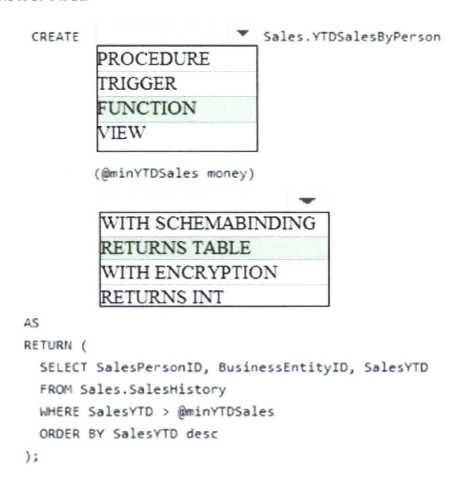

**Solution:** A

**Explanation:**

Explanation: A user defined function can return a table, which can be produces by a SELECT statement. From question: Finance department users must be able to retrieve data from the SalesHistory table for sales persons where the value of the SalesYTD column is above a certain threshold. Incorrect: Not VIEW: The RETURN clause is not used when you create a view. References: https://docs.microsoft.com/en-us/sql/t-sql/statements/create-function-transact-sql?view=sql- server-2017

**Question: 9** *One Answer Is Right*

Note: This question is part of a series of questions that use the same scenario. For your convenience, the scenario is repeated in each question. Each question presents a different goal and answer choices, but the text of the scenario is exactly the same in each question in this series. You have a database that contains the following tables: BlogCategory, BlogEntry, ProductReview, Product, and SalesPerson. The tables were created using the following Transact SQL statements:

```
CREATE TABLE BlogCategory
(
    CategoryID int NOT NULL PRIMARY KEY,
    CategoryName nvarchar (20)
);

CREATE TABLE BlogEntry
(
    Entry int NOT PRIMARY KEY,
    Entrytitle nvarchar (50),
    Category int NOT NULL FOREIGN KEY REFERENCES BlogCategory
(CategoryID)
);

CREATE TABLE dbo.ProductReview
(
    ProductReviewID IDENTITY(1,1) PRIMARY KEY,
    Product int NOT NULL,
    Review varchar (1000) NOT NULL
);

CREATE TABLE dbo.Product
(
    ProductID int Identity(1,1) PRIMARY KEY,
    Name varchar(1000) NOT NULL
);
CREATE TABLE dbo.SalesPerson
(
    SalesPersonID int IDENTITY(1,1) PRIMARY KEY,
    Name varchar (1000) NOT NULL,
    SalesID Money
)
```

You must modify the ProductReview Table to meet the following requirements: 1. The table must reference the ProductID column in the Product table 2. Existing records in the ProductReview table must not be validated with the Product table. 3. Deleting records in the Product table must not be allowed if records are referenced by the ProductReview table. 4. Changes to records in the Product table must propagate to the ProductReview table. You also have the following databse tables: Order, ProductTypes, and SalesHistory, The transact-SQL statements for these tables are not available. You must modify the Orders table to meet the following requirements: 1. Create new rows in the table without granting INSERT permissions to the table. 2. Notify the sales person who places an order whether or not the order was completed. You must add the following constraints to the SalesHistory table: - a constraint on the SaleID column that allows the field to be used as a record identifier - a constant that uses the ProductID column to reference the Product column of the ProductTypes table - a constraint on the CategoryID column that allows one row with a null value in the column - a constraint that limits the SalePrice column to values greater than four Finance department users must be able to retrieve data from the SalesHistory table for sales persons where the value of the SalesYTD column is above a certain threshold. You plan to create a memory-optimized table named SalesOrder. The table must meet the following requirments: - The table must hold 10 million unique sales orders. - The table must use checkpoints to minimize I/O operations and must not use transaction logging. - Data loss is acceptable. Performance for queries against the SalesOrder table that use Where clauses with exact equality operations must be optimized. You need to modify the design of the Orders table. What should you create?

**Answers:**

**A)** a stored procedure with the RETURN statement

**B)** a FOR UPDATE trigger

**C)** an AFTER UPDATE trigger

**D)** a user defined function

**Solution:** D

**Explanation:**

Explanation: Requirements: You must modify the Orders table to meet the following requirements: 1. Create new rows in the table without granting INSERT permissions to the table. 2. Notify the sales person who places an order whether or not the order was completed. References:https://msdn.microsoft.com/en-us/library/ms186755.aspx

**Question: 10** *Multiple Answers Are Right*

HOTSPOT Note: This question is part of a series of questions that use the same scenario. For your convenience, the scenario is repeated in each question. Each question presents a different goal and answer choices, but the text of the scenario is exactly the same in each question in this series. You have a database that contains the following tables: BlogCategory, BlogEntry, ProductReview, Product, and SalesPerson. The tables were created using the following Transact SQL statements:

```
CREATE TABLE BlogCategory
(
    CategoryID int NOT NULL PRIMARY KEY,
    CategoryName nvarchar (20)
);

CREATE TABLE BlogEntry
(
    Entry int NOT PRIMARY KEY,
    Entrytitle nvarchar (50),
    Category int NOT NULL FOREIGN KEY REFERENCES BlogCategory (CategoryID)
);

CREATE TABLE dbo.ProductReview
(
    ProductReviewID IDENTITY(1,1) PRIMARY KEY,
    Product int NOT NULL,
    Review varchar (1000) NOT NULL
);

CREATE TABLE dbo.Product
(
    ProductID int Identity(1,1) PRIMARY KEY,
    Name varchar(1000) NOT NULL
);
CREATE TABLE dbo.SalesPerson
(
    SalesPersonID int IDENTITY(1,1) PRIMARY KEY,
    Name varchar (1000) NOT NULL,
    SalesID Money
)
```

You must modify the ProductReview Table to meet the following requirements: 1. The table must reference the ProductID column in the Product table 2. Existing records in the ProductReview table must not be validated with the Product table. 3. Deleting records in the Product table must not be allowed if records are referenced by the ProductReview table. 4. Changes to records in the Product table must propagate to the ProductReview table. You also have the following databse tables: Order, ProductTypes, and SalesHistory, The transact-SQL statements for these tables are not available. You must modify the Orders table to meet the following requirements: 1. Create new rows in the table without granting INSERT permissions to the table. 2. Notify the sales person who places an order whether or not the order was completed. You must add the following constraints to the SalesHistory table: - a constraint on the SaleID column that allows the field to be used as a record identifier - a constant that uses the ProductID column to reference the Product column of the ProductTypes table - a constraint on the CategoryID column that allows one row with a null value in the column - a constraint that limits the SalePrice column to values greater than four Finance department users must be able to retrieve data from the SalesHistory table for sales persons where the value of the SalesYTD column is above a certain threshold. You plan to create a memory-optimized table named SalesOrder. The table must meet the following requirments: - The table must hold 10 million unique sales orders. - The table must use checkpoints to minimize I/O operations and must not use transaction logging. - Data loss is acceptable. Performance for queries against the SalesOrder table that use Where clauses with exact equality operations must be optimized. You need to update the SalesHistory table How should you complete the Transact_SQL statement? To answer? select the appropriate Transact-SQL, segments in the answer area. Hot Area:

## Answer Area

```
IF OBJECT_id(*SalesHistory*)>0 DROP TABLE SalesHistory
GO
IF OBJECT_ID(*ProductTypes*)>0 DROP TABLE  ProductTypes
GO
CREATE TABLE ProductTypes
(
    ProductID SMALLINT,
    ProductDescripltion VARCHAR(255),
    CONSTRANT pk_ProductID PRIMARY KEY (ProductID)
)
GO
CREATE TABLE [dbp}.{SalesHistoryK]
[SaleID] [int]
```

| ▼ |
|---|
| IDENTITY(1,4) |
| IDENTITY(1,4) NOT NULL PRIMARY KEY |
| UNIQUE |

,

```
[ProductID] SMALLINT NULL ,

[SaleDate] [datetime] NULL

[SalePrice] [money]
```

| ▼ |
|---|
| NOT NULL |
| NULL CHECK (SalesPrice > 4) |
| UNIQUE |

,

```
[CategoryID] [smallint]
```

| ▼ |
|---|
| NOT NULL |
| NULL CHECK (SalesPrice > 4) |
| UNIQUE |

| ▼ |
|---|
| CONSTRAINT fk_SalesHistoryProductID FOREIGN KEY (ProductID) REFERENCES SalesHistory(CategoryID) |
| CONSTRAINT fk_SalesHistoryProductID FOREIGN KEY (ProductID) REFERENCES ProductTypes(ProductD) |

```
)
GO
```

**Answers:**

A)

## Answer Area

```
IF OBJECT_id(*SalesHistory*)>0 DROP TABLE SalesHistory
GO
IF OBJECT_ID(*ProductTypes*)>0 DROP TABLE  ProductTypes
GO
CREATE TABLE ProductTypes
(
    ProductID SMALLINT,
    ProductDescripltion VARCHAR(255),
    CONSTRANT pk_ProductID PRIMARY KEY (ProductID)
)
GO
CREATE TABLE [dbp}.{SalesHistoryK]
[SaleID] [int]
```

| |
|---|
| IDENTITY(1,4) |
| **IDENTITY(1,4) NOT NULL PRIMARY KEY** |
| UNIQUE |

,

`[ProductID] SMALLINT NULL ,`

`[SaleDate] [datetime] NULL`

`[SalePrice] [money]`

| |
|---|
| **NOT NULL** |
| NULL CHECK (SalesPrice > 4) |
| UNIQUE |

,

`[CategoryID] [smallint]`

| |
|---|
| NOT NULL |
| NULL CHECK (SalesPrice > 4) |
| **UNIQUE** |

| |
|---|
| CONSTRAINT fk_SalesHistoryProductID FOREIGN KEY (ProductID) REFERENCES SalesHistory(CategoryID) |
| **CONSTRAINT fk_SalesHistoryProductID FOREIGN KEY (ProductID) REFERENCES ProductTypes(ProductD)** |

```
)
GO
```

**Solution:** A

**Explanation:**

Explanation: Box 1: SaleID must be the primary key, as a constraint on the SaleID column that allows the field to be used as a record identifier is required. Box 2: A constraint that limits the SalePrice column to values greater than four. Box 3: UNIQUE A constraint on the CategoryID column that allows one row with a null value in the column. Box 4: A foreign keyconstraint must be put on the productID referencing the ProductTypes table, as a constraint that uses the ProductID column to reference the Product column of the ProductTypes table is required. Note: Requirements are: You must add the following constraints to the SalesHistory table: - a constraint on the SaleID column that allows the field to be used as a record identifier - a constraint that uses the ProductID column to reference the Product column of the ProductTypes table - a constraint on the CategoryID column that allows one row with a null value in the column - a constraint that limits the SalePrice column to values greater than four

# Chapter 11: 70-778 - Analyzing and Visualizing Data with Microsoft Power BI

## Exam Guide

Analyzing and Visualizing Data with Microsoft Power BI 70-778 Exam:

Analyzing and Visualizing Data with Microsoft Power BI 70-778 Exam which is related to Microsoft Certified Solutions Associate Certification. This exam validates the ability to connect to data sources and perform data transformations, modeling and visualizing data by using Microsoft Power BI Desktop and configure dashboards by using the Power BI service. Microsoft Certified Solutions Associate usually hold or pursue this certification and you can expect the same job role after completion of this certification.

70-778 Exam topics:

Candidates must know the exam topics before they start of preparation. Because it will really help them in hitting the core. Our **70-778 dumps** will include the following topics:

- Consuming and Transforming Data By Using Power BI Desktop
- Modeling and Visualizing Data
- Configure Dashboards, Reports, and Apps in the Power BI Service

Certification Path:

The Analyzing and Visualizing Data with Microsoft Power BI Certification includes only one 70-778 exam.

Who should take the 70-778 exam:

The Analyzing and Visualizing Data with Microsoft Power BI 70-778 Exam certification is an internationally recognized validation that identifies persons who earn it as possessing skilled as a Microsoft Certified Solutions Associate. If candidates want significant improvement in career growth needs enhanced knowledge, skills, and talents. The Analyzing and Visualizing Data with Microsoft Power BI 70-778 Exam certification provides proof of this advanced knowledge and skill. If a candidate has knowledge of associated technologies and skills that are required to pass

Analyzing and Visualizing Data with Microsoft Power BI 70-778 Exam then he should take this exam.

How to study the 70-778 Exam:

Certification-questions.com expert team recommends you to prepare some notes on these topics along with it don't forget to practice Microsoft 70-778 Exam dumps which been written by our expert team, Both these will help you a lot to clear this exam with good marks.

How much 70-778 Exam Cost:

The price of the 70-778 exam is $165 USD.

How to book the 70-778 Exam:

These are following steps for registering the 70-778 exam.
Step 1: Visit to Microsoft Exam Registration
Step 2: Signup/Login to MICROSOFT account
Step 3: Search for MICROSOFT 70-778 Certifications Exam
Step 4: Select Date and Center of examination and confirm with payment value of $165

What is the duration of the 70-778 Exam:

- Format: Multiple choices, multiple answers
- Length of Examination: 150 minutes
- Number of Questions: 45-60
- Passing Score: 700/1000

    The benefit in Obtaining the 70-778 Exam Certification:

- After completion of Microsoft Certified Solutions Associate Certification candidates receive official confirmation from Microsoft that you are now fully certified in their chosen field. This can be now added to their CV, cover letters and job applications.
- When Candidates applying for a job or looking to promotion in their current position, a Microsoft Certified Professional certification in the field in which Candidates are applying will put you at the top of the list and make them a desirable candidate for employers.
- Candidates will get in-depth knowledge by completing the courses along with the access to revision materials for 6 months upon completion means they will have a wider skill set when it comes to the various technologies and systems than an uncertified professional. Certified Professional in this particular skill set is 74% more efficient when it comes to completing their tasks in a timely well-executed manner.
- Organization owners invest a lot in their employees when it comes to their training with the goal of making them quicker, more efficient, and more knowledgeable about their role.

Certified Professional will reduce the time he spends on tasks, meaning he can get more done this could help reduce company downtime when repairing faults on a system or fixing hardware problems.

- Becoming Microsoft Certified Professional means one thing you are worth more to the company and therefore more to yourself in the form of an upgraded pay package. On average a Microsoft Certified Professional member of staff is estimated to be worth 30% more to a company than their uncertified professionals.

Difficulty in writing 70-778 Exam:

There are many problems for the candidates cannot facilitate from the exams preparation and most of the candidates do not know how to prepare their exams and get good marks in their exams. There are a lot of candidates have failed their exams by lack of practice, lack of tension, lack of concentrate and lack of no time. Many candidates want to give a short time to study and get good marks in exams, therefore Certification-questions have a number of ways to prepare and practice for exams in short time through which the candidates will feel relax, a cool mind and ready for exams without any tension. Certification-questions is very much aware of the worth of your time and money that's why Certification-questions give you the most outstanding **Microsoft 70-778 dumps** having all the questions and answers outlined and verified by the Microsoft Professionals. We deliver all those practice questions which will come in the real exam so the candidate can easily get more than 90% marks at first attempt.

For more info visit::

Microsoft 70-778 Exam Reference

# Sample Practice Test for 70-778

**Question: 1** *One Answer Is Right*

Note: This question is part of a series of questions that present the same scenario. Each question in the series contains a unique solution that might meet the stated goals. Some question sets might have more than one correct solution, while others might not have a correct solution. After you answer a question in this section, you will NOT be able to return to it. As a result, these questions will not appear in the review screen. You have a Power BI model that contains two tables named Sales and Date. Sales contains four columns named TotalCost, DueDate, ShipDate, and OrderDate. Date contains one column named Date. The tables have the following relationships: - Sales[DueDate] and Date[Date] - Sales[ShipDate] and Date[Date] - Sales[OrderDate] and Date[Date] The active relationship is on Sales[DueDate]. You need to create measures to count the number of orders by [ShipDate] and the orders by [OrderDate]. You must meet the goal without duplicating data or loading additional data. Solution: You create a calculated table. You create a measure that uses the new table. Does this meet the goal?

**Answers:**

**A)** Yes

**B)** No

**Solution:** B

**Question: 2** *One Answer Is Right*

Note: This question is part of a series of questions that present the same scenario. Each question in the series contains a unique solution that might meet the stated goals. Some question sets might have more than one correct solution, while others might not have a correct solution. After you answer a question in this section, you will NOT be able to return to it. As a result, these questions will not appear in the review screen. You have a Power BI model that contains two tables named Sales and Date. Sales contains four columns named TotalCost, DueDate, ShipDate, and OrderDate. Date contains one column named Date. The tables have the following relationships: - Sales[DueDate] and Date[Date] - Sales[ShipDate] and Date[Date] - Sales[OrderDate] and Date[Date] The active relationship is on Sales[DueDate]. You need to create measures to count the number of orders by [ShipDate] and the orders by [OrderDate]. You must meet the goal without duplicating data or loading additional data. Solution: You create measures that use the CALCULATE, COUNT, and FILTER DAX functions. Does this meet the goal?

**Answers:**

**A)** Yes

**B)** No

**Solution:** A

**Explanation:**

Explanation: References: https://msdn.microsoft.com/en-us/library/ee634966.aspx https://msdn.microsoft.com/en-us/library/ee634825.aspx https://msdn.microsoft.com/en-us/library/ee634791.aspx

**Question: 3** *One Answer Is Right*

Note: This question is part of a series of questions that present the same scenario. Each question in the series contains a unique solution that might meet the stated goals. Some question sets might have more than one correct solution, while others might not have a correct solution. After you answer a question in this section, you will NOT be able to return to it. As a result, these questions will not appear in the review screen. You have a Power BI model that contains two tables named Sales and Date. Sales contains four columns named TotalCost, DueDate, ShipDate, and OrderDate. Date contains one column named Date. The tables have the following relationships: - Sales[DueDate] and Date[Date] - Sales[ShipDate] and Date[Date] - Sales[OrderDate] and Date[Date] The active relationship is on Sales[DueDate]. You need to create measures to count the number of orders by [ShipDate] and the orders by [OrderDate]. You must meet the goal without duplicating data or loading additional data. Solution: You create two copies of the Date table named ShipDate and OrderDateGet. You create a measure that uses the new tables. Does this meet the goal?

**Answers:**

**A)** Yes

**B)** No

**Solution:** B

**Question: 4** *One Answer Is Right*

Note: This question is part of a series of questions that present the same scenario. Each question in the series contains a unique solution that might meet the stated goals. Some question sets might have more than one correct solution, while others might not have a correct solution. After you answer a question in this section, you will NOT be able to return to it. As a result, these questions will not appear in the review screen. You have a user named User1. User1 is a member of a security group named Contoso PowerBI. User1 has access to a workspace named Contoso Workspace. You need to prevent User1 from exporting data from the visualizations in Contoso Workspace. Solution: From the Microsoft Office 365 Admin center, you remove User1 from the All Users security group. Does this meet the goal?

**Answers:**

**A)** Yes

**B)** No

**Solution:** B

**Question: 5** *One Answer Is Right*

Note: This question is part of a series of questions that present the same scenario. Each question in the series contains a unique solution that might meet the stated goals. Some question sets might have more than one correct solution, while others might not have a correct solution. After you answer a question in this section, you will NOT be able to return to it. As a result, these questions will not appear in the review screen. You have a user named User1. User1 is a member of a security group named Contoso PowerBI. User1 has access to a workspace named Contoso Workspace. You need to prevent User1 from exporting data from the visualizations in Contoso Workspace. Solution: From the Microsoft Office 365 Admin center, you modify the properties of Contoso PowerBI. Does this meet the goal?

**Answers:**

**A)** Yes

**B)** No

**Solution:** A

**Explanation:**

Explanation: References: https://docs.microsoft.com/en-us/power-bi/service-manage-app-workspace-in-power-bi-and- office-365

**Question: 6** *One Answer Is Right*

Note: This question is part of a series of questions that present the same scenario. Each question in the series contains a unique solution that might meet the stated goals. Some question sets might have more than one correct solution, while others might not have a correct solution. After you answer a question in this section, you will NOT be able to return to it. As a result, these questions will not appear in the review screen. You have a user named User1. User1 is a member of a security group named Contoso PowerBI. User1 has access to a workspace named Contoso Workspace. You need to prevent User1 from exporting data from the visualizations in Contoso Workspace. Solution: From the PowerBI setting, you modify the Developer Settings. Does this meet the goal?

**Answers:**

**A)** Yes

**B)** No

**Solution:** B

**Question: 7** *One Answer Is Right*

You plan to embed multiple visualizations in a public website. Your Power BI infrastructure contains the visualizations configured as shown in the following table.

| Visualizations name | Characteristic |
| --- | --- |
| Visual 1 | Uses row-level security (RLS) |
| Visual 2 | Uses a dataset that is stored in Microsoft OneDrive for Business |
| Visual 3 | Contained in a report that was shared to your user account |
| Visual 4 | Is a custom visual |
| Visual 5 | Uses a dataset from an on-premises Microsoft SQL Server Analysis Services (SSAS) database |

Which two visualizations can you embed into the website? Each correct answer presents a complete solution. NOTE: Each correct selection is worth one point.

**Answers:**

**A)** Visual 1

**B)** Visual 2

**C)** Visual 3

**D)** Visual 4

**E)** Visual 5

**Solution:** B, D

**Explanation:**

Explanation: References: https://docs.microsoft.com/en-us/power-bi/service-publish-to-web

**Question: 8** *One Answer Is Right*

You have a workspace that contains 10 dashboards. A dashboard named Sales Data displays data from two datasets. You discover that users are unable to find data on the dashboard by using natural language queries. You need to ensure that the users can find data by using natural language queries. What should you do?

**Answers:**

**A)** From the settings of the workspace, modify the Language Settings.

**B)** From the Sales Data dashboard, set the dashboard as a Favorite.

**C)** From the properties of the datasets, modify the Q&A and Cortana settings.

**D)** From the properties of the dashboard, modify the Q&A settings.

**Solution:** C

**Explanation:**

Explanation: References: https://docs.microsoft.com/en-us/power-bi/service-q-and-a-direct-query#limitations-during- public-preview

**Question: 9** *Multiple Answers Are Right*

DRAG DROP You have a Microsoft Excel workbook that contains two tables. From Power BI, you create a dashboard that displays data from the tables. You update the tables each day. You need to ensure that the visualizations in the dashboard are updated daily. Which three actions should you perform in sequence? To answer, move the appropriate actions from the list of actions to the answer area and arrange them in the correct order. NOTE. More than one order of answer choices is correct. You will receive credit for any of the correct orders you select. Select and Place:

**Answers:**

A)

| Actions | | Answer Area | |
|---|---|---|---|
| | | Download and install an on-premises data gateway (personal). | |
| | | Configure the Gateway Connection settings for the dataset. | |
| Add subscriptions for the reports. | ▶ ◀ | Configure the Schedule Refresh settings for the dataset. | ▲ ▼ |
| Download and install Power BI Desktop. | | | |

**Solution:** A

**Explanation:**

Explanation: References: https://docs.microsoft.com/en-us/power-bi/refresh-scheduled-refresh

**Question: 10** *One Answer Is Right*

You manage a Power BI model that has two tables named Sales and Product. You need to ensure that a sales team can view only data that has a CountryRegionName value of Unites States and a ProductCategory value of Clothing. What should you do from Power BI Desktop?

**Answers:**

**A)** Add the following filters to a report. CountryRegionName is United States ProductCategory is Clothing

**B)** From Power BI Desktop, create a new role that has the following filters. [CountryRegionName] = "United States" [ProductCategory] = "Clothing"

**C)** Add the following filters in Query Editor. CountryRegionName is United States ProductCategory is Clothing

**D)** From Power BI Desktop, create a new role that has the following filter. [CountryRegionName] = "United States" && [ProductCategory] = "Clothing"

**Solution:** A

**Explanation:**

Explanation: References: https://docs.microsoft.com/en-us/power-bi/power-bi-how-to-report-filter

# Chapter 12: 98-375 - HTML5 App Development Fundamentals

## Exam Guide

How to Prepare For Microsoft 98-375:HTML5 Application Development Fundamentals Exam

Preparation Guide for Microsoft 98-375:HTML5 Application Development Fundamentals Exam

Introduction

Microsoft 98-375:HTML5 Application Development Fundamentals Exam is designed for professional who are working in the IT industries as well as it focuses on the other candidates who want to prove introductory knowledge of Application Development . There are no specific prerequisites that you must have for HTML5 Application Development Fundamentals Course, but it is recommended that you must be familiar with the concepts and the technologies related to core Application Development of the Microsoft. As a HTML5 Application Development Fundamentals administrator, you are in charge of important Application Development s that span multiple platforms and environments. You are a strong team player who thrives in a fast-paced environment.You Manage the Application Life Cycle, Build the User Interface by Using HTML5, Format the User Interface by Using CSS, Code by Using JavaScript.

This exam checks competency level on topics Core Application Development Concepts, Creating Application Development Objects, and Administering a Application Development

Certification is evidence of your skills, expertise in those areas in which you like to work. There are many vendors in the market that are providing these certifications. If candidate wants to work on Microsoft 98-375:HTML5 Application Development Fundamentals and prove his knowledge, Certification offered by Microsoft. This Microsoft 98-375:HTML5 Application Development Fundamentals Individuals Qualification Certification helps a candidate to validates his skills in **Microsoft 98-375:HTML5 Application Development Fundamentals** Technology.

In this guide, we will cover the Microsoft 98-375:HTML5 Application Development Fundamentals Certification exam, Microsoft 98-375:HTML5 Application Development

Fundamentals Certification salary and all aspects of the Microsoft 98-375:HTML5 Application Development Fundamentals Certification

Introduction to Microsoft 98-375:HTML5 Application Development Fundamentals Exam:

Candidates for this Microsoft 98-375:HTML5 Application Development Fundamentals Exam are seeking to prove core HTML5 client application development skills that will run on today's touch-enabled devices (PCs, tablets, and phones). Although HTML is usually considered as a web technology that is rendered in a browser to generate a UI, this exam targets on using HTML5, CSS3, and JavaScript to develop client applications.

Before taking **Microsoft 98-375:HTML5 Application Development Fundamentals Exam**, candidates should have solid foundational knowledge of the topics outlined in the preparation guide, including CSS and JavaScript. It is suggested that exam aspirants be familiar with the concepts of application life cycle , Debug and test an HTML5-based have some hands-on experience with the related technologies, either by taking relevant training courses or by working with tutorials and samples accessible on MSDN and in Microsoft Visual Studio.

Topics of Microsoft 98-375:HTML5 Application Development Fundamentals Exam:

*1.Manage the application life cycle (20–25%)*

Understand the platform fundamentals

- Packaging and the runtime environment: app package, app container, credentials/permission sets, host process, leverage existing HTML5 skills and content for slate/tablet applications

    Manage the state of an application

- Manage session state, app state, and persist state information; understand states of an application; understand the differences between local and session storage

    Debug and test an HTML5-based, touch-enabled application

- Touch gestures; understand which gestures you test on a device

    *2.Build the user interface (UI) by using HTML5 (25–30%)*

Choose and configure HTML5 tags to display text content

Choose and configure HTML5 tags to display graphics

- When, why, and how to use Canvas; when, why, and how to use scalable vector graphics (SVG)

Choose and configure HTML5 tags to play media

- Video and audio tags

    Choose and configure HTML5 tags to organize content and forms

- Tables, lists, sections; semantic HTML

    Choose and configure HTML5 tags for input and validation

*3. Format the user interface by using Cascading Style Sheets (CSS) (20-25%)*

Understand the core CSS concepts

- Separate presentation from content (create content with HTML and style content with CSS); manage content flow (inline versus block flow); manage positioning of individual elements( float versus absolute positioning); manage content overflow (scrolling, visible, and hidden); basic CSS styling

    Arrange UI content by using CSS

- Use flexible box and grid layouts to establish content alignment, direction, and orientation; proportional scaling and use of "free scale" for elements within a flexible box or grid; order and arrange content; concepts for using flex box for simple layouts and grid for complex layouts; grid content properties for rows and columns; use application templates

    Manage the flow of text content by using CSS

- Regions and using regions to flow text content between multiple sections (content source, content container, dynamic flow, flow-into, flow-from, msRegionUpdate, msRegionOverflow, msGetRegionContent); columns and hyphenation and using these CSS settings to optimize the readability of text; use "positioned floats" to create text flow around a floating object

    Manage the graphical interface by using CSS

- Graphics effects (rounded corners, shadows, transparency, background gradients, typography, and Web Open Font Format); two-dimensional (2-D) and three-dimensional (3-D) transformations (translate, scale, rotate, skew, and 3-D perspective transitions and animations); SVG filter effects; Canvas

    *4. Code by using JavaScript (30-35%)*

Access data access by using JavaScript

- Send and receive data; transmit complex objects and parsing; load and save files; App Cache; datatypes; forms; cookies; local Storage

  Respond to the touch interface

- Gestures, how to capture and respond to gestures

  Code additional HTML5 APIs

- GeoLocation, Web Workers, WebSocket; File API

  Access device and operating system resources

- In memory resources, such as contact lists and calendar; hardware capabilities, such as GPS, accelerometer, and camera

  Who should take the 98-375:HTML5 Application Development Fundamentals Exam:

The Microsoft 98-375:HTML5 Application Development Fundamentals Exam certification is an internationally-recognized certification which help to have validation for those professionals who are keen to make their career in build their career in Microsoft Dynamics 365 domain.

Microsoft Technology Associate (MTA) - HTML5 Application Development Fundamentals exam assess that the candidate possesses the fundamental knowledge and proven skills in the area of Microsoft MTA HTML5 Application Development Fundamentals.

if a candidate/professional seeks a powerful improvement in career growth needs enhanced knowledge, skills, and talents. The Microsoft 98-375:HTML5 Application Development Fundamentals certification provides proof of this advanced knowledge and skill as the skills on below topics are verified Core Application Development Concepts, Creating Application Development Objects, and Administering a Application Development

As per the global Market Survey 2018-2019, there is around 1,12,000 number of jobs available for the Application Development Administration profile. Around 90% of the candidate who are certified in Microsoft 98-375:HTML5 Application Development Fundamentals able to get this job. Every year around 45,000 candidates use to appear for this exam and manage to pass it in their first attempt itself. This open new door of opportunity for them.

How to study the Microsoft 98-375:HTML5 Application Development Fundamentals Exam:

Preparation of certification exams could be covered with two resource types . The first one are the study guides, reference books and study forums that are elaborated and appropriate for building information from ground up. Apart from them video tutorials and lectures are a good option to ease the pain of through study and are relatively make the study process more interesting nonetheless these demand time and concentration from the learner. Smart candidates who wish to create a solid foundation altogether examination topics and connected technologies typically mix video lectures with study guides to reap the advantages of each but practice exams or practice exam engines is one important study tool which goes typically unnoted by most candidates. Practice exams are designed with our experts to make exam prospects test their knowledge on skills attained in course, as well as prospects become comfortable and familiar with the real exam environment. Statistics have indicated exam anxiety plays much bigger role of students failure in exam than the fear of the unknown. Certification-questions expert team recommends preparing some notes on these topics along with it don't forget to practice Microsoft **98-375:HTML5 Application Development Fundamentals Dumps** which had been written by our expert team, each of these can assist you loads to clear this exam with excellent marks.

Microsoft 98-375:HTML5 Application Development Fundamentals Certification Path:

Microsoft 98-375:HTML5 Application Development Fundamentals Exam is foundation level Certification. As such There is no prerequisite for this course. Anyone who is having keen interest and familiar with Microsoft technology are well invited to pursue this certification.

How much 98-375:HTML5 Application Development Fundamentals Exam Cost:

The price of the Microsoft Application Development Fundamentals exam is $127 USD, for more information related to exam price please visit to Microsoft Training website as prices of Microsoft exams fees get varied country wise.

How to book the 98-375:HTML5 Application Development Fundamentals Exam:

These are following steps for registering the 98-375:HTML5 Application Development Fundamentals exam.

- Step 1: Visit to Microsoft Learning and search for 98-375:HTML5 Application Development Fundamentals
- Step 2: Sign up/Login to Pearson VUE account
- Step 3: Select local centre based on your country, date, time and confirm with a payment method.

What is the duration, language, and format of Microsoft 98-375:HTML5 Application Development Fundamentals Exam:

- Length of Examination: 45 mins
- Number of Questions: 40 - 60 (Since Microsoft does not publish this information, the number of exam questions may change without notice.)
- Passing Score 700 / 1000
- Type of Questions: This test format is multiple choice.

Microsoft 98-375:HTML5 Application Development Fundamentals Exam Certified Professional salary:

The average salary of a Microsoft 98-375:HTML5 Application Development Fundamentals Exam Certified Expert in

- United State - 80,247 USD
- India. - 10,00,327 INR
- Europe - 60,347 EURO
- England - 55,632 POUND

The benefit of obtaining the Microsoft 98-375:HTML5 Application Development Fundamentals Exam Certification:

- This certification will be judging your skills and knowledge on your understanding Application Development security concepts & Understanding of need to secure a Application Development , what objects can be secured, what objects ought to be secured, user accounts, roles.
- This certification credential will give you edge over other counterparts. Apart from knowledge from 98-375:HTML5 Application Development Fundamentals Exam.
- It help you to make your career into Application Development Administration and Application Development Administrator use to get respectful plus highly paid jobs into Market. Statistics on the Microsoft Certification website indicate that 91% of hiring managers consider certification as part of their hiring criteria.The main benefit to earning a Microsoft Certification is that it shows potential employers/hiring managers that you have the necessary requirements and skills to be the perfect candidate for the job.

Difficulty in Writing 98-375:HTML5 Application Development Fundamentals Exam:

98-375:HTML5 Application Development Fundamentals is a privileged achievement one could be graced with. But adverse to general notion certifying with Microsoft is not that challenging if the candidates have proper preparation material to pass the 98-375:HTML5 Application Development Fundamentals exam with good grades. Certification questions consist of the foremost phenomenal and noteworthy queries answers and description that consists the complete course content. Certification questions have a brilliant 98-375:HTML5 Application Development Fundamentals dumps with most recent and important questions and answers in PDF files. Certification-questions is sure about the exactness and legitimacy of 98-375:HTML5 Application Development Fundamentals exam dumps and in this manner. Candidates can easily pass the Microsoft 98-375:HTML5 Application Development Fundamentals exam with genuine **98-375:HTML5 Application Development Fundamentals Dumps** and get MICROSOFT certification. These dumps are viewed as the best source to understand the Microsoft 98-375:HTML5 Application Development Fundamentals well by simply pursuing examples questions and answers. If candidate complete practice the exam with certification Microsoft 98-375:HTML5 Application Development Fundamentals dumps along with self-assessment to get the proper idea on MICROSOFT accreditation and to ace the certification exam.

For more info read reference::

Exam 98–375 HTML5 Application Development Fundamentals (Microsoft Official Academic Course) by Microsoft Official Academic CourseMTA 98-375 MOAC (.pdf)
(mta) student study guide for developers 98-375 - Certiport
CSS3 Effects, transitions, and animations
Application Cache API ("AppCache")

# Sample Practice Test for 98-375

**Question: 1** *One Answer Is Right*

Which CSS3 code fragment styles an H2 element only if it is a direct child of a DIV element?

A.
```
div {
background-color: #900;
}
h2 {
background-color: #900;
}
```

B.
```
div > h2 {
background-color: #900;
}
```

C.
```
h2 > div {
background-color: #900;
}
```

D.
```
div, h2 {
background-color: #900;
}
```

Answers:

**A)** Option A

**B)** Option B

**C)** Option C

**D)** Option D

**Solution:** B

**Question: 2** *One Answer Is Right*

Which CSS property defines which sides of an element where other floating elements are not allowed?

Answers:

**A)** float

**B)** position

**C)** display

**D)** clear

**Solution:** D

**Question: 3** *One Answer Is Right*

You write the following code to create a page. (Line numbers are included for reference only.)

```
01 <html>
02 ...
03  <body>
04    <svg xmlns="http://www.w3.org/2000/svg" version="1.1">
05     <defs>
06      <filter id="blur" filterUnits="objectBoundingBox" x="-1" y="-1" width="2.0" height="2.0">
07       <feGaussianBlur stdDeviation="1"/>
08      </filter>
09     </defs>
10     <text x="10" y="50" >Blur Me!</text>
11    </svg>
12   </body>
13 </html>
```

You need to apply the SVG blur filter to the text tag on the page. Which HTML/CSS code should you insert at line 02?

A.
```
<style>
text{font:48px arial bold; fill:blur;}
</style>
```

B.
```
<style>
text{font:48px arial bold; filter:url(#blur);}
</style>
```

C.
```
<style>
text{font:48px arial bold; filter:#blur;}
</style>
```

D.
```
<style>
text{font:48px arial bold; filter:url(blur);}
</style>
```

**Answers:**

**A)** Option A

**B)** Option B

**C)** Option C

**D)** Option D

**Solution:** B

**Question: 4** *One Answer Is Right*

Which layout can you create by using a single CSS3 region?

**Answers:**

**A)** a table layout

**B)** a snaked-column layout

**C)** a multiple column liquid layout

**D)** a multiple column fixed layout

**Solution:** A

**Question: 5** *One Answer Is Right*

In CSS, the flow-into property deposits:

**Answers:**

**A)** the flow into the content.

**B)** the regions into a flow.

**C)** the flow into the regions.

**D)** content into the flow.

**Solution:** D

**Question: 6** *One Answer Is Right*

Which CSS code fragment centers an image horizontally?

A. `img.center { text-align: center; }`

B. `img.center { display: block; text-align: center; }`

C. `img.center { display: block; }`

D. `img.center { display: block; margin-left: auto; margin-right: auto; }`

**Answers:**

**A)** Option A

**B)** Option B

**C)** Option C

**D)** Option D

**Solution:** D

**Question: 7** *Multiple Answers Are Right*

DRAG DROP Match the CSS terms to the corresponding examples. (To answer, drag the appropriate term from the column on the left to its example on the right. Each term may be used once, more than once, or not at all. Each correct match is worth one point.) Select and Place:

| CSS Term | Examples |
|---|---|
| value | 1.8em |
| property | .container |
| id selector | #container |
| declaration | margin-top |
| class selector | font-family: Arial; |

Answers:

A)

| CSS Term | Examples |
|---|---|
| | value — 1.8em |
| | class selector — .container |
| | id selector — #container |
| | property — margin-top |
| | declaration — font-family: Arial; |

**Solution:** A

**Explanation:**

Explanation:

**Question: 8** *One Answer Is Right*

Which positioning scheme places an object in normal document flow?

**Answers:**

**A)** absolute

**B)** relative

**C)** fixed

**D)** float

**Solution:** B

**Question: 9** *One Answer Is Right*

The variable named "ctx" is the context of an HTML5 canvas object. What does the following code fragment draw? ctx.arc(x, y, r, 0, Math.PI, true);

**Answers:**

**A)** a circle at the given point

**B)** a square at the given point

**C)** a semi-circle at the given point

**D)** a line from one point to another

**Solution:** C

**Question: 10** *One Answer Is Right*

Which three are valid JavaScript variables? (Choose three.)

**Answers:**

**A)** xyz1

**B)** .Int

**C)** int1

**D)** _int

**E)** 1xyz

**Solution:** A, C, D

**Explanation:**

Explanation: Variable names must begin with a letter or special variable with either $ or _
Variable names are case sensitive (y and Y are different variables)

# Chapter 13: AI-100 - Designing and Implementing an Azure AI Solution

## Exam Guide

Designing and Implementing an Azure AI Solution AI-100 Exam:

Designing and Implementing an Azure AI Solution AI-100 Exam which is related to Microsoft Azure AI Solution and credits toward Microsoft Certified Azure AI Engineer Associate certifications. This exam validates the ability to use the various services within the Microsoft Azure Artificial Intelligence (AI) portfolio. Candidate must have a strong understanding of basic statistics, data ethics, data privacy, various aspects of the Microsoft Azure AI portfolio, related open source frameworks and technologies, and available data storage options. This exam verifies the Candidates have the ability to use their knowledge of cost models, capacity, and best practices to architect and implement Artificial Intelligence (AI) Solution using Microsoft Azure.

AI-100 Exam topics:

Candidates must know the exam topics before they start of preparation. Because it will really help them in hitting the core. Our **AI-100 dumps** will include the following topics:

- Analyze solution requirements 20-25%
- Design solutions 30-35%
- Integrate AI models into solutions 25-30%
- Deploy and manage solutions 20-25%

Certification Path:

The Microsoft Designing and Implementing an Azure AI Solution Certification includes only one AI-100 Exam.

Who should take the AI-100 exam:

The Designing and Implementing an Azure AI Solution AI-100 Exam certification is an internationally-recognized validation that identifies persons who earn it as possessing skilled as a Microsoft Certified Azure AI Engineer Associate. If candidates want significant improvement in career growth needs enhanced knowledge, skills, and talents. The Designing and Implementing an Azure AI Solution AI-100 Exam certification provides proof of this advanced knowledge and skill. If a candidate has knowledge of associated technologies and skills that are required to pass Designing and Implementing an Azure AI Solution AI-100 Exam then he should take this exam.

How to study the AI-100 Exam:

Certification-questions.com expert team recommends you to prepare some notes on these topics along with it don't forget to practice Microsoft AI-100 Exam dumps which been written by our expert team, Both these will help you a lot to clear this exam with good marks.

How much AI-100 Exam Cost:

The price of the AI-100 exam is $165 USD.

How to book the AI-100 Exam:

These are following steps for registering the AI-100 exam.
Step 1: Visit to Microsoft Exam Registration
Step 2: Signup/Login to MICROSOFT account
Step 3: Search for MICROSOFT AI-100 Certifications Exam
Step 4: Select Date and Center of examination and confirm with payment value of $165

What is the duration of the AI-100 Exam:

- Format: Multiple choices, multiple answers
- Length of Examination: 120 minutes
- Number of Questions: 45-55
- Passing Score: 700/1000

    The benefit in Obtaining the AI-100 Exam Certification:

- After completion of Microsoft Certified Azure AI Engineer Associate Candidates receive official confirmation from Microsoft that you are now fully certified in their chosen field. This can be now added to their CV, cover letters and job applications.
- When Candidates applying for a job or looking to promotion in their current position, a Microsoft Certified Azure AI Engineer Associate certification in the field in which Candidates are applying will put you at the top of the list and make them a desirable candidate for employers.
- Candidates will get in-depth knowledge by completing the courses along with the access to revision materials for 6 months upon completion means they will have a wider skill set when it comes to the various technologies and systems than an uncertified professional.

Certified Professional in this particular skill set is 74% more efficient when it comes to completing their tasks in a timely well-executed manner.
- Organization owners invest a lot in their employees when it comes to their training with the goal of making them quicker, more efficient, and more knowledgeable about their role. Certified Professional will reduce the time he spends on tasks, meaning he can get more done this could help reduce company downtime when repairing faults on a system or fixing hardware problems.
- Becoming Microsoft Certified Azure AI Engineer Associate means one thing you are worth more to the company and therefore more to yourself in the form of an upgraded pay package. On average a Microsoft Certified Azure AI Engineer Associate member of staff is estimated to be worth 30% more to a company than their uncertified professionals.

Difficulty in writing AI-100 Exam:

Microsoft AI-100 exam help Candidates in developing their professionals and academic career and It is a very tough task to pass Microsoft AI-100 exam for those Candidates who have not done hard work and get some relevant Microsoft AI-100 exam preparation material. There are many peoples have passed Microsoft AI-100 exam by following these three things such as look for the latest **Microsoft AI-100 exam dumps**, get relevant **Microsoft AI-100 exam dumps** and develop their knowledge about Microsoft AI-100 exam new questions. At the same time, it can also stress out some people as they found passing Microsoft AI-100 exam a tough task. It is just a wrong assumption as many of the peoples have passed Microsoft AI-100 exam questions. All you have to do is to work hard, get some relevant Microsoft AI-100 exam preparation material and go thoroughly from them. Certification-questions is here to help you with this problem. We have the relevant Microsoft AI-100 exam preparation material which are providing the latest Microsoft AI-100 exam questions with the detailed view of every Microsoft AI-100 exam topic. Certification-questions offered a **Microsoft AI-100 exam dumps** which are more than enough to pass the Microsoft AI-100 exam questions. We are providing all thing such as **Microsoft AI-100 exam dumps**, Microsoft AI-100 practice test, and Microsoft AI-100 pdf dumps that will help the candidate to pass the exam with good grades.

For more info visit::

AI-100 Exam Reference

# Sample Practice Test for AI-100

**Question: 1** *Multiple Answers Are Right*

HOTSPOT You are designing an application to parse images of business forms and upload the data to a database. The upload process will occur once a week. You need to recommend which services to use for the application. The solution must minimize infrastructure costs. Which services should you recommend? To answer, select the appropriate options in the answer area. NOTE: Each correct selection is worth one point. Hot Area:

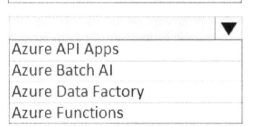

Answers:

A)

## Answer Area

Parse the images: Azure Cognitive Services (selected from: Azure Bot Service, Azure Cognitive Services, Azure Linguistic Analysis API)

Upload the data to the database: Azure Data Factory (selected from: Azure API Apps, Azure Batch AI, Azure Data Factory, Azure Functions)

**Solution:** A

**Explanation:**

Explanation: Box 1: Azure Cognitive Services Azure Cognitive Services include image-processing algorithms to smartly identify, caption, index, and moderate your pictures and videos. Not: Azure Linguistic Analytics API, which provides advanced natural language processing over raw text. Box 2: Azure Data Factory The Azure Data Factory (ADF) is a service designed to allow developers to integrate disparate data sources. It is a platform somewhat like SSIS in the cloud to manage the data you have both on-prem and in the cloud. It provides access to on-premises data in SQL Server and cloud data in Azure Storage (Blob and Tables) and Azure SQL Database. References: https://azure.microsoft.com/en-us/services/cognitive-services/ https://www.jamesserra.com/archive/2014/11/what-is-azure-data-factory/

**Question: 2** *Multiple Answers Are Right*

HOTSPOT You plan to deploy an Azure Data Factory pipeline that will perform the following: - Move data from on-premises to the cloud. - Consume Azure Cognitive Services APIs. You need to recommend which technologies the pipeline should use. The solution must minimize custom code. What should you include in the recommendation? To answer, select the appropriate options in the answer area. NOTE: Each correct selection is worth one point. Hot Area:

## Answer Area

Move data from on-premises to the cloud: ▼
- Azure-SSIS Integration Runtime
- Common language runtime (CLR)
- Integration Runtime (IR)
- Self-hosted integration runtime

Consume Cognitive Services APIs: ▼
- Azure API Management
- Azure Logic Apps
- WebJobs in Azure

**Answers:**

**A)**

## Answer Area

Move data from on-premises to the cloud: ▼
- Azure-SSIS Integration Runtime
- Common language runtime (CLR)
- Integration Runtime (IR)
- **Self-hosted integration runtime**

Consume Cognitive Services APIs: ▼
- Azure API Management
- **Azure Logic Apps**
- WebJobs in Azure

**Solution:** A

**Explanation:**

Explanation: Box 1: Self-hosted Integration Runtime A self-hosted IR is capable of running copy activity between a cloud data stores and a data store in private network. Not Azure-SSIS Integration Runtime, as you would need to write custom code. Box 2: Azure Logic Apps Azure Logic Apps helps you orchestrate and integrate different services by providing 100+ ready-to-use connectors, ranging from on-premises SQL Server or SAP to Microsoft Cognitive Services. Incorrect: Not Azure API Management: Use Azure API Management as a turnkey solution for publishing APIs to external and internal customers. References: https://docs.microsoft.com/en-us/azure/data-factory/concepts-integration-runtime https://docs.microsoft.com/en-us/azure/logic-apps/logic-apps-examples-and-scenarios

**Question: 3** *Multiple Answers Are Right*

HOTSPOT You need to build an interactive website that will accept uploaded images, and then ask a series of predefined questions based on each image. Which services should you use? To answer, select the appropriate options in the answer area. NOTE: Each correct selection is worth one point. Hot Area:

## Answer Area

Dynamically ask questions based on an uploaded image:
- Azure Analysis Services
- Azure Bot Service
- Azure Data Factory
- Azure Linguistic Analysis API

Analyze and classify an image:
- Bing Image Search
- Bing Visual Search
- Computer Vision
- Video Indexer

**Answers:**

A)

## Answer Area

| | |
|---|---|
| Dynamically ask questions based on an uploaded image: | Azure Analysis Services / **Azure Bot Service** / Azure Data Factory / Azure Linguistic Analysis API |
| Analyze and classify an image: | Bing Image Search / Bing Visual Search / **Computer Vision** / Video Indexer |

**Solution:** A

**Explanation:**

Explanation: Box 1: Azure Bot Service Box 2: Computer Vision The Computer Vision Analyze an image feature, returns information about visual content found in an image. Use tagging, domain-specific models, and descriptions in four languages to identify content and label it with confidence. Use Object Detection to get location of thousands of objects within an image. Apply the adult/ racy settings to help you detect potential adult content. Identify image types and color schemes in pictures. References: https://azure.microsoft.com/en-us/services/cognitive-services/computer-vision/

**Question: 4** *One Answer Is Right*

You are designing an AI solution that will analyze millions of pictures by using Azure HDInsight Hadoop cluster. You need to recommend a solution for storing the pictures. The solution must minimize costs. Which storage solution should you recommend?

**Answers:**

**A)** an Azure Data Lake Storage Gen1

**B)** Azure File Storage

**C)** Azure Blob storage

**D)** Azure Table storage

**Solution:** C

**Explanation:**

Explanation: Data Lake will be a bit more expensive although they are in close range of each other. Blob storage has more options for pricing depending upon things like how frequently you need to access your data (cold vs hot storage). Reference: http://blog.pragmaticworks.com/azure-data-lake-vs-azure-blob-storage-in-data-warehousing

**Question: 5** *One Answer Is Right*

You are configuring data persistence for a Microsoft Bot Framework application. The application requires a structured NoSQL cloud data store. You need to identify a storage solution for the application. The solution must minimize costs. What should you identify?

**Answers:**

**A)** Azure Blob storage

**B)** Azure Cosmos DB

**C)** Azure HDInsight

**D)** Azure Table storage

**Solution:** D

**Explanation:**

Explanation: Table Storage is a NoSQL key-value store for rapid development using massive semi-structured datasets You can develop applications on Cosmos DB using popular NoSQL APIs. Both services have a different scenario and pricing model. While Azure Storage Tables is aimed at high capacity on a single region (optional secondary read only region but no failover), indexing by PK/RK and storage-optimized pricing; Azure Cosmos DB Tables aims for high throughput (single-digit millisecond latency), global distribution (multiple failover), SLA-backed predictive performance with automatic indexing of each attribute/property and a pricing model focused on throughput. References: https://db-engines.com/en/system/Microsoft+Azure+Cosmos+DB%3BMicrosoft+Azure+Table+Storage

**Question: 6** *One Answer Is Right*

You have an Azure Machine Learning model that is deployed to a web service. You plan to publish the web service by using the name ml.contoso.com. You need to recommend a solution to ensure that access to the web service is encrypted. Which three actions should you recommend? Each correct answer presents part of the solution. NOTE: Each correct selection is worth one point.

**Answers:**

**A)** Generate a shared access signature (SAS)

**B)** Obtain an SSL certificate

**C)** Add a deployment slot

**D)** Update the web service

**E)** Update DNS

**F)** Create an Azure Key Vault

**Solution:** B, D, E

**Explanation:**

Explanation: The process of securing a new web service or an existing one is as follows: 1. Get a domain name. 2. Get a digital certificate. 3. Deploy or update the web service with the SSL setting enabled. 4. Update your DNS to point to the web service. Note: To deploy (or re-deploy) the service with SSL enabled, set the ssl_enabled parameter to True, wherever applicable. Set the ssl_certificate parameter to the value of the certificate file and the ssl_key to the value of the key file. References: https://docs.microsoft.com/en-us/azure/machine-learning/service/how-to-secure-web-service

**Question: 7** *One Answer Is Right*

You have several AI applications that use an Azure Kubernetes Service (AKS) cluster. The cluster supports a maximum of 32 nodes. You discover that occasionally and unpredictably, the application requires more than 32 nodes. You need to recommend a solution to handle the unpredictable application load. Which scaling methods should you recommend? (Choose two.)

**Answers:**

**A)** horizontal pod autoscaler

**B)** cluster autoscaler

**C)** AKS cluster virtual 32 node autoscaling

**D)** Azure Container Instances

**Solution:** A, B

**Explanation:**

Explanation: B: To keep up with application demands in Azure Kubernetes Service (AKS), you may need to adjust the number of nodes that run your workloads. The cluster autoscaler component can watch for pods in your cluster that can't be scheduled because of resource constraints. When issues are detected, the number of nodes is increased to meet the application demand. Nodes are also regularly checked for a lack of running pods, with the number of nodes then decreased as needed. This ability to automatically scale up or down the number of nodes in your AKS cluster lets you run an efficient, cost-effective cluster. A: You can also use the horizontal pod autoscaler to automatically adjust the number of pods that run your application. Reference: https://docs.microsoft.com/en-us/azure/aks/cluster-autoscaler

**Question: 8** *One Answer Is Right*

You deploy an infrastructure for a big data workload. You need to run Azure HDInsight and Microsoft Machine Learning Server. You plan to set the RevoScaleR compute contexts to run rx function calls in parallel. What are three compute contexts that you can use for Machine Learning Server? Each correct answer presents a complete solution. NOTE: Each correct selection is worth one point.

**Answers:**

**A)** SQL

**B)** Spark

**C)** local parallel

**D)** HBase

**E)** local sequential

**Solution:** A, B, C

**Explanation:**

Explanation: Remote computing is available for specific data sources on selected platforms. The following tables document the supported combinations. - RxInSqlServer, sqlserver: Remote compute context. Target server is a single database node (SQL Server 2016 R Services or SQL Server 2017 Machine Learning Services). Computation is parallel, but not distributed. - RxSpark, spark: Remote compute context. Target is a Spark cluster on Hadoop. - RxLocalParallel, localpar: Compute context is often used to enable controlled, distributed computations relying on instructions you provide rather than a built-in scheduler on Hadoop. You can use compute context for manual distributed computing. References: https://docs.microsoft.com/en-us/machine-learning-server/r/concept-what-is-compute-context

**Question: 9** *One Answer Is Right*

Your company recently deployed several hardware devices that contain sensors. The sensors generate new data on an hourly basis. The data generated is stored on-premises and retained for several years. During the past two months, the sensors generated 300 GB of data. You plan to move the data to Azure and then perform advanced analytics on the data. You need to recommend an Azure storage solution for the data. Which storage solution should you recommend?

**Answers:**

**A)** Azure Queue storage

**B)** Azure Cosmos DB

**C)** Azure Blob storage

**D)** Azure SQL Database

**Solution:** C

**Explanation:**

Explanation: References: https://docs.microsoft.com/en-us/azure/architecture/data-guide/technology-choices/data-storage

**Question: 10** *One Answer Is Right*

You plan to design an application that will use data from Azure Data Lake and perform sentiment analysis by using Azure Machine Learning algorithms. The developers of the application use a mix of Windows- and Linux-based environments. The developers contribute to shared GitHub repositories. You need all the developers to use the same tool to develop the application. What is the best tool to use? More than one answer choice may achieve the goal.

**Answers:**

**A)** Microsoft Visual Studio Code

**B)** Azure Notebooks

**C)** Azure Machine Learning Studio

**D)** Microsoft Visual Studio

**Solution:** C

**Explanation:**

Explanation: References: https://github.com/MicrosoftDocs/azure-docs/blob/master/articles/machine-learning/studio/algorithm- choice.md

# Chapter 14: AZ-103 - Microsoft Azure Administrator

## Exam Guide

Microsoft Azure Administrator AZ-103 Exam:

Microsoft Azure Administrator AZ-103 Exam which is related to Microsoft Certified Azure Administrator certifications. The AZ-103 exam measures the Candidates ability and knowledge in PowerShell and in the Command Line Interface. Candidates should have a basic knowledge of Azure Portal, ARM Templates, Operating Systems, Storage Structures, Networking. IT Professionals, Network Administrators, and Security Administrators usually hold or pursue this certification and you can expect the same job roles after completion of this certification.

AZ-103 Exam topics:

Candidates must know the exam topics before they start of preparation. Because it will really help them in hitting the core. Our **AZ-103 dumps** will include the following topics:

- Manage Azure subscriptions and resources 15-20%
- Implement and manage storage 15-20%
- Deploy and manage virtual machines (VMs) 15-20%
- Configure and manage virtual networks 30-35%
- Manage identities 15-20%

Certification Path:

The Microsoft Certified Azure Administrator Certification includes only one AZ-103 Exam.

Who should take the AZ-103 exam:

The Microsoft Azure Administrator AZ-103 Exam certification is an internationally-recognized validation that identifies persons who earn it as possessing skilled as a Microsoft Certified Azure Administrator. If candidates want significant improvement in career growth needs enhanced knowledge, skills, and talents. The Microsoft Azure Administrator AZ-103 Exam certification provides proof of this advanced knowledge and skill. If a candidate has knowledge of associated technologies and skills that are required to pass Microsoft Azure Administrator AZ-103 Exam then he should take this exam.

How to study the AZ-103 Exam:

Certification-questions.com expert team recommends you to prepare some notes on these topics along with it don't forget to practice Microsoft AZ-103 Exam dumps which been written by our expert team, Both these will help you a lot to clear this exam with good marks.

How much AZ-103 Exam Cost:

The price of the AZ-103 exam is $165 USD.

How to book the AZ-103 Exam:

These are following steps for registering the AZ-103 exam.
Step 1: Visit to Microsoft Exam Registration
Step 2: Signup/Login to MICROSOFT account
Step 3: Search for MICROSOFT AZ-103 Certifications Exam
Step 4: Select Date and Center of examination and confirm with payment value of $165

What is the duration of the AZ-103 Exam:

- Format: Multiple choices, multiple answers
- Length of Examination: 120 minutes
- Number of Questions: 45-55
- Passing Score: 700/1000

   The benefit in Obtaining the AZ-103 Exam Certification:

- After completion of Microsoft Certified Azure Administrator Candidates receive official confirmation from Microsoft that you are now fully certified in their chosen field. This can be now added to their CV, cover letters and job applications.
  When Candidates applying for a job or looking to promotion in their current position, a Microsoft Certified Azure Administrator certification in the field in which Candidates are applying will put you at the top of the list and make them a desirable candidate for employers.
  Candidates will get in-depth knowledge by completing the courses along with the access to revision materials for 6 months upon completion means they will have a wider skill set when it comes to the various technologies and systems than an uncertified professional. Certified Professional in this particular skill set is 74% more efficient when it comes to completing their tasks in a timely well-executed manner.
  Organization owners invest a lot in their employees when it comes to their training with the goal of making them quicker, more efficient, and more knowledgeable about their role.

Certified Professional will reduce the time he spends on tasks, meaning he can get more done this could help reduce company downtime when repairing faults on a system or fixing hardware problems.

Becoming Microsoft Certified Azure Administrator means one thing you are worth more to the company and therefore more to yourself in the form of an upgraded pay package. On average a Microsoft Certified Azure Administrator member of staff is estimated to be worth 30% more to a company than their uncertified professionals.

Difficulty in writing AZ-103 Exam:

The Microsoft AZ-103 exam focuses on many technologies that's why it is getting more and more fame in the IT sector within a short span. Microsoft updates their tech system and introduces new technologies in the market by this value of Microsoft AZ-103 exam increases. Therefore by this increases the difficulty of passing the Microsoft AZ-103 exam. Candidates should pass the Microsoft AZ-103 exam in order to survive in the IT field. Certification-questions provides latest and valid Microsoft AZ-103 exam questions. These **Microsoft AZ-103 exam dumps** have been verified and reviewed by the Microsoft professionals and experts. Certification-questions provides what others won't provide you. Certification-questions **Microsoft AZ-103 exam dumps** have the latest and verified exam questions which will be asked in the real exam. Certification-questions offers you authentic Microsoft AZ-103 exam questions. Apart from this we also provide Microsoft AZ-103 practice test which includes all the practice questions for the Microsoft AZ-103 exam, **Microsoft AZ-103 exam dumps** that that will ensure 100% passing surety and the simple user interface of Microsoft AZ-103 practice test. Our hired professionals who passed their Microsoft AZ-103 exam well contribute to making **Microsoft AZ-103 exam dumps** updated with Microsoft AZ-103 new questions to ensure candidates to clear their Microsoft AZ-103 certification exam at first attempt. Candidates can achieve the best result in the Microsoft AZ-103 exam they need to experience the types of Microsoft AZ-103 exam question they will be asked to answer and prepare for the Microsoft AZ-103 test from Microsoft AZ-103 PDF dumps for each and every topic.

For more info visit::

AZ-103 Exam Reference

# Sample Practice Test for AZ-103

**Question: 1** *One Answer Is Right*

You have an Azure subscription named Subscription1. Subscription1 contains the resource groups in the following table.

| Name | Azure region | Policy |
|------|--------------|--------|
| RG1 | West Europe | Policy1 |
| RG2 | North Europe | Policy2 |
| RG3 | France Central | Policy3 |

RG1 has a web app named WebApp1. WebApp1 is located in West Europe. You move WebApp1 to RG2. What is the effect of the move?

**Answers:**

**A)** The App Service plan for WebApp1 moves to North Europe. Policy2 applies to WebApp1.

**B)** The App Service plan for WebApp1 remains in West Europe. Policy2 applies to WebApp1.

**C)** The App Service plan for WebApp1 moves to North Europe. Policy1 applies to WebApp1.

**D)** The App Service plan for WebApp1 remains in West Europe. Policy1 applies to WebApp1.

**Solution:** B

**Explanation:**

Explanation: You can move an app to another App Service plan, as long as the source plan and the target plan are in the same resource group and geographical region. The region in which your app runs is the region of the App Service plan it's in. However, you cannot change an App Service plan's region. References: https://docs.microsoft.com/en-us/azure/app-service/app-service-plan-manage

**Question: 2** *Multiple Answers Are Right*

HOTSPOT You have an Azure subscription. You plan to use Azure Resource Manager templates to deploy 50 Azure virtual machines that will be part of the same availability set. You need to ensure that as many virtual machines as possible are available if the fabric fails or during servicing. How should you configure the template? To answer, select the appropriate options in the answer area. NOTE: Each correct selection is worth one point. Hot Area:

**Answer Area**

```
{
    "schema": "https://schema.management.azure.com/schemas/2015-01-01/deploymentTemplate.json#",
    "contentVersion": "1.0.0.0",
    "parameters": {},
    "resources": [
        {
            "type": "Microsoft.Compute/availabilitySets",
            "name": "ha",
            "apiVersion": "2017-12-01",
            "location": "eastus",
            "properties": {
                "platformFaultDomainCount":    [ ▼ ],
                                               max value
                                               0
                                               20

                "platfromUpdateDomainCount":   [ ▼ ],
                                               max value
                                               0
                                               20
            }
        }
    ]
}
```

## Answers:

### A)

**Answer Area**

```
{
    "schema": "https://schema.management.azure.com/schemas/2015-01-01/deploymentTemplate.json#",
    "contentVersion": "1.0.0.0",
    "parameters": {},
    "resources": [
        {
            "type": "Microsoft.Compute/availabilitySets",
            "name": "ha",
            "apiVersion": "2017-12-01",
            "location": "eastus",
            "properties": {
                "platformFaultDomainCount":    [ ▼ ],
                                               **max value**
                                               0
                                               **20**

                "platfromUpdateDomainCount":   [ ▼ ],
                                               max value
                                               0
                                               **20**
            }
        }
    ]
}
```

**Solution:** A

**Explanation:**

Explanation: Use two fault domains. 2 or 3 is max value, depending on which region you are in. Use 20 for platformUpdateDomainCount Increasing the update domain (platformUpdateDomainCount) helps with capacity and availability planning when the platform reboots nodes. A higher number for the pool (20 is max) means that fewer of their nodes in any given availability set would be rebooted at once. References: https://www.itprotoday.com/microsoft-azure/check-if-azure-region-supports-2-or-3-fault-domains-managed- disks https://github.com/Azure/acs-engine/issues/1030

**Question: 3** *One Answer Is Right*

Note: This question is part of a series of questions that present the same scenario. Each question in the series contains a unique solution that might meet the stated goals. Some question sets might have more than one correct solution, while others might not have a correct solution. After you answer a question in this section, you will NOT be able to return to it. As a result, these questions will not appear in the review screen. You have an Azure Active Directory (Azure AD) tenant named Adatum and an Azure Subscription named Subscription1. Adatum contains a group named Developers. Subscription1 contains a resource group named Dev. You need to provide the Developers group with the ability to create Azure logic apps in the Dev resource group. Solution: On Dev, you assign the Contributor role to the Developers group. Does this meet the goal?

**Answers:**

**A)** Yes

**B)** No

**Solution:** A

**Explanation:**

Explanation: The Contributor role can manage all resources (and add resources) in a Resource Group.

**Question: 4** *One Answer Is Right*

You have an Azure subscription that contains a resource group named RG1. RG1 contains 100 virtual machines. Your company has three cost centers named Manufacturing, Sales, and Finance. You need to associate each virtual machine to a specific cost center. What should you do?

**Answers:**

**A)** Configure locks for the virtual machine.

**B)** Add an extension to the virtual machines.

**C)** Assign tags to the virtual machines.

**D)** Modify the inventory settings of the virtual machine.

**Solution:** C

**Explanation:**

Explanation: References: https://docs.microsoft.com/en-us/azure/billing/billing-getting-started https://docs.microsoft.com/en-us/azure/azure-resource-manager/resource-group-using-tags

**Question: 5** *One Answer Is Right*

Note: This question is part of a series of questions that present the same scenario. Each question in the series contains a unique solution that might meet the stated goals. Some question sets might have more than one correct solution, while others might not have a correct solution. After you answer a question in this section, you will NOT be able to return to it. As a result, these questions will not appear in the review screen. You have an Azure subscription named Subscription1. Subscription1 contains a resource group named RG1. RG1 contains resources that were deployed by using templates. You need to view the date and time when the resources were created in RG1. Solution: From the Subscriptions blade, you select the subscription, and then click Programmatic deployment. Does this meet the goal?

**Answers:**

**A)** Yes

**B)** No

**Solution:** B

**Question: 6** *One Answer Is Right*

Note: This question is part of a series of questions that present the same scenario. Each question in the series contains a unique solution that might meet the stated goals. Some question sets might have more than one correct solution, while others might not have a correct solution. After you answer a question in this section, you will NOT be able to return to it. As a result, these questions will not appear in the review screen. You have an Azure subscription named Subscription1. Subscription1 contains a resource group named RG1. RG1 contains resources that were deployed by using templates. You need to view the date and time when the resources were created in RG1. Solution: From the Subscriptions blade, you select the subscription, and then click Resource providers. Does this meet the goal?

**Answers:**

**A)** Yes

**B)** No

**Solution:** B

**Question: 7** *One Answer Is Right*

Note: This question is part of a series of questions that present the same scenario. Each question in the series contains a unique solution that might meet the stated goals. Some question sets might have more than one correct solution, while others might not have a correct solution. After you answer a question in this section, you will NOT be able to return to it. As a result, these questions will not appear in the review screen. You have an Azure subscription named Subscription1. Subscription1 contains a resource group named RG1. RG1 contains resources that were deployed by using templates. You need to view the date and time when the resources were created in RG1. Solution: From the RG1 blade, you click Automation script. Does this meet the goal?

**Answers:**

**A)** Yes

**B)** No

**Solution:** B

**Question: 8** *Multiple Answers Are Right*

HOTSPOT You have an Azure Active Directory (Azure AD) tenant that contains three global administrators named Admin1, Admin2, and Admin3. The tenant is associated to an Azure subscription. Access control for the subscription is configured as shown in the Access control exhibit. (Click the Exhibit tab.)

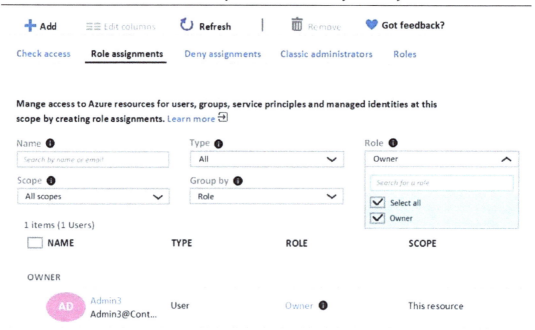

You sign in to the Azure portal as Admin1 and configure the tenant as shown in the Tenant exhibit. (Click the Exhibit tab.)

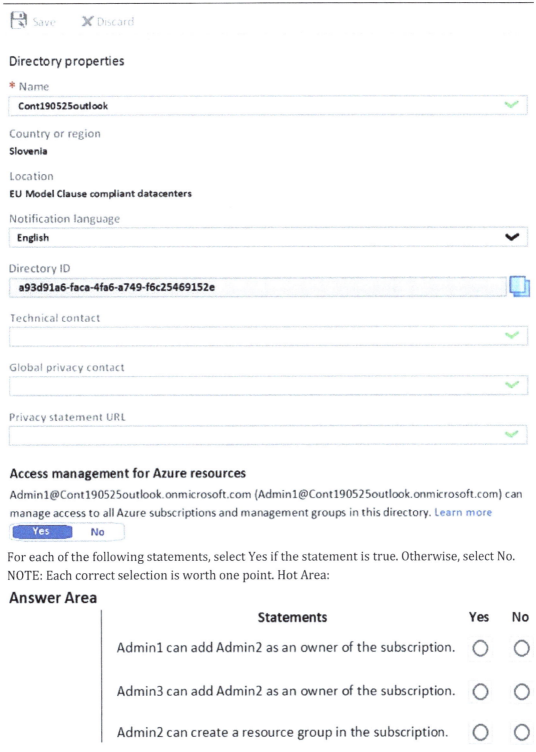

For each of the following statements, select Yes if the statement is true. Otherwise, select No. NOTE: Each correct selection is worth one point. Hot Area:

### Answer Area

| Statements | Yes | No |
| --- | --- | --- |
| Admin1 can add Admin2 as an owner of the subscription. | ○ | ○ |
| Admin3 can add Admin2 as an owner of the subscription. | ○ | ○ |
| Admin2 can create a resource group in the subscription. | ○ | ○ |

Answers:

A)
**Answer Area**

| Statements | Yes | No |
|---|---|---|
| Admin1 can add Admin2 as an owner of the subscription. | ○ | ○ |
| Admin3 can add Admin2 as an owner of the subscription. | ○ | ○ |
| Admin2 can create a resource group in the subscription. | ○ | ○ |

**Solution:** A

**Explanation:**

Explanation:

**Question: 9** *One Answer Is Right*

You have an Azure policy as shown in the following exhibit.

**SCOPE**

* Scope (Learn more about setting the scope)

**Exclusions**
Subscription 1/ Contoso RG1

**BASICS**

* Policy definition
Not allowed resource types

* Assignment name
Not allowed resource types

Assignment ID
/subscriptions/5eb8d0b6-ce3b-4ce0-a631-9f5321bedabb/providers/Microsoft.Authorization/policyAssignments/0e6fb866bf854f54accae2a9

Description

Assigned by
admin1@contoso.com

**PARAMETERS**

* Not allowed resource types
Microsoft.Sql/servers

What is the effect of the policy?

**Answers:**

**A)** You are prevented from creating Azure SQL Servers in ContosoRG1 only.

**B)** You can create Azure SQL servers in ContosoRG1 only.

**C)** You can create Azure SQL servers in any resource group within Subscription 1.

**D)** You are prevented from creating Azure SQL servers anywhere in Subscription 1.

**Solution:** B

**Explanation:**

Explanation: You are prevented from creating Azure SQL servers anywhere in Subscription 1 with the exception of ContosoRG1

**Question: 10** *One Answer Is Right*

You have an Azure Active Directory (Azure AD) tenant named contoso.onmicrosoft.com that contains 100 user accounts. You purchase 10 Azure AD Premium P2 licenses for the tenant. You need to ensure that 10 users can use all the Azure AD Premium features. What should you do?

**Answers:**

**A)** From the Directory role blade of each user, modify the directory role.

**B)** From the Azure AD domain, add an enterprise application.

**C)** From the Groups blade of each user, invite the users to a group.

**D)** From the Licenses blade of Azure AD, assign a license.

**Solution:** D

**Explanation:**

Explanation: Reference: https://docs.microsoft.com/en-us/azure/active-directory/fundamentals/license-users-groups

# Chapter 15: AZ-104 - Microsoft Azure Administrator

## Exam Guide

How to Prepare For AZ-104:Microsoft Azure Administrator Exam

Preparation Guide for AZ-104:Microsoft Azure Administrator Exam

Introduction

Microsoft has created a track for Azure administrator who implements, manages, and monitors identity, governance, storage, compute, and virtual networks in a cloud environment. This certification program will provides Microsoft Azure administrator a way to demonstrate their skills. The assessment is based on a rigorous exam using industry standard methodology to determine whether a candidate meets Microsoft's proficiency standards.

According to Microsoft, a AZ-104 Certified Professional enables organizations will provision, size, monitor, and adjust resources as appropriate.

Certification is evidence of your skills, expertise in those areas in which you like to work. There are many vendors in the market that are providing these certifications. If candidate wants to work on Microsoft Azure administration and prove his knowledge, certification offered by Microsoft. This **AZ-104 Exam** Certification helps a candidate to validates his skills in Microsoft Azure administration.

In this guide, we will cover the AZ-104:Microsoft Azure Administrator Certification exam, AZ-104:Microsoft Azure Administrator Certified professional salary and all aspects of the AZ-104:Microsoft Azure Administrator Certification.

Introduction to AZ-104:Microsoft Azure Administrator Exam:

Candidates for **AZ-104 Exam** are seeking to prove fundamental Microsoft Azure administration knowledge and skills. Before taking this exam, exam aspirants ought to have a solid fundamental information of the concepts shared in preparation guide as well as on Azure.

It is suggested that professionals accustomed to the ideas and also the **technologies represented** here by taking relevant training courses. Candidates are expected to have a strong understanding of core Azure services, Azure workloads, security, and governance . After passing this exam, candidates get a certificate from Microsoft that helps them to **demonstrate their** proficiency in Azure administration to their clients and employers.

Topics of AZ-104:Microsoft Azure Administrator Exam:

Candidates should apprehend the examination topics before they begin of preparation. because it'll extremely facilitate them in touch the core. Our **AZ-104 dumps** will include the following topics:

*1. Manage Azure Identities and Governance (15-20%)*

Manage Azure AD objects

- Create users and groups
- Manage user and group properties
- Manage device settings
- Perform bulk user updates
- Manage guest accounts
- Configure Azure AD Join
- Configure self-service password reset
- NOT: Azure AD Connect; PIM

  Manage role-based access control (RBAC)

- Create a custom role
- Provide access to Azure resources by assigning roles
    - Subscriptions
    - Resource groups
    - Resources (VM, disk, etc.)
- Interpret access assignments
- Manage multiple directories

  Manage subscriptions and governance

- Configure Azure policies
- Configure resource locks
- Apply tags
- Create and manage resource groups
- Manage subscriptions

- Configure Cost Management
- Configure management groups

*2. Implement and Manage Storage (10-15%)*

Manage storage accounts

- Configure network access to storage accounts
- Create and configure storage accounts
- Generate shared access signature
- Manage access keys
- Implement Azure storage replication
- Configure Azure AD Authentication for a storage account

Manage data in Azure Storage

- Export from Azure job
- Import into Azure job
- Install and use Azure Storage Explorer
- Copy data by using AZCopy

Configure Azure files and Azure blob storage

- Create an Azure file share
- Create and configure Azure File Sync service
- Configure Azure blob storage
- Configure storage tiers for Azure blobs

*3. Deploy and Manage Azure Compute Resources (25-30%)*

Configure VMs for high availability and scalability

- Configure high availability
- Deploy and configure scale sets

Automate deployment and configuration of VMs

- Modify Azure Resource Manager (ARM) template
- Configure VHD template
- Deploy from template
- Save a deployment as an ARM template
- Automate configuration management by using custom script extensions

Create and configure VMs

- Configure Azure Disk Encryption
- Move VMs from one resource group to another
- Manage VM sizes
- Add data discs
- Configure networking
- Redeploy VMs

Create and configure containers

- Create and configure Azure Kubernetes Service (AKS)
- Create and configure Azure Container Instances (ACI)
- NOT: selecting an container solution architecture or product; container registry settings

Create and configure Web Apps

- Create and configure App Service
- Create and configure App Service Plans
- NOT: Azure Functions; Logic Apps; Event Grid

*4. Configure and Manage Virtual Networking (30-35%)*

Implement and manage virtual networking

- Create and configure VNET peering
- Configure private and public IP addresses, network routes, network interface, subnets, and virtual network

Configure name resolution

- Configure Azure DNS
- Configure custom DNS settings
- Configure a private or public DNS zone

Secure access to virtual networks

- Create security rules
- Associate an NSG to a subnet or network interface
- Evaluate effective security rules
- Deploy and configure Azure Firewall
- Deploy and configure Azure Bastion Service
- NOT: Implement Application Security Groups; DDoS

Configure load balancing

- Configure Application Gateway
- Configure an internal load balancer
- Configure load balancing rules
- Configure a public load balancer
- Troubleshoot load balancing
- NOT: Traffic Manager and FrontDoor and PrivateLink

Monitor and troubleshoot virtual networking

- Monitor on-premises connectivity
- Use Network resource monitoring
- Use Network Watcher
- Troubleshoot external networking
- Troubleshoot virtual network connectivity

Integrate an on-premises network with an Azure virtual network

- Create and configure Azure VPN Gateway
- Create and configure VPNs
- Configure ExpressRoute
- Verify on premises connectivity
- Configure Azure Virtual WAN

*5. Monitor and back up Azure resources (10-15%)*

Monitor resources by using Azure Monitor

- Configure and interpret metrics
- Configure Log Analytics
- Query and analyze logs
- Set up alerts and actions
- Configure Application Insights

Implement backup and recovery

- Configure and review backup reports
- Perform backup and restore operations by using Azure Backup Service
- Create a Recovery Services Vault use soft delete to recover Azure VMs
- Create and configure backup policy
- Perform site-to-site recovery by using Azure Site Recovery

Who should take the AZ-104:Microsoft Azure Administrator Exam:

The **AZ-104 Exam** certification is an internationally-recognized certification which help to have validation for those professionals who are knowledgeable in the Azure administration process. Candidates should have extensive experience and knowledge of using PowerShell, the Command Line Interface, Azure Portal, and ARM templates. It is good for these candidates:

- Azure administrator
- Fresher

How to study the AZ-104:Microsoft Azure Administrator Exam:

Preparation of certification exams could be covered with two resource types . The first one are the study guides, reference books and study forums that are elaborated and appropriate for building information from ground up. Apart from them video tutorials and lectures are a good option to ease the pain of through study and are relatively make the study process more interesting nonetheless these demand time and concentration from the learner. Smart candidates who wish to create a solid foundation altogether examination topics and connected technologies typically mix video lectures with study guides to reap the advantages of each but practice exams or practice exam engines is one important study tool which goes typically unnoted by most candidates. Practice exams are designed with our experts to make exam prospects test their knowledge on skills attained in course, as well as prospects become comfortable and familiar with the real exam environment. Statistics have indicated exam anxiety plays much bigger role of students failure in exam than the fear of the unknown. Certification-questions expert team recommends preparing some notes on these topics along with it don't forget to practice **AZ-104 dumps** which had been written by our expert team, each of these can assist you loads to clear this exam with excellent marks.

AZ-104:Microsoft Azure Administrator Certification Path:

AZ-104:Microsoft Azure Administrator Exam is Associate level Certification. It is strongly recommended that aspirants for this exam should have completed AZ-900 certification or anyone who is having keen interest and familiar with general Microsoft Azure administration concepts and the technologies. More than 85% of IT support roles require a good foundation of Microsoft Azure administration concepts. Aspirants should have some hands-on experience Azure Portal, ARM templates, operating systems, virtualization, cloud infrastructure, storage structures and networking.

How much AZ-104:Microsoft Azure Administrator Exam Cost:

The price of the Microsoft Azure Administrator Exam exam is $165 USD, for more information related to exam price please visit to Microsoft Training website as prices of Microsoft exams fees get varied country wise.

How to book the AZ-104:Microsoft Azure Administrator Exam:

These are following steps for registering the AZ-104:Microsoft Azure Administrator exam.

- Step 1: Visit to Microsoft Learning and search for AZ-104:Microsoft Azure Administrator.
- Step 2: Sign up/Login to Pearson VUE account
- Step 3: Select local centre based on your country, date, time and confirm with a payment method.

What is the duration, language, and format of AZ-104:Microsoft Azure Administrator Exam:

- Length of Examination: 50 mins
- Number of Questions: 40 to 60 questions(Since Microsoft does not publish this information, the number of exam questions may change without notice.)
- Passing Score: 700 / 1000
- Type of Questions: This test format is multiple choice.
- language: English
- This is beta exam, would be available on or around March 31, 2020.

AZ-104:Microsoft Azure Administrator Exam Certified Professional salary:

The average salary of a AZ-104:Microsoft Azure Administrator Exam Certified Expert in

- United State - 80,000 USD
- India - 12,10,327 INR
- Europe - 60,547 EURO
- England - 60,532 POUND

The benefit of obtaining the AZ-104:Microsoft Azure Administrator Exam Certification:

- This certification will be judging your skills and knowledge on your understanding Microsoft Azure administration concepts & Understanding of how to operate on Microsoft Azure Administrator.
- This certification credential will give you edge over other counterparts. Apart from knowledge from AZ-104:Microsoft Azure Administrator Exam.
- AZ-104 Certification is distinguished among competitors. AZ-104 certification can give them an edge at that time easily when candidates appear for employment interview, employers are very fascinated to note one thing that differentiates the individual from all other candidates.

- AZ-104 certification has more useful and relevant networks that help them in setting career goals for themselves. AZ-104 networks provide them with the correct career guidance than non certified generally are unable to get.
- AZ-104 certified candidates will be confident and stand different from others as their skills are more trained than non-certified professionals.
- **AZ-104 Exam** provide proven knowledge to use the tools to complete the task efficiently and cost effectively than the other non-certified professionals lack in doing so.
- AZ-104 Certification provides practical experience to candidates from all the aspects to be a proficient worker in the organization.
- AZ-104 Certifications provide opportunities to get a job easily in which they are interested in instead of wasting years and ending without getting any experience.
- AZ-104 credential delivers higher earning potential and increased promotion opportunities because it shows a good understanding of azure administration.

Difficulty in Writing AZ-104:Microsoft Azure Administrator Exam:

AZ-104:Microsoft Azure Administrator is a privileged achievement one could be graced with. But adverse to general notion certifying with Microsoft is not that challenging if the candidates have proper preparation material to pass the AZ-104:Microsoft Azure Administrator exam with good grades. Questions answers and clarifications which are designed in form of Certification-questions dumps make sure to cover entire course content. Certification-questions have a brilliant AZ-104:Microsoft Azure Administrator dumps with most recent and important questions and answers in PDF files. Certification-questions is sure about the exactness and legitimacy of AZ-104:Microsoft Azure Administrator dumps and in this manner. Candidates can easily pass the AZ-104:Microsoft Azure Administrator exam with genuine AZ-104:Microsoft Azure Administrator dumps and get MICROSOFT certification. These dumps are viewed as the best source to understand the AZ-104:Microsoft Azure Administrator well by simply pursuing examples questions and answers. If candidate completes practice the exam with certification **AZ-104 Dumps** along with self-assessment to get the proper idea on MICROSOFT accreditation and to ace the certification exam.

For more info read reference::

microsoft learning site
Administer infrastructure resources in Azure
Azure Storage
Azure Network

# Sample Practice Test for AZ-104

**Question: 1** *Multiple Answers Are Right*

You need to the appropriate sizes for the Azure virtual for Server2. What should you do? To answer, select the appropriate options in the answer area. NOTE: Each correct selection is worth one point.

From the Azure portal:

- Create an Azure Migrate project.
- Create a Recovery Services vault.
- Upload a management certificate.
- Create an Azure Import/Export job.

On Server2:

- Enable Hyper-V Replica.
- Install the Azure File Sync agent.
- Create a collector virtual machine.
- Configure Hyper-V storage migration.
- Install the Azure Site Recovery Provider.

**Answers:**

A)

Number of virtual networks: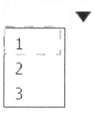

Number of subnets:

**Solution:** A

**Explanation:**

Explanation:

From the Azure portal: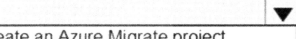

On Server2:

Box 1: Create a Recovery Services vault Create a Recovery Services vault on the Azure Portal.
Box 2: Install the Azure Site Recovery Provider Azure Site Recovery can be used to manage migration of on-premises machines to Azure. Scenario: Migrate the virtual machines hosted on

Server1 and Server2 to Azure. Server2 has the Hyper-V host role. References: https://docs.microsoft.com/en-us/azure/site-recovery/migrate-tutorial-on-premises-azure

**Question: 2** *One Answer Is Right*

You need to meet the technical requirement for VM4. What should you create and configure?

**Answers:**

**A)** an Azure Notification Hub

**B)** an Azure Event Hub

**C)** an Azure Logic App

**D)** an Azure services Bus

**Solution:** B

**Explanation:**

Explanation: Scenario: Create a workflow to send an email message when the settings of VM4 are modified. You can start an automated logic app workflow when specific events happen in Azure resources or third-party resources. These resources can publish those events to an Azure event grid. In turn, the event grid pushes those events to subscribers that have queues, webhooks, or event hubs as endpoints. As a subscriber, your logic app can wait for those events from the event grid before running automated workflows to perform tasks - without you writing any code. References: https://docs.microsoft.com/en-us/azure/event-grid/monitor-virtual-machine-changes-event-grid- logic-app

**Question: 3** *One Answer Is Right*

You need to recommend a solution to automate the configuration for the finance department users. The solution must meet the technical requirements. What should you include in the recommended?

**Answers:**

**A)** Azure AP B2C

**B)** Azure AD Identity Protection

**C)** an Azure logic app and the Microsoft Identity Management (MIM) client

**D)** dynamic groups and conditional access policies

**Solution:** D

**Explanation:**

Explanation: Scenario: Ensure Azure Multi-Factor Authentication (MFA) for the users in the finance department only. The recommendation is to use conditional access policies that can then be targeted to groups of users, specific applications, or other conditions. References: https://docs.microsoft.com/en-us/azure/active-directory/authentication/howto-mfa-userstates Overview Litware, Ltd. is a consulting company that has a main office in Montreal and two branch offices in Seattle and New York. The Montreal office has 2,000 employees. The Seattle office has 1,000 employees. The New York office has 200 employees. All the resources used by Litware are hosted on-premises. Litware creates a new Azure subscription. The Azure Active Directory (Azure AD) tenant uses a domain named Litware.onmicrosoft.com. The tenant uses the P1 pricing tier. Existing Environment The network contains an Active Directory forest named Litware.com. All domain controllers are configured as DNS servers and host the Litware.com DNS zone. Litware has finance, human resources, sales, research, and information technology departments. Each department has an organizational unit (OU) that contains all the accounts of that respective department. All the user accounts have the department attribute set to their respective department. New users are added frequently. Litware.com contains a user named User1. All the offices connect by using private links. Litware has data centers in the Montreal and Seattle offices. Each data center has a firewall that can be configured as a VPN device. All infrastructure servers are virtualized. The virtualization environment contains the servers in the following table.

| Name | Role | Contains virtual machine |
|---|---|---|
| Server1 | VMWare vCenter server | VM1 |
| Server2 | Hyper-V-host | VM2 |

Litware uses two web applications named App1 and App2. Each instance on each web application requires 1GB of memory. The Azure subscription contains the resources in the following table.

| Name | Type |
|---|---|
| VNet1 | Virtual network |
| VM3 | Virtual machine |
| VM4 | Virtual machine |

The network security team implements several network security groups (NSGs). Planned Changes Litware plans to implement the following changes: * Deploy Azure ExpressRoute to the Montreal office. * Migrate the virtual machines hosted on Server1 and Server2 to Azure. * Synchronize on-premises Active Directory to Azure Active Directory (Azure AD). * Migrate App1 and App2 to two Azure web apps named webApp1 and WebApp2. Technical requirements Litware must meet the following technical requirements: * Ensure that WebApp1 can adjust the number of instances automatically based on the load and can scale up to five instance*. * Ensure that VM3 can establish outbound connections over TCP port 8080 to the applications servers in the Montreal office. * Ensure that routing information is exchanged automatically between

Azure and the routers in the Montreal office. * Enable Azure Multi-Factor Authentication (MFA) for the users in the finance department only. * Ensure that webapp2.azurewebsites.net can be accessed by using the name app2.Litware.com. * Connect the New Your office to VNet1 over the Internet by using an encrypted connection. * Create a workflow to send an email message when the settings of VM4 are modified. * Create a custom Azure role named Role1 that is based on the Reader role. * Minimize costs whenever possible.

**Question: 4** *One Answer Is Right*

You discover that VM3 does NOT meet the technical requirements. You need to verify whether the issue relates to the NSGs. What should you use?

**Answers:**

**A)** Diagram in VNet1

**B)** the security recommendations in Azure Advisor

**C)** Diagnostic settings in Azure Monitor

**D)** Diagnose and solve problems in Traffic Manager Profiles

**E)** IP flow verify in Azure Network Watcher

**Solution:** E

**Explanation:**

Explanation: Scenario: Litware must meet technical requirements including: Ensure that VM3 can establish outbound connections over TCP port 8080 to the applications servers in the Montreal office. IP flow verify checks if a packet is allowed or denied to or from a virtual machine. The information consists of direction, protocol, local IP, remote IP, local port, and remote port. If the packet is denied by a security group, the name of the rule that denied the packet is returned. While any source or destination IP can be chosen, IP flow verify helps administrators quickly diagnose connectivity issues from or to the internet and from or to the on-premises environment. References: https://docs.microsoft.com/en-us/azure/network-watcher/network-watcher-ip-flow-verify-overview

**Question: 5** *Multiple Answers Are Right*

You need to meet the connection requirements for the New York office. What should you do? To answer, select the appropriate options in the answer area. NOTE: Each correct selection is worth one point.

**Answer Area**

From the Azure portal:
- Create an ExpressRoute circuit only.
- Create a virtual network gateway only.
- Create a virtual network gateway and a local network gateway.
- Create an ExpressRoute circuit and an on-premises data gateway.
- Create a virtual network gateway and an on-premises data gateway.

In the New York office:
- Deploy ExpressRoute.
- Deploy a DirectAccess server.
- Implement a Web Application Proxy.
- Configure a site-to-site VPN connection.

**Answers:**

**A)**

User1:
- Group1 only
- Group2 only
- Group3 only
- Group1 and Group2 only
- Group1 and Group3 only
- Group2 and Group3 only
- Group1, Group2, and Group3

User2:
- Group1 only
- Group2 only
- Group3 only
- Group1 and Group2 only
- Group1 and Group3 only
- Group2 and Group3 only
- Group1, Group2, and Group3

**Solution:** A

**Explanation:**

Explanation:

From the Azure portal:

- Create an ExpressRoute circuit only.
- Create a virtual network gateway only.
- **Create a virtual network gateway and a local network gateway.**
- Create an ExpressRoute circuit and an on-premises data gateway.
- Create a virtual network gateway and an on-premises data gateway.

In the New York office:

- Deploy ExpressRoute.
- Deploy a DirectAccess server.
- Implement a Web Application Proxy.
- **Configure a site-to-site VPN connection.**

Box 1: Create a virtual network gateway and a local network gateway. Azure VPN gateway. The VPN gateway service enables you to connect the VNet to the on-premises network through a VPN appliance. For more information, see Connect an on-premises network to a Microsoft Azure virtual network. The VPN gateway includes the following elements: * Virtual network gateway. A resource that provides a virtual VPN appliance for the VNet. It is responsible for routing traffic from the on-premises network to the VNet. * Local network gateway. An abstraction of the on-premises VPN appliance. Network traffic from the cloud application to the on-premises network is routed through this gateway. * Connection. The connection has properties that specify the connection type (IPSec) and the key shared with the on-premises VPN appliance to encrypt traffic. * Gateway subnet. The virtual network gateway is held in its own subnet, which is subject to various requirements, described in the Recommendations section below. Box 2: Configure a site-to-site VPN connection On premises create a site-to-site connection for the virtual network gateway and the local network gateway.

Scenario: Connect the New York office to VNet1 over the Internet by using an encrypted connection. ================================================== Topic 1, Humongous Insurance Overview Existing Environment Huongous Insurance is an insurance company that has three offices in Miami, Tokoyo, and Bankok. Each has 5000 users. Active Directory Environment Humongous Insurance has a single-domain Active Directory forest named humongousinsurance.com. The functional level of the forest is Windows Server 2012. You recently provisioned an Azure Active Directory (Azure AD) tenant. Network Infrastructure Each office has a local data center that contains all the servers for that office. Each office has a dedicated connection to the Internet. Each office has several link load balancers that provide access to the servers. Active Directory Issue Several users in humongousinsurance.com have UPNs that contain special characters. You suspect that some of the characters are unsupported in Azure AD. Licensing Issue You attempt to assign a license in Azure to several users and receive the following error message: "Licenses not assigned. License agreement failed for one user." You verify that the Azure subscription has the available licenses. Requirements Planned

Changes Humongous Insurance plans to open a new office in Paris. The Paris office will contain 1,000 users who will be hired during the next 12 months. All the resources used by the Paris office users will be hosted in Azure. Planned Azure AD Infrastructure The on-premises Active Directory domain will be synchronized to Azure AD. All client computers in the Paris office will be joined to an Azure AD domain. Planned Azure Networking Infrastructure You plan to create the following networking resources in a resource group named All_Resources: * Default Azure system routes that will be the only routes used to route traffic * A virtual network named Paris-VNet that will contain two subnets named Subnet1 and Subnet2 * A virtual network named ClientResources-VNet that will contain one subnet named ClientSubnet * A virtual network named AllOffices-VNet that will contain two subnets named Subnet3 and Subnet4 You plan to enable peering between Paris-VNet and AllOffices-VNet. You will enable the Use remote gateways setting for the Paris-VNet peerings. You plan to create a private DNS zone named humongousinsurance.local and set the registration network to the ClientResources-VNet virtual network. Planned Azure Computer Infrastructure Each subnet will contain several virtual machines that will run either Windows Server 2012 R2, Windows Server 2016, or Red Hat Linux. Department Requirements Humongous Insurance identifies the following requirements for the company's departments: * Web administrators will deploy Azure web apps for the marketing department. Each web app will be added to a separate resource group. The initial configuration of the web apps will be identical. The web administrators have permission to deploy web apps to resource groups. * During the testing phase, auditors in the finance department must be able to review all Azure costs from the past week. Authentication Requirements Users in the Miami office must use Azure Active Directory Seamless Single Sign-on (Azure AD Seamless SSO) when accessing resources in Azure.

**Question: 6** *One Answer Is Right*

You need to prepare the environment to meet the authentication requirements. Which two actions should you perform? Each correct answer presents part of the solution. NOTE: Each correct selection is worth one point.

**Answers:**

**A)** Allow inbound TCP port 8080 to the domain controllers in the Miami office.

**B)** Add http://autogon.microsoftazuread-sso.com to the intranet zone of each client computer in the Miami office.

**C)** Join the client computers in the Miami office to Azure AD.

**D)** Install the Active Directory Federation Services (AD FS) role on a domain controller in the Miami office.

**E)** Install Azure AD Connect on a server in the Miami office and enable Pass-through Authentication.

**Solution:** B, E

**Explanation:**

Explanation: B: You can gradually roll out Seamless SSO to your users. You start by adding the following Azure AD URL to all or selected users' Intranet zone settings by using Group Policy in Active Directory: https://autologon.microsoftazuread-sso.com E: Seamless SSO works with any method of cloud authentication - Password Hash Synchronization or Pass-through Authentication, and can be enabled via Azure AD Connect. References: https://docs.microsoft.com/en-us/azure/active-directory/hybrid/how-to-connect-sso-quick-start

**Question: 7** *One Answer Is Right*

You need to resolve the licensing issue before you attempt to assign the license again. What should you do?

**Answers:**

**A)** From the Groups blade, invite the user accounts to a new group.

**B)** From the Profile blade, modify the usage location.

**C)** From the Directory role blade, modify the directory role.

**Solution:** A

**Explanation:**

Explanation: License cannot be assigned to a user without a usage location specified. Scenario: Licensing Issue You attempt to assign a license in Azure to several users and receive the following error message: "Licenses not assigned. License agreement failed for one user." You verify that the Azure subscription has the available licenses.

**Question: 8** *Multiple Answers Are Right*

You need to implement Role1. Which command should you run before you create Role1? To answer, select the appropriate options in the answer area. NOTE: Each correct selection is worth one point.

**Answer Area**

**Answers:**

**A)**

VNET1:
- None
- Department: D1 only
- Department: D1, and RGroup: RG6 only
- Department: D1, and Label: Value1 only
- Department: D1, RGroup: RG6, and Label: Value1

VNET2:
- None
- RGroup: RG6 only
- Label: Value1 only
- RGroup: RG6, and Label: Value1

**Solution:** A

**Explanation:**

Explanation:

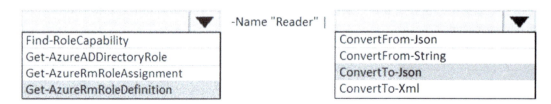

**Question: 9** *Multiple Answers Are Right*

You are evaluating the connectivity between the virtual machines after the planned implementation of the Azure networking infrastructure. For each of the following statements, select Yes if the statement is true. Otherwise, select No.

| Statements | Yes | No |
|---|---|---|
| The virtual machines on Subnet1 will be able to connect to the virtual machines on Subnet3. | ○ | ○ |
| The virtual machines on ClientSubnet will be able to connect to the Internet. | ○ | ○ |
| The virtual machines on Subnet3 and Subnet4 will be able to connect to the Internet. | ○ | ○ |

Answers:

A)

Answer Area

| Statements | Yes | No |
|---|---|---|
| SecAdmin1 must answer the following question if he wants to reset his password: In what city was your first job? | | ☐ |
| BillAdmin1 must answer the following question if he wants to reset his password: What is your favorite food? | ☐ | |
| User1 must answer the following question if he wants to reset his password: What was the name of your first pet? | ☐ | |

Solution: A

Explanation:

Explanation:

| Statements | Yes | No |
|---|---|---|
| The virtual machines on Subnet1 will be able to connect to the virtual machines on Subnet3. | ● | ○ |
| The virtual machines on ClientSubnet will be able to connect to the Internet. | ● | ○ |
| The virtual machines on Subnet3 and Subnet4 will be able to connect to the Internet. | ● | ○ |

**Question: 10** *One Answer Is Right*

Which blade should you instruct the finance department auditors to use?

**Answers:**

**A)** invoices

**B)** partner information

**C)** cost analysis

**D)** External services

**Solution:** A

# Chapter 16: AZ-120 - Planning and Administering Microsoft Azure for SAP Workloads

## Exam Guide

How to Prepare For AZ-120:Planning and Administering Microsoft Azure for SAP Workloads Exam

Preparation Guide for AZ-120:Planning and Administering Microsoft Azure for SAP Workloads Exam

Introduction

Microsoft has created a track for Azure professionals who are knowledgeable in SAP landscape to get certified this platform. This certification program provides Microsoft Azure for SAP Workloads professionals a way to demonstrate their skills. The assessment is based on a rigorous exam using industry standard methodology to determine whether a candidate meets Microsoft's proficiency standards.

According to Microsoft, a Microsoft Certified Professional enables organizations to leverage Microsoft Azure for SAP Workloads technologies with a thorough understanding of generating existing SAP inventories, designing migration strategies, designing Azure infrastructure services, HA models supported in HANA .

Certification is evidence of your skills, expertise in those areas in which you like to work. If candidate wants to work on Microsoft Azure for SAP Workloads and prove his knowledge, certification offered by Microsoft. This **AZ-120 Exam** Certification helps a candidate to validates his skills in Microsoft Azure for SAP Workloads Technology.

In this guide, we will cover the AZ-120:Planning and Administering Microsoft Azure for SAP Workloads Certification exam, AZ-120:Planning and Administering Microsoft Azure for SAP Workloads Certified professional salary and all aspects of the AZ-120:Planning and Administering Microsoft Azure for SAP Workloads Certification.

Introduction to AZ-120:Planning and Administering Microsoft Azure for SAP Workloads Exam:

Candidates for **AZ-120 Exam** are seeking to prove fundamental Microsoft Azure for SAP Workloads knowledge and skills. Before taking this exam, exam aspirants ought to have a solid fundamental information of the concepts shared in preparation guide as well as SAP HANA and LINUX knowledge would give an added edge.

It is suggested that professionals accustomed to the ideas and also the technologies represented here by taking relevant training courses. Candidates are expected to have some hands-on experience with key responsibilities such as recommendations on services and adjust resources as appropriate for optimal resiliency, performance, scale, provision, size, and monitoring. After passing this exam, candidates get a certificate from Microsoft that helps them to demonstrate their proficiency in Mobility and Devices Fundamentals to their clients and employers.

Topics of AZ-120:Planning and Administering Microsoft Azure for SAP Workloads Exam:

Candidates should apprehend the examination topics before they begin of preparation. because it'll extremely facilitate them in touch the core. Our **AZ-120 dumps** will include the following topics:

*1. Migrate SAP Workloads to Azure (10-15%)*

Create an inventory of existing SAP landscapes

- Network inventory
- Security inventory
- Computing inventory
- Operations system inventory
- Resiliency and availability inventory
- SAP Landscape architecture
- SAP workload performance SLA and metrics
- Migration considerations

    Design a migration strategy

- Certified and support SAP Hana hardware directory
- Design criteria for Tailored Datacenter Integration (TDI) v4 and v5 solutions
- Databox with import and export
- HANA System Replication (HSR)
- ASR for SAP
- Backup and restore methods and solutions

- Infrastructure optimization for migration

*2. Design an Azure Solution to Support SAP Workloads (20-25%)*

Design a core infrastructure solution in Azure to support SAP workloads

- Network topology requirements
- Security requirements
- Virtual or bare metal
- Operating system requirements
- Support SAP version
- Storage requirements
- Proximity placement group
- Infrastructure requirements

Design Azure infrastructure services to support SAP workloads

- Backup and restoration requirements
- SLA/High Availability
- Data protection (EFS, LRS/GRS, Availability Zones)
- Compliance
- Monitoring
- Licensing
- Application interfaces
- Dependencies

Design a resilient Azure solution to support SAP workloads

- HA models supported in HANA (N+N, N+0 and N+1)
- Application servers
- SAP Central services
- Availability sets
- Availability zones
- Disaster Recovery (DR) with Hero Regions
- Database HA

*3. Build and Deploy Azure SAP Workloads (35-40%)*

Automate deployment of Virtual Machines (VMs)

- Azure Resource Manager (ARM) template
- Automated configuration of VM

- Scripting with automation tools, including script development, script modification, and deployment dependencies

    Implement and manage virtual networking

- IDS/IPS for Azure
- Routing fundamentals
- Subnetting strategy
- Isolation and segmentation for SAP landscape

    Manage access and authentication on Azure

- Custom domains
- Azure AD Identity Protection
- Azure AD join
- Enterprise state roaming
- Conditional access policies
- Role-based access control (RBAC)
- Service principal
- Just in time access

    Implement and manage identities

- Azure AD Connect
- AD Federation and single sign-on
- LDAP/Kerberos/SSH
- Linux VMs Active Directory domain membership mechanism

    Monitor SAP workloads on Azure

- Azure Enhanced Monitoring Extension for SAP
- Azure Monitor

    *4. Validate Azure Infrastructure for SAP Workloads (10-15%)*

Perform infrastructure validation check

- JMeter, Avalanch, Load Runner
- Test implementation for SAP workloads
- Verify network performance and throughput
- Verify storage
- HANA HW Configuration Check Tool (HWCCT)

- FIO, AnyDB

  Perform operational readiness check

- Backup and restore
- High availability checks
- Failover test
- DR test
- Print test

  *5. Operationalize Azure SAP Architecture (10-15%)*

Optimize performance

- SAP workloads on Azure using ABAPmeter
- Storage structure
- SAP workloads on Azure support pre-requisites
- Scheduled maintenance for planned outages
- Recovery plan for unplanned outages
- SAP application and infrastructure housekeeping
- Bandwidth adjustment for ExpressRoute
- IPtables and GlobalReach for HANA Large Instances (HLI)

  Migrate SAP workloads to Azure

- Migration strategy
- Azure Site Recovery (ASR)
- Private and public IP addresses
- Network routes
- Network interface
- Subnets
- Virtual network
- Storage configuration
- Source and target environments preparation
- Backup and restore of data

Who should take the AZ-120:Planning and Administering Microsoft Azure for SAP Workloads Exam:

The **AZ-120 Exam** certification is an internationally-recognized certification which help to have validation for those professionals who are who are knowledgeable in the SAP Landscape

Certification process and industry standards that are specific to the long-term operation of an SAP solution. Candidates for this exam should be familiar azure administrator, architect, LINUX and SAP HANA concepts. Candidates should have extensive experience and knowledge of SAP applications, SAP workloads migration to Azure, SAP performance SLA, ASR for SAP, HANA System replication (HSR), resilient Azure solution to support SAP workloads. It is good for these candidates:

- Azure administrator
- Azure architect

How to study the AZ-120:Planning and Administering Microsoft Azure for SAP Workloads Exam:

Preparation of certification exams could be covered with two resource types. The first one are the study guides, reference books and study forums that are elaborated and appropriate for building information from ground up. Apart from them video tutorials and lectures are a good option to ease the pain of through study and are relatively make the study process more interesting nonetheless these demand time and concentration from the learner. Smart candidates who wish to create a solid foundation altogether examination topics and connected technologies typically mix video lectures with study guides to reap the advantages of each but practice exams or practice exam engines is one important study tool which goes typically unnoted by most candidates. Practice exams are designed with our experts to make exam prospects test their knowledge on skills attained in course, as well as prospects become comfortable and familiar with the real exam environment. Statistics have indicated exam anxiety plays much bigger role of students failure in exam than the fear of the unknown. Certification-questions expert team recommends preparing some notes on these topics along with it don't forget to practice **AZ-120 dumps** which had been written by our expert team, each of these can assist you loads to clear this exam with excellent marks.

AZ-120:Planning and Administering Microsoft Azure for SAP Workloads Certification Path:

AZ-120:Planning and Administering Microsoft Azure for SAP Workloads Exam is foundation level Certification. It is strongly recommended that aspirants for this exam have an Azure Administrator or Azure Architect certification, in addition to SAP HANA and Linux certifications. Anyone who is having keen interest and familiar with general Microsoft Azure for SAP Workloads concepts and the technologies. More than 85% of IT support roles require a good foundation of Microsoft Azure for SAP Workloads concepts. Aspirants should have some hands-on experience with SAP HANA, S/4HANA, SAP NetWeaver, SAP BW, OS Servers for SAP Applications and Databases, Azure Portal, ARM templates, operating systems, virtualization, cloud infrastructure, storage structures, high availability design, disaster recovery design, data protection concepts, and networking.

How much AZ-120:Planning and Administering Microsoft Azure for SAP Workloads Exam Cost:

The price of the Microsoft Mobility and Devices Fundamentals exam is $165 USD, for more information related to exam price please visit to Microsoft Training website as prices of Microsoft exams fees get varied country wise.

How to book the AZ-120:Planning and Administering Microsoft Azure for SAP Workloads Exam:

These are following steps for registering the AZ-120:Planning and Administering Microsoft Azure for SAP Workloads exam.

- Step 1: Visit to Microsoft Learning and search for AZ-120:Planning and Administering Microsoft Azure for SAP Workloads.
- Step 2: Sign up/Login to Pearson VUE account
- Step 3: Select local centre based on your country, date, time and confirm with a payment method.

What is the duration, language, and format of AZ-120:Planning and Administering Microsoft Azure for SAP Workloads Exam:

- It is a beta exam.
- Length of Examination: 50 mins
- Number of Questions: 100 to 120 questions(Since Microsoft does not publish this information, the number of exam questions may change without notice.)
- Passing Score: 70%
- Type of Questions: This test format is multiple choice.
- language: English

AZ-120:Planning and Administering Microsoft Azure for SAP Workloads Exam Certified Professional salary:

The average salary of a AZ-120:Planning and Administering Microsoft Azure for SAP Workloads Exam Certified Expert in

- United State - 120,000 USD
- India - 20,00,327 INR
- Europe - 90,547 EURO
- England - 90,532 POUND

The benefit of obtaining the AZ-120:Planning and Administering Microsoft Azure for SAP Workloads Exam Certification:

- This certification will be judging your skills and knowledge on your understanding Microsoft Azure for SAP Workloads concepts & Understanding of how to operate on Planning and Administering Microsoft Azure for SAP Workloads .

- This certification credential will give you edge over other counterparts. Apart from knowledge from AZ-120:Planning and Administering Microsoft Azure for SAP Workloads Exam.
- AZ-120 Certification is distinguished among competitors. AZ-120 certification will give them an edge at that time easily when candidates appear for employment interview, employers are very fascinated to note one thing that differentiates the individual from all other candidates.
- AZ-120 certification will be more useful and relevant networks that help them in setting career goals for themselves. AZ-120 networks provide them with the correct career guidance than non certified generally are unable to get.
- AZ-120 certified candidates will be confident and stand different from others as their skills are more trained than non-certified professionals.
- **AZ-120 Exam** provide proven knowledge to use the tools to complete the task efficiently and cost effectively than the other non-certified professionals lack in doing so.
- AZ-120 Certification will provides practical experience to candidates from all the aspects to be a proficient worker in the organization.
- AZ-120 Certifications will provide opportunities to get a job easily in which they are interested in instead of wasting years and ending without getting any experience.
- AZ-120 credentials will delivers higher earning potential and increased promotion opportunities because it shows a good understanding of HP-UX.

Difficulty in Writing AZ-120:Planning and Administering Microsoft Azure for SAP Workloads Exam:

AZ-120:Planning and Administering Microsoft Azure for SAP Workloads is a privileged achievement one could be graced with. But adverse to general notion certifying with Microsoft is not that challenging if the candidates have proper preparation material to pass the AZ-120:Planning and Administering Microsoft Azure for SAP Workloads exam with good grades. Questions answers and clarifications which are designed in form of Certification-questions dumps make sure to cover entire course content. Certification-questions have a brilliant AZ-120:Planning and Administering Microsoft Azure for SAP Workloads dumps with most recent and important questions and answers in PDF files. Certification-questions is sure about the exactness and legitimacy of AZ-120:Planning and Administering Microsoft Azure for SAP Workloads dumps and in this manner. Candidates can easily pass the AZ-120:Planning and Administering Microsoft Azure for SAP Workloads exam with genuine AZ-120:Planning and Administering Microsoft Azure for SAP Workloads dumps and get MICROSOFT certification. These dumps are viewed as the best source to understand the AZ-120:Planning and Administering Microsoft Azure for SAP Workloads well by simply pursuing examples questions and answers. If candidate completes practice the exam with certification **AZ-120 dumps** along with self-assessment to get the proper idea on MICROSOFT accreditation and to ace the certification exam.

For more info read reference::

Microsoft learning site
Planning Azure for SAP workloads
Microsoft Certified: Azure for SAP Workloads Specialty

# Sample Practice Test for AZ-120

**Question: 1** *One Answer Is Right*

You are evaluating which migration method Litware can implement based on the current environment and the business goals. Which migration method will cause the least amount of downtime?

**Answers:**

**A)** Migrate SAP ECC to SAP Business Suite in HANA, and then migrate SAP to Azure.

**B)** Use Near-Zero Downtime (NZDT) to migrate to SAP HANA and Azure during the same maintenance window.

**C)** Use the Database Migration Option (DMO) to migrate to SAP HANA and Azure during the same maintenance window.

**D)** Migrate SAP to Azure, and then migrate SAP ECC to SAP Business Suite on HANA.

**Solution:** C

**Explanation:**

Explanation: The SAP Database Migration Option (DMO) with System Move option of SUM, used as part of the migration allows customer the options to perform the migration in a single step, from source system on-premises, or to the target system residing in Microsoft Azure, minimizing overall downtime. Reference: https://blogs.sap.com/2017/10/05/your-sap-on-azure-part-2-dmo-with-system-move/ Migrate SAP Workloads to Azure

**Question: 2** *Multiple Answers Are Right*

HOTSPOT You are evaluating the proposed backup policy. For each of the following statements, select Yes if the statement is true. otherwise, select No. NOTE: Each correct selection is worth one point. Hot Area:

**Answer Area**

| Statements | Yes | No |
|---|---|---|
| The backup policy meets the technical requirements. | O | O |
| The backup policy meets the business requirements. | O | O |
| If the backup policy is implemented, a deleted file can be restored to the running virtual machine one year after the file was deleted. | O | O |

**Scenario:**

TESTLET-2. Overview Contoso, Ltd. is a manufacturing company that has 15,000 employees. The company uses SAP for sales and manufacturing. Contoso has sales offices in New York and London and manufacturing facilities in Boston and Seattle. Existing Environment Active Directory The network contains an on-premises Active Directory domain named ad.contoso.com. User email addresses use a domain name of contoso.com. SAP Environment The current SAP environment contains the following components: - SAP Solution Manager - SAP ERP Central Component (SAP ECC) - SAP Supply Chain Management (SAP SCM) - SAP application servers that run Windows Server 2008 R2 - SAP HANA database servers that run SUSE Linux Enterprise Server 12 (SLES 12) Problem Statements Contoso identifies the following issues in its current environment: - The SAP HANA environment lacks adequate resources. - The Windows servers are nearing the end of support. - The datacenters are at maximum capacity. Requirements Planned Changes Contoso identifies the following planned changes: - Deploy Azure Virtual WAN. - Migrate the application servers to Windows Server 2016. - Deploy ExpressRoute connections to all of the offices and manufacturing facilities. - Deploy SAP landscapes to Azure for development, quality assurance, and production. All resources for the production landscape will be in a resource group named SAPProduction. Business goals Contoso identifies the following business goals: - Minimize costs whenever possible. - Migrate SAP to Azure without causing downtime. - Ensure that all SAP deployments to Azure are supported by SAP. - Ensure that all the production databases can withstand the failure of an Azure region. - Ensure that all the production application servers can restore daily backups from the last 21 days. Technical Requirements Contoso identifies the following technical requirements: - Inspect all web queries. - Deploy an SAP HANA cluster to two datacenters. - Minimize the bandwidth used for database synchronization. - Use Active Directory accounts to administer Azure resources. - Ensure that each production application server has four 1-TB data disks. - Ensure that an application server can be restored from a backup created during the last five days within 15 minutes. - Implement an approval process to ensure that an SAP administrator is notified before another administrator attempts to make changes to the Azure virtual machines that host SAP. It is estimated that during the migration, the bandwidth required between Azure and the New York office will be 1 Gbps. After the migration, a traffic burst of up to 3 Gbps will occur. Proposed Backup Policy An Azure administrator proposes the backup policy shown in the following exhibit.

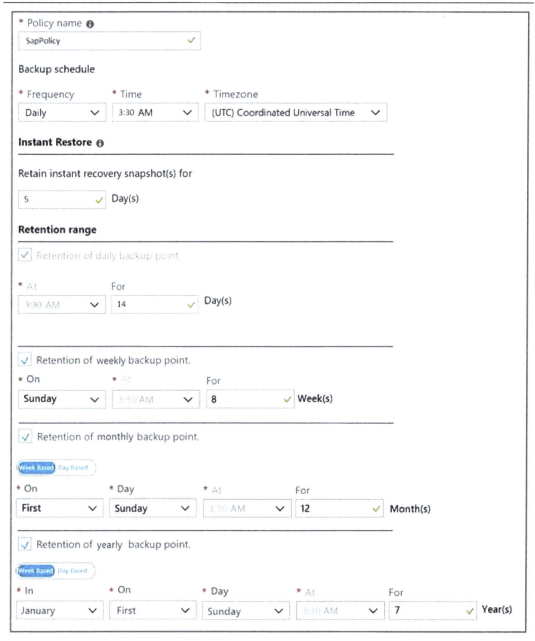

Azure Resource Manager Template An Azure administrator provides you with the Azure Resource Manager template that will be used to provision the production application servers.

```
{
  "apiVersion": "2017-03-30",
  "type": "Microsoft.Compute/virtualMachines",
  "name": "[parameters('vmname')]",

  "location": "EastUS",
  "dependsOn": [
    "[resourceId('Microsoft.Network/networkInterfaces/', parameters('vmname'))]"
  ],
  "properties":{
    "hardwareProfile": {
      "vmSize": "[parameters('vmSize')]"
  },
  "osProfile": {
    "computerName": "[parameters('vmname')]",
    "adminUsername": "[parameters('adminUsername')]",
    "adminPassword": "[parameters('adminPassword')]"
  },
  "storageProfile": {
    "ImageReference": {
      "publisher": "MicrosoftWindowsServer",
      "Offer" : "WindowsServer",
      "sku" : "2016-datacenter",
      "version" : "latest"
    },
    "osDisk": {
      "name": "[concat(parameters('vmname'), '-OS')]",
      "caching": "ReadWrite",
      "createOption": "FromImage",
      "diskSizeGB": 128,
      "managedDisk":{
          "storageAccountType": "[parameters('storageAccountType')]"
      }
    },
    "copy": [
      {
        "name": "DataDisks",
        "count": "[parameters('diskCount')]",
        "input" : {
          "Caching" : "None",
          "diskSizeGB" : 1024,
          "lun": "[copyIndex('datadisks')]",
```

```
          "name": "[concat(parameters('vmname'), '-DD',copyIndex('datadisks'))]",
          "createOption": "Empty"
        }
      }
    ]
  },
  "networkProfile": {
    "networkInterfaces": [
      {
        "id": "[resourceId('Microsoft.Network/networkInterfaces', parameters('vmName'))]"
      }
    ]
  }
},
"resources": [
  {
    "apiVersion": "2017-03-30"
    "type": "Microsoft.Compute/virtualMachines/extensions",
    "name": "[concat(parameters('VMName'), '/joindomain')]",
    "location": "eastus",
    "properties": {
      "publisher": "Microsoft.Compute",
      "type": "JsonADDomainExtension",
      "typeHandlerVersion": "1.3",
      "autoUpgradeMinorVersion": true,
      "settings": {
          "Name": "[parameters('domainName')]",
          "User": "[parameters('domainusername')]",
          "Restart": "true",
          "Options": "3"
      },
      "protectedsettings": {
          "Password": "[parameters('domainPassword')]"
      }
    }
  }
]
}
```

**Answers:**

A)
## Answer Area

| Statements | Yes | No |
|---|---|---|
| The backup policy meets the technical requirements. | ○ | ○ |
| The backup policy meets the business requirements. | ○ | ○ |
| If the backup policy is implemented, a deleted file can be restored to the running virtual machine one year after the file was deleted. | ○ | ○ |

**Solution:** A

**Explanation:**

Explanation: Explanation: Box 1: Yes Scenario: Technical requirements: Ensure that an application server can be restored from a backup created during the last five days within 15 minutes. Instant Restore has 'The instance recovery snapshot(s) for 5 Day(s)'. Box 2: No Scenario: Ensure that all the production application servers can restore daily backups from the last 21 days. The Retention of daily backup point is set to for 14 days only. Box 3: Yes Reference: https://docs.microsoft.com/en-us/azure/backup/backup-instant-restore-capability

**Question: 3** *Multiple Answers Are Right*

HOTSPOT You are planning replication of the SAP HANA database for the disaster recovery environment in Azure. For each of the following statements, select Yes if the statement is true. Otherwise, select No. NOTE: Each correct selection is worth one point. Hot Area:

## Answer Area

| Statements | Yes | No |
|---|---|---|
| You must use synchronous replication. | ○ | ○ |
| You must use delta data shipping for operation mode. | ○ | ○ |
| You must configure an Azure Directory (Azure AD) application to manage the failover. | ○ | ○ |

**Scenario:**

TESTLET-2. Overview Contoso, Ltd. is a manufacturing company that has 15,000 employees. The company uses SAP for sales and manufacturing. Contoso has sales offices in New York and London and manufacturing facilities in Boston and Seattle. Existing Environment Active Directory The network contains an on-premises Active Directory domain named ad.contoso.com. User email addresses use a domain name of contoso.com. SAP Environment The current SAP environment contains the following components: - SAP Solution Manager - SAP ERP Central Component (SAP ECC) - SAP Supply Chain Management (SAP SCM) - SAP application servers that run Windows Server 2008 R2 - SAP HANA database servers that run SUSE Linux Enterprise Server 12 (SLES 12) Problem Statements Contoso identifies the following issues in its current environment: - The SAP HANA environment lacks adequate resources. - The Windows servers are nearing the end of support. - The datacenters are at maximum capacity. Requirements Planned Changes Contoso identifies the following planned changes: - Deploy Azure Virtual WAN. - Migrate the application servers to Windows Server 2016. - Deploy ExpressRoute connections to all of the offices and manufacturing facilities. - Deploy SAP landscapes to Azure for development, quality assurance, and production. All resources for the production landscape will be in a resource group named SAPProduction. Business goals Contoso identifies the following business goals: - Minimize costs whenever possible. - Migrate SAP to Azure without causing downtime. - Ensure that all SAP deployments to Azure are supported by SAP. - Ensure that all the production databases can withstand the failure of an Azure region. - Ensure that all the production application servers can restore daily backups from the last 21 days. Technical Requirements Contoso identifies the following technical requirements: - Inspect all web queries. - Deploy an SAP HANA cluster to two datacenters. - Minimize the bandwidth used for database synchronization. - Use Active Directory accounts to administer Azure resources. - Ensure that each production application server has four 1-TB data disks. - Ensure that an application server can be restored from a backup created during the last five days within 15 minutes. - Implement an approval process to ensure that an SAP administrator is notified before another administrator attempts to make changes to the Azure virtual machines that host SAP. It is estimated that during the migration, the bandwidth required between Azure and the New York office will be 1 Gbps. After the migration, a traffic burst of up to 3 Gbps will occur. Proposed Backup Policy An Azure administrator proposes the backup policy shown in the following exhibit.

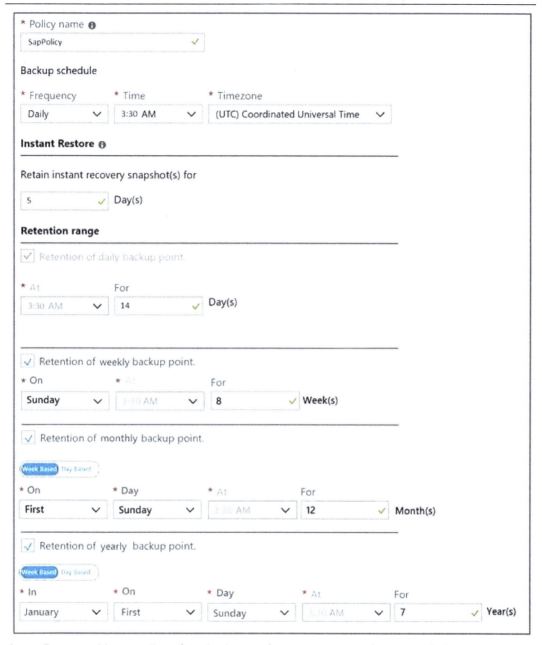

Azure Resource Manager Template An Azure administrator provides you with the Azure Resource Manager template that will be used to provision the production application servers.

```
{
  "apiVersion": "2017-03-30",
  "type": "Microsoft.Compute/virtualMachines",
  "name": "[parameters('vmname')]",

  "location": "EastUS",
  "dependsOn": [
    "[resourceId('Microsoft.Network/networkInterfaces/', parameters('vmname'))]"
  ],
  "properties":{
    "hardwareProfile": {
      "vmSize": "[parameters('vmSize')]"
    },
    "osProfile": {
      "computerName": "[parameters('vmname')]",
      "adminUsername": "[parameters('adminUsername')]",
      "adminPassword": "[parameters('adminPassword')]"
    },
    "storageProfile": {
      "ImageReference": {
        "publisher": "MicrosoftWindowsServer",
        "Offer" : "WindowsServer",
        "sku" : "2016-datacenter",
        "version" : "latest"
      },
      "osDisk": {
        "name": "[concat(parameters('vmname'), '-OS')]",
        "caching": "ReadWrite",
        "createOption": "FromImage",
        "diskSizeGB": 128,
        "managedDisk":{
            "storageAccountType": "[parameters('storageAccountType')]"
        }
      },
      "copy": [
        {
          "name": "DataDisks",
          "count": "[parameters('diskCount')]",
          "input" : {
            "Caching" : "None",
            "diskSizeGB" : 1024,
            "lun": "[copyIndex('datadisks')]",
```

```
            "name": "[concat(parameters('vmname'), '-DD',copyIndex('datadisks'))]",
            "createOption": "Empty"
          }
        }
      ]
    },
    "networkProfile": {
      "networkInterfaces": [
          {
            "id": "[resourceId('Microsoft.Network/networkInterfaces', parameters('vmName'))]"
          }
      ]
    }
  },
  "resources": [
      {
          "apiVersion": "2017-03-30",
          "type": "Microsoft.Compute/virtualMachines/extensions",
          "name": "[concat(parameters('VMName'), '/joindomain')]",
          "location": "eastus",
          "properties": {
            "publisher": "Microsoft.Compute",
            "type": "JsonADDomainExtension",
            "typeHandlerVersion": "1.3",
            "autoUpgradeMinorVersion": true,
            "settings": {
                "Name": "[parameters('domainName')]",
                "User": "[parameters('domainusername')]",
                "Restart": "true",
                "Options": "3"
            },
            "protectedsettings": {
                "Password": "[parameters('domainPassword')]"
            }
          }
      }
  ]
}
```

**Answers:**

A)

## Answer Area

| Statements | Yes | No |
|---|---|---|
| You must use synchronous replication. | ○ | ○ |
| You must use delta data shipping for operation mode. | ○ | ○ |
| You must configure an Azure Directory (Azure AD) application to manage the failover. | ○ | ○ |

Solution: A

Explanation:

Explanation: Explanation: Box 1: No SAP HANA Replication consists of one primary node and at least one secondary node. Changes to the data on the primary node are replicated to the secondary node synchronously or asynchronously. Box 2: No Since SPS11 SAP HANA system replication can be run in two different operation modes: delta_datashipping logreplay Box 3: Yes Reference: https://docs.microsoft.com/en-us/azure/virtual-machines/workloads/sap/sap-hana-high-availability-rhel https://blogs.sap.com/2018/01/08/your-sap-on-azure-part-4-high-availability-for-sap-hana-using-system- replication/ Migrate SAP Workloads to Azure Question Set 3

**Question: 4** *One Answer Is Right*

You are migrating SAP to Azure. The ASCS application servers are in one Azure zone, and the SAP database server in in a different Azure zone. ASCS/ERS is configured for high availability. During performance testing, you discover increased response times in Azure, even though the Azure environment has better computer and memory configurations than the on-premises environment. During the initial analysis, you discover an increased wait time for Enqueue. What are three possible causes of the increased wait time? Each correct answer presents a complete solution. NOTE: Each correct selection is worth one point.

Answers:

A) a missing Enqueue profile

B) disk I/O during Enqueue backup operations

C) misconfigured load balancer rules and health check probes for Enqueue and ASCS

**D)** active Enqueue replication

**E)** network latency between the database server and the SAP application servers

**Solution:** C, D, E

**Explanation:**

Explanation: E: The network latency across Availability Zones is not the same in all Azure regions. In some cases, you can deploy and run the SAP application layer across different zones because the network latency from one zone to the active DBMS VM is acceptable. But in some Azure regions, the latency between the active DBMS VM and the SAP application instance, when deployed in different zones, might not be acceptable for SAP business processes. References: https://docs.microsoft.com/en-us/azure/virtual-machines/workloads/sap/sap-ha-availability-zones

**Question: 5** *One Answer Is Right*

You have an on-premises SAP environment that uses AIX servers and IBM DB2 as the database platform. You plan to migrate SAP to Azure. In Azure, the SAP workloads will use Windows Server and Microsoft SQL Server as the database platform. What should you use to export from DB2 and import the data to SQL Server?

**Answers:**

**A)** R3load

**B)** Azure SQL Data Warehouse

**C)** SQL Server Management Studio (SSMS)

**D)** R3trans

**Solution:** C

**Explanation:**

Explanation: To migrate DB2 databases to SQL Server, you must connect to the DB2 database that you want to migrate. When you connect, SSMA obtains metadata about all DB2 schemas, and then displays it in the DB2 Metadata Explorer pane. References: https://docs.microsoft.com/en-us/sql/ssma/db2/connecting-to-db2-database-db2tosql?view=sql-server- ver15 https://docs.microsoft.com/en-us/biztalk/adapters-and-accelerators/adapter-sap/import-sap-data-using-sql- server-management-studio

**Question: 6** *Multiple Answers Are Right*

HOTSPOT You are designing the backup for an SAP database. You have an Azure Storage account that is configured as shown in the following exhibit.

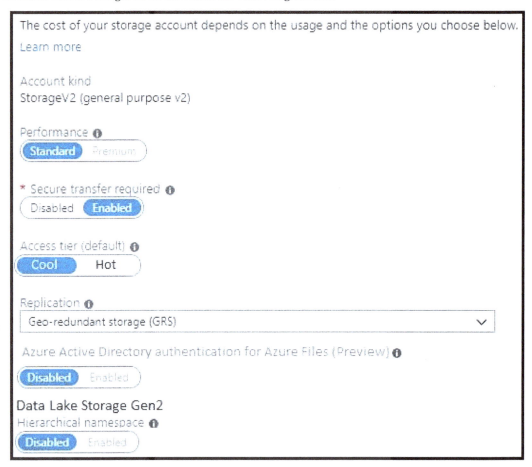

Use the drop-down menus to select the answer choice that completes each statement based on the information presented in the graphic. NOTE: Each correct selection is worth one point. Hot Area:

## Answer Area

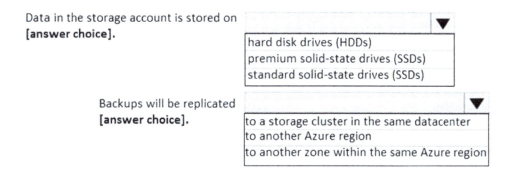

**Answers:**

**A)**

## Answer Area

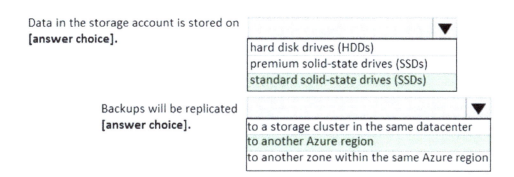

**Solution:** A

**Explanation:**

Explanation: Box 1: standard solid-state drives (SSDs) Standard SSD Managed Disks, a low-cost SSD offering, are optimized for test and entry-level production workloads requiring consistent latency. Box 2: to another Azure region Geo-redundant storage (GRS) copies your data synchronously three times within a single physical location in the primary region using LRS. It then copies your data asynchronously to a single physical location in a secondary region that is hundreds of miles away from the primary region. References: https://azure.microsoft.com/en-us/pricing/details/managed-disks/ https://docs.microsoft.com/en-us/azure/storage/common/storage-redundancy#geo-redundant-storage

**Question: 7** *Multiple Answers Are Right*

DRAG DROP You migrate SAP ERP Central Component (SAP ECC) production and non-production landscapes to Azure. You are licensed for SAP Landscape Management (LaMa). You need to refresh from the production landscape to the non-production landscape. Which four actions should you perform in sequence? To answer, move the appropriate actions from the list of actions to the answer area and arrange them in the correct order. Select and Place:

**Actions**

- From the Azure portal, create a service principal
- From the Cloud Managers tab in LaMa, add an adapter
- From SAP Solution Manager, deploy the LaMa adapter
- Add permissions to the service principal
- Install and configure LaMa on an SAP NetWeaver instance

**Answer Area**

**Answers:**

A)

**Actions**

- From the Azure portal, create a service principal
- From the Cloud Managers tab in LaMa, add an adapter
- From SAP Solution Manager, deploy the LaMa adapter
- Add permissions to the service principal
- Install and configure LaMa on an SAP NetWeaver instance

**Answer Area**

- From the Azure portal, create a service principal
- Add permissions to the service principal
- From the Cloud Managers tab in LaMa, add an adapter
- Install and configure LaMa on an SAP NetWeaver instance

**Solution:** A

**Explanation:**

Explanation: Step 1: From the Azure portal, create a service principal The Azure connector can use a Service Principal to authorize against Microsoft Azure. Follow these steps to create a Service Principal for SAP Landscape Management (LaMa). Step 2: Add permissions to the service principal The Service Principal does not have permissions to access your Azure resources by default. You need to give the Service Principal permissions to access them. Step 3: From the Cloud Managers tab in LaMa, add an adapter Create a new connector in SAP LaMa Open the SAP LaMa website and navigate to Infrastructure. Go to tab Cloud Managers and click on Add. Select the Microsoft Azure Cloud Adapter Step 4: Install and configure LaMA on an SAP NetWeater instance Provision a new adaptive SAP system You can manually deploy a new virtual machine or use one of the Azure templates in the quickstart repository. It contains templates for SAP NetWeaver ASCS, SAP NetWeaver application servers, and the database. You can also use these templates to provision new hosts as part of a system copy/clone etc. Note: To support customers on their journey into a cloud model (hybrid or entirely public cloud), SAP and Microsoft partnered to create an adapter that integrates the SAP management capabilities of LaMa with the IaaS advantages of Microsoft Azure. References: https://docs.microsoft.com/en-us/azure/virtual-machines/workloads/sap/lama-installation

**Question: 8** *Multiple Answers Are Right*

HOTSPOT For each of the following statements, select Yes if the statement is true. Otherwise, select No. NOTE: Each correct selection is worth one point. Hot Area:

Answer Area

| Statements | Yes | No |
|---|---|---|
| Oracle Real Application Clusters (RAC) can be used to provide high availability of SAP databases on Azure. | ○ | ○ |
| You can host SAP databases on Azure by using Oracle on a virtual machine that runs Windows Server 2016. | ○ | ○ |
| You can host SAP databases on Azure by using Oracle on a virtual machine that runs SUSE Linux Enterprise Server 12 (SLES 12). | ○ | ○ |

Answers:

A)

Answer Area

| Statements | Yes | No |
|---|---|---|
| Oracle Real Application Clusters (RAC) can be used to provide high availability of SAP databases on Azure. | ○ | ○ |
| You can host SAP databases on Azure by using Oracle on a virtual machine that runs Windows Server 2016. | ○ | ○ |
| You can host SAP databases on Azure by using Oracle on a virtual machine that runs SUSE Linux Enterprise Server 12 (SLES 12). | ○ | ○ |

Solution: A

Explanation:

Explanation: Box 1: Yes Box 2: Yes Oracle Database 12c Release 2 (12.2) is certified on Microsoft Windows Server 2016 (Standard, Datacenter, and Essentials Editions), which includes support for the database client, server, and Oracle Real Application Clusters. Organizations can run SAP applications with Oracle databases on the same code base on Unix, Linux, and Windows operating systems. Box 3: Yes References: https://docs.microsoft.com/en-us/azure/virtual-

machines/workloads/oracle/oracle-overview
https://docs.oracle.com/en/database/oracle/oracle-database/12.2/ntdbn/index.html#

**Question: 9** *One Answer Is Right*

You have an SAP environment that is managed by using VMware vCenter. You plan to migrate the SAP environment to Azure. You need to gather information to identify which compute resources are required in Azure. What should you use to gather the information?

**Answers:**

**A)** Azure Migrate and SAP EarlyWatch Alert reports

**B)** Azure Site Recovery and SAP Quick Sizer

**C)** SAP Quick Sizer and SAP HANA system replication

**D)** Azure Site Recovery Deployment Planner and SAP HANA Cockpit

**Solution:** A

**Explanation:**

Explanation: Azure Migrate is a Microsoft service that helps an enterprise assess how its on-premises workloads will perform, and how much they will cost to host, in the Azure public cloud. An enterprise can use Azure Migrate to discover information about the VMware VMs running within its own data center, including CPU and memory usage, as well as performance history. SAP EarlyWatch Alert (EWA) is a monitoring service for SAP customers, to monitor SAP systems in the solution landscape. Incorrect Answers: D: SAP HANA Cockpit is an administrative tool with a web interface for a correspondingly named database engine, a part of SAP ERP software. It allows both offline and cloud operations for managing databases, References: https://searchcloudcomputing.techtarget.com/definition/Azure-Migrate

**Question: 10** *One Answer Is Right*

You plan to migrate an SAP ERP Central Component (SAP ECC) production system to Azure. You are reviewing the SAP EarlyWatch Alert report for the system. You need to recommend sizes for the Azure virtual machines that will host the system. Which two sections of the report should you review? Each correct answer presents a complete solution. NOTE: Each correct selection is worth one point.

**Answers:**

**A)** Hardware Capacity

**B)** Patch Levels under SAP Software Configuration

**C)** Hardware Configuration under Landscape

**D)** Database and ABAP Load Optimization

**E)** Data Volume Management

**Solution:** A, D

**Explanation:**

Explanation: It is important to note that there are 2 types of data collected for Hardware Capacity. - Performance Data - e.g. CPU and Memory utilization data. Hardware Capacity data shown in the EWA is measuring CPU and Memory utilization data. This is known as Performance Data. - Configuration Data - e.g. OS information, CPU type. It is also collecting system information about the host such as hardware manufacturer, CPU type etc. This is known as Configuration Data. Incorrect Answers: E: Data Volume Management focuses on whether the collection of DVM content for the EarlyWatch Alert report is not performed, not activated, or not possible because the SAP Solution Manager system does not meet the technical requirements. References: https://wiki.scn.sap.com/wiki/display/SM/Hardware+Capacity+Checks+in+EWA

# Chapter 17: AZ-203 - Developing Solutions for Microsoft Azure

## Exam Guide

Microsoft Azure AZ-203 - Microsoft's Azure Developer Certification Exam:

Developing Solutions for Microsoft Azure AZ-203 Exam is the latest exam introduced by the Microsoft mainly focusing to those candidates who are willing to write line of codes i.e.. those who are in development Job role. Microsoft's Azure Developer certification exam:
AZ-203 which is a combination of AZ-200: Microsoft Azure Developer Core Solutions and Microsoft Azure Developer Advanced Solutions.
Developing Solutions for Microsoft Azure **AZ-203 Exam** for Azure Developers who can design and build cloud solutions such as applications and services.
They should participate in all phases of Applications development, from solution design, to development and deployment, to testing and maintenance.
Candidate should work closely with cloud solution architects, cloud DBAs, cloud administrators, and clients to implement the solution.

Candidates should be proficient in developing apps and services by using Azure tools and technologies, including storage, security, compute, and communications.

Candidates must have at least one year of experience developing scalable solutions through all phases of software development and be skilled in at least one cloud-supported programming language:
For this exam candidate having proficiency in using Power Shell, the Command Line Interface, Azure Portal, ARM templates, operating systems, virtualization, cloud infrastructure, storage structures and networking would be an added advantage.
The online Microsoft Certified Associate: Azure Developer course is ideal for experienced programmers who wish to develop and host solutions in Azure.
Learners should be familiar with designing and building cloud solutions.
This New Certification track introduced by Microsoft i.e.. Developing Solutions for Microsoft Azure AZ-203 is for those passionate developer.

You can expect some enhancement of 15% in the course of the AZ-203 from AZ-200 and AZ-201.

This is the list of the contents in our Developing Solutions for Microsoft Azure **AZ-203 Practice Test**:

- Implement solutions that use virtual machines (VM).
- Develop solutions that use Cosmos DB storage.
- Implement Azure functions.
- Develop code to support scalability of apps and services.
- Implement access control.
- Integrate caching and content delivery within solutions.
- Integrate Azure Search within solutions.
- Instrument solutions to support monitoring and logging.
- Create containerized solutions.

Developing Solutions for Microsoft Azure AZ-203 Dumps:

Developing Solutions for Microsoft Azure AZ-203 Dumps will include below mentioned topics with Exam focused percentage

Develop Azure Infrastructure as Service Compute Solutions 10-15%
Develop Azure Platform as Service Compute Solutions 20-25%
Develop for Azure storage 15-20%
Implement Azure security 10-15%
Monitor, troubleshoot, and optimize Azure solutions 15-20%
Connect to and Consume Azure Services and Third-party Services 20-25%

Developing Solutions for Microsoft Azure AZ-203 Dumps Provided Study Notes:

Certification-questions.com expert team recommend you to prepare some notes on these topics along with it don't forget to practice Developing Solutions for Microsoft Azure AZ-203 Dumps which been written by our expert team.
Both these will help you a lot to clear this exam with good marks.

- Manage APIs by using API Management (APIM)
- Develop solutions using Azure Storages
- Design for hybrid technologies
- Azure Cosmos DB storage
- Implementing authentication
- Implement Data Security Solutions
- Scalability of Apps and Services

- Creating ARM Templates
- Creating Container
- Implementing Azure Batch Services
- Creating mobile apps
- Creating Azure Functions
- Develop Event Based solutions

Overview about MICROSOFT AZ-203 Exam:

Overview about MICROSOFT AZ-203 Exam:

- Format: Multiple choice, multiple answer
- Length of Examination: 150 minutes
- Number of Questions: 40 - 60
- Passing Score: 70-80%
- Registration Fee: 165 USD

Steps for MICROSOFT AZ-203 Certifications Exam booking:

- Visit to website and book your exam. - Signup/Login to MICROSOFT account - Search for MICROSOFT AZ-203 Certifications Exam - Select Date and Center of examination and confirm with payment value of 165$

Benefits of having MICROSOFTAZ-203 Certifications:

Getting a certification like AZ-203 can enhance the value of a job aspirant as a qualified Azure Developer and Administrator.
It'd really attract HR to have a look to your CV and definitely it will help you out to have good salaried job in your hand by the end of the day.
In such a situation, the relevance of a quality AZ-203 Developing Solutions for Microsoft Azure EXAM study material is extremely important.
And so we bring best-in-industry Azure Exam AZ-203 online course and **AZ-203 practice tests** for you to help in your exam preparation.

Difficulty in writing MICROSOFT AZ-203 Exam:

As we already mentioned that **MICROSOFT AZ-203 Exam** is advanced level exam which is coming from AZ-200, AZ-201, AZ-202 exams.
So, going through Microsoft AZ-203 exam would be little bit tough.
Most important thing about this exam is that it is one of the newly introduced exams by the Microsoft so it would be difficult to get proper study material for it. As such, Experts will help you learn to use the Azure platform and prepare for the certification exam.
The successful completion of Azure Developer Practice Papers will allow you to pass the

Microsoft Azure Developer certification exam and get certified Developing Solutions for Microsoft Azure Exam Dumps AZ-203. Having thorough understanding of Azure Development experience along with our provided MICROSOFT AZ-203 dumps will definitely help you out to clear MICROSOFT AZ-203 Exam with very good marks.

For more info visit:

**MICROSOFT AZ-203 Exam** and Reference, Microsoft Documents

# Sample Practice Test for AZ-203

**Question: 1** *One Answer Is Right*

You need to resolve a notification latency issue. Which two actions should you perform? Each correct answer presents part of the solution. NOTE: Each correct selection is worth one point.

**Answers:**

**A)** Set Always On to false.

**B)** Set Always On to true.

**C)** Ensure that the Azure Function is set to use a consumption plan.

**D)** Ensure that the Azure Function is using an App Service plan.

**Solution:** B, D

**Explanation:**

Explanation: Azure Functions can run on either a Consumption Plan or a dedicated App Service Plan. If you run in a dedicated mode, you need to turn on the Always On setting for your Function App to run properly. The Function runtime will go idle after a few minutes of inactivity, so only HTTP triggers will actually "wake up" your functions. This is similar to how WebJobs must have Always On enabled. Scenario: Notification latency: Users report that anomaly detection emails can sometimes arrive several minutes after an anomaly is detected. Anomaly detection service: You have an anomaly detection service that analyzes log information for anomalies. It is implemented as an Azure Machine Learning model. The model is deployed as a web service. If an anomaly is detected, an Azure Function that emails administrators is called by using an HTTP WebHook. References: https://github.com/Azure/Azure-Functions/wiki/Enable-Always-On-when-running-on-dedicated-App-Service- Plan Develop Azure Infrastructure as a Service Compute Solutions

**Question: 2** *Multiple Answers Are Right*

HOTSPOT You need to ensure that you can deploy the LabelMaker application. How should you complete the CLI commands? To answer, select the appropriate options in the answer area. NOTE: Each correct selection is worth one point. Hot Area:

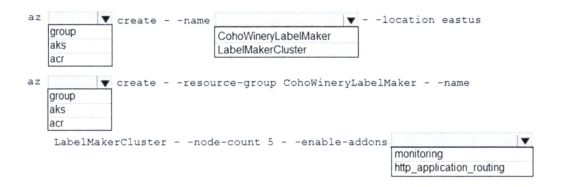

**Answers:**

**A)**

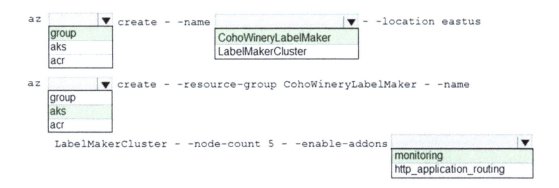

**Solution:** A

**Explanation:**

Explanation: Box 1: group Create a resource group with the az group create command. An Azure resource group is a logical group in which Azure resources are deployed and managed. The following example creates a resource group named myResourceGroup in the westeurope location. az group create --name myResourceGroup --location westeurope Box 2: CohoWinterLabelMaker Use the resource group named, which is used in the second command. Box 3: aks The command az aks create, is used to create a new managed Kubernetes cluster. Box 4: monitoring Scenario: LabelMaker app Azure Monitor Container Health must be used to monitor the performance of workloads that are deployed to Kubernetes environments and hosted on Azure Kubernetes Service (AKS). You must use Azure Container Registry to publish images that support the AKS deployment. Develop Azure Infrastructure as a Service Compute Solutions

**Question: 3** *One Answer Is Right*

You need to support the requirements for the Shipping Logic App. What should you use?

**Scenario:**

TESTLET-3. Case Study This is a case study. Case studies are not timed separately. You can use as much exam time as you would like to complete each case. However, there may be additional case studies and sections on this exam. You must manage your time to ensure that you are able to complete all questions included on this exam in the time provided. To answer the questions included in a case study, you will need to reference information that is provided in the case study. Case studies might contain exhibits and other resources that provide more information about the scenario that is described in the case study. Each question is independent of the other question on this case study. At the end of this case study, a review screen will appear. This screen allows you to review your answers and to make changes before you move to the next sections of the exam. After you begin a new section, you cannot return to this section. To start the case study To display the first question on this case study, click the Next button. Use the buttons in the left pane to explore the content of the case study before you answer the questions. Clicking these buttons displays information such as business requirements, existing environment, and problem statements. If the case study has an All Information tab, note that the information displayed is identical to the information displayed on the subsequent tabs. When you are ready to answer a question, click the Question button to return to the question. Background Wide World Importers is moving all their datacenters to Azure. The company has developed several applications and services to support supply chain operations and would like to leverage serverless computing where possible. Current environment Windows Server 2016 virtual machine This virtual machine (VM) runs Biz Talk Server 2016. The VM runs the following workflows: - Ocean Transport – This workflow gathers and validates container information including container contents and arrival notices at various shipping ports. - Inland Transport – This workflow gathers and validates trucking information including fuel usage, number of stops, and routes. The VM supports the following REST API calls: - Container API – This API provides container information including weight, contents, and other attributes. - Location API – This API provides location information regarding shipping ports of call and truck stops. - Shipping REST API – This API provides shipping information for use and display on the shipping website. Shipping Data The application uses MongoDB JSON document storage database for all container and transport information. Shipping Web Site The site displays shipping container tracking information and container contents. The site is located at http://shipping.wideworldimporters.com Proposed solution The on-premises shipping application must be moved to Azure. The VM has been migrated to a new Standard_D16s_v3 Azure VM by using Azure Site Recovery and must remain running in Azure to complete the BizTalk component migrations. You create a Standard_D16s_v3 Azure VM to host BizTalk Server. The Azure architecture diagram for the proposed solution is shown below:

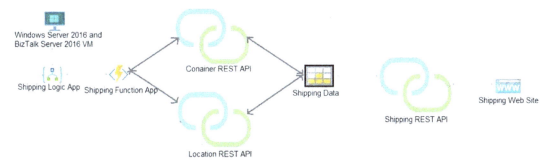

Shipping Logic App The Shipping Logic app must meet the following requirements: - Support the ocean transport and inland transport workflows by using a Logic App. - Support industry-standard protocol X12 message format for various messages including vessel content details and arrival notices. - Secure resources to the corporate VNet and use dedicated storage resources with a fixed costing model. - Maintain on-premises connectivity to support legacy applications and final BizTalk migrations. Shipping Function app Implement secure function endpoints by using app-level security and include Azure Active Directory (Azure AD). REST APIs The REST API's that support the solution must meet the following requirements: - Secure resources to the corporate VNet. - Allow deployment to a testing location within Azure while not incurring additional costs. - Automatically scale to double capacity during peak shipping times while not causing application downtime. - Minimize costs when selecting an Azure payment model. Shipping data Data migration from on-premises to Azure must minimize costs and downtime. Shipping website Use Azure Content Delivery Network (CDN) and ensure maximum performance for dynamic content while minimizing latency and costs. Issues Windows Server 2016 VM The VM shows high network latency, jitter, and high CPU utilization. The VM is critical and has not been backed up in the past. The VM must enable a quick restore from a 7-day snapshot to include in-place restore of disks in case of failure. Shipping website and REST APIs The following error message displays while you are testing the website:

```
Failed to load http://test-shippingapi.wideworldimporters.com/: No 'Access-Control-Allow-Origin'
header is present on the requested resource. Origin 'http://testwideworldimporters.com/' is
therefore not allowed access.
```

Answers:

**A)** Azure Active Directory Application Proxy

**B)** Point-to-Site (P2S) VPN connection

**C)** Site-to-Site (S2S) VPN connection

**D)** On-premises Data Gateway

**Solution:** D

**Explanation:**

Explanation: Explanation: Before you can connect to on-premises data sources from Azure Logic Apps, download and install the on- premises data gateway on a local computer. The gateway works as a bridge that provides quick data transfer and encryption between data sources on premises (not in the cloud) and your logic apps. The gateway supports BizTalk Server 2016. Note: Microsoft have now fully incorporated the Azure BizTalk Services capabilities into Logic Apps and Azure App Service Hybrid Connections. Logic Apps Enterprise Integration pack bring some of the enterprise B2B capabilities like AS2 and X12, EDI standards support Scenario: The Shipping Logic app must meet the following requirements: - Support the ocean transport and inland transport workflows by using a Logic App. - Support industry standard protocol X12 message format for various messages including vessel content details and arrival notices. - Secure resources to the corporate VNet and use dedicated storage resources with a fixed costing model. - Maintain on-premises connectivity to support legacy applications and final BizTalk migrations. References: https://docs.microsoft.com/en-us/azure/logic-apps/logic-apps-gateway-install

**Question: 4** *Multiple Answers Are Right*

HOTSPOT You need to configure Azure App Service to support the REST API requirements. Which values should you use? To answer, select the appropriate options in the answer area. NOTE: Each correct selection is worth one point. Hot Area:

## Answer Area

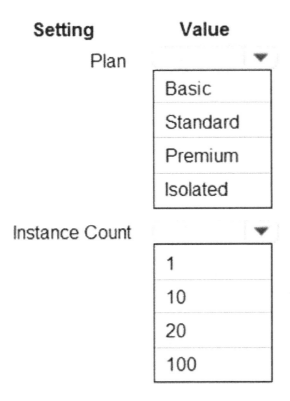

**Scenario:**

TESTLET-3. Case Study This is a case study. Case studies are not timed separately. You can use as much exam time as you would like to complete each case. However, there may be additional case studies and sections on this exam. You must manage your time to ensure that you are able to complete all questions included on this exam in the time provided. To answer the questions included in a case study, you will need to reference information that is provided in the case study. Case studies might contain exhibits and other resources that provide more information about the scenario that is described in the case study. Each question is independent of the other question on this case study. At the end of this case study, a review screen will appear. This screen allows you to review your answers and to make changes before you move to the next sections of the exam. After you begin a new section, you cannot return to this section. To start the case study To display the first question on this case study, click the Next button. Use the buttons in the left pane to explore the content of the case study before you answer the questions. Clicking these buttons displays information such as business requirements, existing environment, and problem statements. If the case study has an All Information tab, note that the information displayed is identical to the information displayed on the subsequent tabs. When you are ready to answer a question, click the Question button to return to the question. Background Wide World Importers is moving all their datacenters to Azure. The company has developed several applications and services to support supply chain operations and would like to leverage serverless computing where possible. Current environment Windows Server 2016 virtual machine This virtual machine (VM) runs Biz Talk Server 2016. The VM runs the following workflows: - Ocean Transport – This workflow gathers and validates container information including container contents and arrival notices at various shipping ports. - Inland Transport – This workflow gathers and validates trucking information including fuel usage, number of stops, and routes. The VM supports the following REST API calls: - Container API – This API provides container information including weight, contents, and other attributes. - Location API – This API provides location information regarding shipping ports of call and truck stops. - Shipping REST API – This API provides shipping information for use and display on the shipping website. Shipping Data The application uses MongoDB JSON document storage database for all container and transport information. Shipping Web Site The site displays shipping container tracking information and container contents. The site is located at http://shipping.wideworldimporters.com Proposed solution The on-premises shipping application must be moved to Azure. The VM has been migrated to a new Standard_D16s_v3 Azure VM by using Azure Site Recovery and must remain running in Azure to complete the BizTalk component migrations. You create a Standard_D16s_v3 Azure VM to host BizTalk Server. The Azure architecture diagram for the proposed solution is shown below:

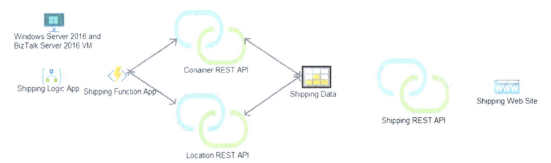

Shipping Logic App The Shipping Logic app must meet the following requirements: - Support the ocean transport and inland transport workflows by using a Logic App. - Support industry-standard protocol X12 message format for various messages including vessel content details and arrival notices. - Secure resources to the corporate VNet and use dedicated storage resources with a fixed costing model. - Maintain on-premises connectivity to support legacy applications and final BizTalk migrations. Shipping Function app Implement secure function endpoints by using app-level security and include Azure Active Directory (Azure AD). REST APIs The REST API's that support the solution must meet the following requirements: - Secure resources to the corporate VNet. - Allow deployment to a testing location within Azure while not incurring additional costs. - Automatically scale to double capacity during peak shipping times while not causing application downtime. - Minimize costs when selecting an Azure payment model. Shipping data Data migration from on-premises to Azure must minimize costs and downtime. Shipping website Use Azure Content Delivery Network (CDN) and ensure maximum performance for dynamic content while minimizing latency and costs. Issues Windows Server 2016 VM The VM shows high network latency, jitter, and high CPU utilization. The VM is critical and has not been backed up in the past. The VM must enable a quick restore from a 7-day snapshot to include in-place restore of disks in case of failure. Shipping website and REST APIs The following error message displays while you are testing the website:

```
Failed to load http://test-shippingapi.wideworldimporters.com/: No 'Access-Control-Allow-Origin' header is present on the requested resource. Origin 'http://testwideworldimporters.com/' is therefore not allowed access.
```

Answers:

A)

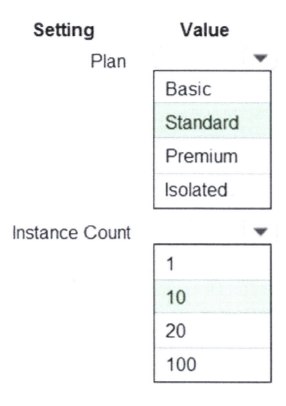

**Solution:** A

**Explanation:**

Explanation: Plan: Standard Standard support auto-scaling Instance Count: 10 Max instances for standard is 10. Scenario: The REST API's that support the solution must meet the following requirements: - Allow deployment to a testing location within Azure while not incurring additional costs. - Automatically scale to double capacity during peak shipping times while not causing application downtime. - Minimize costs when selecting an Azure payment model. References: https://azure.microsoft.com/en-us/pricing/details/app-service/plans/ Develop Azure Infrastructure as a Service Compute Solutions Question Set 4

**Question: 5** *One Answer Is Right*

You are writing code to create and run an Azure Batch job. You have created a pool of compute nodes. You need to choose the right class and its method to submit a batch job to the Batch service. Which method should you use?

**Answers:**

**A)** JobOperations.EnableJobAsync(String, IEnumerable,CancellationToken)

**B)** JobOperations.CreateJob()

**C)** CloudJob.Enable(IEnumerable)

**D)** JobOperations.EnableJob(String,IEnumerable)

**E)** CloudJob.CommitAsync(IEnumerable, CancellationToken)

**Solution:** E

**Explanation:**

Explanation: Explanation: A Batch job is a logical grouping of one or more tasks. A job includes settings common to the tasks, such as priority and the pool to run tasks on. The app uses the BatchClient.JobOperations.CreateJob method to create a job on your pool. The Commit method submits the job to the Batch service. Initially the job has no tasks. { CloudJob job = batchClient.JobOperations.CreateJob(); job.Id = JobId; job.PoolInformation = new PoolInformation { PoolId = PoolId }; job.Commit(); } ... References: https://docs.microsoft.com/en-us/azure/batch/quick-run-dotnet

**Question: 6** *Multiple Answers Are Right*

DRAG DROP You are developing Azure WebJobs. You need to recommend a WebJob type for each scenario. Which WebJob type should you recommend? To answer, drag the appropriate

WebJob types to the correct scenarios. Each WebJob type may be used once, more than once, or not at all. You may need to drag the split bar between panes or scroll to view content. NOTE: Each correct selection is worth one point. Select and Place:

### Answer Area

| WebJob types | Scenario | WebJob type |
|---|---|---|
| Triggered | Run on all instances that the web app runs on. Optionally restrict the WebJob to a single instance. | |
| Continuous | Run on a single instance that Azure select for load balancing. | |
| | Supports remote debugging | |

Answers:

**A)**

### Answer Area

| WebJob types | Scenario | WebJob type |
|---|---|---|
| Triggered | Run on all instances that the web app runs on. Optionally restrict the WebJob to a single instance. | Continuous |
| Continuous | Run on a single instance that Azure select for load balancing. | Triggered |
| | Supports remote debugging | Continuous |

**Solution:** A

**Explanation:**

Explanation: Box 1: Continuous Continuous runs on all instances that the web app runs on. You can optionally restrict the WebJob to a single instance. Box 2: Triggered Triggered runs on a single instance that Azure selects for load balancing. Box 3: Continuous Continuous supports remote debugging. Note: The following table describes the differences between continuous and triggered WebJobs.

| Continuous | Triggered |
|---|---|
| Starts immediately when the WebJob is created. To keep the job from ending, the program or script typically does its work inside an endless loop. If the job does end, you can restart it. | Starts only when triggered manually or on a schedule. |
| Runs on all instances that the web app runs on. You can optionally restrict the WebJob to a single instance. | Runs on a single instance that Azure selects for load balancing. |
| Supports remote debugging. | Doesn't support remote debugging. |

References: https://docs.microsoft.com/en-us/azure/app-service/web-sites-create-web-jobs

**Question: 7** *Multiple Answers Are Right*

DRAG DROP You are developing a software solution for an autonomous transportation system. The solution uses large data sets and Azure Batch processing to simulate navigation sets for entire fleets of vehicles. You need to create compute nodes for the solution on Azure Batch. What should you do? Put the actions in the correct order. Select and Place:

**Select these:**
- In the Azure CLI, run the command: az batch account create
- In Azure CLI, run the command: az batch task create
- In Azure CLI, run the command: az batch pool create
- In Azure CLI, run the command: az batch job create

**Place here:** (empty)

Answers:

A)

**Select these:** (empty)

**Place here:**
- In the Azure CLI, run the command: az batch account create
- In Azure CLI, run the command: az batch pool create
- In Azure CLI, run the command: az batch job create
- In Azure CLI, run the command: az batch task create

**Solution:** A

**Explanation:**

Explanation: With the Azure CLI: Step 1: In the Azure CLI, run the command: az batch account create First we create a batch account. Step 2: In Azure CLI, run the command: az batch pool create Now that you have a Batch account, create a sample pool of Linux compute nodes using the az batch pool create command. Step 3: In Azure CLI, run the command: az batch job create Now that you have a pool, create a job to run on it. A Batch job is a logical group for one or more tasks. A job includes settings common to the tasks, such as priority and the pool to run tasks on. Create a Batch job by using the az batch job create command. Step 4: In Azure CLI, run the command: az batch task create Now use the az batch task create command to create some tasks to run in the job. References: https://docs.microsoft.com/en-us/azure/batch/quick-create-cli

**Question: 8** *Multiple Answers Are Right*

DRAG DROP You are deploying an Azure Kubernetes Services (AKS) cluster that will use multiple containers. You need to create the cluster and verify that the services for the containers are configured correctly and available. Which four commands should you use to develop the solution? To answer, move the appropriate command segments from the list of command segments to the answer area and arrange them in the correct order. Select and Place:

**Command segments**

- az aks get-credentials
- az appservice plan create
- az aks create
- az group create
- kubectl apply

**Answer Area**

Answers:

A)

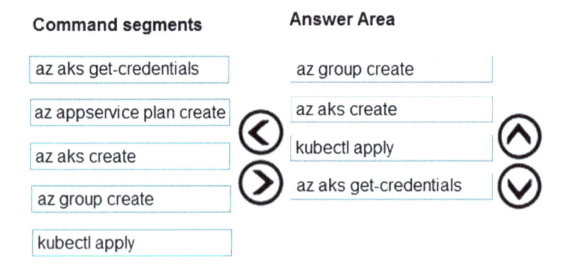

**Solution:** A

**Explanation:**

Explanation: Step 1: az group create Create a resource group with the az group create command. An Azure resource group is a logical group in which Azure resources are deployed and managed. Example: The following example creates a resource group named myAKSCluster in the eastus location. az group create --name myAKSCluster --location eastus Step 2 : az aks create Use the az aks create command to create an AKS cluster. Step 3: kubectl apply To deploy your application, use the kubectl apply command. This command parses the manifest file and creates the defined Kubernetes objects. Step 4: az aks get-credentials Configure it with the credentials for the new AKS cluster. Example: az aks get-credentials --name aks-cluster --resource-group aks-resource-group References: https://docs.bitnami.com/azure/get-started-aks/

**Question: 9** *Multiple Answers Are Right*

DRAG DROP You are preparing to deploy a medical records application to an Azure virtual machine (VM). The application will be deployed by using a VHD produced by an on-premises build server. You need to ensure that both the application and related data are encrypted during and after deployment to Azure. Which three actions should you perform in sequence? To answer, move the appropriate actions from the list of actions to the answer area and arrange them in the correct order. Select and Place:

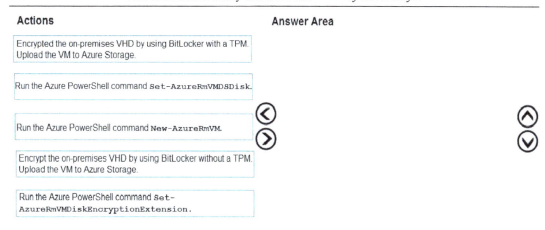

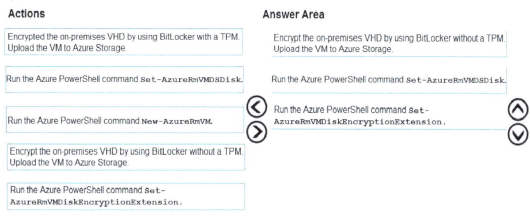

Solution: A

Explanation:

Explanation: Step 1: Encrypt the on-premises VHD by using BitLocker without a TPM. Upload the VM to Azure Storage Step 2: Run the Azure PowerShell command Set-AzureRMVMOSDisk To use an existing disk instead of creating a new disk you can use the Set-AzureRMVMOSDisk command. Example: $osDiskName = $vmname+'_osDisk' $osDiskCaching = 'ReadWrite' $osDiskVhdUri = "https://$stoname.blob.core.windows.net/vhds/"+$vmname+"_os.vhd" $vm = Set-AzureRmVMOSDisk -VM $vm -VhdUri $osDiskVhdUri -name $osDiskName -Create Step 3: Run the Azure PowerShell command Set-AzureRmVMDiskEncryptionExtension Use the Set-AzVMDiskEncryptionExtension cmdlet to enable encryption on a running IaaS virtual machine in Azure. Incorrect: Not TPM: BitLocker can work with or without a TPM. A TPM is a tamper resistant security chip on the system board that will hold the keys for encryption and check the integrity of the boot sequence and allows the most secure BitLocker implementation. A VM does not have a TPM. References: https://www.itprotoday.com/iaaspaas/use-existing-vhd-azurerm-vm

**Question: 10** *Multiple Answers Are Right*

DRAG DROP You plan to create a Docker image that runs as ASP.NET Core application named ContosoApp. You have a setup script named setupScript.ps1 and a series of application files including ContosoApp.dll. You need to create a Dockerfile document that meets the following requirements: - Call setupScript.ps1 when the container is built. - Run ContosoApp.dll when the container starts. The Dockerfile document must be created in the same folder where ContosoApp.dll and setupScript.ps1 are stored. Which four commands should you use to develop the solution? To answer, move the appropriate commands from the list of commands to the answer area and arrange them in the correct order. Select and Place:

**Commands**

- RUN powershell ./setupScript.ps1
  CMD ["dotnet", "ContosoApp.dll"]

- EXPOSE ./ContosoApp/ /apps/ContosoApp

- COPY ./ .

- FROM microsoft/aspnetcore:2.0

- WORKDIR /apps/ContosoApp

- CMD powershell ./setupScript.ps1
  ENTRYPOINT ["dotnet", "ContosoApp.dll"]

**Answer Area**

**Answers:**

A)

**Solution:** A

**Explanation:**

Explanation: Step 1: WORKDIR /apps/ContosoApp Step 2: COPY ./- The Docker document must be created in the same folder where ContosoApp.dll and setupScript.ps1 are stored. Step 3: EXPOSE ./ContosApp/ /app/ContosoApp Step 4: CMD powershell ./setupScript.ps1 ENTRYPOINT ["dotnet", "ContosoApp.dll"] You need to create a Dockerfile document that meets the following requirements: - Call setupScript.ps1 when the container is built. - Run ContosoApp.dll when the container starts. References: https://docs.microsoft.com/en-us/azure/app-service/containers/tutorial-custom-docker-image

# Chapter 18: AZ-204 - Developing Solutions for Microsoft Azure

## Exam Guide

How to Prepare For AZ-204: Developing Solutions for Microsoft Azure Exam

Preparation Guide for AZ-204: Developing Solutions for Microsoft Azure Exam

Introduction

Microsoft has created a track for cloud developers who want to validate foundational knowledge of Developing Solutions for Microsoft Azure landscape to get certified this platform. Cloud developers They partner with cloud DBAs, cloud administrators, and clients to implement solutions. Developing Solutions for Microsoft Azure professionals is a way to demonstrate their skills. The assessment is based on a rigorous exam using industry standard methodology to determine whether a candidate meets Microsoft's proficiency standards.

According to Microsoft, a AZ-204 Certified Professional should be proficient in Azure SDKs, data storage options, data connections, APIs, app authentication and authorization, compute and container deployment, debugging, performance tuning, and monitoring.

Certification is evidence of your skills, expertise in those areas in which you like to work. There are many vendors in the market that are providing these certifications. If candidate wants to work on Developing Solutions for Microsoft Azure and prove his knowledge, certification offered by Microsoft. This **AZ-204 Exam** Certification helps a candidate to validates his skills in Developing Solutions for Microsoft Azure Technology.

In this guide, we will cover the AZ-204: Developing Solutions for Microsoft Azure Certification exam, AZ-204: Developing Solutions for Microsoft Azure Certified professional salary and all aspects of the AZ-204: Developing Solutions for Microsoft Azure Certification.

Introduction to AZ-204: Developing Solutions for Microsoft Azure Exam:

Candidates for **AZ-204 Exam** are seeking to prove fundamental knowledge and skills in Developing Solutions for Microsoft Azure domain. Before taking this exam, aspirants ought to have a solid fundamental information of the concepts shared in preparation guide as well as they must be able to program in an Azure Supported Language which would give an added edge.

It is suggested that professionals accustomed to the ideas and also the technologies represented here by taking relevant training courses. Candidates are expected to have some hands-on experience on implement Iaas , creating ARM templates, creating Azure service web apps. After passing this exam, candidates get a certificate from Microsoft that helps them to demonstrate their proficiency to their clients and employers.

Topics of AZ-204: Developing Solutions for Microsoft Azure Exam:

Candidates should apprehend the examination topics before they begin of preparation. because it'll extremely facilitate them in touch the core. Our **AZ-204 dumps** will include the following topics:

*1. Develop Azure compute solutions (25-30%)*

Implement IaaS solutions

- Provision VMs
- Create ARM templates
- Create container images for solutions
- Publish an image to the Azure Container Registry
- Run containers by using Azure Container Instance

　　Create Azure App Service Web Apps

- Create an Azure App Service Web App
- Enable diagnostics logging
- Deploy code to a web app
- Configure web app settings
- Implement autoscaling rules (schedule, operational/system metrics)

　　Implement Azure functions

- Implement input and output bindings for a function
- Implement function triggers by using data operations, timers, and webhooks
- Implement Azure Durable Functions

　　*2. Develop for Azure storage (10-15%)*

Develop solutions that use Cosmos DB storage

- Select the appropriate API for your solution

- Implement partitioning schemes
- Interact with data using the appropriate SDK
- Set the appropriate consistency level for operations
- Create Cosmos DB containers

   Develop solutions that use blob storage

- Move items in Blob storage between storage accounts or containers
- Set and retrieve properties and metadata
- Interact with data using the appropriate SDK
- Implement data archiving and retention

   *3. Implement Azure security (15-20%)*

Implement user authentication and authorization

- Implement OAuth2 authentication
- Create and implement shared access signatures
- Register apps and use Azure Active Directory to authenticate users

   Implement secure cloud solutions

- Secure app configuration data by using the App Configuration and KeyVault API
- Manage keys, secrets, and certificates by using the KeyVault API
- Implement Managed Identities for Azure resources

   *4. Monitor, troubleshoot, and optimize Azure solutions (10-15%)*

Integrate caching and content delivery within solutions

- Develop code to implement CDN's in solutions
- Configure cache and expiration policies
- Store and retrieve data in Azure Redis cache

   Instrument solutions to support monitoring and logging

- Configure instrumentation in an app or service by using Application Insights
- Analyze and troubleshoot solutions by using Azure Monitor
- Implement Application Insights Web Test and Alerts
- Implement code that handles transient faults

   *5. Connect to and consume Azure services and third-party services (25-30%)*

Develop an App Service Logic App

- Create a Logic App
- Create a custom connector for Logic Apps
- Create a custom template for Logic Apps

  Implement API management

- Create an APIM instance
- Configure authentication for APIs
- Define policies for APIs

  Develop event-based solutions

- Implement solutions that use Azure Event Grid
- Implement solutions that use Azure Notification Hubs
- Implement solutions that use Azure Event Hub

  Develop message-based solutions

- Implement solutions that use Azure Service Bus
- Implement solutions that use Azure Queue Storage queues

  Who should take the AZ-204: Developing Solutions for Microsoft Azure Exam:

The **AZ-204 Exam** certification is an internationally-recognized certification which help to have validation for cloud developers who participate in all phases of development from requirements definition and design, to development and deployment, and maintenance. They partner with cloud DBAs, cloud administrators, and clients to implement solutions. Candidates should be proficient in Azure SDKs, data storage options, data connections, APIs, app authentication and authorization, compute and container deployment, debugging, performance tuning, and monitoring. Candidates must have 1-2 years professional development experience and experience with Microsoft Azure. They must be able to program in an Azure Supported Language.

How to study the AZ-204: Developing Solutions for Microsoft Azure Exam:

Preparation of certification exams could be covered with two resource types . The first one are the study guides, reference books and study forums that are elaborated and appropriate for building information from ground up. Apart from them video tutorials and lectures are a good option to ease the pain of through study and are relatively make the study process more interesting nonetheless these demand time and concentration from the learner. Smart candidates who wish to create a solid foundation altogether examination topics and connected technologies typically mix video lectures with study guides to reap the advantages of each but practice exams or practice exam engines is one important study tool which goes typically unnoted by most candidates. Practice exams are designed with our experts to make exam prospects test their knowledge on skills attained in course, as well as prospects become comfortable and familiar with the real exam environment. Statistics have indicated exam anxiety plays much bigger role of students failure in exam than the fear of the unknown. Certification-questions expert team recommends preparing some notes on these topics along with it don't forget to practice **AZ-204 dumps** which had been written by our expert team, each of these can assist you loads to clear this exam with excellent marks.

AZ-204: Developing Solutions for Microsoft Azure Certification Path:

AZ-204: Developing Solutions for Microsoft Azure Exam is foundation level Certification. This exam can be taken as a precursor to other Dynamics 365 certifications and training.

How much AZ-204: Developing Solutions for Microsoft Azure Exam Cost:

The price of the Microsoft Mobility and Devices Fundamentals exam is $165 USD, for more information related to exam price please visit to Microsoft Training website as prices of Microsoft exams fees get varied country wise.

How to book the AZ-204: Developing Solutions for Microsoft Azure Exam:

These are following steps for registering the AZ-204: Developing Solutions for Microsoft Azure exam.

- Step 1: Visit to Microsoft Learning and search for AZ-204: Developing Solutions for Microsoft Azure.
- Step 2: Sign up/Login to Pearson VUE account
- Step 3: Select local centre based on your country, date, time and confirm with a payment method.

What is the duration, language, and format of AZ-204: Developing Solutions for Microsoft Azure Exam:

- Length of Examination: 50 mins
- Number of Questions: 40 to 60 questions(Since Microsoft does not publish this information, the number of exam questions may change without notice.)
- Passing Score: 700 / 1000
- Type of Questions: This test format is multiple choice.
- Language: English
- This is beta exam.

AZ-204: Developing Solutions for Microsoft Azure Exam Certified Professional salary:

The average salary of a AZ-204: Developing Solutions for Microsoft Azure Exam Certified Expert in

- United State - 120,000 USD
- India - 20,00,327 INR
- Europe - 90,547 EURO
- England - 90,532 POUND

The benefit of obtaining the AZ-204: Developing Solutions for Microsoft Azure Exam Certification:

- This certification will be judging your skills and knowledge on your understanding Developing Solutions for Microsoft Azure concepts & Understanding of how to operate on Planning and Administering Developing Solutions for Microsoft Azure .
- This certification credential will give you edge over other counterparts. Apart from knowledge from AZ-204: Developing Solutions for Microsoft Azure Exam.
- AZ-204 Certification is distinguished among competitors. AZ-204 certification can give them an edge at that time easily when candidates appear for employment interview, employers are very fascinated to note one thing that differentiates the individual from all other candidates.
- AZ-204 certification has more useful and relevant networks that help them in setting career goals for themselves. AZ-204 networks provide them with the correct career guidance than non certified generally are unable to get.
- AZ-204 certified candidates will be confident and stand different from others as their skills are more trained than non-certified professionals.
- **AZ-204 Exam** provide proven knowledge to use the tools to complete the task efficiently and cost effectively than the other non-certified professionals lack in doing so.
- AZ-204 Certification provides practical experience to candidates from all the aspects to be a proficient worker in the organization.
- AZ-204 Certifications provide opportunities to get a job easily in which they are interested in instead of wasting years and ending without getting any experience.
- AZ-204 credential delivers higher earning potential and increased promotion opportunities because it shows a good understanding of Developing Solutions for Microsoft Azure.

Difficulty in Writing AZ-204: Developing Solutions for Microsoft Azure Exam:

AZ-204: Developing Solutions for Microsoft Azure is a privileged achievement one could be graced with. But adverse to general notion certifying with Microsoft is not that challenging if the candidates have proper preparation material to pass the AZ-204: Developing Solutions for Microsoft Azure exam with good grades. Questions answers and clarifications which are designed in form of Certification-questions dumps make sure to cover entire course content. Certification-questions have a brilliant AZ-204: Developing Solutions for Microsoft Azure dumps with most recent and important questions and answers in PDF files. Certification-questions is sure about the exactness and legitimacy of AZ-204: Developing Solutions for Microsoft Azure dumps and in this manner. Candidates can easily pass the AZ-204: Developing Solutions for Microsoft Azure exam with genuine AZ-204: Developing Solutions for Microsoft Azure dumps and get MICROSOFT certification. These dumps are viewed as the best source to understand the AZ-204: Developing Solutions for Microsoft Azure well by simply pursuing examples questions and answers. If candidate completes practice the exam with certification **AZ-204 dumps** along with self-assessment to get the proper idea on MICROSOFT accreditation and to ace the certification exam.

For more info read reference::

microsoft learning site
AZ-204 Skills measured
Create serverless applications

# Sample Practice Test for AZ-204

**Question: 1** *Multiple Answers Are Right*

HOTSPOT You need to configure Azure CDN for the Shipping web site. Which configuration options should you use? To answer, select the appropriate options in the answer area. NOTE: Each correct selection is worth one point. Hot Area:

# Answer Area

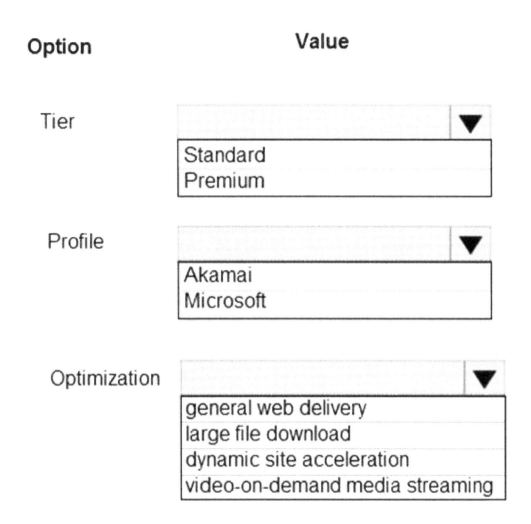

**Scenario:**

TESTLET-1. Case study This is a case study. Case studies are not timed separately. You can use as much exam time as you would like to complete each case. However, there may be additional case studies and sections on this exam. You must manage your time to ensure that you are able to complete all questions included on this exam in the time provided. To answer the questions included in a case study, you will need to reference information that is provided in the case study. Case studies might contain exhibits and other resources that provide more information about the scenario that is described in the case study. Each question is independent of the other questions in this case study. At the end of this case study, a review screen will appear. This screen allows you to review your answers and to make changes before you move to the next section of the exam. After you begin a new section, you cannot return to this section. To start the case study To display the first question in this case study, click the Next button. Use the buttons in the left pane to explore the content of the case study before you answer the questions. Clicking these buttons displays information such as business requirements, existing environment, and problem statements. When you are ready to answer a question, click the Question button to return to the question. Current environment Windows Server 2016 virtual machine This virtual machine (VM) runs BizTalk Server 2016. The VM runs the following workflows: - Ocean Transport – This workflow gathers and validates container information including container contents and arrival notices at various shipping ports. - Inland Transport – This workflow gathers and validates trucking information including fuel usage, number of stops, and routes. The VM supports the following REST API calls: - Container API – This API provides container information including weight, contents, and other attributes. - Location API – This API provides location information regarding shipping ports of call and trucking stops. - Shipping REST API – This API provides shipping information for use and display on the shipping website. Shipping Data The application uses MongoDB JSON document storage database for all container and transport information. Shipping Web Site The site displays shipping container tracking information and container contents. The site is located at http://shipping.wideworldimporters.com/ Proposed solution The on-premises shipping application must be moved to Azure. The VM has been migrated to a new Standard_D16s_v3 Azure VM by using Azure Site Recovery and must remain running in Azure to complete the BizTalk component migrations. You create a Standard_D16s_v3 Azure VM to host BizTalk Server. The Azure architecture diagram for the proposed solution is shown below:

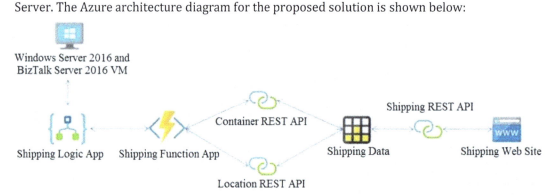

Requirements Shipping Logic app The Shipping Logic app must meet the following requirements: - Support the ocean transport and inland transport workflows by using a Logic App. - Support industry-standard protocol X12 message format for various messages including vessel content details and arrival notices. - Secure resources to the corporate VNet and use dedicated storage resources with a fixed costing model. - Maintain on-premises connectivity to support legacy applications and final BizTalk migrations. Shipping Function app Implement secure function endpoints by using app-level security and include Azure Active Directory (Azure AD). REST APIs The REST API's that support the solution must meet the following requirements: - Secure resources to the corporate VNet. - Allow deployment to a testing location within Azure while not incurring additional costs. - Automatically scale to double capacity during peak shipping times while not causing application downtime. - Minimize costs when selecting an Azure payment model. Shipping data Data migration from on-premises to Azure must minimize costs and downtime. Shipping website Use Azure Content Delivery Network (CDN) and ensure maximum performance for dynamic content while minimizing latency and costs. Issues Windows Server 2016 VM The VM shows high network latency, jitter, and high CPU utilization. The VM is critical and has not been backed up in the past. The VM must enable a quick restore from a 7-day snapshot to include in-place restore of disks in case of failure. Shipping website and REST APIs The following error message displays while you are testing the website: Failed to load http://test-shippingapi.wideworldimporters.com/: No 'Access- Control-Allow-Origin' header is present on the requested resource. Origin 'http://test.wideworldimporters.com/' is therefore not allowed access.

**Answers:**

A)

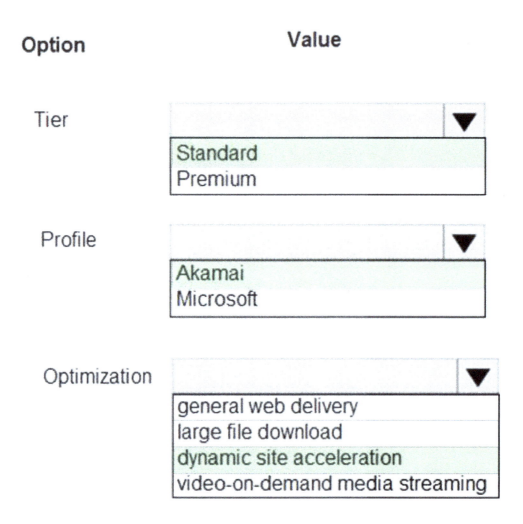

**Solution:** A

**Explanation:**

Explanation: Explanation: Scenario: Shipping website Use Azure Content Delivery Network (CDN) and ensure maximum performance for dynamic content while minimizing latency and costs. Tier: Standard Profile: Akamai Optimization: Dynamic site acceleration Dynamic site acceleration (DSA) is available for Azure CDN Standard from Akamai, Azure CDN Standard from Verizon, and Azure CDN Premium from Verizon profiles. DSA includes various techniques that benefit the latency and performance of dynamic content. Techniques include route and network optimization, TCP optimization, and more. You can use this optimization to accelerate a web app that includes numerous responses that aren't cacheable. Examples are search results, checkout transactions, or real-time data. You can continue to use core Azure CDN caching capabilities for static data. Reference: https://docs.microsoft.com/en-us/azure/cdn/cdn-optimization-overview

**Question: 2** *Multiple Answers Are Right*

HOTSPOT You need to correct the VM issues. Which tools should you use? To answer, select the appropriate options in the answer area. NOTE: Each correct selection is worth one point. Hot Area:

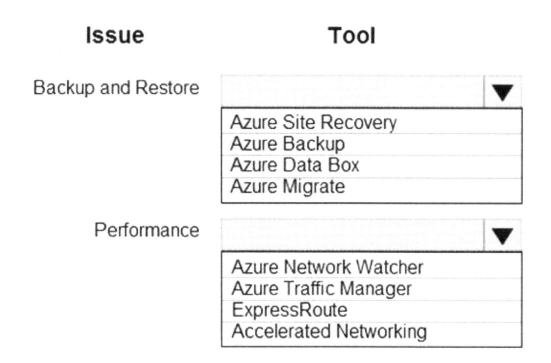

**Scenario:**

TESTLET-1. Case study This is a case study. Case studies are not timed separately. You can use as much exam time as you would like to complete each case. However, there may be additional case studies and sections on this exam. You must manage your time to ensure that you are able to complete all questions included on this exam in the time provided. To answer the questions included in a case study, you will need to reference information that is provided in the case study. Case studies might contain exhibits and other resources that provide more information about the scenario that is described in the case study. Each question is independent of the other questions in this case study. At the end of this case study, a review screen will appear. This screen allows you to review your answers and to make changes before you move to the next section of the exam. After you begin a new section, you cannot return to this section. To start the case study To display the first question in this case study, click the Next button. Use the buttons in the left pane to explore the content of the case study before you answer the questions. Clicking these buttons displays information such as business requirements, existing environment, and problem statements. When you are ready to answer a question, click the Question button to return to the question. Current environment Windows Server 2016 virtual machine This virtual machine (VM) runs BizTalk Server 2016. The VM runs the following workflows: - Ocean Transport – This workflow gathers and validates container information including container contents and arrival notices at various shipping ports. - Inland Transport – This workflow gathers and validates trucking information including fuel usage, number of stops, and routes. The VM supports the following REST API calls: - Container API – This API provides container information including weight, contents, and other attributes. - Location API – This API provides location information regarding shipping ports of call and trucking stops. - Shipping REST API – This API provides shipping information for use and display on the shipping website. Shipping Data The application uses MongoDB JSON document storage database for all container and transport information. Shipping Web Site The site displays shipping container tracking information and container contents. The site is located at http://shipping.wideworldimporters.com/ Proposed solution The on-premises shipping application must be moved to Azure. The VM has been migrated to a new Standard_D16s_v3 Azure VM by using Azure Site Recovery and must remain running in Azure to complete the BizTalk component migrations. You create a Standard_D16s_v3 Azure VM to host BizTalk Server. The Azure architecture diagram for the proposed solution is shown below:

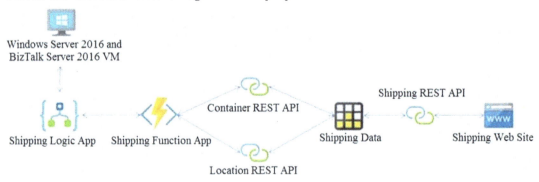

Requirements Shipping Logic app The Shipping Logic app must meet the following requirements: - Support the ocean transport and inland transport workflows by using a Logic App. - Support industry-standard protocol X12 message format for various messages including vessel content details and arrival notices. - Secure resources to the corporate VNet and use dedicated storage resources with a fixed costing model. - Maintain on-premises connectivity to support legacy applications and final BizTalk migrations. Shipping Function app Implement secure function endpoints by using app-level security and include Azure Active Directory (Azure AD). REST APIs The REST API's that support the solution must meet the following requirements: - Secure resources to the corporate VNet. - Allow deployment to a testing location within Azure while not incurring additional costs. - Automatically scale to double capacity during peak shipping times while not causing application downtime. - Minimize costs when selecting an Azure payment model. Shipping data Data migration from on-premises to Azure must minimize costs and downtime. Shipping website Use Azure Content Delivery Network (CDN) and ensure maximum performance for dynamic content while minimizing latency and costs. Issues Windows Server 2016 VM The VM shows high network latency, jitter, and high CPU utilization. The VM is critical and has not been backed up in the past. The VM must enable a quick restore from a 7-day snapshot to include in-place restore of disks in case of failure. Shipping website and REST APIs The following error message displays while you are testing the website: Failed to load http://test-shippingapi.wideworldimporters.com/: No 'Access- Control-Allow-Origin' header is present on the requested resource. Origin 'http://test.wideworldimporters.com/' is therefore not allowed access.

**Answers:**

A)

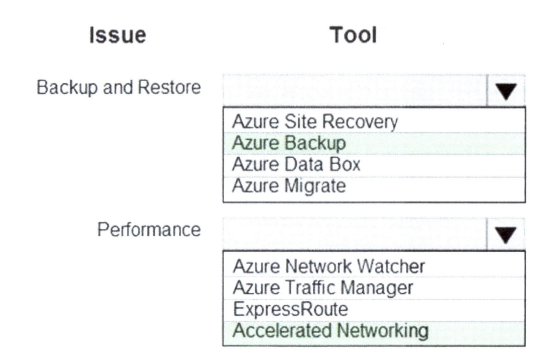

**Solution:** A

**Explanation:**

Explanation: Box 1: Azure Backup The VM is critical and has not been backed up in the past. The VM must enable a quick restore from a 7- day snapshot to include in-place restore of disks in case of failure. In-Place restore of disks in IaaS VMs is a feature of Azure Backup. Performance: Accelerated Networking Scenario: The VM shows high network latency, jitter, and high CPU utilization. Box 2: Accelerated networking The VM shows high network latency, jitter, and high CPU utilization. Accelerated networking enables single root I/O virtualization (SR-IOV) to a VM, greatly improving its networking performance. This high-performance path bypasses the host from the datapath, reducing latency, jitter, and CPU utilization, for use with the most demanding network workloads on supported VM types. Reference: https://azure.microsoft.com/en-us/blog/an-easy-way-to-bring-back-your-azure-vm-with-in-place-restore/ Develop Azure compute solutions Question Set 2

**Question: 3** *One Answer Is Right*

Note: This question is part of a series of questions that present the same scenario. Each question in the series contains a unique solution that might meet the stated goals. Some question sets might have more than one correct solution, while others might not have a correct solution. After you answer a question in this section, you will NOT be able to return to it. As a result, these questions will not appear in the review screen. You develop a software as a service (SaaS) offering to manage photographs. Users upload photos to a web service which then stores the photos in Azure Storage Blob storage. The storage account type is General- purpose V2. When photos are uploaded, they must be processed to produce and save a mobile-friendly version of the image. The process to produce a mobile-friendly version of the image must start in less than one minute. You need to design the process that starts the photo processing. Solution: Move photo processing to an Azure Function triggered from the blob upload. Does the solution meet the goal?

**Answers:**

**A)** Yes

**B)** No

**Solution:** A

**Explanation:**

Explanation: Explanation: Azure Storage events allow applications to react to events. Common Blob storage event scenarios include image or video processing, search indexing, or any file-oriented workflow. Events are pushed using Azure Event Grid to subscribers such as Azure Functions, Azure Logic Apps, or even to your own http listener. Note: Only storage accounts of kind StorageV2 (general purpose v2) and BlobStorage support event integration. Storage (general purpose v1) does not support integration with Event Grid. Reference: https://docs.microsoft.com/en-us/azure/storage/blobs/storage-blob-event-overview

**Question: 4** *One Answer Is Right*

You are developing an application that uses Azure Blob storage. The application must read the transaction logs of all the changes that occur to the blobs and the blob metadata in the storage account for auditing purposes. The changes must be in the order in which they occurred, include only create, update, delete, and copy operations and be retained for compliance reasons. You need to process the transaction logs asynchronously. What should you do?

**Answers:**

**A)** Process all Azure Blob storage events by using Azure Event Grid with a subscriber Azure Function app.

**B)** Enable the change feed on the storage account and process all changes for available events.

**C)** Process all Azure Storage Analytics logs for successful blob events.

**D)** Use the Azure Monitor HTTP Data Collector API and scan the request body for successful blob events.

**Solution:** B

**Explanation:**

Explanation: Explanation: Change feed support in Azure Blob Storage The purpose of the change feed is to provide transaction logs of all the changes that occur to the blobs and the blob metadata in your storage account. The change feed provides ordered, guaranteed, durable, immutable, read-only log of these changes. Client applications can read these logs at any time, either in streaming or in batch mode. The change feed enables you to build efficient and scalable solutions that process change events that occur in your Blob Storage account at a low cost. Reference: https://docs.microsoft.com/en-us/azure/storage/blobs/storage-blob-change-feed

**Question: 5** *Multiple Answers Are Right*

DRAG DROP You are developing an application to use Azure Blob storage. You have configured Azure Blob storage to include change feeds. A copy of your storage account must be created in another region. Data must be copied from the current storage account to the new storage account directly between the storage servers. You need to create a copy of the storage account in another region and copy the data. In which order should you perform the actions? To answer, move all actions from the list of actions to the answer area and arrange them in the correct order. Select and Place:

**Actions**

- Use AZCopy to copy the data to the new storage account.
- Deploy the template to create a new storage account in the target region.
- Export a Resource Manager template.
- Create a new template deployment.
- Modify the template by changing the storage account name and region.

**Answer Area**

**Answers:**

A)

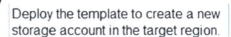

**Actions**
- Use AZCopy to copy the data to the new storage account.
- Deploy the template to create a new storage account in the target region.
- Export a Resource Manager template.
- Create a new template deployment.
- Modify the template by changing the storage account name and region.

**Answer Area**
- Create a new template deployment.
- Export a Resource Manager template.
- Modify the template by changing the storage account name and region.
- Deploy the template to create a new storage account in the target region.
- Use AZCopy to copy the data to the new storage account.

**Solution:** A

**Explanation:**

Explanation: Explanation: To move a storage account, create a copy of your storage account in another region. Then, move your data to that account by using AzCopy, or another tool of your choice. The steps are: - Export a template. - Modify the template by adding the target region and storage account name. - Deploy the template to create the new storage account. - Configure the new storage account. - Move data to the new storage account. - Delete the resources in the source region. Note: You must enable the change feed on your storage account to begin capturing and recording changes. You can enable and disable changes by using Azure Resource Manager templates on Portal or Powershell. Reference: https://docs.microsoft.com/en-us/azure/storage/common/storage-account-move https://docs.microsoft.com/en-us/azure/storage/blobs/storage-blob-change-feed

**Question: 6** *Multiple Answers Are Right*

HOTSPOT You are developing an ASP.NET Core web application. You plan to deploy the application to Azure Web App for Containers. The application needs to store runtime diagnostic data that must be persisted across application restarts. You have the following code:

```
public void SaveDiagData(string data)
{
    var path = Environment.GetEnvironmentVariable("DIAGDATA");
    File.WriteAllText(Path.Combine(path, "data"), data);
}
```

You need to configure the application settings so that diagnostic data is stored as required. How should you configure the web app's settings? To answer, select the appropriate options in the answer area. NOTE: Each correct selection is worth one point. Hot Area:

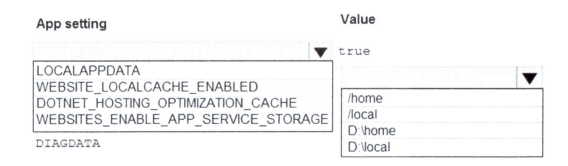

Answers:

A)

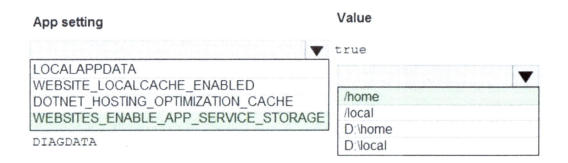

Solution: A

Explanation:

 Explanation: Explanation: Box 1: If WEBSITES_ENABLE_APP_SERVICE_STORAGE If WEBSITES_ENABLE_APP_SERVICE_STORAGE setting is unspecified or set to true, the /home/ directory will be shared across scale instances, and files written will persist across restarts Box 2: /home Reference: https://docs.microsoft.com/en-us/azure/app-service/containers/app-service-linux-faq

**Question: 7** *One Answer Is Right*

You are developing a web app that is protected by Azure Web Application Firewall (WAF). All traffic to the web app is routed through an Azure Application Gateway instance that is used by multiple web apps. The web app address is contoso.azurewebsites.net. All traffic must be secured with SSL. The Azure Application Gateway instance is used by multiple web apps. You need to configure the Azure Application Gateway for the web app. Which two actions should you perform? Each correct answer presents part of the solution. NOTE: Each correct selection is worth one point.

**Answers:**

**A)** In the Azure Application Gateway's HTTP setting, enable the Use for App service setting.

**B)** Convert the web app to run in an Azure App service environment (ASE).

**C)** Add an authentication certificate for contoso.azurewebsites.net to the Azure Application Gateway.

**D)** In the Azure Application Gateway's HTTP setting, set the value of the Override backend path option to contoso22.azurewebsites.net.

**Solution:** A, D

**Explanation:**

Explanation: Explanation: D: The ability to specify a host override is defined in the HTTP settings and can be applied to any back-end pool during rule creation. The ability to derive the host name from the IP or FQDN of the back-end pool members. HTTP settings also provide an option to dynamically pick the host name from a back-end pool member's FQDN if configured with the option to derive host name from an individual back-end pool member. A (not C): SSL termination and end to end SSL with multi-tenant services. In case of end to end SSL, trusted Azure services such as Azure App service web apps do not require whitelisting the backends in the application gateway. Therefore, there is no need to add any authentication certificates.

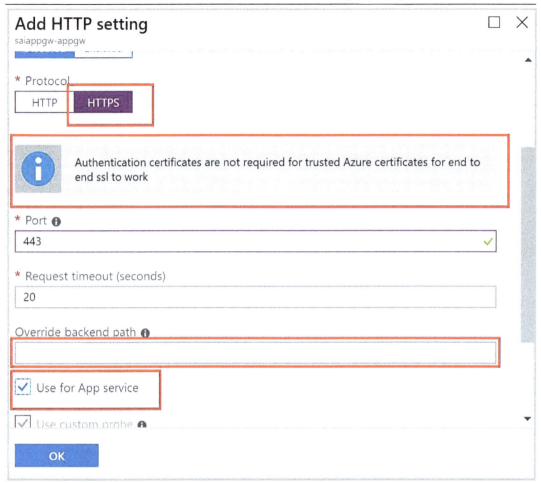

Reference: https://docs.microsoft.com/en-us/azure/application-gateway/application-gateway-web-app-overview

**Question: 8** *Multiple Answers Are Right*

HOTSPOT You are implementing a software as a service (SaaS) ASP.NET Core web service that will run as an Azure Web App. The web service will use an on-premises SQL Server database for storage. The web service also includes a WebJob that processes data updates. Four customers will use the web service. - Each instance of the WebJob processes data for a single customer and must run as a singleton instance. - Each deployment must be tested by using deployment slots prior to serving production data. - Azure costs must be minimized. - Azure resources must be located in an isolated network. You need to configure the App Service plan for the Web App. How should you configure the App Service plan? To answer, select the appropriate settings in the answer area. NOTE: Each correct selection is worth one point. Hot Area:

## Answer Area

| App service plan setting | Value |
|---|---|
| Number of VM instances | ▼ <br> 2 <br> 4 <br> 8 <br> 16 |
| Pricing tier | ▼ <br> Isolated <br> Standard <br> Premium <br> Consumption |

Answers:

A)

## Answer Area

| App service plan setting | Value |
|---|---|
| Number of VM instances | 2 / **4** / 8 / 16 |
| Pricing tier | **Isolated** / Standard / Premium / Consumption |

**Solution:** A

**Explanation:**

Explanation: Number of VM instances: 4 You are not charged extra for deployment slots. Pricing tier: Isolated The App Service Environment (ASE) is a powerful feature offering of the Azure App Service that gives network isolation and improved scale capabilities. It is essentially a deployment of the Azure App Service into a subnet of a customer's Azure Virtual Network (VNet). Reference: https://azure.microsoft.com/sv-se/blog/announcing-app-service-isolated-more-power-scale-and-ease-of-use/

**Question: 9** *Multiple Answers Are Right*

DRAG DROP You are a developer for a software as a service (SaaS) company that uses an Azure Function to process orders. The Azure Function currently runs on an Azure Function app that is triggered by an Azure Storage queue. You are preparing to migrate the Azure Function to Kubernetes using Kubernetes-based Event Driven Autoscaling (KEDA). You need to configure

Kubernetes Custom Resource Definitions (CRD) for the Azure Function. Which CRDs should you configure? To answer, drag the appropriate CRD types to the correct locations. Each CRD type may be used once, more than once, or not at all. You may need to drag the split bar between panes or scroll to view content. NOTE: Each correct selection is worth one point. Select and Place:

**Answer Area**

| CRD types | Setting | CRD type |
|---|---|---|
| Secret | Azure Function code | |
| Deployment | | |
| ScaledObject | Polling interval | |
| TriggerAuthentication | Azure Storage connection string | |

Answers:

A)

**Answer Area**

| CRD types | Setting | CRD type |
|---|---|---|
| Secret | Azure Function code | Deployment |
| Deployment | | |
| ScaledObject | Polling interval | ScaledObject |
| TriggerAuthentication | Azure Storage connection string | Secret |

Solution: A

Explanation:

Explanation: Explanation: Box 1: Deployment To deploy Azure Functions to Kubernetes use the func kubernetes deploy command has several attributes that directly control how our app scales, once it is deployed to Kubernetes. Box 2: ScaledObject With --polling-interval, we can control the interval used by KEDA to check Azure Service Bus Queue for messages. Example of ScaledObject with polling interval apiVersion: keda.k8s.io/v1alpha1 kind: ScaledObject metadata: name: transformer-fn namespace: tt labels: deploymentName: transformer-fn spec: scaleTargetRef: deploymentName: transformer-fn pollingInterval: 5 minReplicaCount: 0 maxReplicaCount: 100 Box 3: Secret Store connection strings in Kubernetes Secrets. Example: to create the Secret in our demo Namespace: # create the k8s demo namespace kubectl create namespace tt # grab connection string from Azure Service Bus KEDA_SCALER_CONNECTION_STRING=$(az servicebus queue authorization-rule keys list \ -g $RG_NAME \ --namespace-name $SBN_NAME \ --queue-name inbound \ -n keda-scaler \ --query "primaryConnectionString" \ -o tsv) # create the kubernetes secret kubectl create secret generic tt-keda-auth \ --from-literal KedaScaler=$KEDA_SCALER_CONNECTION_STRING \ --namespace tt Reference: https://www.thinktecture.com/en/kubernetes/serverless-workloads-with-keda/

**Question: 10** *Multiple Answers Are Right*

HOTSPOT You are creating a CLI script that creates an Azure web app and related services in Azure App Service. The web app uses the following variables:

| Variable name | Value |
|---|---|
| $gitrepo | https://github.com/Contos/webapp |
| $webappname | Webapp1103 |

You need to automatically deploy code from GitHub to the newly created web app. How should you complete the script? To answer, select the appropriate options in the answer area. NOTE: Each correct selection is worth one point. Hot Area:

## Answer Area

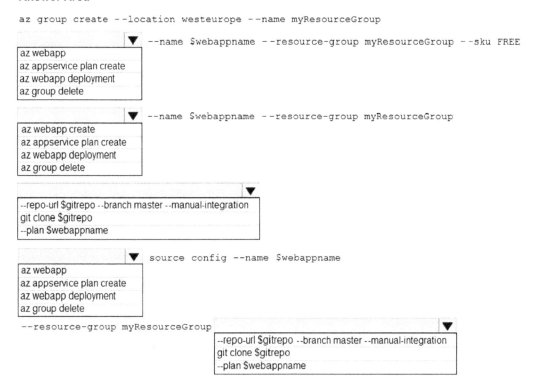

**Answers:**

A)

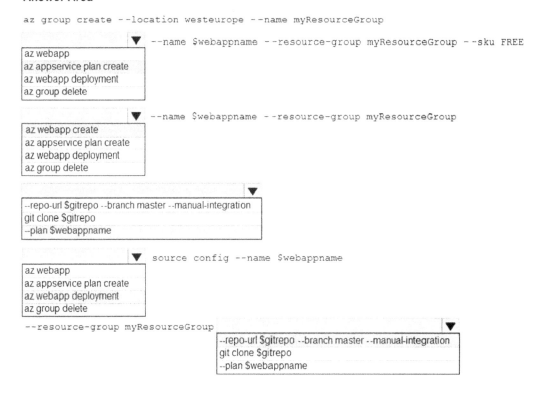

**Solution:** A

**Explanation:**

Explanation: Box 1: az appservice plan create The azure group creates command successfully returns JSON result. Now we can use resource group to create a azure app service plan Box 2: az webapp create Create a new web app.. Box 3: --plan $webappname ..with the serviceplan we created in step 1. Box 4: az webapp deployment Continuous Delivery with GitHub. Example: az webapp deployment source config --name firstsamplewebsite1 --resource-group websites-- repo-url $gitrepo --branch master --git-token $token Box 5: --repo-url $gitrepo --branch master --manual-integration Reference: https://medium.com/@satish1v/devops-your-way-to-azure-web-apps-with-azure-cli-206ed4b3e9b1

# Chapter 19: AZ-220 - Microsoft Azure IoT Developer

## Exam Guide

How to Prepare For AZ-220:Microsoft Azure IoT Developer Exam

Preparation Guide for AZ-220:Microsoft Azure IoT Developer Exam

Introduction

Microsoft has created a track for Azure professionals who are knowledgeable in Azure IoT landscape to get certified this platform. This certification program provides Microsoft Azure IoT developer professionals a way to demonstrate their skills. The assessment is based on a rigorous exam using industry standard methodology to determine whether a candidate meets Microsoft's proficiency standards.

According to Microsoft, a Microsoft AZ-220 Certified Professional enables organizations to leverage Microsoft Azure IoT developer technologies with a thorough implementation and the coding required to create and maintain the cloud and edge portion of an IoT solution. An IoT Developer is responsible for maintaining the devices throughout the life cycle.

Certification is evidence of your skills, expertise in those areas in which you like to work. There are many vendors in the market that are providing these certifications. If candidate wants to work on Microsoft Azure IoT developer and prove his knowledge, certification offered by Microsoft. This **AZ-220 Exam** Certification helps a candidate to validates his skills in Microsoft Azure IoT.

In this guide, we will cover the AZ-220:Microsoft Azure IoT Developer Certification exam, AZ-220:Microsoft Azure IoT Developer Certified professional salary and all aspects of the AZ-220:Microsoft Azure IoT Developer Certification.

Introduction to AZ-220:Microsoft Azure IoT Developer Exam:

Candidates for **AZ-220 Exam** are seeking to prove fundamental knowledge and skills of Microsoft Azure IoT developer domain. Before taking this exam, exam aspirants ought to have a solid fundamental information of the concepts shared in preparation guide as well as designs for IoT solutions implementation knowledge would give an added edge.

It is suggested that professionals accustomed to the ideas and also the technologies represented here by taking relevant training courses. Candidates are expected to have some hands-on experience with key responsibilities such as compute/containers deployment and configures device networking, manage data pipelines, including monitoring.

After passing this exam, candidates get a certificate from Microsoft that helps them to demonstrate their proficiency in Azure IoT development to their clients and employers.

Topics of AZ-220:Microsoft Azure IoT Developer Exam:

Candidates should apprehend the examination topics before they begin of preparation. because it'll extremely facilitate them in touch the core. Our **AZ-220 dumps** will include the following topics:

*1. Implement the IoT solution infrastructure (15-20%)*

Create and configure an IoT Hub

- Create an IoT Hub
- Register a device
- Configure a device twin
- Configure IoT Hub tier and scaling

  Build device messaging and communication

- Build messaging solutions by using SDKs (device and service)
- Implement device-to-cloud communication
- Implement cloud-to-device communication
- Configure file upload for devices

  Configure physical IoT devices

- Recommend an appropriate protocol based on device specifications
- Configure device networking, topology, and connectivity

  *2. Provision and manage devices (20-25%)*

Implement the Device Provisioning Service (DPS)

- Create a Device Provisioning Service
- Create a new enrollment in DPS
- Manage allocation policies by using Azure Functions

- Link an IoT Hub to the DPS

    Manage the device lifecycle

- Provision a device by using DPS
- Deprovision an autoenrollment
- Decommission (disenroll) a device

    Manage IoT devices by using IoT Hub

- Manage devices list in the IoT Hub device registry
- Modify device twin tags and properties
- Trigger an action on a set of devices by using IoT Hub Jobs and Direct Methods
- Set up Automatic Device Management of IoT devices at scale

    Build a solution by using IoT Central

- Define a device type in Azure IoT Central
- Configure rules and actions in Azure IoT Central
- Define the operator view
- Add and manage devices from IoT Central
- Monitor devices

    *3. Implement Edge (15-20%)*

Set up and deploy an IoT Edge device

- Create a device identity in IoT Hub
- Deploy a single IoT device to IoT Edge
- Create a deployment for IoT Edge devices
- Install container runtime on IoT devices
- Define and implement deployment manifest
- Update security daemon and runtime

    Develop modules

- Create and configure an Edge module
- Deploy a module to an Edge device
- Publish an IoT Edge module to an Azure Container Registry

    Configure an IoT Edge device

- Select and deploy an appropriate gateway pattern

- Implement module-to-module communication
- Implement and configure offline support

*4. Process and manage data (15-20%)*

Configure routing in Azure IoT Hub

- Implement message enrichment in IoT Hub
- Configure routing of IoT Device messages to endpoints
- Define and test routing queries
- Integrate with Event Grid

Configure stream processing

- Create ASA for data and stream processing of IoT data
- Process and filter IoT data by using Azure Functions
- Configure Stream Analytics outputs

Configure an IoT solution for Time Series Insights (TSI)

- Implement solutions to handle telemetry and time-stamped data
- Create an Azure Time Series Insights (TSI) environment
- Connect the IoT Hub and the Time Series Insights (TSI)

*5. Monitor, troubleshoot, and optimize IoT solutions (15-20%)*

Configure health monitoring

- Configure metrics in IoT Hub
- Set up diagnostics logs for Azure IoT Hub
- Query and visualize tracing by using Azure monitor

Troubleshoot device communication

- Establish maintenance communication
- Verify device telemetry is received by IoT Hub
- Validate device twin properties, tags and direct methods
- Troubleshoot device disconnects and connects

Perform end-to-end solution testing and diagnostics

- Estimate the capacity required for each service in the solution
- Conduct performance and stress testing
- Set up device D2C message tracing by using Azure Distributed Tracing

### 6. Implement security (15-20%)

Implement device authentication in the IoT Hub

- Choose an appropriate form of authentication
- Manage the X.509 certificates for a device
- Manage the symmetric keys for a device

Implement device security by using DPS

- Configure different attestation mechanisms with DPS
- Generate and manage x.509 certificates for IoT Devices
- Configure enrollment with x.509 certificates
- Generate a TPM endorsements key for a device
- Configure enrollment with symmetric keys

Implement Azure Security Center (ASC) for IoT

- Enable ASC for IoT in Azure IoT Hub
- Create security modules
- Configure custom alerts

Who should take the AZ-220:Microsoft Azure IoT Developer Exam:

The **AZ-220 Exam** certification is an internationally-recognized certification which help to have validation for those IoT developer who implement designs for solutions to including monitoring and data transformation as it relates to IoT. The IoT Developer collaborate with data engineers and other stakeholders to ensure successful business integration.

Candidates for this exam should be familiar implementation of Azure services that form an IoT solution, , including data storage options, data analysis, data processing, and platform-as-a-service options. Candidates should have extensive experience and knowledge of implementation of Edge , provision and manage data.

- Azure IoT Developer
- Fresher

How to study the AZ-220:Microsoft Azure IoT Developer Exam:

Preparation of certification exams could be covered with two resource types . The first one are the study guides, reference books and study forums that are elaborated and appropriate for building information from ground up. Apart from them video tutorials and lectures are a good option to ease the pain of through study and are relatively make the study process more interesting nonetheless these demand time and concentration from the learner. Smart candidates who wish to create a solid foundation altogether examination topics and connected technologies typically mix video lectures with study guides to reap the advantages of each but practice exams or practice exam engines is one important study tool which goes typically unnoted by most candidates. Practice exams are designed with our experts to make exam prospects test their knowledge on skills attained in course, as well as prospects become comfortable and familiar with the real exam environment. Statistics have indicated exam anxiety plays much bigger role of students failure in exam than the fear of the unknown. Certification-questions expert team recommends preparing some notes on these topics along with it don't forget to practice **AZ-220 dumps** which had been written by our expert team, each of these can assist you loads to clear this exam with excellent marks.

AZ-220:Microsoft Azure IoT Developer Certification Path:

AZ-220:Microsoft Azure IoT Developer Exam is foundation level Certification. It is strongly recommended that aspirants for this exam have good command on at least one Azure-supported language, including C#, Node, C, or Python. Anyone who is having keen interest and familiar with general Microsoft Azure IoT developer concepts and the technologies. More than 85% of IoT development role require a good foundation of Microsoft Azure IoT developer concepts.

How much AZ-220:Microsoft Azure IoT Developer Exam Cost:

The price of the Microsoft Mobility and Devices Fundamentals exam is $165 USD, for more information related to exam price please visit to Microsoft Training website as prices of Microsoft exams fees get varied country wise.

How to book the AZ-220:Microsoft Azure IoT Developer Exam:

These are following steps for registering the AZ-220:Microsoft Azure IoT Developer exam.

- Step 1: Visit to Microsoft Learning and search for AZ-220:Microsoft Azure IoT Developer.
- Step 2: Sign up/Login to Pearson VUE account
- Step 3: Select local centre based on your country, date, time and confirm with a payment method.

What is the duration, language, and format of AZ-220:Microsoft Azure IoT Developer Exam:

- Length of Examination: 50 mins
- Number of Questions: 40 to 60 questions(Since Microsoft does not publish this information, the number of exam questions may change without notice.)
- Passing Score: 700 / 1000
- Type of Questions: This test format is multiple choice.

- Language: English
- This is beta exam.

AZ-220:Microsoft Azure IoT Developer Exam Certified Professional salary:

The average salary of a AZ-220:Microsoft Azure IoT Developer Exam Certified Expert in

- United State - 120,000 USD
- India - 20,00,327 INR
- Europe - 90,547 EURO
- England - 90,532 POUND

The benefit of obtaining the AZ-220:Microsoft Azure IoT Developer Exam Certification:

- This certification will be judging your skills and knowledge on your understanding Microsoft Azure IoT developer concepts & Understanding of how to operate on Microsoft Azure IoT Developer .
- This certification credential will give you edge over other counterparts. Apart from knowledge from AZ-220:Microsoft Azure IoT Developer Exam.
- AZ-220 Certification is distinguished among competitors. AZ-220 certification can give them an edge at that time easily when candidates appear for employment interview, employers are very fascinated to note one thing that differentiates the individual from all other candidates.
- AZ-220 certification has more useful and relevant networks that help them in setting career goals for themselves. AZ-220 networks provide them with the correct career guidance than non certified generally are unable to get.
- AZ-220 certified candidates will be confident and stand different from others as their skills are more trained than non-certified professionals.
- **AZ-220 Exam** provide proven knowledge to use the tools to complete the task efficiently and cost effectively than the other non-certified professionals lack in doing so.
- AZ-220 Certification provides practical experience to candidates from all the aspects to be a proficient worker in the organization.
- AZ-220 Certifications provide opportunities to get a job easily in which they are interested in instead of wasting years and ending without getting any experience.
- AZ-220 credential delivers higher earning potential and increased promotion opportunities because it shows a good understanding of Azure IoT .

Difficulty in Writing AZ-220:Microsoft Azure IoT Developer Exam:

AZ-220:Microsoft Azure IoT Developer is a privileged achievement one could be graced with. But adverse to general notion certifying with Microsoft is not that challenging if the candidates have proper preparation material to pass the AZ-220:Microsoft Azure IoT Developer exam with good grades. Questions answers and clarifications which are designed in form of Certification-questions dumps make sure to cover entire course content. Certification-questions have a brilliant AZ-220:Microsoft Azure IoT Developer dumps with most recent and important questions and answers in PDF files. Certification-questions is sure about the exactness and legitimacy of AZ-220:Microsoft Azure IoT Developer dumps and in this manner. Candidates can easily pass the AZ-220:Microsoft Azure IoT Developer exam with genuine AZ-220:Microsoft Azure IoT Developer dumps and get MICROSOFT certification. These dumps are viewed as the best source to understand the AZ-220:Microsoft Azure IoT Developer well by simply pursuing examples questions and answers. If candidate completes practice the exam with certification **AZ-220 dumps** along with self-assessment to get the proper idea on MICROSOFT accreditation and to ace the certification exam.

For more info read reference::

microsoft learning site
Microsoft Certified: Azure IoT Developer Specialty

# Sample Practice Test for AZ-220

**Question: 1** *Multiple Answers Are Right*

HOTSPOT You create a new IoT device named device1 on iothub1. Device1 has a primary key of Uihuih76hbHb. How should you complete the device connection string? To answer, select the appropriate options in the answer area. NOTE: Each correct selection is worth one point. Hot Area:

Answer Area

HostName= [azure-devices.net / criticalep / device1 / iothub1 / tracestate] . [azure-devices.net / criticalep / device1 / iothub1 / tracestate] ;DeviceId= [azure-devices.net / criticalep / device1 / iothub1 / tracestate] ;SharedAccessKey=Uihuih76hbHb

**Answers:**

## A)

**Answer Area**

| HostName= | [iothub1 ▼] | . | [azure-devices.net ▼] | ;DeviceId= | [device1 ▼] | :SharedAccessKey=Uihuih76hbHb |

Dropdown options (each box): azure-devices.net, criticalep, device1, iothub1, tracestate

**Solution:** A

**Explanation:**

Explanation: Box 1: iothub1 The Azure IoT hub is named iothub1. Box 2: azure-devices.net The format of the device connection string looks like: HostName={YourIoTHubName}.azure-devices.net;DeviceId=MyNodeDevice;SharedAccessKey= {YourSharedAccessKey} Box 1: device1 Device1 has a primary key of Uihuih76hbHb. Reference: https://docs.microsoft.com/en-us/azure/iot-hub/quickstart-control-device-dotnet Implement the IoT solution infrastructure Question Set 2

**Question: 2** *One Answer Is Right*

Note: This question is part of a series of questions that present the same scenario. Each question in the series contains a unique solution that might meet the stated goals. Some question sets might have more than one correct solution, while others might not have a correct solution. After you answer a question in this question, you will NOT be able to return to it. As a result, these questions will not appear in the review screen. You have an Azure IoT solution that includes an Azure IoT hub, a Device Provisioning Service instance, and 1,000 connected IoT devices. All the IoT devices are provisioned automatically by using one enrollment group. You need to temporarily disable the IoT devices from the connecting to the IoT hub. Solution: From the Device Provisioning Service, you disable the enrollment group, and you disable device entries in the identity registry of the IoT hub to which the IoT devices are provisioned. Does the solution meet the goal?

**Answers:**

**A)** Yes

**B)** No

**Solution:** A

**Explanation:**

Explanation: Explanation: You may find it necessary to deprovision devices that were previously auto-provisioned through the Device Provisioning Service. In general, deprovisioning a device involves two steps: 1. Disenroll the device from your provisioning service, to prevent future auto-provisioning. Depending on whether you want to revoke access temporarily or permanently, you may want to either disable or delete an enrollment entry. 2. Deregister the device from your IoT Hub, to prevent future communications and data transfer. Again, you can temporarily disable or permanently delete the device's entry in the identity registry for the IoT Hub where it was provisioned. Reference: https://docs.microsoft.com/bs-latn-ba/azure/iot-dps/how-to-unprovision-devices

**Question: 3** *One Answer Is Right*

Note: This question is part of a series of questions that present the same scenario. Each question in the series contains a unique solution that might meet the stated goals. Some question sets might have more than one correct solution, while others might not have a correct solution. After you answer a question in this question, you will NOT be able to return to it. As a result, these questions will not appear in the review screen. You have an Azure IoT solution that includes an Azure IoT hub, a Device Provisioning Service instance, and 1,000 connected IoT devices. All the IoT devices are provisioned automatically by using one enrollment group. You need to temporarily disable the IoT devices from the connecting to the IoT hub. Solution: You delete the enrollment group from the Device Provisioning Service. Does the solution meet the goal?

**Answers:**

**A)** Yes

**B)** No

**Solution:** B

**Explanation:**

Explanation: Explanation: Instead, from the Device Provisioning Service, you disable the enrollment group, and you disable device entries in the identity registry of the IoT hub to which the IoT devices are provisioned. Reference: https://docs.microsoft.com/bs-latn-ba/azure/iot-dps/how-to-unprovision-devices

**Question: 4** *Multiple Answers Are Right*

HOTSPOT You have an Azure IoT hub. You plan to deploy 1,000 IoT devices by using automatic device management. The device twin is shown below.

```
{
  "deviceId": "ContosoHyperDriveEngine1",
  "etag": "AAAAAAAAAw=",
  "deviceEtag": "MTYyNDk20kw",
  "status": "enabled",
  "statusUpdateTime": "0001-01-01t00:00:00Z",
  "connectionTime": "Disconnected",
  "lastActivityTime": "0001-01-01T00:00:00Z",
  "cloudToDeviceMessageCount": 0,
  "authenticationType": "sas",
  "x509Thumbprint": {
    "primaryThumbprint": null,
    "secondaryThumbprint": null
  },
  "version": 13,
  "tags": {
    "engine": {
      "warpCorVersion": "1.2.65b",
      "warpDriveType": "WM105a"
    }
  },
  "properties": {
    "desired": {
      "$metadata": {
        "$lastUpdated": "2019-10-17T18:43:33.7599556Z"
      },
      "$version": 1
    },
    "reported": {
      "$metadata": {
        "$lastUpdated": "2019-10-17T18:43:33.7599556Z"
      },
      "$version": 1
    }
  }
}
```

You need to configure automatic device management for the deployment. Which target Condition and Device Twin Path should you use? To answer, select the appropriate options in the answer area. NOTE: Each correct selection is worth one point. Hot Area:

## Answer Area

**Target Condition:** ▼

- properties.desired.warpDriveType='WM105a'
- properties.reported.warpDriveType='WM105a'
- tags.engine.warpDriveType='WM105a'

**Device Twin Path:** ▼

- properties.desired.warpOperating
- properties.reported.warpOperating
- properties.warpOperating

**Answers:**

**A)**

## Answer Area

**Target Condition:** ▼

- properties.desired.warpDriveType='WM105a'
- properties.reported.warpDriveType='WM105a'
- **tags.engine.warpDriveType='WM105a'**

**Device Twin Path:** ▼

- **properties.desired.warpOperating**
- properties.reported.warpOperating
- properties.warpOperating

**Solution: A**

**Explanation:**

Explanation: Explanation: Box 1: tags.engine.warpDriveType='VM105a' Use tags to target twins. Before you create a configuration, you must specify which devices or modules you want to affect. Azure IoT Hub identifies devices and using tags in the device twin, and identifies modules using tags in the module twin. Box 2: properties.desired.warpOperating The twin path, which is the path to the JSON section within the twin desired properties that will be set. For example, you could set the twin path to properties.desired.chiller-water and then provide the following JSON content: { "temperature": 66, "pressure": 28 } Reference: https://docs.microsoft.com/en-us/azure/iot-hub/iot-hub-automatic-device-management

**Question: 5** *One Answer Is Right*

You plan to deploy a standard tier Azure IoT hub. You need to perform an over-the-air (OTA) update on devices that will connect to the IoT hub by using scheduled jobs. What should you use?

**Answers:**

**A)** a device-to-cloud message

**B)** the device twin reported properties

**C)** a cloud-to-device message

**D)** a direct method

**Solution:** D

**Explanation:**

Explanation: Explanation: Releases via the REST API. All of the operations that can be performed from the Console can also be automated using the REST API. You might do this to automate your build and release process, for example. You can build firmware using the Particle CLI or directly using the compile source code API. Note: Over-the-air (OTA) firmware updates are a vital component of any IoT system. Over-the-air firmware updates refers to the practice of remotely updating the code on an embedded device. Reference: https://docs.particle.io/tutorials/device-cloud/ota-updates/

**Question: 6** *One Answer Is Right*

You have an IoT device that gathers data in a CSV file named Sensors.csv. You deploy an Azure IoT hub that is accessible at ContosoHub.azure-devices.net. You need to ensure that Sensors.csv is uploaded to the IoT hub. Which two actions should you perform? Each correct answer presents part of the solution. NOTE: Each correct selection is worth one point.

**Answers:**

**A)** Upload Sensors.csv by using the IoT Hub REST API.

**B)** From the Azure subscription, select the IoT hub, select Message routing, and then configure a route to storage.

**C)** From the Azure subscription, select the IoT hub, select File upload, and then configure a storage container.

**D)** Configure the device to use a GET request to ContosoHub.azure-devices.net/devices/ContosoDevice1/files/notifications.

**Solution:** A, C

**Explanation:**

Explanation: Explanation: C: To use the file upload functionality in IoT Hub, you must first associate an Azure Storage account with your hub. Select File upload to display a list of file upload properties for the IoT hub that is being modified. For Storage container: Use the Azure portal to select a blob container in an Azure Storage account in your current Azure subscription to associate with your IoT Hub. If necessary, you can create an Azure Storage account on the Storage accounts blade and blob container on the Containers A: IoT Hub has an endpoint specifically for devices to request a SAS URI for storage to upload a file. To start the file upload process, the device sends a POST request to {iot hub}.azure-devices.net/devices/{deviceId}/files with the following JSON body: { "blobName": "{name of the file for which a SAS URI will be generated}" } Incorrect Answers: D: Deprecated: initialize a file upload with a GET. Use the POST method instead. Reference: https://github.com/MicrosoftDocs/azure-docs/blob/master/articles/iot-hub/iot-hub-configure-file-upload.md

**Question: 7** *One Answer Is Right*

You plan to deploy an Azure IoT hub. The IoT hub must support the following: - Three Azure IoT Edge devices - 2,500 IoT devices Each IoT device will spend a 6 KB message every five seconds. You need to size the IoT hub to support the devices. The solution must minimize costs. What should you choose?

**Answers:**

**A)** one unit of the S1 tier

**B)** one unit of the B2 tier

**C)** one unit of the B1 tier

**D)** one unit of the S3 tier

**Solution:** D

**Explanation:**

Explanation: Explanation: 2500* 6 KB * 12 = 180,000 KB/minute = 180 MB/Minute. B3, S3 can handle up to 814 MB/minute per unit. Incorrect Answers: A, C: B1, S1 can only handle up to 1111 KB/minute per unit B: B2, S2 can only handle up to 16 MB/minute per unit. Reference: https://docs.microsoft.com/en-us/azure/iot-hub/iot-hub-scaling

**Question: 8** *Multiple Answers Are Right*

DRAG DROP You deploy an Azure IoT hub. You need to demonstrate that the IoT hub can receive messages from a device. Which three actions should you perform in sequence? To answer, move the appropriate actions from the list of actions to the answer area and arrange them in the correct order. Select and Place:

**Answers:**

**A)**

**Solution:** A

**Explanation:**

Explanation: Explanation: Step 1: Register a device in IoT Hub Before you can use your IoT devices with Azure IoT Edge, you must register them with your IoT hub. Once a device is registered, you can retrieve a connection string to set up your device for IoT Edge workloads. Step 2: Configure the device connection string on a device client. When you're ready to set up your device, you need the connection string that links your physical device with its identity in the IoT hub. Step 3: Trigger a new send event from a device client. Reference: https://docs.microsoft.com/en-us/azure/iot-edge/how-to-register-device

**Question: 9** *Multiple Answers Are Right*

DRAG DROP You have an Azure IoT hub. You plan to attach three types of IoT devices as shown in the following table.

| Name | Specification | Note |
| --- | --- | --- |
| Transparent Field Gateway Device | High-power device with a fast processor and 4 GB of RAM | Will connect to multiple devices, each with its own credentials, by using the same TLS connection. |
| Low Resource Device | Low resource specifications, battery-operated, and 512 KB of RAM | Will connect directly to an IoT hub and will **NOT** connect to any other devices. Will use cloud-to-device messages. |
| Limited Sensor Device | Extremely low-power device with a limited microcontroller (MCU) and 256 KB of RAM | Will **NOT** support the Azure SDK. Messages must be as small as possible. |

You need to select the appropriate communication protocol for each device. What should you select? To answer, drag the appropriate protocols to the correct devices. Each protocol may be used once, more than once, or not at all. You may need to drag the split bar between panes or scroll to view content. NOTE: Each correct selection is worth one point. Select and Place:

## Protocols

- AMQP
- HTTPS
- MQTT

## Answer Area

| Device | Protocol |
|---|---|
| Transparent Field Gateway Device: | Protocol |
| Low Resource Device: | Protocol |
| Limited Sensor Device: | Protocol |

Answers:

A)

## Protocols

- AMQP
- HTTPS
- MQTT

## Answer Area

| Device | Protocol |
|---|---|
| Transparent Field Gateway Device: | AMQP |
| Low Resource Device: | MQTT |
| Limited Sensor Device: | HTTPS |

Solution: A

Explanation:

Explanation: Explanation: Box 1: AMQP Use AMQP on field and cloud gateways to take advantage of connection multiplexing across devices. Box 2: MQTT MQTT is used on all devices that do not require to connect multiple devices (each with its own per-device credentials) over the same TLS connection. Box 3: HTTPS Use HTTPS for devices that cannot support other protocols. Reference: https://docs.microsoft.com/en-us/azure/iot-hub/iot-hub-devguide-protocols

**Question: 10** *One Answer Is Right*

Note: This question is part of a series of questions that present the same scenario. Each question in the series contains a unique solution that might meet the stated goals. Some question sets might have more than one correct solution, while others might not have a correct solution. After you answer a question in this question, you will NOT be able to return to it. As a result, these questions will not appear in the review screen. You have an Azure IoT solution that includes an Azure IoT hub, a Device Provisioning Service instance, and 1,000 connected IoT devices. All the IoT devices are provisioned automatically by using one enrollment group. You need to temporarily disable the IoT devices from the connecting to the IoT hub. Solution: From the IoT hub, you change the credentials for the shared access policy of the IoT devices. Does the solution meet the goal?

**Answers:**

**A)** Yes

**B)** No

**Solution:** B

**Explanation:**

Explanation: Reference: https://docs.microsoft.com/bs-latn-ba/azure/iot-dps/how-to-unprovision-devices

# Chapter 20: AZ-300 - Microsoft Azure Architect Technologies

## Exam Guide

How to Prepare For AZ-300: Microsoft Azure Architect Technologies Exam

Preparation Guide for AZ-300: Microsoft Azure Architect Technologies Exam

Introduction

Microsoft has created a track for Azure Solution architects who guide stakeholders and convert business requirements into scalable, secure, and reliable solutions to get certified this platform. Developing Solutions for Microsoft Azures solution architect a way to demonstrate their skills. The assessment is based on a rigorous exam using the industry-standard methodology to determine whether a candidate meets Microsoft's proficiency standards.

This certification has been designed as a role-based Certification so the candidates who are supposed to deliver and implement Azure Cloud Solutions only those candidates should appear for these certifications.

For this exam candidate having proficiency in using PowerShell, the Command Line Interface, Azure Portal, ARM templates, operating systems, virtualization, cloud infrastructure, storage structures, and networking would be an added advantage.

Certification is evidence of your skills, expertise in those areas in which you like to work. Many vendors in the market are providing these certifications. If a candidate wants to work as an Azure architect and prove his knowledge, certification is offered by Microsoft. This **AZ-300 Exam** Certification helps a candidate to validates his skills in the Azure platform.

In this guide, we will cover the AZ-300: Microsoft Azure Architect Technologies Certification exam, AZ-300: Microsoft Azure Architect Technologies Certified professional salary, and all aspects of the AZ-300: Microsoft Azure Architect Technologies Certification.

Introduction to AZ-300: Microsoft Azure Architect Technologies Exam:

Candidates for **AZ-300 Exam** are seeking to prove fundamental knowledge and skills in the Azure Architect Technologies domain. Before taking this exam, aspirants ought to have a solid fundamental information of the concepts shared in the preparation guide as well as basic understanding of Azure administration, Azure development, and DevOps would give an added edge.

It is suggested that professionals accustomed to the ideas and also the technologies represented here by taking relevant training courses. Candidates are expected to have some hands-on experience in monitoring security, performance, and monitoring performance capacity, Implement virtual networking.

After passing this exam, candidates get a certificate from Microsoft that helps them to demonstrate their proficiency to their clients and employers.

Topics of AZ-300: Microsoft Azure Architect Technologies Exam:

Candidates should apprehend the examination topics before they begin of preparation. because it'll extremely facilitate them in touch the core. Our **AZ-300 dumps** will include the following topics:

*1. Deploy and configure infrastructure (40-45%)*

Analyze resource utilization and consumption

- configure diagnostic settings on resources
- create baseline for resources
- create and test alerts
- analyze alerts across subscription
- analyze metrics across subscription
- create action groups
- monitor for unused resources
- monitor spend
- report on spend
- utilize Log Search query functions
- view Alerts in Azure Monitor logs
- visualize diagnostics data using Azure Monitor Workbooks

  Create and configure storage accounts

- configure network access to the storage account
- create and configure storage account
- generate Shared access signature

- implement Azure AD authentication for storage
- install and use Azure Storage Explorer
- manage access keys
- monitor Activity log by using Azure Monitor logs
- implement Azure storage replication
- implement Azure storage account failover

    Create and configure a VM for Windows and Linux

- configure High Availability
- configure Monitoring
- configure Networking
- configure Storage
- configure Virtual Machine Size
- implement dedicated hosts
- deploy and configure scale sets

    Automate deployment of VMs

- modify Azure Resource Manager template
- configure Location of new VMs
- configure VHD template
- deploy from template
- save a deployment as an Azure Resource Manager template
- deploy Windows and Linux VMs

    Create connectivity between virtual networks

- create and configure Vnet peering
- create and configure Vnet to Vnet connections
- verify virtual network connectivity
- create virtual network gateway

    Implement and manage virtual networking

- configure private IP addressing
- configure public IP addresses
- create and configure network routes
- create and configure network interface
- create and configure subnets

- create and configure virtual network
- create and configure Network Security Groups and Application Security Groups

Manage Azure Active Directory

- add custom domains
- configure Azure AD Identity Protection
- configure Azure AD Join
- configure self-service password reset
- implement conditional access policies
- manage multiple directories
- perform an access review

Implement and manage hybrid identities

- install and configure Azure AD Connect
- configure federation
- configure single sign-on
- manage and troubleshoot Azure AD Connect
- troubleshoot password sync and writeback

Implement solutions that use virtual machines (VM)

- provision VMs
- create Azure Resource Manager templates
- configure Azure Disk Encryption for VMs
- implement Azure Backup for VMs

*2. Implement workloads and security (25-30%)*

Migrate servers to Azure

- migrate servers using Azure Migrate

Configure serverless computing

- create and manage objects
- manage a Logic App Resource
- manage Azure Function app settings
- manage Event Grid
- manage Service Bus

Implement application load balancing

- configure application gateway
- configure Azure Front Door service
- configure Azure Traffic Manager

   Integrate on premises network with Azure virtual network

- create and configure Azure VPN Gateway
- create and configure site to site VPN
- configure ExpressRoute
- configure Virtual WAN
- verify on premises connectivity
- troubleshoot on premises connectivity with Azure

   Implement multi factor authentication

- configure user accounts for MFA
- configure fraud alerts
- configure bypass options
- configure Trusted IPs
- configure verification methods

   Manage role-based access control

- create a custom role
- configure access to Azure resources by assigning roles
- configure management access to Azure
- troubleshoot RBAC
- implement Azure Policies
- assign RBAC Roles

   *3. Create and deploy apps (5-10%)*

Create web apps by using PaaS

- create an Azure app service Web App
- create documentation for the API
- create an App Service Web App for Containers
- create an App Service background task by using WebJobs
- enable diagnostics logging

   Design and develop apps that run in containers

- configure diagnostic settings on resources
- create a container image by using a Dockerfile
- create an Azure Kubernetes Service
- publish an image to the Azure Container Registry
- implement an application that runs on an Azure Container Instance
- manage container settings by using code

*4. Implement authentication and secure data (5-10%)*

Implement authentication

- implement authentication by using certificates, forms-based authentication, tokens, or Windows-integrated authentication
- implement multi-factor authentication by using Azure AD
- implement OAuth2 authentication
- implement Managed Identities for Azure resources Service Principal authentication Implement secure data solutions
- encrypt and decrypt data at rest and in transit
- encrypt data with Always Encrypted
- implement Azure Confidential Compute
- implement SSL/TLS communications
- create, read, update, and delete keys, secrets, and certificates by using the KeyVault API

*5. Develop for the cloud and for Azure storage (15-20%)*

Configure a message-based integration architecture

- configure an app or service to send emails
- configure Event Grid
- configure the Azure Relay service
- create and configure a Notification Hub
- create and configure an Event Hub
- create and configure a Service Bus

Develop for autoscaling

- implement autoscaling rules and patterns (schedule, operational/system metrics)
- implement code that addresses singleton application instances
- implement code that addresses transient state

Develop solutions that use Cosmos DB storage

- create, read, update, and delete data by using appropriate APIs
- implement partitioning schemes
- set the appropriate consistency level for operations

Develop solutions that use a relational database

- provision and configure relational databases
- configure elastic pools for Azure SQL Database
- implement Azure SQL Database managed instances
- create, read, update, and delete data tables by using code

Who should take the AZ-300: Microsoft Azure Architect Technologies Exam:

The AZ-300 Exam certification is an internationally-recognized certification which help to have validation for Azure Solution Architects who participate in all phases of advising stakeholders and translate business requirements into secure, scalable, and reliable solutions. Candidates should be proficient in IT operations, including networking, virtualization, identity, security, business continuity, disaster recovery, data platform, budgeting, and governance.

How to study the AZ-300: Microsoft Azure Architect Technologies Exam:

The preparation of certification exams could be covered with two resource types. The first one is the study guides, reference books, and study forums that are elaborated and appropriate for building information from the ground up. Apart from the video tutorials and lectures are a good option to ease the pain of through study and are relatively make the study process more interesting nonetheless these demand time and concentration from the learner. Smart candidates who wish to create a solid foundation altogether examination topics and connected technologies typically mix video lectures with study guides to reap the advantages of each but practice exams or practice exam engines is one important study tool that goes typically unnoted by most candidates. Practice exams are designed with our experts to make exam prospects test their knowledge on skills attained in the course, as well as prospects become comfortable and familiar with the real exam environment. Statistics have indicated exam anxiety plays a much bigger role in student's failure in the exam than the fear of the unknown. Certification-questions expert team recommends preparing some notes on these topics along with it don't forget to practice **AZ-300 dumps** which had been written by our expert team, each of these can assist you loads to clear this exam with excellent marks.

AZ-300: Microsoft Azure Architect Technologies Certification Path:

AZ-300: Microsoft Azure Architect Technologies Exam is expert level Certification. Aspirants must have expert-level skills in Azure administration and have experience with Azure development processes and DevOps processes.

How much AZ-300: Microsoft Azure Architect Technologies Exam Cost:

The price of the AZ-300: Microsoft Azure Architect Technologies Exam is 165 USD, for more information related to exam price please visit to Microsoft Training website as prices of Microsoft exams fees get varied country wise.

How to book the AZ-300: Microsoft Azure Architect Technologies Exam:

These are the following steps for registering the AZ-300: Microsoft Azure Architect Technologies exam:

- Step 1: Visit to Microsoft Learning and search for AZ-300: Developing Solutions for Microsoft Azure.
- Step 2: Sign up/Login to Pearson VUE account.
- Step 3: Select local centre based on your country, date, time, and confirm with a payment method.

What is the duration, language, and format of AZ-300: Microsoft Azure Architect Technologies Exam:

- Length of Examination: 240 mins
- Number of Questions: 40 to 60 questions(Since Microsoft does not publish this information, the number of exam questions may change without notice.)
- Passing score: 700 / 1000
- Type of Questions: This test format is multiple choice.
- Language: English
- This Exam got expired now and the new AZ-303: Microsoft Azure Architect Technologies Exam has been published now

AZ-300: Microsoft Azure Architect Technologies Exam Certified Professional salary:

The average salary of an AZ-300: Microsoft Azure Architect Technologies Exam Certified Expert in

- United State - 120,000 USD
- India - 20,00,327 INR
- Europe - 90,547 EURO
- England - 90,532 POUND

The benefit of obtaining the AZ-300: Microsoft Azure Architect Technologies Exam Certification:

- This certification will be judging your skills and knowledge on your understanding of Azure Architect Technologies concepts & Understanding of how to operate on Planning and Administering Azure Architect Technologies.

- This certification credential will give you an edge over other counterparts. Apart from knowledge from AZ-300: Microsoft Azure Architect Technologies Exam.

- AZ-300 Certified professionals are distinguished among competitors when appearing for employment or promotion interviews.

- AZ-300 certification has more useful and relevant networks that help them in setting career goals for themselves. AZ-300 networks provide them with the correct career guidance than non certified generally are unable to get.

- **AZ-300 Exam** provide proven knowledge to use the tools to complete the task efficiently and cost-effectively than the other non-certified professionals lack in doing so.

- AZ-300 Certification provides practical experience to candidates from all the aspects to be a proficient worker in the organization.

- AZ-300 credential delivers higher earning opportunity and increases promotion opportunities because it shows a good understanding of Azure Architect Technologies

Difficulty in Writing AZ-300: Microsoft Azure Architect Technologies Exam:

AZ-300: Microsoft Azure Architect Technologies is a privileged achievement one could be graced with. But adverse to the general notion certifying with Microsoft is not that challenging if the candidates have proper preparation material to pass the AZ-300: Microsoft Azure Architect Technologies exam with good grades. Questions answers and clarifications which are designed in form of Certification-questions dumps make sure to cover the entire course content. Certification-questions have a brilliant AZ-300: Microsoft Azure Architect Technologies dumps with most recent and important questions and answers in PDF files. Certification-questions is sure about the exactness and legitimacy of AZ-300: Microsoft Azure Architect Technologies dumps and in this manner. Candidates can easily pass the AZ-300: Microsoft Azure Architect Technologies exam with genuine AZ-300: Microsoft Azure Architect Technologies dumps and get MICROSOFT certification. These dumps are viewed as the best source to understand the AZ-300: Microsoft Azure Architect Technologies well by simply pursuing examples questions and answers. If the candidate completes practice the exam with certification **AZ-300 dumps** along with self-assessment to get the proper idea on MICROSOFT accreditation and to ace the certification exam.

For more info read reference::

microsoft learning site
AZ-300 Skills measured

# Sample Practice Test for AZ-300

**Question: 1** *Multiple Answers Are Right*

HOTSPOT You have an Azure subscription named Subscription1. Subscription1 contains the resources in the following table:

| Name | Type |
|------|------|
| RG1 | Resource group |
| RG2 | Resource group |
| VNet1 | Virtual network |
| VNet2 | Virtual network |

VNet1 is in RG1. VNet2 is in RG2. There is no connectivity between VNet1 and VNet2. An administrator named Admin1 creates an Azure virtual machine VM1 in RG1. VM1 uses a disk named Disk1 and connects to VNet1. Admin1 then installs a custom application in VM1. You need to move the custom application to VNet2. The solution must minimize administrative effort. Which two actions should you perform? To answer, select the appropriate options in the answer area. NOTE: Each correct selection is worth one point. Hot Area:

## Answer Area

First action: [dropdown]
- Create a network interface in RG2.
- Detach a network interface.
- Delete VM1.
- Move a network interface to RG2.

Second action: [dropdown]
- Attach a network interface.
- Create a network interface in RG2.
- Create a new virtual machine.
- Move VM1 to RG2.

Answers:

A)

## Answer Area

First action:
- Create a network interface in RG2.
- Detach a network interface.
- **Delete VM1.**
- Move a network interface to RG2.

Second action:
- Attach a network interface.
- Create a network interface in RG2.
- **Create a new virtual machine.**
- Move VM1 to RG2.

**Solution: A**

**Explanation:**

Explanation: We cannot just move a virtual machine between networks. What we need to do is identify the disk used by the VM, delete the VM itself while retaining the disk, and recreate the VM in the target virtual network and then attach the original disk to it. Reference: https://blogs.technet.microsoft.com/canitpro/2014/06/16/step-by-step-move-a-vm-to-a-different-vnet-on- azure/ https://4sysops.com/archives/move-an-azure-vm-to-another-virtual-network-vnet/#migrate-an-azure-vm- between-vnets

**Question: 2** *One Answer Is Right*

You have two subscriptions named Subscription1 and Subscription2. Each subscription is associated to a different Azure AD tenant. Subscription1 contains a virtual network named VNet1. VNet1 contains an Azure virtual machine named VM1 and has an IP address space of 10.0.0.0/16. Subscription2 contains a virtual network named VNet2. Vnet2 contains an Azure virtual machine named VM2 and has an IP address space of 10.10.0.0/24. You need to connect VNet1 to VNet2. What should you do first?

**Answers:**

**A)** Modify the IP address space of VNet2.

**B)** Move VM1 to Subscription2.

**C)** Provision virtual network gateways.

**D)** Move VNet1 to Subscription2.

**Solution:** C

**Explanation:**

Explanation: We require a virtual network gateway for VNet-to-VNet connectivity. Incorrect Answers: A: There is no need to modify the address space. If you update the address space for one VNet, the other VNet automatically knows to route to the updated address space. Reference: https://docs.microsoft.com/en-us/azure/vpn-gateway/vpn-gateway-howto-vnet-vnet-cli

**Question: 3** *One Answer Is Right*

You have an Azure Active Directory (Azure AD) tenant. You have an existing Azure AD conditional access policy named Policy1. Policy1 enforces the use of Azure AD-joined devices when members of the Global Administrators group authenticate to Azure AD from untrusted locations. You need to ensure that members of the Global Administrators group will also be forced to use multi-factor authentication when authenticating from untrusted locations. What should you do?

**Answers:**

**A)** From the Azure portal, modify session control of Policy1.

**B)** From multi-factor authentication page, modify the user settings.

**C)** From multi-factor authentication page, modify the service settings.

**D)** From the Azure portal, modify grant control of Policy1.

**Solution:** D

**Explanation:**

Explanation: We need to modify the grant control of Policy1. The grant control can trigger enforcement of one or more controls. - Require multi-factor authentication (Azure Multi-Factor

Authentication) - Require device to be marked as compliant (Intune) - Require Hybrid Azure AD joined device - Require approved client app - Require app protection policy Note: It is now possible to explicitly apply the Require MFA for admins rule. Reference: https://docs.microsoft.com/en-us/azure/active-directory/conditional-access/untrusted-networks https://docs.microsoft.com/en-us/azure/active-directory/conditional-access/concept-baseline-protection

**Question: 4** *Multiple Answers Are Right*

HOTSPOT You plan to deploy five virtual machines to a virtual network subnet. Each virtual machine will have a public IP address and a private IP address. Each virtual machine requires the same inbound and outbound security rules. What is the minimum number of network interfaces and network security groups that you require? To answer, select the appropriate options in the answer area. NOTE: Each correct selection is worth one point. Hot Area:

Answer Area

Minimum number of network interfaces:
- 5
- 10
- 15
- 20

Minimum number of network security groups:
- 1
- 2
- 5
- 10

Answers:

A)

### Answer Area

Minimum number of network interfaces: [ 5 / 10 / 15 / 20 ]

Minimum number of network security groups: [ 1 / 2 / 5 / 10 ]

**Solution:** A

**Explanation:**

Explanation: Box 1: 5 We have five virtual machines. Each virtual machine will have a public IP address and a private IP address. Each will require a network interface. Box 2: 1 Each virtual machine requires the same inbound and outbound security rules. We can add tem to one group. Reference: https://blogs.msdn.microsoft.com/igorpag/2016/05/14/azure-network-security-groups-nsg-best-practices- and-lessons-learned/ https://docs.microsoft.com/en-us/azure/virtual-network/security-overview

**Question: 5** *One Answer Is Right*

You have an Azure subscription named Subscription1 that contains an Azure virtual machine named VM1. VM1 is in a resource group named RG1. VM1 runs services that will be used to deploy resources to RG1. You need to ensure that a service running on VM1 can manage the resources in RG1 by using the identity of VM1. What should you do first?

**Answers:**

**A)** From the Azure portal, modify the Access control (IAM) settings of RG1.

**B)** From the Azure portal, modify the Policies settings of RG1.

**C)** From the Azure portal, modify the Access control (IAM) settings of VM1.

**D)** From the Azure portal, modify the value of the Managed Service Identity option for VM1.

**Solution:** D

**Explanation:**

Explanation: Through a create process, Azure creates an identity in the Azure AD tenant that's trusted by the subscription in use. After the identity is created, the identity can be assigned to one or more Azure service instances. Reference: https://docs.microsoft.com/en-us/azure/app-service/overview-managed-identity https://docs.microsoft.com/en-us/azure/active-directory/managed-identities-azure-resources/overview

**Question: 6** *Multiple Answers Are Right*

HOTSPOT You have an Azure subscription named Subscription1. Subscription1 contains the virtual networks in the following table:

| Name | Address space | Subnet name | Subnet address range |
|---|---|---|---|
| VNet1 | 10.1.0.0/16 | Subnet1 | 10.1.1.0/24 |
| VNet2 | 10.10.0.0/16 | Subnet2 | 10.10.1.0/24 |
| VNet3 | 172.16.0.0/16 | Subnet3 | 172.16.1.0/24 |

Subscription1 contains the virtual machines in the following table:

| Name | Network | Subnet | IP address |
|---|---|---|---|
| VM1 | VNet1 | Subnet1 | 10.1.1.4 |
| VM2 | VNet2 | Subnet2 | 10.10.1.4 |
| VM3 | VNet3 | Subnet3 | 172.16.1.4 |

The firewalls on all the virtual machines are configured to allow all ICMP traffic. You add the peerings in the following table:

| Virtual network | Peering network |
|---|---|
| VNet1 | VNet3 |
| VNet2 | VNet3 |
| VNet3 | VNet1 |

For each of the following statements, select Yes if the statement is true. Otherwise, select No.
NOTE: Each correct selection is worth one point. Hot Area:

## Answer Area

| Statements | Yes | No |
|---|---|---|
| VM1 can ping VM3. | ○ | ○ |
| VM2 can ping VM3. | ○ | ○ |
| VM2 can ping VM1. | ○ | ○ |

**Answers:**

A)

## Answer Area

| Statements | Yes | No |
|---|---|---|
| VM1 can ping VM3. | ● | ○ |
| VM2 can ping VM3. | ● | ○ |
| VM2 can ping VM1. | ○ | ● |

**Solution:** A

**Explanation:**

Explanation: VM1 on VNet1 can ping VM3 on VNet3 as VNet1 and VNet3 are peered. VM2 onVNet2 can ping VM3 on VNet3 as VNet2 and VNet3 are peered. VM2 cannot ping VM1 as there is not peering between VNet2 and VNet1. Reference: https://docs.microsoft.com/en-us/azure/virtual-network/tutorial-connect-virtual-networks-portal

**Question: 7** *One Answer Is Right*

You configure Azure AD Connect for Azure Active Directory Seamless Single Sign-On (Azure AD Seamless SSO) for an on-premises network. Users report that when they attempt to access myapps.microsoft.com, they are prompted multiple times to sign in and are forced to use an account name that ends with onmicrosoft.com. You discover that there is a UPN mismatch between Azure AD and the on-premises Active Directory. You need to ensure that the users can use single-sign on (SSO) to access Azure resources. What should you do first?

**Answers:**

A) From on-premises network, deploy Active Directory Federation Services (AD FS).

B) From Azure AD, add and verify a custom domain name.

C) From on-premises network, request a new certificate that contains the Active Directory domain name.

**D)** From the server that runs Azure AD Connect, modify the filtering options.

**Solution:** B

**Explanation:**

Explanation: The UPN is used by Azure AD to allow users to sign-in. The UPN that a user can use, depends on whether or not the domain has been verified. If the domain has been verified, then a user with that suffix will be allowed to sign-in to Azure AD. To do so, you need to add and verify a custom domain in Azure AD before you can start syncing the users. Reference: https://docs.microsoft.com/en-us/azure/active-directory/hybrid/plan-connect-design-concepts#azure-ad- sign-in https://docs.microsoft.com/en-us/azure/active-directory/hybrid/tshoot-connect-objectsync#detect-upn- mismatch-if-object-is-synced-to-azure-active-directory

**Question: 8** *One Answer Is Right*

You have an Active Directory forest named contoso.com. You install and configure Azure AD Connect to use password hash synchronization as the single sign-on (SSO) method. Staging mode is enabled. You review the synchronization results and discover that the Synchronization Service Manager does not display any sync jobs. You need to ensure that the synchronization completes successfully. What should you do?

**Answers:**

**A)** From Azure PowerShell, run Start-AdSyncSyncCycle –PolicyType Initial.

**B)** Run Azure AD Connect and set the SSO method to Pass-through Authentication.

**C)** From Synchronization Service Manager, run a full import.

**D)** Run Azure AD Connect and disable staging mode.

**Solution:** D

**Explanation:**

Explanation: In staging mode, the server is active for import and synchronization, but it does not run any exports. A server in staging mode is not running password sync or password writeback, even if you selected these features during installation. When you disable staging mode, the server starts exporting, enables password sync, and enables password writeback. Reference: https://docs.microsoft.com/en-us/azure/active-directory/hybrid/how-to-connect-sync-staging-server https://docs.microsoft.com/en-us/azure/active-directory/hybrid/how-to-connect-sync-operations

**Question: 9** *Multiple Answers Are Right*

HOTSPOT You have an Azure Active Directory (Azure AD) tenant. You need to create a conditional access policy that requires all users to use multi-factor authentication when they access the Azure portal. Which three settings should you configure? To answer, select the appropriate settings in the answer area. NOTE: Each correct selection is worth one point. Hot Area:

## Answer Area

*Name

[ Policy1                    v ]

### Assignments

---

Users and groups 🛈
0 users and groups selected          >

---

Cloud apps 🛈
0 cloud apps selected                >

---

Conditions 🛈
0 conditions selected                >

---

### Access controls

---

Grant 🛈
0 controls selected                  >

---

Session 🛈
0 controls selected                  >

---

Enable Policy

**Answers:**

A)

## Answer Area

**\*Name**

| Policy1 | ∨ |

**Assignments**

---

**Users and groups** 🛈
0 users and groups selected  >

---

**Cloud apps** 🛈
0 cloud apps selected  >

---

**Conditions** 🛈
0 conditions selected  >

---

**Access controls**

---

**Grant** 🛈
0 controls selected  >

---

**Session** 🛈
0 controls selected  >

---

**Enable Policy**

**Solution:** A

**Explanation:**

Explanation: References: https://docs.microsoft.com/en-us/azure/active-directory/conditional-access/app-based-mfa

**Question: 10** *One Answer Is Right*

You plan to automate the deployment of a virtual machine scale set that uses the Windows Server 2016 Datacenter image. You need to ensure that when the scale set virtual machines are provisioned, they have web server components installed. Which two actions should you perform? Each correct answer presents part of the solution. NOTE: Each correct selection is worth one point.

**Answers:**

**A)** Upload a configuration script.

**B)** Create an automation account.

**C)** Create a new virtual machine scale set in the Azure portal.

**D)** Create an Azure policy.

**E)** Modify the extensionProfile section of the Azure Resource Manager template.

**Solution:** C, E

**Explanation:**

Explanation: References: https://docs.microsoft.com/en-us/azure/virtual-machine-scale-sets/tutorial-install-apps-template

# Chapter 21: AZ-301 - Microsoft Azure Architect Design

## Exam Guide

Microsoft Azure Architect Design Exam with code name AZ-301:

Microsoft has introduced new Role Based Certification i.e.. Microsoft Azure Architect Design Exam with code name AZ-301, it is advance level version of the exam AZ-300 i.e.. Microsoft Azure Architect Technologies.

Actually both AZ-300 and AZ-301 been derived from 70-535 Exam (Architecting Microsoft Azure Solutions).

Few of the new topic and content been introduced into **AZ-301 Exam**.
This Microsoft Azure Architect Design (AZ-301) Exam is validating Candidates knowledge and experience to work as Azure Solution Arhcitect who can manage cloud services that span storage, security, networking, and compute cloud capabilities.

Candidates who are opting for an **AZ-301 exam preparation** must have a deep perception of how each service works on an IT infrastructure.

And he/she should take requests and give recommendations for infrastructure services for using them based on various measures like scale, performance, size, provision, and so on. They make recommendations on services to use for optimal performance and scale, as well as provision, size, monitor, and adjust resources as appropriate.
This certification been actually designed as a Role based Certification so the candidates who are suppose to deliver and implement Azure Cloud Solutions only those candidates should appear for this certifications.

For this exam candidate having proficiency in using PowerShell, the Command Line Interface, Azure Portal, ARM templates, operating systems, virtualization, cloud infrastructure, storage structures and networking would be an added advantage.

if you are the one who having strong eagerness to learn about cloud services willing to provide solution to Customer in terms of Azure Cloud that span security, storage, compute and networking capabilities within Microsoft Azure, this exam been designed for you The AZ-301 Exam requires you to hold a certain skill set that can make you aware of the full IT lifecycle and Enterprise Level Architect. Same is the case with Azure AZ-300 exam which can be considered as base level of AZ-301. While AZ-300 exam preparation consists more of Azure Architect Technologies whereas the AZ-301 deals with Microsoft Azure Architect Design.

if you want to become Certified Azure solution Architect, you need to pass both of these exams (AZ-300 And AZ-301) Microsoft is not having doubt on your skillset just they want to update their Certification track so they came up with Microsoft Azure Architect Design AZ-301 for those passionate candidates who had already shown their expertise by clearing AZ-300 i.e.. Azure Architect Technologies Exam.

This is the list of the contents in our Microsoft Azure Architect Design AZ-301 Practice Test:

- Design an Auditing and Monitoring Strategy.
- Optimizing Consumption Strategy.
- Design Azure Governance.
- Design Data Management Strategy, Flow, Protection.
- Design Identity Management.
- Monitoring Strategy for the Data Platform.
- Design a disaster recovery strategy for individual workloads.
- Design Infrastructure Strategy include storage, compute, Networking.
- Design Migration Strategy.
- Design an API Integration Strategy.
- Design for Risk Prevention for Identity.

Microsoft Azure Architect Design AZ-301 Dumps will include below mentioned topics with Exam focused percentage:

- Determine Workload Requirements 10-15%
- Design for Identity and Security 20-25%
- Design a Data Platform Solution 15-20%
- Design a Business Continuity Strategy 15-20%
- Design for Deployment, Migration, and Integration 10-15%
- Design an Infrastructure Strategy 15-20%

Microsoft Azure Architect Design AZ-301 Dumps Provided Study Notes:

Certification-questions.com expert team recommend you to prepare some notes on these topics along with it don't forget to practice Microsoft Azure Architect Design AZ-301 Dumps which been written by our expert team.

Both these will help you a lot to clear this exam with good marks.

- Virtual Machine (Compute)
- ARM template
- Hybrid identity solution
- Storage Account
- Azure AD
- API/Logic App/Webapp/Functionsapp
- Backup recovery or scaling
- Azure Container Registry
- Azure Virtual Networking
- Azure Governance
- Azure Scaffold
- Azure IOT
- Azure Cognitive Solutions
- Azure Artificial Intelligence
- Azure monitoring
- Azure OMS

Overview about MICROSOFT AZ-301 Exam:

- Format: Multiple choice, multiple answer
- Length of Examination: 150 minutes
- Number of Questions: 40 - 60
- Passing Score: 70-80%
- Registration Fee: 165 USD

Steps for MICROSOFT AZ-301 Certifications Exam booking:

- Visit to website To Book your Exam
- Signup/Login to MICROSOFT account
- Search for MICROSOFT AZ-301 Certifications Exam
- Select Date and Center of examination and confirm with payment value of 165$

Benefits of having MICROSOFT AZ-301 Certifications:

Getting a certification like AZ-301 can enhance the value of a job aspirant as a qualified Azure administrator.
It'd really attract HR to have a look to your CV and definitely it will help you out to have good salaried job in your hand by the end of the day.

In such a situation, the relevance of a quality AZ-301 Microsoft Azure Architect Design EXAM study material is extremely important.

And so we bring best-in-industry Azure Exam AZ-301 online course and **AZ-301 practice tests** for you to help in your exam preparation.

Difficulty in writing MICROSOFT AZ-301 Exam:

**MICROSOFT AZ-301 Exam** i.e. is Expert/Architect level exam in Azure Cloud Technology. Going through this exam is really need enormous effort and dedication.

Most important thing about this exam is that it is one of the newly introduced exam by the Microsoft so it would be little bit tough to get proper study material for it. Having thorough understanding of Azure Architect concepts along with our provided **MICROSOFT AZ-301 dumps** will definitely help you out to clear Microsoft AZ-301 Exam with very good grace. For more info visit:

MICROSOFT AZ-301 Exam Reference, and Microsoft Documents

# Sample Practice Test for AZ-301

**Question: 1** *One Answer Is Right*

You need to recommend a solution for the collection of security logs for the middle tier of the payment processing system. What should you include in the recommendation?

**Answers:**

**A)** Azure Event Hubs

**B)** Azure Notification Hubs

**C)** the Azure Diagnostics agent

**D)** the Microsoft Monitoring agent

**Solution:** C

**Explanation:**

Explanation: Explanation: Scenario: Collect Windows security logs from all the middle-tier servers and retain the logs for a period of seven years. The Azure Diagnostics agent should be used when you want to archive logs and metrics to Azure storage. Reference: https://docs.microsoft.com/en-us/azure/azure-monitor/platform/agents-overview Determine Workload Requirements Question Set 2

**Question: 2** *Multiple Answers Are Right*

HOTSPOT You deploy several Azure SQL Database instances. You plan to configure the Diagnostics settings on the databases as shown in the following exhibit.

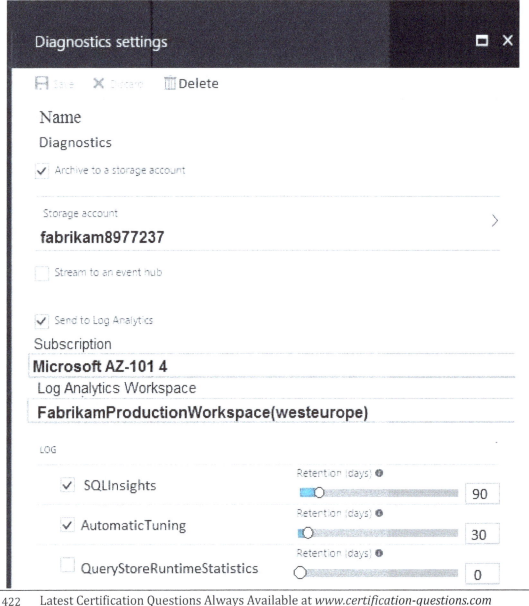

Use the drop-down menus to select the answer choice that completes each statement based on the information presented in the graphic. NOTE: Each correct selection is worth one point. Hot Area:

## Answer Area

The amount of time that SQLInsights data will be stored in blob storage is **[answer choice]**.

- 30 days
- 90 days
- 730 days
- indefinite

The maximum amount of time that SQLInsights data can be stored in Azure Log Analytics is **[answer choice]**.

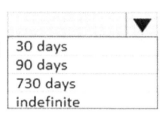

- 30 days
- 90 days
- 730 days
- indefinite

Answers:

A)

## Answer Area

The amount of time that SQLInsights data will be stored in blob storage is **[answer choice]**.

- 30 days
- 90 days
- 730 days
- **indefinite**

The maximum amount of time that SQLInsights data can be stored in Azure Log Analytics is **[answer choice]**.

- 30 days
- 90 days
- **730 days**
- indefinite

**Solution: A**

**Explanation:**

Explanation: In the exhibit, the SQLInsights data is configured to be stored in Azure Log Analytics for 90 days. However, the question is asking for the "maximum" amount of time that the data can be stored which is 730 days.

**Question: 3** *One Answer Is Right*

You have an on-premises Hyper-V cluster. The cluster contains Hyper-V hosts that run Windows Server 2016 Datacenter. The hosts are licensed under a Microsoft Enterprise Agreement that has Software Assurance. The Hyper-V cluster contains 30 virtual machines that run Windows Server 2012 R2. Each virtual machine runs a different workload. The workloads have predictable consumption patterns. You plan to replace the virtual machines with Azure virtual machines that run Windows Server 2016. The virtual machines will be sized according to the consumption pattern of each workload. You need to recommend a solution to minimize the compute costs of the Azure virtual machines. Which two recommendations should you include in the solution? Each correct answer presents part of the solution. NOTE: Each correct selection is worth one point.

**Answers:**

**A)** Purchase Azure Reserved Virtual Machine Instances for the Azure virtual machines

**B)** Create a virtual machine scale set that uses autoscaling

**C)** Configure a spending limit in the Azure account center

**D)** Create a lab in Azure DevTest Labs and place the Azure virtual machines in the lab

**E)** Activate Azure Hybrid Benefit for the Azure virtual machines

**Solution:** A, E

**Explanation:**

Explanation: Explanation: A: With Azure Reserved VM Instances (RIs) you reserve virtual machines in advance and save up to 80 percent. E: For customers with Software Assurance, Azure Hybrid Benefit for Windows Server allows you to use your on-premises Windows Server licenses and run Windows virtual machines on Azure at a reduced cost. You can use Azure Hybrid Benefit for Windows Server to deploy new virtual machines with Windows OS. Reference: https://azure.microsoft.com/en-us/pricing/reserved-vm-instances/ https://docs.microsoft.com/en-us/azure/virtual-machines/windows/hybrid-use-benefit-licensing

**Question: 4** *One Answer Is Right*

You need to recommend a solution to generate a monthly report of all the new Azure Resource Manager resource deployments in your subscription. What should you include in the recommendation?

**Answers:**

**A)** Application Insights

**B)** Azure Activity Log

**C)** Azure Monitor action groups

**D)** Azure Monitor metrics

**Solution:** B

**Explanation:**

Explanation: Explanation: Activity logs are kept for 90 days. You can query for any range of dates, as long as the starting date isn't more than 90 days in the past. Through activity logs, you can determine: - what operations were taken on the resources in your subscription - who started the operation - when the operation occurred - the status of the operation - the values of other properties that might help you research the operation Reference: https://docs.microsoft.com/en-us/azure/azure-resource-manager/management/view-activity-logs

### Question: 5 *One Answer Is Right*

Your company uses Microsoft System Center Service Manager on its on-premises network. You plan to deploy several services to Azure. You need to recommend a solution to push Azure service health alerts to Service Manager. What should you include in the recommendation?

**Answers:**

**A)** Azure Notification Hubs

**B)** Azure Event Hubs

**C)** IT Service Management Connector (ITSM)

**D)** Application Insights Connector

**Solution:** C

**Explanation:**

Explanation: Reference: https://docs.microsoft.com/en-us/azure/azure-monitor/platform/itsmc-overview

### Question: 6 *One Answer Is Right*

You have an on-premises Active Directory forest and an Azure Active Directory (Azure AD) tenant. All Azure AD users are assigned an Azure AD Premium P1 license. You deploy Azure AD Connect. Which two features are available in this environment that can reduce operational overhead for your company's help desk? Each correct answer presents part of the solution. NOTE: Each correct selection is worth one point.

**Answers:**

**A)** Azure AD Privileged Identity Management policies

**B)** access reviews

**C)** self-service password reset

**D)** Microsoft Cloud App Security Conditional Access App Control

**E)** password writeback

**Solution:** C, E

**Question: 7** *One Answer Is Right*

You are planning the implementation of an order processing web service that will contain microservices hosted in an Azure Service Fabric cluster. You need to recommend a solution to provide developers with the ability to proactively identify and fix performance issues. The developers must be able to simulate user connections to the order processing web service from the Internet, as well as simulate user transactions. The developers must be notified if the goals for the transaction response times are not met. What should you include in the recommendation?

**Answers:**

**A)** container health

**B)** Azure Network Watcher

**C)** Application Insights

**D)** Service Fabric Analytics

**Solution:** C

**Question: 8** *Multiple Answers Are Right*

DRAG DROP You have an Azure Active Directory (Azure AD) tenant. All user accounts are synchronized from an on- premises Active Directory domain and are configured for federated authentication. Active Directory Federation Services (AD FS) servers are published for external connections by using a farm of Web Application Proxy servers. You need to recommend a solution to monitor the servers that integrate with Azure AD. The solution must meet the following requirements: - Identify any AD FS issues and their potential resolutions. - Identify any directory synchronization configuration issues and their potential resolutions - Notify administrators when there are any issues affecting directory synchronization or AD FS operations. Which monitoring solution should you recommend for each server type? To answer, drag the appropriate monitoring solutions to the correct server types. Each monitoring solution may be used once, more than once, or not at all. You may need to drag the split bar between panes or scroll to view content. NOTE: Each correct selection is worth one point. Select and Place:

**Monitoring Solutions**

- A Microsoft Office 365 management solution in Azure Monitor
- Active Directory Replication Status Tool
- An Active Directory Health Check solution in Azure Monitor
- An Active Directory Replication Status solution in Azure Monitor
- Azure AD Connect Health
- Azure Security Center

**Answer Area**

| Monitoring Solution | |
|---|---|
| AD FS servers: | |
| Azure AD Connect servers: | |
| Web Application Proxy servers: | |

Answers:

A)

**Monitoring Solutions**

- A Microsoft Office 365 management solution in Azure Monitor
- Active Directory Replication Status Tool
- An Active Directory Health Check solution in Azure Monitor
- An Active Directory Replication Status solution in Azure Monitor
- Azure AD Connect Health
- Azure Security Center

**Answer Area**

| | Monitoring Solution |
|---|---|
| AD FS servers: | Azure AD Connect Health |
| Azure AD Connect servers: | Azure AD Connect Health |
| Web Application Proxy servers: | Azure AD Connect Health |

**Solution:** A

**Explanation:**

Explanation:

**Question: 9** *One Answer Is Right*

You plan to deploy 200 Microsoft SQL Server databases to Azure by using Azure SQL Database and Azure SQL Database Managed Instance. You need to recommend a monitoring solution that provides a consistent monitoring approach for all deployments. The solution must meet the following requirements: - Support current-state analysis based on metrics collected near real-time, multiple times per minute, and maintained for up to one hour - Support longer term analysis based on metrics collected multiple times per hour and maintained for up to two weeks. - Support monitoring of the number of concurrent logins and concurrent sessions. What should you include in the recommendation?

**Answers:**

**A)** dynamic management views

**B)** trace flags

**C)** Azure Monitor

**D)** SQL Server Profiler

**Solution:** C

**Question: 10** *One Answer Is Right*

Please wait while the virtual machine loads. Once loaded, you may proceed to the lab section. This may take a few minutes, and the wait time will not be deducted from your overall test time. When the Next button is available, click it to access the lad section. In this section, you will perform a set of tasks in a live environment. While most functionality will be available to you as it would be in a live environment, some functionality (e.g., copy and paste, ability to navigate to external websites) will not be possible by design. Scoring is based on the outcome of performing the tasks stated in the lab. In other words, it doesn't matter how you accomplish the task, if you successfully perform it, you will earn credit for that task. Labs are not timed separately, and this exam may have more than one lab that you must complete. You can use as much time as you would like to complete each lab. But, you should manage your time appropriately to ensure that you are able to complete the lab(s) and all other sections of the exam in the time provided. Please note that once you submit your work by clicking the Next button within a lab, you will NOT be able to return to the lab. You may now click next to proceed to the lab.

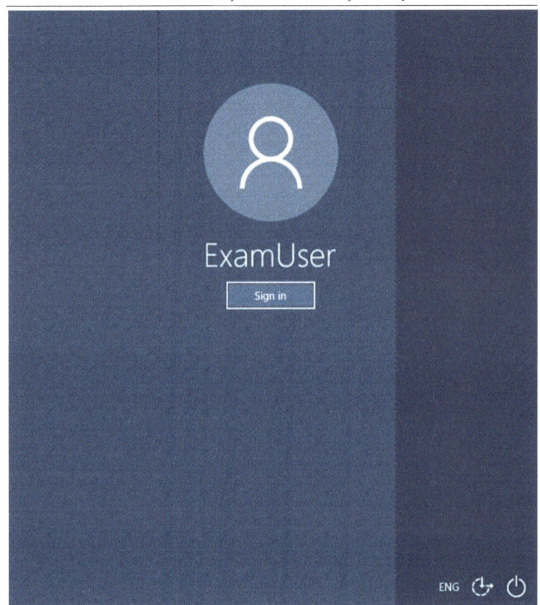

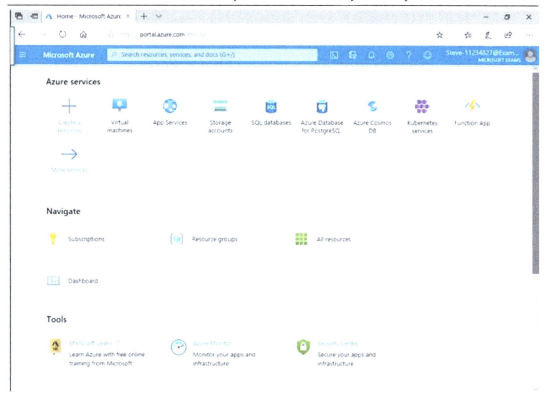

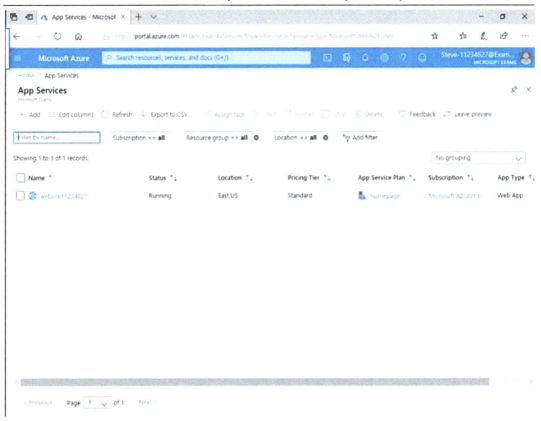

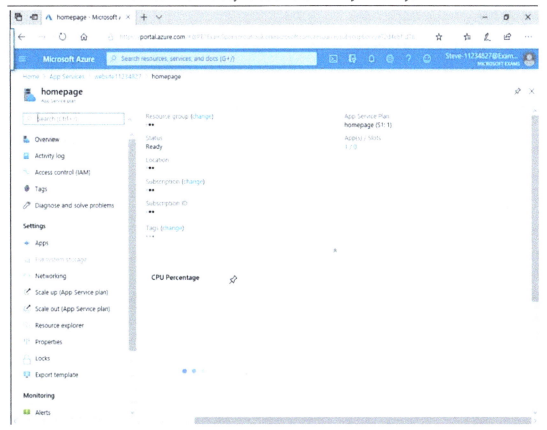

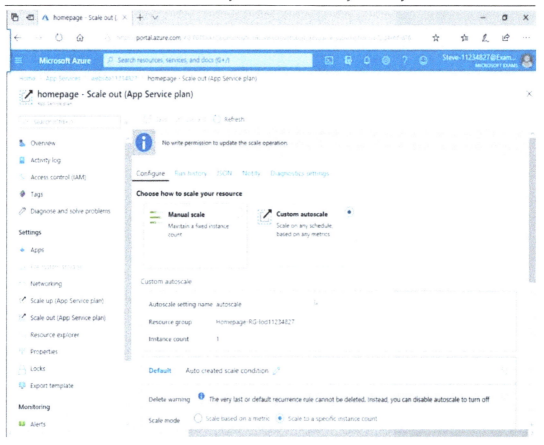

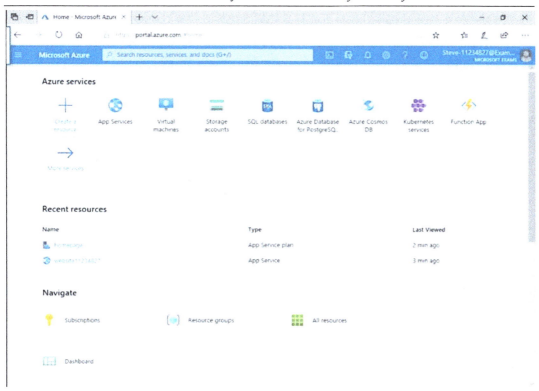

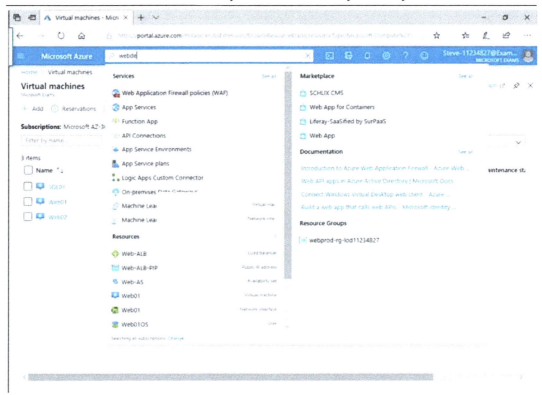

Web01 is used only for testing purposes. You need to reduce the costs to host Web01. What should you modify? NOTE: To answer this question, sign in to the Azure portal and explore the Azure resource groups.

Answers:

A) the disk type of Web01

B) the networking properties of Web01

C) the storage type of the storage account

D) the properties of the storage account

Solution: C

Explanation:

Explanation: Explanation: The storage type can be changed to Block blobs to save money. Reference: https://azure.microsoft.com/en-us/pricing/details/storage/

# Chapter 22: AZ-303 - Microsoft Azure Architect Technologies (beta)

## Exam Guide

How to Prepare For AZ-303: Microsoft Azure Architect Technologies Exam

Preparation Guide for AZ-303: Microsoft Azure Architect Technologies Exam

Introduction

Microsoft has created a track for Azure Solution architects who guide stakeholders and convert business requirements into scalable, secure, and reliable solutions to get certified this platform. Developing Solutions for Microsoft Azures solution architect a way to demonstrate their skills. The assessment is based on a rigorous exam using industry standard methodology to determine whether a candidate meets Microsoft's proficiency standards.

This certification been actually designed as a role based Certification so the candidates who are suppose to deliver and implement Azure Cloud Solutions only those candidates should appear for this certifications.

For this exam candidate having proficiency in using PowerShell, the Command Line Interface, Azure Portal, ARM templates, operating systems, virtualization, cloud infrastructure, storage structures and networking would be an added advantage.

Certification is evidence of your skills, expertise in those areas in which you like to work. There are many vendors in the market that are providing these certifications. If candidate wants to work as Azure architect and prove his knowledge, certification offered by Microsoft. This **AZ-303 Exam** Certification helps a candidate to validates his skills in Azure platform.

In this guide, we will cover the AZ-303: Microsoft Azure Architect Technologies Certification exam, AZ-303: Microsoft Azure Architect Technologies Certified professional salary and all aspects of the AZ-303: Microsoft Azure Architect Technologies Certification.

Introduction to AZ-303: Microsoft Azure Architect Technologies Exam:

Candidates for **AZ-303 Exam** are seeking to prove fundamental knowledge and skills in Azure Architect Technologies domain. Before taking this exam, aspirants ought to have a solid fundamental information of the concepts shared in preparation guide as well as basic understanding of Azure administration, Azure development, and DevOpss would give an added edge.

It is suggested that professionals accustomed to the ideas and also the technologies represented here by taking relevant training courses. Candidates are expected to have some hands-on experience on monitoring security , performance and monitoring performance capacity, Implement virtual networking.

After passing this exam, candidates get a certificate from Microsoft that helps them to demonstrate their proficiency to their clients and employers.

Topics of AZ-303: Microsoft Azure Architect Technologies Exam:

Candidates should apprehend the examination topics before they begin of preparation. because it'll extremely facilitate them in touch the core. Our **AZ-303 dumps** will include the following topics:

*1. Implement and Monitor an Azure Infrastructure (50-55%)*

Implement cloud infrastructure monitoring

- Monitor security
- Monitor performance
- Monitor health and availability
- Monitor cost
- Configure advanced logging
- Configure logging for workloads
- Configure and manage advanced alerts

   Implement storage accounts

- Select storage account options based on a use case
- Configure Azure Files and blob storage
- Configure network access to the storage account
- Implement Shared Access Signatures and access policies
- Implement Azure AD authentication for storage
- Manage access keys
- Implement Azure storage replication
- Implement Azure storage account failover

Implement VMs for Windows and Linux

- Configure High Availability
- Configure storage for VMs
- Select virtual machine size
- Implement Azure Dedicated Hosts
- Deploy and configure scale sets
- Configure Azure Disk Encryption

Automate deployment and configuration of resources

- Save a deployment as an Azure Resource Manager template
- Modify Azure Resource Manager template
- Evaluate location of new resources
- Configure a virtual disk template
- Deploy from a template
- Manage a template library
- Create and execute an automation runbook

Implement virtual networking

- Implement VNet to VNet connections
- Implement VNet peering

Implement Azure Active Directory

- Add custom domains
- Configure Azure AD Identity Protection
- Implement self-service password reset
- Implement Conditional Access including MFA
- Configure user accounts for MFA
- Configure fraud alerts
- Configure bypass options
- Configure Trusted IPs
- Configure verification methods
- Implement and manage guest accounts
- Manage multiple directories

Implement and manage hybrid identities

- Install and configure Azure AD Connect

- Identity synchronization options
- Configure and manage password sync and password writeback
- Configure single sign-on
- Use Azure AD Connect Health

*2. Implement Management and Security Solutions (25-30%)*

Manage workloads in Azure

- Migrate workloads using Azure Migrate
- Implement Azure Backup for VMs
- Implement disaster recovery
- Implement Azure Update Management

Implement load balancing and network security

- Implement Azure Load Balancer
- Implement an application gateway
- Implement a Web Application Firewall
- Implement Azure Firewall
- Implement the Azure Front Door Service
- Implement Azure Traffic Manager
- Implement Network Security Groups and Application Security Groups
- Implement Bastion

Implement and manage Azure governance solutions

- Create and manage hierarchical structure that contains management groups,
- Assign RBAC roles
- Create a custom RBAC role
- Configure access to Azure resources by assigning roles
- Configure management access to Azure
- Interpret effective permissions
- Set up and perform an access review
- Implement and configure an Azure Policy
- Implement and configure an Azure Blueprint

Manage security for applications

- Implement and configure KeyVault
- Implement and configure Azure AD Managed Identities

- Register and manage applications in Azure AD

    *3. Implement Solutions for Apps (10-15%)*

Implement an application infrastructure

- Create and configure Azure App Service
- Create an App Service Web App for Containers
- Create and configure an App Service plan
- Configure an App Service
- Configure networking for an App Service
- Create and manage deployment slots
- Implement Logic Apps
- Implement Azure Functions

    Implement container-based applications

- Create a container image
- Configure Azure Kubernetes Service
- Publish and automate image deployment to the Azure Container Registry
- Publish a solution on an Azure Container Instance

    *4. Implement and Manage Data Platforms (10-15%)*

Implement NoSQL databases

- Configure storage account tables
- Select appropriate CosmosDB APIs
- Set up replicas in CosmosDB

    Implement Azure SQL databases

- Configure Azure SQL database settings
- Implement Azure SQL Database managed instances
- Configure HA for an Azure SQL database
- Publish an Azure SQL database

    Who should take the AZ-303: Microsoft Azure Architect Technologies Exam:

The **AZ-303 Exam** certification is an internationally-recognized certification which help to have validation for Azure Solution Architects who participate in all phases of advising stakeholders and translate business requirements into secure, scalable, and reliable solutions. Candidates should be proficient in IT operations, including networking, virtualization, identity, security, business continuity, disaster recovery, data platform, budgeting, and governance.

How to study the AZ-303: Microsoft Azure Architect Technologies Exam:

Preparation of certification exams could be covered with two resource types. The first one are the study guides, reference books and study forums that are elaborated and appropriate for building information from ground up. Apart from them video tutorials and lectures are a good option to ease the pain of through study and are relatively make the study process more interesting nonetheless these demand time and concentration from the learner. Smart candidates who wish to create a solid foundation altogether examination topics and connected technologies typically mix video lectures with study guides to reap the advantages of each but practice exams or practice exam engines is one important study tool which goes typically unnoted by most candidates. Practice exams are designed with our experts to make exam prospects test their knowledge on skills attained in course, as well as prospects become comfortable and familiar with the real exam environment. Statistics have indicated exam anxiety plays much bigger role of students failure in exam than the fear of the unknown. Certification-questions expert team recommends preparing some notes on these topics along with it don't forget to practice **AZ-303 dumps** which had been written by our expert team, each of these can assist you loads to clear this exam with excellent marks.

AZ-303: Microsoft Azure Architect Technologies Certification Path:

AZ-303: Microsoft Azure Architect Technologies Exam is expert level Certification. Aspirants must have expert-level skills in Azure administration and have experience with Azure development processes and DevOps processes.

How much AZ-303: Microsoft Azure Architect Technologies Exam Cost:

The price of the Microsoft Mobility and Devices Fundamentals exam is $99 USD, for more information related to exam price please visit to Microsoft Training website as prices of Microsoft exams fees get varied country wise.

How to book the AZ-303: Microsoft Azure Architect Technologies Exam:

These are following steps for registering the AZ-303: Microsoft Azure Architect Technologies exam.

- Step 1: Visit to Microsoft Learning and search for AZ-303: Developing Solutions for Microsoft Azure.
- Step 2: Sign up/Login to Pearson VUE account
- Step 3: Select local centre based on your country, date, time and confirm with a payment method.

What is the duration, language, and format of AZ-303: Microsoft Azure Architect Technologies Exam:

- Length of Examination: 50 mins
- Number of Questions: 40 to 60 questions(Since Microsoft does not publish this information, the number of exam questions may change without notice.)
- Passing Score: 700 / 1000
- Type of Questions: This test format is multiple choice.
- Language: English
- This is beta exam, would be available on 28 April 2020

AZ-303: Microsoft Azure Architect Technologies Exam Certified Professional salary:

The average salary of a AZ-303: Microsoft Azure Architect Technologies Exam Certified Expert in

- United State - 120,000 USD
- India - 20,00,327 INR
- Europe - 90,547 EURO
- England - 90,532 POUND

The benefit of obtaining the AZ-303: Microsoft Azure Architect Technologies Exam Certification:

- This certification will be judging your skills and knowledge on your understanding Azure Architect Technologies concepts & Understanding of how to operate on Planning and Administering Azure Architect Technologies .
- This certification credential will give you edge over other counterparts. Apart from knowledge from AZ-303: Microsoft Azure Architect Technologies Exam.
- AZ-303 Certification is distinguished among competitors. AZ-303 certification can give them an edge at that time easily when candidates appear for employment interview, employers are very fascinated to note one thing that differentiates the individual from all other candidates.
- AZ-303 certification has more useful and relevant networks that help them in setting career goals for themselves. AZ-303 networks provide them with the correct career guidance than non certified generally are unable to get.
- AZ-303 certified candidates will be confident and stand different from others as their skills are more trained than non-certified professionals.
- **AZ-303 Exam** provide proven knowledge to use the tools to complete the task efficiently and cost effectively than the other non-certified professionals lack in doing so.

- AZ-303 Certification provides practical experience to candidates from all the aspects to be a proficient worker in the organization.
- AZ-303 Certifications provide opportunities to get a job easily in which they are interested in instead of wasting years and ending without getting any experience.
- AZ-303 credential delivers higher earning potential and increased promotion opportunities because it shows a good understanding of Azure Architect Technologies

Difficulty in Writing AZ-303: Microsoft Azure Architect Technologies Exam:

AZ-303: Microsoft Azure Architect Technologies is a privileged achievement one could be graced with. But adverse to general notion certifying with Microsoft is not that challenging if the candidates have proper preparation material to pass the AZ-303: Microsoft Azure Architect Technologies exam with good grades. Questions answers and clarifications which are designed in form of Certification-questions dumps make sure to cover entire course content. Certification-questions have a brilliant AZ-303: Microsoft Azure Architect Technologies dumps with most recent and important questions and answers in PDF files. Certification-questions is sure about the exactness and legitimacy of AZ-303: Microsoft Azure Architect Technologies dumps and in this manner. Candidates can easily pass the AZ-303: Microsoft Azure Architect Technologies exam with genuine AZ-303: Microsoft Azure Architect Technologies dumps and get MICROSOFT certification. These dumps are viewed as the best source to understand the AZ-303: Microsoft Azure Architect Technologies well by simply pursuing examples questions and answers. If candidate completes practice the exam with certification **AZ-303 dumps** along with self-assessment to get the proper idea on MICROSOFT accreditation and to ace the certification exam.

For more info read reference::

microsoft learning site
AZ-303 Skills measured

# Sample Practice Test for AZ-303

**Question: 1** *Multiple Answers Are Right*

HOTSPOT You plan to create an Azure Storage account in the Azure region of East US 2. You need to create a storage account that meets the following requirements: - Replicates synchronously - Remains available if a single data center in the region fails How should you configure the storage account? To answer, select the appropriate options in the answer area. NOTE: Each correct selection is worth one point. Hot Area:

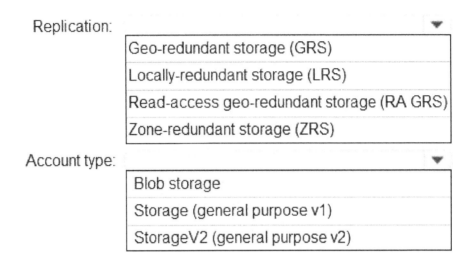

**Answers:**

A)

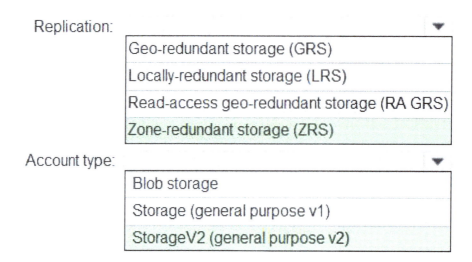

**Solution:** A

**Explanation:**

Explanation: Box 1: Zone-redundant storage (ZRS) Zone-redundant storage (ZRS) replicates your data synchronously across three storage clusters in a single region. LRS would not remain available if a data center in the region fails GRS and RA GRS use asynchronous replication. Box 2: StorageV2 (general purpose V2) ZRS only support GPv2. Reference: https://docs.microsoft.com/en-us/azure/storage/common/storage-redundancy
https://docs.microsoft.com/en-us/azure/storage/common/storage-redundancy-zrs

**Question: 2** *Multiple Answers Are Right*

HOTSPOT You plan to deploy an Azure virtual machine named VM1 by using an Azure Resource Manager template. You need to complete the template. What should you include in the template? To answer, select the appropriate options in the answer area. NOTE: Each correct selection is worth one point. Hot Area:

## Answer Area

```
{
    "type": "Microsoft.Compute/vitualMachines",
    "apiVersion": "2018-10-01",
    "name": "VM1",
    "location": "[parameters('location')]",
    "dependsOn": [
        "[resourceId('Microsoft.Storage/storageAccounts/',   variables('Name3'))]",
        "[resourceId( [_____▼]  variables('Name4'))]"
                      'Microsoft.Network/publicIPAddresses/'
                      'Microsoft.Network/virtualNetworks/'
                      'Microsoft.Network/networkInterfaces/'
                      'Microsoft.Network/virtualNetworks/subnets'
                      'Microsoft.Storage/storageAccounts/'
    ],

{
    "type": "Microsoft.Network/networkInterfaces",
    "apiVersion": "2018-11-01",
    "name": "NIC1",
    "location": "[parameters('location')]",
    "dependsOn": [
        "[resourceId('Microsoft.Network/publicIPAddresses/', variables('Name1'))]",
        "[resourceId( [_____▼]  variables('Name2'))]"
                      'Microsoft.Network/publicIPAddresses/'
                      'Microsoft.Network/virtualNetworks/'
                      'Microsoft.Network/networkInterfaces/'
                      'Microsoft.Network/virtualNetworks/subnets'
                      'Microsoft.Storage/storageAccounts/'
    ],
```

Answers:

## A)
### Answer Area

```
{
    "type": "Microsoft.Compute/vitualMachines",
    "apiVersion": "2018-10-01",
    "name": "VM1",
    "location": "[parameters('location')]",
    "dependsOn": [
        "[resourceId('Microsoft.Storage/storageAccounts/',   variables('Name3'))]",
        "[resourceId(                                     ▼  variables('Name4'))]"
                    'Microsoft.Network/publicIPAddresses/'
                    'Microsoft.Network/virtualNetworks/'
                    'Microsoft.Network/networkInterfaces/'
                    'Microsoft.Network/virtualNetworks/subnets'
                    'Microsoft.Storage/storageAccounts/'
    ],
{
    "type": "Microsoft.Network/networkInterfaces",
    "apiVersion": "2018-11-01",
    "name": "NIC1",
    "location": "[parameters('location')]",
    "dependsOn": [
        "[resourceId('Microsoft.Network/publicIPAddresses/', variables('Name1'))]",
        "[resourceId(                                     ▼  variables('Name2'))]"
                    'Microsoft.Network/publicIPAddresses/'
                    'Microsoft.Network/virtualNetworks/'
                    'Microsoft.Network/networkInterfaces/'
                    'Microsoft.Network/virtualNetworks/subnets'
                    'Microsoft.Storage/storageAccounts/'
    ],
```

**Solution:** A

**Explanation:**

Explanation: Within your template, the dependsOn element enables you to define one resource as a dependent on one or more resources. Its value can be a comma-separated list of resource names. Box 1: 'Microsoft.Network/networkInterfaces' This resource is a virtual machine. It depends on two other resources: Microsoft.Storage/storageAccounts
Microsoft.Network/networkInterfaces Box 2: 'Microsoft.Network/virtualNetworks/' The dependsOn element enables you to define one resource as a dependent on one or more resources. The resource depends on two other resources:
Microsoft.Network/publicIPAddresses Microsoft.Network/virtualNetworks

```
"resources": [
  {
  },
  {
  },
  {
  },
  {
    "type": "Microsoft.Network/networkInterfaces",
    "name": "[variables('nicName')]",
    "location": "[parameters('location')]",
    "apiVersion": "2018-08-01",
    "dependsOn": [
      "[resourceId('Microsoft.Network/publicIPAddresses/', variables('publicIPAddressName'))]",
      "[resourceId('Microsoft.Network/virtualNetworks/', variables('virtualNetworkName'))]"
    ],
    "properties": {
      "ipConfigurations": [
        {
          "name": "ipconfig1",
          "properties": {
            "privateIPAllocationMethod": "Dynamic",
            "publicIPAddress": {
              "id": "[resourceId('Microsoft.Network/publicIPAddresses',variables('publicIPAddressName'))]"
            },
            "subnet": {
              "id": "[variables('subnetRef')]"
            }
          }
        }
      ]
    }
  }
]
```

Reference: https://docs.microsoft.com/en-us/azure/azure-resource-manager/resource-manager-tutorial-create-templates-with-dependent-resources

**Question: 3** *Multiple Answers Are Right*

HOTSPOT Your network contains an Active Directory domain named adatum.com and an Azure Active Directory (Azure AD) tenant named adatum.onmicrosoft.com. Adatum.com contains the user accounts in the following table.

| Name  | Member of                      |
|-------|--------------------------------|
| User1 | Domain Admins                  |
| User2 | Schema Admins                  |
| User3 | Incoming Forest Trust Builders |
| User4 | Replicator                     |
| User5 | Enterprise Admins              |

Adatum.onmicrosoft.com contains the user accounts in the following table.

| Name | Role |
|---|---|
| UserA | Global administrator |
| UserB | User administrator |
| UserC | Security administrator |
| UserD | Service administrator |

You need to implement Azure AD Connect. The solution must follow the principle of least privilege. Which user accounts should you use in Adatum.com and Adatum.onmicrosoft.com to implement Azure AD Connect? To answer select the appropriate options in the answer area. NOTE: Each correct selection is worth one point. Hot Area:

**Answer Area**

Adatum.com:
- User1
- User2
- User3
- User4
- User5

Adatum.onmicrosoft.com:
- UserA
- UserB
- UserC
- UserD

Answers:

A)

## Answer Area

Adatum.com: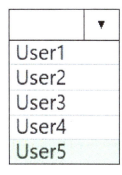

- User1
- User2
- User3
- User4
- User5

Adatum.onmicrosoft.com: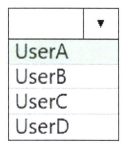

- UserA
- UserB
- UserC
- UserD

**Solution:** A

**Explanation:**

Explanation: Box 1: User5 In Express settings, the installation wizard asks for the following: AD DS Enterprise Administrator credentials Azure AD Global Administrator credentials The AD DS Enterprise Admin account is used to configure your on-premises Active Directory. These credentials are only used during the installation and are not used after the installation has completed. The Enterprise Admin, not the Domain Admin should make sure the permissions in Active Directory can be set in all domains. Box 2: UserA Azure AD Global Admin credentials are only used during the installation and are not used after the installation has completed. It is used to create the Azure AD Connector account used for synchronizing changes to Azure AD. The account also enables sync as a feature in Azure AD. Reference: https://docs.microsoft.com/en-us/azure/active-directory/connect/active-directory-aadconnect-accounts- permissions

**Question: 4** *One Answer Is Right*

You have an Azure subscription that contains 100 virtual machines. You have a set of Pester tests in PowerShell that validate the virtual machine environment. You need to run the tests whenever there is an operating system update on the virtual machines. The solution must minimize implementation time and recurring costs. Which three resources should you use to implement the tests? Each correct answer presents part of the solution. NOTE: Each correct selection is worth one point.

**Answers:**

**A)** Azure Automation runbook

**B)** an alert rule

**C)** an Azure Monitor query

**D)** a virtual machine that has network access to the 100 virtual machines

**E)** an alert action group

**Solution:** A, B, E

**Explanation:**

Explanation: AE: You can call Azure Automation runbooks by using action groups or by using classic alerts to automate tasks based on alerts. B: Alerts are one of the key features of Azure Monitor. They allow us to alert on actions within an Azure subscription Reference: https://docs.microsoft.com/en-us/azure/automation/automation-create-alert-triggered-runbook https://techsnips.io/snips/how-to-create-and-test-azure-monitor-alerts/?page=13

**Question: 5** *Multiple Answers Are Right*

HOTSPOT You have an Azure subscription that contains multiple resource groups. You create an availability set as shown in the following exhibit.

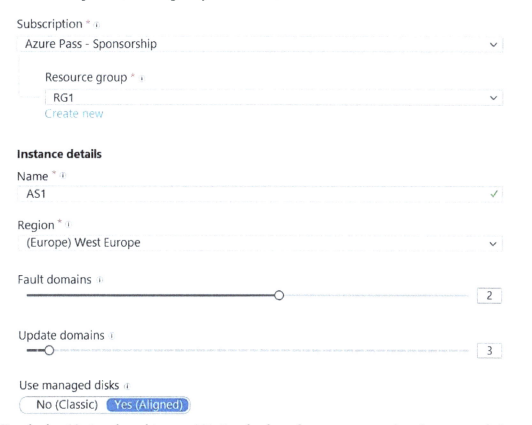

You deploy 10 virtual machines to AS1. Use the drop-down menus to select the answer choice that completes each statement based on the information presented in the graphic. NOTE: Each correct selection is worth one point. Hot Area:

## Answer Area

During planned maintenance, at least **[answer choice]** virtual machines will be available.

| |
|---|
| 4 |
| 5 |
| 6 |
| 8 |

To add another virtual machine to AS1, the virtual machine must be added to **[answer choice]**.

| |
|---|
| any region and the RG1 resource group |
| the West Europe region and any resource group |
| the West Europe region and the RG1 resource group |

Answers:

## A)
## Answer Area

During planned maintenance, at least **[answer choice]** virtual machines will be available.

| |
|---|
| 4 |
| 5 |
| 6 |
| 8 |

To add another virtual machine to AS1, the virtual machine must be added to **[answer choice]**.

| |
|---|
| any region and the RG1 resource group |
| the West Europe region and any resource group |
| **the West Europe region and the RG1 resource group** |

**Solution:** A

**Explanation:**

Explanation: Box 1: 6 Two out of three update domains would be available, each with at least 3 VMs. An update domain is a group of VMs and underlying physical hardware that can be rebooted at the same time. As you create VMs within an availability set, the Azure platform automatically distributes your VMs across these update domains. This approach ensures that at least one instance of your application always remains running as the Azure platform undergoes periodic maintenance. Box 2: the West Europe region and the RG1 resource group Reference: https://docs.microsoft.com/en-us/azure/virtual-machines/windows/regions

**Question: 6** *One Answer Is Right*

You have an Azure subscription that contains an Azure Log Analytics workspace. You have a resource group that contains 100 virtual machines. The virtual machines run Linux. You need to collect events from the virtual machines to the Log Analytics workspace. Which type of data source should you configure in the workspace?

**Answers:**

**A)** Syslog

**B)** Linux performance counters

**C)** custom fields

**Solution:** A

**Explanation:**

Explanation: Explanation: Syslog is an event logging protocol that is common to Linux. Applications will send messages that may be stored on the local machine or delivered to a Syslog collector. When the Log Analytics agent for Linux is installed, it configures the local Syslog daemon to forward messages to the agent. The agent then sends the message to Azure Monitor where a corresponding record is created. Reference: https://docs.microsoft.com/en-us/azure/azure-monitor/platform/data-sources-custom-logs

**Question: 7** *One Answer Is Right*

You have a virtual network named VNet1 as shown in the exhibit. (Click the Exhibit tab.)

**Resource group** (change)
Production

**Address space**
10.2.0.0/16

**Location**
West US

**DNS servers**
Azure provided DNS service

**Subscription** (change)
Production subscription

**Subscription ID**
14d26092-8e42-4ea7-b770-9dcef70fb1ea

**Tags** (change)
Click here to add tags

## Connected devices

Search connected devices

| DEVICE | TYPE | IP ADDRESS | SUBNET |
|---|---|---|---|

No results.

No devices are connected to VNet1. You plan to peer VNet1 to another virtual network named VNet2. VNet2 has an address space of 10.2.0.0/16. You need to create the peering. What should you do first?

**Answers:**

A) Configure a service endpoint on VNet2.

B) Add a gateway subnet to VNet1.

C) Create a subnet on VNEt1 and VNet2.

D) Modify the address space of VNet1.

**Solution:** D

**Explanation:**

Explanation: The virtual networks you peer must have non-overlapping IP address spaces. The exhibit indicates that VNet1 has an address space of 10.2.0.0/16, which is the same as VNet2, and thus overlaps. We need to change the address space for VNet1. Reference: https://docs.microsoft.com/en-us/azure/virtual-network/virtual-network-manage-peering#requirements-and- constraints

**Question: 8** *Multiple Answers Are Right*

HOTSPOT You have an Azure subscription that contains the resource groups shown in the following table.

| Name | Location |
|------|----------|
| RG1  | West US  |
| RG2  | East US  |

You create an Azure Resource Manager template named Template1 as shown in the following exhibit.

```
{
    "$schema": "http://schema.management.azure.com/schemas/2015-01-01/deploymentTemplate.json#",
    "contentVersion": "1.0.0.0",
    "parameters": {
        "name": {
            "type": "String"
        },
        "location": {
            "defaultValue": "westus",
            "type": "String"
        }
    },
    "variables": {
        "location": "[resourceGroup().location]"
    },
    "resources": [
        {
            "type": "Microsoft.Network/publicIPAddresses",
            "apiVersion": "2019-11-01",
            "name": "[parameters('name')]",
            "location": "[variables('location')]",
            "sku": {
                "name": "Basic"
            },
            "properties": {
                "publicIPAddressVersion": "IPv4",
                "publicIPAllocationMethod": "Dynamic",
                "idleTimeoutInMinutes": 4,
                "ipTags": []
            }
        }
    ]
}
```

From the Azure portal, you deploy Template1 four times by using the settings shown in the following table.

| Resource group | Name | Location |
| --- | --- | --- |
| RG1 | IP1 | westus |
| RG1 | IP2 | westus |
| RG2 | IP1 | westus |
| RG2 | IP3 | westus |

What is the result of the deployment? To answer, select the appropriate options in the answer area. NOTE: Each correct selection is worth one point. Hot Area:

## Answer Area

Number of public IP addresses in West US: [dropdown]
- 1
- 2
- 3
- 4

Total number of public IP addresses created: [dropdown]
- 1
- 2
- 3
- 4

Answers:

A)

## Answer Area

Number of public IP addresses in West US: [dropdown]
- 1
- **2** (selected)
- 3
- 4

Total number of public IP addresses created: [dropdown]
- 1
- 2
- 3
- **4** (selected)

Solution: A

Explanation:

Explanation:

**Question: 9** *Multiple Answers Are Right*

HOTSPOT You have an Azure Resource Manager template named Template1 in the library as shown in the following exhibit.

## ARM Template
template 1

```
1   {
2       "$schema": "https://schema.management.azure.com/schemas/2015-01-01/deploymentTemplate.json#",
3       "contentVersion": "1.0.0.0",
4       "parameters": {},
5       "resources": [
6           {
7               "apiVersion": "2016-01-01",
8               "type": "Microsoft.Storage/storageAccounts",
9               "name": "[concat(copyIndex(),'storage',uniqueString(resourceGroup().id))]",
10              "location": "[resourceGroup().location]",
11              "sku": {
12                  "name": "Premium_LRS"
13              },
14              "kind": "Storage",
15              "properties": {},
16              "copy": {
17                  "name": "storagecopy",
18                  "count": 3,
19                  "mode": "Serial",
20                  "batchSize": 1
21              }
22          }
23
24      ]
25  }
26
```

Use the drop-down menus to select the answer choice that completes each statement based on the information presented in the graphic. NOTE: Each correct selection is worth one point. Hot Area:

## Answer Area

During the deployment of Template1, you can specify **[answer choice]**.
- the number of resources to deploy
- the name of the resources to deploy
- the resource group to which to deploy the resources
- the permissions for the resources that will be deployed

Template1 deploys **[answer choice]**.
- a single storage account in one resource group
- three storage accounts in one resource group
- three resource groups that each has one storage account
- three resource groups that each has three storage accounts

**Answers:**

### A)
**Answer Area**

During the deployment of Template1, you can specify **[answer choice]**.
- the number of resources to deploy
- the name of the resources to deploy
- **the resource group to which to deploy the resources** *(selected)*
- the permissions for the resources that will be deployed

Template1 deploys **[answer choice]**.
- a single storage account in one resource group
- **three storage accounts in one resource group** *(selected)*
- three resource groups that each has one storage account
- three resource groups that each has three storage accounts

**Solution:** A

**Explanation:**

Explanation: Reference: https://docs.microsoft.com/en-us/azure/azure-resource-manager/templates/template-syntax

**Question: 10** *Multiple Answers Are Right*

HOTSPOT You are developing an Azure Web App. You configure TLS mutual authentication for the web app. You need to validate the client certificate in the web app. To answer, select the appropriate options in the answer area. NOTE: Each correct selection is worth one point. Hot Area:

## Answer Area

| Property | Value |
|---|---|
| Client certificate location | ▼ <br> HTTP request header <br> Client cookie <br> HTTP message body <br> URL query string |
| Encoding type | ▼ <br> HTML <br> URL <br> Unicode <br> Base64 |

Answers:

A)

## Answer Area

| Property | Value |
|---|---|
| Client certificate location | ▼ <br> **HTTP request header** <br> Client cookie <br> HTTP message body <br> URL query string |
| Encoding type | ▼ <br> HTML <br> URL <br> Unicode <br> **Base64** |

Solution: A

**Explanation:**

Explanation:

# Chapter 23: AZ-400 - Microsoft Azure DevOps Solutions

## Exam Guide

Microsoft Azure AZ-400 - Microsoft Azure DevOps Solutions Exam:

Microsoft Azure DevOps Solutions AZ-400 Exam is a newly introduced role based exam which tests and validates a candidate's expertise as a DevOps Professional around the use of Microsoft Azure technologies for designing and implementing DevOps practices. This exam is a part of the required exams needed to earn the larger Microsoft Certified
Azure DevOps Engineer Expert certification. Exam candidates are expected to be proficient with Agile practices, and must be familiar with both Azure Administration and Azure Development, and should be experts in one of these areas.
They must be able to design and implement DevOps practices for version control, compliance, infrastructure as code (IaC), configuration management, build, release, and testing by using Microsoft Azure technologies.

This Microsoft AZ-400 Exam is a professional exam aiming at candidates who want to make progress in IT area. So, it is desirable to have effective to handle the test.
For this exam candidate having proficiency in using Power Shell, the Command Line Interface, Azure Portal, ARM templates, operating systems, virtualization, cloud infrastructure, storage structures and networking would be an added advantage.
Learners should be familiar with designing and building cloud solutions using CI/CD Tools like Ansible, Azure DevOps, Terraform, Github etc.

This New Certification track introduced by Microsoft i.e.. Microsoft Azure DevOps Solutions Exam is for those passionate DevOps Engineers

We think our Microsoft Azure DevOps Solutions **AZ-400 Exam Practice Test Paper and Dumps** will provide you 100% confidence to make you appear for MICROSOFT AZ-400 Exam. This is the list of the contents in our **Microsoft Azure DevOps Solutions AZ-400 Practice Test**:

- Designing DevOps strategy
- Secure development process

- Design a strategy for integrating monitoring
- Integrate external source control
- Manage target UI test
- Continuous Integration & Delivery
- Implement applications configurations

Microsoft Azure DevOps Solutions AZ-400 Dumps:

Microsoft Azure DevOps Solutions AZ-400 Dumps will include below mentioned topics with Exam focused percentage

Design a DevOps Strategy 20-25%
Implement DevOps Development Processes 20-25%
Implement Continuous Integration 10-15%
Implement Continuous Delivery 10-15%
Implement Dependency Management 5-10%
Implement Application Infrastructure 15-20%
Implement Continuous Feedback 10-15%

Microsoft Azure DevOps Solutions AZ-400 Dumps Provided Study Notes:

Certification-questions.com expert team recommend you to prepare some notes on these topics along with it don't forget to practice **Microsoft Azure DevOps Solutions AZ-400 Dumps** which been written by our expert team
Both these will help you a lot to clear this exam with good marks.

- Multi-agent builds
- Integrate secrets
- Azure Kubernetes Service
- Code technologies
- Terraform
- Azure DevOps
- Ansible
- Puppet
- Code (IaC) strategy
- HockeyApp
- Analyze telemetry

Overview about MICROSOFT AZ-400 Exam:

Overview about MICROSOFT AZ-400 Exam Format: Multiple choice, multiple answer
Length of Examination: 120 minutes

Number of Questions: 40-60
Passing Score: 70-80%
Registration Fee: 165 USD

Steps for MICROSOFT AZ-400 Certifications Exam Booking:

Visit to website Microsoft Exam Registration (it will be available soon)
Signup/Login to MICROSOFT account
Search for MICROSOFT AZ-400 Certifications Exam
Select Date and Center of examination and confirm with payment value of 165 USD

Benefits of having MICROSOFT AZ-400 Certifications:

Getting a certification like AZ-400 can enhance the value of a job aspirant as a qualified Azure DevOps Engineer
It'd really attract HR to have a look to your CV and definitely it will help you out to have good salaried job in your hand by the end of the day.
In such a situation, the relevance of a quality AZ-400 Microsoft Azure DevOps Solutions Exam study material is extremely important.
The relevance of a quality MICROSOFT AZ-400 Exam study material is extremely important.
And so we bring best-in-industry MICROSOFT AZ-400 Exam online course and practice tests for you to help in your exam preparation.

Difficulty in writing MICROSOFT AZ-400 Exam:

This exam is one of the toughest exam in microsoft azure as it require enough experience and knowledge with different CI/CD Tools.

so ignorance & less study can put you in trouble during your first attempt of exam.
Candidates having thorough study and hands-on practice can help you to get prepare for this exam.
It is all up to your decision we mean to say a source which you used for AZ-400 exam preparation it may be a book or an online source which offered you AZ-400.
In these days people mostly prefer to buy their study material from an online platform and there are many online websites who are offering AZ-400 test questions but they are not verified by experts. So, you have to choose a platform which gives you the best & authentic **MICROSOFT AZ-400 practice test paper & MICROSOFT AZ-400 dumps** and i.e. only you can have it at Certification-questions.com because all their exams are verified by the Subject Matter Expert.

For more info visit:

**MICROSOFT AZ-400 Exam Reference**, and **Microsoft Documents**

# Sample Practice Test for AZ-400

**Question: 1** *Multiple Answers Are Right*

How should you configure the release retention policy for the investment planning applications suite? To answer, select the appropriate options in the answer area. NOTE: Each correct selection is worth one point.

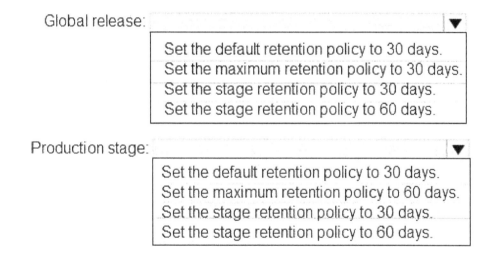

**Answers:**

**A)**

Global release:
- Set the default retention policy to 30 days.
- Set the maximum retention policy to 30 days.
- Set the stage retention policy to 30 days.
- Set the stage retention policy to 60 days.

Production stage:
- Set the default retention policy to 30 days.
- Set the maximum retention policy to 60 days.
- Set the stage retention policy to 30 days.
- Set the stage retention policy to 60 days.

**Solution:** A

**Explanation:**

Explanation:

Global release: **Set the default retention policy to 30 days.**
- Set the maximum retention policy to 30 days.
- Set the stage retention policy to 30 days.
- Set the stage retention policy to 60 days.

Production stage:
- Set the default retention policy to 30 days.
- Set the maximum retention policy to 60 days.
- Set the stage retention policy to 30 days.
- **Set the stage retention policy to 60 days.**

Scenario: By default, all releases must remain available for 30 days, except for production releases, which must be kept for 60 days. Box 1: Set the default retention policy to 30 days The Global default retention policy sets the default retention values for all the build pipelines. Authors of build pipelines can override these values. Box 2: Set the stage retention policy to 60 days You may want to retain more releases that have been deployed to specific stages.
References: https://docs.microsoft.com/en-us/azure/devops/pipelines/policies/retention

**Question: 2** *Multiple Answers Are Right*

Your company wants to use Azure Application Insights to understand how user behaviors affect an application. Which application Insights tool should you use to analyze each behavior? To answer, drag the appropriate tools to the correct behaviors. Each tool may be used once, more than once, or not at all. You may need to drag the split bar between panes or scroll to view content. NOTE: Each correct selection is worth one point.

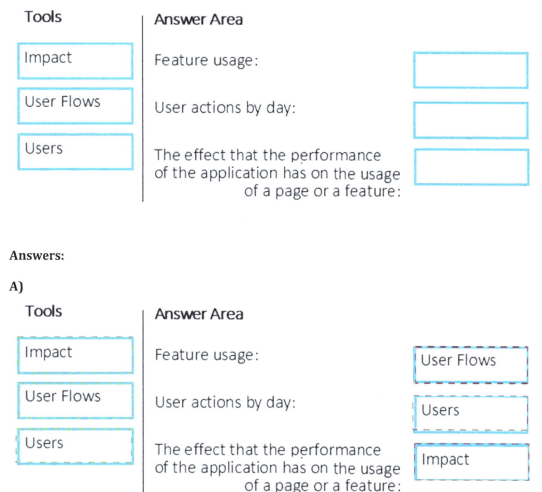

**Answers:**

**A)**

**Solution:** A

**Explanation:**

Explanation:

| | |
|---|---|
| Feature usage: | User Flows |
| User actions by day: | Users |
| The effect that the performance of the application has on the usage of a page or a feature: | Impact |

Box 1: User Flows The User Flows tool visualizes how users navigate between the pages and features of your site. It's great for answering questions like: How do users navigate away from a page on your site? What do users click on a page on your site? Where are the places that users churn most from your site? Are there places where users repeat the same action over and over? Box 2: Users Box 3: Impact Reference: https://docs.microsoft.com/en-us/azure/azure-monitor/app/usage-flows

**Question: 3** *Multiple Answers Are Right*

Your company has a project in Azure DevOps. You plan to create a release pipeline that will deploy resources by using Azure Resource Manager templates. The templates will reference secrets stored in Azure Key Vault. You need to recommend a solution for accessing the secrets stored in the key vault during deployments. The solution must use the principle of least privilege. What should you include in the recommendation? To answer, drag the appropriate configurations to the correct targets. Each configuration may be used once, more than once, or not at all. You may need to drag the split bar between panes or scroll to view content. NOTE: Each correct selection is worth one point.

**Configurations**

- A Key Vault access policy
- A Key Vault advanced access policy
- RBAC

**Answer Area**

- Enable key vaults for template deployment by using: _____
- Restrict access to the secrets in Key Vault by using: _____

**Answers:**

**A)**

Configurations:
- A Key Vault access policy
- A Key Vault advanced access policy
- RBAC

Answer Area:
- Enable key vaults for template deployment by using: A Key Vault advanced access policy
- Restrict access to the secrets in Key Vault by using: RBAC

**Solution:** A

**Explanation:**

Explanation:

Answer Area

- Enable key vaults for template deployment by using: A Key Vault advanced access policy
- Restrict access to the secrets in Key Vault by using: RBAC

Box 1: A key Vault advanced access policy

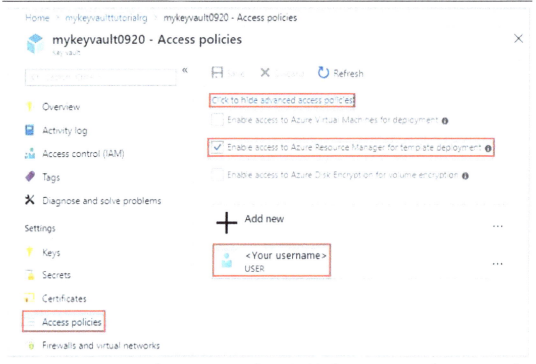

Box 2: RBAC Management plane access control uses RBAC. The management plane consists of operations that affect the key vault itself, such as: * Creating or deleting a key vault. * Getting a list of vaults in a subscription. * Retrieving Key Vault properties (such as SKU and tags). * Setting Key Vault access policies that control user and application access to keys and secrets. References: https://docs.microsoft.com/en-us/azure/azure-resource-manager/resource-manager-tutorial-use- key-vault

**Question: 4** *One Answer Is Right*

You have an Azure DevOps project named Project1 and an Azure subscription named Sub1. You need to prevent releases from being deployed unless the releases comply with the Azure Policy rules assigned to Sub1. What should you do in the release pipeline of Project1?

**Answers:**

**A)** Create a pipeline variable.

**B)** Add a deployment gate.

**C)** Configure a deployment trigger.

**D)** Modify the Deployment queue settings.

**Solution:** A

**Question: 5** *One Answer Is Right*

You have an Azure DevOps organization named Contoso that contains a project named Project 1. You provision an Azure key vault name Keyvault1. You need to reference Keyvault1 secrets in a build pipeline of Project1. What should you do first?

**Answers:**

**A)** Create an XAML build service.

**B)** Create a variable group in Project1.

**C)** Add a secure file to Project1.

**D)** Configure the security policy of Contoso.

**Solution: C**

**Question: 6** *Multiple Answers Are Right*

You are deploying a new application that uses Azure virtual machines. You plan to use the Desired State Configuration (DSC) extension on the virtual machines. You need to ensure that the virtual machines always have the same Windows features installed. Which three actions should you perform in sequence? To answer, move the appropriate actions from the list of actions to the answer area and arrange them in the correct order.

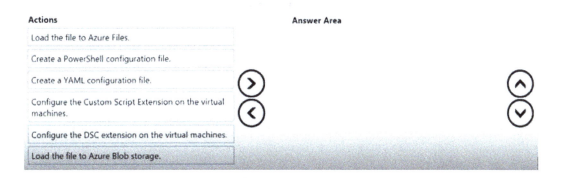

**Answers:**

A)

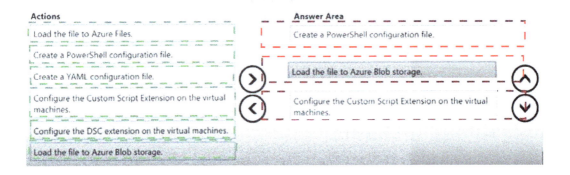

Solution: A

Explanation:

Explanation:

| | Answer Area |
|---|---|
| 1 | Create a PowerShell configuration file. |
| 2 | Load the file to Azure Blob storage. |
| 3 | Configure the Custom Script Extension on the virtual machines. |

Question: 7  One Answer Is Right

Your company uses Azure Artifacts for package management. You need to configure an upstream source in Azure Artifacts for Python packages. Which repository type should you use as an upstream source?

Answers:

A) PyPI

B) npmjs.org

C) Maven Central

D) third-party trusted Python

**Solution:** A

**Question: 8** *One Answer Is Right*

You are developing an iOS application by using Azure DevOps. You need to test the application manually on 10 devices without releasing the application to the public. Which two actions should you perform? Each correct answer presents part of the solution. NOTE: Each correct selection is worth one point.

**Answers:**

**A)** Create a Microsoft Intune device compliance policy.

**B)** Deploy a certificate from an internal certification authority (CA) to each device.

**C)** Register the application in the iTunes store.

**D)** Onboard the devices into Microsoft Intune.

**E)** Distribute a new release of the application.

**F)** Register the IDs of the devices in the Apple Developer portal.

**Solution:** B, F

**Explanation:**

Explanation: References: https://docs.microsoft.com/en-us/appcenter/distribution/auto-provisioning

**Question: 9** *One Answer Is Right*

Your company is concerned that when developers introduce open source libraries, it creates licensing compliance issues. You need to add an automated process to the build pipeline to detect when common open source libraries are added to the code base. What should you use?

**Answers:**

**A)** PDM

**B)** OWASPZAP

**C)** WhiteSource

**D)** Jenkins

**Solution:** C

**Question: 10** *One Answer Is Right*

Note: This question is part of a series of questions that present the same scenario. Each question in the series contains a unique solution that might meet the stated goals. Some question sets might have more than one correct solution, while others might not have a correct solution. After you answer a question in this section, you will NOT be able to return to it. As a result, these questions will not appear in the review screen. You have an approval process that contains a condition. The condition requires that releases be approved by a team leader before they are deployed. You have a policy stating that approvals must occur within eight hours. You discover that deployment fail if the approvals take longer than two hours. You need to ensure that the deployments only fail if the approvals take longer than eight hours. Solution: From Pre-deployment conditions, you modify the Time between re-evaluation of gates option. Does this meet the goal?

**Answers:**

**A)** Yes

**B)** No

**Solution:** B

**Explanation:**

Explanation: References: https://docs.microsoft.com/en-us/azure/devops/pipelines/release/approvals/gates

# Chapter 24: AZ-500 - Microsoft Azure Security Technologies

## Exam Guide

Microsoft Azure Security Technologies AZ-500 Exam:

Microsoft Azure Security Technologies AZ-500 Exam which is related to Microsoft Certified Azure Security Engineer Associate Certification. This AZ-500 exam validates the ability to implementing security controls and maintaining security, and identity, access and protections within Microsoft Azure. This exam also tests the ability to implement security controls, maintain the security posture, manages identity and access, and protects data, applications, and networks. The person usually focuses on the cloud components within the company. Security Engineers usually hold or pursue this certification and you can expect the same job role after completion of this certification.

AZ-500 Exam topics:

Candidates must know the exam topics before they start of preparation. Because it will really help them in hitting the core. Our **AZ-500 dumps** will include the following topics:

- Manage identity and access 20-25%
- Implement platform protection 35-40%
- Manage security operations 15-20%
- Secure data and applications 30-35%

Certification Path:

The Microsoft Azure Security Technologies Certification includes only one AZ-500 Exam.

Who should take the AZ-500 exam:

The Microsoft Azure Security Technologies AZ-500 Exam certification is an internationally-recognized validation that identifies persons who earn it as possessing skilled as a Microsoft Certified Azure Security Engineer. If candidates want significant improvement in career growth needs enhanced knowledge, skills, and talents. The Microsoft Azure Security Technologies AZ-

500 Exam certification provides proof of this advanced knowledge and skill. If a candidate has knowledge of associated technologies and skills that are required to pass Microsoft Azure Security Technologies AZ-500 Exam then he should take this exam.

How to study the AZ-500 Exam:

Certification-questions.com expert team recommends you to prepare some notes on these topics along with it don't forget to practice Microsoft AZ-500 Exam dumps which been written by our expert team, Both these will help you a lot to clear this exam with good marks.

How much AZ-500 Exam Cost:

The price of the AZ-500 exam is $165 USD.

How to book the AZ-500 Exam:

These are following steps for registering the AZ-500 exam.
Step 1: Visit to Microsoft Exam Registration
Step 2: Signup/Login to MICROSOFT account
Step 3: Search for MICROSOFT AZ-500 Certifications Exam
Step 4: Select Date and Center of examination and confirm with payment value of $165

What is the duration of the AZ-500 Exam:

- Format: Multiple choices, multiple answers
- Length of Examination: 150 minutes
- Number of Questions: 45-60
- Passing Score: 700/1000

The benefit in Obtaining the AZ-500 Exam Certification:

- After completion of Microsoft Certified Azure Security Engineer, Associate Certification candidates receive official confirmation from Microsoft that you are now fully certified in their chosen field. This can be now added to their CV, cover letters and job applications.
- When Candidates applying for a job or looking to promotion in their current position, a Microsoft Certified Azure Security Engineer, Associate certification in the field in which Candidates are applying will put you at the top of the list and make them a desirable candidate for employers.
- Candidates will get in-depth knowledge by completing the courses along with the access to revision materials for 6 months upon completion means they will have a wider skill set when it comes to the various technologies and systems than an uncertified professional. Certified Professional in this particular skill set is 74% more efficient when it comes to completing their tasks in a timely well-executed manner.

- Organization owners invest a lot in their employees when it comes to their training with the goal of making them quicker, more efficient, and more knowledgeable about their role. Certified Professional will reduce the time he spends on tasks, meaning he can get more done this could help reduce company downtime when repairing faults on a system or fixing hardware problems.
- Becoming Microsoft Certified Azure Security Engineer, Associate means one thing you are worth more to the company and therefore more to yourself in the form of an upgraded pay package. On average a Microsoft Certified Azure Security Engineer, Associate member of staff is estimated to be worth 30% more to a company than their uncertified professionals.

Difficulty in writing AZ-500 Exam:

Microsoft Certified Azure Security Engineer Associate Certification helps Candidates in developing their professionals and academic career and It is a very tough task to pass Microsoft AZ-500 exam for those Candidates who have not done hard work and get some relevant Microsoft AZ-500 exam preparation material. There are many peoples have passed Microsoft AZ-500 exam by following these three things such as look for the latest Microsoft AZ-500 exam dumps, get relevant **Microsoft AZ-500 exam dumps** and develop their knowledge about Microsoft AZ-500 exam new questions. At the same time, it can also stress out some people as they found passing Microsoft AZ-500 exam a tough task. It is just a wrong assumption as many of the peoples have passed Microsoft AZ-500 exam questions. All you have to do is to work hard, get some relevant Microsoft AZ-500 exam preparation material and go thoroughly from them. Certification-questions is here to help you with this problem. We have the relevant Microsoft AZ-500 exam preparation material which are providing the latest Microsoft AZ-500 exam questions with the detailed view of every Microsoft AZ-500 exam topic. Certification-questions offered **Microsoft AZ-500 exam dumps** which are more than enough to pass the Microsoft AZ-500 exam questions. We are providing all thing such as **Microsoft AZ-500 exam dumps**, Microsoft AZ-500 practice test, and **Microsoft AZ-500 pdf dumps** that will help the candidate to pass the exam with good grades.

For more info visit::

Microsoft AZ-500 Exam Reference

# Sample Practice Test for AZ-500

**Question: 1** *One Answer Is Right*

You need to meet the identity and access requirements for Group1. What should you do?

**Scenario:**

TESTLET-1. Overview Litware, Inc. is a digital media company that has 500 employees in the Chicago area and 20 employees in the San Francisco area. Existing Environment Litware has an Azure subscription named Sub1 that has a subscription ID of 43894a43-17c2-4a39-8cfc-3540c2653ef4. Sub1 is associated to an Azure Active Directory (Azure AD) tenant named litwareinc.com. The tenant contains the user objects and the device objects of all the Litware employees and their devices. Each user is assigned an Azure AD Premium P2 license. Azure AD Privileged Identity Management (PIM) is activated. The tenant contains the groups shown in the following table.

| Name | Type | Description |
|---|---|---|
| Group1 | Security group | A group that has the Dynamic User membership type, contains all the San Francisco users, and provides access to many Azure AD applications and Azure resources. |
| Group2 | Security group | A group that has the Dynamic User membership type and contains the Chicago IT team |

The Azure subscription contains the objects shown in the following table.

| Name | Type | Description |
|---|---|---|
| VNet1 | Virtual network | VNet1 is a virtual network that contains security-sensitive IT resources. VNet1 contains three subnets named Subnet0, Subnet1, and AzureFirewallSubnet. |
| VM0 | Virtual machine | VM0 is an Azure virtual machine that runs Windows Server 2016, connects to Subnet0, and has just in time (JIT) VM access configured. |
| VM1 | Virtual machine | VM1 is an Azure virtual machine that runs Windows Server 2016 and connects to Subnet0. |
| SQLDB1 | Azure SQL Database | SQLDB1 is an Azure SQL database on a SQL Database server named LitwareSQLServer1. |
| WebApp1 | Web app | WebApp1 is an Azure web app that is accessible by using https://www.litwareinc.com and http://www.litwareinc.com. |
| RG1 | Resource group | RG1 is a resource group that contains VNet1, VM0, and VM1. |
| RG2 | Resource group | RG2 is a resource group that contains shared IT resources. |

Azure Security Center is set to the Standard tier. Requirements Planned Changes Litware plans to deploy the Azure resources shown in the following table.

| Name | Type | Description |
|---|---|---|
| Firewall1 | Azure Firewall | An Azure firewall on VNet1. |
| RT1 | Route table | A route table that will contain a route pointing to Firewall1 as the default gateway and will be assigned to Subnet0. |
| AKS1 | Azure Kubernetes Service (AKS) | A managed AKS cluster |

Identity and Access Requirements Litware identifies the following identity and access requirements: - All San Francisco users and their devices must be members of Group1. - The members of Group2 must be assigned the Contributor role to RG2 by using a permanent eligible assignment. - Users must be prevented from registering applications in Azure AD and from consenting to applications that access company information on the users' behalf. Platform Protection Requirements Litware identifies the following platform protection requirements: - Microsoft Antimalware must be installed on the virtual machines in RG1. - The members of Group2 must be assigned the Azure Kubernetes Service Cluster Admin Role. -Azure AD users must be able to authenticate to AKS1 by using their Azure AD credentials.- Following the implementation of the planned changes, the IT team must be able to connect to VM0 by using JIT VM access. - A new custom RBAC role named Role1 must be used to delegate the administration of the managed disks in RG1. Role1 must be available only for RG1. Security Operations Requirements Litware must be able to customize the operating system security configurations in Azure Security Center. Data and Application Requirements Litware identifies the following data and applications requirements: - The users in Group2 must be able to authenticate to SQLDB1 by using their Azure AD credentials. - WebApp1 must enforce mutual authentication. General Requirements Litware identifies the following general requirements: - Whenever possible, administrative effort must be minimized. - Whenever possible, use of automation must be maximized.

**Answers:**

**A)** Add a membership rule to Group1.

**B)** Delete Group1. Create a new group named Group1 that has a group type of Office 365. Add users and devices to the group.

**C)** Modify the membership rule of Group1.

**D)** Change the membership type of Group1 to Assigned. Create two groups that have dynamic memberships. Add the new groups to Group1.

**Solution:** B

**Explanation:**

Explanation: Incorrect Answers: A, C: You can create a dynamic group for devices or for users, but you can't create a rule that contains both users and devices. D: For assigned group you can only add individual members. Scenario: Litware identifies the following identity and access requirements: All San Francisco users and their devices must be members of Group1. The tenant currently contain this group:

| Name | Type | Description |
| --- | --- | --- |
| Group1 | Security group | A group that has the Dynamic User membership type, contains all the San Francisco users, and provides access to many Azure AD applications and Azure resources. |

References: https://docs.microsoft.com/en-us/azure/active-directory/users-groups-roles/groups-dynamic-membership https://docs.microsoft.com/en-us/azure/active-directory/fundamentals/active-directory-groups-create-azure- portal

**Question: 2** *One Answer Is Right*

You need to ensure that User2 can implement PIM. What should you do first?

**Scenario:**

TESTLET-1. Overview Litware, Inc. is a digital media company that has 500 employees in the Chicago area and 20 employees in the San Francisco area. Existing Environment Litware has an Azure subscription named Sub1 that has a subscription ID of 43894a43-17c2-4a39-8cfc-3540c2653ef4. Sub1 is associated to an Azure Active Directory (Azure AD) tenant named litwareinc.com. The tenant contains the user objects and the device objects of all the Litware employees and their devices. Each user is assigned an Azure AD Premium P2 license. Azure AD Privileged Identity Management (PIM) is activated. The tenant contains the groups shown in the following table.

| Name | Type | Description |
| --- | --- | --- |
| Group1 | Security group | A group that has the Dynamic User membership type, contains all the San Francisco users, and provides access to many Azure AD applications and Azure resources. |
| Group2 | Security group | A group that has the Dynamic User membership type and contains the Chicago IT team |

The Azure subscription contains the objects shown in the following table.

| Name | Type | Description |
| --- | --- | --- |
| VNet1 | Virtual network | VNet1 is a virtual network that contains security-sensitive IT resources. VNet1 contains three subnets named Subnet0, Subnet1, and AzureFirewallSubnet. |
| VM0 | Virtual machine | VM0 is an Azure virtual machine that runs Windows Server 2016, connects to Subnet0, and has just in time (JIT) VM access configured. |
| VM1 | Virtual machine | VM1 is an Azure virtual machine that runs Windows Server 2016 and connects to Subnet0. |
| SQLDB1 | Azure SQL Database | SQLDB1 is an Azure SQL database on a SQL Database server named LitwareSQLServer1. |
| WebApp1 | Web app | WebApp1 is an Azure web app that is accessible by using https://www.litwareinc.com and http://www.litwareinc.com. |
| RG1 | Resource group | RG1 is a resource group that contains VNet1, VM0, and VM1. |
| RG2 | Resource group | RG2 is a resource group that contains shared IT resources. |

Azure Security Center is set to the Standard tier. Requirements Planned Changes Litware plans to deploy the Azure resources shown in the following table.

| Name | Type | Description |
|---|---|---|
| Firewall1 | Azure Firewall | An Azure firewall on VNet1. |
| RT1 | Route table | A route table that will contain a route pointing to Firewall1 as the default gateway and will be assigned to Subnet0. |
| AKS1 | Azure Kubernetes Service (AKS) | A managed AKS cluster |

Identity and Access Requirements Litware identifies the following identity and access requirements: - All San Francisco users and their devices must be members of Group1. - The members of Group2 must be assigned the Contributor role to RG2 by using a permanent eligible assignment. - Users must be prevented from registering applications in Azure AD and from consenting to applications that access company information on the users' behalf. Platform Protection Requirements Litware identifies the following platform protection requirements: - Microsoft Antimalware must be installed on the virtual machines in RG1. - The members of Group2 must be assigned the Azure Kubernetes Service Cluster Admin Role. -Azure AD users must be able to authenticate to AKS1 by using their Azure AD credentials.- Following the implementation of the planned changes, the IT team must be able to connect to VM0 by using JIT VM access. - A new custom RBAC role named Role1 must be used to delegate the administration of the managed disks in RG1. Role1 must be available only for RG1. Security Operations Requirements Litware must be able to customize the operating system security configurations in Azure Security Center. Data and Application Requirements Litware identifies the following data and applications requirements: - The users in Group2 must be able to authenticate to SQLDB1 by using their Azure AD credentials. - WebApp1 must enforce mutual authentication. General Requirements Litware identifies the following general requirements: - Whenever possible, administrative effort must be minimized. - Whenever possible, use of automation must be maximized.

**Answers:**

**A)** Assign User2 the Global administrator role.

**B)** Configure authentication methods for contoso.com.

**C)** Configure the identity secure score for contoso.com.

**D)** Enable multi-factor authentication (MFA) for User2.

**Solution:** A

**Explanation:**

Explanation: Explanation: To start using PIM in your directory, you must first enable PIM. 1. Sign in to the Azure portal as a Global Administrator of your directory. You must be a Global Administrator with an organizational account (for example, @yourdomain.com), not a Microsoft account (for example, @outlook.com), to enable PIM for a directory. Scenario: Technical requirements include: Enable Azure AD Privileged Identity Management (PIM) for contoso.com References: https://docs.microsoft.com/bs-latn-ba/azure/active-directory/privileged-identity-management/pim-getting- started Manage identity and access Question Set 3

**Question: 3** *One Answer Is Right*

Note: This question is part of a series of questions that present the same scenario. Each question in the series contains a unique solution that might meet the stated goals. Some question sets might have more than one correct solution, while others might not have a correct solution. After you answer a question in this section, you will NOT be able to return to it. As a result, these questions will not appear in the review screen. You have an Azure subscription named Sub1. You have an Azure Storage account named sa1 in a resource group named RG1. Users and applications access the blob service and the file service in sa1 by using several shared access signatures (SASs) and stored access policies. You discover that unauthorized users accessed both the file service and the blob service. You need to revoke all access to sa1. Solution: You create a new stored access policy. Does this meet the goal?

**Answers:**

**A)** Yes

**B)** No

**Solution:** A

**Explanation:**

Explanation: Explanation: To revoke a stored access policy, you can either delete it, or rename it by changing the signed identifier. Changing the signed identifier breaks the associations between any existing signatures and the stored access policy. Deleting or renaming the stored access policy immediately effects all of the shared access signatures associated with it. References: https://docs.microsoft.com/en-us/rest/api/storageservices/Establishing-a-Stored-Access-Policy

**Question: 4** *One Answer Is Right*

Note: This question is part of a series of questions that present the same scenario. Each question in the series contains a unique solution that might meet the stated goals. Some question sets might have more than one correct solution, while others might not have a correct solution. After you answer a question in this section, you will NOT be able to return to it. As a result, these questions will not appear in the review screen. You have a hybrid configuration of Azure Active Directory (Azure AD). You have an Azure HDInsight cluster on a virtual network. You plan to allow users to authenticate to the cluster by using their on-premises Active Directory credentials. You need to configure the environment to support the planned authentication. Solution: You deploy the On-premises data gateway to the on-premises network. Does this meet the goal?

**Answers:**

**A)** Yes

**B)** No

**Solution:** B

**Explanation:**

Explanation: Explanation: Instead, you connect HDInsight to your on-premises network by using Azure Virtual Networks and a VPN gateway. Note: To allow HDInsight and resources in the joined network to communicate by name, you must perform the following actions: - Create Azure Virtual Network. - Create a custom DNS server in the Azure Virtual Network. - Configure the virtual network to use the custom DNS server instead of the default Azure Recursive Resolver. - Configure forwarding between the custom DNS server and your on-premises DNS server. References: https://docs.microsoft.com/en-us/azure/hdinsight/connect-on-premises-network

**Question: 5** *One Answer Is Right*

Note: This question is part of a series of questions that present the same scenario. Each question in the series contains a unique solution that might meet the stated goals. Some question sets might have more than one correct solution, while others might not have a correct solution. After you answer a question in this section, you will NOT be able to return to it. As a result, these questions will not appear in the review screen. You have a hybrid configuration of Azure Active Directory (Azure AD). You have an Azure HDInsight cluster on a virtual network. You plan to allow users to authenticate to the cluster by using their on-premises Active Directory credentials. You need to configure the environment to support the planned authentication. Solution: You create a site-to-site VPN between the virtual network and the on-premises network. Does this meet the goal?

**Answers:**

**A)** Yes

**B)** No

**Solution:** A

**Explanation:**

Explanation: Explanation: You can connect HDInsight to your on-premises network by using Azure Virtual Networks and a VPN gateway. Note: To allow HDInsight and resources in the joined network to communicate by name, you must perform the following actions: - Create Azure Virtual Network. - Create a custom DNS server in the Azure Virtual Network. - Configure the virtual network to use the custom DNS server instead of the default Azure Recursive Resolver. - Configure forwarding between the custom DNS server and your on-premises DNS server. References: https://docs.microsoft.com/en-us/azure/hdinsight/connect-on-premises-network

## Question: 6 *One Answer Is Right*

Your network contains an Active Directory forest named contoso.com. The forest contains a single domain. You have an Azure subscription named Sub1 that is associated to an Azure Active Directory (Azure AD) tenant named contoso.com. You plan to deploy Azure AD Connect and to integrate Active Directory and the Azure AD tenant. You need to recommend an integration solution that meets the following requirements: - Ensures that password policies and user logon restrictions apply to user accounts that are synced to the tenant - Minimizes the number of servers required for the solution. Which authentication method should you include in the recommendation?

**Answers:**

**A)** federated identity with Active Directory Federation Services (AD FS)

**B)** password hash synchronization with seamless single sign-on (SSO)

**C)** pass-through authentication with seamless single sign-on (SSO)

**Solution:** B

**Explanation:**

Explanation: Explanation: Password hash synchronization requires the least effort regarding deployment, maintenance, and infrastructure. This level of effort typically applies to organizations that only need their users to sign in to Office 365, SaaS apps, and other Azure AD-based resources. When turned on, password hash synchronization is part of the Azure AD Connect sync process and runs every two minutes. Incorrect Answers: A: A federated authentication system relies on an external trusted system to authenticate users. Some companies want to reuse their existing federated system investment with their Azure AD hybrid identity solution. The maintenance and management of the federated system falls outside the control of Azure AD. It's up to the organization by using the federated system to make sure it's deployed securely and can handle the authentication load. C: For pass-through authentication, you need one or more (we recommend three) lightweight agents installed on existing servers. These agents must have access to your on-premises Active Directory Domain Services, including

your on-premises AD domain controllers. They need outbound access to the Internet and access to your domain controllers. For this reason, it's not supported to deploy the agents in a perimeter network. Pass-through Authentication requires unconstrained network access to domain controllers. All network traffic is encrypted and limited to authentication requests.
References: https://docs.microsoft.com/en-us/azure/active-directory/hybrid/how-to-connect-pta

**Question: 7** *Multiple Answers Are Right*

DRAG DROP You are implementing conditional access policies. You must evaluate the existing Azure Active Directory (Azure AD) risk events and risk levels to configure and implement the policies. You need to identify the risk level of the following risk events: - Users with leaked credentials - Impossible travel to atypical locations - Sign-ins from IP addresses with suspicious activity Which level should you identify for each risk event? To answer, drag the appropriate levels to the correct risk events. Each level may be used once, more than once, or not at all. You may need to drag the split bar between panes or scroll to view content. NOTE: Each correct selection is worth one point. Select and Place:

**Levels**         **Answer Area**

| High |    Impossible travel to atypical locations:                 |   |

| Low  |    Users with leaked credentials:                            |   |

| Medium |  Sign-ins from IP addresses with suspicious activity:       |   |

**Answers:**

A)

| Levels | Answer Area | |
|---|---|---|
| High | Impossible travel to atypical locations: | Medium |
| Low | Users with leaked credentials: | High |
| Medium | Sign-ins from IP addresses with suspicious activity: | Low |

**Solution:** A

**Explanation:**

Explanation: Azure AD Identity protection can detect six types of suspicious sign-in activities: - Users with leaked credentials - Sign-ins from anonymous IP addresses - Impossible travel to atypical locations - Sign-ins from infected devices - Sign-ins from IP addresses with suspicious activity - Sign-ins from unfamiliar locations These six types of events are categorized in to 3 levels of risks – High, Medium & Low:

| Sign-in Activity | Risk Level |
|---|---|
| Users with leaked credentials | High |
| Sign-ins from anonymous IP addresses | Medium |
| Impossible travel to atypical locations | Medium |
| Sign-ins from infected devices | Medium |
| Sign-ins from IP addresses with suspicious activity | Low |
| Sign-ins from unfamiliar locations | Medium |

References: http://www.rebeladmin.com/2018/09/step-step-guide-configure-risk-based-azure-conditional-access- policies/

## Question: 8 *Multiple Answers Are Right*

HOTSPOT You create and enforce an Azure AD Identity Protection user risk policy that has the following settings:- Assignment: Include Group1, Exclude Group2 - Conditions: Sign-in risk of Medium and above - Access: Allow access, Require password change You have an Azure Active Directory (Azure AD) tenant named contoso.com that contains the users shown in the following table.

| Name | Member of | Mobile phone | Multi-factor authentication (MFA) status |
|---|---|---|---|
| User1 | Group1 | 123 555 7890 | Disabled |
| User2 | Group1, Group2 | None | Enabled |
| User3 | Group1 | 123 555 7891 | Required |

For each of the following statements, select Yes if the statement is true. Otherwise, select No. NOTE: Each correct selection is worth one point. Hot Area:

### Answer Area

| Statements | Yes | No |
|---|---|---|
| If User1 signs in from an unfamiliar location, he must change his password. | ○ | ○ |
| If User2 signs in from an anonymous IP address, she must change her password. | ○ | ○ |
| If User3 signs in from a computer containing malware that is communicating with known bot servers, he must change his password. | ○ | ○ |

Answers:

A)

## Answer Area

| Statements | Yes | No |
|---|---|---|
| If User1 signs in from an unfamiliar location, he must change his password. | O | |
| If User2 signs in from an anonymous IP address, she must change her password. | O | |
| If User3 signs in from a computer containing malware that is communicating with known bot servers, he must change his password. | | O |

**Solution:** A

**Explanation:**

Explanation: Box 1: Yes User1 is member of Group1. Sign in from unfamiliar location is risk level Medium. Box 2: Yes User2 is member of Group1. Sign in from anonymous IP address is risk level Medium. Box 3: No Sign-ins from IP addresses with suspicious activity is low. Note:

| Sign-in Activity | Risk Level |
|---|---|
| Users with leaked credentials | High |
| Sign-ins from anonymous IP addresses | Medium |
| Impossible travel to atypical locations | Medium |
| Sign-ins from infected devices | Medium |
| Sign-ins from IP addresses with suspicious activity | Low |
| Sign-ins from unfamiliar locations | Medium |

Azure AD Identity protection can detect six types of suspicious sign-in activities: - Users with leaked credentials - Sign-ins from anonymous IP addresses - Impossible travel to atypical locations - Sign-ins from infected devices - Sign-ins from IP addresses with suspicious activity - Sign-ins from unfamiliar locations These six types of events are categorized in to 3 levels of risks – High, Medium & Low: References: http://www.rebeladmin.com/2018/09/step-step-guide-configure-risk-based-azure-conditional-access- policies/

**Question: 9** *Multiple Answers Are Right*

HOTSPOT You need to ensure that the Azure AD application registration and consent configurations meet the identity and access requirements. What should you use in the Azure portal? To answer, select the appropriate options in the answer area. NOTE: Each correct selection is worth one point. Hot Area:

**Answer Area**

To configure the registration settings:
- Azure AD – User settings
- Azure AD – App registrations settings
- Enterprise Applications – User settings

To configure the consent settings:
- Azure AD – User settings
- Azure AD – App registrations settings
- Enterprise Applications – User settings

**Scenario:**

TESTLET-1. Overview Litware, Inc. is a digital media company that has 500 employees in the Chicago area and 20 employees in the San Francisco area. Existing Environment Litware has an Azure subscription named Sub1 that has a subscription ID of 43894a43-17c2-4a39-8cfc-3540c2653ef4. Sub1 is associated to an Azure Active Directory (Azure AD) tenant named litwareinc.com. The tenant contains the user objects and the device objects of all the Litware employees and their devices. Each user is assigned an Azure AD Premium P2 license. Azure AD Privileged Identity Management (PIM) is activated. The tenant contains the groups shown in the following table.

| Name | Type | Description |
|---|---|---|
| Group1 | Security group | A group that has the Dynamic User membership type, contains all the San Francisco users, and provides access to many Azure AD applications and Azure resources. |
| Group2 | Security group | A group that has the Dynamic User membership type and contains the Chicago IT team |

The Azure subscription contains the objects shown in the following table.

| Name | Type | Description |
|---|---|---|
| VNet1 | Virtual network | VNet1 is a virtual network that contains security-sensitive IT resources. VNet1 contains three subnets named Subnet0, Subnet1, and AzureFirewallSubnet. |
| VM0 | Virtual machine | VM0 is an Azure virtual machine that runs Windows Server 2016, connects to Subnet0, and has just in time (JIT) VM access configured. |
| VM1 | Virtual machine | VM1 is an Azure virtual machine that runs Windows Server 2016 and connects to Subnet0. |
| SQLDB1 | Azure SQL Database | SQLDB1 is an Azure SQL database on a SQL Database server named LitwareSQLServer1. |
| WebApp1 | Web app | WebApp1 is an Azure web app that is accessible by using https://www.litwareinc.com and http://www.litwareinc.com. |
| RG1 | Resource group | RG1 is a resource group that contains VNet1, VM0, and VM1. |
| RG2 | Resource group | RG2 is a resource group that contains shared IT resources. |

Azure Security Center is set to the Standard tier. Requirements Planned Changes Litware plans to deploy the Azure resources shown in the following table.

| Name | Type | Description |
|---|---|---|
| Firewall1 | Azure Firewall | An Azure firewall on VNet1. |
| RT1 | Route table | A route table that will contain a route pointing to Firewall1 as the default gateway and will be assigned to Subnet0. |
| AKS1 | Azure Kubernetes Service (AKS) | A managed AKS cluster |

Identity and Access Requirements Litware identifies the following identity and access requirements: - All San Francisco users and their devices must be members of Group1. - The members of Group2 must be assigned the Contributor role to RG2 by using a permanent eligible assignment. - Users must be prevented from registering applications in Azure AD and from consenting to applications that access company information on the users' behalf. Platform Protection Requirements Litware identifies the following platform protection requirements: - Microsoft Antimalware must be installed on the virtual machines in RG1. - The members of Group2 must be assigned the Azure Kubernetes Service Cluster Admin Role. -Azure AD users must be able to authenticate to AKS1 by using their Azure AD credentials.- Following the implementation of the planned changes, the IT team must be able to connect to VM0 by using JIT VM access. - A new custom RBAC role named Role1 must be used to delegate the administration of the managed disks in RG1. Role1 must be available only for RG1. Security Operations Requirements Litware must be able to customize the operating system security configurations in Azure Security Center. Data and Application Requirements Litware identifies the following data and applications requirements: - The users in Group2 must be able to authenticate to SQLDB1 by using their Azure AD credentials. - WebApp1 must enforce mutual authentication. General Requirements Litware identifies the following general requirements: - Whenever possible, administrative effort must be minimized. - Whenever possible, use of automation must be maximized.

Answers:

A)

### Answer Area

To configure the registration settings: [dropdown]
- Azure AD – User settings
- Azure AD – App registrations settings
- Enterprise Applications – User settings

To configure the consent settings: [dropdown]
- Azure AD – User settings
- Azure AD – App registrations settings
- Enterprise Applications – User settings

Solution: A

Explanation:

Explanation: Reference: https://docs.microsoft.com/en-us/azure/active-directory/manage-apps/configure-user-consent Manage identity and access

**Question: 10** *One Answer Is Right*

Your network contains an Active Directory forest named contoso.com. You have an Azure Directory (Azure AD) tenant named contoso.com. You plan to configure synchronization by using the Express Settings installation option in Azure AD Connect. You need to identify which roles and groups are required to perform the planned configuration. The solution must use the principle of least privilege. Which two roles and groups should you identify? Each correct answer presents part of the solution. NOTE: Each correct selection is worth one point.

Answers:

**A)** the Domain Admins group in Active Directory

**B)** the Security administrator role in Azure AD

**C)** the Global administrator role in Azure AD

**D)** the User administrator role in Azure AD

**E)** the Enterprise Admins group in Active Directory

**Solution:** C, E

**Explanation:**

Explanation: References: https://docs.microsoft.com/en-us/azure/active-directory/hybrid/reference-connect-accounts-permissions

# Chapter 25: AZ-900 - Microsoft Azure Fundamentals

## Exam Guide

Microsoft Azure Fundamentals AZ-900 Exam:

**Microsoft Azure Fundamentals AZ-900 Exam** provides learners with an in-depth knowledge of the concepts of Microsoft Azure to effectively perform various tasks in the capacity of an administrator, developer, or database administrator. With Microsoft Azure Fundamentals AZ-900 Exam Candidates can Gain knowledge of the principles of cloud computing, and how these principles have been implemented in Microsoft Azure. Learn how to create the most common Azure services, including Azure virtual machines (VMs), Web Apps, SQL Databases, features of Azure Active Directory (Azure AD) and methods of integrating it with on-premises Active Directory. Candidates will have understanding about Azure Cloud and their different types of services like IaaS, PaaS, SaaS along with it they will be having some understanding of deployment model in Azure Cloud i.e. Public cloud, Private Cloud, Community Cloud & Hybrid Cloud. Microsoft is not having doubt on your skill set just they came up with Microsoft Azure Fundamentals AZ-900 for that passionate candidate who willing to have their career in Cloud Technology. It is foundational level Certification which can introduce you to different certification path in Azure Cloud like for Administrator, Developer or Architect. It will be totally depend on candidate how they want to make their career in Azure Cloud Technology after having AZ-900 Certifications.

This is the list of the contents in our **Microsoft Azure Fundamentals AZ-900 Practice Test:**

- Describe cloud computing, Azure, and Azure subscriptions
- Describe and create Azure Web Apps
- Create and configure VMs in Microsoft Azure
- Create an Azure virtual network
- Describe Azure storage
- Describe and deploy databases in Azure
- Describe Azure AD

Microsoft Azure Fundamentals AZ-900 Dumps will include below mentioned topics with Exam focused percentage:

- Understand Cloud Concepts: 15-20%
- Understand Core Azure Services: 30-35%
- Understand Security, Privacy, Compliance, and Trust: 25-30%
- Understand Azure Pricing and Support: 25-30%

Microsoft Azure Fundamentals AZ-900 Dumps Provided Study Notes:

Certification-questions.com expert team recommend you to prepare some notes on these topics along with it don't forget to practice **Microsoft Azure Fundamentals AZ-900 Dumps** which been written by our expert team, Both these will help you a lot to clear this exam with good marks.

- Virtual Machine
- Web Apps and Cloud Services
- Virtual Networks
- Cloud Storage
- Azure Pricing
- Network Security in Azure
- Microsoft Azure Databases
- Creating and Managing Azure AD

Overview about MICROSOFTAZ-900 Exam:

- Format: Multiple choice, multiple answer
- Length of Examination: 150 minutes
- Number of Questions: 40-60
- Passing Score: 70-80%
- Registration Fee: 99 USD

How to book MICROSOFTAZ-900 Certifications Exam?:

- Visit to Microsoft Exam Registration
- Signup/Login to MICROSOFT account
- Search for MICROSOFTAZ-900 Certifications Exam
- Select Date and Center of examination and confirm with payment value of 99$

Benefits of having MICROSOFT AZ-900 Certifications:

Cloud Technology is one of the fastest growing field in the IT, You can expect better life and position with Azure Cloud Certifications. Getting certification AZ-900 is a good exam if you are just starting with Azure and the cloud. It is not just a marketing and sales exam, even do it is a very light exam. You will need to have some technical know-how. If you are planning to take this exam we have some recommendations for you. Understand the benefits of cloud computing and the different cloud models. Go through the list of Azure services, make sure you know what services are available and for what you would use them. Also make sure that you understand the concepts of Azure in general and in Azure governance, like Subscriptions, Management Groups, Azure Policies, Azure Resource Groups, Role-Based Access Control and many more. In such a situation, the relevance of a quality AZ-900 Microsoft Azure Fundamental EXAM study material is extremely important. And so we bring best-in-industry Azure Exam AZ-900 online course and AZ-900 practice tests for you to help in your exam preparation.

Difficulty in writing MICROSOFT AZ-900 Exam:

As we already mentioned that MICROSOFT AZ-900 Exam is a foundation exam before you introduce yourself in the Azure Cloud Technology So going through this exam won't be hard enough still ignorance can put you in trouble but if you really want to get ready for the cloud and especially for Microsoft Azure, and exam AZ-900, check out Microsoft Learn. Microsoft Learn is a great free learning platform. Most important thing about this exam is that it is one of the newly introduced exams by the Microsoft so it would be little bit tough to get proper study material for it. As such, our Experts will help you to learn how to use the Azure platform and prepare for the certification exam. Having basic understanding of Azure Cloud concepts along with our provided MICROSOFT AZ-900 dumps will definitely help you out to clear MICROSOFT AZ-900 Exam and start your career in the Azure Cloud Technology.

**For more info visit:**

MICROSOFT **AZ-900 Exam** Reference, Microsoft Documents

# Sample Practice Test for AZ-900

**Question: 1** *Multiple Answers Are Right*

HOTSPOT For each of the following statements, select Yes if the statement is true. Otherwise, select No. NOTE: Each correct selection is worth one point. Hot Area:

## Answer Area

| Statements | Yes | No |
|---|---|---|
| A platform as a service (PaaS) solution that hosts web apps in Azure provides full control of the operating systems that host applications. | ○ | ○ |
| A platform as a service (PaaS) solution that hosts web apps in Azure provides the ability to scale the platform automatically. | ○ | ○ |
| A platform as a service (PaaS) solution that hosts web apps in Azure provides professional development services to continuously add features to custom applications. | ○ | ○ |

**Answers:**

## A)

### Answer Area

| Statements | Yes | No |
|---|---|---|
| A platform as a service (PaaS) solution that hosts web apps in Azure provides full control of the operating systems that host applications. | ○ | ● |
| A platform as a service (PaaS) solution that hosts web apps in Azure provides the ability to scale the platform automatically. | ● | ○ |
| A platform as a service (PaaS) solution that hosts web apps in Azure provides professional development services to continuously add features to custom applications. | ● | ○ |

**Solution:** A

**Explanation:**

Explanation: Box 1: No A PaaS solution does not provide access to the operating system. The Azure Web Apps service provides an environment for you to host your web applications. Behind the scenes, the web apps are hosted on virtual machines running IIS. However, you have no direct access to the virtual machine, the operating system or IIS. Box 2: Yes A PaaS solution that hosts web apps in Azure does provide the ability to scale the platform automatically. This is known as autoscaling. Behind the scenes, the web apps are hosted on virtual machines running IIS. Autoscaling means adding more load balanced virtual machines to host the web apps. Box 3: Yes PaaS provides a framework that developers can build upon to develop or customize cloud-based applications. PaaS development tools can cut the time it takes to code new apps with pre-coded application components built into the platform, such as workflow, directory services, security features, search and so on. References: https://azure.microsoft.com/en-gb/overview/what-is-paas/

**Question: 2** *Multiple Answers Are Right*

HOTSPOT For each of the following statements, select Yes if the statement is true. Otherwise, select No. NOTE: Each correct selection is worth one point. Hot Area:

## Answer Area

| Statements | Yes | No |
|---|---|---|
| Azure provides flexibility between capital expenditure (CapEx) and operational exponditure (OpEx). | ○ | ○ |
| If you create two Azure virtual machines that use the B2S size, each virtual machine will always generate the same monthly costs. | ○ | ○ |
| When an Azure virtual machine is stopped, you continue to pay storage costs associated to the virtual machine. | ○ | ○ |

**Answers:**

A)

## Answer Area

| Statements | Yes | No |
|---|---|---|
| Azure provides flexibility between capital expenditure (CapEx) and operational exponditure (OpEx). | O | O |
| If you create two Azure virtual machines that use the B2S size, each virtual machine will always generate the same monthly costs. | O | O |
| When an Azure virtual machine is stopped, you continue to pay storage costs associated to the virtual machine. | O | O |

**Solution:** A

**Explanation:**

Explanation: Box 1: Yes Traditionally, IT expenses have been considered a Capital Expenditure (CapEx). Today, with the move to the cloud and the pay-as-you-go model, organizations have the ability to stretch their budgets and are shifting their IT CapEx costs to Operating Expenditures (OpEx) instead. This flexibility, in accounting terms, is now an option due to the "as a Service" model of purchasing software, cloud storage and other IT related resources. Box 2: No Two virtual machines using the same size could have different disk configurations. Therefore, the monthly costs could be different. Box 3: Yes When an Azure virtual machine is stopped, you don't pay for the virtual machine. However, you do still pay for the storage costs associated to the virtual machine. The most common storage costs are for the disks attached to the virtual machines. There are also other storage costs associated with a virtual machine such as storage for diagnostic data and virtual machine backups. References: https://meritsolutions.com/capex-vs-opex-cloud-computing-blog/

**Question: 3** *Multiple Answers Are Right*

HOTSPOT To complete the sentence, select the appropriate option in the answer area. Hot Area:

**Answer Area**

When you are implementing a Software as a Service (SaaS) solution, you are responsible for

- configuring high availability.
- defining scalability rules.
- installing the SaaS solution.
- configuring the SaaS solution.

Answers:

A)
**Answer Area**

When you are implementing a Software as a Service (SaaS) solution, you are responsible for

- configuring high availability.
- defining scalability rules.
- installing the SaaS solution.
- **configuring the SaaS solution.**

**Solution:** A

**Explanation:**

Explanation: When you are implementing a Software as a Service (SaaS) solution, you are responsible for configuring the SaaS solution. Everything else is managed by the cloud provider. SaaS requires the least amount of management. The cloud provider is responsible for managing everything, and the end user just uses the software. Software as a service (SaaS) allows users to connect to and use cloud-based apps over the Internet. Common examples are email, calendaring and office tools (such as Microsoft Office 365). SaaS provides a complete software solution which you purchase on a pay-as-you-go basis from a cloud service provider. You rent the use of an app for your organization and your users connect to it over the Internet, usually with a web browser. All of the underlying infrastructure, middleware, app software and app data are located in the service provider's data center. The service provider manages the hardware and software and with the appropriate service agreement, will ensure the availability and the security of the app and your data as well. References: https://azure.microsoft.com/en-in/overview/what-is-saas/ https://docs.microsoft.com/en-gb/learn/modules/principles-cloud-computing/5-types-of-cloud-services

**Question: 4** *One Answer Is Right*

You have an on-premises network that contains several servers. You plan to migrate all the servers to Azure. You need to recommend a solution to ensure that some of the servers are available if a single Azure data center goes offline for an extended period. What should you include in the recommendation?

**Answers:**

**A)** fault tolerance

**B)** elasticity

**C)** scalability

**D)** low latency

**Solution:** A

**Explanation:**

Explanation: Fault tolerance is the ability of a system to continue to function in the event of a failure of some of its components. In this question, you could have servers that are replicated across datacenters. Availability zones expand the level of control you have to maintain the availability of the applications and data on your VMs. Availability Zones are unique physical locations within an Azure region. Each zone is made up of one or more datacenters equipped with independent power, cooling, and networking. To ensure resiliency, there are a minimum of three separate zones in all enabled regions. The physical separation of Availability Zones within a region protects applications and data from datacenter failures. With Availability Zones, Azure offers industry best 99.99% VM uptime SLA. By architecting your solutions to use replicated VMs in zones, you can protect your applications and data from the loss of a datacenter. If one zone is compromised, then replicated apps and data are instantly available in another zone. References: https://docs.microsoft.com/en-us/azure/virtual-machines/windows/manage-availability

**Question: 5** *One Answer Is Right*

This question requires that you evaluate the underlined text to determine if it is correct. An organization that hosts its infrastructure in a private cloud can close its data center. Instructions: Review the underlined text. If it makes the statement correct, select "No change is needed". If the statement is incorrect, select the answer choice that makes the statement correct.

**Answers:**

**A)** No change is needed.

**B)** in a hybrid cloud

**C)** in the public cloud

**D)** on a Hyper-V host

**Solution:** C

**Explanation:**

Explanation: A private cloud is hosted in your datacenter. Therefore, you cannot close your datacenter if you are using a private cloud. A public cloud is hosted externally, for example, in Microsoft Azure. An organization that hosts its infrastructure in a public cloud can close its data center. Public cloud is the most common deployment model. In this case, you have no local hardware to manage or keep up-to-date – everything runs on your cloud provider's hardware. Microsoft Azure is an example of a public cloud provider. In a private cloud, you create a cloud environment in your own datacenter and provide self-service access to compute resources to users in your organization. This offers a simulation of a public cloud to your users, but you remain completely responsible for the purchase and maintenance of the hardware and software services you provide. References: https://docs.microsoft.com/en-gb/learn/modules/principles-cloud-computing/4-cloud-deployment-models

**Question: 6** *One Answer Is Right*

What are two characteristics of the public cloud? Each correct answer presents a complete solution. NOTE: Each correct selection is worth one point.

**Answers:**

**A)** dedicated hardware

**B)** unsecured connections

**C)** limited storage

**D)** metered pricing

**E)** self-service management

**Solution:** D, E

## Explanation:

Explanation: With the public cloud, you get pay-as-you-go pricing – you pay only for what you use, no CapEx costs. With the public cloud, you have self-service management. You are responsible for the deployment and configuration of the cloud resources such as virtual machines or web sites. The underlying hardware that hosts the cloud resources is managed by the cloud provider. Incorrect Answers: A: You don't have dedicated hardware. The underlying hardware is shared so you could have multiple customers using cloud resources hosted on the same physical hardware. B: Connections to the public cloud are secure. C: Storage is not limited. You can have as much storage as you like. References: https://docs.microsoft.com/en-gb/learn/modules/principles-cloud-computing/4-cloud-deployment-models

### Question: 7 *One Answer Is Right*

Note: This question is part of a series of questions that present the same scenario. Each question in the series contains a unique solution that might meet the stated goals. Some question sets might have more than one correct solution, while others might not have a correct solution. After you answer a question in this section, you will NOT be able to return to it. As a result, these questions will not appear in the review screen. Your company plans to migrate all its data and resources to Azure. The company's migration plan states that only Platform as a Service (PaaS) solutions must be used in Azure. You need to deploy an Azure environment that meets the company migration plan. Solution: You create an Azure App Service and Azure virtual machines that have Microsoft SQL Server installed. Does this meet the goal?

### Answers:

A) Yes

B) No

### Solution: B

### Explanation:

Explanation: Azure App Service is a PaaS (Platform as a Service) service. However, Azure virtual machines are an IaaS (Infrastructure as a Service) service. Therefore, this solution does not meet the goal.

### Question: 8 *One Answer Is Right*

Note: This question is part of a series of questions that present the same scenario. Each question in the series contains a unique solution that might meet the stated goals. Some question sets might have more than one correct solution, while others might not have a correct solution. After you answer a question in this section, you will NOT be able to return to it. As a result, these questions will not appear in the review screen. Your company plans to migrate all its data and resources to Azure. The company's migration plan states that only Platform as a Service (PaaS) solutions must be used in Azure. You need to deploy an Azure environment that meets the company migration plan. Solution: You create an Azure App Service and Azure Storage accounts. Does this meet the goal?

**Answers:**

**A)** Yes

**B)** No

**Solution:** B

**Explanation:**

Explanation: Azure App Service is a PaaS (Platform as a Service) service. However, Azure Storage accounts are an IaaS (Infrastructure as a Service) service. Therefore, this solution does not meet the goal.

**Question: 9** *Multiple Answers Are Right*

HOTSPOT To complete the sentence, select the appropriate option in the answer area. Hot Area:

**Answer Area**

When planning to migrate a public website to Azure, you must plan to

- deploy a VPN.
- pay monthly usage costs.
- pay to transfer all the website data to Azure.
- reduce the number of connections to the website.

**Answers:**

A)
**Answer Area**

When planning to migrate a public website to Azure, you must plan to ▼

- deploy a VPN.
- **pay monthly usage costs.**
- pay to transfer all the website data to Azure.
- reduce the number of connections to the website.

**Solution:** A

**Explanation:**

Explanation: When planning to migrate a public website to Azure, you must plan to pay monthly usage costs. This is because Azure uses the pay-as-you-go model.

**Question: 10** *One Answer Is Right*

Note: This question is part of a series of questions that present the same scenario. Each question in the series contains a unique solution that might meet the stated goals. Some question sets might have more than one correct solution, while others might not have a correct solution. After you answer a question in this section, you will NOT be able to return to it. As a result, these questions will not appear in the review screen. Your company plans to migrate all its data and resources to Azure. The company's migration plan states that only Platform as a Service (PaaS) solutions must be used in Azure. You need to deploy an Azure environment that meets the company migration plan. Solution: You create an Azure App Service and Azure SQL databases. Does this meet the goal?

**Answers:**

A) Yes

B) No

**Solution:** A

**Explanation:**

Explanation: Azure App Service and Azure SQL databases are examples of Azure PaaS solutions. Therefore, this solution does meet the goal.

# Chapter 26: DP-100 - Designing and Implementing a Data Science Solution on Azure

## Exam Guide

Designing and Implementing a Data Science Solution on Azure (beta) DP-100 Exam:

Designing and Implementing a Data Science Solution on Azure (beta) DP-100 Exam which is related to Microsoft Certified Azure Data Scientist Associate Certification. This DP-100 exam validates the ability to apply scientific rigor and data exploration techniques to gain actionable insights and communicate results to stakeholders. This DP-100 exam also tests the Candidate knowledge to use machine learning techniques to train, evaluate, and deploy models to build AI solutions that satisfy business objectives. Candidates must have skills to use applications that involve natural language processing, speech, computer vision, and predictive analytics. Azure Data Scientist usually hold or pursue this certification and you can expect the same job role after completion of this certification.

DP-100 Exam topics:

Candidates must know the exam topics before they start of preparation. Because it will really help them in hitting the core. Our **DP-100 dumps** will include the following topics:

- Define and prepare the development environment 15-20%
- Prepare data for modeling 25-30%
- Perform feature engineering 15-20%
- Develop models 40-45%

Certification Path:

The Microsoft Certified Azure Data Scientist Associate Certification includes only one DP-100 Exam.

Who should take the DP-100 exam:

The Designing and Implementing a Data Science Solution on Azure (beta) DP-100 Exam certification is an internationally-recognized validation that identifies persons who earn it as possessing skilled as a Microsoft Certified Azure Data Scientist Associate. If candidates want significant improvement in career growth needs enhanced knowledge, skills, and talents. The Designing and Implementing a Data Science Solution on Azure (beta) DP-100 Exam certification provides proof of this advanced knowledge and skill. If a candidate has knowledge of associated technologies and skills that are required to pass Designing and Implementing a Data Science Solution on Azure (beta) DP-100 Exam then he should take this exam.

How to study the DP-100 Exam:

Certification-questions.com expert team recommends you to prepare some notes on these topics along with it don't forget to practice Microsoft DP-100 Exam dumps which been written by our expert team, Both these will help you a lot to clear this exam with good marks.

How much DP-100 Exam Cost:

The price of the DP-100 exam is $165 USD.

How to book the DP-100 Exam:

These are following steps for registering the DP-100 exam.
Step 1: Visit to Microsoft Exam Registration
Step 2: Signup/Login to MICROSOFT account
Step 3: Search for MICROSOFT DP-100 Certifications Exam
Step 4: Select Date and Center of examination and confirm with payment value of $165

What is the duration of the DP-100 Exam:

- Format: Multiple choices, multiple answers
- Length of Examination: 150 minutes
- Number of Questions: 45-60
- Passing Score: 700/1000

   The benefit in Obtaining the DP-100 Exam Certification:

- After completion of Microsoft Certified Azure Data Scientist Associate Certification candidates receive official confirmation from Microsoft that you are now fully certified in their chosen field. This can be now added to their CV, cover letters and job applications.
- When Candidates applying for a job or looking to promotion in their current position, a Microsoft Certified Azure Data Scientist Associate certification in the field in which Candidates are applying will put you at the top of the list and make them a desirable candidate for employers.

- Candidates will get in-depth knowledge by completing the courses along with the access to revision materials for 6 months upon completion means they will have a wider skill set when it comes to the various technologies and systems than an uncertified professional. Certified Professional in this particular skill set is 74% more efficient when it comes to completing their tasks in a timely well-executed manner.
- Organization owners invest a lot in their employees when it comes to their training with the goal of making them quicker, more efficient, and more knowledgeable about their role. Certified Professional will reduce the time he spends on tasks, meaning he can get more done this could help reduce company downtime when repairing faults on a system or fixing hardware problems.
- Becoming Microsoft Certified Azure Data Scientist Associate means one thing you are worth more to the company and therefore more to yourself in the form of an upgraded pay package. On average a Microsoft Certified Azure Data Scientist Associate member of staff is estimated to be worth 30% more to a company than their uncertified professionals.

Difficulty in writing DP-100 Exam:

Microsoft Certified Azure Data Scientist Associate Certification exam has a higher rank in the Information Technology sector. Candidate can add the most powerful Microsoft DP-100 certification on their resume by passing Microsoft DP-100 exam. Microsoft DP-100 is a very challenging exam Candidate will have to work hard to pass this exam. With the help of Certification-questions provided the right focus and preparation material passing this exam is an achievable goal. Certification-Questions provide the most relevant and updated Microsoft DP-100 exam dumps. Furthermore, We also provide the Microsoft DP-100 practice test that will be much beneficial in the preparation. Our aims to provide the best **Microsoft DP-100 pdf dumps**. We are providing all useful preparation materials such as **Microsoft DP-100 dumps** that had been verified by the Microsoft experts, Microsoft DP-100 braindumps and customer care service in case of any problem. These are things are very helpful in passing the exam with good grades.

For more info visit::

Microsoft DP-100 Exam Reference

# Sample Practice Test for DP-100

**Question: 1** *One Answer Is Right*

You are developing a hands-on workshop to introduce Docker for Windows to attendees. You need to ensure that workshop attendees can install Docker on their devices. Which two prerequisite components should attendees install on the devices? Each correct answer presents part of the solution. NOTE: Each correct selection is worth one point.

**Answers:**

**A)** Microsoft Hardware-Assisted Virtualization Detection Tool

**B)** Kitematic

**C)** BIOS-enabled virtualization

**D)** VirtualBox

**E)** Windows 10 64-bit Professional

**Solution:** C, E

**Explanation:**

Explanation: C: Make sure your Windows system supports Hardware Virtualization Technology and that virtualization is enabled. Ensure that hardware virtualization support is turned on in the BIOS settings. For example:

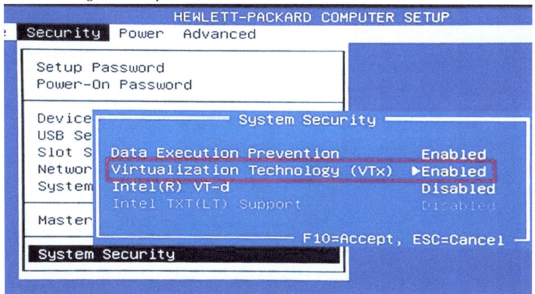

E: To run Docker, your machine must have a 64-bit operating system running Windows 7 or higher. References: https://docs.docker.com/toolbox/toolbox_install_windows/

https://blogs.technet.microsoft.com/canitpro/2015/09/08/step-by-step-enabling-hyper-v-for-use-on-windows- 10/

**Question: 2** *One Answer Is Right*

Your team is building a data engineering and data science development environment. The environment must support the following requirements: - support Python and Scala - compose data storage, movement, and processing services into automated data pipelines - the same tool should be used for the orchestration of both data engineering and data science - support workload isolation and interactive workloads - enable scaling across a cluster of machines You need to create the environment. What should you do?

**Answers:**

**A)** Build the environment in Apache Hive for HDInsight and use Azure Data Factory for orchestration.

**B)** Build the environment in Azure Databricks and use Azure Data Factory for orchestration.

**C)** Build the environment in Apache Spark for HDInsight and use Azure Container Instances for orchestration.

**D)** Build the environment in Azure Databricks and use Azure Container Instances for orchestration.

**Solution:** B

**Explanation:**

Explanation: Explanation: In Azure Databricks, we can create two different types of clusters. - Standard, these are the default clusters and can be used with Python, R, Scala and SQL - High-concurrency Azure Databricks is fully integrated with Azure Data Factory. Incorrect Answers: D: Azure Container Instances is good for development or testing. Not suitable for production workloads. References: https://docs.microsoft.com/en-us/azure/architecture/data-guide/technology-choices/data-science-and- machine-learning

**Question: 3** *Multiple Answers Are Right*

DRAG DROP You are building an intelligent solution using machine learning models. The environment must support the following requirements: - Data scientists must build notebooks in a cloud environment - Data scientists must use automatic feature engineering and model building in machine learning pipelines. - Notebooks must be deployed to retrain using Spark instances with dynamic worker allocation. - Notebooks must be exportable to be version controlled locally. You need to create the environment. Which four actions should you perform in sequence? To answer, move the appropriate actions from the list of actions to the answer area and arrange them in the correct order. Select and Place:

**Actions**

- Install the Azure Machine Learning SDK for Python on the cluster.
- When the cluster is ready, export Zeppelin notebooks to a local environment.
- Create and execute a Jupyter notebook by using automated machine learning (AutoML) on the cluster.
- Install Microsoft Machine Learning for Apache Spark.
- When the cluster is ready and has processed the notebook, export your Jupyter notebook to a local environment.
- Create an Azure HDInsight cluster to include the Apache Spark MLib library.
- Create and execute the Zeppelin notebooks on the cluster.
- Create an Azure Databricks cluster.

**Answer area**

## Answers:

### A)

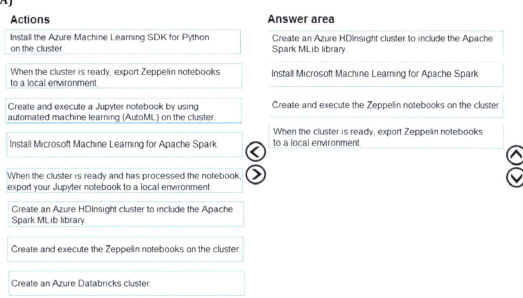

**Solution:** A

**Explanation:**

Explanation: Step 1: Create an Azure HDInsight cluster to include the Apache Spark Mlib library Step 2: Install Microsot Machine Learning for Apache Spark You install AzureML on your Azure HDInsight cluster. Microsoft Machine Learning for Apache Spark (MMLSpark) provides a number of deep learning and data science tools for Apache Spark, including seamless integration of Spark Machine Learning pipelines with Microsoft Cognitive Toolkit (CNTK) and OpenCV, enabling you to quickly create powerful, highly-scalable predictive and analytical models for large image and text datasets. Step 3: Create and execute the Zeppelin notebooks on the cluster Step 4: When the cluster is ready, export Zeppelin notebooks to a local environment. Notebooks must be exportable to be version controlled locally. References: https://docs.microsoft.com/en-us/azure/hdinsight/spark/apache-spark-zeppelin-notebook https://azuremlbuild.blob.core.windows.net/pysparkapi/intro.html

**Question: 4** *One Answer Is Right*

You plan to build a team data science environment. Data for training models in machine learning pipelines will be over 20 GB in size. You have the following requirements: - Models must be built using Caffe2 or Chainer frameworks. - Data scientists must be able to use a data science environment to build the machine learning pipelines and train models on their personal devices in both connected and disconnected network environments. Personal devices must support updating machine learning pipelines when connected to a network. You need to select a data science environment. Which environment should you use?

**Answers:**

**A)** Azure Machine Learning Service

**B)** Azure Machine Learning Studio

**C)** Azure Databricks

**D)** Azure Kubernetes Service (AKS)

**Solution:** A

**Explanation:**

Explanation: Explanation: The Data Science Virtual Machine (DSVM) is a customized VM image on Microsoft's Azure cloud built specifically for doing data science. Caffe2 and Chainer are supported by DSVM. DSVM integrates with Azure Machine Learning. Incorrect Answers: B: Use Machine Learning Studio when you want to experiment with machine learning models quickly and easily, and the built-in machine learning algorithms are sufficient for your solutions. References: https://docs.microsoft.com/en-us/azure/machine-learning/data-science-virtual-machine/overview

**Question: 5** *One Answer Is Right*

You are implementing a machine learning model to predict stock prices. The model uses a PostgreSQL database and requires GPU processing. You need to create a virtual machine that is pre-configured with the required tools. What should you do?

**Answers:**

**A)** Create a Data Science Virtual Machine (DSVM) Windows edition.

**B)** Create a Geo Al Data Science Virtual Machine (Geo-DSVM) Windows edition.

**C)** Create a Deep Learning Virtual Machine (DLVM) Linux edition.

**D)** Create a Deep Learning Virtual Machine (DLVM) Windows edition.

**Solution:** A

**Explanation:**

Explanation: Explanation: In the DSVM, your training models can use deep learning algorithms on hardware that's based on graphics processing units (GPUs). PostgreSQL is available for the following operating systems: Linux (all recent distributions), 64-bit installers available for macOS (OS X) version 10.6 and newer – Windows (with installers available for 64-bit version; tested on latest versions and back to Windows 2012 R2. Incorrect Answers: B: The Azure Geo AI Data Science VM (Geo-DSVM) delivers geospatial analytics capabilities from Microsoft's Data Science VM. Specifically, this VM extends the AI and data science toolkits in the Data Science VM by adding ESRI's market-leading ArcGIS Pro Geographic Information System. C, D: DLVM is a template on top of DSVM image. In terms of the packages, GPU drivers etc are all there in the DSVM image. Mostly it is for convenience during creation where we only allow DLVM to be created on GPU VM instances on Azure. Reference: https://docs.microsoft.com/en-us/azure/machine-learning/data-science-virtual-machine/overview

**Question: 6** *One Answer Is Right*

You are developing deep learning models to analyze semi-structured, unstructured, and structured data types. You have the following data available for model building: - Video recordings of sporting events - Transcripts of radio commentary about events - Logs from related social media feeds captured during sporting events You need to select an environment for creating the model. Which environment should you use?

**Answers:**

**A)** Azure Cognitive Services

**B)** Azure Data Lake Analytics

**C)** Azure HDInsight with Spark MLib

D) Azure Machine Learning Studio

**Solution:** A

**Explanation:**

Explanation: Explanation: Azure Cognitive Services expand on Microsoft's evolving portfolio of machine learning APIs and enable developers to easily add cognitive features – such as emotion and video detection; facial, speech, and vision recognition; and speech and language understanding – into their applications. The goal of Azure Cognitive Services is to help developers create applications that can see, hear, speak, understand, and even begin to reason. The catalog of services within Azure Cognitive Services can be categorized into five main pillars - Vision, Speech, Language, Search, and Knowledge. References: https://docs.microsoft.com/en-us/azure/cognitive-services/welcome

**Question: 7** *One Answer Is Right*

You are moving a large dataset from Azure Machine Learning Studio to a Weka environment. You need to format the data for the Weka environment. Which module should you use?

**Answers:**

A) Convert to CSV

B) Convert to Dataset

C) Convert to ARFF

D) Convert to SVMLight

**Solution:** C

**Explanation:**

Explanation: Explanation: Use the Convert to ARFF module in Azure Machine Learning Studio, to convert datasets and results in Azure Machine Learning to the attribute-relation file format used by the Weka toolset. This format is known as ARFF. The ARFF data specification for Weka supports multiple machine learning tasks, including data preprocessing, classification, and feature selection. In this format, data is organized by entites and their attributes, and is contained in a single text file. References: https://docs.microsoft.com/en-us/azure/machine-learning/studio-module-reference/convert-to-arff

**Question: 8** *One Answer Is Right*

You plan to create a speech recognition deep learning model. The model must support the latest version of Python. You need to recommend a deep learning framework for speech recognition to include in the Data Science Virtual Machine (DSVM). What should you recommend?

**Answers:**

**A)** Rattle

**B)** TensorFlow

**C)** Weka

**D)** Scikit-learn

**Solution:** B

**Explanation:**

Explanation: Explanation: TensorFlow is an open source library for numerical computation and large-scale machine learning. It uses Python to provide a convenient front-end API for building applications with the framework TensorFlow can train and run deep neural networks for handwritten digit classification, image recognition, word embeddings, recurrent neural networks, sequence-to-sequence models for machine translation, natural language processing, and PDE (partial differential equation) based simulations. Incorrect Answers: A: Rattle is the R analytical tool that gets you started with data analytics and machine learning. C: Weka is used for visual data mining and machine learning software in Java. D: Scikit-learn is one of the most useful library for machine learning in Python. It is on NumPy, SciPy and matplotlib, this library contains a lot of effiecient tools for machine learning and statistical modeling including classification, regression, clustering and dimensionality reduction. Reference: https://www.infoworld.com/article/3278008/what-is-tensorflow-the-machine-learning-library-explained.html

**Question: 9** *One Answer Is Right*

You plan to provision an Azure Machine Learning Basic edition workspace for a data science project. You need to identify the tasks you will be able to perform in the workspace. Which three tasks will you be able to perform? Each correct answer presents a complete solution. NOTE: Each correct selection is worth one point.

**Answers:**

**A)** Create a Compute Instance and use it to run code in Jupyter notebooks.

**B)** Create an Azure Kubernetes Service (AKS) inference cluster.

**C)** Use the designer to train a model by dragging and dropping pre-defined modules.

**D)** Create a tabular dataset that supports versioning.

**E)** Use the Automated Machine Learning user interface to train a model.

**Solution:** A, B, D

**Explanation:**

Explanation: Incorrect Answers: C, E: The UI is included the Enterprise edition only. Reference: https://azure.microsoft.com/en-us/pricing/details/machine-learning/

**Question: 10** *One Answer Is Right*

You train and register a model in your Azure Machine Learning workspace. You must publish a pipeline that enables client applications to use the model for batch inferencing. You must use a pipeline with a single ParallelRunStep step that runs a Python inferencing script to get predictions from the input data. You need to create the inferencing script for the ParallelRunStep pipeline step. Which two functions should you include? Each correct answer presents part of the solution. NOTE: Each correct selection is worth one point.

**Answers:**

**A)** run(mini_batch)

**B)** main()

**C)** batch()

**D)** init()

**E)** score(mini_batch)

**Solution:** A, D

**Explanation:**

Explanation: Reference: https://github.com/Azure/MachineLearningNotebooks/tree/master/how-to-use-azureml/machine-learning- pipelines/parallel-run

# Chapter 27: DP-200 - Implementing an Azure Data Solution

## Exam Guide

Implementing an Azure Data Solution DP-200 Exam:

Implementing an Azure Data Solution DP-200 Exam which is related to Microsoft Certified Azure Data Engineer Associate Certification. The DP-200 exam validates the ability to designing and implementing data-driven solutions using the full stack of Azure services. Data engineers, Developers, and Administrators usually hold or pursue this certification and you can expect the same job role after completion of this certification.

DP-200 Exam topics:

Candidates must know the exam topics before they start of preparation. Because it will really help them in hitting the core. Our **DP-200 dumps** will include the following topics:

- Implement data storage solutions 25-30%
- Manage and develop data processing 30-35%
- Manage data security 15-20%
- Monitor data solutions 10-15%
- Manage and troubleshoot Azure data solutions 10-15%

Certification Path:

The Microsoft Certified Azure Data Engineer Associate Certification include DP-200 and DP-201 exams.

Who should take the DP-200 exam:

The Implementing an Azure Data Solution (beta) DP-200 Exam certification is an internationally-recognized validation that identifies persons who earn it as possessing skilled as a Microsoft Certified Azure Data Engineer Associate. If candidates want significant improvement in career growth needs enhanced knowledge, skills, and talents. Implementing an Azure Data Solution (beta) DP-200 Exam certification provides proof of this advanced knowledge and skill. If a candidate has knowledge of associated technologies and skills that are required to pass Implementing an Azure Data Solution (beta) DP-200 Exam then he should take this exam.

How to study the DP-200 Exam:

Certification-questions.com expert team recommends you to prepare some notes on these topics along with it don't forget to practice Microsoft DP-200 Exam dumps which been written by our expert team, Both these will help you a lot to clear this exam with good marks.

How much DP-200 Exam Cost:

The price of the DP-200 exam is $165 USD.

How to book the DP-200 Exam:

These are following steps for registering the DP-200 exam.
Step 1: Visit to Microsoft Exam Registration
Step 2: Signup/Login to MICROSOFT account
Step 3: Search for MICROSOFT DP-200 Certifications Exam
Step 4: Select Date and Center of examination and confirm with payment value of $165

What is the duration of the DP-200 Exam:

- Format: Multiple choices, multiple answers
- Length of Examination: 150 minutes
- Number of Questions: 45-60
- Passing Score: 700/1000

    The benefit in Obtaining the DP-200 Exam Certification:

- After completion of Microsoft Certified Azure Data Engineer, Associate Certification candidates receive official confirmation from Microsoft that you are now fully certified in their chosen field. This can be now added to their CV, cover letters and job applications.
- When Candidates applying for a job or looking to promotion in their current position, a Microsoft Certified Azure Data Engineer Associate certification in the field in which Candidates are applying will put you at the top of the list and make them a desirable candidate for employers.
- Candidates will get in-depth knowledge by completing the courses along with the access to revision materials for 6 months upon completion means they will have a wider skill set when it comes to the various technologies and systems than an uncertified professional. Certified Professional in this particular skill set is 74% more efficient when it comes to completing their tasks in a timely well-executed manner.

- Organization owners invest a lot in their employees when it comes to their training with the goal of making them quicker, more efficient, and more knowledgeable about their role. Certified Professional will reduce the time he spends on tasks, meaning he can get more done this could help reduce company downtime when repairing faults on a system or fixing hardware problems.
- Becoming Microsoft Certified Azure Data Engineer Associate means one thing you are worth more to the company and therefore more to yourself in the form of an upgraded pay package. On average a Microsoft Certified Azure Data Engineer Associate member of staff is estimated to be worth 30% more to a company than their uncertified professionals.

Difficulty in writing DP-200 Exam:

This Microsoft DP-200 exam is very difficult to prepare. Because it requires all candidate attention with practice. So, if Candidate wants to pass this Microsoft DP-200 exam with good grades then he has to choose the right preparation material. By passing the Microsoft DP-200 exam can make a lot of difference in your career. Many Candidates wants to achieve success in the Microsoft DP-200 exam but they are failing in it. Because of their wrong selection but if the candidate can get valid and latest Microsoft DP-200 study material then he can easily get good grades in the Microsoft DP-200 exam. Certification-questions providing many Microsoft DP-200 exam questions that help the candidate to get success in the Microsoft DP-200 test. Our **Microsoft DP-200 dumps** specially designed for those who want to get their desired results in the just first attempt. Microsoft DP-200 braindump questions provided by Certification-questions make candidate preparation material more impactful and the best part is that the training material provided by Certification-questions for Microsoft DP-200 exams are designed by our experts in the several fields of the IT industry.

For more info visit::

Microsoft DP-200 Exam Reference

# Sample Practice Test for DP-200

**Question: 1** *One Answer Is Right*

You are a data engineer implementing a lambda architecture on Microsoft Azure. You use an open-source big data solution to collect, process, and maintain data. The analytical data store performs poorly. You must implement a solution that meets the following requirements: - Provide data warehousing - Reduce ongoing management activities - Deliver SQL query responses in less than one second You need to create an HDInsight cluster to meet the requirements. Which type of cluster should you create?

**Answers:**

**A)** Interactive Query

**B)** Apache Hadoop

**C)** Apache HBase

**D)** Apache Spark

**Solution:** D

**Explanation:**

Explanation: Lambda Architecture with Azure: Azure offers you a combination of following technologies to accelerate real-time big data analytics: 1. Azure Cosmos DB, a globally distributed and multi-model database service. 2. Apache Spark for Azure HDInsight, a processing framework that runs large-scale data analytics applications. 3. Azure Cosmos DB change feed, which streams new data to the batch layer for HDInsight to process. 4. The Spark to Azure Cosmos DB Connector

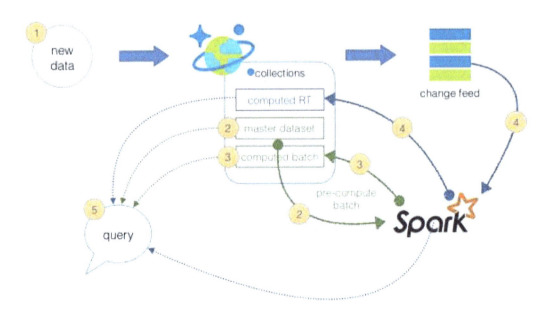

Note: Lambda architecture is a data-processing architecture designed to handle massive quantities of data by taking advantage of both batch processing and stream processing methods, and minimizing the latency involved in querying big data. References: https://sqlwithmanoj.com/2018/02/16/what-is-lambda-architecture-and-what-azure-offers-with-its-new- cosmos-db/

**Question: 2** *Multiple Answers Are Right*

DRAG DROP You develop data engineering solutions for a company. You must migrate data from Microsoft Azure Blob storage to an Azure SQL Data Warehouse for further transformation. You need to implement the solution. Which four actions should you perform in sequence? To answer, move the appropriate actions from the list of actions to the answer area and arrange them in the correct order. Select and Place:

**Actions**

- Provision an Azure SQL Data Warehouse instance.
- Connect to the Blob storage container by using SQL Server Management Studio.
- Provision an Azure Blob storage container.
- Run Transact-SQL statements to load data.
- Connect to the Azure SQL Data Warehouse by using SQL Server Management Studio.
- Build external tables by using Azure portal.
- Build external tables by using SQL Server Management Studio.

**Answer Area**

**Answers:**

## A)

**Actions**

- Provision an Azure SQL Data Warehouse instance.
- Connect to the Blob storage container by using SQL Server Management Studio.
- Provision an Azure Blob storage container.
- Run Transact-SQL statements to load data.
- Connect to the Azure SQL Data Warehouse by using SQL Server Management Studio.
- Build external tables by using Azure portal.
- Build external tables by using SQL Server Management Studio.

**Answer Area**

- Provision an Azure SQL Data Warehouse instance.
- Connect to the Blob storage container by using SQL Server Management Studio.
- Build external tables by using SQL Server Management Studio.
- Run Transact-SQL statements to load data.

**Solution:** A

**Explanation:**

Explanation: Step 1: Provision an Azure SQL Data Warehouse instance. Create a data warehouse in the Azure portal. Step 2: Connect to the Azure SQL Data warehouse by using SQL Server Management Studio Connect to the data warehouse with SSMS (SQL Server Management Studio) Step 3: Build external tables by using the SQL Server Management Studio Create external tables for data in Azure blob storage. You are ready to begin the process of loading data into your new data warehouse. You use external tables to load data from the Azure storage blob. Step 4: Run Transact-SQL statements to load data. You can use the CREATE TABLE AS SELECT (CTAS) T-SQL statement to load the data from Azure Storage Blob into new tables in your data warehouse. References: https://github.com/MicrosoftDocs/azure-docs/blob/master/articles/sql-data-warehouse/load-data-from- azure-blob-storage-using-polybase.md

### Question: 3 *One Answer Is Right*

You develop data engineering solutions for a company. The company has on-premises Microsoft SQL Server databases at multiple locations. The company must integrate data with Microsoft Power BI and Microsoft Azure Logic Apps. The solution must avoid single points of failure during connection and transfer to the cloud. The solution must also minimize latency. You need to secure the transfer of data between on-premises databases and Microsoft Azure. What should you do?

**Answers:**

**A)** Install a standalone on-premises Azure data gateway at each location

**B)** Install an on-premises data gateway in personal mode at each location

**C)** Install an Azure on-premises data gateway at the primary location

**D)** Install an Azure on-premises data gateway as a cluster at each location

**Solution:** D

**Explanation:**

Explanation: You can create high availability clusters of On-premises data gateway installations, to ensure your organization can access on-premises data resources used in Power BI reports and dashboards. Such clusters allow gateway administrators to group gateways to avoid single points of failure in accessing on- premises data resources. The Power BI service always uses the primary gateway in the cluster, unless it's not available. In that case, the service switches to the next gateway in the cluster, and so on. References: https://docs.microsoft.com/en-us/power-bi/service-gateway-high-availability-clusters

**Question: 4** *One Answer Is Right*

You are a data architect. The data engineering team needs to configure a synchronization of data between an on-premises Microsoft SQL Server database to Azure SQL Database. Ad-hoc and reporting queries are being overutilized the on-premises production instance. The synchronization process must: - Perform an initial data synchronization to Azure SQL Database with minimal downtime - Perform bi-directional data synchronization after initial synchronization You need to implement this synchronization solution. Which synchronization method should you use?

**Answers:**

**A)** transactional replication

**B)** Data Migration Assistant (DMA)

**C)** backup and restore

**D)** SQL Server Agent job

**E)** Azure SQL Data Sync

**Solution:** E

**Explanation:**

Explanation: SQL Data Sync is a service built on Azure SQL Database that lets you synchronize the data you select bi- directionally across multiple SQL databases and SQL Server instances. With Data Sync, you can keep data synchronized between your on-premises databases and Azure SQL databases to enable hybrid applications. Compare Data Sync with Transactional Replication

|  | Data Sync | Transactional Replication |
| --- | --- | --- |
| Advantages | - Active-active support<br>- Bi-directional between on-premises and Azure SQL Database | - Lower latency<br>- Transactional consistency<br>- Reuse existing topology after migration |
| Disadvantages | - 5 min or more latency<br>- No transactional consistency<br>- Higher performance impact | - Can't publish from Azure SQL Database single database or pooled database<br>- High maintenance cost |

References: https://docs.microsoft.com/en-us/azure/sql-database/sql-database-sync-data

**Question: 5** *One Answer Is Right*

An application will use Microsoft Azure Cosmos DB as its data solution. The application will use the Cassandra API to support a column-based database type that uses containers to store items. You need to provision Azure Cosmos DB. Which container name and item name should you use? Each correct answer presents part of the solutions. NOTE: Each correct answer selection is worth one point.

**Answers:**

**A)** collection

**B)** rows

**C)** graph

**D)** entities

**E)** table

**Solution:** B, E

**Explanation:**

Explanation: B: Depending on the choice of the API, an Azure Cosmos item can represent either a document in a collection, a row in a table or a node/edge in a graph. The following table shows the mapping between API- specific entities to an Azure Cosmos item:

| Cosmos entity | SQL API | Cassandra API | Azure Cosmos DB's API for MongoDB | Gremlin API | Table API |
|---|---|---|---|---|---|
| Azure Cosmos item | Document | Row | Document | Node or Edge | Item |

E: An Azure Cosmos container is specialized into API-specific entities as follows:

| Azure Cosmos entity | SQL API | Cassandra API | Azure Cosmos DB's API for MongoDB | Gremlin API | Table API |
|---|---|---|---|---|---|
| Azure Cosmos container | Collection | Table | Collection | Graph | Table |

References: https://docs.microsoft.com/en-us/azure/cosmos-db/databases-containers-items

**Question: 6** *One Answer Is Right*

A company has a SaaS solution that uses Azure SQL Database with elastic pools. The solution contains a dedicated database for each customer organization. Customer organizations have peak usage at different periods during the year. You need to implement the Azure SQL Database elastic pool to minimize cost. Which option or options should you configure?

**Answers:**

**A)** Number of transactions only

**B)** eDTUs per database only

**C)** Number of databases only

**D)** CPU usage only

**E)** eDTUs and max data size

**Solution:** E

**Explanation:**

Explanation: The best size for a pool depends on the aggregate resources needed for all databases in the pool. This involves determining the following: - Maximum resources utilized by all databases in the pool (either maximum DTUs or maximum vCores depending on your choice of resourcing model). - Maximum storage bytes utilized by all databases in the pool. Note: Elastic pools enable the developer to purchase resources for a pool shared by multiple databases to accommodate unpredictable periods of usage by individual databases. You can configure resources for the pool based either on the DTU-based purchasing model or the vCore-based purchasing model. References: https://docs.microsoft.com/en-us/azure/sql-database/sql-database-elastic-pool

**Question: 7** *Multiple Answers Are Right*

HOTSPOT You are a data engineer. You are designing a Hadoop Distributed File System (HDFS) architecture. You plan to use Microsoft Azure Data Lake as a data storage repository. You must provision the repository with a resilient data schema. You need to ensure the resiliency of the Azure Data Lake Storage. What should you use? To answer, select the appropriate options in the answer area. NOTE: Each correct selection is worth one point. Hot Area:

**Answer Area**

| Requirement | Node |
|---|---|
| Provide data access to clients. | DataNode / NameNode |
| Run operations on files and directories of the file system. | DataNode / NameNode |
| Perform block creation, deletion, and replication. | DataNode / NameNode |

Answers:

A)

### Answer Area

| Requirement | Node |
|---|---|
| Provide data access to clients. | DataNode / **NameNode** |
| Run operations on files and directories of the file system. | DataNode / **NameNode** |
| Perform block creation, deletion, and replication. | **DataNode** / NameNode |

**Solution:** A

**Explanation:**

Explanation: Box 1: NameNode An HDFS cluster consists of a single NameNode, a master server that manages the file system namespace and regulates access to files by clients. Box 2: DataNode The DataNodes are responsible for serving read and write requests from the file system's clients. Box 3: DataNode The DataNodes perform block creation, deletion, and replication upon instruction from the NameNode. Note: HDFS has a master/slave architecture. An HDFS cluster consists of a single NameNode, a master server that manages the file system namespace and regulates access to files by clients. In addition, there are a number of DataNodes, usually one per node in the cluster, which manage storage attached to the nodes that they run on. HDFS exposes a file system namespace and allows user data to be stored in files. Internally, a file is split into one or more blocks and these blocks are stored in a set of DataNodes. The NameNode executes file system namespace operations like opening, closing, and renaming files and directories. It also determines the mapping of blocks to DataNodes. The DataNodes are responsible for serving read and write requests from the file system's clients. The DataNodes also perform block creation, deletion, and replication upon instruction from the NameNode. References:
https://hadoop.apache.org/docs/r1.2.1/hdfs_design.html#NameNode+and+DataNodes

**Question: 8** *Multiple Answers Are Right*

DRAG DROP You are developing the data platform for a global retail company. The company operates during normal working hours in each region. The analytical database is used once a week for building sales projections. Each region maintains its own private virtual network. Building the sales projections is very resource intensive are generates upwards of 20 terabytes (TB) of data. Microsoft Azure SQL Databases must be provisioned. - Database provisioning must maximize performance and minimize cost - The daily sales for each region must be stored in an Azure SQL Database instance - Once a day, the data for all regions must be loaded in an analytical Azure SQL Database instance You need to provision Azure SQL database instances. How should you provision the database instances? To answer, drag the appropriate Azure SQL products to the correct databases. Each Azure SQL product may be used once, more than once, or not at all. You may need to drag the split bar between panes or scroll to view content. NOTE: Each correct selection is worth one point. Select and Place:

**Answer area**

| Azure SQL products | Database | Azure SQL product |
|---|---|---|
| Azure SQL Database elastic pools | Daily Sales | Azure SQL product |
| Azure SQL Database Premium | Weekly Analysis | Azure SQL product |
| Azure SQL Database Managed Instance | | |
| Azure SQL Database Hyperscale | | |

Answers:

A)

**Answer area**

| Azure SQL products | Database | Azure SQL product |
|---|---|---|
| Azure SQL Database elastic pools | Daily Sales | Azure SQL Database elastic pools |
| Azure SQL Database Premium | Weekly Analysis | Azure SQL Database Hyperscale |
| Azure SQL Database Managed Instance | | |
| Azure SQL Database Hyperscale | | |

**Solution: A**

**Explanation:**

Explanation: Box 1: Azure SQL Database elastic pools SQL Database elastic pools are a simple, cost-effective solution for managing and scaling multiple databases that have varying and unpredictable usage demands. The databases in an elastic pool are on a single Azure SQL Database server and share a set number of resources at a set price. Elastic pools in Azure SQL Database enable SaaS developers to optimize the price performance for a group of databases within a prescribed budget while delivering performance elasticity for each database. Box 2: Azure SQL Database Hyperscale A Hyperscale database is an Azure SQL database in the Hyperscale service tier that is backed by the Hyperscale scale-out storage technology. A Hyperscale database supports up to 100 TB of data and provides high throughput and performance, as well as rapid scaling to adapt to the workload requirements. Scaling is transparent to the application – connectivity, query processing, and so on, work like any other SQL database. Incorrect Answers: Azure SQL Database Managed Instance: The managed instance deployment model is designed for customers looking to migrate a large number of apps from on-premises or IaaS, self-built, or ISV provided environment to fully managed PaaS cloud environment, with as low migration effort as possible. References:
https://docs.microsoft.com/en-us/azure/sql-database/sql-database-elastic-pool
https://docs.microsoft.com/en-us/azure/sql-database/sql-database-service-tier-hyperscale-faq

**Question: 9** *One Answer Is Right*

A company manages several on-premises Microsoft SQL Server databases. You need to migrate the databases to Microsoft Azure by using a backup process of Microsoft SQL Server. Which data technology should you use?

**Answers:**

**A)** Azure SQL Database single database

**B)** Azure SQL Data Warehouse

**C)** Azure Cosmos DB

**D)** Azure SQL Database Managed Instance

**Solution:** D

**Explanation:**

Explanation: Managed instance is a new deployment option of Azure SQL Database, providing near 100% compatibility with the latest SQL Server on-premises (Enterprise Edition) Database Engine, providing a native virtual network (VNet) implementation that addresses common security concerns, and a business model favorable for on-premises SQL Server customers. The managed instance deployment model allows existing SQL Server customers to lift and shift their

on-premises applications to the cloud with minimal application and database changes.
References: https://docs.microsoft.com/en-us/azure/sql-database/sql-database-managed-instance

**Question: 10** *One Answer Is Right*

The data engineering team manages Azure HDInsight clusters. The team spends a large amount of time creating and destroying clusters daily because most of the data pipeline process runs in minutes. You need to implement a solution that deploys multiple HDInsight clusters with minimal effort. What should you implement?

**Answers:**

**A)** Azure Databricks

**B)** Azure Traffic Manager

**C)** Azure Resource Manager templates

**D)** Ambari web user interface

**Solution:** C

**Explanation:**

Explanation: A Resource Manager template makes it easy to create the following resources for your application in a single, coordinated operation: - HDInsight clusters and their dependent resources (such as the default storage account). - Other resources (such as Azure SQL Database to use Apache Sqoop). In the template, you define the resources that are needed for the application. You also specify deployment parameters to input values for different environments. The template consists of JSON and expressions that you use to construct values for your deployment. References: https://docs.microsoft.com/en-us/azure/hdinsight/hdinsight-hadoop-create-linux-clusters-arm-templates

# Chapter 28: DP-201 - Designing an Azure Data Solution

## Exam Guide

Designing an Azure Data Solution DP-201 Exam:

Designing an Azure Data Solution DP-201 Exam which is related to Microsoft Certified Azure Data Engineer Associate Certification. The DP-201 exam validates the ability to ingesting, egressing, and transforming data from multiple sources using various services and tools. This exam also tests the knowledge of designing and implementing the management, monitoring, security, and privacy of data using the full stack of Azure services to satisfy business needs. Data engineers, Developers, and Administrators usually hold or pursue this certification and you can expect the same job role after completion of this certification.

DP-201 Exam topics:

Candidates must know the exam topics before they start of preparation. Because it will really help them in hitting the core. Our **DP-201 dumps** will include the following topics:

- Design Azure data storage solutions 30-35%
- Design data processing solutions 25-30%
- Design for data security and compliance 15-20%
- Design for high availability and disaster recovery 20-25%

Certification Path:

The Microsoft Certified Azure Data Engineer Associate Certification include DP-200 and DP-201 exams.

Who should take the DP-201 exam:

The Designing an Azure Data Solution DP-201 Exam certification is an internationally recognized validation that identifies persons who earn it as possessing skilled as a Microsoft Certified Azure Data Engineer Associate. If candidates want significant improvement in career growth needs enhanced knowledge, skills, and talents. The Designing an Azure Data Solution

DP-201 Exam certification provides proof of this advanced knowledge and skill. If a candidate has knowledge of associated technologies and skills that are required to pass Designing an Azure Data Solution DP-201 Exam then he should take this exam.

How to study the DP-201 Exam:

Certification-questions.com expert team recommends you to prepare some notes on these topics along with it don't forget to practice Microsoft DP-201 Exam dumps which been written by our expert team, Both these will help you a lot to clear this exam with good marks.

How much DP-201 Exam Cost:

The price of the DP-201 exam is $165 USD.

How to book the DP-201 Exam:

These are following steps for registering the DP-201 exam.
Step 1: Visit to Microsoft Exam Registration
Step 2: Signup/Login to MICROSOFT account
Step 3: Search for MICROSOFT DP-201 Certifications Exam
Step 4: Select Date and Center of examination and confirm with payment value of $165

What is the duration of the DP-201 Exam:

- Format: Multiple choices, multiple answers
- Length of Examination: 150 minutes
- Number of Questions: 45-60
- Passing Score: 700/1000

    The benefit in Obtaining the DP-201 Exam Certification:

- After completion of Microsoft Certified Azure Data Engineer, Associate Certification candidates receive official confirmation from Microsoft that you are now fully certified in their chosen field. This can be now added to their CV, cover letters and job applications.
- When Candidates applying for a job or looking to promotion in their current position, a Microsoft Certified Azure Data Engineer Associate certification in the field in which Candidates are applying will put you at the top of the list and make them a desirable candidate for employers.
- Candidates will get in-depth knowledge by completing the courses along with the access to revision materials for 6 months upon completion means they will have a wider skill set when it comes to the various technologies and systems than an uncertified professional. Certified Professional in this particular skill set is 74% more efficient when it comes to completing their tasks in a timely well-executed manner.

- Organization owners invest a lot in their employees when it comes to their training with the goal of making them quicker, more efficient, and more knowledgeable about their role. Certified Professional will reduce the time he spends on tasks, meaning he can get more done this could help reduce company downtime when repairing faults on a system or fixing hardware problems.
- Becoming Microsoft Certified Azure Data Engineer Associate means one thing you are worth more to the company and therefore more to yourself in the form of an upgraded pay package. On average a Microsoft Certified Azure Data Engineer Associate member of staff is estimated to be worth 30% more to a company than their uncertified professionals.

Difficulty in writing DP-201 Exam:

Microsoft Certified Azure Data Engineer Associate Certification is a most privileged achievement one could be graced with. But contrary to common views and opinions certifying with Microsoft is not that difficult. If the candidates have proper preparation material to pass the Microsoft DP-201 exam with good grades. Certification questions contain the most exceptional questions answers and clarifications which cover the entire course content. Certification questions have a brilliant Microsoft DP-201 exam dumps with most recent and important questions and answers in PDF files. Certification-questions is sure about the exactness and legitimacy of **Microsoft DP-201 exam dumps** and in this manner. Candidates can easily pass the Microsoft DP-201 exam with genuine Microsoft DP-201 dumps and get Microsoft certification skillful surely. These dumps are viewed as the best source to understand the Microsoft Certified Azure Data Engineer Associate Certification well by simply perusing these example questions and answers. If candidate complete practice the exam with certification Microsoft DP-201 dumps along with self-assessment to get the proper idea on Microsoft accreditation questions and answers for successful completion of the certification exam. Then he can pass the exam with good grades easily.

For more info visit::

Microsoft DP-201 Exam Reference

# Sample Practice Test for DP-201

**Question: 1** *One Answer Is Right*

You need to design the vehicle images storage solution. What should you recommend?

**Scenario:**

TESTLET-1. Case study This is a case study. Case studies are not timed separately. You can use as much exam time as you would like to complete each case. However, there may be additional case studies and sections on this exam. You must manage your time to ensure that you are able to complete all questions included on this exam in the time provided. To answer the questions included in a case study, you will need to reference information that is provided in the case study. Case studies might contain exhibits and other resources that provide more information about the scenario that is described in the case study. Each question is independent of the other questions in this case study. At the end of this case study, a review screen will appear. This screen allows you to review your answers and to make changes before you move to the next section of the exam. After you begin a new section, you cannot return to this section. To start the case study To display the first question in this case study, click the Next button. Use the buttons in the left pane to explore the content of the case study before you answer the questions. Clicking these buttons displays information such as business requirements, existing environment, and problem statements. If the case study has an All Information tab, note that the information displayed is identical to the information displayed on the subsequent tabs. When you are ready to answer a question, click the Question button to return to the question. Background Trey Research is a technology innovator. The company partners with regional transportation department office to build solutions that improve traffic flow and safety. The company is developing the following solutions:

| Solution | Comments |
| --- | --- |
| Real Time Response | This solution will detect sudden changes in traffic flow including slow downs and stops that persist for more than one minute. The system will automatically dispatch emergency response vehicles to investigate issues. <br> The solution will use a PySpark script to detect traffic flow changes. Script performance will be limited by available memory. |
| Backtrack | This solution will allow public safety officials to locate vehicles on roadways that implement traffic sensors. The solution must report changes in real time. |
| Planning Assistance | Transportation organizations will use Planning Assistance to analyze traffic data. The solution will allow users to define reports based on queries of the traffic data. The reports can be used for the following analyses:<br>• current traffic load<br>• correlation with recent local events susch as sporting events<br>• historical traffic<br>• tracking the travel of a single vehicle |

Regional transportation departments installed traffic sensor systems on major highways across North America. Sensors record the following information each time a vehicle passes in front of a sensor: - Time - Location in latitude and longitude -Speed in kilometers per second (kmps)- License plate number - Length of vehicle in meters Sensors provide data by using the following structure:

```
{
   "time" : "2014-09-15T23:14:25.72511732",
    "location" : {
       "type": "Point",
       "coordinates": [
            31.9.
            -4.8
       ]
    },
    "speed": 66.2,
    "license_plate": "WA-AJ0072W",
    "vehicle_length": 4.5
}
```

Traffic sensors will occasionally capture an image of a vehicle for debugging purposes. You must optimize performance of saving/storing vehicle images. Traffic sensor data - Sensors must have permission only to add items to the SensorData collection. - Traffic data insertion rate must be maximized. - Once every three months all traffic sensor data must be analyzed to look for data patterns that indicate sensor malfunctions. - Sensor data must be stored in a Cosmos DB named treydata in a collection named SensorData - The impact of vehicle images on sensor data throughout must be minimized. Backtrack This solution reports on all data related to a specific vehicle license plate. The report must use data from the SensorData collection. Users must be able to filter vehicle data in the following ways: - vehicles on a specific road - vehicles driving above the speed limit Planning Assistance Data used for Planning Assistance must be stored in a sharded Azure SQL Database. Data from the Sensor Data collection will automatically be loaded into the Planning Assistance database once a week by using Azure Data Factory. You must be able to manually trigger the data load process. Privacy and security policy - Azure Active Directory must be used for all services where it is available. - For privacy reasons, license plate number information must not be accessible in Planning Assistance. - Unauthorized usage of the Planning Assistance data must be detected as quickly as possible. Unauthorized usage is determined by looking for an unusual pattern of usage. - Data must only be stored for seven years. Performance and availability - The report for Backtrack must execute as quickly as possible. - The SLA for Planning Assistance is 70 percent, and multiday outages are permitted. - All data must be replicated to multiple geographic regions to prevent data loss.- You must maximize the performance of the Real Time Response system. Financial requirements Azure resource costs must be minimized where possible.

**Answers:**

**A)** Azure Media Services

**B)** Azure Premium Storage account

**C)** Azure Redis Cache

**D)** Azure Cosmos DB

**Solution:** B

**Explanation:**

Explanation: Premium Storage stores data on the latest technology Solid State Drives (SSDs) whereas Standard Storage stores data on Hard Disk Drives (HDDs). Premium Storage is designed for Azure Virtual Machine workloads which require consistent high IO performance and low latency in order to host IO intensive workloads like OLTP, Big Data, and Data Warehousing on platforms like SQL Server, MongoDB, Cassandra, and others. With Premium Storage, more customers will be able to lift-and-shift demanding enterprise applications to the cloud. Scenario: Traffic sensors will occasionally capture an image of a vehicle for debugging purposes. You must optimize performance of saving/storing vehicle images. The impact of vehicle images on sensor data throughout must be minimized. Reference: https://azure.microsoft.com/es-es/blog/introducing-premium-storage-high-performance-storage-for-azure- virtual-machine-workloads/

**Question: 2** *One Answer Is Right*

You need to design a sharding strategy for the Planning Assistance database. What should you recommend?

**Scenario:**

TESTLET-1. Case study This is a case study. Case studies are not timed separately. You can use as much exam time as you would like to complete each case. However, there may be additional case studies and sections on this exam. You must manage your time to ensure that you are able to complete all questions included on this exam in the time provided. To answer the questions included in a case study, you will need to reference information that is provided in the case study. Case studies might contain exhibits and other resources that provide more information about the scenario that is described in the case study. Each question is independent of the other questions in this case study. At the end of this case study, a review screen will appear. This screen allows you to review your answers and to make changes before you move to the next section of the exam. After you begin a new section, you cannot return to this section. To start the case study To display the first question in this case study, click the Next button. Use the buttons in the left pane to explore the content of the case study before you answer the questions.

Clicking these buttons displays information such as business requirements, existing environment, and problem statements. If the case study has an All Information tab, note that the information displayed is identical to the information displayed on the subsequent tabs. When you are ready to answer a question, click the Question button to return to the question. Background Trey Research is a technology innovator. The company partners with regional transportation department office to build solutions that improve traffic flow and safety. The company is developing the following solutions:

| Solution | Comments |
|---|---|
| Real Time Response | This solution will detect sudden changes in traffic flow including slow downs and stops that persist for more than one minute. The system will automatically dispatch emergency response vehicles to investigate issues. The solution will use a PySpark script to detect traffic flow changes. Script performance will be limited by available memory. |
| Backtrack | This solution will allow public safety officials to locate vehicles on roadways that implement traffic sensors. The solution must report changes in real time. |
| Planning Assistance | Transportation organizations will use Planning Assistance to analyze traffic data. The solution will allow users to define reports based on queries of the traffic data. The reports can be used for the following analyses:<br>• current traffic load<br>• correlation with recent local events susch as sporting events<br>• historical traffic<br>• tracking the travel of a single vehicle |

Regional transportation departments installed traffic sensor systems on major highways across North America. Sensors record the following information each time a vehicle passes in front of a sensor: - Time - Location in latitude and longitude -Speed in kilometers per second (kmps)- License plate number - Length of vehicle in meters Sensors provide data by using the following structure:

```
{
  "time" : "2014-09-15T23:14:25.72511732",
  "location" : {
    "type": "Point",
    "coordinates": [
        31.9.
        -4.8
    ]
  },
  "speed": 66.2,
  "license_plate": "WA-AJ0072W",
  "vehicle_length": 4.5
}
```

Traffic sensors will occasionally capture an image of a vehicle for debugging purposes. You must optimize performance of saving/storing vehicle images. Traffic sensor data - Sensors must have permission only to add items to the SensorData collection. - Traffic data insertion rate must be maximized. - Once every three months all traffic sensor data must be analyzed to look for data patterns that indicate sensor malfunctions. - Sensor data must be stored in a Cosmos DB named treydata in a collection named SensorData - The impact of vehicle images on sensor data throughout must be minimized. Backtrack This solution reports on all data related to a specific vehicle license plate. The report must use data from the SensorData collection. Users must be able to filter vehicle data in the following ways: - vehicles on a specific road - vehicles driving above the speed limit Planning Assistance Data used for Planning Assistance must be stored in a sharded Azure SQL Database. Data from the Sensor Data collection will automatically be loaded into the Planning Assistance database once a week by using Azure Data Factory. You must be able to manually trigger the data load process. Privacy and security policy - Azure Active Directory must be used for all services where it is available. - For privacy reasons, license plate number information must not be accessible in Planning Assistance. - Unauthorized usage of the Planning Assistance data must be detected as quickly as possible. Unauthorized usage is determined by looking for an unusual pattern of usage. - Data must only be stored for seven years. Performance and availability - The report for Backtrack must execute as quickly as possible. - The SLA for Planning Assistance is 70 percent, and multiday outages are permitted. - All data must be replicated to multiple geographic regions to prevent data loss.- You must maximize the performance of the Real Time Response system. Financial requirements Azure resource costs must be minimized where possible.

### Answers:

**A)** a list mapping shard map on the binary representation of the License Plate column

**B)** a range mapping shard map on the binary representation of the speed column

**C)** a list mapping shard map on the location column

**D)** a range mapping shard map on the time column

**Solution:** A

**Explanation:**

Explanation: Data used for Planning Assistance must be stored in a sharded Azure SQL Database. A shard typically contains items that fall within a specified range determined by one or more attributes of the data. These attributes form the shard key (sometimes referred to as the partition key). The shard key should be static. It shouldn't be based on data that might change. Reference: https://docs.microsoft.com/en-us/azure/architecture/patterns/sharding

**Question: 3** *Multiple Answers Are Right*

HOTSPOT You need to design the SensorData collection. What should you recommend? To answer, select the appropriate options in the answer area. NOTE: Each correct selection is worth one point. Hot Area:

## Answer Area

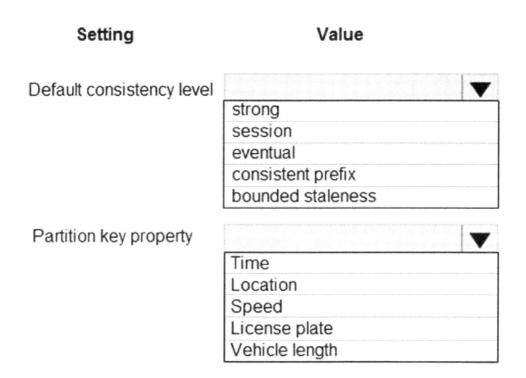

| Setting | Value |
|---|---|
| Default consistency level | strong / session / eventual / consistent prefix / bounded staleness |
| Partition key property | Time / Location / Speed / License plate / Vehicle length |

**Scenario:**

TESTLET-1. Case study This is a case study. Case studies are not timed separately. You can use as much exam time as you would like to complete each case. However, there may be additional case studies and sections on this exam. You must manage your time to ensure that you are able to complete all questions included on this exam in the time provided. To answer the questions included in a case study, you will need to reference information that is provided in the case study. Case studies might contain exhibits and other resources that provide more information about the scenario that is described in the case study. Each question is independent of the other questions in this case study. At the end of this case study, a review screen will appear. This screen allows you to review your answers and to make changes before you move to the next section of the exam. After you begin a new section, you cannot return to this section. To start the case study To display the first question in this case study, click the Next button. Use the buttons in the left pane to explore the content of the case study before you answer the questions. Clicking these buttons displays information such as business requirements, existing environment, and problem statements. If the case study has an All Information tab, note that the information displayed is identical to the information displayed on the subsequent tabs. When you are ready to answer a question, click the Question button to return to the question. Background Trey Research is a technology innovator. The company partners with regional transportation department office to build solutions that improve traffic flow and safety. The company is developing the following solutions:

| Solution | Comments |
| --- | --- |
| Real Time Response | This solution will detect sudden changes in traffic flow including slow downs and stops that persist for more than one minute. The system will automatically dispatch emergency response vehicles to investigate issues.<br>The solution will use a PySpark script to detect traffic flow changes. Script performance will be limited by available memory. |
| Backtrack | This solution will allow public safety officials to locate vehicles on roadways that implement traffic sensors. The solution must report changes in real time. |
| Planning Assistance | Transportation organizations will use Planning Assistance to analyze traffic data. The solution will allow users to define reports based on queries of the traffic data. The reports can be used for the following analyses:<br>• current traffic load<br>• correlation with recent local events susch as sporting events<br>• historical traffic<br>• tracking the travel of a single vehicle |

Regional transportation departments installed traffic sensor systems on major highways across North America. Sensors record the following information each time a vehicle passes in front of a sensor: - Time - Location in latitude and longitude -Speed in kilometers per second (kmps)- License plate number - Length of vehicle in meters Sensors provide data by using the following structure:

```
{
  "time" : "2014-09-15T23:14:25.72511732",
    "location" : {
      "type": "Point",
      "coordinates": [
          31.9.
          -4.8
      ]
    },
  "speed": 66.2,
  "license_plate": "WA-AJ0072W",
  "vehicle_length": 4.5
}
```

Traffic sensors will occasionally capture an image of a vehicle for debugging purposes. You must optimize performance of saving/storing vehicle images. Traffic sensor data - Sensors must have permission only to add items to the SensorData collection. - Traffic data insertion rate must be maximized. - Once every three months all traffic sensor data must be analyzed to look for data patterns that indicate sensor malfunctions. - Sensor data must be stored in a Cosmos DB named treydata in a collection named SensorData - The impact of vehicle images on sensor data throughout must be minimized. Backtrack This solution reports on all data related to a specific vehicle license plate. The report must use data from the SensorData collection. Users must be able to filter vehicle data in the following ways: - vehicles on a specific road - vehicles driving above the speed limit Planning Assistance Data used for Planning Assistance must be stored in a sharded Azure SQL Database. Data from the Sensor Data collection will automatically be loaded into the Planning Assistance database once a week by using Azure Data Factory. You must be able to manually trigger the data load process. Privacy and security policy - Azure Active Directory must be used for all services where it is available. - For privacy reasons, license plate number information must not be accessible in Planning Assistance. - Unauthorized usage of the Planning Assistance data must be detected as quickly as possible. Unauthorized usage is determined by looking for an unusual pattern of usage. - Data must only be stored for seven years. Performance and availability - The report for Backtrack must execute as quickly as possible. - The SLA for Planning Assistance is 70 percent, and multiday outages are permitted. - All data must be replicated to multiple geographic regions to prevent data loss.- You must maximize the performance of the Real Time Response system. Financial requirements Azure resource costs must be minimized where possible.

**Answers:**

A)

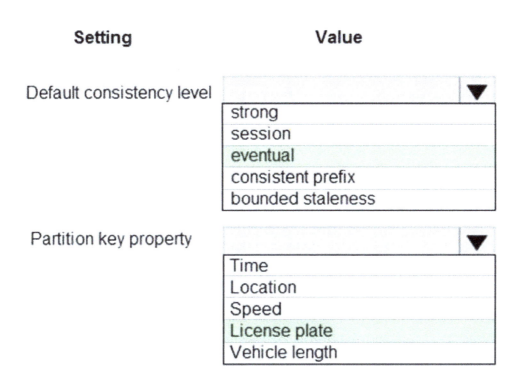

**Solution:** A

**Explanation:**

Explanation: Box 1: Eventual Traffic data insertion rate must be maximized. Sensor data must be stored in a Cosmos DB named treydata in a collection named SensorData With Azure Cosmos DB, developers can choose from five well-defined consistency models on the consistency spectrum. From strongest to more relaxed, the models include strong, bounded staleness, session, consistent prefix, and eventual consistency. Box 2: License plate This solution reports on all data related to a specific vehicle license plate. The report must use data from the SensorData collection. Reference: https://docs.microsoft.com/en-us/azure/cosmos-db/consistency-levels

**Question: 4** *One Answer Is Right*

You need to recommend an Azure SQL Database pricing tier for Planning Assistance. Which pricing tier should you recommend?

**Scenario:**

TESTLET-1. Case study This is a case study. Case studies are not timed separately. You can use as much exam time as you would like to complete each case. However, there may be additional case studies and sections on this exam. You must manage your time to ensure that you are able to complete all questions included on this exam in the time provided. To answer the questions included in a case study, you will need to reference information that is provided in the case study. Case studies might contain exhibits and other resources that provide more information about the scenario that is described in the case study. Each question is independent of the other questions in this case study. At the end of this case study, a review screen will appear. This screen allows you to review your answers and to make changes before you move to the next section of the exam. After you begin a new section, you cannot return to this section. To start the case study To display the first question in this case study, click the Next button. Use the buttons in the left pane to explore the content of the case study before you answer the questions. Clicking these buttons displays information such as business requirements, existing environment, and problem statements. If the case study has an All Information tab, note that the information displayed is identical to the information displayed on the subsequent tabs. When you are ready to answer a question, click the Question button to return to the question. Background Trey Research is a technology innovator. The company partners with regional transportation department office to build solutions that improve traffic flow and safety. The company is developing the following solutions:

| Solution | Comments |
|---|---|
| Real Time Response | This solution will detect sudden changes in traffic flow including slow downs and stops that persist for more than one minute. The system will automatically dispatch emergency response vehicles to investigate issues.<br>The solution will use a PySpark script to detect traffic flow changes. Script performance will be limited by available memory. |
| Backtrack | This solution will allow public safety officials to locate vehicles on roadways that implement traffic sensors. The solution must report changes in real time. |
| Planning Assistance | Transportation organizations will use Planning Assistance to analyze traffic data. The solution will allow users to define reports based on queries of the traffic data. The reports can be used for the following analyses:<br>• current traffic load<br>• correlation with recent local events susch as sporting events<br>• historical traffic<br>• tracking the travel of a single vehicle |

Regional transportation departments installed traffic sensor systems on major highways across

North America. Sensors record the following information each time a vehicle passes in front of a sensor: - Time - Location in latitude and longitude -Speed in kilometers per second (kmps)- License plate number - Length of vehicle in meters Sensors provide data by using the following structure:

```
{
  "time" : "2014-09-15T23:14:25.72511732",
    "location" : {
      "type": "Point",
      "coordinates": [
          31.9.
          -4.8
      ]
    },
    "speed": 66.2,
    "license_plate": "WA-AJ0072W",
    "vehicle_length": 4.5
}
```

Traffic sensors will occasionally capture an image of a vehicle for debugging purposes. You must optimize performance of saving/storing vehicle images. Traffic sensor data - Sensors must have permission only to add items to the SensorData collection. - Traffic data insertion rate must be maximized. - Once every three months all traffic sensor data must be analyzed to look for data patterns that indicate sensor malfunctions. - Sensor data must be stored in a Cosmos DB named treydata in a collection named SensorData - The impact of vehicle images on sensor data throughout must be minimized. Backtrack This solution reports on all data related to a specific vehicle license plate. The report must use data from the SensorData collection. Users must be able to filter vehicle data in the following ways: - vehicles on a specific road - vehicles driving above the speed limit Planning Assistance Data used for Planning Assistance must be stored in a sharded Azure SQL Database. Data from the Sensor Data collection will automatically be loaded into the Planning Assistance database once a week by using Azure Data Factory. You must be able to manually trigger the data load process. Privacy and security policy - Azure Active Directory must be used for all services where it is available. - For privacy reasons, license plate number information must not be accessible in Planning Assistance. - Unauthorized usage of the Planning Assistance data must be detected as quickly as possible. Unauthorized usage is determined by looking for an unusual pattern of usage. - Data must only be stored for seven years. Performance and availability - The report for Backtrack must execute as quickly as possible. - The SLA for Planning Assistance is 70 percent, and multiday outages are permitted. - All data must be replicated to multiple geographic regions to prevent data loss.- You must maximize the performance of the Real Time Response system. Financial requirements Azure resource costs must be minimized where possible.

**Answers:**

**A)** Business critical Azure SQL Database single database

**B)** General purpose Azure SQL Database Managed Instance

**C)** Business critical Azure SQL Database Managed Instance

**D)** General purpose Azure SQL Database single database

**Solution:** B

**Explanation:**

Explanation: Azure resource costs must be minimized where possible. Data used for Planning Assistance must be stored in a sharded Azure SQL Database. The SLA for Planning Assistance is 70 percent, and multiday outages are permitted.

**Question: 5** *Multiple Answers Are Right*

HOTSPOT You need to design the Planning Assistance database. For each of the following statements, select Yes if the statement is true. Otherwise, select No. NOTE: Each correct selection is worth one point. Hot Area:

## Answer Area

| Statement | Yes | No |
| --- | --- | --- |
| Including a clustered columnstore index in the design will benefit performance. | ○ | ○ |
| Including a nonclustered columnstore index in the design will benefit performance. | ○ | ○ |
| Including an index on the License Plate column will benefit performance. | ○ | ○ |

**Scenario:**

TESTLET-1. Case study This is a case study. Case studies are not timed separately. You can use as much exam time as you would like to complete each case. However, there may be additional case studies and sections on this exam. You must manage your time to ensure that you are able to complete all questions included on this exam in the time provided. To answer the questions included in a case study, you will need to reference information that is provided in the case study. Case studies might contain exhibits and other resources that provide more information about the scenario that is described in the case study. Each question is independent of the other questions in this case study. At the end of this case study, a review screen will appear. This screen allows you to review your answers and to make changes before you move to the next section of the exam. After you begin a new section, you cannot return to this section. To start the case study To display the first question in this case study, click the Next button. Use the buttons in the left pane to explore the content of the case study before you answer the questions. Clicking these buttons displays information such as business requirements, existing environment, and problem statements. If the case study has an All Information tab, note that the information displayed is identical to the information displayed on the subsequent tabs. When you are ready to answer a question, click the Question button to return to the question. Background Trey Research is a technology innovator. The company partners with regional transportation department office to build solutions that improve traffic flow and safety. The company is developing the following solutions:

| Solution | Comments |
|---|---|
| Real Time Response | This solution will detect sudden changes in traffic flow including slow downs and stops that persist for more than one minute. The system will automatically dispatch emergency response vehicles to investigate issues. The solution will use a PySpark script to detect traffic flow changes. Script performance will be limited by available memory. |
| Backtrack | This solution will allow public safety officials to locate vehicles on roadways that implement traffic sensors. The solution must report changes in real time. |
| Planning Assistance | Transportation organizations will use Planning Assistance to analyze traffic data. The solution will allow users to define reports based on queries of the traffic data. The reports can be used for the following analyses:<br>• current traffic load<br>• correlation with recent local events susch as sporting events<br>• historical traffic<br>• tracking the travel of a single vehicle |

Regional transportation departments installed traffic sensor systems on major highways across North America. Sensors record the following information each time a vehicle passes in front of a sensor: - Time - Location in latitude and longitude -Speed in kilometers per second (kmps)- License plate number - Length of vehicle in meters Sensors provide data by using the following structure:

```
{
  "time" : "2014-09-15T23:14:25.72511732",
  "location" : {
    "type": "Point",
    "coordinates": [
        31.9,
        -4.8
    ]
  },
  "speed": 66.2,
  "license_plate": "WA-AJ0072W",
  "vehicle_length": 4.5
}
```

Traffic sensors will occasionally capture an image of a vehicle for debugging purposes. You must optimize performance of saving/storing vehicle images. Traffic sensor data - Sensors must have permission only to add items to the SensorData collection. - Traffic data insertion rate must be maximized. - Once every three months all traffic sensor data must be analyzed to look for data patterns that indicate sensor malfunctions. - Sensor data must be stored in a Cosmos DB named treydata in a collection named SensorData - The impact of vehicle images on sensor data throughput must be minimized. Backtrack This solution reports on all data related to a specific vehicle license plate. The report must use data from the SensorData collection. Users must be able to filter vehicle data in the following ways: - vehicles on a specific road - vehicles driving above the speed limit Planning Assistance Data used for Planning Assistance must be stored in a sharded Azure SQL Database. Data from the Sensor Data collection will automatically be loaded into the Planning Assistance database once a week by using Azure Data Factory. You must be able to manually trigger the data load process. Privacy and security policy - Azure Active Directory must be used for all services where it is available. - For privacy reasons, license plate number information must not be accessible in Planning Assistance. - Unauthorized usage of the Planning Assistance data must be detected as quickly as possible. Unauthorized usage is determined by looking for an unusual pattern of usage. - Data must only be stored for seven years. Performance and availability - The report for Backtrack must execute as quickly as possible. - The SLA for Planning Assistance is 70 percent, and multiday outages are permitted. - All data must be replicated to multiple geographic regions to prevent data loss.- You must maximize the performance of the Real Time Response system. Financial requirements Azure resource costs must be minimized where possible.

**Answers:**

A)

## Answer Area

| Statement | Yes | No |
|---|---|---|
| Including a clustered columnstore index in the design will benefit performance. | ○ | ● |
| Including a nonclustered columnstore index in the design will benefit performance. | ● | ○ |
| Including an index on the License Plate column will benefit performance. | ○ | ○ |

**Solution:** A

**Explanation:**

Explanation: Box 1: No Data used for Planning Assistance must be stored in a sharded Azure SQL Database. Box 2: Yes Box 3: Yes Planning Assistance database will include reports tracking the travel of a single vehicle Design Azure data storage solutions

**Question: 6** *One Answer Is Right*

You need to recommend a solution for storing the image tagging data. What should you recommend?

**Scenario:**

TESTLET-2. Overview You develop data engineering solutions for Graphics Design Institute, a global media company with offices in New York City, Manchester, Singapore, and Melbourne. The New York office hosts SQL Server databases that stores massive amounts of customer data. The company also stores millions of images on a physical server located in the New York office. More than 2 TB of image data is added each day. The images are transferred from customer devices to the server in New York. Many images have been placed on this server in an unorganized manner, making it difficult for editors to search images. Images should automatically have object and color tags generated. The tags must be stored in a document database, and be queried by SQL. You are hired to design a solution that can store, transform, and visualize customer data. Requirements Business The company identifies the following business requirements: - You must transfer all images and customer data to cloud storage and remove on-premises servers. - You must develop an analytical processing solution for transforming customer data. - You must develop an image object and color tagging solution. - Capital expenditures must be minimized. - Cloud resource costs must be minimized. Technical The solution has the following technical requirements: - Tagging data must be uploaded to the cloud from the New York office location. - Tagging data must be replicated to regions that are geographically close to company office locations. - Image data must be stored in a single data store at minimum cost. - Customer data must be analyzed using managed Spark clusters. - Power BI must be used to visualize transformed customer data.- All data must be backed up in case disaster recovery is required. Security and optimization All cloud data must be encrypted at rest and in transit. The solution must support: - parallel processing of customer data - hyper-scale storage of images - global region data replication of processed image data

**Answers:**

**A)** Azure File Storage

**B)** Azure Cosmos DB

**C)** Azure Blob Storage

**D)** Azure SQL Database

**E)** Azure Synapse Analytics

**Solution:** C

**Explanation:**

Explanation: Image data must be stored in a single data store at minimum cost. Note: Azure Blob storage is Microsoft's object storage solution for the cloud. Blob storage is optimized for storing massive amounts of unstructured data. Unstructured data is data that does not adhere to a particular data model or definition, such as text or binary data. Blob storage is designed for: - Serving images or documents directly to a browser. - Storing files for distributed access. - Streaming video and audio. - Writing to log files. - Storing data for backup and restore, disaster recovery, and archiving. - Storing data for analysis by an on-premises or Azure-hosted service. Reference: https://docs.microsoft.com/en-us/azure/storage/blobs/storage-blobs-introduction

**Question: 7** *One Answer Is Right*

You need to recommend a solution for storing customer data. What should you recommend?

**Scenario:**

TESTLET-2. Overview You develop data engineering solutions for Graphics Design Institute, a global media company with offices in New York City, Manchester, Singapore, and Melbourne.

The New York office hosts SQL Server databases that stores massive amounts of customer data. The company also stores millions of images on a physical server located in the New York office. More than 2 TB of image data is added each day. The images are transferred from customer devices to the server in New York. Many images have been placed on this server in an unorganized manner, making it difficult for editors to search images. Images should automatically have object and color tags generated. The tags must be stored in a document database, and be queried by SQL. You are hired to design a solution that can store, transform, and visualize customer data. Requirements Business The company identifies the following business requirements: - You must transfer all images and customer data to cloud storage and remove on-premises servers. - You must develop an analytical processing solution for transforming customer data. - You must develop an image object and color tagging solution. - Capital expenditures must be minimized. - Cloud resource costs must be minimized. Technical The solution has the following technical requirements: - Tagging data must be uploaded to the cloud from the New York office location. - Tagging data must be replicated to regions that are geographically close to company office locations. - Image data must be stored in a single data store at minimum cost. - Customer data must be analyzed using managed Spark clusters. -Power BI must be used to visualize transformed customer data.- All data must be backed up in case disaster recovery is required. Security and optimization All cloud data must be encrypted at rest and in transit. The solution must support: - parallel processing of customer data - hyper-scale storage of images - global region data replication of processed image data

**Answers:**

**A)** Azure Synapse Analytics

**B)** Azure Stream Analytics

**C)** Azure Databricks

**D)** Azure SQL Database

**Solution:** C

**Explanation:**

Explanation: From the scenario: Customer data must be analyzed using managed Spark clusters. All cloud data must be encrypted at rest and in transit. The solution must support: parallel processing of customer data. Reference: https://www.microsoft.com/developerblog/2019/01/18/running-parallel-apache-spark-notebook-workloads- on-azure-databricks/

**Question: 8** *Multiple Answers Are Right*

HOTSPOT You need to design storage for the solution. Which storage services should you recommend? To answer, select the appropriate configuration in the answer area. NOTE: Each correct selection is worth one point. Hot Area:

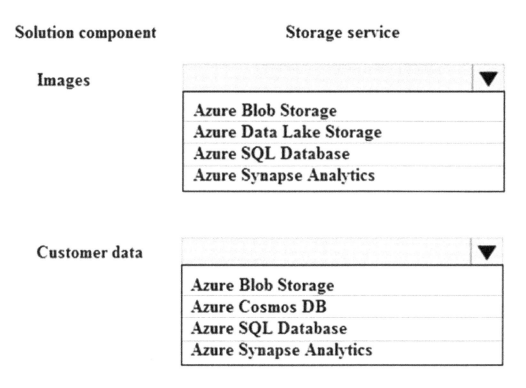

**Scenario:**

TESTLET-2. Overview You develop data engineering solutions for Graphics Design Institute, a global media company with offices in New York City, Manchester, Singapore, and Melbourne. The New York office hosts SQL Server databases that stores massive amounts of customer data. The company also stores millions of images on a physical server located in the New York office. More than 2 TB of image data is added each day. The images are transferred from customer devices to the server in New York. Many images have been placed on this server in an unorganized manner, making it difficult for editors to search images. Images should automatically have object and color tags generated. The tags must be stored in a document database, and be queried by SQL. You are hired to design a solution that can store, transform, and visualize customer data. Requirements Business The company identifies the following business requirements: - You must transfer all images and customer data to cloud storage and remove on-premises servers. - You must develop an analytical processing solution for transforming customer data. - You must develop an image object and color tagging solution. - Capital expenditures must be minimized. - Cloud resource costs must be minimized. Technical The solution has the following technical requirements: - Tagging data must be uploaded to the cloud from the New York office location. - Tagging data must be replicated to regions that are geographically close to company office locations. - Image data must be stored in a single data store at minimum cost. - Customer data must be analyzed using managed Spark clusters. -Power BI must be used to visualize transformed customer data.- All data must be backed up in case disaster recovery is required. Security and optimization All cloud data must be encrypted at rest and in transit. The solution must support: - parallel processing of customer data - hyper-scale storage of images - global region data replication of processed image data

**Answers:**

A)

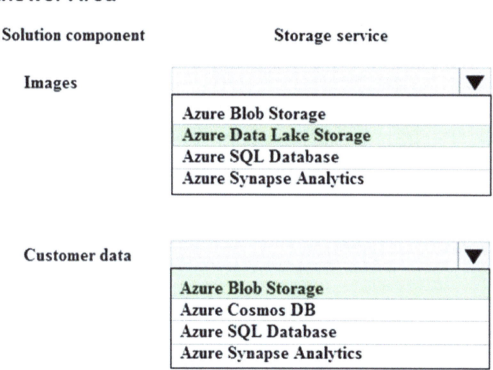

**Solution:** A

**Explanation:**

Explanation: Explanation: Images: Azure Data Lake Storage Scenario: Image data must be stored in a single data store at minimum cost. Customer data: Azure Blob Storage Scenario: Customer data must be analyzed using managed Spark clusters. Spark clusters in HDInsight are compatible with Azure Storage and Azure Data Lake Storage. Azure Storage includes these data services: Azure Blob, Azure Files, Azure Queues, and Azure Tables. Reference: https://docs.microsoft.com/en-us/azure/hdinsight/spark/apache-spark-overview Design Azure data storage solutions

**Question: 9** *One Answer Is Right*

You need to design a solution to meet the SQL Server storage requirements for CONT_SQL3. Which type of disk should you recommend?

**Scenario:**

TESTLET-3. Case study This is a case study. Case studies are not timed separately. You can use as much exam time as you would like to complete each case. However, there may be additional case studies and sections on this exam. You must manage your time to ensure that you are able to complete all questions included on this exam in the time provided. To answer the questions included in a case study, you will need to reference information that is provided in the case study. Case studies might contain exhibits and other resources that provide more information about the scenario that is described in the case study. Each question is independent of the other questions in this case study. At the end of this case study, a review screen will appear. This screen allows you to review your answers and to make changes before you move to the next section of the exam. After you begin a new section, you cannot return to this section. To start the case study To display the first question in this case study, click the Next button. Use the buttons in the left pane to explore the content of the case study before you answer the questions. Clicking these buttons displays information such as business requirements, existing environment, and problem statements. If the case study has an All Information tab, note that the information displayed is identical to the information displayed on the subsequent tabs. When you are ready to answer a question, click the Question button to return to the question. Background Current environment The company has the following virtual machines (VMs):

| VM | Roles | Database size | VM type | Destination |
|---|---|---|---|---|
| CONT_SQL1 | Microsoft SQL Server | 2 TB | Hyper-V | Azure SQL Database |
| CONT_SQL2 | Microsoft SQL Server | 2 TB | Hyper-V | Azure SQL Database |
| CONT_SQL3 | Microsoft SQL Server | 100 GB | Hyper-V | Azure VM |
| CONT_SAP1 | SAP | 1 TB | Vmware | On-premises |
| CONT_SAP2 | SAP | 1 TB | Vmware | On-premises |
| CPNT_SSRS | Microsoft SQL Server Reporting Services | 1 TB | Hyper-V | Azure VM |

Requirements Storage and processing You must be able to use a file system view of data stored in a blob. You must build an architecture that will allow Contoso to use the DB FS filesystem layer over a blob store. The architecture will need to support data files, libraries, and images. Additionally, it must provide a web- based interface to documents that contain runnable command, visualizations, and narrative text such as a notebook. CONT_SQL3 requires an initial scale of 35000 IOPS. CONT_SQL1 and CONT_SQL2 must use the vCore model and should include replicas. The solution must support 8000 IOPS. The storage should be configured to optimized storage for database OLTP workloads. Migration - You must be able to independently scale compute and storage resources. -You must migrate all SQL Server workloads to Azure. You must identify related machines in the on- premises environment, get disk size data usage information. - Data from SQL Server must include zone redundant storage. - You need to ensure that app components can reside on-premises while interacting with components that run in the Azure public cloud. - SAP data must remain on-premises. - The Azure Site Recovery (ASR) results should contain per-machine data. Business requirements - You must design a regional disaster recovery topology. - The database backups have regulatory purposes and must be retained for seven years. - CONT_SQL1 stores customers sales data that requires ETL operations for data analysis. A solution is required that reads data from SQL, performs ETL, and outputs to Power BI. The solution should use managed clusters to minimize costs. To optimize logistics, Contoso needs to analyze customer sales data to see if certain products are tied to specific times in the year. - The analytics solution for customer sales data must be available during a regional outage. Security and auditing - Contoso requires all corporate computers to enable Windows Firewall. - Azure servers should be able to ping other Contoso Azure servers. - Employee PII must be encrypted in memory, in motion, and at rest. Any data encrypted by SQL Server must support equality searches, grouping, indexing, and joining on the encrypted data. - Keys must be secured by using hardware security modules (HSMs). - CONT_SQL3 must not communicate over the default ports Cost - All solutions must minimize cost and resources. - The organization does not want any unexpected charges. - The data engineers must set the SQL Data Warehouse compute resources to consume 300 DWUs. - CONT_SQL2 is not fully utilized during non-peak hours. You must minimize resource costs for during non-peak hours.

**Answers:**

**A)** Standard SSD Managed Disk

**B)** Premium SSD Managed Disk

**C)** Ultra SSD Managed Disk

**Solution:** C

**Explanation:**

Explanation: CONT_SQL3 requires an initial scale of 35000 IOPS. Ultra SSD Managed Disk Offerings

| Disk size (GiB) | 4 | 8 | 16 | 32 | 64 | 128 | 256 | 512 | 1,024-65,536 (in increments of 1 TiB) |
|---|---|---|---|---|---|---|---|---|---|
| IOPS range | 100-1,200 | 100-2,400 | 100-4,800 | 100-9,600 | 100-19,200 | 100-38,400 | 100-76,800 | 100-153,600 | 100-160,000 |
| Throughput Cap (MBps) | 300 | 600 | 1,200 | 2,000 | 2,000 | 2,000 | 2,000 | 2,000 | 2,000 |

The following table provides a comparison of ultra solid-state-drives (SSD) (preview), premium SSD, standard SSD, and standard hard disk drives (HDD) for managed disks to help you decide what to use.

| | Ultra SSD (preview) | Premium SSD | Standard SSD | Standard HDD |
|---|---|---|---|---|
| Disk type | SSD | SSD | SSD | HDD |
| Scenario | IO-intensive workloads such as SAP HANA, top tier databases (for example, SQL, Oracle), and other transaction-heavy workloads. | Production and performance sensitive workloads | Web servers, lightly used enterprise applications and dev/test | Backup, non-critical, infrequent access |
| Disk size | 65,536 gibibyte (GiB) (Preview) | 32,767 GiB | 32,767 GiB | 32,767 GiB |
| Max throughput | 2,000 MiB/s (Preview) | 900 MiB/s | 750 MiB/s | 500 MiB/s |
| Max IOPS | 160,000 (Preview) | 20,000 | 6,000 | 2,000 |

Reference: https://docs.microsoft.com/en-us/azure/virtual-machines/windows/disks-types

**Question: 10** *One Answer Is Right*

A company manufactures automobile parts. The company installs IoT sensors on manufacturing machinery. You must design a solution that analyzes data from the sensors. You need to recommend a solution that meets the following requirements: - Data must be analyzed in real-time. - Data queries must be deployed using continuous integration. - Data must be visualized by using charts and graphs. - Data must be available for ETL operations in the future. - The solution must support high-volume data ingestion. Which three actions should you recommend? Each correct answer presents part of the solution. NOTE: Each correct selection is worth one point.

**Answers:**

**A)** Use Azure Analysis Services to query the data. Output query results to Power BI.

**B)** Configure an Azure Event Hub to capture data to Azure Data Lake Storage.

**C)** Develop an Azure Stream Analytics application that queries the data and outputs to Power BI. Use Azure Data Factory to deploy the Azure Stream Analytics application.

**D)** Develop an application that sends the IoT data to an Azure Event Hub.

**E)** Develop an Azure Stream Analytics application that queries the data and outputs to Power BI. Use Azure Pipelines to deploy the Azure Stream Analytics application.

**F)** Develop an application that sends the IoT data to an Azure Data Lake Storage container.

**Solution:** B, C, D

# Chapter 29: MB-200 - Microsoft Power Platform + Dynamics 365 Core

## Exam Guide

Microsoft Power Platform + Dynamics 365 Core MB-200 Exam:

Microsoft Power Platform + Dynamics 365 Core MB-200 Exam validates the Candidate ability to configure the system to meet client needs, perform design tasks related to implementing new features and functionality, and implement and test system changes.

MB-200 Exam topics:

Candidates must know the exam topics before they start of preparation. Because it will really help them in hitting the core. Our **Microsoft MB-200 dumps** will include the following topics:

- Perform discovery, planning, and analysis 5-10%
- Manage user experience design 20-25%
- Manage entities and data 15-20%
- Implement Security 5-10%
- Implement integration 15-20%
- Perform solutions deployment and testing 25-30%

Certification Path:

There is no prerequisite for this Microsoft MB-200 exam.

Who should take the MB-200 exam:

The Microsoft MB-200 Exam is an internationally recognized validation that identifies persons who earn it as possessing skilled in Microsoft Dynamics 365 Customer Engagement Core. If candidates want significant improvement in career growth needs enhanced knowledge, skills, and talents. The Microsoft MB-200 Exam provides proof of this advanced knowledge and skill. If a candidate has knowledge of associated technologies and skills that are required to pass the Microsoft MB-200 Exam then he should take this exam.

How to study the MB-200 Exam:

There are two main types of resources for preparation of certification exams first there are the study guides and the books that are detailed and suitable for building knowledge from ground up then there are video tutorial and lectures that can somehow ease the pain of through study and are comparatively less boring for some candidates yet these demand time and concentration from the learner. Smart Candidates who want to build a solid foundation in all exam topics and related technologies usually combine video lectures with study guides to reap the benefits of both but there is one crucial preparation tool as often overlooked by most candidates the practice exams. Practice exams are built to make students comfortable with the real exam environment. Statistics have shown that most students fail not due to that preparation but due to exam anxiety the fear of the unknown. Certification-questions.com expert team recommends you to prepare some notes on these topics along with it don't forget to practice **Microsoft MB-200 dumps** which have been written by our expert team, Both these will help you a lot to clear this exam with good marks.

How much MB-200 Exam Cost:

The price of the Microsoft MB-200 exam is $165 USD.

How to book the MB-200 Exam:

These are following steps for registering the Microsoft MB-200 exam.
Step 1: Visit to Microsoft Exam Registration
Step 2: Signup/Login to MICROSOFT account
Step 3: Search for MICROSOFT MB-200 Certifications Exam
Step 4: Select Date and Center of examination and confirm with payment value of $165

What is the duration of the MB-200 Exam:

- Format: Multiple choices, multiple answers
- Length of Examination: 150 minutes
- Number of Questions: 45-60
- Passing Score: 700/1000

    The benefit in Obtaining the MB-200 Exam Certification:

- After completion of Microsoft Dynamics 365 Customer Engagement Core Certification candidates receive official confirmation from Microsoft that you are now fully certified in their chosen field. This can be now added to their CV, cover letters and job applications.
- When Candidates applying for a job or looking to promotion in their current position, a Microsoft Dynamics 365 Customer Engagement Core certification in the field in which Candidates are applying will put you at the top of the list and make them a desirable candidate for employers.

- Candidates will get in-depth knowledge by completing the courses along with the access to revision materials for 6 months upon completion means they will have a wider skill set when it comes to the various technologies and systems than an uncertified professional. Certified Professional in this particular skill set is 74% more efficient when it comes to completing their tasks in a timely well-executed manner.
- Organization owners invest a lot in their employees when it comes to their training with the goal of making them quicker, more efficient, and more knowledgeable about their role. Certified Professional will reduce the time he spends on tasks, meaning he can get more done this could help reduce company downtime when repairing faults on a system or fixing hardware problems.
- Becoming a Microsoft Dynamics 365 Customer Engagement Core means one thing you are worth more to the company and therefore more to yourself in the form of an upgraded pay package. On average a Microsoft Dynamics 365 Customer Engagement Core member of staff is estimated to be worth 30% more to a company than their uncertified professionals.

Difficulty in writing MB-200 Exam:

Candidates face many problems when they start preparing for the Microsoft MB-200 exam. If a candidate wants to prepare his for the Microsoft MB-200 exam without any problem and get good grades in the exam. Then they have to choose the best **Microsoft MB-200 dumps** for real exam questions practice. There are many websites that are offering the latest Microsoft MB-200 exam questions and answers but these questions are not verified by Microsoft certified experts and that's why many are failed in their just first attempt. Certification-questions is the best platform which provides the candidate with the necessary Microsoft MB-200 questions that will help him to pass the Microsoft MB-200 exam on the first time. The candidate will not have to take the Microsoft MB-200 exam twice because with the help of **Microsoft MB-200 dumps** Candidate will have every valuable material required to pass the Microsoft MB-200 exam. We are providing the latest and actual questions and that is the reason why this is the one that he needs to use and there are no chances to fail when a candidate will have valid braindumps from Certification-questions. We have the guarantee that the questions that we have will be the ones that will pass candidate in the Microsoft MB-200 exam in the very first attempt.

For more info visit::

Microsoft MB-200 Exam Reference

# Sample Practice Test for MB-200

**Question: 1** *One Answer Is Right*

You are a Dynamics 365 for Customer Service system administrator. Compliance standards require that entities and fields with Auditing set to On are recorded. You have configured all settings to the default settings and have set Global Auditing to On. You need to verify compliance standards. Which data items will be included in the audit log?

**Answers:**

**A)** Microsoft Office 365 activities

**B)** all entities and fields

**C)** entities and fields with auditing enabled

**D)** user access information only

**Solution:** C

**Question: 2** *One Answer Is Right*

A company identifies a new opportunity. Sales associates must collaborate to convert the opportunity to a sale. All associates have access to Microsoft SharePoint, but some associates do not have access to Dynamics 365 for Sales. You need to ensure that users can collaborate on a single platform that directly integrates with Dynamics 365 data. Which tool should you use?

**Answers:**

**A)** Microsoft OneDrive for Business

**B)** Microsoft Skype for Business

**C)** Microsoft Office 365 Delve

**D)** Yammer

**E)** Microsoft Office 365 Groups

**Solution:** E

**Explanation:**

Explanation: References: https://docs.microsoft.com/en-us/dynamics365/customer-engagement/basics/collaborate-with-colleagues- using-office-365-groups

**Question: 3** *One Answer Is Right*

You are a Dynamics 365 for Customer Service system administrator. A user experiences slow performance when using Dynamics 365. You need to check the latency of the environment. What should you do?

**Answers:**

**A)** Use the organization Insights tool.

**B)** View the Health section of Microsoft Office 365 Admin portal.

**C)** View the Power platform Admin center.

**D)** Run the Dynamics 365 Diagnostics tool.

**Solution:** D

**Explanation:**

Explanation: References: https://community.dynamics.com/365/customerservice/f/763/t/285347

**Question: 4** *One Answer Is Right*

You are a Dynamics 365 for Customer Service system administrator. You need to implement a Dynamics 365 portal that allows customers to perform the following tasks: - Post product experience information to forums. - Enter issues in an online support center. - Enter ideas for future products. Which type of portal should you implement?

**Answers:**

**A)** Partner

**B)** Customer Self-Service

**C)** Employee Self-Service

**D)** Community

**E)** Custom

**Solution:** B

**Question: 5** *Multiple Answers Are Right*

DRAG DROP You have a Dynamics 365 for Customer Service tenant that has one Sandbox instance and multiple Production instances. You need to import changes from the Sandbox instance to each of the Production instances with different requirements. Which types of solutions should you use? To answer, drag the appropriate solution types to the correct requirements. Each solution type may be used once, more than once, or not at all. You may need to drag the split bar between panes or scroll to view content. NOTE: Each correct selection is worth one point. Select and Place:

| Solution types | Answer Area | |
|---|---|---|
| managed | Requirement | Solution type |
| unmanaged | Include changes as part of the default solution. | |
| | Remove changes by uninstalling the solution. | |
| | Ensure ability to maintain customizations of needed. | |
| | Prevent others from making changes to the solution. | |

**Answers:**

**A)**

| Solution types | Answer Area | |
|---|---|---|
| managed | Requirement | Solution type |
| unmanaged | Include changes as part of the default solution. | unmanaged |
| | Remove changes by uninstalling the solution. | managed |
| | Ensure ability to maintain customizations of needed. | unmanaged |
| | Prevent others from making changes to the solution. | managed |

**Solution:** A

**Explanation:**

Explanation:

**Question: 6** *Multiple Answers Are Right*

DRAG DROP A hospital uses Dynamics 365 Customer Engagement. The scheduling department schedules doctors for surgeries. You need to configure relationships between doctor and patient records. From the doctor entity, which relationship types should you use? To answer, drag the relationship types for the correct scenarios. Each relationship type may be used once, more than once, or not at all. You may need to drag the split bar between panes or scroll to view content. NOTE: Each correct selection is worth one point. Select and Place:

**Relationship types**
- N : N
- 1 : N
- N : 1

**Answer Area**

| Scenario | Relationship type |
|---|---|
| A doctor with multiple patients | |
| Operating rooms and doctors | |

**Answers:**

**A)**

**Relationship types**
- N : 1

**Answer Area**

| Scenario | Relationship type |
|---|---|
| A doctor with multiple patients | 1 : N |
| Operating rooms and doctors | N : N |

**Solution: A**

**Explanation:**

Explanation: References: https://docs.microsoft.com/en-us/dynamics365/customer-engagement/customize/create-and-edit-1n- relationships Perform Discovery, Planning, and Analysis

**Question: 7** *One Answer Is Right*

You need to simplify the registration process for repeat guests. Which entity component should you use?

**Answers:**

**A)** fields

**B)** workflows

**C)** relationships

**D)** business rules

**Solution:** C

**Explanation:**

Explanation: Manage user experience design Question Set 1

**Question: 8** *Multiple Answers Are Right*

DRAG DROP You are a Dynamics 365 administrator. A manager creates an Excel template with a pivot table to tracking opportunities. When a salesperson opens the Excel template in the My Opportunities view, they observe the following issues: - The salesperson can view information for all salespeople. - The salesperson does not see their current data. You need ensure the salesperson can only see their information. Which Excel PivotTable attributes should you use? To answer, drag the appropriate attributes to the correct settings. Each attribute may be used once, more than once, or not at all. You may need to drag the split bar between panes or scroll to view content. NOTE: Each correct selection is worth one point. Select and Place:

**Answers:**

**A)**

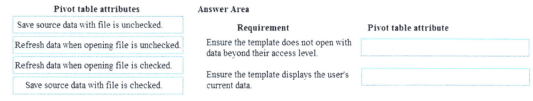

**Solution:** A

**Explanation:**

Explanation:

**Question: 9** *One Answer Is Right*

You are a Dynamics 365 for Customer Service system administrator. You create an app for the sales team. Members of the sales team cannot access the app. You need to ensure that sales team members can access the app. Where should you configure app permissions?

**Answers:**

**A)** Dynamics administration center

**B)** Manage Roles

**C)** Dynamics 365 home

**D)** Security Roles

**Solution:** B

**Explanation:**

Explanation: References: https://docs.microsoft.com/en-us/dynamics365/customer-engagement/customize/manage-access-apps- security-roles

**Question: 10** *Multiple Answers Are Right*

HOTSPOT You are a Dynamics 365 for Customer Service system administrator. You are unable to import a translation file. You need to determine if the file being imported is of the right type and format, and that the file conforms to maximum field length requirements. Which parameter should you use? To answer, select the appropriate options in the answer area. NOTE: Each correct selection is worth one point. Hot Area:

## Answer Area

| Requirement | Parameter |
|---|---|
| File type | ▼ .csv / .zip / .xml / .xlsx |
| File format | ▼ single file formatted with translation and entity field information / same format as the exported file / two files formatted the same as exports but imported in the correct order / same format as the Content_Types file |
| Maximum field length | ▼ 50 / 100 / 250 / 500 |

## Answers:

### A)

**Answer Area**

| Requirement | Parameter |
|---|---|
| File type | .csv / **.zip** / .xml / .xlsx |
| File format | single file formatted with translation and entity field information / **same format as the exported file** / two files formatted the same as exports but imported in the correct order / same format as the Content_Types file |
| Maximum field length | 50 / 100 / 250 / **500** |

**Solution:** A

**Explanation:**

Explanation:

# Chapter 30: MB-300 - Microsoft Dynamics 365: Core Finance and Operations

## Exam Guide

How can you start preparation for Microsoft MB-300 Exam

Get the best study guide For Microsoft MB-300 Exam

Instant guide if you don't have time to read whole the page

Certification is evidence of your skills, expertise in those areas in which you like to work. There are many vendors in the market that are providing these certifications. Microsoft exams assist you to distinguish yourself and verify your education and abilities. Describe your expertise in Microsoft 365 technologies moreover improve your work by earning one of the new Microsoft 365 role-based certifications for business administrators or an Office 365 certification. Verify your abilities in sectors such as relocation and management of cloud-hosted business apps with Microsoft 365 and move your business to the cloud. If Candidate wants to work on Microsoft and prove his knowledge, there are Microsoft Dynamics 365: Core Finance and Operations Certification offered by Microsoft.In this guide, we will cover the Microsoft MB-300 Exam, Microsoft 365 Certification Salary and all aspects of the Microsoft MB-300 Exam Certification.

Microsoft MB-300 Exam:

Microsoft MB-300 Exam covers Microsoft Dynamics 365: Core Finance and Operations. Candidates for this exam are functional specialists who analyze business needs and translate them into fully performed business solutions and processes that implement industry best practices. Candidates are a key resource for deploying and configuring applications to meet the needs of the business.

Read the Microsoft MB-300 Exam topics below:

Candidates must know the exam topics before they start of preparation. Because it will really help them in hitting the core. Our **Microsoft MB-300 Exam dumps** will include the following topics:

- Use common functionality and implementation tools (20-25%)
- Configure security, processes, and options (45-50%)
- Perform data migration (15-20%)
- Validate and support the solution (15-20%)

Read the Microsoft MB-300 Exam Requirements below:

Candidates for this exam have a basic understanding of the concepts of corporate accounting and finance, customer service, field service, manufacturing, retail, and supply chain management.

Applicants for this exam usually train in one or more sets of Microsoft Dynamics 365 Finance functions, including finance, manufacturing, and supply chain management. Applicants must have knowledge of basic accounting principles and practices

- Microsoft Certified: Dynamics 365 Finance Functional Consultant Associate
- Microsoft Certified: Dynamics 365 Supply Chain Management,
- Manufacturing Functional Consultant Associate

Here is the cost of Microsoft MB-300 Exam:

- The cost of Microsoft MB-300 Exam is $165

Read the registration procedure of the Microsoft MB-300 Exam:

The registration for the Microsoft MB-300 Exam follows the steps given below.

Step 1: Visit to Microsoft Exam Registration
Step 2: Signup/Login to MICROSOFT account
Step 3: Search for Microsoft MB-300 Exam
Step 4: Select Date and Center of examination and confirm with payment value of $165

Read the Microsoft MB-300 Exam formate below:

- Format: Multiple choices, multiple answers
- Length of Examination: 120 minutes
- Number of Questions: 40-60
- Passing score: 70%
- Language: English, Japanese

Read the Microsoft MB-300 Exam Certified salary below:

The Average Salary of a Microsoft Dynamics 365: Core Finance and Operations Expert in

- United State - 47000 USD
- India - 3600905 INR
- Europe - 43233 EURO
- England - 37630 POUND

Read the Microsoft MB-300 ExamExam advantages below:

- Microsoft Dynamics 365: Core Finance and Operations is distinguished among competitors. Microsoft MB-300 Exam certification can give them an edge at that time easily when candidates appear for a job interview employers seek to notify something which differentiates the individual to another.

- Microsoft Dynamics 365: Core Finance and Operations has more useful and relevant networks that help them in setting career goals for themselves.Microsoft Dynamics 365 networks provide them with the right career direction than non certified usually are unable to get.

- Microsoft MB-300 Exam will be confident and stand different from others as their skills are more trained than non-certified professionals.

- Microsoft Dynamics 365 has the knowledge to use the tools to complete the task efficiently and cost effectively than the other non-certified professionals lack in doing so.

- Microsoft MB-300 Exam Certification provides practical experience to candidates from all the aspects to be a proficient worker in the organization.

- Microsoft MB-300 Exam Certifications provide opportunities to get a job easily in which they are interested in instead of wasting years and ending without getting any experience.

Solution to prepare Microsoft MB-300 Exam:

if you are a certified professional and are excited to polish your abilities and advance your credentials to further advance your career, then you must take the certification exam for Microsoft Dynamics 365: Core Finance and Operations. For example, Microsoft is considered the career-oriented provider in constant change that gives a boost to your profession. The Microsoft Dynamics 365: Core Finance and Operations tops at the list and is gaining popularity among the professionals and IT industries. But professionals are reluctant to not have enough time to devote to recommended books. But here is the good news for valuable and potential candidates, now certifications-questions offers you the best solution, which helps you to pass and solve your Microsoft MB-300 certification exam in a week. certifications-questions offers you the best and most valid question and answer of exams and exam dump for preparing the Microsoft MB-300 certification exam. To get a well-paying job, you should consider taking one of the famous certification exams. If you need to pass the certification exam on the first try and become a certified expert, you should think of finding the most reliable source that will help you pass multiple certification exams. Certification-questions.com can assist you to improve your chances of passing any certification exam. We have worked hard to create great preparation stuff for anyone who wants to take a certification exam to improve the possibilities of getting a well-paying job in the industry. To increase your possibilities, you should consider using the exam dumps provided by us.

To get a well-paying job, you should consider taking one of the famous certification exams. If you need to pass the certification exam on the first try and become a certified expert, you should think of finding the most reliable source that will help you pass multiple certification exams. Certification-questions.com can assist you to improve your chances of passing any certification exam. We have worked hard to create great preparation stuff for anyone who wants to take a certification exam to improve the possibilities of getting a well-paying job in the industry. To increase your possibilities, you should consider using the exam dumps provided by us.

With the assist of the exam dumps given by Certification-questions.com, you can get 100% success guaranteed on the certification exam. We have created pdf dumps for all those looking to become certified specialists. If you also want to pass the certification exam on the first try, you should think using valid questions given by us. We have a 100% assured success rate and you can get all the referrals you want from us. All our clients are completely satisfied with our exam dumps downloads and our preparation stuff. Certification-questions.com will provide you with up-to-date practical questions so you can quickly prepare for the next exam and pass the exam on the first try.

**Microsoft MB-300 Exam dump** is expected to be valid for the practice to offer you the kind of multiple questions that could be asked in your Microsoft MB-300 certification exam. The Practice test software is intuitive and simulates a real exam, familiarizing you with the real exam questions.

For more information visit::

Microsoft MB-300 Exam Reference

# Sample Practice Test for MB-300

**Question: 1** *One Answer Is Right*

You are responsible for regulatory compliance for a Dynamics 365 Finance environment. You need to be able to search for regulatory features in Microsoft Dynamics Lifecycle Services (LCS). What should you use?

**Answers:**

**A)** Intelligent Data Management Framework (IDMF)

**B)** System diagnostics

**C)** Application Object Tree (AOT)

**D)** Issue search

**Solution:** D

**Explanation:**

Explanation: Reference: https://docs.microsoft.com/en-us/dynamics365/unified-operations/dev-itpro/lifecycle-services/issue-search- lcs

**Question: 2** *Multiple Answers Are Right*

DRAG DROP A company is migrating to Dynamics 365 Finance from a legacy system. The company is creating new questionnaires for customers. When the survey responses come in, the company wants to provide ratings as a foundation for a further discussion. You set up questionnaire types, question types, and questionnaire parameters. You need to design the questionnaire. In which order should you perform the actions? To answer, move all actions to the answer area and arrange them in the correct order. Select and Place:

**Actions**

- Attach questions to the questionnaire
- Set up the questionnaire
- Set up questions and their association
- Set up answer groups and answers

**Answer Area**

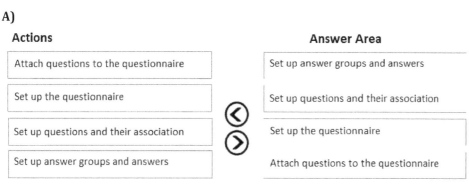

Answers:

**A)**

**Actions**

- Attach questions to the questionnaire
- Set up the questionnaire
- Set up questions and their association
- Set up answer groups and answers

**Answer Area**

- Set up answer groups and answers
- Set up questions and their association
- Set up the questionnaire
- Attach questions to the questionnaire

**Solution:** A

**Explanation:**

Explanation: Reference: https://docs.microsoft.com/en-us/dynamics365/unified-operations/talent/design-questionnaires

**Question: 3** *Multiple Answers Are Right*

DRAG DROP An organization implements Dynamics 365 Finance. You need to determine where work items originate. From which module do the following work items originate? To answer, drag the appropriate modules to the correct work items. Each module may be used once, more than once, or not at all. You may need to drag the split bar between panes or scroll to view content. NOTE: Each correct selection is worth one point. Select and Place:

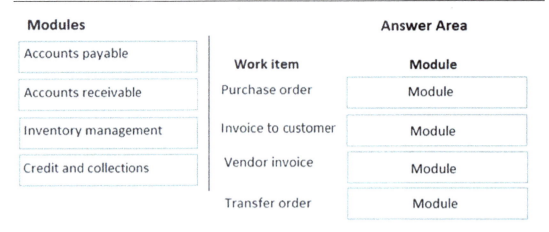

## Answers:

### A)

**Solution:** A

**Explanation:**

Explanation:

**Question: 4** *Multiple Answers Are Right*

HOTSPOT You are tasked with enhancing usability in the Dynamics 365 Finance deployment for an organization. The organization is evaluating different approaches, including using workspaces. You need to identify the goals of using workspaces. Which goals should you identify? To answer, select the appropriate options in the answer area. NOTE: Each correct selection is worth one point. Hot Area:

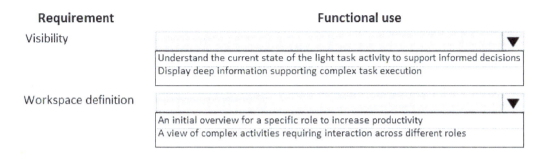

Answers:

A)

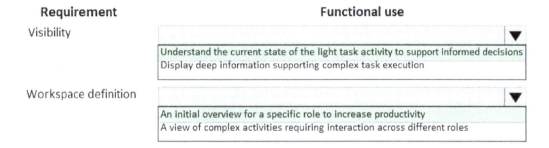

Solution: A

Explanation:

Explanation:

**Question: 5** *Multiple Answers Are Right*

HOTSPOT A company is standardizing its business processes. You plan to facilitate business process alignment by using the Business Process Modeler (BPM) tool in Lifecycle Services (LCS). You need to identify the main capabilities of BPM. Which of the following can you accomplish with the BPM tool in LCS? To answer, select the appropriate options in the answer area. NOTE: Each correct selection is worth one point. Hot Area:

## Answer Area

| Capability | Tasks |
|---|---|
| Integration | ▼ |
| | Upload flowcharts from Task recorder |
| | Pull master data |
| | Pull reference data |
| | Connect to external databases |
| All functionality except | ▼ |
| | Modify flowcharts |
| | Attach video |
| | Push process configurations to instances |
| | Generate gap analysis |

**Answers:**

**A)**

### Answer Area

| Capability | Tasks |
|---|---|
| Integration | Upload flowcharts from Task recorder / Pull master data / Pull reference data / **Connect to external databases** |
| All functionality except | Modify flowcharts / Attach video / **Push process configurations to instances** / Generate gap analysis |

**Solution:** A

**Explanation:**

Explanation:

**Question: 6** *One Answer Is Right*

You are a Dynamics 365 Finance system administrator. Microsoft recently released a new feature for public preview that would add significant value to your organization without licensing adjustments. You need to enable the feature. Where can you enable the preview feature?

**Answers:**

**A)** Solution management

**B)** Lifecycle Services

**C)** Organizational administration module

**D)** experience.dynamics.com

**Solution:** B

**Explanation:**

Explanation: References: https://docs.microsoft.com/en-us/dynamics365/fin-ops-core/fin-ops/get-started/public-preview-releases

**Question: 7** *Multiple Answers Are Right*

HOTSPOT You are a Dynamics 365 Finance system administrator. Data must be filtered based on given criteria to help users quickly reduce the number of records. You need to identify the appropriate syntax to solve user requirements. Which query filter syntax should you use? To answer, select the appropriate options in the answer area. NOTE: Each correct selection is worth one point. Hot Area:

### Answer Area

| Filter requirements | Syntax |
| --- | --- |
| Today's date in a date field | D / Day(1) / T / Today |
| Customers with the names Tina and Tyna | T?na / T!na / T..na |

**Answers:**

**A)**

## Answer Area

| Filter requirements | Syntax |
|---|---|
| Today's date in a date field | ▼ D / Day(1) / T / **Today** |
| Customers with the names Tina and Tyna | ▼ **T?na** / T!na / T..na |

**Solution:** A

**Explanation:**

Explanation: References: https://docs.microsoft.com/en-us/dynamics365/fin-ops-core/fin-ops/get-started/advanced-filtering-query- options

**Question: 8** *One Answer Is Right*

A client runs Dynamics 365 Finance. The client wants to implement supply chain functionality that is fully integrated with the current Dynamics 365 Retail instance. You need to implement the new functionality. What should you do?

**Answers:**

**A)** Integrate Dynamics 365 Retail with Dynamics 365 Finance by using Common Data Service.

**B)** Place the Dynamics 365 Retail instance into maintenance mode by using the Dynamics 365 Instance Management portal.

**C)** Select the Dynamics 365 Finance configuration in Lifecycle Services.

**D)** Clear the Dynamics 365 Retail configuration in the License configuration form.

**Solution:** A

**Question: 9** *Multiple Answers Are Right*

HOTSPOT You are a business process analyst using Dynamics 365 Finance. You develop business processes for your organization. You need to review standard business processes from similar industries and make modifications for your organization. Which business process libraries in Lifecycle Services should you use? To answer, select the appropriate options in the answer area. NOTE: Each correct selection is worth one point. Hot Area:

**Answer Area**

| Requirements | Tools |
|---|---|
| Find standard business processes used by other corporations and industries. | Global libraries / Corporate libraries / My libraries / Core business processes |
| Find processes from other departments. | Corporate libraries / Support processes / My libraries / Global libraries |

**Answers:**

A)

## Answer Area

| Requirements | Tools |
|---|---|
| Find standard business processes used by other corporations and industries. | 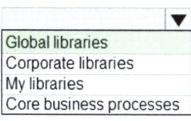 Global libraries / Corporate libraries / My libraries / Core business processes |
| Find processes from other departments. | 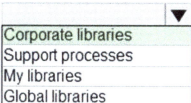 Corporate libraries / Support processes / My libraries / Global libraries |

**Solution:** A

**Explanation:**

Explanation: References: https://docs.microsoft.com/en-us/dynamics365/fin-ops-core/dev-itpro/lifecycle-services/creating-editing- browsing

**Question: 10** *One Answer Is Right*

A company implements Dynamics 365 Finance. The implementation team must build acceptance scripts to make sure that common business use cases can be performed in the new system. They must test use cases by stepping through required tasks, organized by functional hierarchy. You need to create User Acceptance Testing (UAT) tests in Lifecycle Services (LCS) that can be easily repeatable. What should you use?

**Answers:**

A) Task recorder

B) APQC Unified Library

C) Asset library

**D)** Configuration data manager

**Solution:** A

**Explanation:**

Explanation: Reference: https://docs.microsoft.com/en-us/dynamics365/fin-ops-core/dev-itpro/lifecycle-services/using-task-guides- and-bpm-to-create-user-acceptance-tests

# Chapter 31: MB-310 - Microsoft Dynamics 365 Finance

## Exam Guide

How do you start to study for the Microsoft MB-310 Certification Exam

Get the guide For Microsoft MB-310 Certification Exam

Quick study guide if you don't have time to read complete the page

Microsoft exams assist you to distinguish yourself and verify your education and abilities. Describe your expertise in Microsoft 365 technologies moreover improve your work by earning one of the new Microsoft 365 role-based certifications for business administrators or an Office 365 certification. Verify your abilities in sectors such as relocation and management of cloud-hosted business apps with Microsoft 365 and move your business to the cloud. In this guide, we will cover the Microsoft MB-310 Exam, Microsoft Dynamics 365 Finance Certification Salary and all aspects of the Microsoft MB-310 Exam Certification.

Microsoft MB-310 Exam:

Microsoft Dynamics 365 Finance is a certification exam that is conducted by Microsoft to validates Candidate knowledge and skills of Dynamics 365 Finance. Candidates for this exam are functional specialists who analyze business needs and translate them into fully performed business solutions and processes that implement industry best practices. Candidates are a key resource for deploying and configuring applications to meet the needs of the business. After passing this exam, Candidates get a certificate from Microsoft that helps them to demonstrate their proficiency in Microsoft Dynamics 365 to their clients and employers

You can read the Microsoft MB-310 Certification Exam topics below:

Candidates must know the exam topics before they start of preparation. Because it will really help them in hitting the core. Our **Microsoft MB-310 dumps** will include the following topics:

- Set up and configure financial management (35-40%)
- Manage and apply common processes (20-25%)
- Implement and manage accounts payable and receivable (20-25%)

- Manage budgeting and fixed assets (15-20%)

    You can read the Microsoft MB-310 Certification Exam Requirements:

Candidates for this exam have a basic understanding of the concepts of corporate accounting and finance, customer service, field service, manufacturing, retail, and supply chain management.

Applicants for this exam usually train in one or more sets of Microsoft Dynamics 365 Finance functions, including finance, manufacturing, and supply chain management. Applicants must have knowledge of basic accounting principles and practices.

- Microsoft Certified: Dynamics 365 Finance Functional Consultant Associate

    You can read the Microsoft MB-310 Certification Exam cost:

- The cost of the Microsoft MB-310 Exam is $165.

    You can read the Registration procedure of the Microsoft MB-310 Certification Exam:

Step 1: Visit to Microsoft Exam Registration
Step 2: Signup/Login to MICROSOFT account
Step 3: Search for Microsoft MB-310 Certifications Exam
Step 4: Select Date and Center of examination and confirm with payment value of $165

You can read the Microsoft MB-310 Certification Exam format below:

- Format: Multiple choices, multiple answers
- Length of Examination: 120 minutes
- Number of Questions: 40-60
- Passing score: 700
- Language: English

    You can read the Microsoft MB-310 Certification Exam certified salary below:

The average Salary of a Microsoft MB310 Certified Expert in

- United State - 98,000 USD
- India - 3192750 INR
- Europe - 38452 EURO
- England - 35111 POUND

    You can read the Microsoft MB-310 Certification Exam advantages below:

- A candidate might have incredible IT skills. Employers that do the hiring need to make decisions based on limited information and as it always. When they view the official Microsoft Dynamics 365 Finance certification, they can be guaranteed that a candidate has achieved a certain level of competence.
- If the Candidate has the desire to move up to a higher-paying position in an organization. This certification will help as always.
- When an organization hiring or promotion an employee, then the decision is made by human resources. Now while Candidate may have an IT background, they do their decisions in a way that takes into record many different factors. One thing is candidates have formal credentials, such as the Microsoft MB-310 .
- After completing the Microsoft Certified Dynamics 365 Finance certification, Candidate becomes a solid, well-rounded Microsoft Certified MB-310 Exam.

You can read the Best Solution to prepare Microsoft MB-310 Certification Exam:

There are many methods by which a person can prepare for the Microsoft MB-310 Certification exam. Some people prefer to watch tutorials and courses online, while others prefer to answer the questions from the Microsoft MB-310 Exam from the previous year, and some people use appropriate preparation materials to prepare. All methods are valid, but the most useful way is to use Microsoft . The preparation stuff is a complete set that allows people to know every detail about the certification and fully prepare the candidates. Certifications-questions is one of the reliable, verified and highly valued website that provides its online clients with highly detailed and related online exam preparation materials. Our specialists have created the best quality exam dumps for all specialists who need to pass the exam the first time. The success of all our clients speaks for us and we are very proud to have the greatest success rate. All of our clients have used our exam preparation stuff for various certification exams and passed the actual exam after using our practice test software and answers to exam questions. If you need help, you can always contact our technical support team so we can assist you to solve your issues.

To get a well-paying job, you should consider taking one of the famous certification exams. If you need to pass the certification exam on the first try and become a certified expert, you should think of finding the most reliable source that will help you pass multiple certification exams. Certification-questions.com can assist you to improve your chances of passing any certification exam. We have worked hard to create great preparation stuff for anyone who wants to take a certification exam to improve the possibilities of getting a well-paying job in the industry. To increase your possibilities, you should consider using the exam dumps provided by us.

To become a certified expert and acquire skills that will assist you in your future plans, you should think about focusing on your training. Expert certification exams can help you improve your performance and increase job opportunities in the IT sector. If you've worked in a company and want to take a certification exam, Certification-questions.com can help you prepare for the exam. You can quickly remove any exam using the exam dumps provided by Certification-questions. Our specialists are regularly working to improve your expertise and knowledge by creating valid test preparation stuff.

Certification-questions offer you self-assessment tools that help you estimate yourself. Intuitive software interface The practical assessment tool for Microsoft includes several self-assessment features, such as timed exams, randomized questions, multiple types of questions, test history, and test results, etc. You can change the question mode according to your skill level. This will help you to prepare for a valid **Microsoft MB-310 Exam dumps**.

For more information visit::

Microsoft MB-310 Exam Reference

# Sample Practice Test for MB-310

**Question: 1** *One Answer Is Right*

Note: This question is part of a series of questions that present the same scenario. Each question in the series contains a unique solution that might meet the stated goals. Some question sets might have more than one correct solution, while others might not have a correct solution. After you answer a question in this section, you will NOT be able to return to it. As a result, these questions will not appear in the review screen. You are configuring the year-end setup in Dynamics 365 Finance. You need to configure the year-end setup to meet the following requirements: - The accounting adjustments that are received in the first quarter must be able to be posted into the previous year's Period 13. - The fiscal year closing can be run again, but only the most recent closing entry will remain in the transactions. - All dimensions from profit and loss must carry over into the retained earnings. - All future and previous periods must have an On Hold status. Solution: - Configure General ledger parameters. - Set the Delete close of year transactions option to Yes. - Set the Create closing transactions during transfer option to Yes. - Set the Fiscal year status to permanently closed option to No. - Define the Year-end close template. - Designate a retained earnings main account for each legal entity. - Set the Financial dimensions will be used on the Opening transactions option to No. - Set the Transfer profit and loss dimensions' option to Close All. - Set future Ledger periods to a status of On Hold. Does the solution meet the goal?

**Answers:**

**A)** Yes

**B)** No

**Solution:** A

**Explanation:**

Explanation: Reference: https://docs.microsoft.com/en-us/dynamics365/unified-operations/financials/general-ledger/year-end-close

**Question: 2** *One Answer Is Right*

Note: This question is part of a series of questions that present the same scenario. Each question in the series contains a unique solution that might meet the stated goals. Some question sets might have more than one correct solution, while others might not have a correct solution. After you answer a question in this section, you will NOT be able to return to it. As a result, these questions will not appear in the review screen. You are configuring the year-end setup in Dynamics 365 Finance. You need to configure the year-end setup to meet the following requirements: - The accounting adjustments that are received in the first quarter must be able to be posted into the previous year's Period 13. - The fiscal year closing can be run again, but only the most recent closing entry will remain in the transactions. - All dimensions from profit and loss must carry over into the retained earnings. - All future and previous periods must have an On Hold status. Solution: - Configure General ledger parameters. - Set the Delete close of year transactions option to Yes. - Set the Create closing transactions during transfer option to Yes. - Set the Fiscal year status to permanently closed option to Yes. - Define the Year-end close template. - Designate a retained earnings main account for each legal entity. - Set the Financial dimensions will be used on the Opening transactions option to Yes. - Set the Transfer profit and loss dimensions to Close All. - Set all prior and future Ledger periods to a status of On Hold. Does the solution meet the goal?

**Answers:**

**A)** Yes

**B)** No

**Solution:** B

**Explanation:**

Explanation: Reference: https://docs.microsoft.com/en-us/dynamics365/unified-operations/financials/general-ledger/year-end-close

**Question: 3** *One Answer Is Right*

Note: This question is part of a series of questions that present the same scenario. Each question in the series contains a unique solution that might meet the stated goals. Some question sets might have more than one correct solution, while others might not have a correct solution. After you answer a question in this section, you will NOT be able to return to it. As a result, these questions will not appear in the review screen. You are configuring the year-end setup in Dynamics 365 Finance. You need to configure the year-end setup to meet the following requirements: - The accounting adjustments that are received in the first quarter must be able to be posted into the previous year's Period 13. - The fiscal year closing can be run again, but only the most recent closing entry will remain in the transactions. - All dimensions from profit and loss must carry over into the retained earnings. - All future and previous periods must have an On Hold status. Solution: - Configure General ledger parameters. - Set the Delete close of year transactions option to No. - Set the Create closing transactions during transfer option to No. - Set the Fiscal year status to permanently closed option to No. - Define the Year-end close template. - Designate a retained earnings main account for each legal entity. - Set the Financial dimensions will be used on the Opening transactions option to No. - Set the Transfer profit and loss dimensions to Close All. - Set all prior and future Ledger periods to a status of On Hold. Does the solution meet the goal?

**Answers:**

**A)** Yes

**B)** No

**Solution:** B

**Explanation:**

Explanation: Reference: https://docs.microsoft.com/en-us/dynamics365/unified-operations/financials/general-ledger/year-end-close

**Question: 4** *Multiple Answers Are Right*

HOTSPOT You are implementing a Dynamics 365 Finance general ledger module for a client that has multiple legal entities. The client has the following requirements: - Post journal entries for all companies from one legal entity. - Configure automatic creation of due to/due from transactions based on when LegalEntityA transacts with LegalEntityB. - Automatically split the dollar amount in half between DimensionA and DimensionB when the journal is posted. - Set up fixed or variable allocations, and then review the allocations in a journal before posting. - Automatically post year-end results to account 30016 during year-end close. You need to configure the system. Which system capability should you configure? To answer, select the appropriate configuration in the answer area. NOTE: Each correct selection is worth one point.

Hot Area:

## Answer Area

| Client requirement | System capability |
|---|---|
| You must configure automatic creation of due to/due from transactions based on when LegalEntityA transacts with LegalEntityB. | intercompany journal / global journal entry / ledger allocation rules / accounts for automatic transactions |
| You must automatically split the dollar amount in half between DimensionA and DimensionB when the journal is posted. | ledger allocation rules / allocation terms / accounts for automatic transactions / intercompany journal |
| You must set up fixed or variable allocations, and then review the allocations in a journal before posting. | intercompany journal / ledger allocation rules / allocation terms / accounts for automatic transactions |
| The system must automatically post year-end results to account 30016 during year-end close. | ledger allocation rules / allocation terms / accounts for automatic transactions / intercompany journal |

**Answers:**

## A)

### Answer Area

| Client requirement | System capability |
|---|---|
| You must configure automatic creation of due to/due from transactions based on when LegalEntityA transacts with LegalEntityB. | **intercompany journal**<br>global journal entry<br>ledger allocation rules<br>accounts for automatic transactions |
| You must automatically split the dollar amount in half between DimensionA and DimensionB when the journal is posted. | ledger allocation rules<br>**allocation terms**<br>accounts for automatic transactions<br>intercompany journal |
| You must set up fixed or variable allocations, and then review the allocations in a journal before posting. | intercompany journal<br>**ledger allocation rules**<br>allocation terms<br>accounts for automatic transactions |
| The system must automatically post year-end results to account 30016 during year-end close. | ledger allocation rules<br>allocation terms<br>**accounts for automatic transactions**<br>intercompany journal |

**Solution:** A

**Explanation:**

Explanation:

**Question: 5** *One Answer Is Right*

A company is preparing to complete a year-end close process. You need to configure the Dynamics 365 Finance General ledger module. Which three configurations must you use? Each correct answer presents part of the solution. NOTE: Each correct selection is worth one point.

**Answers:**

**A)** Configure the Fiscal year close parameters

**B)** Configure the ledger calendar for the new fiscal year

**C)** Configure the transfer balance

**D)** Validate the main account type

**E)** Create the next fiscal year

**Solution:** A, D, E

**Explanation:**

Explanation: References: https://docs.microsoft.com/en-us/dynamics365/unified-operations/financials/general-ledger/year-end-close

**Question: 6** *One Answer Is Right*

A client has unique accounting needs that sometimes require posting definitions. You need to implement posting definitions. In which situation should you implement posting definitions?

**Answers:**

**A)** when financial dimensions need to default from the vendor record onto an invoice

**B)** when only certain dimensions are allowed to post with certain main account combinations

**C)** when creating multiple balanced ledger entries based on transaction types or accounts

**D)** when the system needs to automatically post a transaction to the accounts receivable account on invoice posting

**Solution:** D

**Question: 7** *One Answer Is Right*

An organization is setting up a cost accounting. You need to set up fiscal calendars for Dynamics 365 Finance. What are three uses for fiscal calendars? Each correct answer presents a complete solution. NOTE: Each correct selection is worth one point.

**Answers:**

**A)** standard work hours

**B)** financial transactions

**C)** fixed asset depreciation

**D)** budget cycles

**E)** shift work hours

**Solution:** B, C, D

**Explanation:**

Explanation: Reference: https://docs.microsoft.com/en-us/dynamics365/unified-operations/financials/budgeting/fiscal-calendars- fiscal-years-periods

**Question: 8** *One Answer Is Right*

You are configuring automatic bank reconciliation functionality for a company that has multiple bank accounts. The company wants to import their bank statements. You need to import electronic bank statements to reconcile the bank accounts. Which three actions can you perform? Each correct answer presents a complete solution. NOTE: Each correct selection is worth one point.

**Answers:**

**A)** Select all the bank accounts for the bank statement files, and then upload all files

**B)** Select Account reconciliation on the bank account form

**C)** Import bank statements from the Data management workspace

**D)** Navigate to Import statement on the Bank Statements page of Cash and Bank Management

**E)** Select Import statement for multiple bank accounts in all legal entities, and then upload a zip file

**Solution:** B, D, E

**Explanation:**

Explanation: Reference: https://docs.microsoft.com/en-us/dynamics365/unified-operations/financials/cash-bank-management/ reconcile-bank-statements-advanced-bank-reconciliation

**Question: 9** *One Answer Is Right*

A company plans to create a new allocation rule for electric utilities expenses. The allocation rule must meet the following requirements: - Distribute overhead utility expense to each department. - Define how and in what proportion the source amounts must be distributed on various destination lines. You need to configure the allocation rule. Which allocation method should you use?

**Answers:**

**A)** Distribute the source document amount equally

**B)** Fixed weight

**C)** Equally

**D)** Basis

**Solution:** D

**Explanation:**

Explanation: Reference: https://docs.microsoft.com/en-us/dynamics365/unified-operations/financials/general-ledger/ledger- allocation-rules

**Question: 10** *Multiple Answers Are Right*

HOTSPOT A food manufacturer uses commodities such as beans, corn, and chili peppers as raw materials. The prices of the commodities fluctuate frequently. The manufacturer wants to use cost versions to simulate these fluctuations. You need to set up cost versions and prices to accomplish the manufacturer's goal. For which purpose should you use each costing type? To answer, select the appropriate options in the answer area. NOTE: Each correct selection is worth one point. Hot Area:

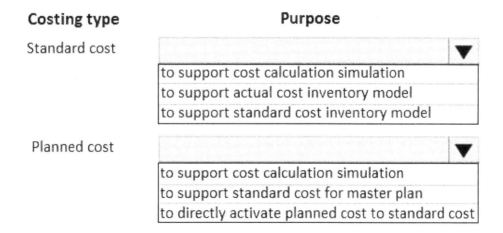

**Answers:**

A)

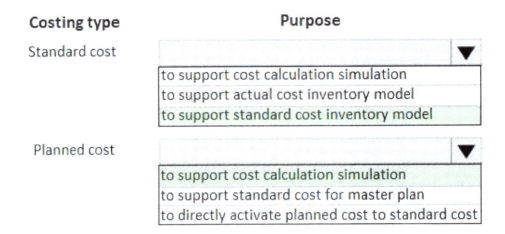

Solution: A

Explanation:

Explanation: Reference: https://docs.microsoft.com/en-us/dynamics365/unified-operations/supply-chain/cost-management/costing- versions

# Chapter 32: MB-330 - Microsoft Dynamics 365 Supply Chain Management

## Exam Guide

How can you begin study for the Microsoft MB-330 Certification Exam

Best guide For Microsoft MB-330 Certification Exam

Quick preparation guide if you don't have time to read complete the page

There are Dynamics 365 Supply Chain Management Certification offered by Microsoft.Microsoft Certified certification helps a candidate to validates his skills in Microsoft Technology.Microsoft exams assist you to distinguish yourself and verify your education and abilities. Describe your expertise in Microsoft 365 technologies moreover improve your work by earning one of the new Microsoft 365 role-based certifications for business administrators or an Office 365 certification. Verify your abilities in sectors such as relocation and management of cloud-hosted business apps with Microsoft 365 and move your business to the cloud.In this guide, we will cover the Microsoft MB-330 Exam, Microsoft Dynamics 365 Supply Chain Management Certification Salary and all aspects of the Microsoft MB-330 Exam Certification.

Microsoft MB-330 Exam Introduction:

Microsoft MB-330 Exam covers Microsoft Dynamics 365 Supply Chain Management.Supply Chain Management in Microsoft Dynamics 365 enables the candidates to implement inventory management,implement and manage supply chain processes ,implement warehouse management and transportation management ,carry out business processes.

Microsoft MB-330 Certification Exam topics are as follow:

Candidates must know the exam topics before they start of preparation. Because it will really help them in hitting the core. Our **Microsoft MB-330 dumps** will include the following topics:

- implement Product information management (25-30%)

- Implement Inventory management (20-25%)
- Implement and manage Supply Chain processes (25-30%)
- Implement Warehouse management and Transportation management and perform business processes (25-30%)

Microsoft MB-330 Certification Exam Requirements are as follow:

- Candidates for this exam have a basic understanding of the concepts of corporate accounting and finance, customer service, field service, manufacturing, retail, and supply chain management concepts.
- Candidates for this exam are usually trained in one or more Microsoft Dynamics 365 feature sets, including finance, manufacturing, and supply chain management.
- Applicants should have some knowledge of supply chain management practices, including procurement, trade, logistics, warehouse management, and transportation management.

Registration procedure of the Microsoft MB-330 Certification Exam are as follow:

These are following steps for registering the Microsoft MB-330 exam.
Step 1: Visit to Microsoft Exam Registration
Step 2: Signup/Login to MICROSOFT account
Step 3: Search for Microsoft MB-330 Certifications Exam
Step 4: Select Date and Center of examination and confirm with payment value of $165

Microsoft MB-330 Certification Exam formate are as follow:

Format: Multiple choices, multiple answers

- Length of Examination: 120 minutes
- Number of Questions: 40-60
- Passing score: 700
- Language: English

Microsoft MB-330 Certification Exam certified salary is as follow:

- United States: 50000 USD
- India: 3712500 INR
- Europe: 44729 Euro
- England: 40816 Pound

Microsoft MB-330 Certification Exam cost is as follow:

- The price of Microsoft MB-330 exam is $165 USD.

Microsoft MB-330 Certification Exam advantages are as follow:

- Improve your earning potential to get higher salaries.
- Learn to perform practical and complex activities through laboratory, practice sessions, study and.
- Develop your experience base and validate your skills to attract potential employers.
- Obtain a safe digital badge that you can attach to your social media profiles.
- Gain visibility of a wide range of features, functions and important activities to use in the workplace.

Great Solution to prepare Microsoft MB-330 Certification Exam:

The study guide of Certification-questions for the Microsoft MB-330 is the best solution for exam preparation. It contains knowledge on each subject of the program and is simply the best in all aspects. The information contained in these dumps of Microsoft MB-330 is transmitted using a very simple and interactive form of questions and answers. This study guide is really wondrous and contains everything you need to know. Candidates for the Microsoft MB-330 should have a thorough knowledge and understanding of all the questions and answers of the Microsoft MB-330 in our guide. In addition to our comprehensive study guide, we also offer dumps of certified Microsoft MB-330 exam, if you want a quick and exam-oriented preparation. Any information in this **Microsoft MB-330 exam dumps** is valuable. Eventually, if you opt for one of the top certifications like Cisco, Microsoft, Oracle, you should visit Certification-questions.com. This will hugely assist you to find all the equipment you need to prepare for the certification exam. The site is user-managed and individuals share their struggles and answers to questions like PDF files at no cost to create a free community. Study stuff for all major certifications such as Cisco, Microsoft, CompTIA, IBM, Oracle, Apple, etc. is accessible here.

Our exam dumps also cover practice test software. PDF file format that allows passage to preparation material anyplace, anytime on various devices. On the other hand, the online practice test engine will assist you to practice your learning content by providing you with practice tests just like the actual exam environment. A free demo can be viewed before purchasing these dumps.

To become a certified expert and acquire skills that will assist you in your future plans, you should think about focusing on your training. Expert certification exams can help you improve your performance and increase job opportunities in the IT sector. If you've worked in a company and want to take a certification exam, Certification-questions.com can help you prepare for the exam. You can quickly remove any exam using the exam dumps provided by Certification-questions. Our specialists are regularly working to improve your expertise and knowledge by creating valid test preparation stuff.

By using certifications-questions.com study materials you can earn great grades that are sure to make your career brighter and open new doors for success and opportunity. You don't have to seek for other websites and waste time because you are in the right site now.

Have you ever thought about taking the real exam in 24 hours? Certifications-questions.com is the best in giving the latest exam dumps and helping IT learners to become certified for the first time. We provide answers to practice exam questions to prepare you for the exam quickly and easily. With our exam dumps, you will have the confidence to pass the real exam. We offer download passage for updated questions, exam dumps answers in PDF format.

The need for qualified and certified experts increases day by day. In a very competitive market, you must stand out for a certification that authenticates your technical skills. When you think of a very requested certification, in general, the first point that comes to mind for most individuals is how to prepare for the certification exam.

Eventually, if you opt for one of the top certifications like Cisco, Microsoft, Oracle, you should visit Certification-questions.com. This will hugely assist you to find all the equipment you need to prepare for the certification exam. The site is user-managed and individuals share their struggles and answers to questions like PDF files at no cost to create a free community. Study stuff for all major certifications such as Cisco, Microsoft, CompTIA, IBM, Oracle, Apple, etc. is accessible here.

With the assist of the exam dumps given by Certification-questions.com, you can get 100% success guaranteed on the certification exam. We have created pdf dumps for all those looking to become certified specialists. If you also want to pass the certification exam on the first try, you should think using valid questions given by us. We have a 100% assured success rate and you can get all the referrals you want from us. All our clients are completely satisfied with our exam dumps downloads and our preparation stuff. Certification-questions.com will provide you with up-to-date practical questions so you can quickly prepare for the next exam and pass the exam on the first try.

Questions and answers from the Microsoft MB-330 Exam include important topics from the Microsoft MB-330 Certification Program and provides easy-to-learn information for easy access. To enable you to further tighten the original exam model and face the challenges of the Microsoft MB-330, they offer you the best solution. They show you the true nature and style of the questions asked by the Microsoft MB-330 Exam . Trying these practice tests will give you confidence. Identifying your weaknesses will guide you to prepare them and improve your chances of success.

To get more details visit::

Microsoft MB-330 Exam Reference

# Sample Practice Test for MB-330

**Question: 1** *One Answer Is Right*

A company needs to create new items that can be company owned or vendor owned. You need to create and set up the items so that they can be used as company owned or consignment. What should you do?

**Answers:**

A) Assign a non-stock service item model group

B) Assign a moving average costing inventory model

C) Activate batch dimension and assign a standard costing inventory model

D) Activate owner dimension and assign a standard costing inventory model

**Solution:** D

**Question: 2** *Multiple Answers Are Right*

DRAG DROP You manage a Dynamics 365 Supply Chain Management system for a company. You need to configure agreements in the system. Which agreement types should you use? To answer, drag the appropriate agreement types to the appropriate scenarios. Each agreement type may be used once, more than once, or not at all. You may need to drag the split bar between panes or scroll to view content. NOTE: Each correct selection is worth one point. Select and Place:

| Agreement types | Answer Area | |
|---|---|---|
| purchase | **Scenario** | **Agreement type** |
| sales | Customers who purchase between 51 and 100 units of Product A receive a $10.00 discont per unit. Customers who purchase over 100 units receive a $12.00 discount per unit. | Agreement type |
| trade | A customer agrees to purchase 500 laptops over the next six months. | Agreement type |
| | Your company agrees to purchase $150,000 worth of office supplies within a year. | Agreement type |

**Answers:**

## A)

**Agreement types**

| purchase |
| sales |
| trade |

**Answer Area**

| Scenario | Agreement type |
|---|---|
| Customers who purchase between 51 and 100 units of Product A receive a $10.00 discont per unit. Customers who purchase over 100 units receive a $12.00 discount per unit. | trade |
| A customer agrees to purchase 500 laptops over the next six months. | sales |
| Your company agrees to purchase $150,000 worth of office supplies within a year. | purchase |

**Solution:** A

**Explanation:**

Explanation:

**Question: 3** *One Answer Is Right*

A company uses trade agreements for their customers. Prices for some customers must round to the nearest US dollar. A customer reports that prices do not round to the nearest US dollar as required. You need to resolve the issue. In Trade agreement journals, which option should you use?

**Answers:**

**A)** Adjustment

**B)** View smart rounding

**C)** Validate all lines

**D)** Apply smart rounding

**Solution:** D

**Question: 4** *Multiple Answers Are Right*

DRAG DROP A company manufactures wood furniture. Cabinets can be purchased with different wood finishes including oak and maple. You need to configure a product attribute to characterize the types of cabinet finishes. Which three actions should you perform in sequence? To answer, move the appropriate actions from the list of actions to the answer area and arrange them in the correct order. Select and Place:

**Actions**

- Add an attribute to the procurement category
- Create an attribute of type Boolean and define the different types of wood finishes
- Assign the attribute to the retail category
- Create style dimensions for the different types of wood finishes
- Create an attribute type of type Text and define the different types of wood finishes
- Create an attribute associated with an attribute type for Cabinet Finishing

**Answer Area**

Answers:

A)

**Actions**

- Add an attribute to the procurement category
- Create an attribute of type Boolean and define the different types of wood finishes
- Assign the attribute to the retail category
- Create style dimensions for the different types of wood finishes
- Create an attribute type of type Text and define the different types of wood finishes
- Create an attribute associated with an attribute type for Cabinet Finishing

**Answer Area**

- Create an attribute type of type Text and define the different types of wood finishes
- Create an attribute associated with an attribute type for Cabinet Finishing
- Assign the attribute to the retail category

**Solution:** A

**Explanation:**

Explanation: References: https://docs.microsoft.com/en-us/dynamics365/unified-operations/retail/attribute-attributegroups-lifecycle

**Question: 5** *One Answer Is Right*

A company creates several item costing versions. All new and existing items have costs associated with them. After applying the costs, the company notices the activation date has not been updated. You need to update the items to the current date for activation. What should you do?

**Answers:**

**A)** Set the item cost record status to Active

**B)** Set the from date to today and leave the item cost record status at Pending

**C)** Set the item cost record status to Pending

**D)** Set the cost price and date of price on the released product

**Solution:** A

**Explanation:**

Explanation: References: https://docs.microsoft.com/en-us/dynamics365/unified-operations/supply-chain/cost-management/costing- versions

**Question: 6** *One Answer Is Right*

An employee at a company releases a new product from the Released product maintenance workspace. An employee in another department is unable to add the product to a sales order. You determine that dimension groups have not been applied to the product. You need to ensure that the product can be added to the sales order. Which two inventory dimension groups should you add to the product? Each correct answer presents part of the solution. NOTE: Each correct selection is worth one point.

**Answers:**

**A)** Tracking dimension group

**B)** Coverage group

**C)** Product dimension group

**D)** Storage dimension group

**Solution:** C, D

**Question: 7** *Multiple Answers Are Right*

DRAG DROP You are the product manager at a distribution company. You are responsible for managing product compliance standards and reporting. Chemical product C0001 can be sold in all parts of the United States except for the state of California. You need to set up these compliance requirements for C0001. Which four actions should be performed in sequence? To answer, move the appropriate actions from the list of actions to the answer area and arrange them in the correct order. Select and Place:

**Actions**

- Create an inclusive list type for New York, United States
- Create an exclusive list type for California, United States
- Add item C0001 to the restricted product lists
- Open the Restricted products regional lists form
- Create an inclusive list type for the United States
- Create a regulated products regional list for California, United States. Add item C0001 to the list
- Open the Regulated products regional lists

**Answer Area**

Answers:

A)

**Actions**

- Create an inclusive list type for New York, United States
- Create an exclusive list type for California, United States
- Add item C0001 to the restricted product lists
- Open the Restricted products regional lists form
- Create an inclusive list type for the United States
- Create a regulated products regional list for California, United States. Add item C0001 to the list
- Open the Regulated products regional lists

**Answer Area**

- Open the Restricted products regional lists form
- Create an inclusive list type for the United States
- Create an exclusive list type for California, United States
- Add item C0001 to the restricted product lists

**Solution:** A

**Explanation:**

Explanation:

**Question: 8** *One Answer Is Right*

An employee at a company needs to lay out the various component to build custom bicycles. You need to identify which constraints the employee should use to set up the bicycles. Which two types of constraints the employee use? Each correct answer presents a complete solution. NOTE: Each correct selection is worth one point.

**Answers:**

**A)** table constraints that are used generically among product configuration models

**B)** expression constraints that are used generically among product configuration models

**C)** expression constraints that are unique to each product configuration model

**D)** table constraints that are always unique to each product configuration model

**Solution:** A, C

**Explanation:**

Explanation: References: https://docs.microsoft.com/en-us/dynamics365/unified-operations/supply-chain/pim/expression-constraints-table-constraints-product-configuration-models

**Question: 9** *Multiple Answers Are Right*

HOTSPOT You are configuring pricing for a new item. Wholesale customers must pay $10.00 for order quantities of up to 9 units. All other customers receive a static price of $14.00 regardless of quantity. You need to configure sales trade agreements. In Trade Agreement Setup, which actions should you perform? To answer, select the appropriate options in the answer area. NOTE: Each correct selection is worth one point. Hot Area:

## Answer Area

| Requirement | Action |
|---|---|
| Create price groups | ▼ |
| | Create and assign a customer group to the trade agreement line |
| | Set up and link a price group to the customer group |
| | Set up and link a price group to each customer |
| | Set up a price group on the trade agreement line and link the line to the customer |
| Create a sales price for a group of customers by quantity | ▼ |
| | Add a trade agreement line by customer group for quantity of 0-9 for $10.00 |
| | Add a trade agreement line by price group for quantity of 1-9 for $10.00 |
| | Add a trade agreement line for quantity of 0 for $14.00 |
| | Add a trade agreement line for quantity of 10-100 at $10.00 |
| Create a sales price for all customers by any quantity | ▼ |
| | Create a trade agreement for all items at $14.00 |
| | Create a trade agreement line for customer group All for $14.00 |
| | Create a trade agreement line for Part code type set to All and price of $14.00 |
| | Create a trade agreement line for wholesale customers at $14.00 |

## Answers:

### A)

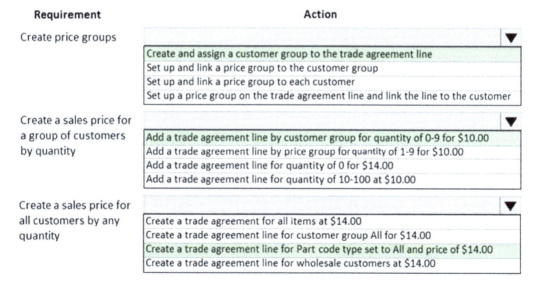

**Solution:** A

**Explanation:**

Explanation: References: https://docs.microsoft.com/en-us/dynamics365/unified-operations/supply-chain/sales-marketing/tasks/ create-new-trade-agreement

**Question: 10** *Multiple Answers Are Right*

HOTSPOT An airport uses Dynamics 365 Supply Chain Management. You purchase new baggage-sorting hardware. You must add both the hardware and the service contract for the hardware to the product hierarchy. You need to configure the category node. What should you do? To answer, select the appropriate options in the answer area. NOTE: Each correct selection is worth one point. Hot Area:

### Answer Area

| Item | Action |
|---|---|
| Baggage system hardware | Create a new category node and select Classify as tangible / Add to an existing category node and select Classify as tangible / Add to an existing category node and clear Classify as tangible |
| Service agreement | Create a new category node and select Classify as tangible / Add to an existing category node and select Classify as tangible / Add to an existing category node and clear Classify as tangible |

**Answers:**

**A)**

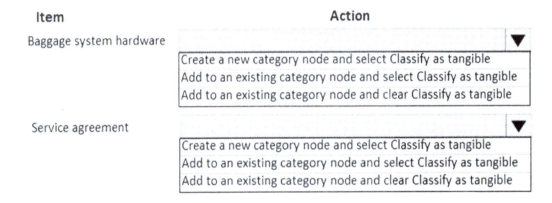

**Solution:** A

**Explanation:**

Explanation:

# Chapter 33: MB-901 - Microsoft Dynamics 365 Fundamentals

## Exam Guide

How to Prepare For MB-901: Microsoft Dynamics 365 Fundamentals (beta) Exam

Preparation Guide for MB-901: Microsoft Dynamics 365 Fundamentals (beta) Exam

Introduction

Microsoft has created a track for professionals who want to validate foundational knowledge of Microsoft Dynamics 365 landscape to get certified this platform. This certification program provides the considerations and benefits of adopting Dynamics 365 and cloud services in general. Microsoft Dynamics 365 Fundamentals (beta) professionals a way to demonstrate their skills. The assessment is based on a rigorous exam using industry standard methodology to determine whether a candidate meets Microsoft's proficiency standards.

According to Microsoft, a MB-900 Certified Professional enables organizations to leverage Microsoft Dynamics 365 Fundamentals (beta) technologies with a thorough understanding of cloud security; the role-based security model in Dynamics 365; and how, and with which products, both the model-driven apps and the Finance and Operations apps integrate.

Certification is evidence of your skills, expertise in those areas in which you like to work. There are many vendors in the market that are providing these certifications. If candidate wants to work on Microsoft Dynamics 365 Fundamental and prove his knowledge, certification offered by Microsoft. This **MB-901 Exam** Certification helps a candidate to validates his skills in Microsoft Dynamics 365 Fundamental Technology.

In this guide, we will cover the MB-901: Microsoft Dynamics 365 Fundamentals (beta) Certification exam, MB-901: Microsoft Dynamics 365 Fundamentals (beta) Certified professional salary and all aspects of the MB-901: Microsoft Dynamics 365 Fundamentals (beta) Certification.

Introduction to MB-901: Microsoft Dynamics 365 Fundamentals (beta) Exam:

Candidates for **MB-901 Exam** are seeking to prove fundamental knowledge and skills in Microsoft Dynamics 365 Fundamental domain. Before taking this exam, aspirants ought to have a solid fundamental information of the concepts shared in preparation guide as well as basic understanding of business scenarios would give an added edge.

It is suggested that professionals accustomed to the ideas and also the technologies represented here by taking relevant training courses. Candidates are expected to have some hands-on experience on Microsoft Dynamics 365; artificial intelligence (AI); mixed reality (MR); the Power Platform
After passing this exam, candidates get a certificate from Microsoft that helps them to demonstrate their proficiency to their clients and employers.

Topics of MB-901: Microsoft Dynamics 365 Fundamentals (beta) Exam:

Candidates should apprehend the examination topics before they begin of preparation. because it'll extremely facilitate them in touch the core. Our **MB-901 dumps** will include the following topics:

*1. Identify Microsoft platform components for Dynamics 365 (30-35%)*

Describe integration capabilities

- Integration across Dynamics 365 apps
- Integration across Microsoft products
- Integration with third-party apps
- Custom integrations in Dynamics 365

    Describe Dynamics 365 cloud security

- Encryption
- Authentication
- Data ownership
- Data center access
- SSO
- Data loss protection (DLP)
- Industry standard certifications (GDPR, etc)

    Understand the benefits of role based security

- App role-based security

- Leveraging security roles

- Streamlined user experience

- Out-of-the-box security roles Identify the business value of the Microsoft cloud

- Azure features used by Dynamics 365

- PaaS

- Life Cycle Services (LCS)

    Understand the use of Power Platform in Dynamics 365

- Power Apps
- Power BI
- Power Automate
- AI Builder
- Common Data Service

    Understand the benefits of the Common Data Model

- Analytics
- Extensibility
- Interoperability
- Consistency

    Identify Dynamics 365 reporting capabilities

- Built in reporting
- Role-based reporting
- Extensible reporting

    *2. Understand AI and Mixed Reality for Dynamics 365 (10-15%)*

Leverage AI for data insights

- Fraud protection
- Virtual agents
- Sales insights
- Customer insights
- Relationship insights
- Customer service insights

    Leverage mixed reality

- Remote assist

- Guides
- Layouts

*3. Understand Customer Engagement apps (25-30%)*

Understand the capabilities of Dynamics 365 Sales

- Dynamics 365 sales automation
- Pipeline management
- Contact management
- Customer requests and follow up
- LinkedIn Sales Navigator

Understand the capabilities of Dynamics 365 Marketing

- Lead generation and qualifications
- Customer journey
- Surveys
- Landing pages
- Segmentation
- Event management
- Dynamics 365 for marketing

Understand the capabilities of Dynamics 365 Field Service

- Resource Scheduling Optimization (RSO)
- Connected Field Service
- Service resource scheduling
- Proactive customer service
- Field Service Mobile

Understand the capabilities of Dynamics 365 Customer Service

- Account management
- Omni channel service
- Case life cycle
- Knowledge articles

*3. Understand Dynamics 365 Finance and Operations apps (25-30%)*

Understand the capabilities of Dynamics 365 Finance

- General Ledger

- Accounts Payable
- Accounts Receivable
- Project accounting
- Budgeting
- Global attributes
- End to end business processes
- Real time cash flow visibility
- Enterprise asset management

Understand the capabilities of Dynamics 365 Human Resources Core HR

- Employee self-service
- Personnel management
- Benefits management
- Employee development

Understand the capabilities of Dynamics 365 Business Central

- Finance
- Supply chain
- Project management
- Sales and service
- Budgeting
- When to use Business Central vs other Dynamics 365 products

Understand the capabilities of Dynamics 365 Supply Chain Management

- Project accounting
- Modernize operations
- Procurement and sourcing
- Manufacturing
- Warehouse management
- Master planning
- Product information

Understand the capabilities of Dynamics 365 Retail

- Retail capability
- Channel Management
- Point of Sale (POS)

- Mobile commerce

    Who should take the MB-901: Microsoft Dynamics 365 Fundamentals (beta) Exam:

The **MB-901 Exam** certification is an internationally-recognized certification which help to have validation for those professionals who should have general knowledge or relevant working experience in an Information Technology (IT) environment. Candidates should also have a basic understanding of business scenarios and experience in addressing business, legal, and security requirements for IT projects.

How to study the MB-901: Microsoft Dynamics 365 Fundamentals (beta) Exam:

Preparation of certification exams could be covered with two resource types . The first one are the study guides, reference books and study forums that are elaborated and appropriate for building information from ground up. Apart from them video tutorials and lectures are a good option to ease the pain of through study and are relatively make the study process more interesting nonetheless these demand time and concentration from the learner. Smart candidates who wish to create a solid foundation altogether examination topics and connected technologies typically mix video lectures with study guides to reap the advantages of each but practice exams or practice exam engines is one important study tool which goes typically unnoted by most candidates. Practice exams are designed with our experts to make exam prospects test their knowledge on skills attained in course, as well as prospects become comfortable and familiar with the real exam environment. Statistics have indicated exam anxiety plays much bigger role of students failure in exam than the fear of the unknown. Certification-questions expert team recommends preparing some notes on these topics along with it don't forget to practice **MB-901 dumps** which had been written by our expert team, each of these can assist you loads to clear this exam with excellent marks.

MB-901: Microsoft Dynamics 365 Fundamentals (beta) Certification Path:

MB-901: Microsoft Dynamics 365 Fundamentals (beta) Exam is foundation level Certification. This exam can be taken as a precursor to other Dynamics 365 certifications and training.

How much MB-901: Microsoft Dynamics 365 Fundamentals (beta) Exam Cost:

The price of the Microsoft Mobility and Devices Fundamentals exam is $99 USD, for more information related to exam price please visit to Microsoft Training website as prices of Microsoft exams fees get varied country wise.

How to book the MB-901: Microsoft Dynamics 365 Fundamentals (beta) Exam:

These are following steps for registering the MB-901: Microsoft Dynamics 365 Fundamentals (beta) exam.

- Step 1: Visit to Microsoft Learning and search for MB-901: Microsoft Dynamics 365 Fundamentals (beta).
- Step 2: Sign up/Login to Pearson VUE account
- Step 3: Select local centre based on your country, date, time and confirm with a payment method.

What is the duration, language, and format of MB-901: Microsoft Dynamics 365 Fundamentals (beta) Exam:

- Length of Examination: 50 mins
- Number of Questions: 40 to 60 questions(Since Microsoft does not publish this information, the number of exam questions may change without notice.)
- Passing Score: 700 / 1000
- Type of Questions: This test format is multiple choice.
- Language: English
- This is beta exam.

MB-901: Microsoft Dynamics 365 Fundamentals (beta) Exam Certified Professional salary:

The average salary of a MB-901: Microsoft Dynamics 365 Fundamentals (beta) Exam Certified Expert in

- United State - 120,000 USD
- India - 20,00,327 INR
- Europe - 90,547 EURO
- England - 90,532 POUND

The benefit of obtaining the MB-901: Microsoft Dynamics 365 Fundamentals (beta) Exam Certification:

- This certification will be judging your skills and knowledge on your understanding Microsoft Dynamics 365 Fundamental concepts & Understanding of how to operate on Planning and Administering Microsoft Dynamics 365 Fundamental .
- This certification credential will give you edge over other counterparts. Apart from knowledge from MB-901: Microsoft Dynamics 365 Fundamentals (beta) Exam.
- MB-901 Certification is distinguished among competitors. MB-901 certification can give them an edge at that time easily when candidates appear for employment interview, employers are very fascinated to note one thing that differentiates the individual from all other candidates.

- MB-901 certification has more useful and relevant networks that help them in setting career goals for themselves. MB-901 networks provide them with the correct career guidance than non certified generally are unable to get.
- MB-901 certified candidates will be confident and stand different from others as their skills are more trained than non-certified professionals.
- **MB-901 Exam** provide proven knowledge to use the tools to complete the task efficiently and cost effectively than the other non-certified professionals lack in doing so.
- MB-901 Certification provides practical experience to candidates from all the aspects to be a proficient worker in the organization.
- MB-901 Certifications provide opportunities to get a job easily in which they are interested in instead of wasting years and ending without getting any experience.
- MB-901 credential delivers higher earning potential and increased promotion opportunities because it shows a good understanding of Microsoft Dynamics 365 Fundamentals (beta).

Difficulty in Writing MB-901: Microsoft Dynamics 365 Fundamentals (beta) Exam:

MB-901: Microsoft Dynamics 365 Fundamentals (beta) is a privileged achievement one could be graced with. But adverse to general notion certifying with Microsoft is not that challenging if the candidates have proper preparation material to pass the MB-901: Microsoft Dynamics 365 Fundamentals (beta) exam with good grades. Questions answers and clarifications which are designed in form of Certification-questions dumps make sure to cover entire course content. Certification-questions have a brilliant MB-901: Microsoft Dynamics 365 Fundamentals (beta) dumps with most recent and important questions and answers in PDF files. Certification-questions is sure about the exactness and legitimacy of MB-901: Microsoft Dynamics 365 Fundamentals (beta) dumps and in this manner. Candidates can easily pass the MB-901: Microsoft Dynamics 365 Fundamentals (beta) exam with genuine MB-901: Microsoft Dynamics 365 Fundamentals (beta) dumps and get MICROSOFT certification. These dumps are viewed as the best source to understand the MB-901: Microsoft Dynamics 365 Fundamentals (beta) well by simply pursuing examples questions and answers. If candidate completes practice the exam with certification **MB-901 dumps** along with self-assessment to get the proper idea on MICROSOFT accreditation and to ace the certification exam.

For more info read reference::

Microsoft learning site
Microsoft Dynamics 365 Fundamentals (beta)
Introduction to Dynamics 365 Marketing

# Sample Practice Test for MB-901

**Question: 1** *Multiple Answers Are Right*

HOTSPOT A company uses one system for sales and one system for order management. When quotes are accepted in the sales system, the customer and order are reentered into the order management system. What is a benefit of using the Common Data Model, and who can manage the model? To answer, select the appropriate options in the answer area. NOTE: Each correct selection is worth one point. Hot Area:

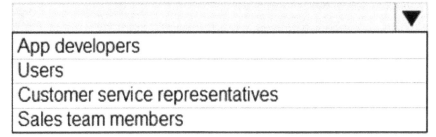

Answers:

**A)**

### Answer Area

What is a benefit of using the Common Data Model?

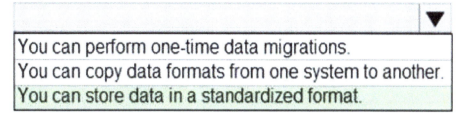

- You can perform one-time data migrations.
- You can copy data formats from one system to another.
- **You can store data in a standardized format.**

Who can manage Common Data Model models?

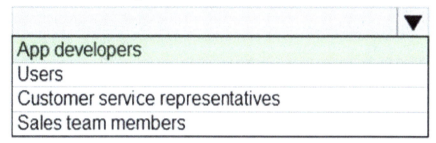

- **App developers**
- Users
- Customer service representatives
- Sales team members

**Solution:** A

**Explanation:**

Explanation: Reference: https://docs.microsoft.com/en-us/common-data-model/

**Question: 2** *One Answer Is Right*

You are implementing Dynamics 365 Customer Service. Company executives need to decide whether to put the data on-premises or in the cloud. You need to explain the data security benefits of the cloud. What should you communicate to the executives?

**Answers:**

**A)** Active Directory keeps data secure.

**B)** Data is in a government cloud.

**C)** Data on-premises is encrypted by default.

**D)** Data online is encrypted by default.

**Solution:** D

**Explanation:**

Explanation: Reference: https://docs.microsoft.com/en-us/microsoft-365/compliance/office-365-encryption-in-microsoft-dynamics- 365?view=o365-worldwide

**Question: 3** *Multiple Answers Are Right*

HOTSPOT A company uses Dynamics 365 Sales. The company plans to create custom reports and dashboards. The company does not want to manage security for reporting separately. For each of the following statements, select Yes if the statement is true. Otherwise, select No. NOTE: Each correct selection is worth one point. Hot Area:

### Answer Area

| Statement | Yes | No |
|---|---|---|
| An administrator imports data from Dynamics 365 Sales into Power BI. Power BI reports use the same security as Dynamics 365 Sales. | ○ | ○ |
| SQL Server Reporting Services reports use the same security as Dynamics 365 Sales. | ○ | ○ |
| Sales Insights uses the same security as Dynamics 365 Sales. | ○ | ○ |

Answers:

A)

### Answer Area

| Statement | Yes | No |
|---|---|---|
| An administrator imports data from Dynamics 365 Sales into Power BI. Power BI reports use the same security as Dynamics 365 Sales. | ○ | ● |
| SQL Server Reporting Services reports use the same security as Dynamics 365 Sales. | ● | ○ |
| Sales Insights uses the same security as Dynamics 365 Sales. | ● | ○ |

**Solution:** A

**Explanation:**

Explanation:

**Question: 4** *Multiple Answers Are Right*

HOTSPOT A non-profit company is considering moving their Dynamics 365 solution from on-premises to online. You need to help the company understand where their data will be stored after the move and who will own the data. How should you respond? To answer, select the appropriate options in the answer area. NOTE: Each correct selection is worth one point. Hot Area:

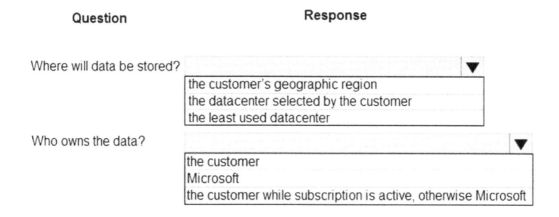

**Answers:**

**A)**

## Answer Area

| Question | Response |
|---|---|
| Where will data be stored? | the customer's geographic region / **the datacenter selected by the customer** / the least used datacenter |
| Who owns the data? | **the customer** / Microsoft / the customer while subscription is active, otherwise Microsoft |

**Solution:** A

**Explanation:**

Explanation:

**Question: 5** *Multiple Answers Are Right*

DRAG DROP A company plans to deploy Dynamics 365 Sales. Match each term to its definition. Instructions: To answer, drag the appropriate deployment type from the column on the left to its definition on the right. Each deployment type may be used once, more than once, or not at all. Each correct match is worth one point. NOTE: Each correct selection is worth one point. Select and Place:

## Answer Area

| Deployment types | Benefit | Deployment type |
|---|---|---|
| online | Remove the dependence on internal IT staff to perform backups. | |
| on-premises | Simplify investments in licenses. | |
| | Production and test environment can be provisioned without using internal resources. | |

**Answers:**

**A)**

**Answer Area**

| Deployment types | Benefit | Deployment type |
|---|---|---|
| online | Remove the dependence on internal IT staff to perform backups. | online |
| on-premises | Simplify investments in licenses. | on-premises |
| | Production and test environment can be provisioned without using internal resources. | online |

**Solution:** A

**Explanation:**

Explanation:

**Question: 6** *Multiple Answers Are Right*

HOTSPOT A company wants to ensure they comply with common data privacy standards and regulations. For each of the following statements, select Yes if the statement is true. Otherwise, select No. NOTE: Each correct selection is worth one point. Hot Area:

**Answer Area**

| Statement | Yes | No |
|---|---|---|
| An administrator can export personal user data at the request of the user. | ○ | ○ |
| Both Microsoft and the company are responsible for breaches of personal data. | ○ | ○ |
| Compliance Manager is a third-party tool that assesses the compliance of a company's cloud solution. | ○ | ○ |

**Answers:**

A)

## Answer Area

| Statement | Yes | No |
|---|---|---|
| An administrator can export personal user data at the request of the user. | O | O |
| Both Microsoft and the company are responsible for breaches of personal data. | O | O |
| Compliance Manager is a third-party tool that assesses the compliance of a company's cloud solution. | O | O |

**Solution:** A

**Explanation:**

Explanation:

**Question: 7** *One Answer Is Right*

A company uses Microsoft Exchange Online. Sales team members want to use Microsoft Outlook to view items that were created in Dynamics 365 Sales. Which three components are synchronized between Dynamics 365 Sales and Outlook? Each correct answer presents a complete solution. NOTE: Each correct selection is worth one point.

**Answers:**

**A)** Tasks

**B)** Appointments

**C)** Phone calls

**D)** Accounts

**E)** Contacts

**Solution:** A, B, E

**Explanation:**

Explanation: Reference: https://docs.microsoft.com/en-us/dynamics365/outlook-addin/admin-guide/configure-synchronization- appointments-contacts-tasks

**Question: 8** *One Answer Is Right*

A company uses Dynamics 365 Sales. You plan to use Power Apps to create a customized app that allows sales team members to enter data for customer, leads, and opportunities. Sales team members must be able to enter the information from desktops, laptops, tablets, and mobile devices. All salespeople need access to the same forms, views and reports. What is the minimum number of Power Apps that you must create?

**Answers:**

**A)** 1

**B)** 2

**C)** 3

**D)** 4

**Solution:** A

**Question: 9** *One Answer Is Right*

There are complex services being used with your Dynamics 365 instance in which you own and manage the software applications as well as the data hosted in Azure. You need to determine which type of cloud service model is being used by your organization. Which cloud service model is being used?

**Answers:**

**A)** platform as a service (PaaS)

**B)** infrastructure as a service (IaaS)

**C)** software as a service (SaaS)

**Solution:** A

**Question: 10** *One Answer Is Right*

You are discussing the benefits of hosting a Dynamics 365 development sandbox on Microsoft Azure. What are two benefits? Each correct answer presents a complete solution. NOTE: Each correct selection is worth one point.

**Answers:**

**A)** ability to adhere to static cost requirements

**B)** a higher level of system availability in the event of a disaster

**C)** ability to easily scale for increased growth

**D)** physical control over server hardware

**Solution:** B, C

# Chapter 34: MD-100 - Windows 10

## Exam Guide

Windows 10 MD-100 Exam:

Windows 10 MD-100 Exam which is related to Microsoft 365 Certified Modern Desktop Administrator Associate Certification. This exam validates the Candidates ability to deploy Windows, manage devices and data, configure connectivity and maintain Windows. Microsoft IT Professionals usually hold or pursue this certification and you can expect the same job roles after completion of this certification.

MD-100 Exam topics:

Candidates must know the exam topics before they start of preparation. Because it will really help them in hitting the core. Our **MD-100 dumps** will include the following topics:

- Deploy Windows 15-20%
- Manage devices and data 35-40%
- Configure connectivity 15-20%
- Maintain Windows 25-30%

Certification Path:

The Microsoft Windows 10 (beta) Certification includes only one MD-100 exam.

Who should take the MD-100 exam:

The Microsoft Windows 10 (beta) MD-100 Exam certification is an internationally recognized validation that identifies persons who earn it as possessing skills in a Microsoft Windows 10. If candidates want significant improvement in career growth needs enhanced knowledge, skills, and talents. The Microsoft Windows 10 (beta) MD-100 Exam certification provides proof of this advanced knowledge and skill. If a candidate has given below knowledge and skills that are required to pass Microsoft Windows 10 (beta) MD-100 Exam then he should take this exam.

- Configure Language Packs
- Migrate User Data
- Perform a clean installation

- Configure Networking
- Remote Connectivity
- Monitor and Manage Windows.

How to study the MD-100 Exam:

Certification-questions.com expert team recommends you to prepare some notes on these topics along with it don't forget to practice Microsoft MD-100 Exam dumps which been written by our expert team, Both these will help you a lot to clear this exam with good marks.

How much MD-100 Exam Cost:

The price of the MD-100 exam is $165 USD.

How to book the MD-100 Exam:

These are following steps for registering the MD-100 exam.
Step 1: Visit to Microsoft Exam Registration
Step 2: Signup/Login to MICROSOFT account
Step 3: Search for MICROSOFT MD-100 Certifications Exam
Step 4: Select Date and Center of examination and confirm with payment value of $165

What is the duration of the MD-100 Exam:

- Format: Multiple choices, multiple answers
- Length of Examination: 150 minutes
- Number of Questions: 45-60
- Passing Score: 700/1000

The benefit in Obtaining the MD-100 Exam Certification:

- After completion of Microsoft 365 Certified Modern Desktop Administrator Associate Certification candidates receive official confirmation from Microsoft that you are now fully certified in their chosen field. This can be now added to their CV, cover letters and job applications.
- When Candidates applying for a job or looking to promotion in their current position, a Microsoft 365 Certified Modern Desktop Administrator Associate certification in the field in which Candidates are applying will put you at the top of the list and make them a desirable candidate for employers.
- Candidates will get in-depth knowledge by completing the courses along with the access to revision materials for 6 months upon completion means they will have a wider skill set when it comes to the various technologies and systems than an uncertified professional.

Certified Professional in this particular skill set is 74% more efficient when it comes to completing their tasks in a timely well-executed manner.
- Organization owners invest a lot in their employees when it comes to their training with the goal of making them quicker, more efficient, and more knowledgeable about their role. Certified Professional will reduce the time he spends on tasks, meaning he can get more done this could help reduce company downtime when repairing faults on a system or fixing hardware problems.
- Becoming Microsoft 365 Certified Modern Desktop Administrator Associate means one thing you are worth more to the company and therefore more to yourself in the form of an upgraded pay package. On average a Microsoft 365 Certified Modern Desktop Administrator Associate member of staff is estimated to be worth 30% more to a company than their uncertified professionals.

Difficulty in writing MD-100 Exam:

Microsoft MD-100 exam help Candidates in developing their professionals and academic career and It is a very tough task to pass Microsoft MD-100 exam for those Candidates who have not done hard work and get some relevant Microsoft MD-100 exam preparation material. There are many peoples have passed Microsoft MD-100 exam by following these three things such as look for the latest **Microsoft MD-100 exam dumps**, get relevant Microsoft MD-100 exam dumps and develop their knowledge about Microsoft MD-100 exam new questions. At the same time, it can also stress out some people as they found passing Microsoft MD-100 exam a tough task. It is just a wrong assumption as many of the peoples have passed Microsoft MD-100 exam questions. All you have to do is to work hard, get some relevant Microsoft MD-100 exam preparation material and go thoroughly from them. Certification-questions is here to help you with this problem. We have the relevant Microsoft MD-100 exam preparation material which are providing the latest Microsoft MD-100 exam questions with the detailed view of every Microsoft MD-100 exam topic. Certification-questions offered a Microsoft MD-100 exam dumps which are more than enough to pass the Microsoft MD-100 exam questions. We are providing all thing such as **Microsoft MD-100 exam dumps**, Microsoft MD-100 practice test, and **Microsoft MD-100 pdf dumps** that will help the candidate to pass the exam with good grades.

For more info visit::

Microsoft MD-100 Exam Reference

# Sample Practice Test for MD-100

**Question: 1** *Multiple Answers Are Right*

HOTSPOT You need to implement a solution to configure the contractors' computers. What should you do? To answer, select the appropriate options in the answer area. NOTE: Each correct selection is worth one point. Hot Area:

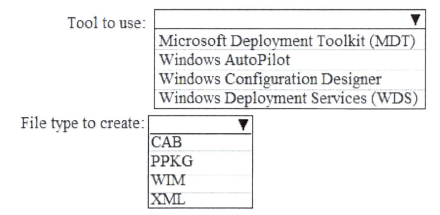

**Scenario:**

TESTLET-1. Overview Existing Environment Fabrikam, Inc. is a distribution company that has 500 employees and 100 contractors. Active Directory The network contains an Active Directory forest named fabrikam.com. The forest is synced to Microsoft Azure Active Directory (Azure AD). All the employees are assigned Microsoft 365 E3 licenses. The domain contains a user account for an employee named User10. Client Computers All the employees have computers that run Windows 10 Enterprise. All the computers are installed without Volume License Keys. Windows 10 license keys are never issued. All the employees register their computer to Azure AD when they first receive the computer. User10 has a computer named Computer10. All the contractors have their own computer that runs Windows 10. None of the computers are joined to Azure AD. Operational Procedures Fabrikam has the following operational procedures: - Updates are deployed by using Windows Update for Business. - When new contractors are hired, administrators must help the contactors configure the following settings on their computer: - User certificates - Browser security and proxy settings - Wireless network connection settings Security policies The following security policies are enforced on all the client computers in the domain:- All the computers are encrypted by using BitLocker Drive Encryption (BitLocker). BitLocker recovery information is stored in Active Directory and Azure AD. - The local Administrators group on each computer contains an enabled account named LocalAdmin. - The LocalAdmin account is managed by using Local Administrator Password Solution (LAPS). Problem Statements Fabrikam identifies the following issues: - Employees in the finance department use an application named Application1. Application1 frequently crashes due to a memory error. When Application1 crashes, an event is written to the application log and an administrator runs a script to delete the temporary files and restart the application. - When employees attempt to connect to the network from their home computer, they often cannot establish a VPN connection because of misconfigured VPN settings. - An employee has a computer named Computer11. Computer11 has a hardware failure that prevents the computer from connecting to the network. - User10 reports that Computer10 is not activated. Technical requirements Fabrikam identifies the following technical requirements for managing the client computers: - Provide employees with a configuration file to configure their VPN connection. - Use the minimum amount of administrative effort to implement the technical requirements. - Identify which employees' computers are noncompliant with the Windows Update baseline of the company. - Ensure that the service desk uses Quick Assist to take remote control of an employee's desktop during support calls. - Automate the configuration of the contractors' computers. The solution must provide a configuration file that the contractors can open from a Microsoft SharePoint site to apply the required configurations.

**Answers:**

**A)**

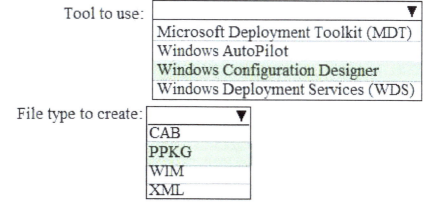

**Solution:** A

## Explanation:

Explanation: The requirement states: Automate the configuration of the contractors' computers. The solution must provide a configuration file that the contractors can open from a Microsoft SharePoint site to apply the required configurations. The 'configuration file' in this case is known as a 'provisioning package'. A provisioning package (.ppkg) is a container for a collection of configuration settings. With Windows 10, you can create provisioning packages that let you quickly and efficiently configure a device without having to install a new image. The tool for creating provisioning packages is renamed Windows Configuration Designer, replacing the Windows Imaging and Configuration Designer (ICD) tool. References: https://docs.microsoft.com/en-us/windows/configuration/provisioning-packages/provisioning-install-icd https://docs.microsoft.com/en-us/windows/configuration/provisioning-packages/provisioning-packages

**Question: 2** *One Answer Is Right*

You need to ensure that User10 can activate Computer10. What should you do?

## Scenario:

TESTLET-1. Overview Existing Environment Fabrikam, Inc. is a distribution company that has 500 employees and 100 contractors. Active Directory The network contains an Active Directory forest named fabrikam.com. The forest is synced to Microsoft Azure Active Directory (Azure AD). All the employees are assigned Microsoft 365 E3 licenses. The domain contains a user account for an employee named User10. Client Computers All the employees have computers that run Windows 10 Enterprise. All the computers are installed without Volume License Keys. Windows 10 license keys are never issued. All the employees register their computer to Azure AD when they first receive the computer. User10 has a computer named Computer10. All the contractors have their own computer that runs Windows 10. None of the computers are joined to Azure AD. Operational Procedures Fabrikam has the following operational procedures: - Updates are deployed by using Windows Update for Business. - When new contractors are hired, administrators must help the contactors configure the following settings on their computer: - User certificates - Browser security and proxy settings - Wireless network connection settings Security policies The following security policies are enforced on all the client computers in the domain:- All the computers are encrypted by using BitLocker Drive Encryption (BitLocker). BitLocker recovery information is stored in Active Directory and Azure AD. - The local Administrators group on each computer contains an enabled account named LocalAdmin. - The LocalAdmin account is managed by using Local Administrator Password Solution (LAPS). Problem Statements Fabrikam identifies the following issues: - Employees in the finance department use an application named Application1. Application1 frequently crashes due to a memory error. When Application1 crashes, an event is written to the application log and an administrator runs a script to delete the temporary files and restart the application. -

When employees attempt to connect to the network from their home computer, they often cannot establish a VPN connection because of misconfigured VPN settings. - An employee has a computer named Computer11. Computer11 has a hardware failure that prevents the computer from connecting to the network. - User10 reports that Computer10 is not activated. Technical requirements Fabrikam identifies the following technical requirements for managing the client computers: - Provide employees with a configuration file to configure their VPN connection. - Use the minimum amount of administrative effort to implement the technical requirements. - Identify which employees' computers are noncompliant with the Windows Update baseline of the company. - Ensure that the service desk uses Quick Assist to take remote control of an employee's desktop during support calls. - Automate the configuration of the contractors' computers. The solution must provide a configuration file that the contractors can open from a Microsoft SharePoint site to apply the required configurations.

**Answers:**

**A)** Request that a Windows 10 Enterprise license be assigned to User10, and then activate Computer10.

**B)** From the Microsoft Deployment Toolkit (MDT), add a Volume License Key to a task sequence, and then redeploy Computer10.

**C)** From System Properties on Computer10, enter a Volume License Key, and then activate Computer10.

**D)** Request that User10 perform a local AutoPilot Reset on Computer10, and then activate Computer10.

**Solution:** D

**Explanation:**

Explanation: The case study states: User10 reports that Computer10 is not activated. The solution is to perform a local AutoPilot Reset on the computer. This will restore the computer settings to a fully-configured or known IT-approved state. When User10 signs in to the computer after the reset, the computer should activate. You can use Autopilot Reset to remove personal files, apps, and settings from your devices. The devices remain enrolled in Intune and are returned to a fully-configured or known IT-approved state. You can Autopilot Reset a device locally or remotely from the Intune for Education portal. Incorrect Answers: A: All users have Microsoft 365 E3 licenses. This license includes Windows 10 Enterprise so we don't need to assign a Windows 10 Enterprise license to User10. B: Volume License Keys aren't required. C: Volume License Keys aren't required. References: https://docs.microsoft.com/en-us/windows/deployment/windows-autopilot/windows-autopilot-requirements- licensing https://docs.microsoft.com/en-us/intune-education/autopilot-reset Deploy Windows

**Question: 3** *One Answer Is Right*

You need to meet the technical requirements for the San Diego office computers. Which Windows 10 deployment method should you use?

**Scenario:**

TESTLET-2. Overview Contoso, Ltd. is a consulting company that has a main office in Montreal and two branch offices in Seattle and New York. Contoso has IT, human resources (HR), and finance departments. Contoso recently opened a new branch office in San Diego. All the users in the San Diego office work from home. Existing environment Contoso uses Microsoft 365. The on-premises network contains an Active Directory domain named contoso.com. The domain is synced to Microsoft Azure Active Directory (Azure AD). All computers run Windows 10 Enterprise. You have four computers named Computer1, Computer2, Computer3, and ComputerA. ComputerA is in a workgroup on an isolated network segment and runs the Long Term Servicing Channel version of Windows 10. ComputerA connects to a manufacturing system and is business critical. All the other computers are joined to the domain and run the Semi-Annual Channel version of Windows 10. In the domain, you create four groups named Group1, Group2, Group3, and Group4. Computer2 has the local Group Policy settings shown in the following table.

| Policy | Security Setting |
|---|---|
| Access this computer from the network | Group1 |
| Deny access to this computer from the network | Group2 |
| Allow log on through Remote Desktop Services | Group3 |
| Deny log on through Remote Desktop Services | Group4 |

The computers are updated by using Windows Update for Business. The domain has the users shown in the following table.

| Name | Member of |
|---|---|
| User1 | Domain Admins, Domain Users |
| User2 | Administrators, Domain Users |
| User3 | Account Operators, Domain Users |
| User4 | Domain Users |
| User5 | Domain Users, Guests |
| User6 | Group2, Group3, Domain Users |

Computer1 has the local users shown in the following table.

| Name | Member of |
|---|---|
| User11 | Administrators |
| User12 | Users |
| User13 | Guests |

Requirements Planned Changes Contoso plans to purchase computers preinstalled with Windows 10 Pro for all the San Diego office users. Technical requirements Contoso identifies the following technical requirements: - The computers in the San Diego office must be upgraded automatically to Windows 10 Enterprise and must be joined to Azure AD the first time a user starts each new computer. End users must not be required to accept the End User License Agreement (EULA). - Helpdesk users must be able to troubleshoot Group Policy object (GPO) processing on the Windows 10 computers. The helpdesk users must be able to identify which Group Policies are applied to the computers. - Users in the HR department must be able to view the list of files in a folder named D:\Reports on Computer3. - ComputerA must be configured to have an Encrypting File System (EFS) recovery agent. - Quality update installations must be deferred as long as possible on ComputerA. - Users in the IT department must use dynamic lock on their primary device. - User6 must be able to connect to Computer2 by using Remote Desktop. - The principle of least privilege must be used whenever possible. - Administrative effort must be minimized whenever possible. - Kiosk (assigned access) must be configured on Computer1.

**Answers:**

**A)** wipe and load refresh

**B)** in-place upgrade

**C)** provisioning packages

**D)** Windows Autopilot

**Solution:** D

**Explanation:**

Explanation: The requirement states: The computers in the San Diego office must be upgraded automatically to Windows 10 Enterprise and must be joined to Azure AD the first time a user starts each new computer. End users must not be required to accept the End User License Agreement (EULA). Windows Autopilot is a collection of technologies used to set up and pre-configure new devices, getting them ready for productive use. You can also use Windows Autopilot to reset, repurpose and recover devices. The OEM Windows 10 installation on the new computers can be transformed into a "business-ready" state, applying settings and policies, installing apps, and even changing the edition of Windows 10 being used (e.g. from Windows 10

Pro to Windows 10 Enterprise) to support advanced features. The only interaction required from the end user is to connect to a network and to verify their credentials. Everything beyond that is automated. References: https://docs.microsoft.com/en-us/windows/deployment/windows-autopilot/windows-autopilot

**Question: 4** *Multiple Answers Are Right*

HOTSPOT You need to meet the technical requirement for Computer1. What should you do? To answer, select the appropriate options in the answer area. NOTE: Each correct selection is worth one point. Hot Area:

## Answer Area

User who should configure Kiosk (assigned access):
- User1
- User2
- User3
- User11
- User12

Configure Kiosk (assigned access) for:
- User4
- User5
- User12
- User13

**Scenario:**

TESTLET-2. Overview Contoso, Ltd. is a consulting company that has a main office in Montreal and two branch offices in Seattle and New York. Contoso has IT, human resources (HR), and finance departments. Contoso recently opened a new branch office in San Diego. All the users in the San Diego office work from home. Existing environment Contoso uses Microsoft 365. The on-premises network contains an Active Directory domain named contoso.com. The domain is synced to Microsoft Azure Active Directory (Azure AD). All computers run Windows 10 Enterprise. You have four computers named Computer1, Computer2, Computer3, and ComputerA. ComputerA is in a workgroup on an isolated network segment and runs the Long Term Servicing Channel version of Windows 10. ComputerA connects to a manufacturing system and is business critical. All the other computers are joined to the domain and run the Semi-Annual Channel version of Windows 10. In the domain, you create four groups named Group1, Group2, Group3, and Group4. Computer2 has the local Group Policy settings shown in the following table.

| Policy | Security Setting |
|---|---|
| Access this computer from the network | Group1 |
| Deny access to this computer from the network | Group2 |
| Allow log on through Remote Desktop Services | Group3 |
| Deny log on through Remote Desktop Services | Group4 |

The computers are updated by using Windows Update for Business. The domain has the users shown in the following table.

| Name | Member of |
|---|---|
| User1 | Domain Admins, Domain Users |
| User2 | Administrators, Domain Users |
| User3 | Account Operators, Domain Users |
| User4 | Domain Users |
| User5 | Domain Users, Guests |
| User6 | Group2, Group3, Domain Users |

Computer1 has the local users shown in the following table.

| Name | Member of |
|---|---|
| User11 | Administrators |
| User12 | Users |
| User13 | Guests |

Requirements Planned Changes Contoso plans to purchase computers preinstalled with Windows 10 Pro for all the San Diego office users. Technical requirements Contoso identifies the following technical requirements: - The computers in the San Diego office must be upgraded automatically to Windows 10 Enterprise and must be joined to Azure AD the first time a user starts each new computer. End users must not be required to accept the End User License Agreement (EULA). - Helpdesk users must be able to troubleshoot Group Policy object (GPO) processing on the Windows 10 computers. The helpdesk users must be able to identify which Group Policies are applied to the computers. - Users in the HR department must be able to view the list of files in a folder named D:\Reports on Computer3. - ComputerA must be configured to have an Encrypting File System (EFS) recovery agent. - Quality update installations must be deferred as long as possible on ComputerA. - Users in the IT department must use dynamic lock on their primary device. - User6 must be able to connect to Computer2 by using Remote Desktop. - The principle of least privilege must be used whenever possible. - Administrative effort must be minimized whenever possible. - Kiosk (assigned access) must be configured on Computer1.

**Answers:**

**A)**

**Answer Area**

| User who should configure Kiosk (assigned access): | ▼ |
|---|---|
| | User1 |
| | User2 |
| | User3 |
| | **User11** |
| | User12 |

| Configure Kiosk (assigned access) for: | ▼ |
|---|---|
| | User4 |
| | User5 |
| | **User12** |
| | User13 |

**Solution:** A

**Explanation:**

Explanation: The requirement states: Kiosk (assigned access) must be configured on Computer1. Kiosk (assigned access) is a feature on Windows 10 that allows you to create a lockdown environment that lets users interact with only one app when they sign into a specified account. With Kiosk (assigned access), users won't be able to get to the desktop, Start menu, or any other app, including the Settings app. Box 1: User 11 Kiosk (assigned access) must be configured by a user who is a member of the Local Administrators group on the Computer. Box 2: User 12. Kiosk (assigned access) must be configured for a user account that is a member of the Users group. References: https://www.windowscentral.com/how-set-assigned-access-windows-10 Deploy Windows Question Set 3

**Question: 5** *One Answer Is Right*

Your company has an isolated network used for testing. The network contains 20 computers that run Windows 10. The computers are in a workgroup. During testing, the computers must remain in the workgroup. You discover that none of the computers are activated. You need to recommend a solution to activate the computers without connecting the network to the Internet. What should you include in the recommendation?

**Answers:**

**A)** Volume Activation Management Tool (VAMT)

**B)** Key Management Service (KMS)

**C)** Active Directory-based activation

**D)** the Get-WindowsDeveloperLicense cmdlet

**Solution:** B

**Explanation:**

Explanation: You can configure one of the computers as a Key Management Service (KMS) host and activate the KMS host by phone. The other computers in the isolated network can then activate using the KMS host. Installing a KMS host key on a computer running Windows 10 allows you to activate other computers running Windows 10 against this KMS host and earlier versions of the client operating system, such as Windows 8.1 or Windows 7. Clients locate the KMS server by using resource records in DNS, so some configuration of DNS may be required. This scenario can be beneficial if your organization uses volume activation for clients and MAK-based activation for a smaller number of servers. To enable KMS functionality, a KMS key is installed on a KMS host; then, the host is activated over the Internet or by phone using Microsoft's activation services. References: https://docs.microsoft.com/en-us/windows/deployment/volume-activation/activate-using-key-management- service-vamt

**Question: 6** *One Answer Is Right*

You plan to deploy Windows 10 to 100 secure computers. You need to select a version of Windows 10 that meets the following requirements: - Uses Microsoft Edge as the default browser - Minimizes the attack surface on the computer - Supports joining Microsoft Azure Active Directory (Azure AD) - Only allows the installation of applications from the Microsoft Store What is the best version to achieve the goal? More than one answer choice may achieve the goal. Select the BEST answer.

**Answers:**

**A)** Windows 10 Pro in S mode

**B)** Windows 10 Home in S mode

**C)** Windows 10 Pro

**D)** Windows 10 Enterprise

**Solution:** A

**Explanation:**

Explanation: Windows 10 in S mode is a version of Windows 10 that's streamlined for security and performance, while providing a familiar Windows experience. To increase security, it allows only apps from the Microsoft Store, and requires Microsoft Edge for safe browsing. Azure AD Domain join is available for Windows 10 Pro in S mode and Windows 10 Enterprise in S mode. It's not available in Windows 10 Home in S mode. References: https://support.microsoft.com/en-gb/help/4020089/windows-10-in-s-mode-faq

**Question: 7** *Multiple Answers Are Right*

DRAG DROP You have a computer named Computer1 that runs Windows 7. Computer1 has a local user named User1 who has a customized profile. On Computer1, you perform a clean installation of Windows 10 without formatting the drives. You need to migrate the settings of User1 from Windows7 to Windows 10. Which two actions should you perform? To answer, drag the appropriate actions to the correct targets. Each action may be used once, more than once, or not at all. You may need to drag the split bar between panes or scroll to view content. NOTE: Each correct selection is worth one point. Select and Place:

**Actions**

- Run scanstate.exe and specify the C:\Users subfolder.
- Run loadstate.exe and specify the C:\Users subfolder.
- Run scanstate.exe and specify the C:\Windows.old subfolder.
- Run loadstate.exe and specify the C:\Windows.old subfolder.
- Run usmutils.exe and specify the C:\Users subfolder.
- Run usmutils.exe and specify the C:\Windows.old subfolder.

**Answer Area**

First action: *Action*

Second action: *Action*

**Answers:**

## A)

**Actions**

- Run scanstate.exe and specify the C:\Users subfolder.
- Run loadstate.exe and specify the C:\Users subfolder.
- Run scanstate.exe and specify the C:\Windows.old subfolder.
- Run loadstate.exe and specify the C:\Windows.old subfolder.
- Run usmutils.exe and specify the C:\Users subfolder.
- Run usmutils.exe and specify the C:\Windows.old subfolder.

**Answer Area**

- First action: Run loadstate.exe and specify the C:\Windows.old subfolder.
- Second action: Run loadstate.exe and specify the C:\Users subfolder.

**Solution:** A

**Explanation:**

Explanation: The User State Migration Tool (USMT) includes two tools that migrate settings and data: ScanState and LoadState. ScanState collects information from the source computer, and LoadState applies that information to the destination computer. In this case the source and destination will be the same computer. As we have performed a clean installation of Windows 10 without formatting the drives, User1's customized Windows 7 user profile will be located in the \Windows.old folder. Therefore, we need to run scanstate.exe on the \Windows.old folder. User1's Windows 10 profile will be in the C:\Users folder so we need to run loadstate.exe to apply the changes in the C:\Users folder. References: https://docs.microsoft.com/en-us/windows/deployment/usmt/usmt-how-it-works https://docs.microsoft.com/en-us/windows/deployment/usmt/usmt-common-migration-scenarios#bkmk- fourpcrefresh

**Question: 8** *One Answer Is Right*

Note: This question is part of a series of questions that present the same scenario. Each question in the series contains a unique solution that might meet the stated goals. Some question sets might have more than one correct solution, while others might not have a correct solution. After you answer a question in this section, you will NOT be able to return to it. As a result, these questions will not appear in the review screen. You have a computer named Computer1 that runs Windows10. A service named Application1 is configured as shown in the exhibit.

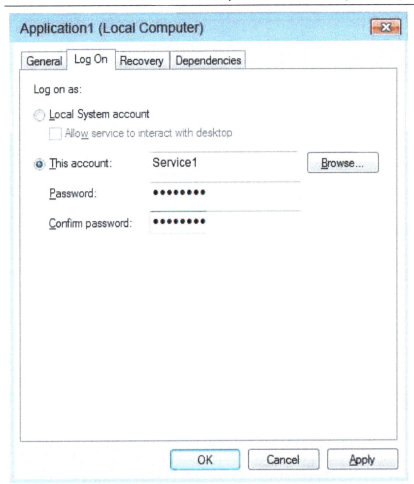

You discover that a user used the Service1 account to sign in to Computer1 and deleted some files. You need to ensure that the identity used by Application1 cannot be used by a user to sign in to sign in to the desktop on Computer1. The solution must use the principle of least privilege. Solution: On Computer1, you configure Application1 to sign in as the LocalSystem account and select the Allow service to interact with desktop check box. You delete the Service1 account. Does this meet the goal?

**Answers:**

**A)** Yes

**B)** No

**Solution:** B

**Explanation:**

Explanation: Configuring Application1 to sign in as the LocalSystem account would ensure that the identity used by Application1 cannot be used by a user to sign in to the desktop on Computer1. However, this does not use the principle of least privilege. The LocalSystem account has full access to the system. Therefore, this solution does not meet the goal. Reference: https://docs.microsoft.com/en-us/windows/security/threat-protection/security-policy-settings/deny-log-on- locally

**Question: 9** *One Answer Is Right*

Note: This question is part of a series of questions that present the same scenario. Each question in the series contains a unique solution that might meet the stated goals. Some question sets might have more than one correct solution, while others might not have a correct solution. After you answer a question in this section, you will NOT be able to return to it. As a result, these questions will not appear in the review screen. You have a computer named Computer1 that runs Windows 10. A service named Application1 is configured as shown in the exhibit.

You discover that a user used the Service1 account to sign in to Computer1 and deleted some

files. You need to ensure that the identity used by Application1 cannot be used by a user to sign in to sign in to the desktop on Computer1. The solution must use the principle of least privilege. Solution: On Computer1, you assign Service1 the Deny log on locally user right. Does this meet the goal?

**Answers:**

**A)** Yes

**B)** No

**Solution:** A

**Explanation:**

Explanation: By using the Service1 account as the identity used by Application1, we are applying the principle of least privilege as required in this question. However, the Service1 account could be used by a user to sign in to the desktop on the computer. To sign in to the desktop on the computer, an account needs the log on locally right which all user accounts have by default. Therefore, we can prevent this by assigning Service1 the deny log on locally user right. References: https://docs.microsoft.com/en-us/windows/security/threat-protection/security-policy-settings/deny-log-on- locally

**Question: 10** *One Answer Is Right*

Note: This question is part of a series of questions that present the same scenario. Each question in the series contains a unique solution that might meet the stated goals. Some question sets might have more than one correct solution, while others might not have a correct solution. After you answer a question in this section, you will NOT be able to return to it. As a result, these questions will not appear in the review screen. You have a computer named Computer1 that runs Windows 10. A service named Application1 is configured as shown in the exhibit.

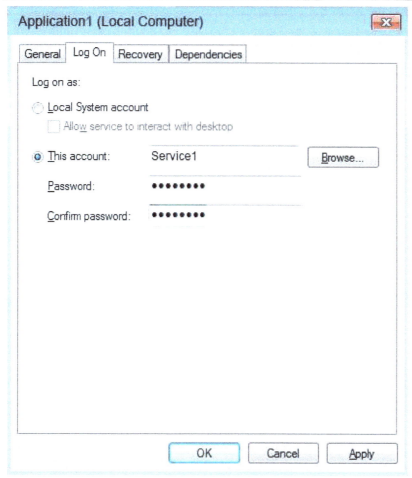

You discover that a user used the Service1 account to sign in to Computer1 and deleted some files. You need to ensure that the identity used by Application1 cannot be used by a user to sign in to sign in to the desktop on Computer1. The solution must use the principle of least privilege. Solution: On Computer1, you assign Service1 the Deny log on as a service user right. Does this meet the goal?

**Answers:**

**A)** Yes

**B)** No

**Solution:** B

**Explanation:**

Explanation: A service account needs the log on as a service user right. When you assign an account to be used by a service, that account is granted the log on as a service user right. Therefore, assigning Service1 the deny log on as a service user right would mean the service would not function. To sign in to the desktop on the computer, an account needs the log on locally right which all user accounts have by default. To meet the requirements of this question, we need to assign Service1 the deny log on locally user right, not the deny log on as a service user right. References: https://docs.microsoft.com/en-us/windows/security/threat-protection/security-policy-settings/deny-log-on-as- a-service

# Chapter 35: MD-101 - Managing Modern Desktops

## Exam Guide

Managing Modern Desktops MD-101 Exam:

Managing Modern Desktops MD-101 Exam which is related to Microsoft 365 Certified Modern Desktop Administrator Associate Certification. This exam measures the Candidate ability to configure, deploy, manage, secure and monitor devices and client applications in an enterprise environment. This exam also tests the Candidates have the knowledge to manage identity, access, policies, updates, and apps.

MD-101 Exam topics:

Candidates must know the exam topics before they start of preparation. Because it will really help them in hitting the core. Our **MD-101 dumps** will include the following topics:

- Deploy and update operating systems (15-20%)
- Manage policies and profiles (35-40%)
- Manage and protect devices (15-20%)
- Manage apps and data (25-30%)

Certification Path:

The Managing Modern Desktops (beta) Certification includes only one MD-101 exam.

Who should take the MD-101 exam:

The Managing Modern Desktops (beta) MD-101 Exam certification is an internationally recognized validation that identifies persons who earn it as possessing skilled as a Microsoft 365 Certified Modern Desktop Administrator Associate. If candidates want significant improvement in career growth needs enhanced knowledge, skills, and talents. The Managing Modern Desktops (beta) MD-101 Exam certification provides proof of this advanced knowledge and skill. If a candidate has knowledge of associated technologies and skills that are required to pass Managing Modern Desktops (beta) MD-101 Exam then he should take this exam.

How to study the MD-101 Exam:

Certification-questions.com expert team recommends you to prepare some notes on these topics along with it don't forget to practice Microsoft MD-101 Exam dumps which been written by our expert team, Both these will help you a lot to clear this exam with good marks.

How much MD-101 Exam Cost:

The price of the MD-101 exam is $165 USD.

How to book the MD-101 Exam:

These are following steps for registering the MD-101 exam.
Step 1: Visit to Microsoft Exam Registration
Step 2: Signup/Login to MICROSOFT account
Step 3: Search for MICROSOFT MD-101 Certifications Exam
Step 4: Select Date and Center of examination and confirm with payment value of $165

What is the duration of the MD-101 Exam:

- Format: Multiple choices, multiple answers
- Length of Examination: 150 minutes
- Number of Questions: 45-60
- Passing Score: 700/1000

The benefit in Obtaining the MD-101 Exam Certification:

- After completion of Microsoft 365 Certified Modern Desktop Administrator Associate Certification candidates receive official confirmation from Microsoft that you are now fully certified in their chosen field. This can be now added to their CV, cover letters and job applications.
- When Candidates applying for a job or looking to promotion in their current position, a Microsoft 365 Certified Modern Desktop Administrator Associate certification in the field in which Candidates are applying will put you at the top of the list and make them a desirable candidate for employers.
- Candidates will get in-depth knowledge by completing the courses along with the access to revision materials for 6 months upon completion means they will have a wider skill set when it comes to the various technologies and systems than an uncertified professional. Certified Professional in this particular skill set is 74% more efficient when it comes to completing their tasks in a timely well-executed manner.
- Organization owners invest a lot in their employees when it comes to their training with the goal of making them quicker, more efficient, and more knowledgeable about their role. Certified Professional will reduce the time he spends on tasks, meaning he can get more

done this could help reduce company downtime when repairing faults on a system or fixing hardware problems.
- Becoming Microsoft 365 Certified Modern Desktop Administrator Associate means one thing you are worth more to the company and therefore more to yourself in the form of an upgraded pay package. On average a Microsoft 365 Certified Modern Desktop Administrator Associate member of staff is estimated to be worth 30% more to a company than their uncertified professionals.

Difficulty in writing MD-101 Exam:

There are many problems for the candidates cannot facilitate from the exams preparation and most of the candidates do not know how to prepare their exams and get good marks in their exams. There are a lot of candidates have failed their exams by lack of practice, lack of tension, lack of concentrate and lack of no time. Many candidates want to give a short time to study and get good marks in exams, therefore Certification-questions have a number of ways to prepare and practice for exams in short time through which the candidates will feel relax, a cool mind and ready for exams without any tension. Certification-questions is very much aware of the worth of your time and money that's why Certification-questions give you the most outstanding **Microsoft MD-101 dumps** having all the questions and answers outlined and verified by the Microsoft Professionals. We deliver all those practice questions which will come in the real exam so the candidate can easily get more than 90% marks at first attempt.

For more info visit::

Microsoft MD-101 Exam Reference

# Sample Practice Test for MD-101

**Question: 1** *One Answer Is Right*

You need to prepare for the deployment of the Phoenix office computers. What should you do first?

**Scenario:**

TESTLET-2. Overview Contoso, Ltd, is a consulting company that has a main office in Montreal and two branch offices in Seattle and New York. Contoso has the users and computers shown in the following table.

| Location | Users | Laptops | Desktop computers | Mobile devices |
|---|---|---|---|---|
| Montreal | 2,500 | 2,800 | 300 | 3,100 |
| Seattle | 1,000 | 1,100 | 200 | 1,500 |
| New York | 300 | 320 | 30 | 400 |

The company has IT, human resources (HR), legal (LEG), marketing (MKG) and finance (FIN) departments. Contoso uses Microsoft Store for Business and recently purchased a Microsoft 365 subscription. The company is opening a new branch office in Phoenix. Most of the users in the Phoenix office will work from home. Existing Environment The network contains an Active Directory domain named contoso.com that is synced to Microsoft Azure Active Directory (Azure AD). All member servers run Windows Server 2016. All laptops and desktop computers run Windows 10 Enterprise. The computers are managed by using Microsoft Endpoint Configuration Manager. The mobile devices are managed by using Microsoft Intune. The naming convention for the computers is the department acronym, followed by a hyphen, and then four numbers, for example, FIN-6785. All the computers are joined to the on-premises Active Directory domain. Each department has an organizational unit (OU) that contains a child OU named Computers. Each computer account is in the Computers OU of its respective department. Intune Configuration The domain has the users shown in the following table.

| Name | Role | Member of |
|---|---|---|
| User1 | Intune administrator | GroupA |
| User2 | None | GroupB |

User2 is a device enrollment manager (DEM) in Intune. The devices enrolled in Intune are shown in the following table.

| Name | Platform | Encryption | Member of |
|---|---|---|---|
| Device1 | Android | Disabled | Group1 |
| Device2 | iOS | Not applicable | Group2, Group3 |
| Device3 | Android | Disabled | Group2, Group3 |
| Device4 | iOS | Not applicable | Group2 |

The device compliance policies in Intune are configured as shown in the following table.

| Name | Platform | Require encryption | Assigned |
|---|---|---|---|
| Policy1 | Android | Not configured | Yes |
| Policy2 | iOS | Not applicable | Yes |
| Policy3 | Android | Require | Yes |

The device compliance policies have the assignments shown in the following table.

| Name | Include | Exclude |
|---|---|---|
| Policy1 | Group3 | None |
| Policy2 | Group2 | Group3 |
| Policy3 | Group1 | None |

The device limit restrictions in Intune are configured as shown in the following table.

| Priority | Name | Device limit | Assigned to |
|---|---|---|---|
| 1 | Restriction1 | 15 | GroupB |
| 2 | Restriction2 | 10 | GroupA |
| Default | All users | 5 | All users |

Requirements Planned Changes Contoso plans to implement the following changes:- Provide new computers to the Phoenix office users. The new computers have Windows 10 Pro preinstalled and were purchased already. - Start using a free Microsoft Store for Business app named App1. - Implement co-management for the computers. Technical Requirements Contoso must meet the following technical requirements: - Ensure that the users in a group named Group4 can only access Microsoft Exchange Online from devices that are enrolled in Intune. - Deploy Windows 10 Enterprise to the computers of the Phoenix office users by using Windows Autopilot. - Monitor the computers in the LEG department by using Windows Analytics. - Create a provisioning package for new computers in the HR department. - Block iOS devices from sending diagnostic and usage telemetry data. - Use the principle of least privilege whenever possible. - Enable the users in the MKG department to use App1. - Pilot co-management for the IT department.

Answers:

A) Extract the hardware ID information of each computer to a CSV file and upload the file from the Devices settings in Microsoft Store for Business.

B) Extract the serial number information of each computer to a XML file and upload the file from the Microsoft Intune blade in the Azure portal.

C) Extract the serial number information of each computer to a CSV file and upload the file from the Microsoft Intune blade in the Azure portal.

D) Extract the hardware ID information of each computer to an XLSX file and upload the file from the Devices settings in Microsoft Store for Business.

**Solution:** A

**Explanation:**

Explanation: To manage devices through Microsoft Store for Business and Education, you'll need a .csv file that contains specific information about the devices. You should be able to get this from your Microsoft account contact, or the store where you purchased the devices. Upload the .csv file to Microsoft Store to add the devices. Reference: https://docs.microsoft.com/en-us/microsoft-store/add-profile-to-devices Deploy and Update Operating Systems Question Set 3

**Question: 2** *One Answer Is Right*

You need to capture the required information for the sales department computers to meet the technical requirements. Which Windows PowerShell command should you run first?

**Scenario:**

TESTLET-1. Overview Litware, Inc. is an international manufacturing company that has 3,000 employees. The company has sales, marketing, research, human resources (HR), development, and IT departments. Litware has two main offices in New York and Los Angeles. Litware has five branch offices in Asia. Existing Environment Current Business Model The Los Angeles office has 500 developers. The developers work flexible hours ranging from 11 AM to 10 PM. Litware has a Microsoft System Center 2012 R2 Configuration Manager deployment. During discovery, the company discovers a process where users are emailing bank account information of its customers to internal and external recipients. Current Environment The network contains an Active Directory domain that is synced to Microsoft Azure Active Directory (Azure AD). The functional level of the forest and the domain is Windows Server 2012 R2. All domain controllers run Windows Server 2012 R2. Litware has the computers shown in the following table.

| Department | Windows version | Management platform | Domain-joined |
|---|---|---|---|
| Marketing | 8.1 | Configuration Manager | Hybrid Azure AD-joined |
| Research | 10 | Configuration Manager | Hybrid Azure AD-joined |
| HR | 8.1 | Configuration Manager | Hybrid Azure AD-joined |
| Developers | 10 | Microsoft Intune | Azure AD-joined |
| Sales | 10 | Microsoft Intune | Azure AD-joined |

The development department uses projects in Azure DevOps to build applications. Most of the employees in the sales department are contractors. Each contractor is assigned a computer that runs Windows 10. At the end of each contract, the computer is assigned to a different contractor. Currently, the computers are re-provisioned manually by the IT department. Problem Statements Litware identifies the following issues on the network: - Employees in the Los Angeles office report slow Internet performance when updates are downloading. The employees also report that the updates frequently consume considerable resources when they are installed. The Update settings are configured as shown in the Updates exhibit. (Click the Updates button.) - Management suspects that the source code for the proprietary applications in Azure DevOps in being shared externally. - Re-provisioning the sales department computers is too time consuming. Requirements Business Goals Litware plans to transition to co-management for all the company-owned Windows 10 computers. Whenever possible, Litware wants to minimize hardware and software costs. Device Management Requirements Litware identifies the following device management requirements: - Prevent the sales department employees from forwarding email that contains bank account information. - Ensure that Microsoft Edge Favorites are accessible from all computers to which the developers sign in. - Prevent employees in the research department from copying patented information from trusted applications to untrusted applications. Technical Requirements Litware identifies the following technical requirements for the planned deployment: - Re-provision the sales department computers by using Windows AutoPilot. - Ensure that the projects in Azure DevOps can be accessed from the corporate network only. - Ensure that users can sign in to the Azure AD-joined computers by using a PIN. The PIN must expire every 30 days. - Ensure that the company name and logo appears during the Out of Box Experience (OOBE) when using Windows AutoPilot. Exhibits Updates

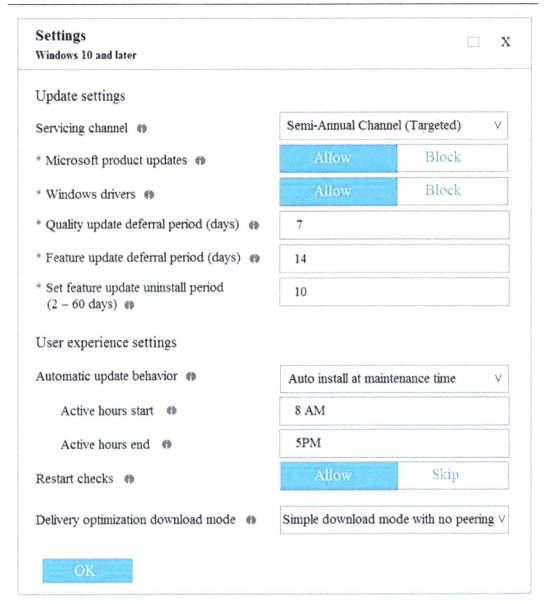

**Answers:**

**A)** Install-Module WindowsAutoPilotIntune

**B)** Install-Script Get-WindowsAutoPilotInfo

**C)** Import-AutoPilotCSV

**D)** Get-WindowsAutoPilotInfo

**Solution:** A

**Explanation:**

Explanation: References: https://docs.microsoft.com/en-us/windows/deployment/windows-autopilot/existing-devices

**Question: 3** *One Answer Is Right*

What should you configure to meet the technical requirements for the Azure AD-joined computers?

**Scenario:**

TESTLET-1. Overview Litware, Inc. is an international manufacturing company that has 3,000 employees. The company has sales, marketing, research, human resources (HR), development, and IT departments. Litware has two main offices in New York and Los Angeles. Litware has five branch offices in Asia. Existing Environment Current Business Model The Los Angeles office has 500 developers. The developers work flexible hours ranging from 11 AM to 10 PM. Litware has a Microsoft System Center 2012 R2 Configuration Manager deployment. During discovery, the company discovers a process where users are emailing bank account information of its customers to internal and external recipients. Current Environment The network contains an Active Directory domain that is synced to Microsoft Azure Active Directory (Azure AD). The functional level of the forest and the domain is Windows Server 2012 R2. All domain controllers run Windows Server 2012 R2. Litware has the computers shown in the following table.

| Department | Windows version | Management platform | Domain-joined |
|---|---|---|---|
| Marketing | 8.1 | Configuration Manager | Hybrid Azure AD-joined |
| Research | 10 | Configuration Manager | Hybrid Azure AD-joined |
| HR | 8.1 | Configuration Manager | Hybrid Azure AD-joined |
| Developers | 10 | Microsoft Intune | Azure AD-joined |
| Sales | 10 | Microsoft Intune | Azure AD-joined |

The development department uses projects in Azure DevOps to build applications. Most of the employees in the sales department are contractors. Each contractor is assigned a computer that runs Windows 10. At the end of each contract, the computer is assigned to a different contractor. Currently, the computers are re-provisioned manually by the IT department. Problem Statements Litware identifies the following issues on the network: - Employees in the Los Angeles office report slow Internet performance when updates are downloading. The employees also report that the updates frequently consume considerable resources when they are installed. The Update settings are configured as shown in the Updates exhibit. (Click the Updates button.) - Management suspects that the source code for the proprietary applications in Azure DevOps in being shared externally. - Re-provisioning the sales department computers is too time consuming. Requirements Business Goals Litware plans to transition to co-management for all the company-owned Windows 10 computers. Whenever possible, Litware wants to minimize hardware and software costs. Device Management Requirements Litware identifies the following device management requirements: - Prevent the sales department employees from forwarding email that contains bank account information. - Ensure that Microsoft Edge Favorites are accessible from all computers to which the developers sign in. - Prevent employees in the research department from copying patented information from trusted applications to untrusted applications. Technical Requirements Litware identifies the following technical requirements for the planned deployment: - Re-provision the sales department computers by using Windows AutoPilot. - Ensure that the projects in Azure DevOps can be accessed from the corporate network only. - Ensure that users can sign in to the Azure AD-joined computers by using a PIN. The PIN must expire every 30 days. - Ensure that the company name and logo appears during the Out of Box Experience (OOBE) when using Windows AutoPilot. Exhibits Updates

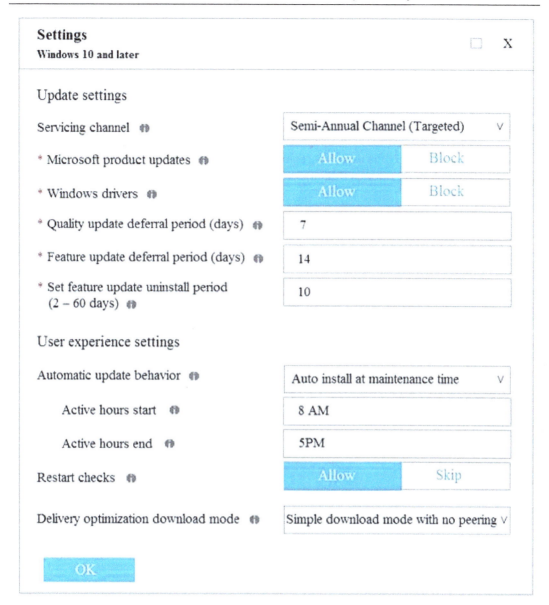

**Answers:**

**A)** Windows Hello for Business from the Microsoft Intune blade in the Azure portal.

**B)** The Accounts options in an endpoint protection profile.

**C)** The Password Policy settings in a Group Policy object (GPO).

**D)** A password policy from the Microsoft Office 365 portal.

**Solution:** A

**Explanation:**

Explanation: References: https://docs.microsoft.com/en-us/windows/security/identity-protection/hello-for-business/hello-manage-in- organization

**Question: 4** *Multiple Answers Are Right*

HOTSPOT You need to meet the technical requirements for the new HR department computers. How should you configure the provisioning package? To answer, select the appropriate options in the answer area. NOTE: Each correct selection is worth one point. Hot Area:

Answer Area

Specify ComputerName as:
- "HR"+ RAND(4)
- "HumanResources-"+ RAND(????)
- HR-%RAND:4%
- HR-????
- HumanResources-%RAND:4%

Specify AccountOU as:
- CN=Computers, CN=HR, DC=Contoso, DC=com
- Computers/HumanResources/Contoso.com
- Contoso.com/HR/Computers
- OU=Computers, OU=HR, DC=Contoso, DC=com

**Scenario:**

TESTLET-2. Overview Contoso, Ltd, is a consulting company that has a main office in Montreal and two branch offices in Seattle and New York. Contoso has the users and computers shown in the following table.

| Location | Users | Laptops | Desktop computers | Mobile devices |
|---|---|---|---|---|
| Montreal | 2,500 | 2,800 | 300 | 3,100 |
| Seattle | 1,000 | 1,100 | 200 | 1,500 |
| New York | 300 | 320 | 30 | 400 |

The company has IT, human resources (HR), legal (LEG), marketing (MKG) and finance (FIN) departments. Contoso uses Microsoft Store for Business and recently purchased a Microsoft 365 subscription. The company is opening a new branch office in Phoenix. Most of the users in the

Phoenix office will work from home. Existing Environment The network contains an Active Directory domain named contoso.com that is synced to Microsoft Azure Active Directory (Azure AD). All member servers run Windows Server 2016. All laptops and desktop computers run Windows 10 Enterprise. The computers are managed by using Microsoft Endpoint Configuration Manager. The mobile devices are managed by using Microsoft Intune. The naming convention for the computers is the department acronym, followed by a hyphen, and then four numbers, for example, FIN-6785. All the computers are joined to the on-premises Active Directory domain. Each department has an organizational unit (OU) that contains a child OU named Computers. Each computer account is in the Computers OU of its respective department. Intune Configuration The domain has the users shown in the following table.

| Name | Role | Member of |
|---|---|---|
| User1 | Intune administrator | GroupA |
| User2 | None | GroupB |

User2 is a device enrollment manager (DEM) in Intune. The devices enrolled in Intune are shown in the following table.

| Name | Platform | Encryption | Member of |
|---|---|---|---|
| Device1 | Android | Disabled | Group1 |
| Device2 | iOS | Not applicable | Group2, Group3 |
| Device3 | Android | Disabled | Group2, Group3 |
| Device4 | iOS | Not applicable | Group2 |

The device compliance policies in Intune are configured as shown in the following table.

| Name | Platform | Require encryption | Assigned |
|---|---|---|---|
| Policy1 | Android | Not configured | Yes |
| Policy2 | iOS | Not applicable | Yes |
| Policy3 | Android | Require | Yes |

The device compliance policies have the assignments shown in the following table.

| Name | Include | Exclude |
|---|---|---|
| Policy1 | Group3 | None |
| Policy2 | Group2 | Group3 |
| Policy3 | Group1 | None |

The device limit restrictions in Intune are configured as shown in the following table.

| Priority | Name | Device limit | Assigned to |
|---|---|---|---|
| 1 | Restriction1 | 15 | GroupB |
| 2 | Restriction2 | 10 | GroupA |
| Default | All users | 5 | All users |

Requirements Planned Changes Contoso plans to implement the following changes:- Provide new computers to the Phoenix office users. The new computers have Windows 10 Pro preinstalled and were purchased already. - Start using a free Microsoft Store for Business app named App1. - Implement co-management for the computers. Technical Requirements Contoso must meet the following technical requirements: - Ensure that the users in a group named Group4 can only access Microsoft Exchange Online from devices that are enrolled in Intune. - Deploy Windows 10 Enterprise to the computers of the Phoenix office users by using Windows Autopilot. - Monitor the computers in the LEG department by using Windows Analytics. - Create a provisioning package for new computers in the HR department. - Block iOS devices from sending diagnostic and usage telemetry data. - Use the principle of least privilege whenever possible. - Enable the users in the MKG department to use App1. - Pilot co-management for the IT department.

**Answers:**

**A)**

Answer Area

Specify ComputerName as:
- "HR"+ RAND(4)
- "HumanResources-"+ RAND(????)
- HR-%RAND:4%
- HR-????
- HumanResources-%RAND:4%

Specify AccountOU as:
- CN=Computers, CN=HR, DC=Contoso, DC=com
- Computers/HumanResources/Contoso.com
- Contoso.com/HR/Computers
- OU=Computers, OU=HR, DC=Contoso, DC=com

**Solution:** A

**Explanation:**

Explanation: Reference: https://docs.microsoft.com/en-us/windows/configuration/wcd/wcd-accounts

## Question: 5  *One Answer Is Right*

You manage 1,000 computers that run Windows 10. All the computers are enrolled in Microsoft Intune. You manage the servicing channel settings of the computers by using Intune. You need to review the servicing status of a computer. What should you do?

**Answers:**

**A)** From Device configuration - Profiles, view the device status.

**B)** From Device compliance, view the device compliance.

**C)** From Software updates, view the audit logs.

**D)** From Software updates, view the Per update ring deployment state.

**Solution:** D

**Explanation:**

Explanation: References: https://docs.microsoft.com/en-us/intune/windows-update-compliance-reports

## Question: 6  *One Answer Is Right*

Note: This question is part of a series of questions that present the same scenario. Each question in the series contains a unique solution that might meet the stated goals. Some question sets might have more than one correct solution, while others might not have a correct solution. After you answer a question in this section, you will NOT be able to return to it. As a result, these questions will not appear in the review screen. Your company uses Windows Autopilot to configure the computer settings of computers issued to users. A user named User1 has a computer named Computer1 that runs Windows 10. User1 leaves the company. You plan to transfer the computer to a user named User2. You need to ensure that when User2 first starts the computer, User2 is prompted to select the language setting and to agree to the license agreement. Solution: You perform a remote Windows AutoPilot Reset. Does this meet the goal?

**Answers:**

**A)** Yes

**B)** No

**Solution:** B

**Explanation:**

Explanation: Reference: https://docs.microsoft.com/en-us/windows/deployment/windows-autopilot/windows-autopilot-reset-remote

**Question: 7** *One Answer Is Right*

Note: This question is part of a series of questions that present the same scenario. Each question in the series contains a unique solution that might meet the stated goals. Some question sets might have more than one correct solution, while others might not have a correct solution. After you answer a question in this section, you will NOT be able to return to it. As a result, these questions will not appear in the review screen. Your company uses Windows Autopilot to configure the computer settings of computers issued to users. A user named User1 has a computer named Computer1 that runs Windows 10. User1 leaves the company. You plan to transfer the computer to a user named User2. You need to ensure that when User2 first starts the computer, User2 is prompted to select the language setting and to agree to the license agreement. Solution: You create a new Windows AutoPilot user-driven deployment profile. Does this meet the goal?

**Answers:**

**A)** Yes

**B)** No

**Solution:** A

**Explanation:**

Explanation: Reference: https://docs.microsoft.com/en-us/windows/deployment/windows-autopilot/user-driven

**Question: 8** *One Answer Is Right*

Note: This question is part of a series of questions that present the same scenario. Each question in the series contains a unique solution that might meet the stated goals. Some question sets might have more than one correct solution, while others might not have a correct solution. After you answer a question in this section, you will NOT be able to return to it. As a result, these questions will not appear in the review screen. Your company uses Windows Autopilot to configure the computer settings of computers issued to users. A user named User1 has a computer named Computer1 that runs Windows 10. User1 leaves the company. You plan to transfer the computer to a user named User2. You need to ensure that when User2 first starts the computer, User2 is prompted to select the language setting and to agree to the license agreement. Solution: You create a new Windows AutoPilot self-deploying deployment profile. Does this meet the goal?

**Answers:**

**A)** Yes

**B)** No

**Solution:** B

**Explanation:**

Explanation: Reference: https://docs.microsoft.com/en-us/windows/deployment/windows-autopilot/self-deploying

**Question: 9** *One Answer Is Right*

Note: This question is part of a series of questions that present the same scenario. Each question in the series contains a unique solution that might meet the stated goals. Some question sets might have more than one correct solution, while others might not have a correct solution. After you answer a question in this section, you will NOT be able to return to it. As a result, these questions will not appear in the review screen. You need to ensure that feature and quality updates install automatically on a Windows 10 computer during a maintenance window. Solution: In Group policy, from the Maintenance Scheduler settings, you configure Automatic Maintenance Random Delay. Does this meet the goal?

**Answers:**

**A)** Yes

**B)** No

**Solution:** A

**Explanation:**

Explanation: Reference: https://docs.microsoft.com/en-us/sccm/sum/deploy-use/automatically-deploy-software-updates

**Question: 10** *One Answer Is Right*

Note: This question is part of a series of questions that present the same scenario. Each question in the series contains a unique solution that might meet the stated goals. Some question sets might have more than one correct solution, while others might not have a correct solution. After you answer a question in this section, you will NOT be able to return to it. As a result, these questions will not appear in the review screen. You need to ensure that feature and quality updates install automatically on a Windows 10 computer during a maintenance window. Solution: In Group policy, from the Windows Update settings, you enable Configure Automatic

Updates, select 4-Auto download and schedule the install, and then enter a time. Does this meet the goal?

**Answers:**

**A)** Yes

**B)** No

**Solution:** B

**Explanation:**

Explanation: Reference: https://docs.microsoft.com/en-us/sccm/sum/deploy-use/automatically-deploy-software-updates

# Chapter 36: MS-100 - Microsoft 365 Identity and Services

## Exam Guide

Microsoft 365 Identity and Services MS-100 Exam:

Microsoft 365 Identity and Services MS-100 Exam which is related to Microsoft 365 Certified Enterprise Administrator Expert Certification. This exam validates the ability to evaluate, plan, migrate, develop, and market Microsoft 365 services. Candidate can perform Microsoft 365 tenant management tasks, for an enterprise, including its identities, security, compliance and supporting technologies. This exam also verifies the working knowledge of Candidate in Microsoft 365 workloads and must have experience in administration for at least one Microsoft 365 workload (Exchange, SharePoint, Skype for Business, Windows as a Service). Candidates must have a strong understanding of networking, server administration and IT fundamentals such as DNS, Active Directory and PowerShell.

MS-100 Exam topics:

Candidates must know the exam topics before they start of preparation. Because it will really help them in hitting the core. Our **MS-100 dumps** will include the following topics:

- Design and Implement Microsoft 365 Services 25-30%
- Manage User Identity and Roes 35-40%
- Manage Access and Authentication 20-25%
- Plan Microsoft 365 Workloads and Applications 10-15%

Certification Path:

The Microsoft 365 Identity and Services Certification includes only one MS-100 exam.

Who should take the MS-100 exam:

The Microsoft 365 Identity and Services MS-100 Exam certification is an internationally recognized validation that identifies persons who earn it as possessing skilled as a Microsoft 365 Certified Enterprise Administrator Expert. If candidates want significant improvement in career growth needs enhanced knowledge, skills, and talents. The Microsoft 365 Identity and Services MS-100 Exam certification provides proof of this advanced knowledge and skill. If a candidate has knowledge of associated technologies and skills that are required to pass Microsoft 365 Identity and Services MS-100 Exam then he should take this exam.

How to study the MS-100 Exam:

Certification-questions.com expert team recommends you to prepare some notes on these topics along with it don't forget to practice Microsoft MS-100 Exam dumps which been written by our expert team, Both these will help you a lot to clear this exam with good marks.

How much MS-100 Exam Cost:

The price of the MS-100 exam is $165 USD.

How to book the MS-100 Exam:

These are following steps for registering the MS-100 exam.
Step 1: Visit to Microsoft Exam Registration
Step 2: Signup/Login to MICROSOFT account
Step 3: Search for MICROSOFT MS-100 Certifications Exam
Step 4: Select Date and Center of examination and confirm with payment value of $165

What is the duration of the MS-100 Exam:

- Format: Multiple choices, multiple answers
- Length of Examination: 150 minutes
- Number of Questions: 45-60
- Passing Score: 700/1000

The benefit in Obtaining the MS-100 Exam Certification:

- After completion of Microsoft 365 Certified Enterprise Administrator Expert Certification candidates receive official confirmation from Microsoft that you are now fully certified in their chosen field. This can be now added to their CV, cover letters and job applications.
- When Candidates applying for a job or looking to promotion in their current position, a Microsoft 365 Certified Enterprise Administrator Expert certification in the field in which Candidates are applying will put you at the top of the list and make them a desirable candidate for employers.
- Candidates will get in-depth knowledge by completing the courses along with the access to revision materials for 6 months upon completion means they will have a wider skill set when it comes to the various technologies and systems than an uncertified professional. Certified Professional in this particular skill set is 74% more efficient when it comes to completing their tasks in a timely well-executed manner.

- Organization owners invest a lot in their employees when it comes to their training with the goal of making them quicker, more efficient, and more knowledgeable about their role. Certified Professional will reduce the time he spends on tasks, meaning he can get more done this could help reduce company downtime when repairing faults on a system or fixing hardware problems.
- Becoming Microsoft 365 Certified Enterprise Administrator Expert means one thing you are worth more to the company and therefore more to yourself in the form of an upgraded pay package. On average a Microsoft 365 Certified Enterprise Administrator Expert member of staff is estimated to be worth 30% more to a company than their uncertified professionals.

Difficulty in writing MS-100 Exam:

Now, these days the significance of Microsoft MS-100 is increasing day by day then the difficulty of passing Microsoft MS-100 exam questions is also advancing. Candidates can only be passed Microsoft MS-100 exam if they practice daily, prepare from quality preparation material and believe in yourself. This is always a tough task for the candidates to pass Microsoft MS-100 exam because Microsoft MS-100 exam syllabus has some tricky concepts and the candidates find it hard to understand these topics. To overcome these problems candidates should have to keep these points in mind. First of all look for some updated and in detailed exam preparation material. They will really help you in understanding the very small to the small concept of the Microsoft MS-100 exam. The second point look for Microsoft experts helps, as they have the experience of the Microsoft MS-100 exam and they can tell you the real exam scenario. The third point is candidates should practice from quality Microsoft MS-100 exam practice tests. Certification-questions provides you internationally recognized **Microsoft MS-100 dumps** that will ensure hundred percent passing surety at the first attempt. These Microsoft MS-100 questions answers have been made by Microsoft professionals and experts. The most important thing Certification-questions also provides Microsoft MS-100 practice test with updated and latest questions that will help candidates a lot from the prospect of preparation.

For more info visit::

Microsoft MS-100 Exam Reference

# Sample Practice Test for MS-100

## Question: 1 *One Answer Is Right*

Note: This question is part of a series of questions that present the same scenario. Each question in the series contains a unique solution that might meet the stated goals. Some question sets might have more than one correct solution, while others might not have a correct solution. After you answer a question in this section, you will NOT be able to return to it. As a result, these questions will not appear in the review screen. Your company has a Microsoft Office 365 tenant. You suspect that several Office 365 features were recently updated. You need to view a list of the features that were recently updated in the tenant. Solution: You use the View service requests option in the Microsoft 365 admin center. Does this meet the goal?

**Answers:**

**A)** Yes

**B)** No

**Solution:** B

**Explanation:**

Explanation: A service request is a support ticket. Therefore, the View service requests option in the Microsoft 365 admin center displays a list of support tickets. It does not display a list of the features that were recently updated in the tenant so this solution does not meet the goal. To meet the goal, you need to use Message center in the Microsoft 365 admin center. Reference: https://docs.microsoft.com/en-us/office365/admin/manage/message-center?view=o365-worldwide

## Question: 2 *One Answer Is Right*

Note: This question is part of a series of questions that present the same scenario. Each question in the series contains a unique solution that might meet the stated goals. Some question sets might have more than one correct solution, while others might not have a correct solution. After you answer a question in this section, you will NOT be able to return to it. As a result, these questions will not appear in the review screen. Your company has a Microsoft Office 365 tenant. You suspect that several Office 365 features were recently updated. You need to view a list of the features that were recently updated in the tenant. Solution: You use Dashboard in Security & Compliance. Does this meet the goal?

**Answers:**

**A)** Yes

**B)** No

**Solution:** B

**Explanation:**

Explanation: Depending on what your organization's Office 365 subscription includes, the Dashboard in Security & Compliance includes several widgets, such as Threat Management Summary, Threat Protection Status, Global Weekly Threat Detections, Malware, etc. It does not display a list of the features that were recently updated in the tenant so this solution does not meet the goal. To meet the goal, you need to use Message center in the Microsoft 365 admin center. Reference: https://docs.microsoft.com/en-us/microsoft-365/security/office-365-security/security-dashboard https://docs.microsoft.com/en-us/office365/admin/manage/message-center?view=o365-worldwide

**Question: 3** *One Answer Is Right*

Note: This question is part of a series of questions that present the same scenario. Each question in the series contains a unique solution that might meet the stated goals. Some question sets might have more than one correct solution, while others might not have a correct solution. After you answer a question in this section, you will NOT be able to return to it. As a result, these questions will not appear in the review screen. Your company has a Microsoft Office 365 tenant. You suspect that several Office 365 features were recently updated. You need to view a list of the features that were recently updated in the tenant. Solution: You use Message center in the Microsoft 365 admin center. Does this meet the goal?

**Answers:**

**A)** Yes

**B)** No

**Solution:** A

**Explanation:**

Explanation: The Message center in the Microsoft 365 admin center is where you would go to view a list of the features that were recently updated in the tenant. This is where Microsoft posts official messages with information including new and changed features, planned maintenance, or other important announcements. Reference: https://docs.microsoft.com/en-us/office365/admin/manage/message-center?view=o365-worldwide

**Question: 4** *One Answer Is Right*

Note: This question is part of a series of questions that present the same scenario. Each question in the series contains a unique solution that might meet the stated goals. Some question sets might have more than one correct solution, while others might not have a correct solution. After you answer a question in this section, you will NOT be able to return to it. As a result, these questions will not appear in the review screen. Your company has a Microsoft Office 365 tenant. You suspect that several Office 365 features were recently updated. You need to view a list of the features that were recently updated in the tenant. Solution: You review the Security & Compliance report in the Microsoft 365 admin center. Does this meet the goal?

**Answers:**

**A)** Yes

**B)** No

**Solution:** B

**Explanation:**

Explanation: The Security & Compliance reports in the Microsoft 365 admin center are reports regarding security and compliance for your Office 365 Services. For example, email usage reports, Data Loss Prevention reports etc. They do not display a list of the features that were recently updated in the tenant so this solution does not meet the goal. To meet the goal, you need to use Message center in the Microsoft 365 admin center. Reference: https://docs.microsoft.com/en-us/microsoft-365/security/office-365-security/download-existing-reports

**Question: 5** *One Answer Is Right*

You recently migrated your on-premises email solution to Microsoft Exchange Online and are evaluating which licenses to purchase. You want the members of two groups named IT and Managers to be able to use the features shown in the following table.

| Feature | Available to |
|---|---|
| Microsoft Azure Active Directory (Azure AD) conditional access | IT group, Managers group |
| Microsoft Azure Active Directory (Azure AD) Privileged Identity Management | IT group |

The IT group contains 50 users. The Managers group contains 200 users. You need to recommend which licenses must be purchased for the planned solution. The solution must minimize licensing costs. Which licenses should you recommend?

**Answers:**

**A)** 250 Microsoft 365 E3 only

**B)** 50 Microsoft 365 E3 and 200 Microsoft 365 E5

**C)** 250 Microsoft 365 E5 only

**D)** 200 Microsoft 365 E3 and 50 Microsoft 365 E5

**Solution:** D

**Explanation:**

Explanation: Microsoft Azure Active Directory Privileged Identity Management requires an Azure AD Premium P2 license. This license comes as part of the Microsoft 365 E5 license. Therefore, we need 50 Microsoft 365 E5 licenses for the IT group. Conditional Access requires the Azure AD Premium P1 license. This comes as part of the Microsoft E3 license. Therefore, we need 200 Microsoft 365 E3 licenses for the Managers group. Reference: https://docs.microsoft.com/en-us/azure/active-directory/privileged-identity-management/subscription- requirements

**Question: 6** *One Answer Is Right*

You have a Microsoft 365 tenant that contains Microsoft Exchange Online. You plan to enable calendar sharing with a partner organization named adatum.com. The partner organization also has a Microsoft 365 tenant. You need to ensure that the calendar of every user is available to the users in adatum.com immediately. What should you do?

**Answers:**

**A)** From the Exchange admin center, create a sharing policy.

**B)** From the Exchange admin center, create a new organization relationship.

**C)** From the Microsoft 365 admin center, modify the Organization profile settings.

**D)** From the Microsoft 365 admin center, configure external site sharing.

**Solution:** B

**Explanation:**

Explanation: You need to set up an organization relationship to share calendar information with an external business partner. Office 365 admins can set up an organization relationship with another Office 365 organization or with an Exchange on-premises organization. Reference: https://docs.microsoft.com/en-us/exchange/sharing/organization-relationships/create-an-organization- relationship

**Question: 7** *Multiple Answers Are Right*

DRAG DROP Your company has a Microsoft Azure Active Directory (Azure AD) tenant named contoso.onmicrosoft.com. You purchase a domain named contoso.com from a registrar and add all the required DNS records. You create a user account named User1. User1 is configured to sign in as user1@contoso.onmicrosoft.com. You need to configure User1 to sign in as user1@contoso.com. Which three actions should you perform in sequence? To answer, move the appropriate actions from the list of actions to the answer area and arrange them in the correct order. Select and Place:

**Actions**

- Run `Set-MsolDomainAuthentication -TenantID contoso.com`
- Modify the email address of User1.
- Modify the username of User1.
- Verify the custom domain.
- Add contoso.com as a SAN for an X.509 certificate.
- Add a custom domain name.

**Answer Area**

Answers:

**A)**

**Actions**

- Run `Set-MsolDomainAuthentication -TenantID contoso.com`
- Modify the email address of User1.
- Modify the username of User1.
- Verify the custom domain.
- Add contoso.com as a SAN for an X.509 certificate.
- Add a custom domain name.

**Answer Area**

- Add a custom domain name.
- Verify the custom domain.
- Modify the username of User1.

**Solution:** A

**Explanation:**

Explanation: The first step is to add the contoso.com domain to Office 365. You do this by adding a custom domain. When you add a custom domain to office 365, you can use the domain as your email address or to sign in to Office 365. The second step is to verify the custom domain. This is to prove that you own the domain. You can verify the custom domain by adding a DNS record to the domain DNS zone. When you have added and verified the domain, you can configure the user accounts to use it. To configure User1 to sign in as user1@contoso.com, you need to change the username of User1. In Office 365, the username is composed of two parts. The first part is the actual username (User1) and the second part is the domain. You need to modify the username of User1 by selecting the contoso.com domain from the dropdown list of domains. The dropdown list of domains contains the .onmicrosoft.com domain and any custom domains that have been added. Reference: https://docs.microsoft.com/en-us/office365/admin/setup/add-domain?view=o365-worldwide

**Question: 8** *One Answer Is Right*

Your company has an on-premises Microsoft Exchange Server 2016 organization and a Microsoft 365 Enterprise subscription. You plan to migrate mailboxes and groups to Exchange Online. You start a new migration batch. Users report slow performance when they use the on-premises Exchange Server organization. You discover that the migration is causing the slow performance. You need to reduce the impact of the mailbox migration on the end-users. What should you do?

**Answers:**

A) Create a mail flow rule.

B) Configure back pressure.

C) Modify the migration endpoint settings.

D) Create a throttling policy.

**Solution: C**

**Explanation:**

Explanation: The migration is causing the slow performance. This suggests that the on-premise Exchange server is struggling under the load of copying the mailboxes to Exchange Online. You can reduce the load on the on- premise server by reducing the maximum number of concurrent mailbox migrations. Migrating just a few mailboxes at a time will have less of a performance impact than migrating many mailboxes concurrently. Reference: https://support.microsoft.com/en-gb/help/2797784/how-to-manage-the-maximum-concurrent-migration- batches-in-exchange-onl

**Question: 9** *One Answer Is Right*

You have a Microsoft 365 subscription. You need to prevent phishing email messages from being delivered to your organization. What should you do?

**Answers:**

**A)** From the Exchange admin center, create an anti-malware policy.

**B)** From Security & Compliance, create a DLP policy.

**C)** From Security & Compliance, create a new threat management policy.

**D)** From the Exchange admin center, create a spam filter policy.

**Solution:** C

**Explanation:**

Explanation: Anti-phishing protection is part of Office 365 Advanced Threat Protection (ATP). To prevent phishing email messages from being delivered to your organization, you need to configure a threat management policy. ATP anti-phishing is only available in Advanced Threat Protection (ATP). ATP is included in subscriptions, such as Microsoft 365 Enterprise, Microsoft 365 Business, Office 365 Enterprise E5, Office 365 Education A5, etc. Reference: https://docs.microsoft.com/en-us/office365/securitycompliance/set-up-anti-phishing-policies

**Question: 10** *One Answer Is Right*

Your company has a Microsoft 365 subscription. All identities are managed in the cloud. The company purchases a new domain name. You need to ensure that all new mailboxes use the new domain as their primary email address. What are two possible ways to achieve the goal? Each correct answer presents a complete solution. NOTE: Each correct selection is worth one point.

**Answers:**

**A)** Run the Update-EmailAddressPolicy Windows PowerShell command

**B)** From the Exchange admin center, select mail flow, and then configure the email address policies.

**C)** From the Microsoft 365 admin center, select Setup, and then configure the domains.

**D)** Run the Set-EmailAddressPolicy Windows PowerShell command.

**E)** From the Azure Active Directory admin center, configure the custom domain names.

**Solution:** B, D

**Explanation:**

Explanation: Email address policies define the rules that create email addresses for recipients in your Exchange organization whether this is Exchange on-premise or Exchange online. You can configure email address policies using the graphical interface of the Exchange Admin Center or by using PowerShell with the Set-EmailAddressPolicy cmdlet. The Set-EmailAddressPolicy cmdlet is used to modify an email address policy. The Update- EmailAddressPolicy cmdlet is used to apply an email address policy to users. Reference: https://docs.microsoft.com/en-us/exchange/email-addresses-and-address-books/email-address-policies/ email-address-policies?view=exchserver-2019

# Chapter 37: MS-101 - Microsoft 365 Mobility and Security

## Exam Guide

Microsoft 365 Mobility and Security MS-101 Exam:

Microsoft 365 Mobility and Security MS-101 Exam which is related to Microsoft 365 Certified Enterprise Administrator Expert Certification. This exam validates Candidates ability to implement modern device services, Microsoft 365 Security and threat management manage Microsoft 365 Governance and Compliance. Microsoft IT Professionals usually hold or pursue this certification and you can expect the same job role after completion of this certification.

MS-101 Exam topics:

Candidates must know the exam topics before they start of preparation. Because it will really help them in hitting the core. Our **MS-101 dumps** will include the following topics:

- Implement Modern Device Services 30-35%
- Implement Microsoft 365 Security and Threat Management 30-35%
- Manage Microsoft 365 Governance and Compliance 35-40%

Certification Path:

The Microsoft 365 Mobility and Security Certification includes only one MS-101 exam.

Who should take the MS-101 exam:

The Microsoft 365 Mobility and Security MS-101 Exam certification is an internationally recognized validation that identifies persons who earn it as possessing skilled as a Microsoft 365 Certified Enterprise Administrator Expert. If candidates want significant improvement in career growth needs enhanced knowledge, skills, and talents. The Microsoft 365 Mobility and Security MS-101 Exam certification provides proof of this advanced knowledge and skill. If a candidate has knowledge of associated technologies and skills that are required to pass Microsoft 365 Mobility and Security MS-101 Exam then he should take this exam.

How to study the MS-101 Exam:

Certification-questions.com expert team recommends you to prepare some notes on these topics along with it don't forget to practice Microsoft MS-101 Exam dumps which been written by our expert team, Both these will help you a lot to clear this exam with good marks.

How much MS-101 Exam Cost:

The price of the MS-101 exam is $165 USD.

How to book the MS-101 Exam:

These are following steps for registering the MS-101 exam.
Step 1: Visit to Microsoft Exam Registration
Step 2: Signup/Login to MICROSOFT account
Step 3: Search for MICROSOFT MS-101 Certifications Exam
Step 4: Select Date and Center of examination and confirm with payment value of $165

What is the duration of the MS-101 Exam:

- Format: Multiple choices, multiple answers
- Length of Examination: 150 minutes
- Number of Questions: 45-60
- Passing Score: 700/1000

The benefit in Obtaining the MS-101 Exam Certification:

- After completion of Microsoft 365 Certified Enterprise Administrator Expert Certification candidates receive official confirmation from Microsoft that you are now fully certified in their chosen field. This can be now added to their CV, cover letters and job applications.
- When Candidates applying for a job or looking to promotion in their current position, a Microsoft 365 Certified Enterprise Administrator Expert certification in the field in which Candidates are applying will put you at the top of the list and make them a desirable candidate for employers.
- Candidates will get in-depth knowledge by completing the courses along with the access to revision materials for 6 months upon completion means they will have a wider skill set when it comes to the various technologies and systems than an uncertified professional. Certified Professional in this particular skill set is 74% more efficient when it comes to completing their tasks in a timely well-executed manner.
- Organization owners invest a lot in their employees when it comes to their training with the goal of making them quicker, more efficient, and more knowledgeable about their role. Certified Professional will reduce the time he spends on tasks, meaning he can get more done this could help reduce company downtime when repairing faults on a system or fixing hardware problems.

- Becoming Microsoft 365 Certified Enterprise Administrator Expert means one thing you are worth more to the company and therefore more to yourself in the form of an upgraded pay package. On average a Microsoft 365 Certified Enterprise Administrator Expert member of staff is estimated to be worth 30% more to a company than their uncertified professionals.

    Difficulty in writing MS-101 Exam:

Microsoft 365 Certified Enterprise Administrator Expert Certification helps Candidates in developing their professionals and academic career and It is a very tough task to pass Microsoft MS-101 exam for those Candidates who have not done hard work and get some relevant Microsoft MS-101 exam preparation material. There are many peoples have passed Microsoft MS-101 exam by following these three things such as look for the latest **Microsoft MS-101 exam dumps**, get relevant **Microsoft MS-101 exam dumps** and develop their knowledge about Microsoft MS-101 exam new questions. At the same time, it can also stress out some people as they found passing Microsoft MS-101 exam a tough task. It is just a wrong assumption as many of the peoples have passed Microsoft MS-101 exam questions. All you have to do is to work hard, get some relevant Microsoft MS-101 exam preparation material and go thoroughly from them. Certification-questions is here to help you with this problem. We have the relevant Microsoft MS-101 exam preparation material which are providing the latest Microsoft MS-101 exam questions with the detailed view of every Microsoft MS-101 exam topic. Certification-questions offered **Microsoft MS-101 exam dumps** which are more than enough to pass the Microsoft MS-101 exam questions. We are providing all thing such as **Microsoft MS-101 exam dumps**, Microsoft MS-101 practice test, and Microsoft MS-101 pdf dumps that will help the candidate to pass the exam with good grades.

For more info visit::

Microsoft MS-101 Exam Reference

# Sample Practice Test for MS-101

**Question: 1** *One Answer Is Right*

Note: This question is part of a series of questions that present the same scenario. Each question in the series contains a unique solution that might meet the stated goals. Some question sets might have more than one correct solution, while others might not have a correct solution. After you answer a question in this section, you will NOT be able to return to it. As a result, these questions will not appear in the review screen. You are deploying Microsoft Intune. You successfully enroll Windows 10 devices in Intune. When you try to enroll an iOS device in Intune, you get an error. You need to ensure that you can enroll the iOS device in Intune. Solution: You add your user account as a device enrollment manager. Does this meet the goal?

**Answers:**

**A)** Yes

**B)** No

**Solution:** B

**Question: 2** *One Answer Is Right*

Note: This question is part of a series of questions that present the same scenario. Each question in the series contains a unique solution that might meet the stated goals. Some question sets might have more than one correct solution, while others might not have a correct solution. After you answer a question in this section, you will NOT be able to return to it. As a result, these questions will not appear in the review screen. You are deploying Microsoft Intune. You successfully enroll Windows 10 devices in Intune. When you try to enroll an iOS device in Intune, you get an error. You need to ensure that you can enroll the iOS device in Intune. Solution: You configure the Apple MDM Push certificate. Does this meet the goal?

**Answers:**

**A)** Yes

**B)** No

**Solution:** A

**Explanation:**

Explanation: References: https://docs.microsoft.com/en-us/intune/apple-mdm-push-certificate-get

**Question: 3** *One Answer Is Right*

Note: This question is part of a series of questions that present the same scenario. Each question in the series contains a unique solution that might meet the stated goals. Some question sets might have more than one correct solution, while others might not have a correct solution. After you answer a question in this section, you will NOT be able to return to it. As a result, these questions will not appear in the review screen. You are deploying Microsoft Intune. You successfully enroll Windows 10 devices in Intune. When you try to enroll an iOS device in Intune, you get an error. You need to ensure that you can enroll the iOS device in Intune. Solution: You create an Apple Configurator enrollment profile. Does this meet the goal?

**Answers:**

**A)** Yes

**B)** No

**Solution:** B

**Question: 4** *One Answer Is Right*

Note: This question is part of a series of questions that present the same scenario. Each question in the series contains a unique solution that might meet the stated goals. Some question sets might have more than one correct solution, while others might not have a correct solution. After you answer a question in this section, you will NOT be able to return to it. As a result, these questions will not appear in the review screen. Your network contains an Active Directory domain named contoso.com that is synced to Microsoft Azure Active Directory (Azure AD). You manage Windows 10 devices by using Microsoft System Center Configuration Manager (Current Branch). You configure pilot co-management. You add a new device named Device1 to the domain. You install the Configuration Manager client on Device1. You need to ensure that you can manage Device1 by using Microsoft Intune and Configuration Manager. Solution: You create a device configuration profile from the Device Management admin center. Does this meet the goal?

**Answers:**

**A)** Yes

**B)** No

**Solution:** B

**Question: 5** *One Answer Is Right*

Note: This question is part of a series of questions that present the same scenario. Each question in the series contains a unique solution that might meet the stated goals. Some question sets might have more than one correct solution, while others might not have a correct solution. After you answer a question in this section, you will NOT be able to return to it. As a result, these questions will not appear in the review screen. Your network contains an Active Directory domain named contoso.com that is synced to Microsoft Azure Active Directory (Azure AD). You manage Windows 10 devices by using Microsoft System Center Configuration Manager (Current Branch). You configure pilot co-management. You add a new device named Device1 to the domain. You install the Configuration Manager client on Device1. You need to ensure that you can manage Device1 by using Microsoft Intune and Configuration Manager. Solution: You add Device1 to an Active Directory group. Does this meet the goal?

**Answers:**

**A)** Yes

**B)** No

**Solution:** A

**Explanation:**

Explanation: References: https://www.scconfigmgr.com/2017/11/30/how-to-setup-co-management-part-6/

**Question: 6** *One Answer Is Right*

Note: This question is part of a series of questions that present the same scenario. Each question in the series contains a unique solution that might meet the stated goals. Some question sets might have more than one correct solution, while others might not have a correct solution. After you answer a question in this section, you will NOT be able to return to it. As a result, these questions will not appear in the review screen. Your network contains an Active Directory domain named contoso.com that is synced to Microsoft Azure Active Directory (Azure AD). You manage Windows 10 devices by using Microsoft System Center Configuration Manager (Current Branch). You configure pilot co-management. You add a new device named Device1 to the domain. You install the Configuration Manager client on Device1. You need to ensure that you can manage Device1 by using Microsoft Intune and Configuration Manager. Solution: You unjoin Device1 from the Active Directory domain. Does this meet the goal?

**Answers:**

**A)** Yes

**B)** No

**Solution:** B

**Question: 7** *Multiple Answers Are Right*

HOTSPOT Your network contains an Active Directory forest named contoso.com that is synced to Microsoft Azure Active Directory (Azure AD). You use Microsoft Endpoint Configuration Manager for device management. You have the Windows 10 devices shown in the following table.

| Name | Collection |
|---|---|
| Device1 | Collection1 |
| Device2 | Collection2 |

You configure Endpoint Configuration Manager co-management as follows: - Automatic enrollment in Intune: Pilot - Pilot collection for all workloads: Collection2 You configure co-management workloads as shown in the following exhibit.

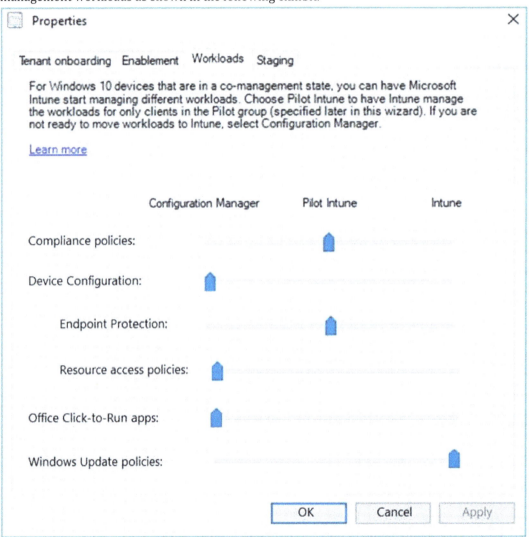

For each of the following statements, select Yes if the statement is true. Otherwise, select No. NOTE: Each correct selection is worth one point. Hot Area:

**Answer Area**

| Statements | Yes | No |
|---|---|---|
| Microsoft Intune manages the compliance policies for Device1. | ○ | ○ |
| Configuration Manager manages the Windows Update policies for Device1. | ○ | ○ |
| Microsoft Intune manages Endpoint Protection for Device2. | ○ | ○ |

Answers:

A)

**Answer Area**

| Statements | Yes | No |
|---|---|---|
| Microsoft Intune manages the compliance policies for Device1. | ○ | ◉ |
| Configuration Manager manages the Windows Update policies for Device1. | ○ | ◉ |
| Microsoft Intune manages Endpoint Protection for Device2. | ◉ | ○ |

Solution: A

Explanation:

Explanation:

**Question: 8** *Multiple Answers Are Right*

HOTSPOT You have three devices enrolled in Microsoft Intune as shown in the following table.

| Name | Platform | Member of |
|---|---|---|
| Device1 | Windows 10 | Group1 |
| Device2 | Android | Group2, Group3 |
| Device3 | Windows 10 | Group2, Group3 |

The device compliance policies in Intune are configured as shown in the following table.

| Name | Platform | Assigned |
|---|---|---|
| Policy1 | Windows 10 and later | Yes |
| Policy2 | Android | No |
| Policy3 | Windows 10 and later | Yes |

The device compliance policies have the assignments shown in the following table.

| Name | Include | Exclude |
|---|---|---|
| Policy1 | Group3 | None |
| Policy2 | Group2 | Group3 |

For each of the following statements, select Yes if the statement is true. Otherwise, select No. NOTE: Each correct selection is worth one point. Hot Area:

Answer Area

| Statements | Yes | No |
|---|---|---|
| Policy1 applies to Device3. | ○ | ○ |
| Policy2 applies to Device2. | ○ | ○ |

Answers:

A)

Answer Area

| Statements | Yes | No |
|---|---|---|
| Policy1 applies to Device3. | ○ | ○ |
| Policy2 applies to Device2. | ○ | ○ |

Solution: A

Explanation:

Explanation:

Question: 9 *One Answer Is Right*

You have Windows 10 Pro devices that are joined to an Active Directory domain. You plan to create a Microsoft 365 tenant and to upgrade the devices to Windows 10 Enterprise. You are evaluating whether to deploy Windows Hello for Business. What are two prerequisites of the deployment? Each correct answer presents a complete solution. NOTE: Each correct selection is worth one point.

Answers:

A) Microsoft Intune enrollment

B) Microsoft Azure Active Directory (Azure AD)

C) smartcards

**D)** TPM-enabled devices

**Solution:** A, B

**Explanation:**

Explanation: Reference: https://docs.microsoft.com/en-us/windows/security/identity-protection/hello-for-business/hello-hybrid-aadj- sso-base

**Question: 10** *One Answer Is Right*

You have a Microsoft 365 tenant. All users are assigned the Enterprise Mobility + Security license. You need to ensure that when users join their device to Microsoft Azure Active Directory (Azure AD), the device is enrolled in Microsoft Intune automatically. What should you configure?

**Answers:**

**A)** Enrollment restrictions from the Device Management admin center

**B)** device enrollment managers from the Device Management admin center

**C)** MAM User scope from the Azure Active Directory admin center

**D)** MDM User scope from the Azure Active Directory admin center

**Solution:** D

**Explanation:**

Explanation: References: https://docs.microsoft.com/en-us/intune/windows-enroll

# Chapter 38: MS-201 - Implementing a Hybrid and Secure Messaging Platform

## Exam Guide

Implementing a Hybrid and Secure Messaging Platform MS-201 Exam:

Implementing a Hybrid and Secure Messaging Platform MS-201 Exam which is related to Microsoft 365 Certified Messaging Administrator Associate. This exam validates the Candidates ability to deploy, configure, manage, troubleshoot, and monitor recipients, permissions, mail protection, mail flow, and public folders in both on-premises and cloud enterprise environments. This exam also verifies the Candidate working knowledge of managing hygiene, messaging infrastructure, hybrid configuration, migration, disaster recovery, high availability, and client access.

MS-201 Exam topics:

Candidates must know the exam topics before they start of preparation. Because it will really help them in hitting the core. Our **MS-201 dumps** will include the following topics:

- Plan and implement a hybrid configuration and migration 35-40%
- Secure the messaging environment 40-45%
- Manage organizational settings 15-20%

Certification Path:

Implementing a Hybrid and Secure Messaging Platform Certification includes only one MS-201 exam.

Who should take the MS-201 exam:

The Implementing a Hybrid and Secure Messaging Platform MS-201 Exam certification is an internationally recognized validation that identifies persons who earn it as possessing skilled as a Microsoft 365 Certified Messaging Administrator Associate. If candidates want significant improvement in career growth needs enhanced knowledge, skills, and talents. The Implementing a Hybrid and Secure Messaging Platform MS-201 Exam certification provides proof of this advanced knowledge and skill. If a candidate has knowledge of associated technologies and skills that are required to pass Implementing a Hybrid and Secure Messaging Platform MS-201 Exam then he should take this exam.

How to study the MS-201 Exam:

Certification-questions.com expert team recommends you to prepare some notes on these topics along with it don't forget to practice Microsoft MS-201 Exam dumps which been written by our expert team, Both these will help you a lot to clear this exam with good marks.

How much MS-201 Exam Cost:

The price of the MS-201 exam is $165 USD.

How to book the MS-201 Exam:

These are following steps for registering the MS-201 exam.
Step 1: Visit to Microsoft Exam Registration
Step 2: Signup/Login to MICROSOFT account
Step 3: Search for MICROSOFT MS-201 Certifications Exam
Step 4: Select Date and Center of examination and confirm with payment value of $165

What is the duration of the MS-201 Exam:

- Format: Multiple choices, multiple answers
- Length of Examination: 150 minutes
- Number of Questions: 45-60
- Passing Score: 700/1000

The benefit in Obtaining the MS-201 Exam Certification:

- After completion of Microsoft 365 Certified Messaging Administrator Associate Certification candidates receive official confirmation from Microsoft that you are now fully certified in their chosen field. This can be now added to their CV, cover letters and job applications.
- When Candidates applying for a job or looking to promotion in their current position, a Microsoft 365 Certified Messaging Administrator Associate certification in the field in which Candidates are applying will put you at the top of the list and make them a desirable candidate for employers.
- Candidates will get in-depth knowledge by completing the courses along with the access to revision materials for 6 months upon completion means they will have a wider skill set when it comes to the various technologies and systems than an uncertified professional. Certified Professional in this particular skill set is 74% more efficient when it comes to completing their tasks in a timely well-executed manner.

- Organization owners invest a lot in their employees when it comes to their training with the goal of making them quicker, more efficient, and more knowledgeable about their role. Certified Professional will reduce the time he spends on tasks, meaning he can get more done this could help reduce company downtime when repairing faults on a system or fixing hardware problems.
- Becoming Microsoft 365 Certified Messaging Administrator Associate means one thing you are worth more to the company and therefore more to yourself in the form of an upgraded pay package. On average a Microsoft 365 Certified Messaging Administrator Associate member of staff is estimated to be worth 30% more to a company than their uncertified professionals.

Difficulty in writing MS-201 Exam:

This Microsoft MS-201 exam is very difficult to prepare. Because it requires all candidate attention with practice. So, if Candidate wants to pass this Microsoft MS-201 exam with good grades then he has to choose the right preparation material. By passing the Microsoft MS-201 exam can make a lot of difference in your career. Many Candidates wants to achieve success in the Microsoft MS-201 exam but they are failing in it. Because of their wrong selection but if the candidate can get valid and latest Microsoft MS-201 study material then he can easily get good grades in the Microsoft MS-201 exam. Certification-questions providing many Microsoft MS-201 exam questions that help the candidate to get success in the Microsoft MS-201 test. Our **Microsoft MS-201 exam dumps** specially designed for those who want to get their desired results in the just first attempt. Microsoft MS-201 braindump questions provided by Certification-questions make candidate preparation material more impactful and the best part is that the training material provided by Certification-questions for Microsoft MS-201 exams are designed by our experts in the several fields of the IT industry.

For more info visit::

Microsoft MS-201 Exam Reference

# Sample Practice Test for MS-201

**Question: 1** *Multiple Answers Are Right*

HOTSPOT You have a Microsoft Exchange Server 2019 hybrid deployment. You are migrating mailboxes from the on-premises organization to Exchange Online. From the Exchange admin center, you create a new migration batch that includes 25 mailboxes, and then you select Manual Complete the batch. Later, you must complete the migration of a mailbox named user1@litware.com in the batch as soon as possible. You discover that the status of the migration batch is Syncing, but the status of the move request for user1@litware.com is Synced. You need to complete the migration of the user1@litware.com mailbox to Exchange Online as soon as possible. How should you complete the command? To answer, select the appropriate options in the answer area. NOTE: Each correct selection is worth one point. Hot Area:

**Answer Area**

Answers:

A)

**Answer Area**

**Solution:** A

**Explanation:**

Explanation: References: https://docs.microsoft.com/en-us/powershell/module/exchange/move-and-migration/set-moverequest?view=exchange-ps

### Question: 2 *One Answer Is Right*

You have a Microsoft Exchange Server 2019 organization. You purchase an Exchange Online subscription. You plan to implement an Exchange hybrid deployment that supports the following features: - Federated sharing of free/busy information between organizations. - Single-sign on (SSO) access to both on-premises and Exchange Online mailboxes. - Secured access to mailboxes by using Microsoft Azure Active Directory (Azure AD) conditional access policies. - A unified global address list (GAL) that contains all the mailboxes in the on-premises and Exchange Online organizations. You plan to run the Microsoft Office 365 Hybrid Configuration wizard. You are evaluating whether to use Exchange Classic Hybrid or Exchange Modern Hybrid. Which requirement can only be met by using the Exchange Modern Hybrid connection option?

**Answers:**

**A)** the federated sharing of free/busy information between organizations

**B)** SSO access to both on-premises and Exchange Online mailboxes

**C)** a unified GAL list that contains all the mailboxes in the on-premises and Exchange Online organizations

**D)** secured access to mailboxes by using Azure AD conditional access policies.

**Solution:** A

**Explanation:**

Explanation: References: https://docs.microsoft.com/en-us/exchange/hybrid-deployment/hybrid-agent

**Question: 3** *Multiple Answers Are Right*

HOTSPOT You have a Microsoft Exchange Server 2019 organization that contains the Mailbox servers shown in the following table.

| Name | Member of | Database |
|---|---|---|
| EX1 | Site1 | Mail1 |
| EX2 | Site2 | Mail2 |
| EX3 | Site3 | Mail3 |

The organization contains the mailboxes shown in the following table.

| Name | Database |
|---|---|
| User1 | Mail1 |
| User2 | Mail2 |
| User3 | Mail3 |

You create the public folder mailboxes shown in the following table.

| Mailbox | Database | Hierarchy |
|---------|----------|-----------|
| PF1 | Mail1 | Primary |
| PF2 | Mail2 | Secondary |
| PF3 | Mail3 | Secondary |

You set the DefaultPublicFolderMailbox property of each user mailbox to the public folder mailbox closest to the user. For each of the following statements, select Yes if the statement is true. Otherwise, select No. NOTE: Each correct selection is worth one point. Hot Area:

| Statements | Yes | No |
|---|---|---|
| If User3 creates a public folder, the folder hierarchy will be updated first on EX3. | ○ | ○ |
| When User2 views the folder hierarchy, the user will use EX2. | ○ | ○ |
| If User3 accesses a public folder from PF1, and then EX1 goes offline, User3 can still access the content in the public folder. | ○ | ○ |

**Answers:**

**A)**

| Statements | Yes | No |
|---|---|---|
| If User3 creates a public folder, the folder hierarchy will be updated first on EX3. | ○ | ● |
| When User2 views the folder hierarchy, the user will use EX2. | ● | ○ |
| If User3 accesses a public folder from PF1, and then EX1 goes offline, User3 can still access the content in the public folder. | ● | ○ |

**Solution:** A

**Explanation:**

Explanation: References: https://docs.microsoft.com/en-us/exchange/collaboration/public-folders/public-folders?view=exchserver- 2019

**Question: 4** *Multiple Answers Are Right*

HOTSPOT You have a Microsoft Exchange Server 2019 hybrid deployment. You have the on-premises mailboxes shown in the following table.

| Name | Forwarding address |
|---|---|
| User1 | User6 |
| User2 | None |
| User3 | None |
| User4 | None |
| User5 | None |
| User6 | None |

You add the mailbox permissions shown in the following table.

| Mailbox | Permission |
|---|---|
| User2 | Send As for User4 |
| User4 | Full Access for User3 |
| User6 | Send on Behalf for User5 |

You plan to migrate the mailboxes to Exchange Online by using remote mailbox move requests. The mailboxes will be migrated according to the schedule shown in the following table.

| Week | Mailbox |
|---|---|
| 1 | User1, User2, User3, User6 |
| 2 | User4, User5 |

Mailboxes migrated the same week will have their mailbox move requests included in the same batch and will be cut over simultaneously. For each of the following statements, select Yes if the statement is true. Otherwise, select No. NOTE: Each correct selection is worth one point. Hot Area:

| Statements | Yes | No |
|---|---|---|
| The mail forwarding settings of the User1 mailbox will be preserved automatically after the migration. | ○ | ○ |
| The permissions granted to the User4 mailbox for the User2 mailbox will be preserved automatically after the migration. | ○ | ○ |
| The permissions granted to the User3 mailbox for the User4 mailbox will be preserved automatically after the migration. | ○ | ○ |

**Answers:**

**A)**

| Statements | Yes | No |
|---|---|---|
| The mail forwarding settings of the User1 mailbox will be preserved automatically after the migration. | ○ | ○ |
| The permissions granted to the User4 mailbox for the User2 mailbox will be preserved automatically after the migration. | ○ | ○ |
| The permissions granted to the User3 mailbox for the User4 mailbox will be preserved automatically after the migration. | ○ | ○ |

**Solution:** A

**Explanation:**

Explanation: References: https://docs.microsoft.com/en-us/exchange/exchange-hybrid
https://practical365.com/exchange-online/configuring-exchange-hybrid-cross-forest-permissions/

**Question: 5** *One Answer Is Right*

Your network contains an Active Directory domain named fabrikam.com. You have a Microsoft Exchange Server 2019 organization that contains two Mailbox servers in a database availability group (DAG). You plan to implement a hybrid deployment by using the Exchange Modern Hybrid connection option. Which three configurations will be transferred automatically from the on-premises organization to Exchange Online? Each correct answer presents part of the solution. NOTE: Each correct selection is worth one point.

**Answers:**

**A)** the device access rules

**B)** the address lists

**C)** the address book policies (ABPs)

**D)** the Messaging Records Management (MRM) settings

**E)** the mail flow rules

**Solution:** A, B, E

**Explanation:**

Explanation: References: https://practical365.com/exchange-online/hybrid-exchange-making-it-easier-and-faster-to-move-to-the- cloud/

**Question: 6** *One Answer Is Right*

You have a Microsoft Exchange Server 2019 organization that contains 5,000 mailboxes. You purchase a Microsoft 365 E5 subscription and create a hybrid deployment. You configure all MX records to point to Exchange Online. You purchase 2,000 Microsoft 365 E5 licenses, and you migrate 2,000 mailboxes to Exchange Online. You need to identify which additional licenses must be purchased. The solution must minimize costs. Which licenses should you identify?

**Answers:**

A) Enterprise Mobility + Security E5 licenses for the Exchange Online users

B) Microsoft Office 365 Enterprise E1 licenses for the on-premises users

C) Microsoft Azure Active Directory Premium P2 licenses for all users

D) an Exchange Online Protection (EOP) license for each on-premises mailbox

**Solution:** C

**Explanation:**

Explanation: References: https://docs.microsoft.com/en-us/azure/active-directory/fundamentals/active-directory-whatis

**Question: 7** *One Answer Is Right*

You have a Microsoft Exchange Server 2019 organization. You plan to purchase a Microsoft 365 E5 subscription and create a hybrid deployment. You are evaluating the security requirements for communication between the on-premises organization and Exchange Online. You need to ensure that Exchange Online services can access the necessary on-premises virtual directories. Which two on-premises virtual directories should be accessible to Exchange Online services? Each correct answer presents part of the solution. NOTE: Each correct selection is worth one point.

**Answers:**

A) Rpc

B) EWS

C) PowerShell

D) ecp

**E)** mapi

**F)** Autodiscover

**Solution:** E, F

**Explanation:**

Explanation: References: https://docs.microsoft.com/en-us/office365/enterprise/configure-exchange-server-for-hybrid-modern- authentication

**Question: 8** *Multiple Answers Are Right*

HOTSPOT You have a Microsoft Exchange Server 2019 hybrid deployment. You plan to enable Hybrid Modern Authentication (HMA). You run the Get-MapiVirtualDirectory cmdlet and receive the output shown in the following exhibit.

```
[PS] C:\>Get-MapiVirtualDirectory -Server EX01 | fl 'auth','url'

IISAuthenticationMethods      : {Ntlm, Negotiate}
InternalAuthenticationMethod  : {Ntlm, Negotiate}
ExternalAuthenticationMethod  : {Ntlm, Negotiate}
InternalUrl                   : https//mail.contoso.com/mapi
ExternalUrl                   : https//mail.contoso.com/mapi
```

Use the drop-down menus to select the answer choice that completes each statement based on the information presented in the graphic. NOTE: Each correct selection is worth one point. Hot Area:

**Answer Area**

Before you can enable HMA, you must enable **[answer choice]** authentication on the virtual directory.

| certificate-based |
| Digest |
| OAuth |
| WS-Security |

Before you can enable HMA, a service principal name (SPN) for **[answer choice]** must exist in Microsoft Azure Directory (Azure AD).

| https://mail.contoso.com |
| https://mail.contoso.com/mapi |
| mail.contoso.com |
| mail.contoso.com/mapi |

**Answers:**

A)

**Answer Area**

Before you can enable HMA, you must enable **[answer choice]** authentication on the virtual directory.

| certificate-based |
|---|
| Digest |
| OAuth |
| WS-Security |

Before you can enable HMA, a service principal name (SPN) for **[answer choice]** must exist in Microsoft Azure Directory (Azure AD).

| https://mail.contoso.com |
|---|
| https://mail.contoso.com/mapi |
| mail.contoso.com |
| mail.contoso.com/mapi |

**Solution: A**

**Explanation:**

Explanation: References: https://docs.microsoft.com/en-us/office365/enterprise/configure-exchange-server-for-hybrid-modern- authentication

**Question: 9** *Multiple Answers Are Right*

DRAG DROP You have a Microsoft Exchange Server 2019 hybrid deployment. All user mailboxes are migrated to Exchange Online. You need to migrate the public folders from the on-premises organization to Exchange Online. Which three actions should you perform in sequence before you create the migration batch? To answer, move the appropriate actions from the list of actions to the answer area and arrange them in the correct order. Select and Place:

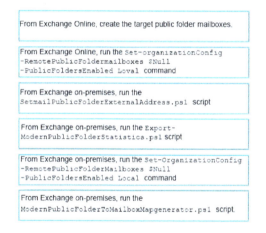

## Answers:

### A)

**Solution:** A

**Explanation:**

Explanation: References: https://docs.microsoft.com/en-us/Exchange/collaboration/public-folders/migrate-to-exchange-online?view=exchserver-2019

**Question: 10** *One Answer Is Right*

You have a Microsoft Exchange Server 2019 organization. You purchase a Microsoft 365 subscription and configure Active Directory synchronization. You use a smart host for all communication between the organization and the Internet. The smart host performs email hygiene and alters message headers. You plan to run the Hybrid Configuration wizard to create an Exchange hybrid deployment and change the MX record to point to Exchange Online. You need to decommission the smart host from the organization. What should you do first?

**Answers:**

**A)** Modify the InternalSmtpServer value by running the Set-TransportConfig cmdlet.

**B)** Modify the Send connector to use DNS delivery.

**C)** Modify the TLSReceiveDomainSecureList value by running the Set-TransportConfig cmdlet.

**D)** Create a Receive connector that allows anonymous authentication.

**Solution:** C

**Explanation:**

Explanation: References: https://docs.microsoft.com/en-us/powershell/module/exchange/mail-flow/set-transportconfig? view=exchange-ps

# Chapter 39: MS-300 - Deploying Microsoft 365 Teamwork

## Exam Guide

Deploying Microsoft 365 Teamwork (beta) MS-300 Exam:

Deploying Microsoft 365 Teamwork (beta) MS-300 Exam which is related to Microsoft 365 Certified Teamwork Administrator Associate Certification. This exam validates the Candidates ability to configure and manage SharePoint online, manage OneDrive for business, configure and manage teams, Integrate M365 Workloads. Microsoft Teamwork Administrator usually holds or pursue this certification and you can expect the same job roles after completion of this certification.

MS-300 Exam topics:

Candidates must know the exam topics before they start of preparation. Because it will really help them in hitting the core. Our **MS-300 dumps** will include the following topics:

- Configure and manage SharePoint Online 35-40%
- Configure and manage OneDrive for Business 25-30%
- Configure and manage Teams 20-25%
- Configure and manage workload integrations 15-20%

Certification Path:

The Microsoft 365 Messaging Administrator Certification Transition (beta) Certification includes only one MS-300 exam.

Who should take the MS-300 exam:

The Deploying Microsoft 365 Teamwork (beta) MS-300 Exam certification is an internationally recognized validation that identifies persons who earn it as possessing skilled as a Microsoft 365 Certified Teamwork Administrator Associate. If candidates want significant improvement in career growth needs enhanced knowledge, skills, and talents. The Deploying Microsoft 365 Teamwork (beta) MS-300 Exam certification provides proof of this advanced knowledge and skill. If a candidate has knowledge of associated technologies and skills that are required to pass Deploying Microsoft 365 Teamwork (beta) MS-300 Exam then he should take this exam.

How to study the MS-300 Exam:

Certification-questions.com expert team recommends you to prepare some notes on these topics along with it don't forget to practice Microsoft MS-300 Exam dumps which been written by our expert team, Both these will help you a lot to clear this exam with good marks.

How much MS-300 Exam Cost:

The price of the MS-300 exam is $165 USD.

How to book the MS-300 Exam:

These are following steps for registering the MS-300 exam.
Step 1: Visit to Microsoft Exam Registration
Step 2: Signup/Login to MICROSOFT account
Step 3: Search for MICROSOFT MS-300 Certifications Exam
Step 4: Select Date and Center of examination and confirm with payment value of $165

What is the duration of the MS-300 Exam:

- Format: Multiple choices, multiple answers
- Length of Examination: 150 minutes
- Number of Questions: 45-60
- Passing Score: 700/1000

The benefit in Obtaining the MS-300 Exam Certification:

- After completion of Microsoft 365 Certified Teamwork Administrator Associate Certification candidates receive official confirmation from Microsoft that you are now fully certified in their chosen field. This can be now added to their CV, cover letters and job applications.
- When Candidates applying for a job or looking to promotion in their current position, a Microsoft 365 Certified Teamwork Administrator Associate certification in the field in which Candidates are applying will put you at the top of the list and make them a desirable candidate for employers.
- Candidates will get in-depth knowledge by completing the courses along with the access to revision materials for 6 months upon completion means they will have a wider skill set when it comes to the various technologies and systems than an uncertified professional. Certified Professional in this particular skill set is 74% more efficient when it comes to completing their tasks in a timely well-executed manner.

- Organization owners invest a lot in their employees when it comes to their training with the goal of making them quicker, more efficient, and more knowledgeable about their role. Certified Professional will reduce the time he spends on tasks, meaning he can get more done this could help reduce company downtime when repairing faults on a system or fixing hardware problems.
- Becoming Microsoft 365 Certified Teamwork Administrator Associate means one thing you are worth more to the company and therefore more to yourself in the form of an upgraded pay package. On average a Microsoft 365 Certified Teamwork Administrator Associate member of staff is estimated to be worth 30% more to a company than their uncertified professionals.

Difficulty in writing MS-300 Exam:

This is exam is very difficult for those candidates who don't practice during preparation and candidates need a lab for practicing. Then practical exposure is much required to understand the contents of the exam. So, if anyone is associated with some kinds of an organization where he has opportunities to practice but if you can't afford the lab and don't have time to practice. So, Certification-questions is the solution to this problem. We provide the best **Microsoft MS-300 exam dumps** and practice test for your preparation. **Microsoft MS-300 exam dumps** to ensure your success in Microsoft 365 Certified Teamwork Administrator Associate Certification Exam at first attempt. Our **Microsoft MS-300 dumps** are updated on regular basis. Certification-questions has the combination of PDF and VCE file that will be much helpful for candidates in passing the exam. Certification-questions provides verified questions with relevant answers which will be asked from candidates in their final exam. So, it makes it for candidates to get good grades in the final exam and one of the best features is we also provide **Microsoft MS-300 dumps** in PDF format which is candidates can download and study offline.

For more info visit::

Microsoft MS-300 Exam Reference

# Sample Practice Test for MS-300

**Question: 1** *One Answer Is Right*

You need to confirm whether the performance issues experienced by the HR department site collection are due to the large images. What should you do?

**Scenario:**

TESTLET-2. Overview Contoso, Ltd. is a pharmaceutical company that has 750 users. Contoso has departmental teams spread across offices in North America. The company has a main office in Seattle and four branch offices in New York, New Jersey, Boston, and Florida. Existing Environment Active Directory Environment The network contains an on-premises Active Directory domain. All users are created in the domain and are organized in organizational units (OUs). All the users use their domain credentials to sign in to their computer. Microsoft Office 365 Environment Contoso has a Microsoft Office 365 subscription and uses the following services: - OneDrive for Business - SharePoint Online - Exchange Online - Yammer - Teams Currently, the identity of each user is maintained separately in both on-premises Active Directory and Office 365. Contoso implements SharePoint site collections for the following departments: - Research & development - Human resources (HR) - Marketing -Finance - IT Each department assigns a site owner to manage its site collection and to manage access. The site collection of each department contains multiple subsites. Sharing is allowed across different site collections by default. External sharing is enabled for the organization. Current Business Model Contoso has the following business model: - The HR department has a branded site collection - Currently, the default storage limit is set for all the site collections - The marketing department uses multiple site collections created by an administrator named Admin1. - Contoso has a strategic partnership with a company name Litware, Inc. Litware has an Office 365 subscription. All users at Litware have a user account in the litwareinc.com domain. Problem Statements Contoso identifies the following issues: - Non-site owners invite external users to access the content in SharePoint Online. - Users upload audio, video, and executable program files to OneDrive for Business. - The company manages two separate identities for each user, which creates more administrative work. - Users in the HR department report performance issues affecting their site collection. You suspect that the issues are due to large images on the home page. Technical Requirements Contoso has the following technical requirements for the Office 365 environment: - Add a Yammer feed to new communication sites. - Prevent non-site owners from inviting external users. - Troubleshoot the performance issues of the HR department site collection. - Implement a 100-GB storage limit for the site collection of the marketing department. - Prevent users from syncing media files, such as MP3 and MP4 files, from OneDrive. - Restrict users from sharing content from the finance department site collection to the Litware users. - Ensure that SharePoint administrators do not have administrative permissions to the site collections. - Ensure that the managers in the marketing department can view the storage metrics of the marketing department sites. - Maintain all user identities in on-premises Active Directory. Sync passwords to Microsoft Azure Active Directory (Azure AD). - Ensure that when users are deleted from Microsoft 365 their associated OneDrive content is retained for 90 days. After 90 days, the content must be deleted permanently.

**Answers:**

**A)** From Site Settings for the site collection, select Storage Metrics

**B)** From Site Settings for the site collection, select Site collection health checks

**C)** From the Microsoft 365 admin center, view the service status of SharePoint Online

**D)** From Microsoft Edge, open the site. Run the developer tools

**Solution:** D

**Explanation:**

Explanation: Scenario: Users in the HR department report performance issues affecting their site collection. You suspect that the issues are due to large images on the home page. You can diagnose common issues with your SharePoint Online site using Internet Explorer developer tools. There are three different ways that you can identify that a page on a SharePoint Online site has a performance problem with the customizations. - The F12 tool bar network monitor - Comparison to a non-customized baseline - SharePoint Online response header metrics References: https://docs.microsoft.com/en-us/office365/enterprise/diagnosing-performance-issues-with-sharepoint- online

**Question: 2** *One Answer Is Right*

What should you configure to meet the licensing requirements for Admin1?

**Scenario:**

TESTLET-1. Overview Litware, Inc. is a design and manufacturing company that has 4,500 users. The company has sales, marketing, design, research, field test, and human resources (HR) departments. Litware has a main office in California, three branch offices in the United States, and five branch offices in Europe. Existing Environment On-premises Infrastructure The network contains an Active Directory forest named litwareinc.com that contains a child domain for each region. All domain controllers run Windows Server 2012. The main office syncs identities to Microsoft Azure Active Directory (Azure AD) by using Azure AD Connect. All user accounts are created in the on-premises Active Directory and sync to Azure AD. Each office contains the following servers and client computers: - A domain controller that runs Windows Server 2012 - A file server that runs Windows Server 2012 - Client computers that run Windows 10 Currently, all content created by users is stored locally on file servers. Cloud Infrastructure Litware is moving the content from the file servers to Microsoft Office 365. The company purchases 4,500 Microsoft 365 E5 licenses. Litware uses Microsoft Exchange Online for email. Problem Statements Litware identifies the following issues:- Finding content and people within the organization is difficult. - Users cannot access company data from outside the corporate network. - Content recovery is slow because all the content is still on-premises. - Data security is compromised because users can copy company content to USB drives. - The locally stored content is not classified as confidential and users can email documents to external people. - Users must frequently contact the HR department to find employees within the organization who have relevant skills. - Users can delete content indiscriminately and without resource as they have full control of the content of the file servers. Requirements Business Goals Litware identifies the following strategic initiatives to remain competitive: - All content must be stored centrally - Access to content must be based on the user's: 1. Department 2. Security level 3. Physical location - Users must be able to work on content offline - Users must be able to share content externally - Content classifications must be accessible from mobile devices - Content classifications must include a physical location - Content must be retained and protected based on its type - Litware must adhere to highly confidential regulatory standards that include: 1. The ability to restrict the copying of all content created internally and externally 2. Including accurate time zone reporting in audit trails - Users must be able to search for content and people across the entire organization. - Content classification metadata must adhere to naming conventions specified by the IT department. - Users must be able to access content quickly without having to review many pages of search results to find documents. - Security rules must be implemented so that user access can be revoked if a user shares confidential content with external users. Planned Changes Litware plans to implement the following changes: - Move all department content to Microsoft SharePoint Online - Move all user content to Microsoft OneDrive for Business - Restrict user access based on location and device Technical Requirements Litware identifies the following technical requirements: - All on-premises documents (approximately one million documents) must be migrated to the SharePoint document library of their respective department. - Each department must have its own term store group. Stakeholders must be notified when term sets are moved or deleted. - All the OneDrive content of a user must be retained for a minimum of 180 days after the user has left the organization. - All external users must be added explicitly to Office 365 groups to give the users access to SharePoint team sites. - Office 365 groups must be used as the primary membership service for Microsoft Yammer, Teams, and SharePoint. - A user named Admin1 must be allowed to consume apps in the App Catalog and to add additional app license. - Viewers must be prevented from printing documents that are stored in a modern site named Finance. - Users must be prevented from printing content accessed in OneDrive from iOS and Android devices. -Retention, protection, and security policies must be implemented for all content stored online.- All offices must use the Managed Metadata Service to classify documents uploaded to SharePoint. - The Azure Information Protection client must be deployed to all domain-joined computers. - Searches must show results only when the result set is complete. - OneDrive must be used to work with documents offline. - Solutions must use the principle of least privilege whenever possible.

Answers:

**A)** Add Admin1 to the App Catalog site owners group of the App Requests list.

**B)** Assign Admin1 the SharePoint administrators of the App Catalog site

**C)** Add Admin1 to the site collection administrators of the App Catalog site

**D)** Add Admin1 as a License Manager of the apps.

**E)** Assign Admin1 the SharePoint administrator role.

**Solution:** A

**Explanation:**

Explanation: References: https://docs.microsoft.com/en-us/sharepoint/administration/manage-the-app-catalog

**Question: 3** *One Answer Is Right*

You need to recommend a solution for the documents stored in the Finance site. What should you recommend?

**Scenario:**

TESTLET-1. Overview Litware, Inc. is a design and manufacturing company that has 4,500 users. The company has sales, marketing, design, research, field test, and human resources (HR) departments. Litware has a main office in California, three branch offices in the United States, and five branch offices in Europe. Existing Environment On-premises Infrastructure The network contains an Active Directory forest named litwareinc.com that contains a child domain for each region. All domain controllers run Windows Server 2012. The main office syncs identities to Microsoft Azure Active Directory (Azure AD) by using Azure AD Connect. All user accounts are created in the on-premises Active Directory and sync to Azure AD. Each office contains the following servers and client computers: - A domain controller that runs Windows Server 2012 - A file server that runs Windows Server 2012 - Client computers that run Windows 10 Currently, all content created by users is stored locally on file servers. Cloud Infrastructure Litware is moving the content from the file servers to Microsoft Office 365. The company purchases 4,500 Microsoft 365 E5 licenses. Litware uses Microsoft Exchange Online for email. Problem Statements Litware identifies the following issues:- Finding content and people within the organization is difficult. - Users cannot access company data from outside the corporate network. - Content recovery is slow because all the content is still on-premises. - Data security is compromised because users can copy company content to USB drives. - The locally stored content is not classified as confidential and users can email documents to external people. - Users must frequently contact the HR department to find employees within the organization who have relevant skills. - Users can delete content indiscriminately and without resource as they have full control of the content of the file servers. Requirements Business Goals Litware identifies the following strategic initiatives to remain competitive: - All content must be stored centrally - Access to content must be based on the user's: 1. Department 2. Security level 3. Physical location - Users must be able to work on content offline - Users must be able to share content externally - Content classifications must be accessible from mobile devices - Content classifications must include a physical location - Content must be retained and protected based on its type - Litware must adhere to highly confidential regulatory standards that include: 1. The ability to restrict the copying of all content created internally and externally 2. Including accurate time zone reporting in audit trails - Users must be able to search for content and people across the entire organization. - Content classification metadata must adhere to naming conventions specified by the IT department. - Users must be able to access content quickly without having to review many pages of search results to find documents. - Security rules must be implemented so that user access can be revoked if a user shares confidential content with external users. Planned Changes Litware plans to implement the following changes: - Move all department content to Microsoft SharePoint Online - Move all user content to Microsoft OneDrive for Business - Restrict user access based on location and device Technical Requirements Litware identifies the following technical requirements: - All on-premises documents (approximately one million documents) must be migrated to the SharePoint document library of their respective department. - Each department must have its own term store group. Stakeholders must be notified when term sets are moved or deleted. - All the OneDrive content of a user must be retained for a minimum of 180 days after the user has left the organization. - All external users must be added explicitly to Office 365 groups to give the users access to SharePoint team sites. - Office 365 groups must be used as the primary membership service for Microsoft Yammer, Teams, and SharePoint. - A user named Admin1 must be allowed to consume apps in the App Catalog and to add additional app license. - Viewers must be prevented from printing documents that are stored in a modern site named Finance. - Users must be prevented from printing content accessed in OneDrive from iOS and Android devices. -Retention, protection, and security policies must be implemented for all content stored online.- All offices must use the Managed Metadata Service to classify documents uploaded to SharePoint. - The Azure Information Protection client must be deployed to all domain-joined computers. - Searches must show results only when the result set is complete. - OneDrive must be used to work with documents offline. - Solutions must use the principle of least privilege whenever possible.

**Answers:**

**A)** Enable Azure Information Protection policy labeling.

**B)** For each library, enable sensitivity labeling that uses protection.

**C)** From Settings in the SharePoint admin center, enable Information Rights Management (IRM) for SharePoint Online.

**D)** Enable an Information Rights Management (IRM) policy for the libraries.

**Solution:** D

**Explanation:**

Explanation: References: https://support.office.com/en-us/article/apply-information-rights-management-to-a-list-or-library-3bdb5c4e- 94fc-4741-b02f-4e7cc3c54aa1

**Question: 4** *One Answer Is Right*

You need to grant an external user guest access to the SharePoint site of the design department. What should you do?

**Scenario:**

TESTLET-1. Overview Litware, Inc. is a design and manufacturing company that has 4,500 users. The company has sales, marketing, design, research, field test, and human resources (HR) departments. Litware has a main office in California, three branch offices in the United States, and five branch offices in Europe. Existing Environment On-premises Infrastructure The network contains an Active Directory forest named litwareinc.com that contains a child domain for each region. All domain controllers run Windows Server 2012. The main office syncs identities to Microsoft Azure Active Directory (Azure AD) by using Azure AD Connect. All user accounts are created in the on-premises Active Directory and sync to Azure AD. Each office contains the following servers and client computers: - A domain controller that runs Windows Server 2012 - A file server that runs Windows Server 2012 - Client computers that run Windows 10 Currently, all content created by users is stored locally on file servers. Cloud Infrastructure Litware is moving the content from the file servers to Microsoft Office 365. The company purchases 4,500 Microsoft 365 E5 licenses. Litware uses Microsoft Exchange Online for email. Problem Statements Litware identifies the following issues:- Finding content and people within the organization is difficult. - Users cannot access company data from outside the corporate network. - Content recovery is slow because all the content is still on-premises. - Data security is compromised because users can copy company content to USB drives. - The locally stored content is not classified as confidential and users can email documents to external people. - Users must frequently contact the HR department to find employees within the organization who have relevant skills. - Users can delete content indiscriminately and without resource as they have full control of the content of the file servers. Requirements Business Goals Litware identifies the following strategic initiatives to remain competitive: - All content must be stored centrally - Access to content must be based on the user's: 1. Department 2. Security level 3. Physical location - Users must be able to work on content offline - Users must be able to share content externally - Content classifications must be accessible from mobile devices - Content classifications must include a physical location - Content must be retained and protected based on its type - Litware must adhere to highly confidential regulatory standards that include: 1. The ability to restrict the copying of all content created internally and externally 2. Including accurate time zone reporting in audit trails - Users must be able to search for content and people across the entire organization. - Content classification metadata must adhere to naming conventions specified by the IT department. - Users must be able to access content quickly without having to review many pages of search results to find documents. - Security rules must be implemented so that user access can be revoked if a user shares confidential content with external users. Planned Changes Litware plans to implement the following changes: - Move all department content to Microsoft SharePoint Online - Move all user content to Microsoft OneDrive for Business - Restrict user access based on location and device Technical Requirements Litware identifies the following technical requirements: - All on-premises documents (approximately one million documents) must be migrated to the SharePoint document library of their respective department. - Each department must have its own term store group. Stakeholders must be notified when term sets are moved or deleted. - All the OneDrive content of a user must be retained for a minimum of 180 days after the user has left the organization. - All external users must be added explicitly to Office 365 groups to give the users access to SharePoint team sites. - Office 365 groups must be used as the primary membership service for Microsoft Yammer, Teams, and SharePoint. - A user named Admin1 must be allowed to consume apps in the App Catalog and to add additional app license. - Viewers must be prevented from printing documents that are stored in a modern site named Finance. - Users must be prevented from printing content accessed in OneDrive from iOS and Android devices. -Retention, protection, and security policies must be implemented for all content stored online.- All offices must use the Managed Metadata Service to classify documents uploaded to SharePoint. - The Azure Information Protection client must be deployed to all domain-joined computers. - Searches must show results only when the result set is complete. - OneDrive must be used to work with documents offline. - Solutions must use the principle of least privilege whenever possible.

**Answers:**

**A)** From the SharePoint team site, modify the Visitors group.

**B)** From the SharePoint team site, modify the Members group

**C)** From Microsoft Outlook, add a member to a group.

**Solution:** B

**Question: 5** *One Answer Is Right*

You need to minimize the number of documents returned during searches. The solution must meet the technical requirements. What should you configure?

**Scenario:**

TESTLET-1. Overview Litware, Inc. is a design and manufacturing company that has 4,500 users. The company has sales, marketing, design, research, field test, and human resources (HR)

departments. Litware has a main office in California, three branch offices in the United States, and five branch offices in Europe. Existing Environment On-premises Infrastructure The network contains an Active Directory forest named litwareinc.com that contains a child domain for each region. All domain controllers run Windows Server 2012. The main office syncs identities to Microsoft Azure Active Directory (Azure AD) by using Azure AD Connect. All user accounts are created in the on-premises Active Directory and sync to Azure AD. Each office contains the following servers and client computers: - A domain controller that runs Windows Server 2012 - A file server that runs Windows Server 2012 - Client computers that run Windows 10 Currently, all content created by users is stored locally on file servers. Cloud Infrastructure Litware is moving the content from the file servers to Microsoft Office 365. The company purchases 4,500 Microsoft 365 E5 licenses. Litware uses Microsoft Exchange Online for email. Problem Statements Litware identifies the following issues:- Finding content and people within the organization is difficult. - Users cannot access company data from outside the corporate network. - Content recovery is slow because all the content is still on-premises. - Data security is compromised because users can copy company content to USB drives. - The locally stored content is not classified as confidential and users can email documents to external people. - Users must frequently contact the HR department to find employees within the organization who have relevant skills. - Users can delete content indiscriminately and without resource as they have full control of the content of the file servers. Requirements Business Goals Litware identifies the following strategic initiatives to remain competitive: - All content must be stored centrally - Access to content must be based on the user's: 1. Department 2. Security level 3. Physical location - Users must be able to work on content offline - Users must be able to share content externally - Content classifications must be accessible from mobile devices - Content classifications must include a physical location - Content must be retained and protected based on its type - Litware must adhere to highly confidential regulatory standards that include: 1. The ability to restrict the copying of all content created internally and externally 2. Including accurate time zone reporting in audit trails - Users must be able to search for content and people across the entire organization. - Content classification metadata must adhere to naming conventions specified by the IT department. - Users must be able to access content quickly without having to review many pages of search results to find documents. - Security rules must be implemented so that user access can be revoked if a user shares confidential content with external users. Planned Changes Litware plans to implement the following changes: - Move all department content to Microsoft SharePoint Online - Move all user content to Microsoft OneDrive for Business - Restrict user access based on location and device Technical Requirements Litware identifies the following technical requirements: - All on-premises documents (approximately one million documents) must be migrated to the SharePoint document library of their respective department. - Each department must have its own term store group. Stakeholders must be notified when term sets are moved or deleted. - All the OneDrive content of a user must be retained for a minimum of 180 days after the user has left the organization. - All external users must be added explicitly to Office 365 groups to give the users access to SharePoint team sites. - Office 365 groups must be used as the primary membership service for Microsoft Yammer, Teams, and SharePoint. - A user named Admin1 must be allowed to consume apps in the App Catalog and to add additional app license. - Viewers must be prevented from printing documents that are stored in a modern site named Finance. - Users must be prevented from printing content accessed in OneDrive from iOS and Android devices. -Retention, protection, and security policies must be implemented for all content stored online.- All offices must use the Managed Metadata Service to classify documents uploaded to SharePoint. - The Azure Information Protection client must be deployed to all domain-joined computers. - Searches must show results only when the result set is complete. - OneDrive must be used to work with documents offline. - Solutions must use the principle of least privilege whenever possible.

**Answers:**

A) Add a result source and prevent partial search results from being returned.

B) Create a managed property for each document type.

C) Create a crawled property for each document type.

D) Add a query transform to restrict results to certain documents types.

**Solution: A**

**Explanation:**

Explanation: References: https://docs.microsoft.com/en-us/sharepoint/search/understanding-result-sources-for-search

**Question: 6** *Multiple Answers Are Right*

DRAG DROP You need to configure the term store group to meet the requirements. Which three actions should you perform in sequence? To answer, move the appropriate actions from the list of actions to the answer area and arrange them in the correct order. Select and Place:

**Actions**

- From the SharePoint admin center, create term groups.
- Select **Use this Term Set for Faceted Navigation**
- Set Submission Policy to **Open**
- Add Stakeholders
- Create a term set

**Answer Area**

## Scenario:

TESTLET-1. Overview Litware, Inc. is a design and manufacturing company that has 4,500 users. The company has sales, marketing, design, research, field test, and human resources (HR) departments. Litware has a main office in California, three branch offices in the United States, and five branch offices in Europe. Existing Environment On-premises Infrastructure The network contains an Active Directory forest named litwareinc.com that contains a child domain for each region. All domain controllers run Windows Server 2012. The main office syncs identities to Microsoft Azure Active Directory (Azure AD) by using Azure AD Connect. All user accounts are created in the on-premises Active Directory and sync to Azure AD. Each office contains the following servers and client computers: - A domain controller that runs Windows Server 2012 - A file server that runs Windows Server 2012 - Client computers that run Windows 10 Currently, all content created by users is stored locally on file servers. Cloud Infrastructure Litware is moving the content from the file servers to Microsoft Office 365. The company purchases 4,500 Microsoft 365 E5 licenses. Litware uses Microsoft Exchange Online for email. Problem Statements Litware identifies the following issues:- Finding content and people within the organization is difficult. - Users cannot access company data from outside the corporate network. - Content recovery is slow because all the content is still on-premises. - Data security is compromised because users can copy company content to USB drives. - The locally stored content is not classified as confidential and users can email documents to external people. - Users must frequently contact the HR department to find employees within the organization who have relevant skills. - Users can delete content indiscriminately and without resource as they have full control of the content of the file servers. Requirements Business Goals Litware identifies the following strategic initiatives to remain competitive: - All content must be stored centrally - Access to content must be based on the user's: 1. Department 2. Security level 3. Physical location - Users must be able to work on content offline - Users must be able to share content externally - Content classifications must be accessible from mobile devices - Content classifications must include a physical location - Content must be retained and protected based on its type - Litware must adhere to highly confidential regulatory standards that include: 1. The ability to restrict the copying of all content created internally and externally 2. Including accurate time zone reporting in audit trails - Users must be able to search for content and people across the entire organization. - Content classification metadata must adhere to naming conventions specified by the IT department. - Users must be able to access content quickly without having to review many pages of search results to find documents. - Security rules must be implemented so that user access can be revoked if a user shares confidential content with external users. Planned Changes Litware plans to implement the following changes: - Move all department content to Microsoft SharePoint Online - Move all user content to Microsoft OneDrive for Business - Restrict user access based on location and device Technical Requirements Litware identifies the following technical requirements: - All on-premises documents (approximately one million documents) must be migrated to the SharePoint document library of their respective department. - Each department must have its own term store group. Stakeholders must be notified when term sets are moved or deleted. - All the OneDrive content of a user must be retained for a minimum of 180 days after the user has left the organization. - All external users must be added explicitly to Office 365 groups to give the users access to SharePoint team sites. - Office 365 groups must be used as the primary membership service for Microsoft Yammer, Teams, and SharePoint. - A user named Admin1 must be allowed to consume apps in the App Catalog and to add additional app license. - Viewers must be prevented from printing documents that are stored in a modern site named Finance. - Users must be prevented from printing content accessed in OneDrive from iOS and Android devices. -Retention, protection, and security policies must be implemented for all content stored online.- All offices must use the Managed Metadata Service to classify documents uploaded to SharePoint. - The Azure Information Protection client must be deployed to all domain-joined computers. - Searches must show results only when the result set is complete. - OneDrive must be used to work with documents offline. - Solutions must use the principle of least privilege whenever possible.

**Answers:**

## A)

**Actions**

- Select **Use this Term Set for Faceted Navigation**
- Set Submission Policy to **Open**

**Answer Area**

- From the SharePoint admin center, create term groups.
- Create a term set
- Add Stakeholders

**Solution:** A

**Explanation:**

Explanation:

**Question: 7** *One Answer Is Right*

An administrator creates a new user named User5. Users report that they cannot find the User5 account. Thirty minutes later, the users report that User5 now appears. What was a possible cause of the delay?

**Scenario:**

TESTLET-1. Overview Litware, Inc. is a design and manufacturing company that has 4,500 users. The company has sales, marketing, design, research, field test, and human resources (HR) departments. Litware has a main office in California, three branch offices in the United States, and five branch offices in Europe. Existing Environment On-premises Infrastructure The network contains an Active Directory forest named litwareinc.com that contains a child domain for each region. All domain controllers run Windows Server 2012. The main office syncs identities to Microsoft Azure Active Directory (Azure AD) by using Azure AD Connect. All user accounts are created in the on-premises Active Directory and sync to Azure AD. Each office contains the following servers and client computers: - A domain controller that runs Windows Server 2012 - A file server that runs Windows Server 2012 - Client computers that run Windows 10 Currently, all content created by users is stored locally on file servers. Cloud Infrastructure Litware is moving the content from the file servers to Microsoft Office 365. The company purchases 4,500 Microsoft 365 E5 licenses. Litware uses Microsoft Exchange Online for email. Problem Statements Litware identifies the following issues:- Finding content and people within the organization is difficult. - Users cannot access company data from outside the corporate network. - Content recovery is slow because all the content is still on-premises. - Data security is compromised because users can copy company content to USB drives. - The locally stored content is not classified as confidential and users can email documents to external people. - Users must frequently contact the HR department to find employees within the organization who have relevant skills. - Users can delete content indiscriminately and without resource as they have full control of the content of the file servers. Requirements Business Goals Litware identifies the following strategic initiatives to remain competitive: - All content must be stored centrally - Access to content must be based on the user's: 1. Department 2. Security level 3. Physical location - Users must be able to work on content offline - Users must be able to share content externally - Content classifications must be accessible from mobile devices - Content classifications must include a physical location - Content must be retained and protected based on its type - Litware must adhere to highly confidential regulatory standards that include: 1. The ability to restrict the copying of all content created internally and externally 2. Including accurate time zone reporting in audit trails - Users must be able to search for content and people across the entire organization. - Content classification metadata must adhere to naming conventions specified by the IT department. - Users must be able to access content quickly without having to review many pages of search results to find documents. - Security rules must be implemented so that user access can be revoked if a user shares confidential content with external users. Planned Changes Litware plans to implement the following changes: - Move all department content to Microsoft SharePoint Online - Move all user content to Microsoft OneDrive for Business - Restrict user access based on location and device Technical Requirements Litware identifies the following technical requirements: - All on-premises documents (approximately one million documents) must be migrated to the SharePoint document library of their respective department. - Each department must have its own term store group. Stakeholders must be notified when term sets are moved or deleted. - All the OneDrive content of a user must be retained for a minimum of 180 days after the user has left the organization. - All external users must be added explicitly to Office 365 groups to give the users access to SharePoint team sites. - Office 365 groups must be used as the primary membership service for Microsoft Yammer, Teams, and SharePoint. - A user named Admin1 must be allowed to consume apps in the App Catalog and to add additional app license. - Viewers must be prevented from printing documents that are stored in a modern site named Finance. - Users must be prevented from printing content accessed in OneDrive from iOS and Android devices. -Retention, protection, and security policies must be implemented for all content stored online.- All offices must use the Managed Metadata Service to classify documents uploaded to SharePoint. - The Azure Information Protection client must be deployed to all domain-joined computers. - Searches must show results only when the result set is complete. - OneDrive must be used to work with documents offline. - Solutions must use the principle of least privilege whenever possible.

**Answers:**

**A)** the Azure AD Connect synchronization schedule

**B)** Global Catalog replication

**C)** the Status of the User Profile Synchronization Service

**D)** an Azure AD conditional access policy

**Solution:** A

**Explanation:**

Explanation: Configure and Manage SharePoint Online

**Question: 8** *Multiple Answers Are Right*

DRAG DROP You need to meet the site requirements for the marketing department managers. Which three actions should you perform in sequence? To answer, move the appropriate actions from the list of actions to the answer area and arrange them in the correct order. Select and Place:

**Actions**

- Select Sharing.
- Select the site collections.
- One the SharePoint admin center.
- Open the marketing department site collections.
- Configure the owners.
- Open Site Settings.

**Answer Area**

**Scenario:**

TESTLET-2. Overview Contoso, Ltd. is a pharmaceutical company that has 750 users. Contoso has departmental teams spread across offices in North America. The company has a main office in Seattle and four branch offices in New York, New Jersey, Boston, and Florida. Existing

Environment Active Directory Environment The network contains an on-premises Active Directory domain. All users are created in the domain and are organized in organizational units (OUs). All the users use their domain credentials to sign in to their computer. Microsoft Office 365 Environment Contoso has a Microsoft Office 365 subscription and uses the following services: - OneDrive for Business - SharePoint Online - Exchange Online - Yammer - Teams Currently, the identity of each user is maintained separately in both on-premises Active Directory and Office 365. Contoso implements SharePoint site collections for the following departments: - Research & development - Human resources (HR) - Marketing -Finance - IT Each department assigns a site owner to manage its site collection and to manage access. The site collection of each department contains multiple subsites. Sharing is allowed across different site collections by default. External sharing is enabled for the organization. Current Business Model Contoso has the following business model: - The HR department has a branded site collection - Currently, the default storage limit is set for all the site collections - The marketing department uses multiple site collections created by an administrator named Admin1. - Contoso has a strategic partnership with a company name Litware, Inc. Litware has an Office 365 subscription. All users at Litware have a user account in the litwareinc.com domain. Problem Statements Contoso identifies the following issues: - Non-site owners invite external users to access the content in SharePoint Online. - Users upload audio, video, and executable program files to OneDrive for Business. - The company manages two separate identities for each user, which creates more administrative work. - Users in the HR department report performance issues affecting their site collection. You suspect that the issues are due to large images on the home page. Technical Requirements Contoso has the following technical requirements for the Office 365 environment: - Add a Yammer feed to new communication sites. - Prevent non-site owners from inviting external users. - Troubleshoot the performance issues of the HR department site collection. - Implement a 100-GB storage limit for the site collection of the marketing department. - Prevent users from syncing media files, such as MP3 and MP4 files, from OneDrive. - Restrict users from sharing content from the finance department site collection to the Litware users. - Ensure that SharePoint administrators do not have administrative permissions to the site collections. - Ensure that the managers in the marketing department can view the storage metrics of the marketing department sites. - Maintain all user identities in on-premises Active Directory. Sync passwords to Microsoft Azure Active Directory (Azure AD). - Ensure that when users are deleted from Microsoft 365 their associated OneDrive content is retained for 90 days. After 90 days, the content must be deleted permanently.

**Answers:**

## A)

**Actions**

- Select **Sharing**.
- Select the site collections.
- One the SharePoint admin center.
- Open the marketing department site collections.
- Configure the owners.
- Open Site Settings.

**Answer Area**

- One the SharePoint admin center.
- Open the marketing department site collections.
- Configure the owners.

**Solution:** A

**Explanation:**

Explanation:

**Question: 9** *One Answer Is Right*

You need to recommend an identity model that meets the technical requirements. Which identity model should you recommend?

**Scenario:**

TESTLET-2. Overview Contoso, Ltd. is a pharmaceutical company that has 750 users. Contoso has departmental teams spread across offices in North America. The company has a main office in Seattle and four branch offices in New York, New Jersey, Boston, and Florida. Existing Environment Active Directory Environment The network contains an on-premises Active Directory domain. All users are created in the domain and are organized in organizational units (OUs). All the users use their domain credentials to sign in to their computer. Microsoft Office 365 Environment Contoso has a Microsoft Office 365 subscription and uses the following services: - OneDrive for Business - SharePoint Online - Exchange Online - Yammer - Teams Currently, the identity of each user is maintained separately in both on-premises Active Directory and Office 365. Contoso implements SharePoint site collections for the following departments: - Research & development - Human resources (HR) - Marketing -Finance - IT Each department assigns a site owner to manage its site collection and to manage access. The site collection of each department contains multiple subsites. Sharing is allowed across different site collections by default. External sharing is enabled for the organization. Current Business Model Contoso has the following business model: - The HR department has a branded site collection - Currently, the default storage limit is set for all the site collections - The marketing department uses multiple site collections created by an administrator named Admin1. - Contoso has a strategic partnership with a company name Litware, Inc. Litware has an Office 365 subscription. All users at Litware have a user account in the litwareinc.com domain. Problem Statements Contoso identifies the following issues: - Non-site owners invite external users to access the content in SharePoint Online. - Users upload audio, video, and executable program files to OneDrive for Business. - The company manages two separate identities for each user, which creates more administrative work. - Users in the HR department report performance issues affecting their site collection. You suspect that the issues are due to large images on the home page. Technical Requirements Contoso has the following technical requirements for the Office 365 environment: - Add a Yammer feed to new communication sites. - Prevent non-site owners from inviting external users. - Troubleshoot the performance issues of the HR department site collection. - Implement a 100-GB storage limit for the site collection of the marketing department. - Prevent users from syncing media files, such as MP3 and MP4 files, from OneDrive. - Restrict users from sharing content from the finance department site collection to the Litware users. - Ensure that SharePoint administrators do not have administrative permissions to the site collections. - Ensure that the managers in the marketing department can view the storage metrics of the marketing department sites. - Maintain all user identities in on-premises Active Directory. Sync passwords to Microsoft Azure Active Directory (Azure AD). - Ensure that when users are deleted from Microsoft 365 their associated OneDrive content is retained for 90 days. After 90 days, the content must be deleted permanently.

**Answers:**

**A)** Cloud Identity

**B)** Synchronized Identity

**C)** Federated Identity

**Solution:** B

**Question: 10** *Multiple Answers Are Right*

DRAG DROP You need to meet the technical requirements for the managers of the marketing department. Which three actions should you perform in sequence? To answer, move the appropriate actions from the list of actions to the answer area and arrange them in the correct order. Select and Place:

**Actions**

- Select **Sharing**
- Open Site Settings
- Navigate to the marketing department site collections
- Configure the owners
- Select the marketing department site collections
- Open the SharePoint admin center

**Answer Area**

**Scenario:**

TESTLET-2. Overview Contoso, Ltd. is a pharmaceutical company that has 750 users. Contoso has departmental teams spread across offices in North America. The company has a main office in Seattle and four branch offices in New York, New Jersey, Boston, and Florida. Existing Environment Active Directory Environment The network contains an on-premises Active Directory domain. All users are created in the domain and are organized in organizational units (OUs). All the users use their domain credentials to sign in to their computer. Microsoft Office 365 Environment Contoso has a Microsoft Office 365 subscription and uses the following services: - OneDrive for Business - SharePoint Online - Exchange Online - Yammer - Teams Currently, the identity of each user is maintained separately in both on-premises Active Directory and Office 365. Contoso implements SharePoint site collections for the following departments: - Research & development - Human resources (HR) - Marketing -Finance - IT Each department assigns a site owner to manage its site collection and to manage access. The site collection of each department contains multiple subsites. Sharing is allowed across different site collections by default. External sharing is enabled for the organization. Current Business Model Contoso has the following business model: - The HR department has a branded site collection - Currently, the default storage limit is set for all the site collections - The marketing department uses multiple site collections created by an administrator named Admin1. - Contoso has a strategic partnership with a company name Litware, Inc. Litware has an Office 365 subscription. All users at Litware have a user account in the litwareinc.com domain. Problem Statements Contoso identifies the following issues: - Non-site owners invite external users to access the content in SharePoint Online. - Users upload audio, video, and executable program files to OneDrive for Business. - The company manages two separate identities for each user, which creates more administrative work. - Users in the HR department report performance issues affecting their site collection. You suspect that the issues are due to large images on the home page. Technical Requirements Contoso has the following technical requirements for the Office 365 environment: - Add a Yammer feed to new communication sites. - Prevent non-site owners from inviting external users. - Troubleshoot the performance issues of the HR department site collection. - Implement a 100-GB storage limit for the site collection of the marketing department. - Prevent users from syncing media files, such as MP3 and MP4 files, from OneDrive. - Restrict users from sharing content from the finance department site collection to the Litware users. - Ensure that SharePoint administrators do not have administrative permissions to the site collections. - Ensure that the managers in the marketing department can view the storage metrics of the marketing department sites. - Maintain all user identities in on-premises Active Directory. Sync passwords to Microsoft Azure Active Directory (Azure AD). - Ensure that when users are deleted from Microsoft 365 their associated OneDrive content is retained for 90 days. After 90 days, the content must be deleted permanently.

Answers:

A)

| Actions | Answer Area |
|---|---|
| Select **Sharing** | Open the SharePoint admin center |
| Open Site Settings | Navigate to the marketing department site collections |
| | Configure the owners |
| Select the marketing department site collections | |

Solution: A

Explanation:

Explanation: Scenario: Ensure that the managers in the marketing department can view the storage metrics of the marketing department sites.

# Chapter 40: MS-301 - Deploying SharePoint Server Hybrid

## Exam Guide

Deploying SharePoint Server Hybrid MS-301 Exam:

Deploying SharePoint Server Hybrid MS-301 Exam which is related to Microsoft 365 Certified Teamwork Administrator Associate Certification. This exam validates the Candidates ability to configure and manage SharePoint online, manage OneDrive for business, configure and manage teams, Integrate M365 Workloads. This exam also tests the working knowledge of the Candidate to configure, deploy, and manage Office 365 and Azure workloads that focus on efficient and effective collaboration and adoption. Microsoft Teamwork Administrator usually holds or pursue this certification and you can expect the same job roles after completion of this certification.

MS-301 Exam topics:

Candidates must know the exam topics before they start of preparation. Because it will really help them in hitting the core. Our **MS-301 dumps** will include the following topics:

- Configure and manage SharePoint on-premises 55-60%
- Configure and manage hybrid scenarios 30-35%
- Migrate to SharePoint Online 5-10%

Certification Path:

The Deploying SharePoint Server Hybrid Certification includes only one MS-301 exam.

Who should take the MS-301 exam:

The Microsoft Deploying SharePoint Server Hybrid MS-301 Exam certification is an internationally recognized validation that identifies persons who earn it as possessing skilled as a Microsoft 365 Certified Teamwork Administrator Associate. If candidates want significant improvement in career growth needs enhanced knowledge, skills, and talents. The Microsoft Deploying SharePoint Server Hybrid MS-301 Exam certification provides proof of this advanced knowledge and skill. If a candidate has knowledge of associated technologies and skills that are required to pass Microsoft Deploying SharePoint Server Hybrid MS-301 Exam then he should take this exam.

How to study the MS-301 Exam:

Certification-questions.com expert team recommends you to prepare some notes on these topics along with it don't forget to practice Microsoft MS-301 Exam dumps which been written by our expert team, Both these will help you a lot to clear this exam with good marks.

How much MS-301 Exam Cost:

The price of the MS-301 exam is $165 USD.

How to book the MS-301 Exam:

These are following steps for registering the MS-301 exam.
Step 1: Visit to Microsoft Exam Registration
Step 2: Signup/Login to MICROSOFT account
Step 3: Search for MICROSOFT MS-301 Certifications Exam
Step 4: Select Date and Center of examination and confirm with payment value of $165

What is the duration of the MS-301 Exam:

- Format: Multiple choices, multiple answers
- Length of Examination: 150 minutes
- Number of Questions: 45-60
- Passing Score: 700/1000

The benefit in Obtaining the MS-301 Exam Certification:

- After completion of Microsoft 365 Certified Teamwork Administrator Associate Certification candidates receive official confirmation from Microsoft that you are now fully certified in their chosen field. This can be now added to their CV, cover letters and job applications.
- When Candidates applying for a job or looking to promotion in their current position, a Microsoft 365 Certified Teamwork Administrator Associate certification in the field in which Candidates are applying will put you at the top of the list and make them a desirable candidate for employers.
- Candidates will get in-depth knowledge by completing the courses along with the access to revision materials for 6 months upon completion means they will have a wider skill set when it comes to the various technologies and systems than an uncertified professional. Certified Professional in this particular skill set is 74% more efficient when it comes to completing their tasks in a timely well-executed manner.

- Organization owners invest a lot in their employees when it comes to their training with the goal of making them quicker, more efficient, and more knowledgeable about their role. Certified Professional will reduce the time he spends on tasks, meaning he can get more done this could help reduce company downtime when repairing faults on a system or fixing hardware problems.
- Becoming Microsoft 365 Certified Teamwork Administrator Associate means one thing you are worth more to the company and therefore more to yourself in the form of an upgraded pay package. On average a Microsoft 365 Certified Teamwork Administrator Associate member of staff is estimated to be worth 30% more to a company than their uncertified professionals.

Difficulty in writing MS-301 Exam:

There are many problems for the candidates cannot facilitate from the exams preparation and most of the candidates do not know how to prepare their exams and get good marks in their exams. There are a lot of candidates have failed their exams by lack of practice, lack of tension, lack of concentrate and lack of no time. Many candidates want to give a short time to study and get good marks in exams, therefore Certification-questions have a number of ways to prepare and practice for exams in short time through which the candidates will feel relax, a cool mind and ready for exams without any tension. Certification-questions is very much aware of the worth of your time and money that's why Certification-questions give you the most outstanding **Microsoft MS-301 dumps** having all the questions and answers outlined and verified by the Microsoft Professionals. We deliver all those practice questions which will come in the real exam so the candidate can easily get more than 90% marks at first attempt.

For more info visit::

Microsoft MS-301 Exam Reference

# Sample Practice Test for MS-301

**Question: 1** *One Answer Is Right*

Which feature should you activate for the sales department?

**Scenario:**

TESTLET-1. Overview Litware, Inc. is an international manufacturing company that has 3,000 users. The company has sales, marketing, research, IT, and human resources (HR) departments. Litware has two main offices located in New York and London. The company has five branch offices located in Asia. Existing Environment Active Directory The network contains an Active Directory forest named litwareinc.com. The forest contains a single domain. All domain controllers run Windows Server 2016. SharePoint Server Environment Litware has a SharePoint Server 2019 farm that contains the servers shown in the following table.

| Name | Configuration |
|---|---|
| SPWEB1 | Front-end server |
| SPWEB2 | Front-end server |
| SPCACHE1 | Distributed cache server |
| SPAPP1 | Application server |
| SPSEARCH1 | Search server |
| SPSEARCH2 | Search server |
| SQLSVR1 | Microsoft SQL Server |
| SQLSVR2 | Microsoft SQL Server |

Central Administration has a URL of http://spweb1.litwareinc.com. The HR department currently uses a SharePoint web application that uses only forms authentication. The sales department has a SharePoint site that is available anonymously to display product information. Line-of-Business Application You have a line-of-business application named LOBApp. LOBApp stores content in a SQL Server database named LOBAppDB. LOBApp has a service account named LobAppSA. Problem Statements Litware identifies the following issues: - None of the SharePoint sites use TLS. - The Distributed Cache service uses the farm account. - When users perform searches from the SharePoint site of the HR department, they receive no results. - You discover that the user names and passwords configured for managed services were transmitted on the network in plain text. Requirements Business Goals All the components in the SharePoint Server farm must be highly available by using the least number of servers possible. Each document stored in the HR department site must have the following pieces of metadata: CONID, CONNO, CONDate, and CONApproved. Security The farm uses the managed service accounts shown in the following table.

| Account name | Description |
|---|---|
| Spfarm | Farm account |
| SpContent | SharePoint content database account |
| SpServices | SharePoint service account |
| SpSecureStore | SharePoint Secure Store Service account |
| SpBI | SharePoint Business Intelligence |
| LOBAppSA | Content access account for LOBApp |

Technical Requirements Litware identifies the following technical requirements: - LOBApp content must be visible in search results. - The principle of least privilege must be used whenever possible. - All SharePoint service applications must use the SpServices account. - Information for each product must be displayed as a separate webpage for the sales department. - Search crawling must start every 10 minutes, regardless of whether the prior session is complete. - The Cloud Search Service Application must crawl on-premises content in a cloud hybrid search solution. - The Secure Store Service application must use LitwareAppID as the target application to access LOBAppDB.

Answers:

**A)** SharePoint Server Standard Site Collection features

**B)** Site Policy feature

**C)** SharePoint Server Enterprise Site Collection features

**D)** SharePoint Server Publishing Infrastructure

**Solution:** D

**Question: 2** *Multiple Answers Are Right*

HOTSPOT You need to configure the crawl settings to meet the technical requirements. How should you complete the PowerShell script? To answer, select the appropriate options in the answer area. NOTE: Each correct selection is worth one point. Hot Area:

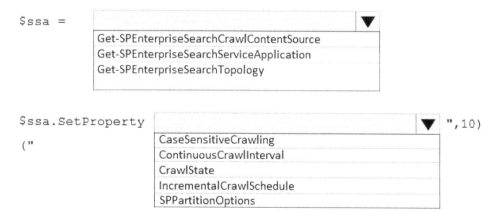

Scenario:

TESTLET-1. Overview Litware, Inc. is an international manufacturing company that has 3,000 users. The company has sales, marketing, research, IT, and human resources (HR) departments. Litware has two main offices located in New York and London. The company has five branch offices located in Asia. Existing Environment Active Directory The network contains an Active Directory forest named litwareinc.com. The forest contains a single domain. All domain controllers run Windows Server 2016. SharePoint Server Environment Litware has a SharePoint Server 2019 farm that contains the servers shown in the following table.

| Name | Configuration |
|---|---|
| SPWEB1 | Front-end server |
| SPWEB2 | Front-end server |
| SPCACHE1 | Distributed cache server |
| SPAPP1 | Application server |
| SPSEARCH1 | Search server |
| SPSEARCH2 | Search server |
| SQLSVR1 | Microsoft SQL Server |
| SQLSVR2 | Microsoft SQL Server |

Central Administration has a URL of http://spweb1.litwareinc.com. The HR department currently uses a SharePoint web application that uses only forms authentication. The sales department has a SharePoint site that is available anonymously to display product information. Line-of-Business Application You have a line-of-business application named LOBApp. LOBApp stores content in a SQL Server database named LOBAppDB. LOBApp has a service account named LobAppSA. Problem Statements Litware identifies the following issues: - None of the SharePoint sites use TLS. - The Distributed Cache service uses the farm account. - When users perform searches from the SharePoint site of the HR department, they receive no results. - You discover that the user names and passwords configured for managed services were transmitted on the network in plain text. Requirements Business Goals All the components in the SharePoint Server farm must be highly available by using the least number of servers possible. Each document stored in the HR department site must have the following pieces of metadata: CONID, CONNO, CONDate, and CONApproved. Security The farm uses the managed service accounts shown in the following table.

| Account name | Description |
|---|---|
| Spfarm | Farm account |
| SpContent | SharePoint content database account |
| SpServices | SharePoint service account |
| SpSecureStore | SharePoint Secure Store Service account |
| SpBI | SharePoint Business Intelligence |
| LOBAppSA | Content access account for LOBApp |

Technical Requirements Litware identifies the following technical requirements: - LOBApp content must be visible in search results. - The principle of least privilege must be used whenever possible. - All SharePoint service applications must use the SpServices account. - Information for each product must be displayed as a separate webpage for the sales department. - Search crawling must start every 10 minutes, regardless of whether the prior session is complete. - The Cloud Search Service Application must crawl on-premises content in a cloud hybrid search solution. - The Secure Store Service application must use LitwareAppID as the target application to access LOBAppDB.

**Answers:**

A)

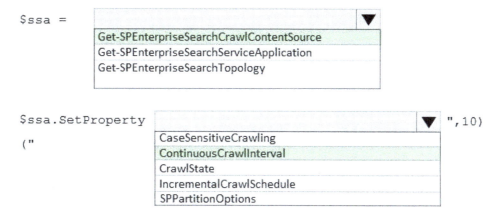

**Solution:** A

**Explanation:**

Explanation:

**Question: 3** *Multiple Answers Are Right*

DRAG DROP You need to meet the technical requirements for searching the LOBApp content. Which three actions should you perform in sequence? To answer, move the appropriate actions from the list of actions to the answer area and arrange them in the correct order. Select and Place:

**Actions**

- Create an external content source
- Create an external content type
- Create a content type hub
- Create a document set
- Configure permissions for the search crawl account

**Answer Area**

---

**Scenario:**

TESTLET-1. Overview Litware, Inc. is an international manufacturing company that has 3,000 users. The company has sales, marketing, research, IT, and human resources (HR) departments. Litware has two main offices located in New York and London. The company has five branch offices located in Asia. Existing Environment Active Directory The network contains an Active Directory forest named litwareinc.com. The forest contains a single domain. All domain controllers run Windows Server 2016. SharePoint Server Environment Litware has a SharePoint Server 2019 farm that contains the servers shown in the following table.

| Name | Configuration |
|---|---|
| SPWEB1 | Front-end server |
| SPWEB2 | Front-end server |
| SPCACHE1 | Distributed cache server |
| SPAPP1 | Application server |
| SPSEARCH1 | Search server |
| SPSEARCH2 | Search server |
| SQLSVR1 | Microsoft SQL Server |
| SQLSVR2 | Microsoft SQL Server |

Central Administration has a URL of http://spweb1.litwareinc.com. The HR department currently uses a SharePoint web application that uses only forms authentication. The sales department has a SharePoint site that is available anonymously to display product information. Line-of-Business Application You have a line-of-business application named LOBApp. LOBApp stores content in a SQL Server database named LOBAppDB. LOBApp has a service account named LobAppSA. Problem Statements Litware identifies the following issues: - None of the

SharePoint sites use TLS. - The Distributed Cache service uses the farm account. - When users perform searches from the SharePoint site of the HR department, they receive no results. - You discover that the user names and passwords configured for managed services were transmitted on the network in plain text. Requirements Business Goals All the components in the SharePoint Server farm must be highly available by using the least number of servers possible. Each document stored in the HR department site must have the following pieces of metadata: CONID, CONNO, CONDate, and CONApproved. Security The farm uses the managed service accounts shown in the following table.

| Account name | Description |
|---|---|
| Spfarm | Farm account |
| SpContent | SharePoint content database account |
| SpServices | SharePoint service account |
| SpSecureStore | SharePoint Secure Store Service account |
| SpBI | SharePoint Business Intelligence |
| LOBAppSA | Content access account for LOBApp |

Technical Requirements Litware identifies the following technical requirements: - LOBApp content must be visible in search results. - The principle of least privilege must be used whenever possible. - All SharePoint service applications must use the SpServices account. - Information for each product must be displayed as a separate webpage for the sales department. - Search crawling must start every 10 minutes, regardless of whether the prior session is complete. - The Cloud Search Service Application must crawl on-premises content in a cloud hybrid search solution. - The Secure Store Service application must use LitwareAppID as the target application to access LOBAppDB.

**Answers:**

A)

| Actions | Answer Area |
|---|---|
| Create an external content source | Create an external content type |
| Create an external content type | Configure permissions for the search crawl account |
| Create a content type hub | Create an external content source |
| Create a document set | |
| Configure permissions for the search crawl account | |

**Solution:** A

**Explanation:**

Explanation: References: http://prairiedeveloper.com/2016/04/setup-sharepoint-search-crawl-bcs/

**Question: 4** *One Answer Is Right*

You need to recommend changes to the existing environment to support the minimum high-availability SharePoint Server farm. The solution must minimize costs. Which three changes should you recommend? Each correct answer presents part of the solution. NOTE: Each correct selection is worth one point.

**Scenario:**

TESTLET-1. Overview Litware, Inc. is an international manufacturing company that has 3,000 users. The company has sales, marketing, research, IT, and human resources (HR) departments. Litware has two main offices located in New York and London. The company has five branch offices located in Asia. Existing Environment Active Directory The network contains an Active Directory forest named litwareinc.com. The forest contains a single domain. All domain controllers run Windows Server 2016. SharePoint Server Environment Litware has a SharePoint Server 2019 farm that contains the servers shown in the following table.

| Name | Configuration |
|---|---|
| SPWEB1 | Front-end server |
| SPWEB2 | Front-end server |
| SPCACHE1 | Distributed cache server |
| SPAPP1 | Application server |
| SPSEARCH1 | Search server |
| SPSEARCH2 | Search server |
| SQLSVR1 | Microsoft SQL Server |
| SQLSVR2 | Microsoft SQL Server |

Central Administration has a URL of http://spweb1.litwareinc.com. The HR department currently uses a SharePoint web application that uses only forms authentication. The sales department has a SharePoint site that is available anonymously to display product information. Line-of-Business Application You have a line-of-business application named LOBApp. LOBApp stores content in a SQL Server database named LOBAppDB. LOBApp has a service account named LobAppSA. Problem Statements Litware identifies the following issues: - None of the SharePoint sites use TLS. - The Distributed Cache service uses the farm account. - When users perform searches from the SharePoint site of the HR department, they receive no results. - You discover that the user names and passwords configured for managed services were transmitted on the network in plain text. Requirements Business Goals All the components in the SharePoint Server farm must be highly available by using the least number of servers possible. Each document stored in the HR department site must have the following pieces of metadata: CONID, CONNO, CONDate, and CONApproved. Security The farm uses the managed service accounts shown in the following table.

| Account name | Description |
|---|---|
| Spfarm | Farm account |
| SpContent | SharePoint content database account |
| SpServices | SharePoint service account |
| SpSecureStore | SharePoint Secure Store Service account |
| SpBI | SharePoint Business Intelligence |
| LOBAppSA | Content access account for LOBApp |

Technical Requirements Litware identifies the following technical requirements: - LOBApp content must be visible in search results. - The principle of least privilege must be used whenever possible. - All SharePoint service applications must use the SpServices account. - Information for each product must be displayed as a separate webpage for the sales department. - Search crawling must start every 10 minutes, regardless of whether the prior session is complete. - The Cloud Search Service Application must crawl on-premises content in a cloud hybrid search solution. - The Secure Store Service application must use LitwareAppID as the target application to access LOBAppDB.

**Answers:**

**A)** Change the role of SPWEB1 and SPWEB2 to Front-end with Distributed Cache.

**B)** Change the role of SPSEARCH1 and SPSEARCH2 to Application with Search.

**C)** Remove SPCACHE1 and SPAPP1 from the farm.

**D)** Change the role of SPCACHE1 to Single-Server Farm.

**E)** Change the role of SPAPP1 to Single-Server Farm.

**F)** Remove SPWEB1 and SPSEARCH1 from the farm.

**Solution:** A, B, C

**Question: 5** *One Answer Is Right*

You need to resolve the issues related to passwords being transmitted over the network in plain text. What should you do?

**Scenario:**

TESTLET-1. Overview Litware, Inc. is an international manufacturing company that has 3,000 users. The company has sales, marketing, research, IT, and human resources (HR) departments. Litware has two main offices located in New York and London. The company has five branch offices located in Asia. Existing Environment Active Directory The network contains an Active Directory forest named litwareinc.com. The forest contains a single domain. All domain controllers run Windows Server 2016. SharePoint Server Environment Litware has a SharePoint Server 2019 farm that contains the servers shown in the following table.

| Name | Configuration |
|---|---|
| SPWEB1 | Front-end server |
| SPWEB2 | Front-end server |
| SPCACHE1 | Distributed cache server |
| SPAPP1 | Application server |
| SPSEARCH1 | Search server |
| SPSEARCH2 | Search server |
| SQLSVR1 | Microsoft SQL Server |
| SQLSVR2 | Microsoft SQL Server |

Central Administration has a URL of http://spweb1.litwareinc.com. The HR department currently uses a SharePoint web application that uses only forms authentication. The sales department has a SharePoint site that is available anonymously to display product information. Line-of-Business Application You have a line-of-business application named LOBApp. LOBApp stores content in a SQL Server database named LOBAppDB. LOBApp has a service account named LobAppSA. Problem Statements Litware identifies the following issues: - None of the SharePoint sites use TLS. - The Distributed Cache service uses the farm account. - When users perform searches from the SharePoint site of the HR department, they receive no results. - You discover that the user names and passwords configured for managed services were transmitted on the network in plain text. Requirements Business Goals All the components in the SharePoint Server farm must be highly available by using the least number of servers possible. Each document stored in the HR department site must have the following pieces of metadata: CONID, CONNO, CONDate, and CONApproved. Security The farm uses the managed service accounts shown in the following table.

| Account name | Description |
|---|---|
| Spfarm | Farm account |
| SpContent | SharePoint content database account |
| SpServices | SharePoint service account |
| SpSecureStore | SharePoint Secure Store Service account |
| SpBI | SharePoint Business Intelligence |
| LOBAppSA | Content access account for LOBApp |

Technical Requirements Litware identifies the following technical requirements: - LOBApp content must be visible in search results. - The principle of least privilege must be used whenever possible. - All SharePoint service applications must use the SpServices account. - Information for each product must be displayed as a separate webpage for the sales department. - Search crawling must start every 10 minutes, regardless of whether the prior session is complete. - The Cloud Search Service Application must crawl on-premises content in a cloud hybrid search solution. - The Secure Store Service application must use LitwareAppID as the target application to access LOBAppDB.

Answers:

A) Configure the SQL servers to use TLS.

B) Configure Central Administration to use forms authentication.

C) On SPWEB1, configure a firewall rule that allows outbound traffic on TCP port 443.

D) Configure Central Administration to use Secure Sockets Layer (SSL).

Solution: A

Question: 6 *One Answer Is Right*

You need to implement the business goals for the HR department. What should you do?

**Scenario:**

TESTLET-1. Overview Litware, Inc. is an international manufacturing company that has 3,000 users. The company has sales, marketing, research, IT, and human resources (HR) departments. Litware has two main offices located in New York and London. The company has five branch offices located in Asia. Existing Environment Active Directory The network contains an Active Directory forest named litwareinc.com. The forest contains a single domain. All domain controllers run Windows Server 2016. SharePoint Server Environment Litware has a SharePoint Server 2019 farm that contains the servers shown in the following table.

| Name | Configuration |
|---|---|
| SPWEB1 | Front-end server |
| SPWEB2 | Front-end server |
| SPCACHE1 | Distributed cache server |
| SPAPP1 | Application server |
| SPSEARCH1 | Search server |
| SPSEARCH2 | Search server |
| SQLSVR1 | Microsoft SQL Server |
| SQLSVR2 | Microsoft SQL Server |

Central Administration has a URL of http://spweb1.litwareinc.com. The HR department currently uses a SharePoint web application that uses only forms authentication. The sales department has a SharePoint site that is available anonymously to display product information. Line-of-Business Application You have a line-of-business application named LOBApp. LOBApp stores content in a SQL Server database named LOBAppDB. LOBApp has a service account named LobAppSA. Problem Statements Litware identifies the following issues: - None of the SharePoint sites use TLS. - The Distributed Cache service uses the farm account. - When users perform searches from the SharePoint site of the HR department, they receive no results. - You discover that the user names and passwords configured for managed services were transmitted on the network in plain text. Requirements Business Goals All the components in the SharePoint Server farm must be highly available by using the least number of servers possible. Each document stored in the HR department site must have the following pieces of metadata: CONID, CONNO, CONDate, and CONApproved. Security The farm uses the managed service accounts shown in the following table.

| Account name | Description |
|---|---|
| Spfarm | Farm account |
| SpContent | SharePoint content database account |
| SpServices | SharePoint service account |
| SpSecureStore | SharePoint Secure Store Service account |
| SpBI | SharePoint Business Intelligence |
| LOBAppSA | Content access account for LOBApp |

Technical Requirements Litware identifies the following technical requirements: - LOBApp content must be visible in search results. - The principle of least privilege must be used whenever possible. - All SharePoint service applications must use the SpServices account. - Information for each product must be displayed as a separate webpage for the sales department. - Search crawling must start every 10 minutes, regardless of whether the prior session is complete. - The Cloud Search Service Application must crawl on-premises content in a cloud hybrid search solution. - The Secure Store Service application must use LitwareAppID as the target application to access LOBAppDB.

**Answers:**

**A)** Create a content type that contains site columns. Add the content type to the document libraries.

**B)** Add site columns to a document library. Save the document library as a template.

**C)** Enable enterprise metadata and keywords for the document libraries.

**D)** Activate Content Type Syndication Hub. Update the Column default value settings for the document libraries.

**Solution:** C

**Question: 7** *Multiple Answers Are Right*

DRAG DROP You need to resolve the issue for the Distributed Cache service. How should you complete the command? To answer, select the appropriate options in the answer area. NOTE: Each correct selection is worth one point. Select and Place:

| Values | Answer Area |
|---|---|
| ADUser | $farm = Get-SPfarm |
| AppFabricCachingService | $cacheService = $farm.Services \| where {$_.Name -eq" [Value] "} |
| LocalService | $accnt = Get- [Value] -Identity Litwareinc\SpServices |
| NetworkService | $cacheService.ProcessIdentity.CurrentIdentityType = " [Value] " |
| SpecificUser | $cacheService.ProcessIdentity.ManagedAccount = $accnt |
| SPManagedAccount | $cacheService.ProcessIdentity.Update() |
| SPUser | $cacheService.ProcessIdentity.Deploy() |

**Scenario:**

TESTLET-1. Overview Litware, Inc. is an international manufacturing company that has 3,000 users. The company has sales, marketing, research, IT, and human resources (HR) departments. Litware has two main offices located in New York and London. The company has five branch offices located in Asia. Existing Environment Active Directory The network contains an Active Directory forest named litwareinc.com. The forest contains a single domain. All domain controllers run Windows Server 2016. SharePoint Server Environment Litware has a SharePoint Server 2019 farm that contains the servers shown in the following table.

| Name | Configuration |
|---|---|
| SPWEB1 | Front-end server |
| SPWEB2 | Front-end server |
| SPCACHE1 | Distributed cache server |
| SPAPP1 | Application server |
| SPSEARCH1 | Search server |
| SPSEARCH2 | Search server |
| SQLSVR1 | Microsoft SQL Server |
| SQLSVR2 | Microsoft SQL Server |

Central Administration has a URL of http://spweb1.litwareinc.com. The HR department currently uses a SharePoint web application that uses only forms authentication. The sales department has a SharePoint site that is available anonymously to display product information. Line-of-Business Application You have a line-of-business application named LOBApp. LOBApp stores content in a SQL Server database named LOBAppDB. LOBApp has a service account named LobAppSA. Problem Statements Litware identifies the following issues: - None of the SharePoint sites use TLS. - The Distributed Cache service uses the farm account. - When users perform searches from the SharePoint site of the HR department, they receive no results. - You discover that the user names and passwords configured for managed services were transmitted on the network in plain text. Requirements Business Goals All the components in the SharePoint Server farm must be highly available by using the least number of servers possible. Each document stored in the HR department site must have the following pieces of metadata: CONID, CONNO, CONDate, and CONApproved. Security The farm uses the managed service accounts shown in the following table.

| Account name | Description |
|---|---|
| Spfarm | Farm account |
| SpContent | SharePoint content database account |
| SpServices | SharePoint service account |
| SpSecureStore | SharePoint Secure Store Service account |
| SpBI | SharePoint Business Intelligence |
| LOBAppSA | Content access account for LOBApp |

Technical Requirements Litware identifies the following technical requirements: - LOBApp content must be visible in search results. - The principle of least privilege must be used whenever possible. - All SharePoint service applications must use the SpServices account. - Information for each product must be displayed as a separate webpage for the sales department. - Search crawling must start every 10 minutes, regardless of whether the prior session is complete. - The Cloud Search Service Application must crawl on-premises content in a cloud hybrid search solution. - The Secure Store Service application must use LitwareAppID as the target application to access LOBAppDB.

**Answers:**

**A)**

**Solution:** A

**Explanation:**

Explanation: References: https://docs.microsoft.com/en-us/sharepoint/administration/manage-the-distributed-cache-service#change-the-service-account

**Question: 8** *One Answer Is Right*

You need to resolve the search issues for the HR department site. What should you do?

**Scenario:**

TESTLET-1. Overview Litware, Inc. is an international manufacturing company that has 3,000 users. The company has sales, marketing, research, IT, and human resources (HR) departments. Litware has two main offices located in New York and London. The company has five branch offices located in Asia. Existing Environment Active Directory The network contains an Active Directory forest named litwareinc.com. The forest contains a single domain. All domain controllers run Windows Server 2016. SharePoint Server Environment Litware has a SharePoint Server 2019 farm that contains the servers shown in the following table.

| Name | Configuration |
| --- | --- |
| SPWEB1 | Front-end server |
| SPWEB2 | Front-end server |
| SPCACHE1 | Distributed cache server |
| SPAPP1 | Application server |
| SPSEARCH1 | Search server |
| SPSEARCH2 | Search server |
| SQLSVR1 | Microsoft SQL Server |
| SQLSVR2 | Microsoft SQL Server |

Central Administration has a URL of http://spweb1.litwareinc.com. The HR department currently uses a SharePoint web application that uses only forms authentication. The sales department has a SharePoint site that is available anonymously to display product information. Line-of-Business Application You have a line-of-business application named LOBApp. LOBApp stores content in a SQL Server database named LOBAppDB. LOBApp has a service account named LobAppSA. Problem Statements Litware identifies the following issues: - None of the SharePoint sites use TLS. - The Distributed Cache service uses the farm account. - When users perform searches from the SharePoint site of the HR department, they receive no results. - You discover that the user names and passwords configured for managed services were transmitted on the network in plain text. Requirements Business Goals All the components in the SharePoint Server farm must be highly available by using the least number of servers possible. Each document stored in the HR department site must have the following pieces of metadata: CONID, CONNO, CONDate, and CONApproved. Security The farm uses the managed service accounts shown in the following table.

| Account name | Description |
|---|---|
| Spfarm | Farm account |
| SpContent | SharePoint content database account |
| SpServices | SharePoint service account |
| SpSecureStore | SharePoint Secure Store Service account |
| SpBI | SharePoint Business Intelligence |
| LOBAppSA | Content access account for LOBApp |

Technical Requirements Litware identifies the following technical requirements: - LOBApp content must be visible in search results. - The principle of least privilege must be used whenever possible. - All SharePoint service applications must use the SpServices account. - Information for each product must be displayed as a separate webpage for the sales department. - Search crawling must start every 10 minutes, regardless of whether the prior session is complete. - The Cloud Search Service Application must crawl on-premises content in a cloud hybrid search solution. - The Secure Store Service application must use LitwareAppID as the target application to access LOBAppDB.

**Answers:**

**A)** Extend the HR department web application. Set the default zone to forms authentication and the extended zone to NTLM.

**B)** Extend the HR department web application. Set the default zone to NTLM and the extended zone to forms authentication.

**C)** Create an alternate access mapping for the HR department web application and set the default URL to an intranet zone.

**D)** Create an alternate access mapping for the HR department web application and set the default URL to an extranet zone.

**Solution:** B

**Explanation:**

Explanation: Configure and Manage SharePoint On-Premises

**Question: 9** *One Answer Is Right*

You need to investigate the cause of the search issues reported by the users. What should you use?

**Scenario:**

TESTLET-1. Overview Litware, Inc. is an international manufacturing company that has 3,000 users. The company has sales, marketing, research, IT, and human resources (HR) departments. Litware has two main offices located in New York and London. The company has five branch offices located in Asia. Existing Environment Active Directory The network contains an Active Directory forest named litwareinc.com. The forest contains a single domain. All domain controllers run Windows Server 2016. SharePoint Server Environment Litware has a SharePoint Server 2019 farm that contains the servers shown in the following table.

| Name | Configuration |
|---|---|
| SPWEB1 | Front-end server |
| SPWEB2 | Front-end server |
| SPCACHE1 | Distributed cache server |
| SPAPP1 | Application server |
| SPSEARCH1 | Search server |
| SPSEARCH2 | Search server |
| SQLSVR1 | Microsoft SQL Server |
| SQLSVR2 | Microsoft SQL Server |

Central Administration has a URL of http://spweb1.litwareinc.com. The HR department currently uses a SharePoint web application that uses only forms authentication. The sales department has a SharePoint site that is available anonymously to display product information. Line-of-Business Application You have a line-of-business application named LOBApp. LOBApp stores content in a SQL Server database named LOBAppDB. LOBApp has a service account named LobAppSA. Problem Statements Litware identifies the following issues: - None of the SharePoint sites use TLS. - The Distributed Cache service uses the farm account. - When users perform searches from the SharePoint site of the HR department, they receive no results. - You discover that the user names and passwords configured for managed services were transmitted on the network in plain text. Requirements Business Goals All the components in the SharePoint Server farm must be highly available by using the least number of servers possible. Each document stored in the HR department site must have the following pieces of metadata: CONID, CONNO, CONDate, and CONApproved. Security The farm uses the managed service accounts shown in the following table.

| Account name | Description |
|---|---|
| Spfarm | Farm account |
| SpContent | SharePoint content database account |
| SpServices | SharePoint service account |
| SpSecureStore | SharePoint Secure Store Service account |
| SpBI | SharePoint Business Intelligence |
| LOBAppSA | Content access account for LOBApp |

Technical Requirements Litware identifies the following technical requirements: - LOBApp content must be visible in search results. - The principle of least privilege must be used whenever possible. - All SharePoint service applications must use the SpServices account. - Information for each product must be displayed as a separate webpage for the sales department. - Search crawling must start every 10 minutes, regardless of whether the prior session is complete. - The Cloud Search Service Application must crawl on-premises content in a cloud hybrid search solution. - The Secure Store Service application must use LitwareAppID as the target application to access LOBAppDB.

Answers:

**A)** usage reports

**B)** query health reports

**C)** a SharePoint activity report

**D)** crawl health reports

**Solution:** D

**Explanation:**

Explanation: Configure and Manage SharePoint On-Premises Question Set 3

**Question: 10** *One Answer Is Right*

Note: This question is part of a series of questions that present the same scenario. Each question in the series contains a unique solution that might meet the stated goals. Some question sets might have more than one correct solution, while others might not have a correct solution. After you answer a question in this section, you will NOT be able to return to it. As a result, these questions will not appear in the review screen. You have a SharePoint Server farm. You create an external content type named ECT1 for a Microsoft SQL Server database. You implement cloud hybrid search. You create a Line of Business Data content source and run a full crawl. Users in SharePoint Online report that the search results do not contain any data from ECT1. You need to ensure that searches can return data from ECT1. Solution: You grant the Default content access account Full control permissions to the Central Administration web application. Does this meet the goal?

Answers:

**A)** Yes

**B)** No

**Solution:** B

# Chapter 41: MS-500 - Microsoft 365 Security Administration

## Exam Guide

Microsoft 365 Security Administration MS-500 Exam:

Microsoft 365 Security Administration MS-500 Exam which is related to Microsoft 365 Certified Security Administrator Associate Certification. This exam validates the Candidates ability to Implement and manage identity and access, Azure AD identity protection, Azure AD privileged identity management (PIM), implement and manage threat protection, manage Governance and compliance features in Microsoft. Microsoft 365 Security Administrator usually hold or pursue this certification and you can expect the same job role after completion of this certification.

MS-500 Exam topics:

Candidates must know the exam topics before they start of preparation. Because it will really help them in hitting the core. Our **MS-500 dumps** will include the following topics:

- Implement and manage identity and access 30-35%
- Implement and manage threat protection 20-25%
- Implement and manage information protection 15-20%
- Manage governance and compliance features in Microsoft 365 25-30%

Certification Path:

The Microsoft 365 Security Administration Certification includes only one MS-500 exam.

Who should take the MS-500 exam:

The Microsoft 365 Security Administration MS-500 Exam certification is an internationally recognized validation that identifies persons who earn it as possessing skilled as a Microsoft 365 Certified Security Administrator Associate. If candidates want significant improvement in career growth needs enhanced knowledge, skills, and talents. The Microsoft 365 Security Administration MS-500 Exam certification provides proof of this advanced knowledge and skill.

If a candidate has knowledge of associated technologies and skills that are required to pass Microsoft 365 Security Administration MS-500 Exam then he should take this exam.

How to study the MS-500 Exam:

Certification-questions.com expert team recommends you to prepare some notes on these topics along with it don't forget to practice Microsoft MS-500 Exam dumps which been written by our expert team, Both these will help you a lot to clear this exam with good marks.

How much MS-500 Exam Cost:

The price of the MS-500 exam is $165 USD.

How to book the MS-500 Exam:

These are following steps for registering the MS-500 exam.
Step 1: Visit to Microsoft Exam Registration
Step 2: Signup/Login to MICROSOFT account
Step 3: Search for MICROSOFT MS-500 Certifications Exam
Step 4: Select Date and Center of examination and confirm with payment value of $165

What is the duration of the MS-500 Exam:

- Format: Multiple choices, multiple answers
- Length of Examination: 150 minutes
- Number of Questions: 45-60
- Passing Score: 700/1000

The benefit in Obtaining the MS-500 Exam Certification:

- After completion of Microsoft 365 Certified Security Administrator Associate Certification candidates receive official confirmation from Microsoft that you are now fully certified in their chosen field. This can be now added to their CV, cover letters and job applications.
- When Candidates applying for a job or looking to promotion in their current position, a Microsoft 365 Certified Security Administrator Associate certification in the field in which Candidates are applying will put you at the top of the list and make them a desirable candidate for employers.
- Candidates will get in-depth knowledge by completing the courses along with the access to revision materials for 6 months upon completion means they will have a wider skill set when it comes to the various technologies and systems than an uncertified professional. Certified Professional in this particular skill set is 74% more efficient when it comes to completing their tasks in a timely well-executed manner.

- Organization owners invest a lot in their employees when it comes to their training with the goal of making them quicker, more efficient, and more knowledgeable about their role. Certified Professional will reduce the time he spends on tasks, meaning he can get more done this could help reduce company downtime when repairing faults on a system or fixing hardware problems.
- Becoming Microsoft 365 Certified Security Administrator Associate means one thing you are worth more to the company and therefore more to yourself in the form of an upgraded pay package. On average a Microsoft 365 Certified Security Administrator Associate member of staff is estimated to be worth 30% more to a company than their uncertified professionals.

Difficulty in writing MS-500 Exam:

Now, these days the significance of Microsoft MS-500 is increasing day by day then the difficulty of passing Microsoft MS-500 exam questions is also advancing. Candidates can only be passed Microsoft MS-500 exam if they practice daily, prepare from quality preparation material and believe in yourself. This is always a tough task for the candidates to pass Microsoft MS-500 exam because Microsoft MS-500 exam syllabus has some tricky concepts and the candidates find it hard to understand these topics. To overcome these problems candidates should have to keep these points in mind. First of all look for some updated and in detailed exam preparation material. They will really help you in understanding the very small to the small concept of the Microsoft MS-500 exam. The second point look for Microsoft experts helps, as they have the experience of the Microsoft MS-500 exam and they can tell you the real exam scenario. The third point is candidates should practice from quality Microsoft MS-500 exam practice tests. Certification-questions provides you internationally recognized **Microsoft MS-500 dumps** that will ensure hundred percent passing surety at the first attempt. These Microsoft MS-500 questions answers have been made by Microsoft professionals and experts. The most important thing Certification-questions also provides Microsoft MS-500 practice test with updated and latest questions that will help candidates a lot from the prospect of preparation.

For more info visit::

Microsoft MS-500 Exam Reference

# Sample Practice Test for MS-500

**Question: 1** *One Answer Is Right*

An administrator configures Azure AD Privileged Identity Management as shown in the following exhibit.

What should you do to meet the security requirements?

**Scenario:**

TESTLET-1. Overview Fabrikam, Inc. is manufacturing company that sells products through partner retail stores. Fabrikam has 5,000 employees located in offices throughout Europe. Existing Environment Network Infrastructure The network contains an Active Directory forest named fabrikam.com. Fabrikam has a hybrid Microsoft Azure Active Directory (Azure AD) environment. The company maintains some on-premises servers for specific applications, but most end-user applications are provided by a Microsoft 365 E5 subscription. Problem Statements Fabrikam identifies the following issues: - Since last Friday, the IT team has been receiving automated email messages that contain "Unhealthy Identity Synchronization Notification" in the subject line. - Several users recently opened email attachments that contained malware. The process to remove the malware was time consuming. Requirements Planned Changes Fabrikam plans to implement the following changes: - Fabrikam plans to monitor and investigate suspicious sign-ins to Active Directory - Fabrikam plans to provide partners with access to some of the data stored in Microsoft 365 Application Administration Fabrikam identifies the following application requirements for managing workload applications: - User administrators will work from different countries - User administrators will use the Azure Active Directory admin center - Two new administrators named Admin1 and Admin2 will be responsible for managing Microsoft Exchange Online only Security Requirements Fabrikam identifies the following security requirements:- Access to the Azure Active Directory admin center by the user administrators must be reviewed every seven days. If an administrator fails to respond to an access request within three days, access must be removed - Users who manage Microsoft 365 workloads must only be allowed to perform administrative tasks for up to three hours at a time. Global administrators must be exempt from this requirement - Users must be prevented from inviting external users to view company data. Only global administrators and a user named User1 must be able to send invitations - Azure Advanced Threat Protection (ATP) must capture security group modifications for sensitive groups, such as Domain Admins in Active Directory - Workload administrators must use multi-factor authentication (MFA) when signing in from an anonymous or an unfamiliar location - The location of the user administrators must be audited when the administrators authenticate to Azure AD - Email messages that include attachments containing malware must be delivered without the attachment - The principle of least privilege must be used whenever possible

**Answers:**

**A)** Change the Assignment Type for Admin2 to Permanent

**B)** From the Azure Active Directory admin center, assign the Exchange administrator role to Admin2

**C)** From the Azure Active Directory admin center, remove the Exchange administrator role to Admin1

**D)** Change the Assignment Type for Admin1 to Eligible

**Solution:** D

**Question: 2** *One Answer Is Right*

You need to recommend a solution for the user administrators that meets the security requirements for auditing. Which blade should you recommend using from the Azure Active Directory admin center?

**Scenario:**

TESTLET-1. Overview Fabrikam, Inc. is manufacturing company that sells products through partner retail stores. Fabrikam has 5,000 employees located in offices throughout Europe. Existing Environment Network Infrastructure The network contains an Active Directory forest named fabrikam.com. Fabrikam has a hybrid Microsoft Azure Active Directory (Azure AD) environment. The company maintains some on-premises servers for specific applications, but most end-user applications are provided by a Microsoft 365 E5 subscription. Problem Statements Fabrikam identifies the following issues: - Since last Friday, the IT team has been receiving automated email messages that contain "Unhealthy Identity Synchronization Notification" in the subject line. - Several users recently opened email attachments that contained malware. The process to remove the malware was time consuming. Requirements Planned Changes Fabrikam plans to implement the following changes: - Fabrikam plans to monitor and investigate suspicious sign-ins to Active Directory - Fabrikam plans to provide partners with access to some of the data stored in Microsoft 365 Application Administration Fabrikam identifies the following application requirements for managing workload applications: - User administrators will work from different countries - User administrators will use the Azure Active Directory admin center - Two new administrators named Admin1 and Admin2 will be responsible for managing Microsoft Exchange Online only Security Requirements Fabrikam identifies the following security requirements:- Access to the Azure Active Directory admin center by the user administrators must be reviewed every seven days. If an administrator fails to respond to an access request within three days, access must be removed - Users who manage Microsoft 365 workloads must only be allowed to perform administrative tasks for up to three hours at a time. Global administrators must be exempt from this requirement - Users must be prevented from inviting external users to view company data. Only global administrators and a user named User1 must be able to send invitations - Azure Advanced Threat Protection (ATP) must capture security group modifications for sensitive groups, such as Domain Admins in Active Directory - Workload administrators must use multi-factor authentication (MFA) when signing in from an anonymous or an unfamiliar location - The location of the user administrators must be audited when the administrators authenticate to Azure AD - Email messages that include attachments containing malware must be delivered without the attachment - The principle of least privilege must be used whenever possible

**Answers:**

**A)** Sign-ins

**B)** Azure AD Identity Protection

**C)** Authentication methods

**D)** Access review

**Solution:** A

**Explanation:**

Explanation: References: https://docs.microsoft.com/en-us/azure/active-directory/reports-monitoring/concept-sign-ins

**Question: 3** *Multiple Answers Are Right*

HOTSPOT You plan to configure an access review to meet the security requirements for the workload administrators. You create an access review policy and specify the scope and a group. Which other settings should you configure? To answer, select the appropriate options in the answer area. NOTE: Each correct selection is worth one point. Hot Area:

Set the frequency to:

| One time | V |
| Weekly | |
| Monthly | |

To ensure that access is removed if an administrator fails to respond, configure the:

| Upon completion settings | V |
| Advanced settings | |
| Programs | |
| Reviewers | |

**Scenario:**

TESTLET-1. Overview Fabrikam, Inc. is manufacturing company that sells products through partner retail stores. Fabrikam has 5,000 employees located in offices throughout Europe. Existing Environment Network Infrastructure The network contains an Active Directory forest named fabrikam.com. Fabrikam has a hybrid Microsoft Azure Active Directory (Azure AD) environment. The company maintains some on-premises servers for specific applications, but most end-user applications are provided by a Microsoft 365 E5 subscription. Problem Statements Fabrikam identifies the following issues: - Since last Friday, the IT team has been receiving automated email messages that contain "Unhealthy Identity Synchronization Notification" in the subject line. - Several users recently opened email attachments that contained malware. The process to remove the malware was time consuming. Requirements Planned Changes Fabrikam plans to implement the following changes: - Fabrikam plans to monitor and investigate suspicious sign-ins to Active Directory - Fabrikam plans to provide partners with access to some of the data stored in Microsoft 365 Application Administration Fabrikam identifies the following application requirements for managing workload applications: - User administrators will work from different countries - User administrators will use the Azure Active Directory admin center - Two new administrators named Admin1 and Admin2 will be responsible for managing Microsoft Exchange Online only Security Requirements Fabrikam identifies the following security requirements:- Access to the Azure Active Directory admin center by the user administrators must be reviewed every seven days. If an administrator fails to respond to an access request within three days, access must be removed - Users who manage Microsoft 365 workloads must only be allowed to perform administrative tasks for up to three hours at a time. Global administrators must be exempt from this requirement - Users must be prevented from inviting external users to view company data. Only global administrators and a user named User1 must be able to send invitations - Azure Advanced Threat Protection (ATP) must capture security group modifications for sensitive groups, such as Domain Admins in Active Directory - Workload administrators must use multi-factor authentication (MFA) when signing in from an anonymous or an unfamiliar location - The location of the user administrators must be audited when the administrators authenticate to Azure AD - Email messages that include attachments containing malware must be delivered without the attachment - The principle of least privilege must be used whenever possible

**Answers:**

**A)**

Set the frequency to:

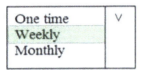

To ensure that access is removed if an administrator fails to respond, configure the:

| Upon completion settings | V |
| Advanced settings | |
| Programs | |
| Reviewers | |

**Solution:** A

**Explanation:**

Explanation:

**Question: 4** *One Answer Is Right*

You need to recommend a solution to protect the sign-ins of Admin1 and Admin2. What should you include in the recommendation?

**Scenario:**

TESTLET-1. Overview Fabrikam, Inc. is manufacturing company that sells products through partner retail stores. Fabrikam has 5,000 employees located in offices throughout Europe. Existing Environment Network Infrastructure The network contains an Active Directory forest named fabrikam.com. Fabrikam has a hybrid Microsoft Azure Active Directory (Azure AD) environment. The company maintains some on-premises servers for specific applications, but most end-user applications are provided by a Microsoft 365 E5 subscription. Problem Statements Fabrikam identifies the following issues: - Since last Friday, the IT team has been receiving automated email messages that contain "Unhealthy Identity Synchronization

Notification" in the subject line. - Several users recently opened email attachments that contained malware. The process to remove the malware was time consuming. Requirements Planned Changes Fabrikam plans to implement the following changes: - Fabrikam plans to monitor and investigate suspicious sign-ins to Active Directory - Fabrikam plans to provide partners with access to some of the data stored in Microsoft 365 Application Administration Fabrikam identifies the following application requirements for managing workload applications: - User administrators will work from different countries - User administrators will use the Azure Active Directory admin center - Two new administrators named Admin1 and Admin2 will be responsible for managing Microsoft Exchange Online only Security Requirements Fabrikam identifies the following security requirements:- Access to the Azure Active Directory admin center by the user administrators must be reviewed every seven days. If an administrator fails to respond to an access request within three days, access must be removed - Users who manage Microsoft 365 workloads must only be allowed to perform administrative tasks for up to three hours at a time. Global administrators must be exempt from this requirement - Users must be prevented from inviting external users to view company data. Only global administrators and a user named User1 must be able to send invitations - Azure Advanced Threat Protection (ATP) must capture security group modifications for sensitive groups, such as Domain Admins in Active Directory - Workload administrators must use multi-factor authentication (MFA) when signing in from an anonymous or an unfamiliar location - The location of the user administrators must be audited when the administrators authenticate to Azure AD - Email messages that include attachments containing malware must be delivered without the attachment - The principle of least privilege must be used whenever possible

**Answers:**

**A)** a device compliance policy

**B)** an access review

**C)** a user risk policy

**D)** a sign-in risk policy

**Solution:** C

**Explanation:**

Explanation: References: https://docs.microsoft.com/en-us/azure/active-directory/identity-protection/howto-user-risk-policy

**Question: 5** *One Answer Is Right*

You need to resolve the issue that generates the automated email messages to the IT team. Which tool should you run first?

## Scenario:

TESTLET-1. Overview Fabrikam, Inc. is manufacturing company that sells products through partner retail stores. Fabrikam has 5,000 employees located in offices throughout Europe. Existing Environment Network Infrastructure The network contains an Active Directory forest named fabrikam.com. Fabrikam has a hybrid Microsoft Azure Active Directory (Azure AD) environment. The company maintains some on-premises servers for specific applications, but most end-user applications are provided by a Microsoft 365 E5 subscription. Problem Statements Fabrikam identifies the following issues: - Since last Friday, the IT team has been receiving automated email messages that contain "Unhealthy Identity Synchronization Notification" in the subject line. - Several users recently opened email attachments that contained malware. The process to remove the malware was time consuming. Requirements Planned Changes Fabrikam plans to implement the following changes: - Fabrikam plans to monitor and investigate suspicious sign-ins to Active Directory - Fabrikam plans to provide partners with access to some of the data stored in Microsoft 365 Application Administration Fabrikam identifies the following application requirements for managing workload applications: - User administrators will work from different countries - User administrators will use the Azure Active Directory admin center - Two new administrators named Admin1 and Admin2 will be responsible for managing Microsoft Exchange Online only Security Requirements Fabrikam identifies the following security requirements:- Access to the Azure Active Directory admin center by the user administrators must be reviewed every seven days. If an administrator fails to respond to an access request within three days, access must be removed - Users who manage Microsoft 365 workloads must only be allowed to perform administrative tasks for up to three hours at a time. Global administrators must be exempt from this requirement - Users must be prevented from inviting external users to view company data. Only global administrators and a user named User1 must be able to send invitations - Azure Advanced Threat Protection (ATP) must capture security group modifications for sensitive groups, such as Domain Admins in Active Directory - Workload administrators must use multi-factor authentication (MFA) when signing in from an anonymous or an unfamiliar location - The location of the user administrators must be audited when the administrators authenticate to Azure AD - Email messages that include attachments containing malware must be delivered without the attachment - The principle of least privilege must be used whenever possible

## Answers:

A) Synchronization Service Manager

B) Azure AD Connect wizard

C) Synchronization Rules Editor

D) IdFix

**Solution:** B

**Explanation:**

Explanation: References: https://docs.microsoft.com/en-us/office365/enterprise/fix-problems-with-directory-synchronization Implement and manage identity and access

**Question: 6** *One Answer Is Right*

You need to create Group2. What are two possible ways to create the group?

**Scenario:**

TESTLET-2. Overview Litware, Inc. is a financial company that has 1,000 users in its main office in Chicago and 100 users in a branch office in San Francisco. Existing Environment Internal Network Infrastructure The network contains a single domain forest. The forest functional level is Windows Server 2016. Users are subject to sign-in hour restrictions as defined in Active Directory. The network has the IP address ranges shown in the following table.

| Location | IP address range |
|---|---|
| Chicago office internal network | 192.168.0.0/20 |
| Chicago office perimeter network | 172.16.0.0/24 |
| Chicago office external network | 131.107.83.0/28 |
| San Francisco office internal network | 192.168.16.0/20 |
| San Francisco office perimeter network | 172.16.16.0/24 |
| San Francisco office external network | 131.107.16.218/32 |

The offices connect by using Multiprotocol Label Switching (MPLS). The following operating systems are used on the network: - Windows Server 2016 - Windows 10 Enterprise - Windows 8.1 Enterprise The internal network contains the systems shown in the following table.

| Office | Name | Configuration |
|---|---|---|
| Chicago | DC1 | Domain controller |
| Chicago | DC2 | Domain controller |
| San Francisco | DC3 | Domain controller |
| Chicago | Server1 | SIEM-server |

Litware uses a third-party email system. Cloud Infrastructure Litware recently purchased Microsoft 365 subscription licenses for all users. Microsoft Azure Active Directory (Azure AD) Connect is installed and uses the default authentication settings. User accounts are not yet synced to Azure AD. You have the Microsoft 365 users and groups shown in the following table.

| Name | Object type | Description |
|---|---|---|
| Group1 | Security group | A group for testing Azure and Microsoft 365 functionality |
| User1 | User | A test user who is a member of Group1 |
| User2 | User | A test user who is a member of Group1 |
| User3 | User | A test user who is a member of Group1 |
| User4 | User | An administrator |
| Guest1 | Guest user | A guest user |

Requirements Planned Changes Litware plans to implement the following changes: - Migrate the email system to Microsoft Exchange Online - Implement Azure AD Privileged Identity Management Security Requirements Litware identifies the following security requirements: - Create a group named Group2 that will include all the Azure AD user accounts. Group2 will be used to provide limited access to Windows Analytics - Create a group named Group3 that will be used to apply Azure Information Protection policies to pilot users. Group3 must only contain user accounts - Use Azure Advanced Threat Protection (ATP) to detect any security threats that target the forest - Prevent users locked out of Active Directory from signing in to Azure AD and Active Directory - Implement a permanent eligible assignment of the Compliance administrator role for User1 - Configure domain-joined servers to ensure that they report sensor data to Microsoft Defender ATP - Prevent access to Azure resources for the guest user accounts by default - Ensure that all domain-joined computers are registered to Azure AD Multi-factor authentication (MFA) Requirements Security features of Microsoft Office 365 and Azure will be tested by using pilot Azure user accounts. You identify the following requirements for testing MFA: - Pilot users must use MFA unless they are signing in from the internal network of the Chicago office. MFA must NOT be used on the Chicago office internal network. - If an authentication attempt is suspicious, MFA must be used, regardless of the user location. -Any disruption of legitimate authentication attempts must be minimized. General Requirements Litware wants to minimize the deployment of additional servers and services in the Active Directory forest.

**Answers:**

A) an Office 365 group in the Microsoft 365 admin center

B) a mail-enabled security group in the Microsoft 365 admin center

C) a security group in the Microsoft 365 admin center

D) a distribution list in the Microsoft 365 admin center

E) a security group in the Azure AD admin center

**Solution:** C, E

**Question: 7** *One Answer Is Right*

Which IP address space should you include in the Trusted IP MFA configuration?

**Scenario:**

TESTLET-2. Overview Litware, Inc. is a financial company that has 1,000 users in its main office in Chicago and 100 users in a branch office in San Francisco. Existing Environment Internal Network Infrastructure The network contains a single domain forest. The forest functional level is Windows Server 2016. Users are subject to sign-in hour restrictions as defined in Active Directory. The network has the IP address ranges shown in the following table.

| Location | IP address range |
|---|---|
| Chicago office internal network | 192.168.0.0/20 |
| Chicago office perimeter network | 172.16.0.0/24 |
| Chicago office external network | 131.107.83.0/28 |
| San Francisco office internal network | 192.168.16.0/20 |
| San Francisco office perimeter network | 172.16.16.0/24 |
| San Francisco office external network | 131.107.16.218/32 |

The offices connect by using Multiprotocol Label Switching (MPLS). The following operating systems are used on the network: - Windows Server 2016 - Windows 10 Enterprise - Windows 8.1 Enterprise The internal network contains the systems shown in the following table.

| Office | Name | Configuration |
|---|---|---|
| Chicago | DC1 | Domain controller |
| Chicago | DC2 | Domain controller |
| San Francisco | DC3 | Domain controller |
| Chicago | Server1 | SIEM-server |

Litware uses a third-party email system. Cloud Infrastructure Litware recently purchased Microsoft 365 subscription licenses for all users. Microsoft Azure Active Directory (Azure AD) Connect is installed and uses the default authentication settings. User accounts are not yet synced to Azure AD. You have the Microsoft 365 users and groups shown in the following table.

| Name | Object type | Description |
|---|---|---|
| Group1 | Security group | A group for testing Azure and Microsoft 365 functionality |
| User1 | User | A test user who is a member of Group1 |
| User2 | User | A test user who is a member of Group1 |
| User3 | User | A test user who is a member of Group1 |
| User4 | User | An administrator |
| Guest1 | Guest user | A guest user |

Requirements Planned Changes Litware plans to implement the following changes: - Migrate the email system to Microsoft Exchange Online - Implement Azure AD Privileged Identity Management Security Requirements Litware identifies the following security requirements: - Create a group named Group2 that will include all the Azure AD user accounts. Group2 will be used to provide limited access to Windows Analytics - Create a group named Group3 that will be used to apply Azure Information Protection policies to pilot users. Group3 must only contain user accounts - Use Azure Advanced Threat Protection (ATP) to detect any security threats that target the forest - Prevent users locked out of Active Directory from signing in to Azure AD and Active Directory - Implement a permanent eligible assignment of the Compliance administrator role for User1 - Configure domain-joined servers to ensure that they report sensor data to Microsoft Defender ATP - Prevent access to Azure resources for the guest user accounts by default - Ensure that all domain-joined computers are registered to Azure AD Multi-factor authentication (MFA) Requirements Security features of Microsoft Office 365 and Azure will be tested by using pilot Azure user accounts. You identify the following requirements for testing MFA: - Pilot users must use MFA unless they are signing in from the internal network of the Chicago office. MFA must NOT be used on the Chicago office internal network. - If an authentication attempt is suspicious, MFA must be used, regardless of the user location. -Any disruption of legitimate authentication attempts must be minimized. General Requirements Litware wants to minimize the deployment of additional servers and services in the Active Directory forest.

**Answers:**

**A)** 131.107.83.0/28

**B)** 192.168.16.0/20

**C)** 172.16.0.0/24

**D)** 192.168.0.0/20

**Solution:** B

**Question: 8** *Multiple Answers Are Right*

HOTSPOT How should you configure Group3? To answer, select the appropriate options in the answer area. NOTE: Each correct selection is worth one point. Hot Area:

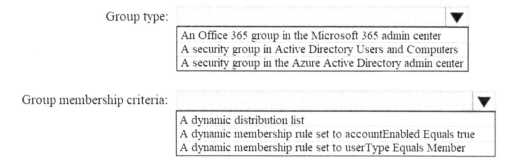

Scenario:

TESTLET-2. Overview Litware, Inc. is a financial company that has 1,000 users in its main office in Chicago and 100 users in a branch office in San Francisco. Existing Environment Internal Network Infrastructure The network contains a single domain forest. The forest functional level is Windows Server 2016. Users are subject to sign-in hour restrictions as defined in Active Directory. The network has the IP address ranges shown in the following table.

| Location | IP address range |
| --- | --- |
| Chicago office internal network | 192.168.0.0/20 |
| Chicago office perimeter network | 172.16.0.0/24 |
| Chicago office external network | 131.107.83.0/28 |
| San Francisco office internal network | 192.168.16.0/20 |
| San Francisco office perimeter network | 172.16.16.0/24 |
| San Francisco office external network | 131.107.16.218/32 |

The offices connect by using Multiprotocol Label Switching (MPLS). The following operating systems are used on the network: - Windows Server 2016 - Windows 10 Enterprise - Windows 8.1 Enterprise The internal network contains the systems shown in the following table.

| Office | Name | Configuration |
|---|---|---|
| Chicago | DC1 | Domain controller |
| Chicago | DC2 | Domain controller |
| San Francisco | DC3 | Domain controller |
| Chicago | Server1 | SIEM-server |

Litware uses a third-party email system. Cloud Infrastructure Litware recently purchased Microsoft 365 subscription licenses for all users. Microsoft Azure Active Directory (Azure AD) Connect is installed and uses the default authentication settings. User accounts are not yet synced to Azure AD. You have the Microsoft 365 users and groups shown in the following table.

| Name | Object type | Description |
|---|---|---|
| Group1 | Security group | A group for testing Azure and Microsoft 365 functionality |
| User1 | User | A test user who is a member of Group1 |
| User2 | User | A test user who is a member of Group1 |
| User3 | User | A test user who is a member of Group1 |
| User4 | User | An administrator |
| Guest1 | Guest user | A guest user |

Requirements Planned Changes Litware plans to implement the following changes: - Migrate the email system to Microsoft Exchange Online - Implement Azure AD Privileged Identity Management Security Requirements Litware identifies the following security requirements: - Create a group named Group2 that will include all the Azure AD user accounts. Group2 will be used to provide limited access to Windows Analytics - Create a group named Group3 that will be used to apply Azure Information Protection policies to pilot users. Group3 must only contain user accounts - Use Azure Advanced Threat Protection (ATP) to detect any security threats that target the forest - Prevent users locked out of Active Directory from signing in to Azure AD and Active Directory - Implement a permanent eligible assignment of the Compliance administrator role for User1 - Configure domain-joined servers to ensure that they report sensor data to Microsoft Defender ATP - Prevent access to Azure resources for the guest user accounts by default - Ensure that all domain-joined computers are registered to Azure AD Multi-factor authentication (MFA) Requirements Security features of Microsoft Office 365 and Azure will be tested by using pilot Azure user accounts. You identify the following requirements for testing MFA: - Pilot users must use MFA unless they are signing in from the internal network of the Chicago office. MFA must NOT be used on the Chicago office internal network. - If an authentication attempt is suspicious, MFA must be used, regardless of the user location. -Any disruption of legitimate authentication attempts must be minimized. General Requirements Litware wants to minimize the deployment of additional servers and services in the Active Directory forest.

**Answers:**

**A)**

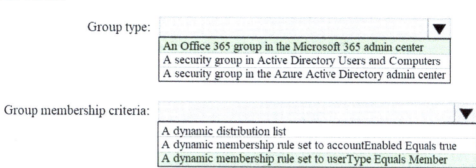

**Solution:** A

**Explanation:**

Explanation: Reference: https://docs.microsoft.com/en-us/azure/information-protection/prepare

**Question: 9** *Multiple Answers Are Right*

HOTSPOT How should you configure Azure AD Connect? To answer, select the appropriate options in the answer area. NOTE: Each correct selection is worth one point. Hot Area:

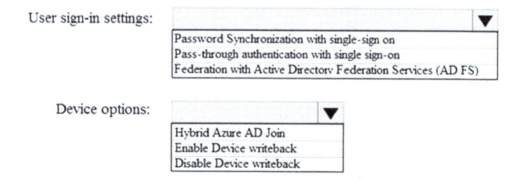

**Scenario:**

TESTLET-2. Overview Litware, Inc. is a financial company that has 1,000 users in its main office in Chicago and 100 users in a branch office in San Francisco. Existing Environment Internal Network Infrastructure The network contains a single domain forest. The forest functional level is Windows Server 2016. Users are subject to sign-in hour restrictions as defined in Active Directory. The network has the IP address ranges shown in the following table.

| Location | IP address range |
|---|---|
| Chicago office internal network | 192.168.0.0/20 |
| Chicago office perimeter network | 172.16.0.0/24 |
| Chicago office external network | 131.107.83.0/28 |
| San Francisco office internal network | 192.168.16.0/20 |
| San Francisco office perimeter network | 172.16.16.0/24 |
| San Francisco office external network | 131.107.16.218/32 |

The offices connect by using Multiprotocol Label Switching (MPLS). The following operating systems are used on the network: - Windows Server 2016 - Windows 10 Enterprise - Windows 8.1 Enterprise The internal network contains the systems shown in the following table.

| Office | Name | Configuration |
|---|---|---|
| Chicago | DC1 | Domain controller |
| Chicago | DC2 | Domain controller |
| San Francisco | DC3 | Domain controller |
| Chicago | Server1 | SIEM-server |

Litware uses a third-party email system. Cloud Infrastructure Litware recently purchased Microsoft 365 subscription licenses for all users. Microsoft Azure Active Directory (Azure AD) Connect is installed and uses the default authentication settings. User accounts are not yet synced to Azure AD. You have the Microsoft 365 users and groups shown in the following table.

| Name | Object type | Description |
|---|---|---|
| Group1 | Security group | A group for testing Azure and Microsoft 365 functionality |
| User1 | User | A test user who is a member of Group1 |
| User2 | User | A test user who is a member of Group1 |
| User3 | User | A test user who is a member of Group1 |
| User4 | User | An administrator |
| Guest1 | Guest user | A guest user |

Requirements Planned Changes Litware plans to implement the following changes: - Migrate the email system to Microsoft Exchange Online - Implement Azure AD Privileged Identity Management Security Requirements Litware identifies the following security requirements: - Create a group named Group2 that will include all the Azure AD user accounts. Group2 will be used to provide limited access to Windows Analytics - Create a group named Group3 that will be used to apply Azure Information Protection policies to pilot users. Group3 must only contain user accounts - Use Azure Advanced Threat Protection (ATP) to detect any security threats that target the forest - Prevent users locked out of Active Directory from signing in to Azure AD and Active Directory - Implement a permanent eligible assignment of the Compliance administrator role for User1 - Configure domain-joined servers to ensure that they report sensor data to Microsoft Defender ATP - Prevent access to Azure resources for the guest user accounts by default - Ensure that all domain-joined computers are registered to Azure AD Multi-factor authentication (MFA) Requirements Security features of Microsoft Office 365 and Azure will be tested by using pilot Azure user accounts. You identify the following requirements for testing MFA: - Pilot users must use MFA unless they are signing in from the internal network of the Chicago office. MFA must NOT be used on the Chicago office internal network. - If an authentication attempt is suspicious, MFA must be used, regardless of the user location. -Any disruption of legitimate authentication attempts must be minimized. General Requirements Litware wants to minimize the deployment of additional servers and services in the Active Directory forest.

Answers:

A)

**Answer Area**

User sign-in settings:
- Password Synchronization with single-sign on
- Pass-through authentication with single sign-on
- Federation with Active Directory Federation Services (AD FS)

Device options:
- Hybrid Azure AD Join
- Enable Device writeback
- Disable Device writeback

**Solution:** A

**Explanation:**

Explanation:

**Question: 10** *One Answer Is Right*

You need to create Group3. What are two possible ways to create the group?

**Scenario:**

TESTLET-2. Overview Litware, Inc. is a financial company that has 1,000 users in its main office in Chicago and 100 users in a branch office in San Francisco. Existing Environment Internal Network Infrastructure The network contains a single domain forest. The forest functional level is Windows Server 2016. Users are subject to sign-in hour restrictions as defined in Active Directory. The network has the IP address ranges shown in the following table.

| Location | IP address range |
|---|---|
| Chicago office internal network | 192.168.0.0/20 |
| Chicago office perimeter network | 172.16.0.0/24 |
| Chicago office external network | 131.107.83.0/28 |
| San Francisco office internal network | 192.168.16.0/20 |
| San Francisco office perimeter network | 172.16.16.0/24 |
| San Francisco office external network | 131.107.16.218/32 |

The offices connect by using Multiprotocol Label Switching (MPLS). The following operating systems are used on the network: - Windows Server 2016 - Windows 10 Enterprise - Windows 8.1 Enterprise The internal network contains the systems shown in the following table.

| Office | Name | Configuration |
|---|---|---|
| Chicago | DC1 | Domain controller |
| Chicago | DC2 | Domain controller |
| San Francisco | DC3 | Domain controller |
| Chicago | Server1 | SIEM-server |

Litware uses a third-party email system. Cloud Infrastructure Litware recently purchased Microsoft 365 subscription licenses for all users. Microsoft Azure Active Directory (Azure AD) Connect is installed and uses the default authentication settings. User accounts are not yet synced to Azure AD. You have the Microsoft 365 users and groups shown in the following table.

| Name | Object type | Description |
|---|---|---|
| Group1 | Security group | A group for testing Azure and Microsoft 365 functionality |
| User1 | User | A test user who is a member of Group1 |
| User2 | User | A test user who is a member of Group1 |
| User3 | User | A test user who is a member of Group1 |
| User4 | User | An administrator |
| Guest1 | Guest user | A guest user |

Requirements Planned Changes Litware plans to implement the following changes: - Migrate the email system to Microsoft Exchange Online - Implement Azure AD Privileged Identity Management Security Requirements Litware identifies the following security requirements: - Create a group named Group2 that will include all the Azure AD user accounts. Group2 will be used to provide limited access to Windows Analytics - Create a group named Group3 that will be used to apply Azure Information Protection policies to pilot users. Group3 must only contain user accounts - Use Azure Advanced Threat Protection (ATP) to detect any security threats that target the forest - Prevent users locked out of Active Directory from signing in to Azure AD and Active Directory - Implement a permanent eligible assignment of the Compliance administrator role for User1 - Configure domain-joined servers to ensure that they report sensor data to Microsoft Defender ATP - Prevent access to Azure resources for the guest user accounts by default - Ensure that all domain-joined computers are registered to Azure AD Multi-factor authentication (MFA) Requirements Security features of Microsoft Office 365 and Azure will be tested by using pilot Azure user accounts. You identify the following requirements for testing MFA: - Pilot users must use MFA unless they are signing in from the internal network of the Chicago office. MFA must NOT be used on the Chicago office internal network. - If an authentication attempt is suspicious, MFA must be used, regardless of the user location. -Any disruption of legitimate authentication attempts must be minimized. General Requirements Litware wants to minimize the deployment of additional servers and services in the Active Directory forest.

## Answers:

A) an Office 365 group in the Microsoft 365 admin center

B) a mail-enabled security group in the Microsoft 365 admin center

C) a security group in the Microsoft 365 admin center

D) a distribution list in the Microsoft 365 admin center

E) a security group in the Azure AD admin center

**Solution:** A, D

**Explanation:**

Explanation: Implement and manage identity and access

# Chapter 42: MS-700 - Managing Microsoft Teams

## Exam Guide

How to Prepare For MS-700: Managing Microsoft Teams (beta) Exam

Preparation Guide for MS-700: Managing Microsoft Teams (beta) Exam

Introduction

Microsoft has created a track for Microsoft Teams Administrators who are knowledgeable to plan, manage and deploy Teams apps, chat, channels, meetings, live events, audio conferencing, and calling. The Teams Administrator is also responsible for upgrading from Skype for Business to Teams. This certification program provides Microsoft Teams Administrators a way to demonstrate their skills. The assessment is based on a rigorous exam using industry standard methodology to determine whether a candidate meets Microsoft's proficiency standards.

According to Microsoft, a Microsoft Certified Professional enables organizations to leverage integration of advanced voice features into Microsoft Teams. Certification is evidence of your skills, expertise in those areas in which you like to work. If candidate wants to work on Microsoft Teams management and prove his knowledge, certification offered by Microsoft. This **MS-700 Exam** Certification helps a candidate to validates his skills in Microsoft Azure for SAP Workloads Technology.

In this guide, we will cover the MS-700: Managing Microsoft Teams (beta) Certification exam, MS-700: Managing Microsoft Teams (beta) Certified professional salary and all aspects of the MS-700: Managing Microsoft Teams (beta) Certification.

Introduction to MS-700: Managing Microsoft Teams (beta) Exam:

Candidates for **MS-700 Exam** are seeking to prove fundamental Microsoft teams management knowledge and skills. Before taking this exam, exam aspirants ought to have a solid fundamental information of the concepts shared in preparation guide as well as upgradation of SFB to Microsoft Teams.

It is suggested that professionals accustomed to the ideas and also the technologies represented here by taking relevant training courses. Candidates are expected to have some hands-on experience with key responsibilities such as integration points with apps and services, including but not limited to SharePoint, OneDrive for Business, Exchange, Azure AD, and Office 365 Groups. The Teams Administrator understands how to integrate external apps and services. After passing this exam, candidates get a certificate from Microsoft that helps them to demonstrate their proficiency in Microsoft Teams to their clients and employers.

Topics of MS-700: Managing Microsoft Teams (beta) Exam:

Candidates should apprehend the examination topics before they begin of preparation. because it'll extremely facilitate them in touch the core. Our **MS-700 dumps** will include the following topics:

*1. Plan and Configure a Microsoft Teams Environment (45-50%)*

Upgrade from Skype for Business to Microsoft Teams

- Choose an appropriate upgrade path and coexistence mode to meet specific requirements
- Plan and troubleshoot meeting migration
- Configure Microsoft Teams upgrade notification and meeting app choices
- Configure coexistence mode for the organization and per-user

    Plan and configure network settings for Microsoft Teams

- Plan for successful network deployment by using Network Planner
- Calculate network bandwidth capacity for Microsoft Teams voice, video, meetings and Live Events
- Assess network readiness by using the Network Testing Companion
- Configure network ports and protocols used by Microsoft Teams client application
- Configure media optimizations by using QoS

    Implement Governance and Lifecycle Management for Microsoft Teams

- Create team templates
- Set up policies for Office 365 Groups creation
- Configure Office 365 Groups for Microsoft Teams classifications, expiration policy, and naming policy
- Archive, restore, and delete a team

    Configure and manage guest access

- Configure guest users for Microsoft Teams

- Configure guest permissions for a team
- Configure meeting, messaging, and calling options for guests
- Remove guests
- Manage Azure AD access review for guests
- Configure guest access from Azure AD portal

  Manage security and compliance

- Assign Microsoft Teams Admin roles
- Create and manage compliance features, including retention and sensitivity policies
- Create security and compliance alerts for Microsoft Teams
- Create an information barrier policy
- Interpret security reports for Microsoft Teams

  Deploy and manage Microsoft Teams endpoints

- Deploy Microsoft Teams clients to devices, including Windows, VDI (Virtual Desktop), MacOS, and mobile devices
- Manage configuration profiles
- Manage device settings and firmware
- Configure Microsoft Teams Rooms

  Monitor and analyze service usage

- Interpret Microsoft Teams usage reports
- Interpret Microsoft 365 usage reports
- Optimize call quality by using Call Analytics
- Analyze organization-wide call quality by using Call Quality Dashboard

  *3. Manage Chat, Calling, and Meetings (30-35%)*

Manage chat and collaboration experiences

- Configure messaging policies
- Manage external access
- Manage channels for a team
- Manage private channel creation policies
- Manage email integration
- Configure external access for SharePoint and OneDrive for Business
- Manage cloud file storage options for collaboration

  Manage meeting experiences

- Configure meeting settings
- Create and manage meeting policies
- Configure settings for live events
- Create and manage policies for live events
- Configure conference bridge settings

  Manage phone numbers

- Recommend a PSTN connectivity solution based on specific business requirements
- order phone numbers
- Manage service numbers
- Add, change, or remove an emergency address for your organization
- Assign, change, or remove a phone number for a user
- Manage voice settings for users

  Manage Phone System

- Manage resource accounts
- Create and configure call queues
- Create and configure auto attendants
- Manage call park policies
- Manage calling policies
- Manage caller ID policies
- Interpret the Direct Routing health dashboard

   *4. Manage Teams and App Policies (20-25%)*

Manage a team

- Create a team
- Upgrade an existing resource to a team
- Manage privacy levels for a team
- Manage org-wide teams

  Manage membership in a team

- Manage users in a team
- Configure dynamic membership
- Manage access review for team members

  Implement policies for Microsoft Teams apps

- Create and manage app permission policies
- Create and manage app setup policies

Who should take the MS-700: Managing Microsoft Teams (beta) Exam:

The MS-700 Exam certification is an internationally-recognized certification which help to have validation for those professionals who are manages Office 365 workloads for Microsoft Teams that focus on efficient and effective collaboration and communication in an enterprise environment. It is good for these candidates:

- Microsoft Teams Administrator

How to study the MS-700: Managing Microsoft Teams (beta) Exam:

Preparation of certification exams could be covered with two resource types. The first one are the study guides, reference books and study forums that are elaborated and appropriate for building information from ground up. Apart from them video tutorials and lectures are a good option to ease the pain of through study and are relatively make the study process more interesting nonetheless these demand time and concentration from the learner. Smart candidates who wish to create a solid foundation altogether examination topics and connected technologies typically mix video lectures with study guides to reap the advantages of each but practice exams or practice exam engines is one important study tool which goes typically unnoted by most candidates. Practice exams are designed with our experts to make exam prospects test their knowledge on skills attained in course, as well as prospects become comfortable and familiar with the real exam environment. Statistics have indicated exam anxiety plays much bigger role of students failure in exam than the fear of the unknown. Certification-questions expert team recommends preparing some notes on these topics along with it don't forget to practice **MS-700 dumps** which had been written by our expert team, each of these can assist you loads to clear this exam with excellent marks.

MS-700: Managing Microsoft Teams (beta) Certification Path:

MS-700: Managing Microsoft Teams (beta) Exam is foundation level Certification. Anyone who is having keen interest and familiar with general Microsoft team administrator concepts and the technologies. Aspirants should have some hands-on experience should be proficient at managing Teams settings by using PowerShell.

How much MS-700: Managing Microsoft Teams (beta) Exam Cost:

The price of the Microsoft Mobility and Devices Fundamentals exam is $165 USD, for more information related to exam price please visit to Microsoft Training website as prices of Microsoft exams fees get varied country wise.

How to book the MS-700: Managing Microsoft Teams (beta) Exam:

These are following steps for registering the MS-700: Managing Microsoft Teams (beta) exam.

- Step 1: Visit to Microsoft Learning and search for MS-700: Managing Microsoft Teams (beta).
- Step 2: Sign up/Login to Pearson VUE account
- Step 3: Select local centre based on your country, date, time and confirm with a payment method.

What is the duration, language, and format of MS-700: Managing Microsoft Teams (beta) Exam:

- Length of Examination: 50 mins
- Number of Questions: 40 to 60 questions(Since Microsoft does not publish this information, the number of exam questions may change without notice.)
- Passing Score: 700 / 1000
- Type of Questions: This test format is multiple choice.
- language: English
- It is a Beta exam.

MS-700: Managing Microsoft Teams (beta) Exam Certified Professional salary:

The average salary of a MS-700: Managing Microsoft Teams (beta) Exam Certified Expert in

- United State - 100,000 USD
- India - 20,00,327 INR
- Europe - 90,547 EURO
- England - 90,532 POUND

The benefit of obtaining the MS-700: Managing Microsoft Teams (beta) Exam Certification:

- This certification will be judging your skills and knowledge on your understanding Microsoft Azure for SAP Workloads concepts & Understanding of how to operate on Planning and Administering Microsoft Azure for SAP Workloads .
- This certification credential will give you edge over other counterparts. Apart from knowledge from MS-700: Managing Microsoft Teams (beta) Exam.
- MS-700 Certification is distinguished among competitors. MS-700 certification can give them an edge at that time easily when candidates appear for employment interview, employers are very fascinated to note one thing that differentiates the individual from all other candidates.

- MS-700 certification has more useful and relevant networks that help them in setting career goals for themselves. MS-700 networks provide them with the correct career guidance than non certified generally are unable to get.
- MS-700 certified candidates will be confident and stand different from others as their skills are more trained than non-certified professionals.
- **MS-700 Exam** provide proven knowledge to use the tools to complete the task efficiently and cost effectively than the other non-certified professionals lack in doing so.
- MS-700 Certification provides practical experience to candidates from all the aspects to be a proficient worker in the organization.
- MS-700 Certifications provide opportunities to get a job easily in which they are interested in instead of wasting years and ending without getting any experience.
- MS-700 credential delivers higher earning potential and increased promotion opportunities because it shows a good understanding of HP-UX.

Difficulty in Writing MS-700: Managing Microsoft Teams (beta) Exam:

MS-700: Managing Microsoft Teams (beta) is a privileged achievement one could be graced with. But adverse to general notion certifying with Microsoft is not that challenging if the candidates have proper preparation material to pass the MS-700: Managing Microsoft Teams (beta) exam with good grades. Questions answers and clarifications which are designed in form of Certification-questions dumps make sure to cover entire course content. Certification-questions have a brilliant MS-700: Managing Microsoft Teams (beta) dumps with most recent and important questions and answers in PDF files. Certification-questions is sure about the exactness and legitimacy of MS-700: Managing Microsoft Teams (beta) dumps and in this manner. Candidates can easily pass the MS-700: Managing Microsoft Teams (beta) exam with genuine MS-700: Managing Microsoft Teams (beta) dumps and get MICROSOFT certification. These dumps are viewed as the best source to understand the MS-700: Managing Microsoft Teams (beta) well by simply pursuing examples questions and answers. If candidate completes practice the exam with certification **MS-700 dumps** along with self-assessment to get the proper idea on MICROSOFT accreditation and to ace the certification exam.

For more info read reference::

microsoft learning site
Microsoft Teams PowerShell documentation
Microsoft Teams technical documentation

# Sample Practice Test for MS-700

**Question: 1** *One Answer Is Right*

Note: This question is part of a series of questions that present the same scenario. Each question in the series contains a unique solution that might meet the stated goals. Some question sets might have more than one correct solution, while others might not have a correct solution. After you answer a question in this section, you will NOT be able to return to it. As a result, these questions will not appear in the review screen. Your company has a Microsoft 365 subscription. You plan to configure the environment to allow external users to collaborate in Microsoft Teams by using guest access. The company implements a new security policy that has the following requirements: - Only guest users from specific domains must be allowed to connect to collaborate by using Microsoft Teams. - Guest users must be prevented from inviting other guests. You need to recommend a solution to meet the security policy requirements. Solution: From the Microsoft Teams admin center, you modify the global meeting policy. Does this meet the goal?

**Answers:**

**A)** Yes

**B)** No

**Solution:** B

**Question: 2** *One Answer Is Right*

Note: This question is part of a series of questions that present the same scenario. Each question in the series contains a unique solution that might meet the stated goals. Some question sets might have more than one correct solution, while others might not have a correct solution. After you answer a question in this section, you will NOT be able to return to it. As a result, these questions will not appear in the review screen. Your company has a Microsoft 365 subscription. You plan to configure the environment to allow external users to collaborate in Microsoft Teams by using guest access. The company implements a new security policy that has the following requirements: - Only guest users from specific domains must be allowed to connect to collaborate by using Microsoft Teams. - Guest users must be prevented from inviting other guests. You need to recommend a solution to meet the security policy requirements. Solution: From PowerShell, you run the New-AzureADPolicy and Set-AzureADPolicy cmdlets. Does this meet the goal?

**Answers:**

**A)** Yes

**B)** No

**Solution:** B

**Question: 3** *One Answer Is Right*

Note: This question is part of a series of questions that present the same scenario. Each question in the series contains a unique solution that might meet the stated goals. Some question sets might have more than one correct solution, while others might not have a correct solution. After you answer a question in this section, you will NOT be able to return to it. As a result, these questions will not appear in the review screen. Your company has a Microsoft 365 subscription. You plan to configure the environment to allow external users to collaborate in Microsoft Teams by using guest access. The company implements a new security policy that has the following requirements: - Only guest users from specific domains must be allowed to connect to collaborate by using Microsoft Teams. - Guest users must be prevented from inviting other guests. You need to recommend a solution to meet the security policy requirements. Solution: From the Azure Active Directory, you modify the External collaboration settings. Does this meet the goal?

**Answers:**

**A)** Yes

**B)** No

**Solution:** A

**Question: 4** *One Answer Is Right*

Note: This question is part of a series of questions that present the same scenario. Each question in the series contains a unique solution that might meet the stated goals. Some question sets might have more than one correct solution, while others might not have a correct solution. After you answer a question in this section, you will NOT be able to return to it. As a result, these questions will not appear in the review screen. Your company has a Microsoft 365 subscription that uses an Azure Active Directory (Azure AD) tenant named contoso.com. You need to prevent guest users in the tenant from using cameras during Microsoft Teams meetings. Solution: From the Azure Active Directory admin center, you modify the External collaboration settings. Does this meet the goal?

**Answers:**

**A)** Yes

**B)** No

**Solution:** B

**Question: 5** *One Answer Is Right*

Note: This question is part of a series of questions that present the same scenario. Each question in the series contains a unique solution that might meet the stated goals. Some question sets might have more than one correct solution, while others might not have a correct solution. After you answer a question in this section, you will NOT be able to return to it. As a result, these questions will not appear in the review screen. Your company has a Microsoft 365 subscription that uses an Azure Active Directory (Azure AD) tenant named contoso.com. You need to prevent guest users in the tenant from using cameras during Microsoft Teams meetings. Solution: From Microsoft Teams admin center, you modify the External collaboration settings. Does this meet the goal?

**Answers:**

**A)** Yes

**B)** No

**Solution:** A

**Question: 6** *One Answer Is Right*

Note: This question is part of a series of questions that present the same scenario. Each question in the series contains a unique solution that might meet the stated goals. Some question sets might have more than one correct solution, while others might not have a correct solution. After you answer a question in this section, you will NOT be able to return to it. As a result, these questions will not appear in the review screen. Your company has a Microsoft 365 subscription that uses an Azure Active Directory (Azure AD) tenant named contoso.com. You need to prevent guest users in the tenant from using cameras during Microsoft Teams meetings. Solution: From the Microsoft 365 admin center, you modify the Sharing settings. Does this meet the goal?

**Answers:**

**A)** Yes

**B)** No

**Solution:** B

**Question: 7** *One Answer Is Right*

Note: This question is part of a series of questions that present the same scenario. Each question in the series contains a unique solution that might meet the stated goals. Some question sets might have more than one correct solution, while others might not have a correct solution. After you answer a question in this section, you will NOT be able to return to it. As a result, these questions will not appear in the review screen. Your company has a Microsoft 365 subscription. You need to prevent a user named User1 from permanently deleting private chats in Microsoft Teams. Solution: You place the mailbox of User1 on Litigation Hold. Does this meet the goal?

**Answers:**

**A)** Yes

**B)** No

**Solution:** A

**Question: 8** *One Answer Is Right*

Note: This question is part of a series of questions that present the same scenario. Each question in the series contains a unique solution that might meet the stated goals. Some question sets might have more than one correct solution, while others might not have a correct solution. After you answer a question in this section, you will NOT be able to return to it. As a result, these questions will not appear in the review screen. Your company has a Microsoft 365 subscription. You need to prevent a user named User1 from permanently deleting private chats in Microsoft Teams. Solution: You create an In-Place Hold for the Microsoft SharePoint site used by Microsoft Team. Does this meet the goal?

**Answers:**

**A)** Yes

**B)** No

**Solution:** B

**Question: 9** *One Answer Is Right*

Note: This question is part of a series of questions that present the same scenario. Each question in the series contains a unique solution that might meet the stated goals. Some question sets might have more than one correct solution, while others might not have a correct solution. After you answer a question in this section, you will NOT be able to return to it. As a result, these questions will not appear in the review screen. Your company has a Microsoft 365 subscription. You need to prevent a user named User1 from permanently deleting private chats in Microsoft Teams. Solution: You place the group mailboxes used by Microsoft Teams on Litigation Hold. Does this meet the goal?

**Answers:**

**A)** Yes

**B)** No

**Solution:** B

**Question: 10** *One Answer Is Right*

Your company has a Microsoft 365 subscription that contains 20 teams. You need to ensure that a team named Team1 is identified as Highly Confidential in the Microsoft Teams client. What should you use?

**Answers:**

**A)** a teams app setup policy in the Microsoft Teams admin center

**B)** a sensitivity label in the Security & Compliance admin center

**C)** a supervision policy in the Security & Compliance admin center

**D)** a teams policy in the Microsoft Teams admin center

**Solution:** B

# Chapter 43: MS-900 - Microsoft 365 Fundamentals

## Exam Guide

Microsoft 365 Fundamentals MS-900 Exam:

Microsoft 365 Fundamentals MS-900 Exam which is related to Microsoft Certified Professional. This exam is suitable for those who are looking to demonstrate foundational knowledge on the considerations and benefits of adopting cloud services in general and the software as a service (SaaS) Cloud Model. It validates the ability to understand Cloud Concepts, Core Microsoft 365 services and concepts, understand the concepts of Modern Management, security and compliance concepts with Microsoft 365. Microsoft IT Professionals usually hold or pursue this certification and you can expect the same job role after completion of this certification.

MS-900 Exam topics:

Candidates must know the exam topics before they start of preparation. Because it will really help them in hitting the core. Our **MS-900 dumps** will include the following topics:

- Understand cloud concepts 15-20%
- Understand core Microsoft 365 services and concepts 30-35%
- Understand security, compliance, privacy, and trust in Microsoft 365 30-35%
- Understand Microsoft 365 pricing and support 25-30%

Certification Path:

The Microsoft 365 Fundamentals Certification includes only one MS-900 exam.

Who should take the MS-900 exam:

The Microsoft 365 Fundamentals MS-900 Exam certification is an internationally recognized validation that identifies persons who earn it as possessing skilled as a Microsoft Certified Professional. If candidates want significant improvement in career growth needs enhanced knowledge, skills, and talents. The Microsoft 365 Fundamentals MS-900 Exam certification provides proof of this advanced knowledge and skill. If a candidate has knowledge of associated technologies and skills that are required to pass Microsoft 365 Fundamentals MS-900 Exam then he should take this exam.

How to study the MS-900 Exam:

Certification-questions.com expert team recommends you to prepare some notes on these topics along with it don't forget to practice Microsoft MS-900 Exam dumps which been written by our expert team, Both these will help you a lot to clear this exam with good marks.

How much MS-900 Exam Cost:

The price of the MS-900 exam is $165 USD.

How to book the MS-900 Exam:

These are following steps for registering the MS-900 exam.
Step 1: Visit to Microsoft Exam Registration
Step 2: Signup/Login to MICROSOFT account
Step 3: Search for MICROSOFT MS-900 Certifications Exam
Step 4: Select Date and Center of examination and confirm with payment value of $165

What is the duration of the MS-900 Exam:

- Format: Multiple choices, multiple answers
- Length of Examination: 150 minutes
- Number of Questions: 45-60
- Passing Score: 700/1000

   The benefit in Obtaining the MS-900 Exam Certification:

- After completion of Microsoft Certified Professional Certification candidates receive official confirmation from Microsoft that you are now fully certified in their chosen field. This can be now added to their CV, cover letters and job applications.
- When Candidates applying for a job or looking to promotion in their current position, a Microsoft Certified Professional certification in the field in which Candidates are applying will put you at the top of the list and make them a desirable candidate for employers.
- Candidates will get in-depth knowledge by completing the courses along with the access to revision materials for 6 months upon completion means they will have a wider skill set when it comes to the various technologies and systems than an uncertified professional. Certified Professional in this particular skill set is 74% more efficient when it comes to completing their tasks in a timely well-executed manner.
- Organization owners invest a lot in their employees when it comes to their training with the goal of making them quicker, more efficient, and more knowledgeable about their role.

Certified Professional will reduce the time he spends on tasks, meaning he can get more done this could help reduce company downtime when repairing faults on a system or fixing hardware problems.
- Becoming Microsoft Certified Professional means one thing you are worth more to the company and therefore more to yourself in the form of an upgraded pay package. On average a Microsoft Certified Professional member of staff is estimated to be worth 30% more to a company than their uncertified professionals.

Difficulty in writing MS-900 Exam:

Microsoft Certified Professional Certification helps Candidates in developing their professionals and academic career and It is a very tough task to pass Microsoft MS-900 exam for those Candidates who have not done hard work and get some relevant Microsoft MS-900 exam preparation material. There are many peoples have passed Microsoft MS-900 exam by following these three things such as look for the latest **Microsoft MS-900 exam dumps**, get relevant **Microsoft MS-900 exam dumps** and develop their knowledge about Microsoft MS-900 exam new questions. At the same time, it can also stress out some people as they found passing Microsoft MS-900 exam a tough task. It is just a wrong assumption as many of the peoples have passed Microsoft MS-900 exam questions. All you have to do is to work hard, get some relevant Microsoft MS-900 exam preparation material and go thoroughly from them. Certification-questions is here to help you with this problem. We have the relevant Microsoft MS-900 exam preparation material which are providing the latest Microsoft MS-900 exam questions with the detailed view of every Microsoft MS-900 exam topic. Certification-questions offered **Microsoft MS-900 exam dumps** which are more than enough to pass the Microsoft MS-900 exam questions. We are providing all thing such as MS-900 exam dumps, Microsoft MS-900 practice test, and Microsoft MS-900 pdf dumps that will help the candidate to pass the exam with good grades.

For more info visit::

Microsoft MS-900 Exam Reference

# Sample Practice Test for MS-900

**Question: 1** *Multiple Answers Are Right*

DRAG DROP You are implementing cloud services. Match each scenario to its service. To answer, drag the appropriate scenario from the column on the left to its cloud service on the right. Each scenario may be used only once. NOTE: Each correct selection is worth one point. Select and Place:

**Answer Area**

| Scenarios | Service | Scenario |
|---|---|---|
| Exchange Online integrated with on-premises Exchange Server 2019 | Software as a service (SaaS) | |
| Custom web and mobile application securely connected to an on-premises data store | Platform as a service (PaaS) | |
| Server-based workloads on a virtual machine connected to an on-premises nework | Infrastructure as a service (IaaS) | |

Answers:

A)

**Answer Area**

| Scenarios | Service | Scenario |
|---|---|---|
| Exchange Online integrated with on-premises Exchange Server 2019 | Software as a service (SaaS) | Exchange Online integrated with on-premises Exchange Server 2019 |
| Custom web and mobile application securely connected to an on-premises data store | Platform as a service (PaaS) | Custom web and mobile application securely connected to an on-premises data store |
| Server-based workloads on a virtual machine connected to an on-premises nework | Infrastructure as a service (IaaS) | Server-based workloads on a virtual machine connected to an on-premises nework |

**Solution: A**

**Explanation:**

Explanation: References: https://docs.microsoft.com/en-us/office365/enterprise/hybrid-cloud-overview

**Question: 2** *One Answer Is Right*

You need to identify which Microsoft platforms provide hybrid capabilities for migrating from an on-premises deployment. Which two platforms provide hybrid capabilities for migration? Each correct answer provides a complete solution. (Choose two.) NOTE: Each correct selection is worth one point.

**Answers:**

**A)** Microsoft Skype for Business

**B)** Microsoft Yammer

**C)** Microsoft Exchange

**D)** Microsoft Teams

**Solution:** A, C

**Explanation:**

Explanation: References: https://docs.microsoft.com/en-us/office365/enterprise/architecture-of-microsoft-hybrid-cloud-scenarios

**Question: 3** *One Answer Is Right*

A company is moving to Microsoft Azure. Some applications cannot be moved. You need to identify which applications will remain in a hybrid environment after the migration. Which applications will remain in a hybrid environment?

**Answers:**

**A)** applications that manage sensitive information

**B)** applications that use a USB-token device to control access

**C)** legacy applications that use a message-based interface

**D)** a new server that runs several line-of-business applications

**Solution:** A

**Question: 4** *Multiple Answers Are Right*

DRAG DROP You are the Microsoft 365 administrator for a company. You must provide infrastructure recommendations. All proposed solutions must minimize costs. You need to identify the appropriate cloud model for the given scenarios. Which cloud models should you use? To answer, drag the appropriate cloud models to the correct requirements. Each cloud model may be used once, more than once, or not at all. You may need to drag the split bar between panes or scroll to view content. NOTE: Each correct selection is worth one point. Select and Place:

## Answer area

**Cloud models**
- Private
- Public
- Hybrid

| Requirement | Cloud model |
|---|---|
| Provide an on-demand sandbox environment. | Cloud model |
| Provide failover capabilities between resources that you manage and resources in other regions. | Cloud model |
| Deploy virtual machines that supports USB devices. | Cloud model |

### Answers:

**A)**

## Answer area

**Cloud models**
- Private
- Public
- Hybrid

| Requirement | Cloud model |
|---|---|
| Provide an on-demand sandbox environment. | Public |
| Provide failover capabilities between resources that you manage and resources in other regions. | Public |
| Deploy virtual machines that supports USB devices. | Hybrid |

### Solution: A

### Explanation:

Explanation: Reference: https://azure.microsoft.com/en-us/overview/what-are-private-public-hybrid-clouds/ https://www.thinksys.com/cloud/private-vs-public-vs-hybrid-cloud/

### Question: 5 *One Answer Is Right*

You are the Microsoft 365 administrator for a company. The company runs SharePoint Server and Exchange Server in an on-premises datacenter. The site collection for the finance department is currently encrypted using third-party software. You need to move as many services to Microsoft 365 as possible. What should you do?

### Answers:

**A)** Migrate all SharePoint data and Exchange mailboxes to Microsoft 365.

**B)** Leave SharePoint data for finance department users on-premises. Migrate all other SharePoint data and Exchange mailboxes to Microsoft 365.

**C)** Leave mailboxes for finance department users on-premises. Migrate all other SharePoint data and Exchange mailboxes to Microsoft 365.

**D)** Leave SharePoint data and mailboxes for finance department users on-premises. Migrate all other SharePoint data and Exchange mailboxes to Microsoft 365.

**Solution:** A

**Question: 6** *One Answer Is Right*

A company has an Exchange Server environment. The company plans to migrate to the cloud. You need to recommend a cloud model that meets the following requirements: - Upgrade the existing email environment - Minimize server and application maintenance Which model should you recommend?

**Answers:**

**A)** Platform as a service (PaaS)

**B)** Windows as a service (WaaS)

**C)** Software as a service (SaaS)

**D)** Infrastructure as a service (IaaS)

**Solution:** C

**Explanation:**

Explanation: References: https://www.cmswire.com/cms/information-management/cloud-service-models-iaas-saas-paas-how- microsoft-office-365-azure-fit-in-021672.php

**Question: 7** *Multiple Answers Are Right*

DRAG DROP You are the Azure administrator for a company. The company uses only Platform as a Service (PaaS). You need to identify which solution components Microsoft must manage and which solution components your IT staff must manage. Match each management owner to its component. To answer, drag the responsible party from the column on the left to its component on the right. Each party may be used once, more than once, or not at all. NOTE: Each correct selection is worth one point. Select and Place:

## Answer Area

**Responsible parties**

- IT staff
- Microsoft

| Component | Responsible party |
|---|---|
| Applications | |
| Operating systems | |
| Storage | |
| Application data | |

Answers:

A)

## Answer Area

**Responsible parties**

- IT staff
- Microsoft

| Component | Responsible party |
|---|---|
| Applications | IT staff |
| Operating systems | Microsoft |
| Storage | Microsoft |
| Application data | IT staff |

**Solution:** A

**Explanation:**

Explanation: References: https://www.itprotoday.com/industry-perspectives/choosing-cloud-model-saas-versus-paas

**Question: 8** *Multiple Answers Are Right*

DRAG DROP An organization is moving to Microsoft Azure and Microsoft 365. You need to classify the following components: - website hosting - a virtual machine that runs Linux - document storage that uses OneDrive for Business Match each component to its classification. To answer, drag the appropriate components from the column on the left to its classifications on the right. Each component may be used once, more than once, or not at all. NOTE: Each correct selection is worth one point. Select and Place:

| Classifications | Component | Classification |
|---|---|---|
| Platform as a service (PaaS) | website hosting | |
| Software as a service (SaaS) | a virtual machine that runs Linux | |
| Infrastructure as a service (IaaS) | document storage that uses OneDrive for Business | |

**Answers:**

**A)**

| Classifications | Component | Classification |
|---|---|---|
| | website hosting | Platform as a service (PaaS) |
| | a virtual machine that runs Linux | Infrastructure as a service (IaaS) |
| | document storage that uses OneDrive for Business | Software as a service (SaaS) |

**Solution: A**

**Explanation:**

Explanation:

**Question: 9** *Multiple Answers Are Right*

HOTSPOT For each of the following statements, select Yes if the statement is true. Otherwise, select No. NOTE: Each correct selection is worth one point. Hot Area:

## Answer Area

| Statement | Yes | No |
|---|---|---|
| It is possible to connect cloud services to on-premises server resources. | ○ | ○ |
| Scaling cloud-hosted infrastructure components includes expanding Azure server resources and networking components. | ○ | ○ |

Answers:

A)

## Answer Area

| Statement | Yes | No |
|---|---|---|
| It is possible to connect cloud services to on-premises server resources. | ● | ○ |
| Scaling cloud-hosted infrastructure components includes expanding Azure server resources and networking components. | ● | ○ |

**Solution:** A

**Explanation:**

Explanation:

**Question: 10** *Multiple Answers Are Right*

HOTSPOT For each of the following statements, select Yes if the statement is true. Otherwise, select No. NOTE: Each correct selection is worth one point. Hot Area:

## Answer Area

| Statement | Yes | No |
|---|---|---|
| Adopting cloud applications reduces the number of on-premises servers and services to manage. | ○ | ○ |
| For remote users, accessing applications stored in the cloud is easier than accessing applications stored on a company network. | ○ | ○ |
| A loss of internet connectivity will not significantly impact functionality for users accessing applications and services in the cloud. | ○ | ○ |

Answers:

A)

## Answer Area

| Statement | Yes | No |
|---|---|---|
| Adopting cloud applications reduces the number of on-premises servers and services to manage. | ● | ○ |
| For remote users, accessing applications stored in the cloud is easier than accessing applications stored on a company network. | ● | ○ |
| A loss of internet connectivity will not significantly impact functionality for users accessing applications and services in the cloud. | ○ | ● |

**Solution:** A

**Explanation:**

Explanation:

# Chapter 44: PL-900 - Microsoft Power Platform Fundamentals

## Exam Guide

How to Prepare For PL-900: Microsoft Power Platform Fundamentals (beta) Exam

Preparation Guide for PL-900: Microsoft Power Platform Fundamentals (beta) Exam

Introduction

Microsoft has created a track for professionals who aspire towards productivity enhancement by inculcating automation in business process,analyzing data to produce business insights, and acting more effectively by creating simple app experiences. This certification program provides Microsoft Power Platform Fundamentals (beta) a way to demonstrate their skills. The assessment is based on a rigorous exam using industry standard methodology to determine whether a candidate meets Microsoft's proficiency standards.

According to Microsoft, a Microsoft Certified Professional enables organizations to leverage Microsoft Power Platform Fundamentals (beta) technologies by identifying the basic functionality and business value Power Platform components; implement simple solutions with Microsoft Flow, Power BI, and AI Builder.

Certification is evidence of your skills, expertise in those areas in which you like to work. If candidate wants to work on Microsoft Azure for SAP Workloads and prove his knowledge, certification offered by Microsoft. This **PL-900 Exam** Certification helps a candidate to validates his skills in Microsoft Power Platform Technology.

In this guide, we will cover the PL-900: Microsoft Power Platform Fundamentals (beta) Certification exam, PL-900: Microsoft Power Platform Fundamentals (beta) Certified professional salary and all aspects of the PL-900: Microsoft Power Platform Fundamentals (beta) Certification.

Introduction to PL-900: Microsoft Power Platform Fundamentals (beta) Exam:

Candidates for **PL-900 Exam** are seeking to prove fundamental Microsoft Power Platform knowledge and skills. Before taking this exam, exam aspirants ought to have a solid fundamental information of the concepts shared in preparation guide as well as Power Platform components: Power Apps, Power BI, Microsoft Flow, Common Data Service connectors.

It is suggested that professionals accustomed to the ideas and also the technologies represented here by taking relevant training courses. Candidates are expected to have some expert knowledge on components of power BI, business value of Power BI, building of basic dashboard, business value of Power Automate.

After passing this exam, candidates get a certificate from Microsoft that helps them to demonstrate their proficiency to their clients and employers.

Topics of PL-900: Microsoft Power Platform Fundamentals (beta) Exam:

Candidates should apprehend the examination topics before they begin of preparation. because it'll extremely facilitate them in touch the core. Our **PL-900 dumps** will include the following topics:

*1. Understand the business value of Power Platform (20-25%)*

Describe the value of Power Platform applications

- Analyze data by using Power BI
- Act with Power Apps
- Build solutions that use Common Data Service (CDS)
- Automate with Power Automate
- Interoperate with external systems and data

Describe the value of connecting business solutions

- Dynamics 365
- Microsoft 365
- Microsoft Azure
- Third-party services and apps

Understand Power Platform administration and security

- Understand how Power Platform implements security
- Understand Power Platform as a service
- Describe how to manage apps and users
- Describe admin centers
- Understand how the platform supports compliance

*2. Understand the Core Components of Power Platform (20-25%)*

Understand Common Data Services

- User experience vs unique job role using Power Apps
- Identify entities, fields, and relationships
- Describe environments
- Describe use cases and limitations of Business process flows
- Describe use cases and limitations of business rules
- Describe the Common Data Model (CDM)
- Identify common standard entities

  Understand Connectors

- Describe uses for and types of triggers
- Describe actions
- Describe connectors
- Identify use cases for custom connectors

  Understand AI Builder

- Identify the business value of AI Builder
- Describe models
- Consumption by the Power Platform

  *3. Demonstrate the business value of Power BI (15-20%)*

Understand common components in Power BI

- Identify and describe uses for visualization controls
- Describe types of filters
- Describe Tabs
- Custom visuals
- Compare and contrast dashboards and workspaces
- Compare and contrast Power BI Desktop and Power BI Service

  Connect to and consume data

- Combine multiple data sources
- Clean and transform data
- Describe and implement aggregate functions
- Identify available types of data sources
- Describe and consume shared datasets and template apps

  Build a basic dashboard using Power BI

- Design a Power BI dashboard
- Design data layout and mapping
- Publish and share reports and dashboards

*4. Demonstrate the business value of Power Apps (20-25%)*

Understand common components in Power Apps

- Describe canvas apps
- Describe model-driven apps
- Identify and describe controls
- Understand uses for templates
- Understand use cases for formulas

Build a basic canvas app

- Connect to data
- Use controls to design the user experience
- Describe the customer journey
- Publish and share an app

Understand Power Apps portals

- Describe use case for and the business value of portals
- Describe how to extend CDS data, use controls, and embed Power BI objects

*5. Demonstrate the business value of Power Automate (15-20%)*

Understand the common components of Power Automate

- Flow types
- Templates
- Connectors
- Triggers
- Conditions
- Expressions
- Approvals

Build a basic flow

- Create a business process flow
- Implement a Power Automate template
- Modify a flow

- Run a flow
- Export a flow to Logic Apps

Who should take the PL-900: Microsoft Power Platform Fundamentals (beta) Exam:

The **PL-900 Exam** certification is an internationally-recognized certification which help to have validation for those professionals who are looking forward to improve productivity by automating business process. Candidates for this exam should be familiar with business value of power platform applications, analyzing data by using power BI, value of connecting business solutions, act with power apps.

How to study the PL-900: Microsoft Power Platform Fundamentals (beta) Exam:

Preparation of certification exams could be covered with two resource types. The first one are the study guides, reference books and study forums that are elaborated and appropriate for building information from ground up. Apart from them video tutorials and lectures are a good option to ease the pain of through study and are relatively make the study process more interesting nonetheless these demand time and concentration from the learner. Smart candidates who wish to create a solid foundation altogether examination topics and connected technologies typically mix video lectures with study guides to reap the advantages of each but practice exams or practice exam engines is one important study tool which goes typically unnoted by most candidates. Practice exams are designed with our experts to make exam prospects test their knowledge on skills attained in course, as well as prospects become comfortable and familiar with the real exam environment. Statistics have indicated exam anxiety plays much bigger role of students failure in exam than the fear of the unknown. Certification-questions expert team recommends preparing some notes on these topics along with it don't forget to practice **PL-900 dumps** which had been written by our expert team, each of these can assist you loads to clear this exam with excellent marks.

PL-900: Microsoft Power Platform Fundamentals (beta) Certification Path:

PL-900: Microsoft Power Platform Fundamentals (beta) Exam is foundation level Certification. Anyone who is having keen interest and familiar with general concepts and the technologies of Microsoft Power Platform Fundamentals (beta). Aspirants should have some hands-on experience with Dynamics 365, Microsoft 365, Microsoft Azure, core components of power platform, common data model.

How much PL-900: Microsoft Power Platform Fundamentals (beta) Exam Cost:

The price of the Microsoft Mobility and Devices Fundamentals exam is $99 USD, for more information related to exam price please visit to Microsoft Training website as prices of Microsoft exams fees get varied country wise.

How to book the PL-900: Microsoft Power Platform Fundamentals (beta) Exam:

These are following steps for registering the PL-900: Microsoft Power Platform Fundamentals (beta) exam.

- Step 1: Visit to Microsoft Learning and search for PL-900: Microsoft Power Platform Fundamentals (beta).
- Step 2: Sign up/Login to Pearson VUE account
- Step 3: Select local centre based on your country, date, time and confirm with a payment method.

What is the duration, language, and format of PL-900: Microsoft Power Platform Fundamentals (beta) Exam:

- Length of Examination: 50 mins
- Number of Questions: 40 to 60 questions(Since Microsoft does not publish this information, the number of exam questions may change without notice.)
- Passing Score: 700 / 1000
- Type of Questions: This test format is multiple choice.
- language: English

PL-900: Microsoft Power Platform Fundamentals (beta) Exam Certified Professional salary:

The average salary of a PL-900: Microsoft Power Platform Fundamentals (beta) Exam Certified Expert in

- United State - 120,000 USD
- India - 20,00,327 INR
- Europe - 90,547 EURO
- England - 90,532 POUND

The benefit of obtaining the PL-900: Microsoft Power Platform Fundamentals (beta) Exam Certification:

- This certification will be judging your skills and knowledge on your understanding Microsoft Azure for SAP Workloads concepts & Understanding of how to operate on Planning and Administering Microsoft Azure for SAP Workloads .
- This certification credential will give you edge over other counterparts. Apart from knowledge from PL-900: Microsoft Power Platform Fundamentals (beta) Exam.
- PL-900 Certification is distinguished among competitors. PL-900 certification can give them an edge at that time easily when candidates appear for employment interview, employers are very fascinated to note one thing that differentiates the individual from all other candidates.

- PL-900 certification has more useful and relevant networks that help them in setting career goals for themselves. PL-900 networks provide them with the correct career guidance than non certified generally are unable to get.
- PL-900 certified candidates will be confident and stand different from others as their skills are more trained than non-certified professionals.
- **PL-900 Exam** provide proven knowledge to use the tools to complete the task efficiently and cost effectively than the other non-certified professionals lack in doing so.
- PL-900 Certification provides practical experience to candidates from all the aspects to be a proficient worker in the organization.
- PL-900 Certifications provide opportunities to get a job easily in which they are interested in instead of wasting years and ending without getting any experience.
- PL-900 credential delivers higher earning potential and increased promotion opportunities.

Difficulty in Writing PL-900: Microsoft Power Platform Fundamentals (beta) Exam:

PL-900: Microsoft Power Platform Fundamentals (beta) is a privileged achievement one could be graced with. But adverse to general notion certifying with Microsoft is not that challenging if the candidates have proper preparation material to pass the PL-900: Microsoft Power Platform Fundamentals (beta) exam with good grades. Questions answers and clarifications which are designed in form of Certification-questions dumps make sure to cover entire course content. Certification-questions have a brilliant PL-900: Microsoft Power Platform Fundamentals (beta) dumps with most recent and important questions and answers in PDF files. Certification-questions is sure about the exactness and legitimacy of PL-900: Microsoft Power Platform Fundamentals (beta) dumps and in this manner. Candidates can easily pass the PL-900: Microsoft Power Platform Fundamentals (beta) exam with genuine PL-900: Microsoft Power Platform Fundamentals (beta) dumps and get MICROSOFT certification. These dumps are viewed as the best source to understand the PL-900: Microsoft Power Platform Fundamentals (beta) well by simply pursuing examples questions and answers. If candidate completes practice the exam with certification **PL-900 dumps** along with self-assessment to get the proper idea on MICROSOFT accreditation and to ace the certification exam.

For more info read reference::

microsoft learning site
Microsoft Power Platform Fundamentals (beta)
Introduction to PowerApps

# Sample Practice Test for PL-900

**Question: 1** *One Answer Is Right*

This question requires that you evaluate the underlined text to determine if it is correct. You have a Power Apps app. You create a new version of the app and then publish the new version. A customer goes through the process of restoring the previous version of the app. In the Version tab for the app, you will see two versions of the app. Review the underlined text. If it makes the statement correct, select "No change is needed." If the statement is incorrect, select the answer choice that makes the statement correct.

**Answers:**

**A)** No change is needed.

**B)** one

**C)** three

**D)** four

**Solution:** C

**Explanation:**

Explanation: Restore a canvas app to a previous version in PowerApps. 1. Open powerapps.com, and then click or tap Apps in the left navigation bar. 2. Near the right edge, click or tap the info icon for the app that you want to restore. 3. Click or tap the Versions tab, and then click or tap Restore for the version that you want to restore.

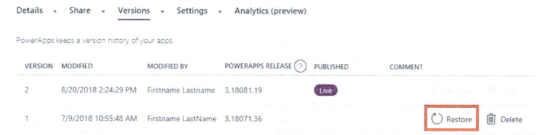

4. In the confirmation dialog box, click or tap Restore. A new version is added to your list.

Reference: https://docs.microsoft.com/en-us/powerapps/maker/canvas-apps/restore-an-app

**Question: 2** *One Answer Is Right*

A company uses Dynamics 365 Sales. The company uses a browser-based app named Sales Hub. You need to ensure that users can access data from mobile devices. Which app should users install?

**Answers:**

**A)** Dynamics 365 Remote Assist

**B)** Dynamics 365 Finance

**C)** Dynamics 365 Business Central

**D)** Dynamics 365 for Phones

**Solution:** D

**Explanation:**

Explanation: Use the Dynamics 365 for phones and Dynamics 365 for tablets apps for your sales, customer service, field service, and other tasks when you're on the go. With one download from your app store, you'll automatically have access to all the apps you need for your role. You will see apps with the new Unified Interface on your mobile device. Reference: https://docs.microsoft.com/en-us/dynamics365/mobile-app/dynamics-365-phones-tablets-users-guide

**Question: 3** *One Answer Is Right*

You are a customer service manager. You need to implement a Power Apps portal that allows customers to submit cases. Which type of data source is used?

**Answers:**

**A)** Dynamics 365 Connector

**B)** Microsoft SharePoint

**C)** Microsoft Azure Storage

**D)** Common Data Service

**Solution:** B

**Explanation:**

Explanation: SharePoint can be set up to setup customer feedback. Note: The PowerApp uses Finance and Operations connector to grab sales order information and SharePoint connector to connect and write the data to SharePoint list. Reference: https://powerapps.microsoft.com/en-us/blog/scenario-2-collect-customer-feedback-in-sharepoint-after- order-delivery/

**Question: 4** *Multiple Answers Are Right*

HOTSPOT You create a user-owned custom entity by using Common Data Service. For each of the following statements, select Yes if the statement is true. Otherwise, select No. NOTE: Each correct selection is worth one point. Hot Area:

## Answer Area

| Statement | Yes | No |
|---|---|---|
| You can change the entity ownership from User to Organization-owned. | ○ | ○ |
| You can create a business rule for a custom entity that can be used in a Flow. | ○ | ○ |

**Answers:**

A)

## Answer Area

| Statement | Yes | No |
|---|---|---|
| You can change the entity ownership from User to Organization-owned. | ○ | ○ |
| You can create a business rule for a custom entity that can be used in a Flow. | ○ | ○ |

**Solution:** A

**Explanation:**

Explanation: Box 1: No Common Data Service supports two types of record ownership. Organization owned, and User or Team owned. This is a choice that happens at the time the entity is created and can't be changed. Box 2: Yes By combining conditions and actions, you can do any of the following with business rules: Set field values Clear field values Set field requirement levels Show or hide fields Enable or disable fields Validate data and show error messages Create business recommendations based on business intelligence. Reference: https://docs.microsoft.com/en-us/power-platform/admin/wp-security-cds

**Question: 5** *Multiple Answers Are Right*

DRAG DROP You need to explain the major components of the Common Data Model (CDM) and their functions. Match each term to its definition. Instructions: To answer, drag the appropriate term from the column on the left to its definition on the right. Each term may be used once, more than once, or not at all. Each correct match is worth one point. NOTE: Each correct selection is worth one point. Select and Place:

**Tools**
- Entities
- Data connectors
- Common Data Service
- Common Data Model
- Microsoft Power Platform
- Workflows

**Answer Area**

| Purpose | Tool |
|---|---|
| Helps jumpstart application development by leveraging business logic, security, and integrations. | Tool |
| A set of records used to store data. | Tool |

## Answers:

### A)

**Tools**
- Entities
- Data connectors
- Common Data Service
- Common Data Model
- Microsoft Power Platform
- Workflows

**Answer Area**

| Purpose | Tool |
|---|---|
| Helps jumpstart application development by leveraging business logic, security, and integrations. | Microsoft Power Platform |
| A set of records used to store data. | Entities |

**Solution:** A

**Explanation:**

Explanation: Box 1: Microsoft Power Platform Power Platform combines the robust power of PowerApps, PowerBI, and Microsoft Flow into one powerful business application platform – providing quick and easy app building and data insights. Each component of the Microsoft Power Platform is built on the Common Data Service for Apps. Each component is dynamic by itself, but brilliant and masterful when combined. The Microsoft Power platform brings all your data together into a common data model. Box 2: Entities An entity is a set of records used to store data, similar to how a table stores data within a database. Reference: https://community.dynamics.com/365/b/encloud9dynamicss365crm/posts/an-introduction-to-the-microsoft- power-platform https://docs.microsoft.com/en-us/powerapps/maker/common-data-service/data-platform-intro

**Question: 6** *Multiple Answers Are Right*

HOTSPOT You are building Power Apps apps that use both Dynamics 365 Sales and Microsoft 365. For each of the following statements, select Yes if the statement is true. Otherwise, select No. NOTE: Each correct selection is worth one point. Hot Area:

## Answer Area

| Statement | Yes | No |
|---|---|---|
| Dynamics 365 Sales and Microsoft 365 must be in the same tenant to allow Single Sign-On (SSO). | ○ | ○ |
| You must download a product from AppSource to ensure that SSO works with Dynamics 365 Sales and Microsoft 365. | ○ | ○ |

Answers:

A)

## Answer Area

| Statement | Yes | No |
|---|---|---|
| Dynamics 365 Sales and Microsoft 365 must be in the same tenant to allow Single Sign-On (SSO). | ○ | ○ |
| You must download a product from AppSource to ensure that SSO works with Dynamics 365 Sales and Microsoft 365. | ○ | ○ |

Solution: A

Explanation:

Explanation: Box 1: No When you offer your application for use by other companies through a purchase or subscription, you make your application available to customers within their own

Azure tenants. This is known as creating a multi- tenant application. Box 2: No Reference: https://docs.microsoft.com/en-us/azure/active-directory/manage-apps/isv-sso-content

**Question: 7** *One Answer Is Right*

You need to implement Microsoft Business Applications along with the Microsoft Power platform. Which three Microsoft products are part of the Power platform? Each correct answer presents a complete solution. NOTE: Each correct selection is worth one point.

**Answers:**

**A)** Microsoft Power Apps

**B)** Azure Active Directory

**C)** Microsoft Flow

**D)** Azure Machine Learning

**E)** Microsoft Power BI

**Solution:** A, C, E

**Explanation:**

Explanation: The Power Platform uses PowerApps, Power BI, and Power Automate (previously named Flow) to customize, extend, and build all the apps you need for your business and unlock the potential of Office 365 and Dynamics 365. Reference: https://docs.microsoft.com/en-us/learn/powerplatform/

**Question: 8** *Multiple Answers Are Right*

HOTSPOT A company plans to implement Power Platform apps. The company does not plan to use any development tools or plug-ins. Which actions can you perform? For each of the following statements, select Yes if the statement is true. Otherwise, select No. NOTE: Each correct selection is worth one point. Hot Area:

## Answer Area

| Statement | Yes | No |
|---|---|---|
| You can synchronize account information from Dynamics 365 Sales with a third-party database. | ○ | ○ |
| You can create invoices from orders and then send the invoices to the customer by using a Power Automate flow. | ○ | ○ |

Answers:

A)
## Answer Area

| Statement | Yes | No |
|---|---|---|
| You can synchronize account information from Dynamics 365 Sales with a third-party database. | ◉ | ○ |
| You can create invoices from orders and then send the invoices to the customer by using a Power Automate flow. | ◉ | ○ |

**Solution:** A

**Explanation:**

Explanation: The Power Platform uses PowerApps, Power BI, and Power Automate (previously named Flow) to customize, extend, and build all the apps you need for your business and unlock the potential of Office 365 and Dynamics 365. Reference: https://docs.microsoft.com/en-us/learn/powerplatform/

**Question: 9** *One Answer Is Right*

A distribution company has multiple warehouses. Tax rates charged on sales orders need to be calculated based on locality and region. You need to recommend a cost-effective solution that can be implemented quickly. What should you recommend?

Answers:

**A)** Check AppSource for a tax add-on.

**B)** Create alerts in Dynamics 365 Finance for tax table changes.

**C)** Implement the Common Data Model.

**D)** Run a Power BI report.

**E)** Write scripts and code tax updates.

**Solution:** B

**Explanation:**

Explanation: Reference: https://docs.microsoft.com/en-us/dynamics365/finance/general-ledger/indirect-taxes-overview

**Question: 10** *Multiple Answers Are Right*

DRAG DROP You manage the support team at a rapidly growing company. Customers and support technicians need a better experience when logging and responding to support requests. You need more visibility into what the support technicians are doing every week. You need to recommend tools to help the company's needs. Which tools should you recommend? To answer, drag the appropriate tools to the correct requirements. Each tool may be used once, more than once, or not at all. You may need to drag the split bar between panes or scroll to view content. NOTE: Each correct selection is worth one point. Select and Place:

| Tools | Answer Area | |
|---|---|---|
| Power Apps portal | **Requirement** | **Tool** |
| Power Automate | Customers must be able to submit support requests by using a website. | |
| Power BI | Support requests must be created and stored. | |
| Common Data Service | Support technicians must be notified when a new support request is entered. | |
| | Support technicians must be able to enter a status report for work completed during the previous week by using a mobile app. | |

**Answers:**

## A)

**Tools**
- Power Apps portal
- Power Automate
- Power BI
- Common Data Service

**Answer Area**

| Requirement | Tool |
|---|---|
| Customers must be able to submit support requests by using a website. | Power BI |
| Support requests must be created and stored. | Common Data Service |
| Support technicians must be notified when a new support request is entered. | Power Automate |
| Support technicians must be able to enter a status report for work completed during the previous week by using a mobile app. | Power Apps portal |

**Solution:** A

**Explanation:**

Explanation:

# SUMMARY

To recap, main stages of certification exam study guide are Introduction to Microsoft Exam , Microsoft Exam topics in which Candidates must know the exam topics before they start of preparation, Microsoft Exam Requirements, Cost of Microsoft Exam, registration procedure of the Microsoft Exam, Microsoft Exam formate, Microsoft Exam Certified salary, MicrosoftExam advantages.

If you are aspirant to pass the cerification exam, start exam preparation with study material provided by Certification-questions.com

# About The Author

## David Mayer

Co-Founder of Certification-Questions.com

David is the Co-founder of Certification-Questions.com, one of the largest Certification practice tests and PDF exams websites on the Internet. They are providing dumps an innovative way by providing Online Web Simulator and Mobile App. He likes to share his knowledge and is active in the Microsoft community.

He has written several books, blogs, and is active in the Microsoft community.

# APPENDIX

## Certification

The action or process of providing someone or something with an official document that accredits a state or level of results.

## Practice test

The practical exam is an alternative, non-scoring version of the intermediate or final exam of the course. The practice exam has the same format as the "real" exam, which means that if the practice exam has 20 multiple-choice questions and four free-answer questions, the "real" exam will be the same.